PERSPECTIVES

IN

PHILOSOPHY

PERSPECTIVES IN PHILOSOPHY

A BOOK OF READINGS

Robert N. Beck
Clark University

HOLT, RINEHART AND WINSTON / NEW YORK

To my students,

with affection and gratitude

PREFACE

A textbook of selections is one of the tools of learning. It will be utilized in a variety of ways by students and instructors. They give the materials form and seek to comprehend the living thought rather than repeat the dead word. But this does not mean that the materials themselves should be relatively formless.

As an alternative to the introductory textbook of selections that is based on a "problems" approach to philosophy, this volume is organized in terms of positions or schools of philosophy. The concept of a philosophical position is admittedly a difficult one and clearly seems to be "open textured." Generally, I think, a position should be defined in terms of a "continuity of intention," to use Professor Urban's phrase, rather than through identity of conclusions. Vague, then, as the idea of a school is bound to be, it nevertheless can like all classificatory devices be a useful pedagogical instrument. If internal differences and variety are not suppressed, and if thinking of "isms" is seen as a means to understanding rather than its end, an introduction to philosophy through the study of major alternative positions will have its unique values.

This does not mean that the problems approach should be dropped, but rather that the approach to problems taken by philosophers should reflect a context or, as we may call it, a philosophic school. Chosen from some of the main areas of philosophic concern, the selections are designed to convey to the student some notion of philosophic schools as well as insight into the nature of philosophic problems and awareness of some of the important answers philosophers have given to them.

All determination is negation, and all selection reflects something of the arbitrary. Teachers will note that not all important philosophic schools have been—or could be—included, and that some major thinkers are not represented. There is also some validity to the viewpoint that the greatest philosophers transcend schools—though in fact such transcendence usually leads to the founding of another school. Generally, the aim of selection in this textbook has been to provide as firm a basis for further study as possible and, for those for whom a "problems" course is the only elective in philosophy, to offer a valid terminal experience.

The general structure of the book is historical in the sense that the first positions studied are relatively older, the later recent. This arrangement allows the student to grasp materials from more traditional philosophy first and then utilize them in the study of positions of more recent origin. Within each position, however, both older and contemporary thinkers are represented. Another feature of the book's structure is the relatively similar organization of selections within each perspective.

Thus the value of the problems approach is not lost and, because there is emphasis upon the context within which these problems are developed, may in fact be enriched.

Introductory material is provided to guide students in their reading and understanding of the selections. Brief bibliographical notes follow each section to aid in further reading, should students desire to pursue beyond the introductory level the ideas presented in the selections. A selected glossary of some of the important terms used by authors is included at the end of the book.

Words of thanks are due many people, including the authors and publishers noted throughout the text for their kind permissions to use their materials, and the many students who have helped me to learn —if even a little—the art of introduction. Finally, but not least, I want to express appreciation for the countless chores done by my wife in the task of bringing this book to print.

R. N. B.

Worcester, Massachusetts
January, 1961

CONTENTS

INTRODUCTION: THE NATURE OF PHILOSOPHY

JAMES / MONTAGUE / SCHLICK
DEWEY / RUSSELL

Philosophy, like religion, seems to defy precise definition. The subject is complex and diverse, an initial difficulty; and a second difficulty arises from the fact that individual philosophers see the task of philosophy differently, and usually make their definitions of it part of their general philosophic positions. Nor is etymology fully helpful: "philosophy" is derived from the Greek *philein*, to love, and *sophia*, wisdom; but the meaning of wisdom is somewhat obscure, and of course the definition reflects Greek rather than other views of philosophy. Perhaps one should ask "what is philosophy" after, rather than before, exposure to the field.

Yet a general characterization of philosophy, even if tentative, will help to delineate our field of study and to distinguish it from other inquiries. Here our main clues are taken from the history of philosophy. Looking back over that history, we discover that philosophy has attempted to do four distinguishable though interrelated things. It has sought to work out some inclusive conception of the universe in all its aspects, including man's place in it. Here philosophy has been synthetic. Making use of the beliefs of common sense and the results of science, and adding to them the insights of our moral, esthetic, and religious experiences, it has undertaken to "see life steadily and see it whole." It has also been speculative, advancing hypotheses that seem, at least, to transcend the deliverances of ordinary experience. To put it briefly, philosophy in this activity is the attempt to give a comprehensive theory of reality as a whole.

A second philosophical activity has been called technically "phenomenological." Here the interest of the philosopher has been not so much speculative as descriptive, and descriptive in a complete and, at least initially, uninterpreted sense. Many facets of our experience are not immediately obvious, and some are neither clear to common sense nor studied by the natural sciences. Still others may be so muddied by inherited beliefs and interpretations that the philosopher feels obliged to return to the data, to the facts themselves. Facts must be revealed, the implicit made explicit, and the misinterpreted or uninterpreted brought forward for examination.

Besides these two activities, there has been yet a third that, unlike the others, is close to the etymology of "philosophy." Philosophers have sometimes tried to provide not only a vision of the world in which we live, but standards and guides for individual and social action as well. The principles of right and wrong, the norms of associative life, the meaning of the good life—such concerns have been central to the philosopher's search for "wisdom."

In pursuit of the real and the ideal, synoptically and descriptively, philosophers have usually engaged in a fourth activity that we shall call criticism or analysis. Perhaps less exciting, yet essential to the philosophic spirit, analysis has included a critical assessment of the assumptions or presuppositions and of the methods upon which common sense, the sciences, and even philosophy rely. Analytic inquiries have also been directed toward key terms like "real," "true," "good," "matter," "mind," "space," and "time," which play a central role in all systematic thinking. Here the philosopher—whatever his ultimate goal may be— is simply searching for fundamental clarity and understanding.

These four activities, then—the speculative, the descriptive, the normative, and the analytic—seem to describe the philosopher's work. But how shall we view these activities in their interrelationship? Some philosophers would answer that they are all *parts* of an inclusive philosophic activity, and any philosophy that aims to be truly adequate must include all of them, as did those of the great classical philosophers like Plato, Aristotle, Spinoza, and Hegel. Another group of philosophers would regard these activities not as parts but as different *kinds* of philosophy, the implication being that the student must choose one kind from among them. This is the view held by many philosophers today. Some follow the lead of men like Ludwig Wittgenstein, arguing that philosophy can be neither speculative, descriptive, nor normative, and that it should therefore limit itself to the activity of analysis. Others, such as the followers of John Dewey, contend that philosophy's chief business is normative, that it should be primarily "a search for the ends and values that give direction to our collective human activities." Only a relatively few contemporary thinkers, such for example as those influenced by Alfred North Whitehead, urge that philosophy should return to its original speculative interests as well.

The selections in this introduction present a variety of views about the nature of philosophy and of these various philosophic activities. They should be read as introductory statements, subject to later development and articulation. Following them is the presentation of the first of the six major movements or positions in philosophy that are our main subjects of study. Each of the six begins with a brief definition of the position represented, followed by an examination of the chief historical sources of the movement, and then a tracing of the development of that position through its treatment of a variety of problems of philosophic interest. The goal of our study is not only to understand the meaning of philosophy, but also to grasp something of the spirit of a general perspective in philosophy and to examine the solutions to problems of human concern that these perspectives offer.

These problems provide a basis for distinguishing the divisions of philosophy that are recognized by most if not all philosophers, regardless of their commitments about the nature of philosophy itself, their manner in treating them, or the conclusions reached in them. Here again we shall give only introductory statements about these divisions, and allow the selections to develop them. First is the discipline named *metaphysics*. Metaphysics can be defined as the general theory of reality. Among the questions it has traditionally asked are, What is the nature of reality? Is reality one or many? and, Is reality purposive or mechanical? It is usually subdivided into the following fields: *ontology*, or theory of being; *cosmology*, or theory of the cosmos; *rational psychology*, or theory of mind and mind's place in nature; *rational theology*, or theory of divinity; and *axiology*, or theory of values and of the place of values in reality. Generally, the methods in metaphysical investigation have been speculative rather than experimental; frequently, in fact, metaphysics and speculation have been taken as synonymous.

The second major subdivision of philosophy is *epistemology*, or theory of knowledge. Among its questions are, What is the nature of knowledge? What is the source of knowledge? and, What is the criterion of knowledge? A third subdivision is usually called the *normative sciences*, chiefly because it deals with problems of value in relation to rules or standards. The major normative sciences are *logic*, the study of arguments; *ethics*, the study of the individual good; *social philosophy*, the study of the social good; *esthetics*, the normative science of art and the beautiful; and *philosophy of religion*, the philosophic examination of religious beliefs and practices. Last is a group of studies to which no special name has been traditionally given, but which we shall call the "philosophies of." They are alike in that each of them begins with some limited area of experience and then seeks to relate that area to a general philosophic position. The philosophy of science is one study from this group that is included in this volume.

Such, then, are the major activities and fields of philosophy. We turn now from talk about philosophy to talk in philosophy. In so doing, we will meet problems which are among the most important a human being can face, and with which many of the best minds of Western culture have wrestled. The struggle for understanding will not always be easy, nor will the conclusions examined be satisfactory; but always the activity will be important. Whoever has "wondered," as Aristotle put it, about man, truth, and reality will find the study of philosophy a priceless adventure—even though, with Spinoza, we must conclude by observing that "all good things are as difficult as they are rare."

1. PHILOSOPHY AND ITS CRITICS
William James (1842-1910)

Philosophy must not only define itself, but must consider objections to its activities as well. In this selection the well-known American psychologist and philosopher William James addresses himself both to definition and defense. James' definition of philosophy follows the etymology of the word, emphasizing philosophy's concern for the general and universal, but noting also that it expresses a personal temper and purpose rather than a neatly bounded discipline. The objections James examines are among those commonly raised against philosophy. He finds them partly, but not necessarily, valid.

The progress of society is due to the fact that individuals vary from the human average in all sorts of directions, and that the originality is often so attractive or useful that they are recognized by their tribe as leaders, and become objects of envy or admiration, and setters of new ideals.

Among the variations, every generation of men produces some individuals exceptionally preoccupied with theory. Such men find matter for puzzle and astonishment where no one else does. Their imagination invents explanations and combines them. They store up the learning of their time, utter prophecies and warnings, and are regarded as sages. Philosophy, etymologically meaning the love of wisdom, is the work of this class of minds, regarded with an indulgent relish, if not with admiration, even by those who do not understand them or believe much in the truth which they proclaim.

The selection is from Chapter I of William James, *Some Problems of Philosophy* (New York: Longmans, Green & Co., 1911), pp. 3-27, with omissions. Copyright © 1911 by Longmans, Green & Company. Reprinted by permission of Paul R. Reynolds & Son, 599 Fifth Avenue, New York 17, N. Y.

Philosophy, thus become a race-heritage, forms in its totality a monstrously unwieldy mass of learning. So taken, there is no reason why any special science like chemistry, or astronomy, should be excluded from it. By common consent, however, special sciences are today excluded, for reasons presently to be explained; and what remains is manageable enough to be taught under the name of philosophy by one man if his interests be broad enough.

If this were a German textbook I should first give my abstract definition of the topic, thus limited by usage, then proceed to display its *"Begriff, und Eintheilung* [concept and division]," and its *"Aufgabe und Methode* [task and method]." But as such displays are usually unintelligible to beginners, and unnecessary after reading the book, it will conduce to brevity to omit that chapter altogether, useful though it might possibly be to more advanced readers as a summary of what is to follow.

I will tarry a moment, however, over the matter of definition. Limited by the omission of the special sciences, the name of philosophy has come more and more to denote ideas of universal scope exclusively.

The principles of explanation that underlie all things without exception, the elements common to gods and men and animals and stones, the first *whence* and the last *whither* of the whole cosmic procession, the conditions of all knowing, and the most general rules of human action—these furnish the problems commonly deemed philosophic *par excellence;* and the philosopher is the man who finds the most to say about them. Philosophy is defined in the usual scholastic textbooks as "the knowledge of things in general by their ultimate causes, so far as natural reason can attain to such knowledge." This means that explanation of the universe at large, not description of its details, is what philosophy must aim at; and so it happens that a view of anything is termed philosophic just in proportion as it is broad and connected with other views, and as it uses principles not proximate, or intermediate, but ultimate and all-embracing, to justify itself. Any very sweeping view of the world is a philosophy in this sense, even though it may be a vague one. It is a *Weltanschauung,* an intellectualized attitude towards life. Professor Dewey well describes the constitution of all the philosophies that actually exist, when he says that philosophy expresses a certain attitude, purpose and temper of conjoined intellect and will, rather than a discipline whose boundaries can be neatly marked off.

To know the chief rival attitudes towards life, as the history of human thinking has developed them, and to have heard some of the reasons they can give for themselves, ought to be considered an essential part of liberal education. Philosophy, indeed, in one sense of the term is only a compendious name for the spirit in education which the word "college" stands for in America. Things can be taught in dry dogmatic ways or in a philosophic way. At a technical school a man may grow into a first-rate instrument for doing a certain job, but he may miss all the graciousness of mind suggested by the term liberal culture. He may remain a cad, and not a gentleman, intellectually pinned down to his one narrow subject, literal, unable to suppose anything different from what he has seen, without imagination, atmosphere, or mental perspective.

Philosophy, beginning in wonder, as Plato and Aristotle said, is able to fancy everything different from what it is. It sees the familiar as if it were strange, and the strange as if it were familiar. It can take things up and lay them down again. Its mind is full of air that plays round every subject. It rouses us from our native dogmatic slumber and breaks up our caked prejudices. Historically it has always been a sort of fecundation of four different human interests, science, poetry, religion, and logic, by one another. It has sought by hard reasoning for results emotionally valuable. To have some contact with it, to catch its influence, is thus good for both literary and scientific students. By its poetry it appeals to literary minds; but its logic stiffens them up and remedies their softness. By its logic it appeals to the scientific; but softens them by its other aspects, and saves them from too dry a technicality. Both types of student ought to get from philosophy a livelier spirit, more air, more mental background. "Hast any philosophy in thee, Shepherd?"— this question of Touchstone's is the one with which men should always meet one another. A man with no philosophy in him is the most inauspicious and unprofitable of all possible social mates.

I say nothing in all this of what may be called the gymnastic use of philosophic study, the purely intellectual power gained by defining the high and abstract concepts of the philosopher, and discriminating between them.

In spite of the advantages thus enumerated, the study of philosophy has systematic enemies, and they were never as numerous as at the present day. The definite conquests of science and the apparent indefiniteness of philosophy's results partly account for this; to say nothing of man's native rudeness of mind, which maliciously enjoys deriding long words and abstractions. "Scholastic jargon," "medieval dialectics," are for many people synonyms of the word philosophy. With his obscure and uncertain speculations as to the intimate nature and causes of things, the philosopher is likened to a "blind man in a dark room looking for a black cat that is not there." His occupation is described as the art of "endlessly disputing without coming to any conclusion," or more contemptuously still as the "*systematische Misbrauch einer eben zu diesem Zwecke erfundenen Terminologie* [systematic misuse of a terminology produced just for this purpose]."

Only to a very limited degree is this sort of hostility reasonable. I will take up some of the current objections in successive order, since to reply to them will be a convenient way of entering into the interior of our subject.

Objection 1. Whereas the sciences make steady progress and yield applications of matchless utility, philosophy makes no progress and has no practical applications.

Reply. The opposition is unjustly founded, for the sciences are themselves branches of the tree of philosophy. As fast as questions got accurately answered, the answers were called "scientific," and what men call "philosophy" today is but the residuum of questions still unanswered. At this very moment we are seeing two sciences, psychology and general biology, drop off from the parent trunk and take independent root as specialties. The more general philosophy cannot as a rule follow the voluminous details of any special science. . . .

Philosophy in the full sense is only *man thinking,* thinking about generalities rather than about particulars. But whether about generalities or particulars, man thinks always by the same methods. He observes, discriminates, generalizes, classifies, looks for causes, traces analogies, and makes hypotheses. Philosophy, taken as something distinct from science or from practical affairs, follows no method peculiar to itself. All our thinking today has evolved gradually out of primitive human thought, and the only really important changes that have come over its manner (as distinguished from the matters in which it believes) are a greater hesitancy in asserting its convictions, and the habit of seeking verification for them whenever it can. . . .

Objection 2. Philosophy is dogmatic, and pretends to settle things by pure reason, whereas the only fruitful mode of getting at truth is to appeal to concrete experience. Science collects, classes, and analyzes facts, and thereby far outstrips philosophy.

Reply. This objection is historically valid. Too many philosophers have aimed at closed systems, established *a priori,* claiming infallibility, and to be accepted or rejected only as totals. The sciences on the other hand, using hypotheses only, but always seeking to verify them by experiment and observation, open a way for indefinite self-correction and increase. At the present day, it is getting more and more difficult for dogmatists claiming finality for their systems, to get a hearing in educated circles. Hypothesis and verification, the watchwords of science, have set the fashion too strongly in academic minds.

Since philosophers are only men thinking about things in the most comprehensive possible way, they can use any method whatsoever freely. Philosophy must, in any case, complete the sciences, and must incorporate their methods. One cannot see why, if such a policy should appear advisable, philosophy might not end by forswearing all dogmatism whatever, and become as hypothetical in her manners as the most empirical science of them all.

Objection 3. Philosophy is out of touch with real life, for which it substitutes abstractions. The real world is various, tangled, painful. Philosophers have, almost without exception, treated it as noble, simple, and perfect, ignoring the complexity of fact, and indulging in a sort of optimism that exposes their systems to the contempt of common men, and to the satire of such writers as Voltaire and Schopenhauer. The great popular success of Schopenhauer is due to the fact that, first among philosophers, he spoke the concrete truth about the ills of life.

Reply. This objection also is historically valid, but no reason appears why philosophy should keep aloof from reality permanently. Her manners may change as she successfully develops. The thin and noble abstractions may give way to more solid and real constructions, when the materials and methods for making such constructions shall be more and more securely ascertained. In the end philosophers may get into as close contact as realistic novelists with the facts of life.

2. PHILOSOPHY AS VISION

W. P. Montague (1873-1953)

Professor Montague begins this selection by explaining some conventional definitions of philosophy and pointing out its relations with science and religion. His real concern, however, is to determine the true task of philosophy. To do this, he observes that knowledge has two dimensions—breadth and certainty. The ideal of knowledge would be to achieve both of these ends, but in fact the ideal is an impossible one. Philosophy therefore, in his view, must sacrifice certainty for breadth and richness of content.

To make his point in another way, Professor Montague distinguishes two questions: *what* are the possibilities open to an event? and, *which* of these possibilities has actually been realized? The latter question he grants to scientific inquiry, but the former, he feels, is the proper one for philosophy. Philosophy must, that is, leave the domain of fact for the realm of possibility, which is known through a speculative philosophic vision. To this suggestion, Professor Montague well realizes, there will be objections, yet he concludes with the belief that the exploration of significant possibilities has its unique and rewarding values.

There are many kinds of philosophers and many definitions of philosophy. Implicit in all of these definitions is the conception of a domain of inquiry broader and vaguer, deeper and more subtle, than the domain of ordinary knowledge. As I see it there are three main types of question

The selection is from W. P. Montague, *Great Visions of Philosophy* (La Salle, Ill.: Open Court Publishing Co., 1950), pp. 3-7, 11-14, 16-18, 20-21. Used by permission of the Open Court Publishing Company.

which philosophy asks. They are the questions of methodology, of metaphysics, and of kalology.

First: What are the ways in which we should attain and verify our knowledge, and how should we interpret truth when we have attained it—as subjective and dependent upon our minds, or as objective and identical with reality? These are the questions comprising methodology with its two branches, logic and epistemology.

Second: What is the general structure

of our cosmos and what are the fundamental forms and principles which underlie that structure and which are presupposed by the sciences that investigate its parts? These are the questions of metaphysics—of synthetic metaphysics or cosmology, and of analytic metaphysics or ontology.

Third: What are the kinds of things which, whether actually existent or merely ideal, arouse in us the specific attitude of "approval" and to which, in token of that attitude, we apply the name "values"—be they exemplified in the beauty of sensory combinations such as those of tone and color, or in the righteousness or moral goodness of character and conduct? These are the questions of kalology, including ethics and esthetics.

The three groups of questions when considered in themselves and in their relation to one another cover pretty completely the entire field of philosophy.

If the foregoing is an approximately correct account of the meaning of philosophy and of its main departments, the nature of its relations to its nearest neighbors, science and religion, is easy to see. Philosophy differs from science in that its questions are more comprehensive and more fundamental, with the natural result that its answers have none of the definitely verifiable character that scientists demand for their answers. Philosophy resembles science, not in the success of its inquiry but in the spirit in which the inquiry is made. The philosopher, like the scientist, is engaged in an intellectual enterprise. They both seek to attain the truth irrespective of whether that truth shall turn out to be glad or sad, edifying or demoralizing. Dispassionate concern for objective truth governs, or ought to govern, every intellectual quest, whether broadly philosophic or narrowly scientific.

The relation in which philosophy stands to religion is the opposite of that in which it stands to science. Religion and philosophy resemble each other in content but are contrasted in spirit. Both seek answers to ultimate rather than proximate problems concerning the universe and man's place in it; but the way of religion is not the way of philosophy. Instead of the audacious individualistic attempt of the philosopher to plumb the mysteries of nature with his own little mind, the religionist, with humility, piety, and faith, joins up with bands of his fellows in the acceptance and practice of beliefs which he feels to be not his own discovery but a divine revelation to men greater than himself, the saints and prophets of his church. Even when the religiously minded person consents to describe his creed as the one true philosophy, he will stress the fact that it is not his philosophy but God's. And, conversely, when the philosopher arrives by free speculative inquiry at a result identical with the creed of his ancestors, he will stress the fact that his conclusions are vindicated by reason rather than accepted on faith.

Up to this point I hope and believe that I have said nothing very new and nothing that is not in accord with the traditional and acceptable conception of philosophy and its affiliations. I wish now to offer for consideration some ideas that I have deeply at heart as to what might be, and ought to be, the aim and function of the philosopher. These ideas, though not in contradiction to the conventional account already given, involve a reversal of what, if I am not mistaken, has been the main emphasis in the traditional procedure of philosophy.

1. THE QUEST FOR CERTAINTY IN PHILOSOPHY AND SCIENCE

Knowledge or truth is like a magnitude of two dimensions. We wish it to be as broad as possible and we wish it to have as high an approximation to certainty as possible. Breadth and richness of content constitute its extensive dimension, degree of validity its intensive dimension. A system of perfect knowledge would cover the entire range of being, and each of its propositions would possess complete certainty. Now, in the search for knowledge as in most other human undertakings we are forced to recognize not only that perfection in any respect is unattainable, but that even the approach to perfection in some one direction is often incompatible with the approach to perfection in some other direction. He who would master a single trade must resign himself to ignorance of others; a jack-of-all-trades can be master of none. To be deep is to be narrow, and to be broad is to be shallow. This tragic incompatibility of the extensive and the intensive coefficients of success is, to be sure, not always present. In some types of enterprise there is the blessing of a positive rather than a negative correlation between depth and breadth, but usually we must choose the one or the other as the object of our principal emphasis.

Already in philosophy such a choice is forced upon us, however loath we may be to recognize it. If in a moment of detachment from our private preoccupations with this or that phase of philosophy we gaze upon the panorama of mighty systems from Democritus and Plato to Hegel and Bergson we shall, I think, be struck by two facts significant in themselves and still more significant in their relation to each other. First, the value of the great philosophies consists far more in breadth and richness of vision than in cogency or rigor of demonstration. Second, in each of the famous systems there is implicitly or explicitly manifested a pathetic pride on the part of its author in the degree of certainty with which his far-flung theories have been proved.

Now it is common enough to find people who are proud of characteristics in which they are really weak, and correspondingly humble in their appraisal of the virtues which they do possess. But in the case of the great philosophers this familiar and engaging human blindness is not only pathetic and comical but most unfortunate in its effects upon the prosperity of the enterprise to which both they and we are committed. Is it not too obvious to mention that the differing pictures of the cosmos cannot all be true, if only because of their contradictoriness to one another? And is it almost as obvious that no one of them, even if it were true in fact, could be proved to be so for reason? The abysmal gap between a metaphysician's conclusions and the meager data on which they are founded is not to be bridged by any logic of demonstration. If the worth of philosophy were to be measured by its certainty philosophy would be in a very poor way.

Despite this, the claim to cogency is always present. Are we not ourselves, as teachers, obsessed by this claim when we strive to disprove this or that doctrine opposed to our own? And do we not in our courses produce in the minds of many of our students the conviction that philosophy is something of a fraud and a bluff—pretending to have scientific validity while completely lacking in that consensus of agreement that science exhibits? If this were all we could probably bear it, for the disillusionment of students should not be allowed to spoil the games played by their teachers. But unfortunately this is by no means all. Disillusionment and a mood of defeatism is making itself felt throughout our entire guild. How can we go on with speculative theories about the constitution of reality when the winds of scientific knowledge in physics, chemistry, biology, and psychology are sweeping around us and covering the once fertile fields of fancy with the arid sands of fact? The ancient Ionians were not plagued with quantum mechanics, benzene rings, reflex arcs, and "learning curves," and there were few known facts to cramp their style. But for us it is different. . . .

2. A KNOWLEDGE OF THE "WHAT" AND A KNOWLEDGE OF THE "WHICH"

The quest for certainty—happily so christened by John Dewey but by him (also happily) not too meticulously pursued—that is the real source of our trouble. We should rid ourselves once for all of our pre-occupation with proving our theories and engage upon a quite different enterprise. Does this mean that we should give up that search for knowledge without which the love of wisdom is but sentimentality? I think not.

Knowledge possesses two quite different levels. There is knowledge of the *what* and there is knowledge of the *which*. The former usually precedes the latter. Before we can know which of two possibilities is realized in fact, we must know, at least to some extent, what the possibilities are between which a choice is to be made. In any pursuit of truth imaginative anticipation precedes logical proof. The proof may be of the concrete, empirical kind established by observation and experiment; or it may be of the abstract, mathematical kind established by formal demonstration. Proof of this second kind gives that superior sort of actuality that is called "necessity," to distinguish it from "contingent" or "brute" fact—fact merely as such. The necessary facts confirmed by mathematical deduction are thicker and richer than the ordinary kind established by sensory observation, but the realm in which they are found is poorer and thinner, comprising as it does only the domain of abstract forms. But, whether the verification be inductive or deductive, a knowledge of what is to be proved must come before the proof itself. Logic can never create or discover; and its function, however important, is secondary rather than primary. It is the censor and arbiter of our fancies, not their maker. In short, it is imagination that proposes and reason that

disposes. Each quite obviously needs the other, and neither is ever found without something of the other.

Scientists like Faraday or Einstein may be blessed with glorious imaginations, and their fame may rest as much upon the hypotheses that they have constructed as upon the proofs that they have carried out or inspired others to carry out. But for these aristocrats, no less than for their humbler brethren who grub for facts with pick and shovel, miscroscope or camera, the ultimate concern of science as such—whether directed to the concrete field of perceptual events or to the abstract field of conceptual forms—is to find out which are and which are not the actual facts. The quest for certainty is the quest of science, and no domain of actuality whatever can be permanently shut off from those who pursue that quest. In very truth the scientists want the earth; and I suggest that we give it to them, while the giving is good.

For us in philosophy what then will remain? Why, of course, the sea will remain, the ocean of possibilities to be discovered by imagination and vision and enjoyed without limit or surcease by us and by all who love beauty and wonder. But if this proposal be accepted, it should not be accepted sulkily and with a feeling of *faute de mieux*. In leaving behind us forever the dry land of fact we are leaving the scene of a series of battles in which we have been increasingly beaten by the ever-increasing armies of science; and in abandoning the place of our defeat we should abandon also that mood of defeatism which has been steadily growing upon us, weakening our courage, withering our spirit, and shamefully narrowing the field of our activities and ambitions. If philosophers will consent gladly and with right good will to embark on this voyage and sail forever the blue waters, where possible rather than proven truths are to be found, I believe that philosophy herself will suffer a sea change into something which, if not rich and strange, will at least be more like her ancient self and refreshingly different from the doleful and bedraggled creature which, during recent years, she seems to have become.

3. PHILOSOPHY AS VISION: ITS AIM AND SCOPE AND JUSTIFICATION

To the proposal that philosophy abandon the domain of the actual for the domain of the possible and substitute inquiry as to the *what* for inquiry as to the *which,* I shall receive from some of my colleagues a rough response. "Thank you for nothing," they will say. "Is it not bad enough that science has taken all our possessions and left us holding the bag—a bag that once contained all time and existence but which now holds just empty air? Are we to add irony to tragedy and continue as ghosts of our former selves, mere playboys of the intellectual world, blowing vain bubbles of fancy? And because scientists will have none of us there is no reason for supposing that artists will make much of us. The thin and grandiose abstractions of the metaphysicians are even poorer for poetry than for science. Far better that we surrender completely in the knowledge that we have outlasted our time and are needed no longer. We live in a world of science and are ruled by a dictatorship of fact. Under that iron rule there is no place for the free activity of philosophical imagination."

To escape being utterly crushed by such rejoinders to my plan for preserving philosophy by offering to it a new function and a new domain, I beg leave to return for a moment to the shelter of the metaphor that I have been playing with, and to point out that when I urge that philosophers should cruise the seas of possibility it is a quite special cruise that I have in mind. Not the cruise to distant havens, still less the jolly week-end cruise to Nowhere with which prohibition once made us familiar. Rather would I urge a sober and conservative cruise along the shores of fact, keeping within easy distance of the great landmarks of established knowledge and directing our imaginative vision only upon those possibilities which are severely pertinent to the truths already discovered and to the truths that are still to come. In short, philosophy should be concerned not with bare possibilities but with real possibilities—not the golden mountain and the mooncalf or any idle fancy, but the real alternatives between which a later knowledge will or may decide. . . .

To confine one's attention to the actual is to narrow one's spirit to brutish dimensions. The distinctive glory of the human mind is its power to detach itself, not only from the *here* and *now* but from the *there* and *then* of existence, and bathe its tired memories in ideal waters. So it is that the great visions of philosophy, even if considered merely as visions, are precious and imperishable possessions of our culture. Even when their content has been proved false to the world of fact they lend to that world depth and richness of meaning, and norms for appraising its values which otherwise could never come. The pride of philosophy is in its disclosure of significant possibility. This ought to be so in the future and it has been so in the past. We should interpret our subject in this way, not only because there is nothing else that we can do in an age of science, but also because, as I have already said, the best work of our predecessors has exemplified this deal and no other. Great in vision, poor in proof, philosophy at its highest has ever been. . . .

But while lacking the value of their primary intent, the arguments of philosophy often possess a real though secondary importance. They may clarify the meaning of the vision though failing utterly to substantiate its truth. For this reason the study of a philosopher's vision should sometimes include the study of the proofs advanced in its support; and for the same reason a consideration of the biography of a philosopher, and of the age and social setting in which he lived, may be pertinent to an appreciation of his *aperçu*. To that extent and to that extent alone should the facts of philosophic history and the circumstances under which a philosophic vision was produced be of concern to students of philosophy. For the rest, they should be left to the professional historians who, because they are comparatively undistracted by the duties of interpreting and evaluating the meaning of past performances, will be bet-

ter able to describe to us accurately the times and places of their occurrence. . . .

What proof is to science, and what faith is to religion, probability is to philosophy. An elusive, glimmering, dancing light, it nevertheless gives to imagination a sense of proportion; and to the visions of imagination it gives a perspective whereby their greatly varying values can be discovered and appraised. Though probability for the philosopher never rises to certainty, it suffices to keep him in wholesome proximity to the land of fact. That land he has abandoned to science, but he need never lose sight of its snug and sheltering harbors, to which upon occasion he may retreat.

3. PHILOSOPHY AS CLARIFICATION

Moritz Schlick (1882-1936)

Very different indeed is the conception of philosophy offered by Professor Schlick. Philosophy, he believes, cannot be a science in the sense of proposing truths, for there are no specifically philosophical truths at all. If we are dealing with a question of fact, the truth about that fact must be determined by the sciences; and all factual questions are scientific questions. But what then are the problems of philosophy? Professor Schlick sees them as problems of meaning. Philosophy, he argues, is the pursuit of meaning, of the finding and clarification of meaning. And this is an essential step in all inquiry; for we must have a grasp of meaning before we can proceed to determine truth and falsehood. The meaning of an idea is known when we know the circumstances that would make it either true or false. Such a conception reduces philosophy to analytic clarification, and philosophic problems in the end either turn out to be scientific ones or disappear. Yet because of the absolutely fundamental necessity of clarification, philosophy remains the queen of the sciences, even though she is not herself a science.

The study of the history of philosophy is perhaps the most fascinating pursuit for anyone who is eager to understand the civilization and culture of the human race, for all of the different elements of human na-

The selection is from Moritz Schlick, *The Future of Philosophy* (College of the Pacific Publications in Philosophy, 1932), pp. 45-47, 54-62. Used by permission of the Editor.

ture that help to build up the culture of a certain epoch or a nation mirror themselves in one way or another in the philosophy of that epoch or of that nation.

The history of philosophy can be studied from two distinct points of view. The first point of view is that of the historian; the second one is that of the philosopher. They will each approach the study of the history of philosophy with different feelings. The historian will be excited to the greatest enthusiasm by the great works of the thinkers of all times, by the spectacle of the immense mental energy and imagination, zeal and unselfishness which they have devoted to their creations, and the historian will derive the highest enjoyment from all of these achievements. The philosopher, of course, when he studies the history of philosophy will also be delighted, and he cannot help being inspired by the wonderful display of genius throughout all the ages. But he will not be able to rejoice at the sight that philosophy presents to him with exactly the same feelings as the historian. He will not be able to enjoy the thoughts of ancient and modern times without being disturbed by feelings of an entirely different nature.

The philosopher cannot be satisfied to ask, as the historian would ask of all the systems of thought—are they beautiful, are they brilliant, are they historically important? and so on. The only question which will interest him is the question, "What truth is there in these systems?" And the moment he asks it he will be discouraged when he looks at the history of philosophy because, as you all know, there is so much contradiction between the various systems—so much quarreling and strife between the different opinions that have been advanced in different periods by different philosophers belonging to different nations—that it seems at first quite impossible to believe that there is anything like a steady advance in the history of philosophy as there seems to be in other pursuits of the human mind, for example, science or technique. . . .

We want to ask the question, "What will be the future of philosophy?" entirely from the point of view of the philosopher. However, to answer the question we shall have to use the method of the historian because we shall not be able to say what the future of philosophy will be except in so far as our conclusions are derived from our knowledge of its past and its present.

The first effect of a historical consideration of philosophical opinions is that we feel sure we cannot have any confidence in any one system. If this is so—if we cannot be Cartesians, Spinozists, Kantians, and so forth—it seems that the only alternative is that we become skeptics, and we become inclined to believe that there can be no true system of philosophy because if there were any such system it seems that at least it must have been suspected and would have shown itself in some way. However, when we examine the history of philosophy honestly, it seems as if there were no traces of any discovery that might lead to unanimous philosophical opinion.

This skeptical inference, in fact, has been drawn by a good many historians, and even some philosophers have come to the conclusion that there is no such thing as philosophical advancement, and that philosophy itself is nothing but the history of philosophy. This view was advocated by more than one philosopher in the beginning of the century and it has been called "historicism." That philosophy consists only of its own history is a strange view to take, but it has been advocated and defended with apparently striking arguments. However, we shall not find ourselves compelled to take such a skeptical view.

We have thus far considered two possible alternatives that one may believe in. First, that the ultimate truth is really presented in some one system of philosophy and secondly, that there is no philosophy at all, but only a history of thought. I do not tonight propose to choose either of these two alternatives; but I should like to propose a third view which is neither skeptical nor based on the belief that there can be any system of philosophy as a system of ultimate truths. I intend to take an entirely different view of philosophy and it is, of course, my opinion that this view of philosophy will some time in the future be adopted by everybody. . . .

Before I go any farther, let me state shortly and clearly that I believe Science should be defined as the *"pursuit of truth"* and Philosophy as the *"pursuit of meaning."* Socrates has set the example of the true philosophic method for all times. But I shall have to explain this method from the modern point of view.

When we make a statement about anything we do this by pronouncing a sentence and the sentence stands for the proposition. This proposition is either true or false, but before we can know or decide whether it is true or false we must know what this proposition says. We must know the meaning of the proposition first. After we know its sense we may be able to find out whether it is true or not. These two things, of course, are inseparably connected. I cannot find out the truth without knowing the meaning, and if I know the meaning of the proposition I shall at least know the beginning of some path that will lead to the discovery of the truth or falsity of the proposition even if I am unable to find it at present. It is my opinion that the future of philosophy hinges on this distinction between the discovery of sense and the discovery of truth.

How do we decide what the sense of a proposition is, or what we mean by a sentence which is spoken, written, or printed? We try to present to ourselves the significance of the different words that we have learned to use, and then endeavor to find sense in the proposition. Sometimes we can do so and sometimes we cannot; the latter case happens, unfortunately, most frequently with propositions which are supposed to be "philosophical."—But how can we be quite sure that we really know and understand what we mean when we make an assertion? What is the ultimate criterion of its sense? The answer is this: We know the meaning of a proposition when we are able to indicate exactly the circumstances

under which it would be true (or, what amounts to the same, the circumstances which would make it false). The description of these circumstances is absolutely the only way in which the meaning of a sentence can be made clear. After it has been made clear we can proceed to look for the actual circumstances in the world and decide whether they make our proposition true or false. There is no vital difference between the ways we decide about truth and falsity in science and in every-day life. Science develops in the same ways in which does knowledge in daily life. The method of verification is essentially the same; only the facts by which scientific statements are verified are usually more difficult to observe. . . .

From what I have said so far it might seem that philosophy would simply have to be defined as the science of meaning, as, for example, astronomy is the science of the heavenly bodies, or zoology the science of animals, and that philosophy would be a science just as other sciences, only its subject would be different, namely, "Meaning." . . .

But philosophy is not a science in this sense. There can be no science of meaning, because there cannot be any set of true propositions about meaning. The reason for this is that in order to arrive at the meaning of a sentence or of a proposition we must go beyond propositions. For we cannot hope to explain the meaning of a proposition merely by presenting another proposition. When I ask somebody, "What is the meaning of this or that?" he must answer by a sentence that would try to describe the meaning. But he cannot ultimately succeed in this, for his answering sentence would be but another proposition and I would be perfectly justified in asking "What do you mean by *this?*" We would perhaps go on defining what he meant by using different words, and repeat his thought over and over again by using new sentences. I could always go on asking "But what does this new proposition mean?" You see, there would never be any end to this kind of inquiry, the meaning could never be clarified, if there were no other way of arriving at it than by a series of propositions. . . .

Our conclusion is that philosophy was misunderstood when it was thought that philosophical results could be expressed in propositions, and that there could be a system of philosophy consisting of a system of propositions which would represent the answers to "philosophical" questions. There are no specific "philosophical" truths which would contain the solution of specific "philosophical" problems, but philosophy has the task of finding the meaning of *all* problems and their solutions. It must be defined as *the activity of finding meaning*.

Philosophy is an activity, not a science, but this activity, of course, is at work in every single science continually, because before the sciences can discover the truth or falsity of a proposition they have to get at the meaning first. And sometimes in the course of their work they are surprised to find, by the contradictory results at which they arrive, that they have been using words without a perfectly clear meaning, and then they will have to turn to the philosophical activity of clarification, and they cannot go on with the pursuit of truth before the pursuit of meaning has been successful. In this way philosophy is an extremely important factor within science and it very well deserves to bear the name of "The Queen of Sciences."

The Queen of Sciences is not itself a science. It is an activity which is needed by all scientists and pervades all their other activities. But all real problems are scientific questions, there are no others.

And what was the matter with those great questions that have been looked upon —or rather looked up to—as specific "philosophical problems" for so many centuries? Here we must distinguish two cases. In the

first place, there are a great many questions which look like questions because they are formed according to a certain grammatical order but which nevertheless are not real questions, since it can easily be shown that the words, as they are put together, do not make logical sense. . . .

In the second place, there are some "philosophical" problems which prove to be real questions. But of these it can always be shown by proper analysis that they are capable of being solved by the methods of science although we may not be able to apply these methods at present for merely technical reasons. We can at least say what would have to be done in order to answer the question even if we cannot actually do it with the means at our disposal. In other words: problems of this kind have no special "philosophical" character, but are simply scientific questions. They are always answerable in principle, if not in practice, and the answer can be given only by scientific investigation.

Thus the fate of all "philosophical problems" is this: Some of them will disappear by being shown to be mistakes and misunderstandings of our language and the others will be found to be ordinary scientific questions in disguise. These remarks, I think, determine the whole future of philosophy. . . .

It is my hope that the philosophers of the future will see that it is impossible for them to adopt, even in outward appearance, the methods of the scientists. Most books on philosophy seem to be, I must confess, ridiculous when judged from the most elevated point of view. They have all the appearance of being extremely scientific books because they seem to use the scientific language. However, the finding of meaning cannot be done in the same way as the finding of truth. This difference will come out much more clearly in the future. There is a good deal of truth in the way in which Schopenhauer [1] (although his own thinking seems to me to be very imperfect indeed) describes the contrast between the real philosopher and the academic scholar who regards philosophy as a subject of scientific pursuit. Schopenhauer had a very clear instinct when he spoke disparagingly of the "professorial philosophy of the professors of philosophy." His opinion was that one should not try to teach philosophy at all but only the history of philosophy and logic; and a good deal may be said in favor of this view.

I hope I have not been misunderstood as though I were advocating an actual separation of scientific and philosophical work. On the contrary, in most cases future philosophers will have to be scientists because it will be necessary for them to have a certain subject matter on which to work—and

[1 The reference is to Arthur Schopenhauer (1788-1860), brilliant and many-sided German philosopher who propounded a deterministic and pessimistic view. *Ed.*]

they will find cases of confused or vague meaning particularly in the foundations of the sciences. But, of course, clarification of meaning will be needed very badly also in a great many questions with which we are concerned in our ordinary human life. Some thinkers, and perhaps some of the strongest minds among them, may be especially gifted in this practical field. In such instances, the philosopher may not have to be a scientist —but in all cases he will have to be a man of deep understanding. In short he will have to be a *wise* man.

I am convinced that our view of the nature of philosophy will be generally adopted in the future; and the consequence will be that it will no longer be attempted to teach philosophy as a system. We shall teach the special sciences and their history in the true philosophical spirit of searching for clarity and, by doing this, we shall develop the philosophical mind of future generations. This is all we can do, but it will be a great step in the mental progress of our race.

4. PHILOSOPHY AS CRITIC OF ACTION
John Dewey (1859-1952)

The most influential American thinker of the twentieth century, Dewey was the leading spokesman of the philosophy of pragmatism or, as he frequently called it, instrumentalism. Thought, he believed, is essentially related to action and serves "to clarify men's ideas as to the social and moral strifes of their own day." For Dewey, this is also the principal task of philosophy. To emphasize his view, Dewey presents his interpretations of the prephilosophical roots of philosophy and especially of traditional speculative philosophy. The latter, he argues, is a covert substitute for custom as the sanction of moral and social values. He thus tends to deny any validity to the more speculative disciplines of philosophy such as transcendent metaphysics, and rather sees them simply as rationalizations of moral and political beliefs. The result of this interpretation, Dewey concludes, is a changed attitude toward the nature and function of philosophy in modern culture.

The selection is from Chapter I of John Dewey, *Reconstruction In Philosophy* (New York: Henry Holt and Co., Inc., 1920), pp. 1-27, with omissions. Used by permission of the publisher.

To treat the early beliefs and traditions of mankind as if they were attempts at scientific explanation of the world, only erroneous and absurd attempts, is thus to be guilty of a great mistake. The material out of which philosophy finally emerges is irrelevant to science and to explanation. It is figurative, symbolic of fears and hopes, made of imaginations and suggestions, not significant of a world of objective fact intellectually confronted. It is poetry and drama, rather than science, and is apart from scientific truth and falsity, rationality or absurdity of fact in the same way in which poetry is independent of these things.

This original material has, however, to pass through at least two stages before it becomes philosophy proper. One is the stage in which stories and legends and their accompanying dramatizations are consolidated. At first the emotionalized records of experiences are largely casual and transitory. Events that excite the emotions of an individual are seized upon and lived over in tale and pantomime. But some experiences are so frequent and recurrent that they concern the group as a whole. They are socially generalized. The piecemeal adventure of the single individual is built out till it becomes representative and typical of the emotional life of the tribe. Certain incidents affect the weal and woe of the group in its entirety and thereby get an exceptional emphasis and elevation. A certain texture of tradition is built up; the story becomes a social heritage and possession; the pantomime develops into the stated rite. Tradition thus formed becomes a kind of norm to which individual fancy and suggestion conform. An abiding framework of imagination is constructed. A communal way of conceiving life grows up into which individuals are inducted by education. Both unconsciously and by definite social requirement individual memories are assimilated to group memory or tradition, and individual fancies are accommodated to the body of beliefs characteristic of a community. Poetry becomes fixated and systematized. The story becomes a social norm. The original drama which re-enacts an emotionally important experience is institutionalized into a cult. Suggestions previously free are hardened into doctrines. . . .

Although a necessary antecedent, this organization and generalization of ideas and principles of belief is not the sole and sufficient generator of philosophy. There is still lacking the motive for logical system and intellectual proof. This we may suppose to be furnished by the need of reconciling the moral rules and ideals embodied in the traditional code with the matter of fact positivistic knowledge which gradually grows up. For man can never be wholly the creature of suggestion and fancy. The requirements of continued existence make indispensable some attention to the actual facts of the world. Although it is surprising how little check the environment actually puts upon the formation of ideas, since no notions are too absurd not to have been accepted by some people, yet the environment does enforce a certain minimum of correctness under penalty of extinction. That certain things are foods, that they are to be found in certain places, that water drowns, fire burns, that sharp points penetrate and cut, that heavy things fall unless supported, that there is a certain regularity in the changes of day and night and the alteration of hot and cold, wet and dry:—such prosaic facts force themselves upon even primitive attention. . . .

For a long time the imaginative body of beliefs closely connected with the moral habits of a community group and with its emotional indulgences and consolations persists side by side with the growing body of matter of fact knowledge. Wherever possible they are interlaced. At other points, their inconsistencies forbid their interweaving, but the two things are kept apart as if in different compartments. Since one is merely superimposed upon the other their incompatibility is not felt, and there is no need of reconciliation. In most cases, the two kinds of mental products are kept apart because they become the possession of separate social classes. The religious and poetic beliefs having acquired a definite social and political value and function are in the keeping of a higher class directly associated with the ruling elements in the society. The workers and craftsmen who possess the prosaic matter of fact knowledge are likely to occupy a low social status, and their kind of knowledge is affected by the social disesteem entertained for the manual worker who engages in activities useful to the body. It doubtless was this fact in Greece which in spite of the keenness of observation, the extraordinary power of logical reasoning and the great freedom of speculation attained by the Athenian, postponed the general and systematic employment of the experimental method. Since the industrial craftsman was only just above the slave in social rank, his type of knowledge and the method upon which it depended lacked prestige and authority.

Nevertheless, the time came when matter of fact knowledge increased to such bulk and scope that it came into conflict with not merely the detail but with the spirit and temper of traditional and imaginative beliefs. Without going into the vexed question of how and why, there is no doubt that this is just what happened in what we term the sophistic movement in Greece, within which originated philosophy proper in the sense in which the Western world understands that term. The fact that the sophists had a bad name given them by Plato and Aristotle, a name they have never been able to shake off, is evidence that with the sophists the strife between the two types of belief was the emphatic thing, and that the conflict had a disconcerting effect upon the traditional system of religious beliefs and the moral code of conduct bound up with it.

Although Socrates was doubtless sincerely interested in the reconciliation of the two sides, yet the fact that he approached the matter from the side of matter of fact method, giving its canons and criteria primacy, was enough to bring him to the condemnation of death as a contemner of the gods and a corrupter of youth. . . .

Yet the more acute and active minds, like that of Plato himself, could no longer be content to accept, along with the conservative citizen of the time, the old beliefs in the old way. The growth of positive knowledge and of the critical, inquiring spirit undermined these in their old form. The advantages in definiteness, in accuracy, in verifiability were all on the side of the new knowledge. Tradition was noble in aim and scope, but uncertain in foundation. The unquestioned life, said Socrates, was not one fit to be lived by man, who is a questioning being because he is a rational being. Hence he must search out the reason of things, and not accept them from custom and political authority. What was to be done? Develop a method of rational investigation and proof which should place the essential elements of traditional belief upon an unshakable basis; develop a method of thought and knowledge which while purifying tradition should preserve its moral and social values unimpaired; nay, by purifying them, add to their power and authority. To put it in a word, that which had rested upon custom was to be restored, resting no longer upon the habits of the past, but upon the very metaphysics of Being and the Universe. Metaphysics is a substitute for custom as the source and guarantor of higher moral and social values —that is the leading theme of the classic philosophy of Europe, as evolved by Plato and Aristotle—a philosophy, let us always recall, renewed and restated by the Christian philosophy of Medieval Europe.

Out of this situation emerged, if I mistake not, the entire tradition regarding the function and office of philosophy which till very recently has controlled the systematic and constructive philosophies of the Western world. If I am right in my main thesis that the origin of philosophy lay in an attempt to reconcile the two different types of mental product, then the key is in our hands as to the main traits of subsequent philosophy so far as that was not of a negative and heterodox kind. In the first place, philosophy did not develop in an unbiased way from an open and unprejudiced origin. It had its task cut out for it from the start. It had a mission to perform, and it was sworn in advance to that mission. It had to extract the essential moral kernel out of the threatened traditional beliefs of the past. So far so good; the work was critical and in the interests of the only true conservatism—that which will conserve and not waste the values wrought out by humanity. But it was also precommitted to extracting this moral essence in a spirit congenial to the spirit of past beliefs. The association with imagination and with social authority was too intimate to be deeply disturbed. It was not possible to conceive of the content of social institutions in any form radically different from that in which they had existed in the past. It became the work of philosophy to justify on rational grounds the spirit, though not the form, of accepted beliefs and traditional customs. . . .

And this brings us to a second trait of philosophy springing from its origin. Since it aimed at a rational justification of things that had been previously accepted because of their emotional congeniality and social prestige, it had to make much of the apparatus of reason and proof. Because of the lack of intrinsic rationality in the matters with which it dealt, it leaned over backward, so to speak, in parade of logical form. In dealing with matters of fact, simpler and rougher ways of demonstration may be resorted to. It is enough, so to say, to produce the fact in question and point to

it—the fundamental form of all demonstration. But when it comes to convincing men of the truth of doctrines which are no longer to be accepted upon the say-so of custom and social authority, but which also are not capable of empirical verification, there is no recourse save to magnify the signs of rigorous thought and rigid demonstration. Thus arises that appearance of abstract definition and ultra-scientific argumentation which repels so many from philosophy but which has been one of its chief attractions to its devotees.

At the worst, this has reduced philosophy to a show of elaborate terminology, a hair-splitting logic, and a fictitious devotion to the mere external forms of comprehensive and minute demonstration. Even at the best, it has tended to produce an overdeveloped attachment to system for its own sake, and an overpretentious claim to certainty. Bishop Butler [1] declared that probability is the guide of life; but few philosophers have been courageous enough to avow that philosophy can be satisfied with anything that is merely probable. The customs dictated by tradition and desire had claimed finality and immutability. They had claimed to give certain and unvarying laws of conduct. Very early in its history philosophy made pretension to a similar conclusiveness, and something of this temper has clung to classic philosophies ever since. They have insisted that they were more scientific than the sciences—that, indeed, philosophy was necessary because after all the special sciences fail in attaining final and complete truth. There have been a few dissenters who have ventured to assert, as did William James, that "philosophy is vision" and that its chief function is to free men's minds from bias and prejudice and to enlarge their perceptions of the world about them. But in the main philosophy has

[1 Joseph Butler (1692-1752), English divine and bishop, whose judgment that probability is the guide of life is frequently quoted. *Ed.*]

set up much more ambitious pretensions. To say frankly that philosophy can proffer nothing but hypotheses, and that these hypotheses are of value only as they render men's minds more sensitive to life about them, would seem like a negation of philosophy itself.

In the third place, the body of beliefs dictated by desire and imagination and developed under the influence of communal authority into an authoritative tradition, was pervasive and comprehensive. It was, so to speak, omnipresent in all the details of the group life. Its pressure was unremitting and its influence universal. It was then probably inevitable that the rival principle, reflective thought, should aim at a similar universality and comprehensiveness. It would be as inclusive and far-reaching metaphysically as tradition had been socially. Now there was just one way in which this pretension could be accomplished in conjunction with a claim of complete logical system and certainty.

All philosophies of the classic type have made a fixed and fundamental distinction between two realms of existence. One of these corresponds to the religious and supernatural world of popular tradition, which in its metaphysical rendering became the world of highest and ultimate reality. Since the final source and sanction of all important truths and rules of conduct in community life had been found in superior and unquestioned religious beliefs, so the absolute and supreme reality of philosophy afforded the only sure guaranty of truth about empirical matters, and the sole rational guide to proper social institutions and individual behavior. Over against this absolute and noumenal reality which could be apprehended only by the systematic discipline of philosophy itself stood the ordinary empirical, relatively real, phenomenal world of everyday experience. It was with this world that the practical affairs and utilities of men were connected. It was

to this imperfect and perishing world that matter of fact, positivistic science referred.

This is the trait which, in my opinion, has affected most deeply the classic notion about the nature of philosophy. Philosophy has arrogated to itself the office of demonstrating the existence of a transcendent, absolute or inner reality and of revealing to man the nature and features of this ultimate and higher reality. It has therefore claimed that it was in possession of a higher organ of knowledge than is employed by positive science and ordinary practical experience, and that it is marked by a superior dignity and importance—a claim which is undeniable *if* philosophy leads man to proof and intuition of a Reality beyond that open to day-by-day life and the special sciences.

This claim has, of course, been denied by various philosophers from time to time. But for the most part these denials have been agnostic and skeptical. They have contented themselves with asserting that absolute and ultimate reality is beyond human ken. But they have not ventured to deny that such Reality would be the appropriate sphere for the exercise of philosophic knowledge provided only it were within the reach of human intelligence. Only comparatively recently has another conception of the proper office of philosophy arisen. This course of lectures will be devoted to setting forth this different conception of philosophy in some of its main contrasts to what this lecture has termed the classic conception. At this point, it can be referred only to by anticipation and in cursory fashion. It is implied in the account which has been given of the origin of philosophy out of the background of an authoritative tradition; a tradition originally dictated by man's imagination working under the influence of love and hate and in the interest of emotional excitement and satisfaction. Common frankness requires that it be stated that this account of the origin of philosophies claiming to deal with absolute Being in a systematic way has been given with malice prepense. It seems to me that this genetic method of approach is a more effective way of undermining this type of philosophic theorizing than any attempt at logical refutation could be.

If this lecture succeeds in leaving in your minds as a reasonable hypothesis the idea that philosophy originated not out of intellectual material, but out of social and emotional material, it will also succeed in leaving with you a changed attitude toward traditional philosophies. They will be viewed from a new angle and placed in a new light. New questions about them will be aroused and new standards for judging them will be suggested.

If any one will commence without mental reservations to study the history of philosophy not as an isolated thing but as a chapter in the development of civilization and culture; if one will connect the story of philosophy with a study of anthropology, primitive life, the history of religion, literature and social institutions, it is confidently asserted that he will reach his own independent judgment as to the worth of the account which has been presented today. Considered in this way, the history of philosophy will take on a new significance. What is lost from the standpoint of would-be science is regained from the standpoint of humanity. Instead of the disputes of rivals about the nature of reality, we have the scene of human clash of social purpose and aspirations. Instead of impossible attempts to transcend experience, we have the significant record of the efforts of men to formulate the things of experience to which they are most deeply and passionately attached. Instead of imper-

sonal and purely speculative endeavors to contemplate as remote beholders the nature of absolute things-in-themselves, we have a living picture of the choice of thoughtful men about what they would have life to be, and to what ends they would have men shape their intelligent activities.

Any one of you who arrives at such a view of past philosophy will of necessity be led to entertain a quite definite conception of the scope and aim of future philosophizing. He will inevitably be committed to the notion that what philosophy has been unconsciously, without knowing or intending it, and, so to speak, under cover, it must henceforth be openly and deliberately. When it is acknowledged that under disguise of dealing with ultimate reality, philosophy has been occupied with the precious values embedded in social traditions, that it has sprung from a clash of social ends and from a conflict of inherited institutions with incompatible contemporary tendencies, it will be seen that the task of future philosophy is to clarify men's ideas as to the social and moral strifes of their own day. Its aim is to become so far as is humanly possible an organ for dealing with these conflicts. That which may be pretentiously unreal when it is formulated in metaphysical distinctions becomes intensely significant when connected with the drama of the struggle of social beliefs and ideals. Philosophy which surrenders its somewhat barren monopoly of dealings with Ultimate and Absolute Reality will find a compensation in enlightening the moral forces which move mankind and in contributing to the aspirations of men to attain to a more ordered and intelligent happiness.

5. THE VALUE OF PHILOSOPHY

Bertrand Russell (1872-   )

Has the study of philosophy any value? This is the question to which Lord Russell addresses himself in the following selection. It arises, he believes, because philosophy can in no way be likened to the sciences with their certainty, progress, and application. Rather, though aiming to give us knowledge, philosophy ends in uncertainty. But it is precisely this uncertainty that Lord Russell finds to be of value in the study of philosophy. While not of direct utility to the "practical" man, philosophy nevertheless affects the lives of those who do pursue it, for the greatness of its problems fosters greatness of mind and encourages the traditional liberal virtues of freedom and impartiality. That is, philosophy frees us from the tyranny of custom by enlarging our awareness of possibilities, and it leads to impartiality by relating us to the cosmos in which we have our being.

It will be well to consider now, what is the value of philosophy and why it ought to be studied. It is the more necessary to consider this question, in view of the fact that many men, under the influence of science or of practical affairs, are inclined to doubt whether philosophy is anything better than innocent but useless trifling, hair-splitting distinctions, and controversies on matters concerning which knowledge is impossible.

This view of philosophy appears to result, partly from a wrong conception of the ends of life, partly from a wrong conception of the kind of goods which philosophy strives to achieve. Physical science, through the medium of inventions, is useful to innumerable people who are wholly ignorant of it; thus the study of physical science is to be recommended, not only, or primarily, because of the effect on the student, but rather because of the effect on mankind in general. Thus utility does not belong to philosophy. If the study of philosophy has any value at all for others than students of philosophy, it must be only indirectly, through its effects upon the lives of those who study it. It is in these effects, therefore, if anywhere, that the value of philosophy must be primarily sought.

But further, if we are not to fail in our endeavor to determine the value of philosophy, we must first free our minds from the prejudices of what are wrongly called "practical" men. The "practical" man, as this word is often used, is one who recognizes only material needs, who realizes that men must have food for the body, but is oblivious of the necessity of providing food for the mind. If all men were well off, if poverty and disease had been reduced to their lowest possible point, there would still remain much to be done to produce a valuable society; and even in the existing world the goods of the mind are at least as important as the goods of the body. It is exclusively among the goods of the mind that the value of philosophy is to be found; and only those who are not indifferent to these goods can be persuaded that the study of philosophy is not a waste of time.

Philosophy, like all other studies, aims primarily at knowledge. The knowledge it aims at is the kind of knowledge which gives unity and system to the body of the sciences, and the kind which results from a

The selection is from Bertrand Russell, *The Problems of Philosophy* (Oxford: Oxford University Press, 1912), pp. 153-161. Used by permission of the publisher.

critical examination of the grounds of our convictions, prejudices, and beliefs. But it cannot be maintained that philosophy has had any very great measure of success in its attempts to provide definite answers to its questions. If you ask a mathematician, a mineralogist, a historian, or any other man of learning, what definite body of truths has been ascertained by his science, his answer will last as long as you are willing to listen. But if you put the same question to a philosopher, he will, if he is candid, have to confess that his study has not achieved positive results such as have been achieved by other sciences. It is true that this is partly accounted for by the fact that, as soon as definite knowledge concerning any subject becomes possible, this subject ceases to be called philosophy, and becomes a separate science. The whole study of the heavens, which now belongs to astronomy, was once included in philosophy; Newton's great work was called "the mathematical principles of natural philosophy." Similarly, the study of the human mind, which was a part of philosophy, has now been separated from philosophy and has become the science of psychology. Thus, to a great extent, the uncertainty of philosophy is more apparent than real: those questions which are already capable of definite answers are placed in the sciences, while those only to which, at present, no definite answer can be given, remain to form the residue which is called philosophy.

This is, however, only a part of the truth concerning the uncertainty of philosophy. There are many questions—and among them those that are of the profoundest interest to our spiritual life—which, so far as we can see, must remain insoluble to the human intellect unless its powers become of quite a different order from what they are now. Has the universe any unity of plan or purpose, or is it a fortuitous concourse of atoms? Is consciousness a permanent part of the universe, giving hope of

indefinite growth in wisdom, or is it a transitory accident on a small planet on which life must ultimately become impossible? Are good and evil of importance to the universe or only to man? Such questions are asked by philosophy, and variously answered by various philosophers. But it would seem that, whether answers be otherwise discoverable or not, the answers suggested by philosophy are none of them demonstrably true. Yet, however slight may be the hope of discovering an answer, it is part of the business of philosophy to continue the consideration of such questions, to make us aware of their importance, to examine all the approaches to them, and to keep alive that speculative interest in the universe which is apt to be killed by confining ourselves to definitely ascertainable knowledge.

Many philosophers, it is true, have held that philosophy could establish the truth of certain answers to such fundamental questions. They have supposed that what is of most importance in religious beliefs could be proved by strict demonstration to be true. In order to judge of such attempts, it is necessary to take a survey of human knowledge, and to form an opinion as to its methods and its limitations. On such a subject it would be unwise to pronounce dogmatically; but if our investigations do not lead us astray, we shall be compelled to renounce the hope of finding philosophical proofs of religious beliefs. We cannot, therefore, include as part of the value of philosophy any definite set of answers to such questions. Hence, once more, the value of philosophy must not depend upon any supposed body of definitely ascertainable knowledge to be acquired by those who study it.

The value of philosophy is, in fact, to be sought largely in its very uncertainty. The man who has no tincture of philosophy goes through life imprisoned in the prejudices derived from common sense, from

the habitual beliefs of his age or his nation, and from convictions which have
grown up in his mind without the co-opera-
tion or consent of his deliberate reason. To
such a man the world tends to become
definite, finite, obvious; common objects
rouse no questions, and unfamiliar possibilities are contemptuously rejected. As soon
as we begin to philosophize, on the contrary, we find . . . that even the most
everyday things lead to problems to which
only very incomplete answers can be given.
Philosophy, though unable to tell us with
certainty what is the true answer to the
doubts which it raises, is able to suggest
many possibilities which enlarge our
thoughts and free them from the tyranny of
custom. Thus, while diminishing our feeling
of certainty as to what things are, it greatly
increases our knowledge as to what they
may be; it removes the somewhat arrogant
dogmatism of those who have never travelled into the region of liberating doubt,
and it keeps alive our sense of wonder by
showing familiar things in an unfamiliar
aspect.

Apart from its utility in showing unsuspected possibilities, philosophy has a value
—perhaps its chief value—through the
greatness of the objects which it contemplates, and the freedom from narrow and
personal aims resulting from this contemplation. The life of the instinctive man is
shut up within the circle of his private
interests: family and friends may be included, but the outer world is not regarded
except as it may help or hinder what comes
within the circle of instinctive wishes. In
such a life there is something feverish and
confined, in comparison with which the
philosophic life is calm and free. The private
world of instinctive interests is a small one,
set in the midst of a great and powerful
world which must, sooner or later, lay our
private world in ruins. Unless we can so enlarge our interests as to include the whole
outer world, we remain like a garrison in a
beleaguered fortress, knowing that the enemy prevents escape and that ultimate surrender is inevitable. In such a life there is
no peace, but a constant strife between the
insistence of desire and the powerlessness of
will. In one way or another, if our life is to
be great and free, we must escape this
prison and this strife.

One way of escape is by philosophic
contemplation. Philosophic contemplation
does not, in its widest survey, divide the
universe into two hostile camps—friends
and foes, helpful and hostile, good and bad
—it views the whole impartially. Philosophic contemplation, when it is unalloyed,
does not aim at proving that the rest of the
universe is akin to man. All acquisition of
knowledge is an enlargement of the Self,
but this enlargement is best attained when
it is not directly sought. It is obtained when
the desire for knowledge is alone operative,
by a study which does not wish in advance
that its objects should have this or that
character, but adapts the Self to the characters which it finds in its objects. This
enlargement of Self is not obtained when,
taking the Self as it is, we try to show that
the world is so similar to this Self that
knowledge of it is possible without any admission of what seems alien. The desire to
prove this is a form of self-assertion, and
like all self-assertion, it is an obstacle to the
growth of Self which it desires, and of which
the Self knows that it is capable. Self-assertion, in philosophic speculation as elsewhere,
views the world as a means to its own ends;
thus it makes the world of less account
than Self, and the Self sets bounds to the
greatness of its goods. In contemplation, on
the contrary, we start from the not-Self,
and through its greatness the boundaries of
Self are enlarged; through the infinity of
the universe the mind which contemplates
it achieves some share in infinity.

For this reason greatness of soul is not
fostered by those philosophies which assimilate the universe to Man. Knowledge is a

form of union of Self and not-Self; like all union, it is impaired by dominion, and therefore by any attempt to force the universe into conformity with what we find in ourselves. There is a widespread philosophical tendency towards the view which tells us that Man is the measure of all things, that truth is man-made, that space and time and the world of universals are properties of the mind, and that, if there be anything not created by the mind, it is unknowable and of no account for us. This view, if our previous discussions were correct, is untrue; but in addition to being untrue, it has the effect of robbing philosophic contemplation of all that gives it value, since it fetters contemplation to Self. What it calls knowledge is not a union with the not-Self, but a set of prejudices, habits, and desires, making an impenetrable veil between us and the world beyond. The man who finds pleasure in such a theory of knowledge is like the man who never leaves the domestic circle for fear his word might not be law.

The true philosophic contemplation, on the contrary, finds its satisfaction in every enlargement of the not-Self, in everything that magnifies the objects contemplated, and thereby the subject contemplating. Everything, in contemplation, that is personal or private, everything that depends upon habit, self-interest, or desire, distorts the object, and hence impairs the union which the intellect seeks. By thus making a barrier between subject and object, such personal and private things become a prison to the intellect. The free intellect will see as God might see, without a *here* and *now*, without hopes and fears, without the trammels of customary beliefs and traditional prejudices, calmly, dispassionately, in the sole and exclusive desire of knowledge—knowledge as impersonal, as purely contemplative, as it is possible for man to attain. Hence also the free intellect will value more the abstract and universal knowledge into which the ac-

cidents of private history do not enter, than the knowledge brought by the senses, and dependent, as such knowledge must be, upon an exclusive and personal point of view and a body whose sense organs distort as much as they reveal.

The mind which has become accustomed to the freedom and impartiality of philosophic contemplation will preserve something of the same freedom and impartiality in the world of action and emotion. It will view its purposes and desires as parts of the whole, with the absence of insistence that results from seeing them as infinitesimal fragments in a world of which all the rest is unaffected by any one man's deeds. The impartiality which, in contemplation, is the unalloyed desire for truth, is the very same quality of mind which, in action, is justice, and in emotion is that universal love which can be given to all, and not only to those who are judged useful or admirable. Thus contemplation enlarges not only the objects of our thoughts, but also the objects of our actions and our affections: it makes us citizens of the universe, not only of one walled city at war with all the rest. In this citizenship of the universe consists man's true freedom, and his liberation from the thraldom of narrow hopes and fears.

Thus, to sum up our discussion of the value of philosophy; Philosophy is to be studied, not for the sake of any definite answers to its questions, since no definite answers can, as a rule, be known to be true, but rather for the sake of the questions themselves; because these questions enlarge our conception of what is possible, enrich our intellectual imagination, and diminish the dogmatic assurance which closes the mind against speculation; but above all because, through the greatness of the universe which philosophy contemplates, the mind also is rendered great, and becomes capable of that union with the universe which constitutes its highest good.

I

CLASSICAL REALISM

PLATO / ARISTOTLE / COPLESTON

WILD / GILSON / CICERO

MARITAIN / ST. ANSELM / ST. THOMAS AQUINAS

One of the oldest and most continuously active movements in philosophy is classical realism. It is termed "classical" both to indicate its origins in Greek thought and to distinguish it from other realistic movements such as Scottish realism and the American new realism. It is called "realism" because its basic doctrine holds that there is a world of real existence, independent of man, which can be known by the human intellect. Such a proposition may seem to be only "common sense," and the realist would urge that his position is one which acknowledges and remains true to the beliefs of the common man. But realism is not simply common sense; for in its efforts to articulate the deliverances of ordinary experience, it becomes a technically developed philosophy.

The fundamental theses of this philosophy may be divided into three groups.[1] First, realists believe that metaphysics is a valid and important discipline —indeed, that it is the central philosophical activity. They define metaphysics as the science of being, and a concern for being and its principles will be found throughout realist writings. Furthermore, realists believe that experience shows that both material and immaterial beings exist; no reduction of one mode of being to another is possible. In their epistemology realists urge that these beings can be known by the human mind as they are in themselves. Thus truth can be grasped

---

[1] These theses are part of the platform of a contemporary professional organization, the Association for Realistic Philosophy. See John Wild (ed.), *The Return To Reason* (Chicago: Henry Regnery Co., 1953), pp. 357-363.

by man, and it is universal, absolute, and eternal. Truth is achieved through a cognitive union of the intellect and its objects. In the areas of individual and social action, realists find that knowledge—especially that which treats human nature—provides mankind with reliable and unchanging norms of good and evil.

In developing these theses, realists have adopted a common and basic technical vocabulary whose key terms include "substance," "form," "matter," "essence," and "existence." Such terms were utilized by the Greek philosophers Plato and Aristotle, and we find in their writings an effort to define and explain them. Realists through the centuries have been guided by the thought of these Greek thinkers; even today they believe that important truths are contained in the Greek philosophic tradition, and that that tradition merits careful and continuous study. Hence it is necessary for our study of realism to begin with selections from Plato and Aristotle.

1 / INTRODUCTION

The general problem of Plato's dialogue *The Republic,* from which the first selection is taken, is that of justice. In attempting to determine its meaning, Plato is led to assert that justice, which must be based on knowledge, will be achieved only when rulers become philosophers. This however raises the question of the meaning of "philosopher," which leads Plato to a statement of the "Theory of Forms," his most distinctive philosophic tenet.

Socrates, spokesman in the dialogue, defines the philosopher as a lover of wisdom. But what is a lover of wisdom? He is one who has, or loves, knowledge, one who has a passion for truth. But what, again, is the meaning of this reply? Seeking to explain his answer, Socrates points out that there is a difference between one who dreams and one who does not, in that the dreamer mistakes an appearance for a reality. The philosopher as a pursuer of truth has an object before him which his thought is seeking. And that natural object of his thought is the real.

Again we must ask, however, what this real is. It must be something, Socrates asserts, which *is.* But a thing which *is* cannot be something which comes into being, changes, and then passes away and is no more. What *is* is permanent and unchanging. Nothing with these characteristics is found in the world of nature, the world observed by the senses; and this leads Plato to assert that reality belongs not to the sense world which is always in a state of flux, but rather to a world of forms, to a world of intelligible objects known by the "mind's eye," and perfect, immutable, and eternal. Consider a brief illustration of what Plato is saying: a bridge is constructed of materials like steel and concrete; but it is not only material, for it embodies certain laws or principles involving stresses and strains, gravitation, and so on. The bridge itself, belonging to the sense world, may endure for a long time, but it is not eternal. The mathematical and physical laws, however, known and utilized by the engineer, do not perish when the bridge does;

they are eternal and hence, for Plato, they are the real, not the mortar and steel.

Thus in his Theory of Forms, Plato holds a dualistic metaphysics of the real and sense worlds. In maintaining this view, he raises such problems as those of truth, knowledge, form, and reality. His discussions of these problems had a direct influence not only on his famous pupil Aristotle and through him on all realists, but also on the whole course of Western thought.

THE THEORY OF FORMS

Plato (428-348)

[Socrates.] Now, if we are to have a chance of escaping from the assailants you speak of, I think it essential to give them our definition of "philosophers," and shew whom we mean, when we venture to assert that such persons ought to govern; in order that, their character having been made thoroughly apparent, we may be able to defend ourselves by demonstrating that it is the natural province of these men to embrace philosophy, and take the lead in a state, and the province of all others to let philosophy alone, and follow the lead of the former.

[Glaucon.] Yes, it is a fit time, he said, to give this definition.

Come then, follow my steps, and let us try if we can in some way or other satisfactorily expound our notion.

Lead on.

Will it be necessary to remind you, or do you remember without it, that when we state that a man loves some object, we are bound to shew, if the statement be correct, that he does not love one part of that object to the exclusion of another, but that he takes delight in the whole?

I require to be reminded, it seems: for I do not quite understand you.

Such a confession, Glaucon, would have been more appropriate in another person.

A man of your amorous nature ought not to forget that a boy-loving, susceptible person is in some way or other attracted and excited by the charms of all who are in their bloom, and thinks they all deserve his attentions and addresses. Is not this the manner in which you behave to your favorites? You will praise a boy with a turned-up nose as having a winning look; the hooked nose of another you consider king-like; while a third, whose nose is between the two extremes, has a beautifully-proportioned face: the dark, you say, have a manly look, the fair are children of the gods: and who do you suppose coined the phrase "olive-pale" but a lover who could palliate and easily put up with paleness, when he found it on the cheek of youth? In one word, you invent all kinds of excuses, and employ every variety of expression, sooner than reject any that are in the flower and prime of life.

If you wish, replied Glaucon, to found on my case an assertion that the amatively disposed thus act, I will allow you to do so for the argument's sake.

To take another illustration; do you not observe that those who are fond of wine behave in a precisely similar manner, finding some excuse or other to admire every sort of wine?

Yes, certainly.

And you doubtless have seen how persons who love honor will command a company, if they cannot lead an army, and in default of being honored by great and

The selection is from Book V of *The Republic of Plato* (trs. John Llewelyn Davies and David James Vaughan) (London: Macmillan and Company, Ltd., 1895), pp. 187-196.

important personages, are glad to receive the respect of the little and the insignificant; so covetous are they of honor in any shape.

Precisely so.

Then answer me yes or no to this: when we describe a man as having a longing for something, are we to assert that he longs after the whole class that the term includes, or only after one part, to the exclusion of another?

He longs after the whole.

Then shall we not maintain that the philosopher, or the lover of wisdom, is one who longs for wisdom, not partially, but wholly?

True.

So that if a person makes difficulties about his studies, especially while he is young and unable to discriminate between what is profitable and what is not, we shall pronounce him to be no lover of learning or of wisdom; just as when a man is nice about his eating, we deny that he is hungry or desirous of food, and instead of describing him as fond of eating, we call him a bad feeder.

Yes, and we shall be right in doing so.

On the other hand, when a man is ready and willing to taste every kind of knowledge, and addresses himself joyfully to his studies with an appetite which never can be satiated, we shall justly call such a person a philosopher, shall we not?

To which Glaucon replied, You will find your description includes a great number and a strange company. All the lovers of sights, I conclude, are philosophers, because they take pleasure in acquiring knowledge; and those who delight in hearing, are a very singular set to reckon among philosophers,—those, I mean, who will never, if they can help it, be present at a philosophical discussion, or any similar entertainment, but are unfailing attendants at every Dionysian festival, whether held in town or country, and run about as if they had let

out their ears on hire to listen to all the choruses of the season. Are we then to give the title of philosophers to all these people, as well as to others who have a taste for any similar studies, and to the professors of small arts?

Certainly not, I replied: we must call them counterfeit philosophers.

And whom, he asked, do you call genuine philosophers?

Those who love to see truth, I answered.

In that, he said, you cannot be wrong: but will you explain what you mean?

That would be not at all easy, with a different questioner: but you, I imagine, will make me the admission I require.

What is it?

That since beauty is the opposite of deformity, they are two things.

Of course they are.

Then since they are two, each of them taken separately is one thing.

That also is true.

The same thing may be said likewise of justice and injustice, good and evil, and all general conceptions. Each of them in itself is one thing, but by the intermixture with actions and bodies and with one another, through which they are everywhere made visible, each appears to be many things.

You are right.

By the help of this principle, then, I draw a distinction between those whom you described just now as lovers of sights, lovers of arts, and practical persons, on the one hand, and on the other, those about whom we are now inquiring, to whom alone we can rightly give the name of philosophers.

Explain what you mean.

Why, I suppose that those who love seeing and hearing admire beautiful sounds, and colors, and forms, and all artistic products into which these enter; but the nature of beauty in itself their understanding is unable to behold and embrace.

Yes, it certainly is as you say.

But those who are capable of reaching to the independent contemplation of abstract beauty will be rare exceptions, will they not?

They will indeed.

Therefore if a man recognizes the existence of beautiful things, but disbelieves in abstract beauty, and has not the power to follow should another lead the way to the knowledge of it, is his life, think you, a dreaming or a waking one? Just consider. Is it not dreaming when a person, whether asleep or awake, mistakes the likeness of anything for the real thing of which it is a likeness?

I confess I should say that a person in that predicament was dreaming.

Take again the opposite case, of one who acknowledges an abstract beauty, and has the power to discern both this essence and the objects into which it enters, and who never mistakes such objects for the essence, nor the essence for the objects; does such a person, think you, live a dreaming or a waking life?

A waking life, undoubtedly.

If so, shall we not be right in calling the mental process of the latter knowledge, because he really knows; and that of the former, opinion, because he merely opines?

Yes, perfectly right.

Well then, should this person, whom we describe as opining, but not knowing, grow wroth with us, and contend that what we say is not true, shall we be able to appease his indignation and gently convince him, disguising from him the fact that he is in an unsound state?

That were certainly desirable.

Come then, consider what we are to say to him. Would you like us to make certain inquiries of him, premising that if he really does know anything, we shall not in the least grudge him his knowledge?—on the contrary, we shall be truly glad to find that it is so. But answer us this question, we shall say: When a man knows, does he know

something or nothing? Be so good, Glaucon, as to make answer in his behalf.

My answer will be, that he knows something.

Something that exists, or does not exist?

Something that exists: for how could a thing that does not exist be known?

Are we then quite sure of this fact, in whatever variety of ways we might examine it, that what completely exists may be completely known, whereas that which has no existence at all must be wholly unknown?

We are perfectly sure of it.

Good: now, if there be anything so constituted, as at the same time to be and not to be, must it not lie somewhere between the purely existent and the absolutely non-existent?

It must.

Well then, as knowledge is correlative to the existent, and the negation of knowledge necessarily to the non-existent, must we not try to find something intermediate between science and ignorance, if there is anything of the kind, to correspond to this that is intermediate between the existent and the non-existent?

Yes, by all means.

Do we speak of opinion as a something?

Undoubtedly we do.

Do we consider it a faculty distinct from science or identical with it?

Distinct from it.

Therefore opinion is appointed to one province and science to another, each acting according to its own peculiar power.

Just so.

Is it not the nature of science, as correlative to the existent, to know how the existent exists? But first there is a distinction which I think it necessary to establish.

What is that?

We shall hold that faculties, as a certain general class, are the things whereby we, and every other thing, are able to do whatever we can do: for example, I call sight and hearing faculties, if you happen to understand the special conception which I wish to describe.

I do understand it.

Then let me tell you what view I take of them. In a faculty I do not see either color, or form, or any of those qualities that I observe in many other things, by regarding which I can in many cases distinguish to myself between one thing and another. No, in a faculty I look only to its province and its function, and thus I am led to call it in each case by this name, pronouncing those faculties to be identical whose provinces and functions are identical, and those diverse whose provinces and functions are diverse. But pray, how do you proceed?

Just in the same way.

Now then, return with me, my excellent friend. Under what general term do you class science? Do you make it a faculty?

Yes I do; it is of all the faculties the most powerful.

Well, is opinion a faculty; or are we to refer it to some other denomination?

Not to any other: for that whereby we are able to opine, can only be opinion.

Well, but a little while ago you admitted that science and opinion are not identical.

Why how could a sensible man identify the fallible with the infallible?

Very good: so we are clearly agreed that opinion is a thing distinct from science?

It is.

If so, each of them has by its nature a different province, and a different efficacy.

The inference is inevitable.

Science, I believe, has for its province to know the nature of the existent.

Yes.

And the province of opinion is, we say, to opine.

Yes.

Does opinion take cognizance of precisely that material which science knows? In other words, is the object-matter of opinion identical with that of science? or is that impossible?

It is impossible, after the admissions we have made; that is, if it be granted that different faculties have different provinces, and that both opinion and science are faculties, and that the two are distinct,—all which we affirm. These premises make it impossible to identify the object-matter of science and that of opinion.

Then, if the existent is the object-matter of knowledge, that of opinion must be something other than the existent?

It must.

Well then, does opinion exercise itself upon the non-existent, or is it impossible to apprehend even in opinion that which does not exist? Consider—does not the person opining carry his thought towards something? Or is it possible to have an opinion, but an opinon about nothing?

It is impossible.

Then the person who opines has an opinion about some one thing?

Yes.

Well, but the non-existent could not be called some one thing; it might, on the contrary, with the greatest truth be styled nothing.

Just so.

But to the non-existent we were constrained to assign ignorance, and to the existent, knowledge.

And rightly.

Then neither the existent nor the non-existent is the object of opinion?

No.

Therefore opinion cannot be either ignorance or knowledge.

Apparently not.

Then does it lie beyond either of these, so as to surpass either knowledge in certainty or ignorance in uncertainty?

It does neither.

Then tell me, do you look upon opinion as something more dusky than knowledge, more luminous than ignorance?

Yes, it is strongly so distinguished from either.

And does it lie within these extremes?

Yes.

Then opinion must be something between the two.

Precisely so.

Now a little while back, did we not say, that if anything could be found so constituted as at the same time to be and not to be, it must lie between the purely existent and the absolutely not existent, and must be the object neither of science nor yet of ignorance, but of a third faculty, which should be similarly discovered in the interval between science and ignorance?

We did.

But now we have discovered between these two a faculty which we call opinion.

We have.

It will remain then for us, apparently, to find what that is which partakes both of being and of not being, and which cannot be rightly said to be either of these absolutely; in order that, should it discover itself to us, we may justly proclaim it to be the object of opinion; thus assigning extremes to extremes, and means to means. Am I not right?

You are.

These positions then being laid down, I shall proceed to interrogate that worthy man who denies the existence of anything absolutely beautiful, or any form of abstract beauty, which for ever continues the same and unchangeable, though he acknowledges a variety of beautiful objects,—that lover of sights, who cannot endure to be told that beauty is one, and justice one, and so on of the rest:—My good sir, I shall say, of all these beautiful things, is there one which may not appear ugly? Of all these just things, is there one which may not appear unjust? Or of these holy things, one which may not appear unholy?

No, answered Glaucon: they must inevitably appear in a certain sense both fair and foul, both just and unjust, both holy and unholy.

Again, may not the many double things be considered halves just as well as doubles?

Just as well.

In the same way, have the things which we describe as great, small, light, heavy, any better claim to these titles, than to their opposites?

No, they will always be equally entitled to either.

Would it be more correct, then, to predicate of those many objects, that each of them is, or is not, that which it is said to be?

You remind me of the conundrums with a contradiction in them, that are proposed at table, and of the children's riddle * about the eunuch who threw at the bat, hinting darkly with what he hit it, and on what it sat: for the things in question have the same ambiguous character, and one cannot positively conceive of them as either being or not being, as both being and not being, or as neither.

Can you tell then, said I, what to do with them, or where they may be better put than in the interspace between being and not being? For I presume they will not appear either darker than the non-existent, and so more non-existent, or more luminous than the existent, and therefore more existent.

You are perfectly right.

Hence we have discovered, apparently, that the mass of notions, current among the mass of men, about beauty, justice, and the rest, roam about between the confines of pure existence and pure non-existence.

We have.

And we before admitted, that if anything of this kind should be brought to light, it ought to be described as the object of

---

* The riddle is thus given by the Scholiast: "A tale is told, that a man and not a man, seeing and not seeing a bird and not a bird, seated on wood and not on wood, hit it and did not hit it with a stone and not a stone." It is partly explained in the text, and we leave the further solution of it to the reader. [Translators' note.]

opinion, and not of knowledge,—these intermediate rovers being caught by the intermediate faculty.

We did make this admission.

Therefore, when people have an eye for a multitude of beautiful objects, but can neither see beauty in itself, nor follow those who would lead them to it,—when they behold a number of just things, but not justice in itself, and so in every instance, we shall say they have in every case an opinion, but no real knowledge of the things about which they opine.

It is a necessary inference.

But what, on the other hand, must we say of those who contemplate things as they are in themselves, and as they exist ever permanent and immutable? Shall we not speak of them as knowing, not opining?

That also is a necessary inference.

Then shall we not assert that such persons admire and love the objects of knowledge,—the others, the objects of opinion? For we have not forgotten, have we, that we spoke of these latter as loving and looking upon beautiful sounds and colors and the like, while they will not hear of the existence of an abstract beauty?

We have not forgotten it.

Shall we commit any fault then, if we call these people philodoxical rather than philosophical, that is to say, lovers of opinion rather than lovers of wisdom? And will they be very much offended with us for telling them so?

No, not if they will take my advice: for it is wrong to be offended with the truth.

Those therefore that set their affections on that which in each case really exists, we must call not philodoxical, but philosophical?

Yes, by all means.

Known simply as The Philosopher, in the Middle Ages, Aristotle developed one of the truly major philosophies of our civilization. He began his career as a student in Plato's Academy, remaining there for nearly twenty years and undoubtedly accepting the main tenets of Platonism. Toward the end of that period, however, Aristotle began to differ from his master, and upon Plato's death he left the Academy to develop his own position.

There were differences in temperament between the two philosophers which were at least partly responsible for their differences in thought. Plato was more mystical—his philosophy has appealed to mystics through the centuries—whereas Aristotle, perhaps influenced by his birth into a medical family, was more empirical, more scientific, more concerned with the experienced world.

This concern led Aristotle finally to reject the Platonic dualism and to assert that reality is the concrete, individual thing: this man, this stone, this animal. He uses the word "ousia," or substance, to refer to the truly real. But because individuals alone are real, the principles explaining and accounting for them must therefore be intrinsic ones. Aristotle's metaphysical analysis uncovers four factors "that make a thing what it is"—namely, a material, formal, efficient, and final cause. Further, since change is a universal characteristic of things, Aristotle turns to its analysis and finds its explanation in the concepts of potency and actuality.

THE THEORY OF SUBSTANCE

Aristotle (384-322)

[i. *The science of being*.] There is a certain science which makes, as the object of its speculation, being, as far forth as it is being, and the things which are essentially inherent in this. But this is the same with none of those which are called particular sciences; for none of the rest of the sciences examines universally concerning being so far forth as it is being: but, cutting away a certain portion of it, they investigate what is accidental in regard of this; as, for example, the mathematical sciences. But, whereas we are in search of first principles and the topmost causes of being, it is evident that they must needs be absolutely of a certain nature. If, therefore, they, also, who investigate the elements of things were accustomed to investigate these first principles, it is necessary, likewise, that their elements should not have a subsistence according to accident or extrinsically, but rather as intrinsic aspects of being itself. Wherefore, also, must we ascertain the first causes of being, so far as it is being.

[ii. *The meanings of being*.] Now, being is spoken of in various senses, indeed, but in reference to one, and to one certain nature, and not equivocally; but, in like manner, also, as everything conducive to health is termed so in reference to health, partly, indeed, in its preserving that state, and partly in giving rise to it, and partly in being an indication of health, and partly in being receptive of it; and, in like manner, as the medicinal is styled so in reference to the art of medicine; for, indeed, a thing

is called medicinal partly in reference to its possessing the medicinal power, partly in its being by nature adapted for the possession of such, and partly in its being the work of the medicinal art: and we shall receive the predication of other things in a similar manner with these. Thus, however, is being, also, spoken of in various ways indeed, but all in reference to one first meaning: for some things, because they are substances, are styled beings; but others, because they are modifications of substance; and others, because they are on the way to becoming substance, either as corruptions, or privations, or qualities, or things formative or generative, of substance, or of those which are spoken of in reference to substance, or the negations of any of these or of substance. Wherefore, also, even nonbeing we pronounce to "be" nonbeing.

As, then, there is one science of all things pertaining to health, in like manner, also, is this so in the case of other things. For it is the province of one science to speculate concerning not only those things spoken of according to one subject-matter, but also those spoken of in reference to a single nature. For these, also, in a certain manner, are spoken of in accordance with one subject-matter. It is evident, therefore, that it is the province of a single science to speculate concerning beings, so far forth as they are being. But in every respect is the science of ontology strictly a science of that which is first or primary, both on which the other things depend and through which they are denominated. If, then, this is substance, the Philosopher or Metaphysician must needs be in possession of the first principles and causes of substances. . . .

[iii. *The meanings of substance*.] As regards substance, both simple bodies, as, for instance, earth, and fire, and water, and

The selection is from John H. M'Mahon (tr. and ed.), *The Metaphysics of Aristotle* (London: Henry G. Bohn, 1857), pp. 79-80, 127-128, 112-113, 309-311, 236-237, and 241-245. Minor changes have been made from the original text.

such like, are called substances; and, in general, bodies are styled so; and animals consisting of these, and those beings that are of demons, and the parts of these. Now, all these are denominated substances because they are not predicated of a subject, whereas other things are predicated of these. But in another way is that styled substance whatever may be the cause of being, and may be inherent in such as are not predicated of a subject; for example, soul in an animal. Further, as many parts as are inherent in such things that both define and signify "the what" a certain thing is, on the removal of which the whole is taken away,—as, for example, if superficies be taken away body also is destroyed, as some say; and superficies is destroyed by taking away a line; and, in general, number seems too certain to be a thing of this kind: for that if it is removed away nothing can subsist, and that it defines all things,—such parts we may consider substances. Further, the essence of which the formal cause is the definition, this, also, is styled the substance of each thing.

Now, substance happens in two ways to be styled substance, both as the ultimate subject which no longer is predicated of anything else, and as that which may be this certain particular thing, and may be separable; but such is the form and the species of each thing.

[iv. *The four causes of being*.] (1) In one way that is called cause from which, as inherent, anything is produced; as, for example, the brass of a statue, and the silver of a cup, and the genera of these; (2) but, in another way, the form and exemplar are regarded as causes; and this is the reason of the formal cause and the genera of these; as, for instance, in the diapason the cause is the ratio of two to one; and, in general, number and the parts, those that are in the ratio, belong to this order of cause. (3) But, further, that constitutes a cause from whence is the first principle of change or of rest; as, for instance, the designing cause and the father of a child; and, generally speaking, the forming of that which is being formed, and that capable of effecting a change of that which is undergoing a change. (4) Further, a cause is as the end; this, however, is the final cause, as, for instance, health of walking. For why does one walk? we say, that he may have good health; and, saying so, we think that we have assigned the cause. And as many operations, doubtless, as take place between any other source of motion and the end are regarded as causes; for example, of health, tenuity, or purging, or medicines, or instruments, for all these are on account of the end; but they differ from one another in respect of being, some as instruments, and others as things done. Causes, indeed, therefore, are enumerated after this manner.

And seeing that causes are thus multifariously denominated, it happens that many of them are causes of the same thing, not according to accident; for instance, of the statue both the statuary art and the brass, not according to anything that is different, but so far forth as it is a statue; this, however, does not take place in the same manner, but the brass is as matter, and the art as the origin of motion, or the efficient cause. And some things are reciprocally causes of one another; as, for example, labor of a good habit of body, and this latter, again, of labor: yet not in the same manner, but the one is as the end, and the other as the principle of motion. Further, the same thing sometimes is the cause of things that are contrary; for that which when present is the cause of this particular thing, this when absent we sometimes denominate the cause of the contrary: for example, the absence of the pilot is the cause of the capsizing of the boat, the presence of whom is the cause of its preservation. Both, however, as well the presence as the absence of the pilot, are as efficient causes, that is, causes imparting motion. . . .

[v. *The types of change.*] Now, that which undergoes a change is changed partly, indeed, according to accident,—as when we say the musician walks,—and partly when a thing is said simply to be changed in respect of something belonging to this undergoing a change; for example, whatsoever things are changed, are changed according to parts: for the body is reduced to a sound state of health because the eye is restored to a healthy condition. Now, there is something which primarily is moved in itself or essentially, and this is that which may have motion impressed upon it from itself. And there is also something of the same sort in the case of that which imparts motion likewise; for one thing imparts motion according to accident, and another according to a portion, but a third essentially or of itself: and there is something that is the primary source of motion, and there is something that has motion impressed upon it; further is there the time in which, and there is the place from which, and the direction towards which, a thing is moved. But the forms, and passive states, and place into which are moved the things that are being moved, themselves are immovable, as science and heat; but the heat does not constitute motion, yet the process of heating does. The change, however, that does not ensue according to accident does not reside in all things, but in contraries and media, and in contradiction. But a reliance upon this statement may be drawn from induction.

Now, that which undergoes a change is changed either from a subject into a subject, or from that which is not a subject into a subject, or from a subject into a nonsubject, or from a non-subject into a subject: but I mean by a subject that which is made manifest by affirmation. Wherefore, changes must needs be three in number; for that which is from a non-subject into a nonsubject is not properly a change, for it subsists neither between contraries nor between contradiction, because there is not opposition in the case of a transition from a non-subject into a non-subject. The change, indeed, therefore, from that which is a non-subject into a subject, according to contradiction, amounts to generation; and such a change, of course, when simply considered, is simple generation, and when it is partial, it is partial generation: but the change from subject into that which is nonsubject amounts to corruption, which, when it is simply so, is simply corruption; but when it is partial, it is partial corruption.

If, therefore, nonbeing is predicated multifariously, and that according to composition or division does not admit of being put in motion, so neither can it be so with that according to capacity, which is opposed to that which subsists simply; for a thing that is not white, or not good, nevertheless admits of being moved according to accident: for that which is not white may be a man; but this cannot by any means be the case with this particular thing which subsists simply: for it is impossible that nonbeing should be moved; and, if this be admitted, it is impossible, also, that generation amounts to motion; for nonbeing would be produced if it did, for in such a case most especially would it be produced according to accident; yet, nevertheless, it is true to assert of that which is generated simply that a nonbeing has a subsistence. In like manner, also, stands the case with the being in a state of rest. And, doubtless, such are the difficulties that attend on this hypothesis, even on the supposition that everything that is being moved is in place; but what is a nonbeing is not in place, for it would be somewhere. Hence neither does corruption constitute motion, for motion or rest is a thing that is contrary to motion, but corruption is contrary to generation. Since, however, every motion amounts to a certain change, and there are three changes, as just now enumerated, and of these the changes that ensue according to generation and corruption are not motions

—and these are those that subsist according to contradiction—it is necessary that the change from subject into subject should alone constitute motion. Subjects, however, are either contraries or media; and let privation be considered as a thing that is contrary: and it is made manifest by affirmation; for instance, that which is naked and toothless, and that which is black.

[vi. *The nature of actuality*.] But since we have spoken concerning potentiality, such as subsists according to motion, let us frame some definitions and distinctions regarding actuality, both as to what it is, and what sort of a being it has. For the nature of that which is potential, or endued with capacity, likewise, at the same time will be apparent to those who make a division in this matter, because we not only say that this is a thing endued with potentiality or capacity which is fitted by nature to impart motion to something else, or to have motion imparted to itself by something else, either viewed simply or in a certain manner, but we also assert this as being the case after a different mode. Wherefore, in our investigations we shall also treat of these points.

The existence of the thing, however, as actuality, does not subsist in such a way as when we speak of a thing in potentiality; now, we mean by a thing subsisting in potentiality, for instance, mercury in the wood, and the half in the whole, because it can be taken away from the whole: and we term that a scientific person in capacity, even though not actually engaged in speculation, provided only such may be endued with a capacity for speculative pursuits; and we mean by a thing's subsisting in actuality,—now, by an induction of particular cases is the assertion evident which we wish to make, and it is not expedient that we should seek after a definition for everything; but it is sufficient to perceive at a glance that which is analogous,—now, I say, by a thing's subsisting in actuality

we mean that it should be as a person engaged in building stands in relation to that which is fit for being built, and the wakeful to the sleeper, and one who sees to one whose eyes are closed, but who nevertheless possesses the power of vision, and as that which involves a separable subsistence from matter to matter, and as that which has been wrought by art to that which is unwrought. After this mode, then, is actuality compared with capacity or potentiality. By one portion, however, of this difference let actuality be distinguished, and that which is endued with potentiality by the other.

All things, however, are not said to subsist in actuality in a similar way; but either analogically as this thing in this, or relatively to this; and that thing in this particular thing, or relatively to this particular thing. For some things are as motion in respect of potentiality; but other things are as substance in respect of a certain matter. . . .

[vii. *The priority of the actual*.] Since, however, it has been determined in how many ways that which has a priority of subsistence is predicated, it is evident that actuality is prior to potentiality. Now, I mean by potentiality not merely a definite potentiality, which is styled an alternative first principle in another body, so far forth as it is another, but, in general, every first principle which is the originator of motion or rest. For Nature, also, may be ranked in the same genus with potentiality; for she is a first principle which is fit to be the cause of motion, not, however, in another body, but in itself, so far forth as it is itself.

Therefore, prior to every principle of this sort is actuality, both in definition and in substance; but it is, also, in a certain respect prior in duration, and in a certain respect it is not so. That, indeed, therefore, it is prior in definition is evident, for that which is potential in regard of its possibility of actualization, or assuming a state of actuality, such is a thing that is primarily endued with capacity or potentiality; for example, I speak of one that is skilled in building—now, I mean one that has a capacity of building, and I speak of one that is able to see, and I mean one that possesses the capacity of seeing, and of a thing that may be seen, as that which involves the capacity of being seen: and the same reasoning, also, holds good as regards other things. Wherefore, the definition and knowledge of actuality must needs pre-exist the definition and knowledge of potentiality.

But the actual, likewise, is in time prior to potentiality after this mode: namely, the priority of that which actively accomplishes the same thing in species, but not in number. Now, I mean to say this, that, in the case of this particular man existing at present according to actuality, and in the case of the corn, and the horse, and the person who sees, prior in time are the matter, and the seed, and that which is able to see, which in potentiality constitute man, and corn, and one who sees, but are not as yet these in actuality. Prior, however, to these in time are those different things that subsist in actuality, and from which these have been generated; for always from a being in potentiality arises, or is generated, a being in actuality by means of a being in actuality—as man is generated from man, a musician by means of a musician—on the condition of something that is primary in its nature always imparting motion: the moving power at present, however, subsists in actuality. But it has been declared, in our disquisitions concerning substance, that everything that is generated is generated from something, and by something, and that this is the same in species. Wherefore, also, it seems to be impossible that a builder be a person not likely to have built anything, or a harpest to be one who has not harped anything; for one who learns to play upon the harp

learns to play upon the harp by actually playing upon the harp: it is also the case, in like manner, with other artists. . . .

But, unquestionably, it is also prior in substance, at least, in the first place, indeed, then, because those things that are subsequent in generation are prior in form and substance; as a man to a child, and a human being to a seed: for now the one possesses the form, but the other does not. And, in the second place, this is so because everything that is being produced advances towards a first principle and an end; for the final cause is a first principle, and the generation or production is on account of the end. But actuality is an end, and on account of this is potentiality assumed; for not in order that they may have the power of vision do animals see: but they have the power of vision that they may see.

In like manner, also, persons are in possession of the building art, or capacity, that they may actually build, and of the speculative art that they may devise systems of speculation; they do not, however, devise speculative systems that they may have the speculative capacity, unless those who do so for the sake of meditation: yet these by no means speculate absolutely; but they either speculate in this manner, or the fact is so that they have not in any wise an occasion to speculate. . . .

And since of some things that which is ultimate is the use—as, for example, of the power of vision the act of vision, and besides this no other work is produced different from the power of vision—yet in certain things is there something else generated; for example, from the art of housebuilding a house is produced in addition to the act of building, notwithstanding that actuality, nevertheless, will be the end of potentiality, in both instances, to be sure, though it is more the end of it in the latter than in the former. For building is contained in that which is being built, and is generated and exists at the same time with the house. Of as many things, therefore, as there is something different (namely, that which is being produced) from their use, of these does there subsist the actuality in that which is being constructed, just as both the building resides in that which is being built, and the weaving in that which is being woven; in like manner, also, is it the case with other things, and, in general, does motion subsist in that to which motion is being imparted. Of as many things, however, as there is not some different work beside the actuality, in these is actuality inherent; as, for instance, the

act, or power, of seeing resides in the person who sees, and theory in the theoriser, and vitality, or life, in the soul: therefore, also, is happiness resident in the soul, for it also constitutes a certain sort of vitality. Wherefore, is it evident, that substance and form are each of them a certain actuality. And therefore, according to this reasoning, it is evident that in substance actuality is prior to potentiality. And, as we have stated, one actuality invariably is antecedent to another in time, up to that which is primarily and eternally the First Moving Cause.

2 / THEORY OF KNOWLEDGE

Realists hold generally that reality is knowable, that the human mind can therefore attain truth, and that it can do so with certainty. When we know an object, we both know that we know it, and we know it as knowable. To explain these assertions, Fr. Copleston develops in the following selection the classical Thomistic epistemology, which in turn is based largely on the thought of Aristotle.

Knowledge begins in sense and proceeds from the perception through the image to the idea or concept. Corresponding to and responsible for this process are various powers of the soul: the sense organ, the common sense, the imagination, and the active and passive intellects. We may illustrate the process as it occurs within the soul: an object is perceived by the sense of sight, and therewith the sensible form of the object is received. This form is presented by the common sense to the imagination, where an image is developed which bears the intelligible form. Next the active intellect picks out this form or universal concept from the image and impresses it on the passive intellect where it is known as a universal.

In this process there is synthesis, abstraction, and continuity. There is continuity in that the concept or intelligible form is implicit in the sense-perception and is in the end known explicitly in the intellect. There is an act of abstraction, for the intellect knows the object according to the latter's own form or essence. And there is synthesis, for the act of knowing is one in which the powers of the soul work together to achieve the universal concept.

KNOWING AND REALITY

F. C. Copleston (1907-   )

The first stage in the acquisition of knowledge is sense-perception. Our organs of sense are affected by external objects, and we receive sense-impressions. The eye, for example, sees colors or color-patches; but it would not do so unless it were affected by its object acting on it through a medium. It receives an impression, therefore, and undergoes a physical alteration. The process of sensation cannot, however, be reduced to a mere physical change. "If physiological change sufficed for sensation, all natural bodies would have sensations when they underwent change" (*S.T.*, Ia, 78, 3). Sensation is a psycho-physical process in which a sensible "form" is received.

If we consider the level of the individual external senses in itself, it is true to say that there are only discrete sense-impressions. The sense of sight, says Aquinas, is able to distinguish one color from another (the impression of green is different from the impression of blue); but the sense of sight is quite unable to compare and distinguish colors from sounds, since it does not hear. It is obvious, however, that even animals synthesize their sense-impressions. The dog perceives a man and achieves a synthesis of the different sense-impressions of sight, hearing, smell and touch. It is therefore clear that even at the level of purely sensitive life there takes place a synthesis of the data of the different external senses. Aquinas therefore postulates interior "senses" by means of which this synthesis is achieved. The word "sense" may seem peculiar, because we are accustomed to use the word only in reference to what Aquinas calls the five external senses; but by using the word

he intends to indicate that the power or faculty of which he speaks belongs to the level of sensitive life and is found in animals as well as in human beings.

The function of distinguishing and collating the data of the various external senses is performed by the general sense *(sensus communis)*. We must also postulate an imaginative power which conserves the forms received by the senses. Again, the animal is able to apprehend, for example, that something is useful to it. A dog apprehends that a particular man is friendly or unfriendly. We shall thus have to postulate a power or disposition to apprehend these facts (the *vis aestimativa*) and a power of conserving such apprehensions (the *vis memorativa*). In postulating all these powers or faculties Aquinas relied very largely on Aristotle, and we may well ask in what precise sense, if any, we are justified in speaking of different "faculties" or "interior senses." But the point to which I wish to draw attention is Aquinas' insistence on the work of synthesis that goes on in cognition. The synthesis of which I have been speaking takes place at the level of sensitive life, and it must not be taken to mean a conscious, deliberate synthesis; but that a synthesis does take place is a fact which scarcely admits of doubt.

Although, however, the synthesis which takes place on the sensitive level is in some sense common to animals and to men, this does not mean that sensitive cognition is identical in both. I have already quoted a passage from the *De potentia* (3, 11 *ad* 1), where Aquinas says that sensitive life, though generically the same in animals as in men, is not specifically the same, since it is "much higher" in the latter, "as is clear in the case of touch and in the case of the interior senses." Thus according to

The selection is from F. C. Copleston, *Aquinas* (Harmondsworth: Penguin Books, Ltd., 1955), pp. 173-178 and 46-51. Used by permission of the publisher.

Aquinas what corresponds in human beings to the *vis aestimativa* in animals deserves a special name, since more than instinct is involved: and he calls it the *vis cogitativa*. He was aware that in human perception sense and reason are both involved. But it does not follow that an attempt to abstract or isolate what belongs to the level of sense-life from what belongs to the level of reason is misguided or useless.

For Aquinas an explanation is needed of the transition from sensitive to rational or intellectual cognition. The senses apprehend particular objects, and images, even if confused, are particular. The mind, however, has universal concepts; it apprehends in abstraction the forms of things. We therefore have on the one hand sensitive apprehension of the particular and on the other intellectual cognition of the universal. This does not mean that universals as such have any extramental existence. There are, for example, only particular human beings; there is no such thing as an existent universal man, nor can there be. But individual human beings possess, Aquinas was convinced, specifically similar essences, and this similarity of essence is the objective foundation of the universal concept of man, which enables us to predicate the same term of individual human beings, saying, for example, that John is a man and that Peter is also a man. But even when we suppose this view of universals, namely that universals as such exist in the mind and not extramentally, the problem still remains, how is the universal concept formed? What is the process by which the universal concept is formed? It cannot be explained as a purely passive process, passive, that is to say, on the mind's part. For the mind, being immaterial, cannot be directly affected by a material thing or by the image. It is necessary to postulate an activity on the mind's part, in order to explain how the universal concept is formed from the material provided by sense-experience. In other words, on the rational level there

takes place a further stage of the process of synthesis involved in human cognition, and an analysis of this further stage is required.

Aquinas employs the Aristotelian distinction between the active and passive intellects, two distinct functions of the mind. According to him the active intellect "illumines" the image of the object apprehended by the senses; that is to say, it actively reveals the formal and potentially universal element which is implicitly contained in the image. It then abstracts this potentially universal element and produces in the passive intellect what Aquinas calls the *species impressa*. The passive intellect reacts to this determination by the active intellect, and the result is the *species expressa*, the universal concept in the full sense. This language is certainly unfamiliar and therefore difficult to follow; but what Aquinas has in mind is more or less this. The human intellect has no store of innate ideas: it is in potentiality to possessing ideas or concepts. Considered in this light, the intellect is passive. And its concepts must be derived in some way from the data provided by the senses, exterior and interior. But the senses provide particular impressions of particular objects, together with the images to which these impressions give rise, whereas concepts are universal in character. We must suppose, then, that the intellect as active picks out, as it were, the potentially universal element in the image, the synthesized reproduction in the imagination of the data of the different senses. Thus the intellect as active abstracts the universal essence of man from a particular image, leaving out the particularizing notes which confine the image to being the image of this or that particular man, and impresses it on the intellect as passive. And so the universal concept is born.

In the process of synthesis and abstraction there is therefore continuity, from the primary sense-impressions up to the universal concept. The mediating point between the data of sense and the universal concept is for Aquinas the image. And it is important to realize that when he talks about images in this connection he is not speaking of arbitrarily constructed images like the image of a unicorn. In our sense-experience of, say, Peter, the eye sees color-patches, the ear hears sounds, and so on. These sense-impressions are, however, synthesized in the form of the "image." And it is from this synthesis that the universal, "man," is, according to Aquinas, abstracted. That which is primarily known by the mind is, however, the universal, that is the form, as apprehended in Peter. Peter is known as a man. It is only secondarily that the mind apprehends the universal precisely as universal. That is to say, it is only secondarily that it apprehends the universal as predictable not only of Peter but also of James and John and every other individual human being. To speak of "abstraction" is not, therefore, for Aquinas to cut off the life of the intellect from that of the senses and to say that the mind knows only its own ideas. The universal concept is primarily the modification of the intellect by which a thing (Peter for example) is known according to its form or essence.

As we have seen earlier, Aquinas held that the mind is dependent on the image, not only in the formation of its ideas but also in their employment, in the sense that there is no thinking without the use of images or symbols. Since the mind is active and possesses the power of active reflection, it is not confined to the knowledge of material things; but at the same time it can know immaterial things only in so far as material things are related to them and reveal them. Moreover, in thinking about immaterial things we cannot dispense with the use of images or symbols. We can recognize the inadequacy of the images based on sense-experience, but we cannot get rid of them. We cannot conceive immaterial things, even when their existence is known by revelation, except on an analogy with visible things, though we can attempt to purify our ideas of them. "Images necessarily accompany our knowledge in this present life, however spiritual the knowledge may be: for even God is known by us through the images of His effects (in creatures)" (*De malo*, 16, 8, *ad* 3). Again, "the image is a principle of our knowledge. It is that from which our intellectual activity begins, not simply as a transitory stimulus, but as a permanent foundation of intellectual activity . . . And so when the imagination is impeded, so also is our theological knowledge" (*In librum Boethii de Trinitate*, 6, 2, *ad* 5).

A point to be noticed is that truth and falsity are predicated primarily neither of sense-impressions nor of concepts but of judgments. We can hardly speak of error in the case of a particular sense apprehending its own proper object, unless perhaps the organ is impaired; but inasmuch as Aquinas is prepared to speak of the senses "judging," he is also prepared to speak of truth and falsity at the sense-level. We might say, for example, that an animal misjudged the distance, distance being only indirectly apprehended by the senses. But though a "judgment" of sense may be true or false, according as it corresponds or not with reality, its truth or falsity is not reflectively apprehended at the sense-level. "Truth is primarily in the mind . . . It is defined as conformity between the mind and the thing. Hence to know this conformity is to know truth. Sense, however, does not know truth as such. For although sight has the likeness of a visible thing it does not know the correspondence between the thing seen and its perception of it. The mind, however, can know its own conformity with an intelligible thing, not simply by apprehending its essence, but it makes a judgment about the thing . . . It is then that it first knows and enunciates truth . . . And so, strictly speaking, it is in the mind's judgments that truth is found and not in sensation, nor in the intellectual apprehension of an essence"

(*S.T.*, I*a*, 16, 2). I may have a true perception of Peter as white; but it is not of
this perception as such that truth is primarily predicated. It is the judgment that
Peter is white which is strictly speaking
"true." Aquinas does, indeed, speak of
things as "true," as, being, for example, conformed to the mind of the Creator. But in
the *De veritate* and elsewhere he carefully
distinguishes the various senses in which he
uses the word "true" and states that truth
is primarily found in the mind's act of
judging. . . .

According to Aquinas it is in the act of
knowing truth that the mind is aware of
its ability to attain truth. Truth is predicated primarily of propositions; or, as he
puts it, truth is found primarily in the
judgment. Now, there are indubitable propositions, the truth of which cannot really be
doubted, though they can, of course, be
verbally denied. "The whole is greater than
any of its parts" would be a case in point.
And in recognizing the truth of such indubitable propositions the mind recognizes both
the fact that it knows their truth and that
it is its own nature to be conformed to
reality and so to know. In a rather cryptic
passage Aquinas states that truth is a resultant of the activity of the mind, when
the mind's judgment is about the thing as
it is. Truth is known by the mind according
as the mind reflects on its act, not only as
knowing its act but also as knowing the
relation of conformity between the act and
the thing *(proportionem eius ad rem)*. This
indeed cannot be known unless the nature
of the act itself is known; and this in turn
cannot be known unless the nature of the
active principle, that is, of the mind itself,
is known, to whose nature it pertains to be
conformed to reality (to things, *rebus*).
Therefore the mind knows truth according
as it reflects on itself" (*De veritate*, 1, 9).
Thus the mind knows its own power of attaining truth by reflecting on itself in the
act of knowing truth. Aquinas' point of view

was that sometimes at least we know something with certainty, that we know that we
know it and that in knowing it we know
that the object is knowable. It may be objected that this point of view is uncritical
and naïve on the ground that it amounts to
accepting the ordinary man's spontaneous
conviction that he can attain truth and
often does so. But the point is that for
Aquinas the ordinary man's conviction on
this matter is not simply "naïve." It is in
the act of knowing that the mind's ability
to know is recognized; and it is recognized
by the ordinary man. The philosopher can
reflect on this recognition and make explicit
what for the ordinary man is implicit. And
this procedure can be called "second reflection." The passage quoted above is an instance of second reflection. But the "reflection" about which the passage speaks is not
itself philosophic reflection: it is what we
may call "first reflection," the awareness of
knowing truth which at least sometimes accompanies the ordinary man's mental activity. In other words, the philosopher can
reflect on the ordinary man's awareness of
attaining truth, but he has not at his disposal some extraordinary and special means
of proving that we can know truth or that
"knowledge" is knowledge. If a philosopher
were to comment that in this case we can
never prove that we can attain truth and
that if we cannot prove it we can never
know it, Aquinas might reply that the sort
of proof which the philosopher is looking for
is inherently useless and indeed impossible,
but that it does not follow that we cannot
both attain truth and also know that we can
attain it. We do not need any further
guarantee of our ability to attain truth
than our awareness or recognition of the
fact that we do in fact attain it. . . .

It would, however, be a mistake to interpret Aquinas' appeal to the ordinary
man's awareness of attaining truth as equivalent to saying that whenever anyone
thinks that he knows the truth he does in

fact know it. In the case of some propositions there can be no error, but this does not mean that we cannot enunciate false propositions while believing them to be true. If I say "That object in the distance is a tree," my statement may turn out to be false, even though I now believe it to be true. But though error is possible, Aquinas did not regard this possibility as any valid reason for unlimited skepticism. In cases where there is a possibility of error or where there is reason to suspect error Aquinas speaks of a "resolution to first principles." But we must not interpret "first principles" as meaning exclusively the first principles of logic and mathematics. True, if we have reason to suspect that there is an error in our mathematical reasoning, we have to go back and retrace our steps. But under "first principles" in the present connection Aquinas includes actual sense-perception. "Because the first principle of our knowledge is sense, it is necessary to reduce in some way to sense all things about which we judge" (*De veritate*, 1, 2, 3, *ad* 2). If my statement that the object in the field is a tree is open to doubt, the way to resolve the doubt or to correct the error is to look more closely. It may be said that this does not touch the problem whether all sense-perception may not be illusory. But I do not think that Aquinas would have had much patience with a problem of this kind. The term "illusion" has meaning for us only in contrast with what is not illusion and is known not to be illusion, and the word "false" has meaning for us only in contrast with the word "true." And we know the meaning of the word "true" because we enunciate and know that we enunciate true propositions. Again, the word "knowledge" is meaningful for us because we actually know. And to ask whether the knowledge we have is "really" knowledge is to pursue a profitless inquiry. Of course, if when we ask whether what we think to

be knowledge is "really" knowledge, we mean to ask whether knowing that there is a cat under the table is "mathematical knowledge," the answer is that it is not. And if we insist that only the conclusions of mathematical demonstrations can properly be said to be "known," it follows that knowledge of non-mathematical truths is not knowledge. But all we are doing is to propose a peculiar use of the words "know" and "knowledge" which is different from the normal use and which has little, if anything, to recommend it. In other words, I suggest that Aquinas would have considerable sympathy with those modern philosophers who examine with the aid of linguistic analysis what precisely is being asked when it is asked whether all that we take to be knowledge may not be something other than knowledge, whether all sense-perception may not be illusory, whether all experience may not be a dream, and so on.

For Aquinas, therefore, it is in actually knowing something that we know that we know and that the object is knowable. And he was convinced that further reflection shows that the object is knowable or intelligible because and in so far as it has being. The truth that being is intelligible is revealed in the concrete act of knowing anything, though its expression in the form of an abstract proposition is the work of reflection. And this is for Aquinas the reason why the mind goes forward confidently to investigate reality, whether in the sciences or in philosophy. And if his philosophical interpretation of the world forms in some sense a system, the reason why it does so is not for him that reality is forced into a preconceived and presupposed mould but that the world is in itself an intelligible system and that this intelligible system discloses itself to the reflective mind. It is rather that the system is imposed on the mind by reality than that the mind reads a system into phenomena.

3 / METAPHYSICS

The metaphysical analyses of Plato and, especially, Aristotle are utilized by Professor Wild to explain the being of the objects of nature and human experience. His statement is developed through attention to the fact of change, and he incorporates the substance-accident and form-matter distinctions first fully discussed by Aristotle. In the first part of the selection is a review of these concepts. Change, Professor Wild observes, always involves three factors: matter, form, and privative form. The first of these accounts for the continuity present in change, the latter for the change itself. The further distinction between substance and accident is required to analyze changes where a basic structure abides but change happens to it ("accidental change"), and change where the structure itself of something changes ("substantial change").

Yet another distinction is necessary, however—namely, that of essence and existence. These terms received their fullest treatment within the realistic tradition by St. Thomas Aquinas. The immediate data of experience, realists hold, involve more than form and matter, for as beings they all exist in opposition to nonbeing. Hence the need for essence-existence: essence, or what a thing is, separates kinds of entities, whereas the act of existence separates entities from nonbeing. The exploration of these principles is, therefore, Professor Wild's second concern.

BEING, ESSENCE, AND EXISTENCE

John Wild (1902-   )

The object of general metaphysics is being as such. The facts we there observe apply to any being whatsoever, whether finite or infinite, changing or immutable, multiple or one. Now we must turn to an existential analysis of the entities which are presented to us in our immediate experience. How do these entities exist? Are they changing or immutable? Do they exist in themselves or in something else distinct from them? Are they one or many? Is their existence atomic and self-enclosed or incomplete and tendential? Is their existence necessary or contingent? These basic ques-

tions cannot be answered by any of the sciences restricted to non-pervasive data. They are philosophical questions which can be scientifically answered only by a careful description and analysis of the philosophical data which constitutively pervade the whole field of experience. Let us now turn to these peculiar, existential data and attempt such an analysis.

How do the entities of our experience exist? They are evidently finite, mutable, and multiple. We shall start with the data of mutability, then turn to those of multiplicity, and conclude with a brief discussion of the more basic datum of finitude which underlies both.

A. The datum of change. Unlike existence, the datum of change is not all-pervasive. There is nothing about existence as

The selection is from John Wild, "Phenomenology and Metaphysics," in *The Return to Reason,* edited by John Wild, copyright 1953 by Henry Regnery Company. Used by permission of the publisher.

such which requires that any existent entity must be mutable. Nevertheless, change does pervade the data of human experience. The extended objects of nature are constantly undergoing those modes of physical change which are peculiar to them. I feel many kinds of psychophysical change proceeding within myself, and through the agencies of human communication I am aware of those manifold modes of social and cultural change which make up the complex web of human history. From this it is clear that change is too pervasive a datum to fall within the restricted province of any one of the special sciences. Each science studies only a special kind of change from its own special point of view.

Modern philosophy has not been clearly aware of its own peculiar data but has been deeply impressed by the positivistic view that every datum belongs to the special province of some restricted science. Hence when one raises the fundamental question: *What is change?* even in philosophical literature, he looks in vain for an intelligible answer. Many philosophers, like Dewey, insist upon the universal occurrence of what they call process and flux. But they seem almost wholly unaware of the need for a philosophical analysis and explanation of this peculiar and complex, philosophic datum. Instead of analysis, they give us merely synonyms. . . .

In the realistic analysis of change, first suggested by Aristotle, three sources of change are always recognized: two opposed structural principles (such as green and red) to account for the discontinuity, and one potential or dispositional principle (matter) to account for the continuity. When this third, dispositional principle is not clearly recognized, change is reduced to the pure discontinuity of succession, first one specific determination and then another opposed determination, annihilation and creation *ex nihilo*. On this view, the end of a process would have nothing in common with the beginning, and anything could come out of anything. But there is a vast array of empirical evidence against this conclusion. You cannot make a silk purse out of a sow's ear nor a poplar tree from an apple seed. Change is continuous as well as discontinuous.

What, then, are the major kinds of change? If we stick close to the data, we shall be forced to recognize two types in particular which are so important that we shall single them out for a brief analysis.

B. Accidental change and the distinction of substance and accident. At the present time, there are several deep-seated misconceptions of substance and accident. Since this topic is treated more thoroughly elsewhere, we shall confine ourselves here to a brief consideration of these major misunderstandings, which are three in number.

The first is a widespread impression that the distinction of substance from accident is derived primarily from epistemological considerations and must be defended, if it is to be defended at all, on the basis of epistemological evidence. On this view, the accidental properties of a thing are supposed to be directly sensed. The realist is held to believe that back of these accidents, underlying them, is a noumenal x, or substance, in which they inhere like separate pins in an underlying pincushion. This conception is far removed from any realistic conception of substance and accident.

In the first place, this distinction is concerned not with epistemological facts but with dynamic facts. It is required to explain not the structure of knowledge but the structure of change. As we have just noted, there is a factor of continuity in all types of change. But in certain types, this continuous factor is constituted by a complex, formal pattern (or essence) which persists throughout the process. At the level of inorganic nature, where our entitative knowledge is less exact, we cannot clearly grasp the formal unity of what is changing. But in the case of individual plants and animals, we can grasp something of this substantial structure. As the roots are extended, the stalk grows, and the buds ripen and fall, the plant endures as a single, corporeal, living entity.

Somewhere between the simplest physical transformations and the processes of life, certain forms of unified structure have gained sufficient domination over limited bits of matter to enable them to persist through the various accidental transformations to which they are subject. Thus I am directly aware of various evolutions and transformations, resulting in the gain or loss of accidental properties, as long as my life endures. But I am also aware of the fact that I myself persist through these changes as a corporeal, living, human substance. This is an example of accidental change in which the continuity is provided by a unified, formal structure, partially expressed in the specific definition of the entity.

In the second place, substance and accident cannot be accurately understood as separate entities, merely juxtaposed with, or inhering in, one another as pins in a pincushion. This atomistic conception utterly fails to do justice to the situation. Substance is not a *thing*, and accident another *thing*, which happen to be joined. Neither is a thing. Each of them is a correlative principle which exists only by virtue of its fusion with the other. The only thing is the concrete entity constituted by this fusion.

Each principle contributes something to the whole entity. Thus its identity and individuation are derived from the substantial component, its changing qualities from the accidental component. But it is precisely the *whole, composite entity* which is individuated and qualified, not merely a part. It is entirely wrong to think of the substance as a fixed atom, remaining lifeless and inert as the accidental changes sweep by it. This is a complete perversion of the

facts. It is the whole entity which changes, and every constitutive phase of the entity is involved in this change, the substance as providing it with continuity and individuality, the accidents as providing it with novelty and discontinuity.

Finally, in the third place, it is clear from their correlative structure that neither substance nor accident can be known without the other. It is as impossible to know accidents without substance as to know a father without any children. This is a pure figment of atomistic thought. But what of human sensation? Surely it is aware of the pure color green, the middle-C sound, which are accidents, but not of that mysterious something I know not what, which John Locke [1] confused with substance.

This last phrase is correct. Sensation knows nothing of *substance*. But neither does it know anything of *accident*. The color green is the object of a universal concept. It is never sensed. What is sensed is a complex flux of quantitative and qualitative characters confused together in an unanalyzed blur. Substance and accident are implicit in this blur. But they can be clearly apprehended and distinguished only through a rational analysis of this sensory confusion. Substance is the formal unity which persists throughout the concrete change. The accidents come and go.

C. Substantial change and the distinction of matter and form. The accidental changes we have so far been considering affect the whole, concrete, changing entity. They do not affect the formal essence which maintains the substantial unity of the entity throughout these accidental transformations. There is another more radical type of change, however, which results in the generation or destruction of the entity and which, therefore, does penetrate to the very essence. The death of my cat is not an

---

[1 The reference is to the philosopher, John Locke (1632-1714), the first great British empiricist. *Ed.*]

accidental change, for he does not survive the process. My cat has ceased to be. Nevertheless, the data show that this process is not wholly discontinuous. The carcass remains, and while it consists of new substances not in existence before, there is something in them which was once in the cat.

This matter, or capacity to be possessed by different substantial forms, underlies any process of substantial change and supplies it with a minimum continuity. Thus in order to account for the continuity which characterizes even the most radical changes of nature, including the evolution of new species from earlier forms, we must recognize a further composition in the very essence of any natural entity which has come into existence by a process of evolution. On the one hand, its essence must consist of a certain formal structure marking off this entity from other species, which disappears when the entity is destroyed. But there must be another essential part which existed before and which will outlast the entity. This must be a capacity or potency, able to exist under divergent forms and able to unite both essence and accidents together into a single, material unity.

Here again it is most important to notice how this hylomorphic composition in the essence of any evolutionary entity must be distorted by any atomistic mode of analysis. Matter is not one thing, and form another. The essence is no mere addition of quantitative atoms. Matter and form are correlative principles, each of which exists only by virtue of the other. It is true that this matter may exist under some other form than that which now possesses it. But it cannot exist as an atom by itself alone. Similarly, the form can be found apart from *this* matter, but never apart from matter. Each is a vectorial principle, intrinsically correlative to something distinct from itself, and each contributes something to the whole concrete entity which is thus

constituted. The matter sustains the entity and gives it an individual position in nature, while the form specifically characterizes the entity as a whole.

Thus in order to account for the pervasive datum of change, we are forced to recognize a fourfold composition in the structure of the simplest conceivable dynamic entity. First (unless it was created *ex nihilo*), this entity must include a matter from which it continuously evolved. It must also include an essential form, marking it off from other *kinds* of entity, which must be in possession of the matter as long as the entity endures, from the moment of its generation to that of its extinction. The matter, when given existence in union with such a form, is a complete substance, which is then capable of undergoing accidental transformations by which further existent properties are gained or lost without the destruction of the entity. These principles are not entities, but vectorial factors by which a concrete natural entity exists. Matter cannot exist without form, nor form without matter. Substance exists only with accidents, and accidents only in substance.

We must now turn to an even more basic composition which is required by another immediate datum of experience—multiplicity.

D. The problem of the one and the many: essence and existence. An *order* is a unit in multiplicity. The data of change present us with a certain type of order, a temporal multiplicity of determinations united by matter, or by substantial form in the case of accidental change. In order to account for these immediate data, we are forced to recognize in any concrete changing entity the distinct, component principles of matter and form, substance and accident. But at any given moment we are also presented with an even more basic *static* order, as we may call it—a multiplicity of diverse entities, all of which share in existence. On the one hand, each entity is distinct from, and opposed to, the rest. So they are a multiplicity. But on the other hand, they all share in that existence which opposes them all to nothing. In this respect they are one. How can they be both many and one?

Consider my own being. I am directly aware of myself as radically distinct from all the other entities surrounding me. They are not what I am, and I am not what they are. This is an immediate datum of experience, thrust upon me with inexorable constraint. I cannot question it without also questioning, if I am consistent, all other data as well, and thus abandoning the whole attempt to know. But there is another datum also thrust upon me with equal constraint. This is the datum of existence which pervades both self and not-self. The others exist as much as I. Existence is shared in common. But how is this possible? How can the same entity be both diverse and similar to the very same entities? Unless we are to fall into a radical monism which denies the datum of multiplicity, or into a radical, atomistic pluralism which denies the datum of shared existence, we must find an answer to this problem of the one and the many.

There is only one way of solving this problem. That is by inferring another and even more basic composition in the complex structure of a finite entity. This means that an absolutely *simple* Democritean atom, or Humean impression, is impossible. Such a simple, atomic entity cannot exist among others even for an instant. A simple, finite entity cannot be both similar to, and distinct from, the very same entities. But the actual entities now existing at this instant are both similar to, and distinct from, the rest. Hence they are not simple. Each must include something within it, essence, by which it is wholly divorced from other entities, and something else, existence, by which it is opposed to nothing and in this respect similar to the rest.

Each of these principles is correlative.

Neither can be adequately conceived apart from the other. Existence is always the existence *of* something (an essence), and essence is always the distinct character *of* something existent. When we conceive of an essence not actualized, which we call a possibility, we conceive of it as something that *might be* actualized, and therefore in relation to existence. Furthermore, in any actual thing these two principles are fused together in such a way that each determines the entity as a whole. In my concrete totality I am marked off from other entities, and every phase of my being is pervaded by my existence.

The essence as such is atomistic and self-enclosed. In the second place, it is nontendential and inactive. One essence as such does not tend to other essences, nor can it diffuse anything to another. Each is simply *what it is*. Finally, the determinate parts of a concrete essence are more readily grasped by the human mind. Hence, as has been recently noted, there has been a strong tendency in the history of Western thought to emphasize essence at the expense of existence, which is less easily abstracted and fixed by the human mind in clear and distinct definitions by universal concepts. As a result of this tendency, Western thought has been peculiarly prone to philosophies of radical pluralism and logical atomism, which view the world as a set of distinct entities entirely divorced from one another and which have great difficulty in focusing the active, causal phases of being which spring from existence rather than from essence.

This essentialist tendency leads to significant distortions and over-simplifications of philosophical doctrine, for existence is more ultimate and more perfect than essence. Essence without existence, though it may be brought before the mind very easily as a logical abstraction, in reality is nothing at all. It is only by virtue of existence that essence emerges from its causes and ceases to be nothing. Though less easily grasped than essence, existence is actually possessed in common by all the data of experience, indeed by anything whatsoever, whether in human experience or not. Furthermore, it is active and diffusive, never atomistic, self-enclosed, and insular, like the essential aspect of finite being. These active, tendential, and causal phases of concrete entities are due to existence rather than to essence. They are expressed in our language by verbs rather than by nouns. It is to these existential aspects of finite being that we must now turn.

E. Tendency and causation. Activity is a special kind of change, namely, that which originates within a finite entity. The origination and partial completion of such activity within the entity is *tendency*.

The existence of such tendencies within all the entities we experience is confirmed by a vast wealth of direct evidence. First of all, we constantly feel within ourselves such tendencies as hunger, thirst, curiosity, and so forth. Through communication with others, we discover such tendencies in them. In the case of subhuman entities, with which communication is impossible, we find that similar entities act and behave in similar ways. Unless we assume constant, self-originating tendencies, determined by similar, formal structures, we cannot explain the myriad facts revealed by what is called induction.

That these tendencies originate within the entity is confirmed by evidence which shows that a given entity will go on behaving in a constant manner even though the surrounding conditions may vary over a wide range. Otherwise, the prediction of what a given entity will do in a hitherto unobserved situation would be impossible. As long as its structure endures, fire tends to burn, ice to cool, and so on. Every natural entity constantly tends to act in ways which are determined by its essential struc-

ture. What is the explanation of this constant, tendential factor?

It cannot be explained by reference to essence alone, for as we have seen, essence, like a Humean impression, is always insular, self-enclosed, and exclusive. Tendency is an urge that reaches out beyond essence to more being not yet possessed. Hence it is due to existence rather than to essence, for it is by existence that the finity entity is allied to others beyond itself. As soon as existence is fused with a determinate, restricted essence, it bubbles over as an active tendency toward further existence. But the specific form of this tendency is determined by the essence. Each tends beyond its essence because of its existence.

But the character of this tendency is due to its essence. Each divergent kind of thing has correspondingly divergent tendencies. Inorganic things have simpler tendencies, corresponding to their simpler nature. Plants have their constant, vegetative tendencies, and individual human beings all possess tendencies to live in human ways determined by their human nature. This basic urge is the root of what is called human obligation, and the realization of these essential tendencies is the standard of human goodness. Any entity is in a sound or healthy state only in so far it it realizes its essential tendencies. Good is no mere property or essence, but an *existential category* —the active realization of a given nature.[2]

Tendency is, therefore, a necessary result of essence and existence together. It must be recognized as a distinct factor in the complex structure of any finite entity. There are two distinct types of tendency, the immanent and the transitive. Immanent

---

[2] Hence for a realist there is no radical separation of fact from value. What is *universally* and essentially good for man is determined by his tendential nature, certainly a fact. He is in a good condition when this nature is realized, in a bad condition when this is thwarted.

tendencies not only originate but are also completed within the active agent. Thus the tendency to knowledge in man is completed within the knowing agent without any change being produced in the environment. Such purely immanent tendencies are, however, very rare. Most tendencies are transitive in character. Such tendencies originate within a given entity, but then pass out of it to effect changes in surrounding entities by which alone the original tendency is realized.

This transitive realization of tendency, which is diffused to other entities, is commonly referred to as *causal efficacy,* or more properly as *efficient causation.* Many of these causal influences are directly observed. Others are inferred. They are expressed in the natural laws or principles of science, which show the dependence of one kind of entity on another. No finite entity can exist by itself; but it is dependent upon other entities in myriad ways.

This raises an important question concerning the whole collection of finite entities which constitutes the world of nature. Can it exist alone? Or is it dependent on something extrinsic?

4 / ETHICS

Realistic ethics is marked by three basic principles. The first is called the law of nature or the natural law. The natural law, realists hold, prescribes the good for man and, as we shall see later, for society. It is not based simply on subjective interests or desires, but rather on the very nature of man and the universe he inhabits. Therefore realists argue that the natural law is not arbitrarily constructed by any human groups, but rather it is discovered by human reason as embedded in the nature of man and things. This makes the natural law objective or independent of particular circumstance and interest, and universal in the sense that it applies to all men everywhere.

The second principle of realist ethics is happiness or well-being. This principle refers to the perfection of our human nature which is the goal of all moral effort. But such perfection is achieved only by the development of proper habits. Good habits are called virtues; bad habits, vices. Virtue is thus the third principle of realist ethics. It is the primary internal cause of happiness, and human activity in accordance with virtue is the very definition of happiness itself.

The following selection is from Aristotle's major ethical work, the *Nicomachean Ethics.* It includes a discussion of happiness, a description of the virtues related to and derived from Aristotle's view of man, and a statement of man's highest good as the exercise of his highest capacity, contemplative reason. These Aristotelian concepts have remained the basis of realistic ethics to the present day.

HAPPINESS AND VIRTUE

Aristotle (384-322)

BOOK I. THE GOOD OR THE END

1. Every art and every kind of inquiry, and likewise every act and purpose, seems to aim at some good: and so it has been well said that the good is that at which everything aims.

But a difference is observable among these aims or ends. What is aimed at is sometimes the exercise of a faculty, sometimes a certain result beyond that exercise. And where there is an end beyond the act, there the result is better than the exercise of the faculty.

Now since there are many kinds of actions and many arts and sciences, it follows that there are many ends also; *e. g.* health is the end of medicine, ships of shipbuilding, victory of the art of war, and wealth of economy.

But when several of these are subordinated to some one art or science,—as the making of bridles and other trappings to the art of horsemanship, and this in turn, along with all else that the soldier does, to the art of war, and so on,—then the end of the master-art is always more desired than the ends of the subordinate arts, since these are pursued for its sake. And this is equally true whether the end in view be the mere exercise of a faculty or something beyond that, as in the above instances.

2. If then in what we do there be some end which we wish for on its own account, choosing all the others as means to this, but not every end without exception as a means to something else (for so we should go on *ad infinitum,* and desire would be left void and objectless),—this evidently will be the good

or the best of all things. And surely from a practical point of view it much concerns us to know this good; for then, like archers shooting at a definite mark, we shall be more likely to attain what we want.

If this be so, we must try to indicate roughly what it is, and first of all to which of the arts or sciences it belongs.

It would seem to belong to the supreme art or science, that one which most of all deserves the name of master-art or master-science.

Now Politics [1] seems to answer to this description. For it prescribes which of the sciences a state needs, and which each man shall study, and up to what point; and to it we see subordinated even the highest arts, such as economy, rhetoric, and the art of war.

Since then it makes use of the other practical sciences, and since it further ordains what men are to do and from what to refrain, its end must include the ends of the others, and must be the proper good of man.

For though this good is the same for the individual and the state, yet the good of the state seems a grander and more perfect thing both to attain and to secure; and glad as one would be to do this service for a single individual, to do it for a people and for a number of states is nobler and more divine.

This then is the aim of the present inquiry, which is a sort of political inquiry. . . .

4. Since—to resume—all knowledge and all purpose aims at some good, what is this which we say is the aim of Politics; or, in

The selection is from the translation by F. H. Peters, *The Nicomachean Ethics of Aristotle* (7th ed.) (London: Kegan Paul, Trench, Trübner and Co., Ltd., 1898), Books I, II, and VI, with omissions.

[1 Aristotle uses the term "politics" for the general study of human life, of which ethics or the study of the individual good is a part. *Ed.*]

other words, what is the highest of all realizable goods?

As to its name, I suppose nearly all men
are agreed; for the masses and the men of
culture alike declare that it is happiness,
and hold that to "live well" or to "do well"
is the same as to be "happy."

But they differ as to what this happiness
is, and the masses do not give the same
account of it as the philosophers.

The former take it to be something pal-
pable and plain, as pleasure or wealth or
fame; one man holds it to be this, and another that, and often the same man is of
different minds at different times,—after
sickness it is health, and in poverty it is
wealth; while when they are impressed with
the consciousness of their ignorance, they
admire most those who say grand things
that are above their comprehension.

Some philosophers, on the other hand,
have thought that, beside these several
good things, there is an "absolute" good
which is the cause of their goodness.

As it would hardly be worth while to
review all the opinions that have been held,
we will confine ourselves to those which are
most popular, or which seem to have some
foundation in reason. . . .

5. . . . It seems that men not unreason-
ably take their notions of the good or
happiness from the lives actually led, and
that the masses who are the least refined
suppose it to be pleasure, which is the reason why they aim at nothing higher than
the life of enjoyment.

For the most conspicuous kinds of life
are three: this life of enjoyment, the life of
the statesman, and, thirdly, the contemplative life.

The mass of men show themselves utterly slavish in their preference for the life
of brute beasts, but their views receive
consideration because many of those in high
places have the tastes of Sardanapalus.

Men of refinement with a practical turn
prefer honor; for I suppose we may say

that honor is the aim of the statesman's
life.

But this seems too superficial to be the
good we are seeking: for it appears to depend upon those who give rather than upon
those who receive it; while we have a pre-
sentiment that the good is something that
is peculiarly a man's own and can scarce be
taken away from him.

Moreover, these men seem to pursue
honor in order that they may be assured of
their own excellence,—at least, they wish
to be honored by men of sense, and by those
who know them, and on the ground of their
virtue or excellence. It is plain, then, that in
their view, at any rate, virtue or excellence is better than honor; and perhaps
we should take this to be the end of the
statesman's life, rather than honor.

But virtue or excellence also appears too
incomplete to be what we want; for it
seems that a man might have virtue and yet
be asleep or be inactive all his life, and,
moreover, might meet with the greatest disasters and misfortunes; and no one would
maintain that such a man is happy, except
for argument's sake. But we will not dwell
on these matters now, for they are sufficiently discussed in the popular treatises.

The third kind of life is the life of contemplation: we will treat of it further on.

As for the money-making life, it is
something quite contrary to nature; and
wealth evidently is not the good of which
we are in search, for it is merely useful as
a means to something else. So we might
rather take pleasure and virtue or excellence to be ends than wealth; for they are
chosen on their own account. But it seems
that not even they are the end, though
much breath has been wasted in attempts
to show that they are. . . .

7. Leaving these matters, then, let us
return once more to the question, what this
good can be of which we are in search.

It seems to be different in different kinds
of action and in different arts,—one thing

in medicine and another in war, and so on. What then is the good in each of these cases? Surely that for the sake of which all else is done. And that in medicine is health, in war is victory, in building is a house,—a different thing in each different case, but always, in whatever we do and in whatever we choose, the end. For it is always for the sake of the end that all else is done.

If then there be one end of all that man does, this end will be the realizable good, —or these ends, if there be more than one.

By this generalization our argument is brought to the same point as before. This point we must try to explain more clearly.

We see that there are many ends. But some of these are chosen only as means, as wealth, flutes, and the whole class of instruments. And so it is plain that not all ends are final.

But the best of all things must, we conceive, be something final.

If then there be only one final end, this will be what we are seeking,—or if there be more than one, then the most final of them.

Now that which is pursued as an end in itself is more final than that which is pursued as means to something else, and that which is never chosen as means than that which is chosen both as an end in itself and as means, and that is strictly final which is always chosen as an end in itself and never as means.

Happiness seems more than anything else to answer to this description: for we always choose it for itself, and never for the sake of something else; while honor and pleasure and reason, and all virtue or excellence, we choose partly indeed for themselves (for, apart from any result, we should choose each of them), but partly also for the sake of happiness, supposing that they will help to make us happy. But no one chooses happiness for the sake of these things, or as a means to anything else at all. . . .

But perhaps the reader thinks that though no one will dispute the statement that happiness is the best thing in the world, yet a still more precise definition of it is needed.

This will best be gained, I think, by asking, What is the function of man? For as the goodness and the excellence of a piper or a sculptor, or the practicer of any art, and generally of those who have any function or business to do, lies in that function, so man's good would seem to lie in his function, if he has one.

But can we suppose that, while a carpenter or a cobbler has a function and a business of his own, man has no business and no function assigned him by nature? Nay, surely as his several members, eye and hand and foot, plainly have each his own function, so we must suppose that man also has some function over and above all these.

What then is it?

Life evidently he has in common even with the plants, but we want that which is peculiar to him. We must exclude, therefore, the life of mere nutrition and growth.

Next to this comes the life of sense; but this too he plainly shares with horses and cattle and all kinds of animals.

There remains then the life whereby he acts—the life of his rational nature, with its two sides or divisions, one rational as obeying reason, the other rational as having and exercising reason.

But as this expression is ambiguous, we must be understood to mean thereby the life that consists in the exercise of the faculties; for this seems to be more properly entitled to the name.

The function of man, then, is exercise of his vital faculties [or soul] on one side in obedience to reason, and on the other side with reason.

But what is called the function of a man of any profession and the function of a man who is good in that profession are generically the same, *e. g.* of a harper and of a good harper; and this holds in all cases without exception, only that in the case of the latter his superior excellence at his work is added; for we say a harper's function is to harp, and a good harper's to harp well.

(Man's function then being, as we say, a kind of life—that is to say, exercise of his faculties and action of various kinds with reason—the good man's function is to do this well and beautifully [or nobly]. But the function of anything is done well when it is done in accordance with the proper excellence of that thing.)

If this be so the result is that the good of man is exercise of his faculties in accordance with excellence or virtue, or, if there be more than one, in accordance with the best and most complete virtue.

But there must also be a full term of years for this exercise; for one swallow or one fine day does not make a spring, nor does one day or any small space of time make a blessed or happy man. . . .

13. Since happiness is an exercise of the vital faculties in accordance with perfect virtue or excellence, we will now inquire about virtue or excellence; for this will probably help us in our inquiry about happiness. . . .

The virtue or excellence that we are to consider is, of course, the excellence of man; for it is the good of man and the happiness of man that we started to seek. And by the excellence of man I mean excellence not of body, but of soul; for happiness we take to be an activity of the soul.

If this be so, then it is evident that the statesman must have some knowledge of the soul, just as the man who is to heal the eye or the whole body must have some knowledge of them, and that the more in proportion as the science of the state is higher and better than medicine. But all educated physicians take much pains to know about the body.

As statesmen [or students of Politics],

then, we must inquire into the nature of the soul, but in so doing we must keep our special purpose in view and go only so far as that requires; for to go into minuter detail would be too laborious for the present undertaking.

Now, there are certain doctrines about the soul which are stated elsewhere with sufficient precision, and these we will adopt.

Two parts of the soul are distinguished, an irrational and a rational part.

Whether these are separated as are the parts of the body or any divisible thing, or whether they are only distinguishable in thought but in fact inseparable, like concave and convex in the circumference of a circle, makes no difference for our present purpose.

Of the irrational part, again, one division seems to be common to all things that live, and to be possessed by plants—I mean that which causes nutrition and growth; for we must assume that all things that take nourishment have a faculty of this kind, even when they are embryos, and have the same faculty when they are full grown; at least, this is more reasonable than to suppose that they then have a different one.

The excellence of this faculty, then, is plainly one that man shares with other beings, and not specifically human. . . .

But there seems to be another vital principle that is irrational, and yet in some way partakes of reason. In the case of the continent and of the incontinent man alike we praise the reason or the rational part, for it exhorts them rightly and urges them to do what is best; but there is plainly present in them another principle besides the rational one, which fights and struggles against the reason. For just as a paralyzed limb, when you will to move it to the right, moves on the contrary to the left, so is it with the soul; the incontinent man's impulses run counter to his reason. Only whereas we see the refractory member in the case of the body, we do not see it in the case of the soul. But we must nevertheless, I think, hold that in the soul too there is something beside the reason, which opposes and runs counter to it (though in what sense it is distinct from the reason does not matter here).

It seems, however, to partake of reason also, as we said: at least, in the continent man it submits to the reason; while in the temperate and courageous man we may say it is still more obedient; for in him it is altogether in harmony with the reason.

The irrational part, then, it appears, is twofold. There is the vegetative faculty, which has no share of reason; and the faculty of appetite or of desire in general, which in a manner partakes of reason or is rational as listening to reason and submitting to its sway,—rational in the sense in which we speak of rational obedience to father or friends, not in the sense in which we speak of rational apprehension of mathematical truths. But all advice and all rebuke and exhortation testify that the irrational part is in some way amenable to reason.

If then we like to say that this part, too, has a share of reason, the rational part also will have two divisions: one rational in the strict sense as possessing reason in itself, the other rational as listening to reason as a man listens to his father.

Now, on this division of the faculties is based the division of excellence; for we speak of intellectual excellences and of moral excellences; wisdom and understanding and prudence we call intellectual, liberality and temperance we call moral virtues or excellences. When we are speaking of a man's moral character we do not say that he is wise or intelligent, but that he is gentle or temperate. But we praise the wise man, too, for his habit of mind or trained faculty; and a habit or trained faculty that is praiseworthy is what we call an excellence or virtue.

BOOK II. MORAL VIRTUE

1. Excellence, then, being of these two kinds, intellectual and moral, intellectual excellence owes its birth and growth mainly to instruction, and so requires time and experience, while moral excellence is the result of habit or custom (ἔθος), and has accordingly in our language received a name formed by a slight change from ἔθος.

From this it is plain that none of the moral excellences or virtues is implanted in us by nature; for that which is by nature cannot be altered by training. For instance, a stone naturally tends to fall downwards, and you could not train it to rise upwards, though you tried to do so by throwing it up ten thousand times, nor could you train fire to move downwards, nor accustom anything which naturally behaves in one way to behave in any other way.

The virtues, then, come neither by nature nor against nature, but nature gives the capacity for acquiring them, and this is developed by training. . . .

We may safely assert that the virtue or excellence of a thing causes that thing both to be itself in good condition and to perform its function well. The excellence of the eye, for instance, makes both the eye and its work good; for it is by the excellence of the eye that we see well. So the proper excellence of the horse makes a horse what he should be, and makes him good at running, and carrying his rider, and standing a charge.

If, then, this holds good in all cases, the proper excellence or virtue of man will be the habit or trained faculty that makes a man good and makes him perform his function well.

How this is to be done we have already said, but we may exhibit the same conclusion in another way, by inquiring what the nature of this virtue is.

Now, if we have any quantity, whether continuous or discrete, it is possible to take either a larger [or too large], or a smaller [or too small], or an equal [or fair] amount, and that either absolutely or relatively to our own needs.

By an equal or fair amount I understand a mean amount, or ones that lies between excess and deficiency.

By the absolute mean, or mean relatively to the thing itself, I understand that which is equidistant from both extremes, and this is one and the same for all.

By the mean relatively to us I understand that which is neither too much nor too little for us; and this is not one and the same for all.

For instance, if ten be larger [or too large] and two be smaller [or too small], if we take six we take the mean relatively to the thing itself [or the arithmetical mean]; for it exceeds one extreme by the same amount by which it is exceeded by the other extreme; and this is the mean in arithmetical proportion.

But the mean relatively to us cannot be found in this way. If ten pounds of food is too much for a given man to eat, and two pounds too little, it does not follow that the trainer will order him six pounds: for that also may perhaps be too much for the man in question, or too little; too little for Milo, too much for the beginner. The same holds true in running and wrestling.

And so we may say generally that a master in any art avoids what is too much and what is too little, and seeks for the mean and chooses it—not the absolute but the relative mean.

If, then, every art or science perfects its work in this way, looking to the mean and bringing its work up to this standard (so that people are wont to say of a good work that nothing could be taken from it or added to it, implying that excellence is destroyed by excess or deficiency, but secured by observing the mean; and good artists, as we say, do in fact keep their eyes

fixed on this in all that they do), and if virtue, like nature, is more exact and better than any art, it follows that virtue also must aim at the mean—virtue of course meaning moral virtue or excellence; for it has to do with passions and actions, and it is these that admit of excess and deficiency and the mean. For instance, it is possible to feel fear, confidence, desire, anger, pity, and generally to be affected pleasantly and painfully, either too much or too little, in either case wrongly; but to be thus affected at the right times, and on the right occasions, and towards the right persons, and with the right object, and in the right fashion, is the mean course and the best course, and these are characteristics of virtue. And in the same way our outward acts also admit of excess and deficiency, and the mean or due amount.

Virtue, then, has to deal with feelings or passions and with outward acts, in which excess is wrong and deficiency also is blamed, but the mean amount is praised and is right—both of which are characteristics of virtue.

Virtue, then, is a kind of moderation (μεσότης τις), inasmuch as it aims at the mean or moderate amount (τὸ μέσον).

Again, there are many ways of going wrong (for evil is infinite in nature, to use a Pythagorean [2] figure, while good is finite), but only one way of going right; so that the one is easy and the other hard—easy to miss the mark and hard to hit. On this account also, then, excess and deficiency are characteristic of vice, hitting the mean is characteristic of virtue:—

Goodness is simple, ill takes any shape.

Virtue, then, is a habit or trained faculty of choice, the characteristic of which lies in moderation or observance of the

[2 Aristotle refers here to a doctrine of Pythagoras (c. 522-497), a pre-Socratic philosopher, mathematician, and religious leader. *Ed.*]

mean relatively to the persons concerned, as determined by reason, *i. e.* by the reason by which the prudent man would determine it. And it is a moderation, firstly, inasmuch as it comes in the middle or mean between two vices, one on the side of excess, the other on the side of defect; and, secondly, inasmuch as, while these vices fall short of or exceed the due measure in feeling and in action, it finds and chooses the mean, middling, or moderate amount.

Regarded in its essence, therefore, or according to the definition of its nature, virtue is a moderation or middle state, but viewed in its relation to what is best and right it is the extreme of perfection.

But it is not all actions nor all passions that admit of moderation; there are some whose very names imply badness, as malevolence, shamelessness, envy, and, among acts, adultery, theft, murder. These and all other like things are blamed as being bad in themselves, and not merely in their excess or deficiency. It is impossible therefore to go right in them; they are always wrong: rightness and wrongness in such things (*e. g.* in adultery) does not depend upon whether it is the right person and occasion and manner, but the mere doing of any one of them is wrong.

It would be equally absurd to look for moderation or excess or deficiency in unjust, cowardly, or profligate conduct; for then there would be moderation in excess or deficiency, and excess in excess, and deficiency in deficiency.

The fact is that just as there can be no excess or deficiency in temperance or courage, because the mean or moderate amount is, in a sense, an extreme, so in these kinds of conduct also there can be no moderation or excess or deficiency, but the acts are wrong however they be done. For, to put it generally, there cannot be moderation in excess or deficiency, nor excess or deficiency in moderation. . . .

BOOK VI. THE INTELLECTUAL VIRTUES

1. . . . The virtues or excellences of the mind or soul, it will be remembered, we divided into two classes, and called the one moral and the other intellectual. The moral excellences or virtues we have already discussed in detail; let us now examine the other class, the intellectual excellences, after some preliminary remarks about the soul.

We said before that the soul consists of two parts, the rational and the irrational part. We will now make a similar division of the former, and will assume that there are two rational faculties: (1) that by which we know those things that depend on invariable principles, (2) that by which we know those things that are variable. For to generically different objects must correspond generically different faculties, if, as we hold, it is in virtue of some kind of likeness or kinship with their objects that our faculties are able to know them.

Let us call the former the scientific or demonstrative, the latter the calculative or deliberative faculty. For to deliberate is the same as to calculate, and no one deliberates about things that are invariable. One division then of the rational faculty may be fairly called the calculative faculty. . . .

6. Science is a mode of judging that deals with universal and necessary truths; but truths that can be demonstrated depend upon principles, and (since science proceeds by demonstrative reasoning) every science has its principles. The principles, then, on which the truths of science depend cannot fall within the province of science, nor yet of art or prudence; for a scientific truth is one that can be demonstrated, but art and prudence have to do with that which is variable.

Nor can they fall within the province of wisdom; for it is characteristic of the wise man to have a demonstrative knowledge of certain things.

But the habits of mind or formed faculties by which we apprehend truth without any mixture of error, whether in the domain of things invariable or in the domain of things variable, are science, prudence, wisdom, and reason. If then no one of the first three (prudence, science, wisdom) can be the faculty which apprehends these principles, the only possible conclusion is that they are apprehended by reason.

7. The term oophia (wisdom) is sometimes applied in the domain of the arts to those who are consummate masters of their art; *e. g.* it is applied to Phidias as a master of sculpture, and to Polyclitus for his skill in portrait-statues; and in this application it means nothing else than excellence of art or perfect development of the artistic faculty.

But there are also men who are considered wise, not in part nor in any particular thing (as Homer says in the Margites—

Him the gods gave no skill with spade
  or plough,
Nor made him wise in aught),

but generally wise. In this general sense, then, wisdom plainly will be the most perfect of the sciences.

The wise man, then, must not only know what follows from the principles of knowledge, but also know the truth about those principles. Wisdom, therefore, will be the union of [intuitive] reason with [demonstrative] scientific knowledge, or scientific knowledge of the noblest objects with its crowning perfection, so to speak, added to it. For it would be absurd to suppose that the political faculty or prudence is the highest of our faculties, unless indeed man is the best of all things in the universe.

5 / ESTHETICS

Aristotle distinguished three types of science: the theoretical, which deals with knowledge referring to things known; the practical, which deals with knowledge in reference to human action; and the productive, which deals with knowledge of art. The following selection by a well-known contemporary Thomist is concerned with the ontology of painting, and more especially with the problem of artistic creation.

As the art object is an existent, Professor Gilson applies Aristotelian and Thomistic metaphysical concepts to the understanding of that being. The artist, he notes, produces a being: his act is creative, although not in the absolute sense in which God is creative. Yet apart from the creative activity of the artist, the world would lose those existents which he produces and would therefore be a poorer place. This is why the death of a great artist is such a loss to the world, for actual existence is always at stake in the artist's work.

ART AND REALITY

Étienne Gilson (1884-   )

The notion of form is familiar to painters, but it presupposes other notions whose presence in their mind is certain, even though it is not always perceived with complete clarity. The obscurity of these notions is due to their high degree of abstraction, itself inseparable from the mystery of being. Yet the most elementary esthetic experience attests the reality of their objects.

Let us consider music. Its very existence presupposes that of silence. We recognize as nonmusically gifted the well-known class of persons whom music inspires at once with an irresistible urge to talk. The reason for this is that talking is making noise and that to make noise is to make music impossible. Hence, on a larger scale, the many precautions taken by the conductors of orchestras to ensure complete silence at the beginning of any concert or any operatic performance. The existence of musical sounds presupposes the absolute nothingness of all other sounds. In this sense, music can be said to be created *ex nihilo musicae*, just about as the world is said to have been created by God from a nothingness of world, or as being was first created from a nothingness of being. There is nothing paradoxical in such statements. On the contrary, they could rather be reproached with stating what is too obvious to stand in need of restatement—namely, that the nonmusic that is silence is a prerequisite for the creation of music.

Let us now consider the poet. Con-

fronted as he is with his sheet of white paper, he sees it as the place of infinite poetic possibilities, any one of which can materialize precisely because none of them is already there. The same remark applies to the canvas, wood panel, or wall selected by the painter as the support of his future painting. Whatever its nature, the first care of the painter will be to prime it—that is, to lay on it a coating or preparation that will ensure its perfect uniformity and neutrality with respect to any possible pattern of lines and colors it may have later on to receive. This initial nothingness of figures corresponds to the nothingness of sounds that is the silence created by conductors at the beginning of a musical performance. Like music, painting can be said to be, in a certain sense, created from nothing.[1]

After priming his canvas, the first thing usually done by a painter is to sketch an outline of his future work. This, of course, is an extremely complex operation in which intelligence, imagination, and draftsmanship are equally involved, but we can arbitrarily simplify it to facilitate analysis. More precisely, we can consider in it the sole initial motion of the hand whereby a painter (or a child) delineates the first outline on a sheet of white paper. Even reduced to these

---

The selection is from Étienne Gilson, *Painting and Reality*. Bollingen Series XXXV.4, Bollingen Foundation, Inc. (New York: Pantheon Books; London: Routledge & Kegan Paul, Ltd., 1957), pp. 113-121. Used by permission of the Bollingen Foundation and of Routledge & Kegan Paul, Ltd.

[1] It is remarkable that modern artists have sometimes spontaneously resorted to the language of Holy Scripture in expressing their own experience on this point. For instance, speaking of his glass pictures, which he began by drawing with a needle on a blackened piece of glass, Paul Klee found it natural to say: "I begin logically with chaos, that is only natural" (Grohmann, *Paul Klee*, p. 115). Speaking of Piet Mondrian: "To create emptiness is the principal act. And this is true creation, because this emptiness is positive; it contains the germ of the absolutely new." (Michel Seuphor, *L'Art abstrait*, p. 120.)

simple terms, the question evokes at once such a variety of answers that it remains necessary to make a further choice or, at least, to adopt a certain order.

Expressed in the simplest possible terms, the result of this initial operation is to make "some thing" appear where, heretofore, there was "no thing." This is what is meant by the term "creation" when it is applied to works of art. In this, art is unique, and the fact is especially evident in the case of the plastic arts such as design, drawing, engraving, or painting.

In a loose sense, all the productions of the human mind can be called its creations. Science is something added to nature by the minds of scientists, but it is not another thing added by scientists to the world of already existing things. Science is not an artifact. It is not even a mental image of reality that we could conceive as duplicating and enriching it in the mind of the scientist. As a construction of the mind, science remains contained within the very reality it strives to describe. And what is true of science is also true of philosophy, particularly of metaphysics. The aim and scope of philosophy is to know the ultimate nature of reality. At a different level, and by methods different from those of science, metaphysics, too, is essentially speculative; its ultimate aim and purpose is not to produce a new being, or thing, but, rather, to know given reality exactly as it is. To the extent that it is art, painting is an activity specifically different from both scientific and metaphysical cognition.[2]

This does not mean that there is no art in science and that a philosopher cannot be, at the same time, an artist.[3] The unity

of the human mind is such that, just as there is intellectual knowledge in all that man does, or makes, there seldom is complete absence of art in what man knows. Elegance is a quality highly prized in mathematical demonstrations. The same elegance is perceptible in the dialogues of Plato, so much so that some of them—for instance, his *Symposium*—constitute in themselves exceptionally perfect specimens of literary art. But this is not our question. Even if it is truly esthetic in nature, mathematical elegance is entirely at the service of cognition: it aims to achieve an expression of truth highly satisfactory to the mind. As to such works of art as Plato's *Symposium,* what of philosophy they contain could be stated in a much simpler, shorter, and less artistic way without losing any of its truth value, although it would lose all its beauty and much of its persuasive force. But this reduction of art to any kind of cognitive process is particularly impossible in the case of painting. The work of the painter is there, materially present in space, for everyone to see. While a scientist is explaining his science, he himself and his science occupy the same place in the lecture room; when a painter presents his works to the public, he himself and his paintings do not occupy the same space in the exhibition room. This is what we mean in saying that the art of painting is not a particular species included in the genus "cognition."

This point is of decisive importance, and the answers to so many other problems depend upon it that we should not let important difficulties pass unnoticed. One of the best known follows from the popular

[2] See E. Gilson, "Art et métaphysique," *Revue de métaphysique et de morale,* XXIII, No. 1 bis (Jan., 1916), 244-46.
[3] Thomas Aquinas has noted that "even in speculative matters there is something by way of work"; we *make* speeches, reasonings, demonstrations, expositions, etc. The arts related to the operations of the mind, and in

which the body does not share, are called, for this very reason, *liberal* arts: *Summa theologiae,* Ia, IIae, 57, 3, reply to obj. 3.—On the many different answers given to the question "What is art?" see the excellent ch. III, "The Meanings of Art," in Thomas Munro, *The Arts and Their Interrelations,* pp. 49-109.

definition of art commonly attributed to the novelist Émile Zola: art is a fragment of nature seen through a temperament. If this were true, nothing would be more common than artistic creativity, for, indeed, each and every man has a temperament through which he cannot help seeing nature, but very few men are endowed by nature with the gifts that it takes to create works of art worthy of the name. This elementary confusion lies at the origin of many pseudo-artistic vocations. The most exquisite sensitiveness to natural beauty requires neither science, nor philosophy, nor even any kind of intellectual culture in general; between the charm of nature and ourselves, there is nothing, but between our sensibility and any painting that we may attempt to do, there is art. In the case of painting, art is not nature seen through a temperament; rather, it is the ability to create a new being that nobody would ever see, either in nature or otherwise, unless the art of the painter caused it to exist.

A similar formula, attributed to Francis Bacon, defines art as "man added to nature" *(homo additus naturae)*, and it raises similar difficulties. Like so many other brilliant definitions, this one does not bear the acid test of critical examination. Since man is part and parcel of nature, he cannot be added to it. Rather than as man added to nature, art should be conceived as man adding to nature, or, better still, as nature enriching itself by all the additions that it receives at the hands of man. As has been said, the painter is neither a philosopher nor a scientist in whose mind nature mirrors itself; but he is not, at the same time, one of those engineers whose cleverness harnesses the forces of nature and puts them at our disposal; he is one of the creative forces of nature, in this sense at least, that he gives existence to certain beings that, in nature, nothing else than himself could possibly have produced. And not only nothing else, but no one else. It is not evident that, at

the present stage of scientific progress, the premature death of a great scientist renders impossible the scientific discoveries that a longer life would have enabled him to make. On the contrary, the death of an artist certainly brings to a close the production of the kind of painting that bears the imprint of his hand. Many men can now know the paintings and enjoy them, but no other man than himself could cause them to exist. The lineage of these beings, which resemble one another as the children of the same father, is now extinct, and neither the admiration nor the zeal and cleverness of his most faithful pupils will ever increase it by a single unit. The creative artist is for us the only empirically observable example of a force analogous to the still more mysterious one in virtue of which the works of nature come into being. No painting, drawing, or etching done by anyone else will ever replace those which a still longer life would have enabled Matisse himself to create. The death of a great painter is an irretrievable loss of substance for the world.[4]

In the light of what precedes, it may well be asked if paintings should simply be classified among the artifacts. And, indeed, they are artifacts, at least in the sense that they are products of human workmanship; but even granting that all paintings are artifacts, it cannot be granted that all artifacts are works of art. Considered as a genus, artifacts include, besides works of art properly so called, the densely populated class of the many and manifold tools, instruments, and machines due to the inven-

---

[4] See the epigraph (borrowed from Gabriele d'Annunzio's *Il Fuoco*) to our essay of 1915 on "Art et métaphysique": "Ah, Stelio, t'aspettavo! Riccardo Wagner è morto.—Il mondo parve diminuito di valore." ("Ah, Stelio, I was waiting for you! Richard Wagner is dead.—The world seemed to have lost some of its value.")—This page was written on the very day the Toronto radio announced the death of Henri Matisse (November 5, 1954).

tiveness and skill of *homo faber*. Now, whatever their differences, all these tools, instruments, and machines have this in common, that their final cause lies outside themselves. Not one of them is made for its own sake. One does not look at a timepiece (taken precisely qua timepiece) except to know what time it is. An ornamented shotgun may well be considered a work of art, but then it is no longer seen as a shotgun, whose intrinsic qualities, taken precisely qua shotgun, are foreign to the notions of ornamentation and decoration. Not so in the case of paintings. We call "tool" anything that serves as a means to an end, but, precisely, a painting cannot be used as a means to any end extrinsic to itself. A painting is not there to permit any kind of operation to be performed such as carrying goods or persons, talking from a distance, or shooting game. There is nothing that one can do *with* a painting. True enough, there is something that one can do *about* it, but, precisely, there is only one such thing, and it is to look at it. If he considers a painting as a means to any other end than its contemplation, a man does not see it as a work of art. He may look at it as an art dealer looks at the particular brand of merchandise he tries to sell, or as an investor looks at a more or less promising kind of stock. He may even consider it something to be talked about, if he is a lecturer; or something to be written about, if he is an art historian or an art critic.[5] In every one of these cases, the end of the work of art lies outside it, as in money, in a lecture to give, in

an article or in a book to write; consequently, in every one of these cases, the work of art will be used as a means to another end; it will cease to act as a work of art.

We can now return to our question and give it an answer. The question was: in what sense is it true to say that the term "creation" fittingly designates the initial operation of artists, and quite especially of painters? The answer is: because the immediate and direct effect of such an operation is to cause something to be or, in simpler terms, because the effect of such an operation is the actual existence of a new "being." Here again a comparison with theology can help, not at all because we should attempt in any way to deduce esthetics from theology, but rather, on the contrary, because in certain matters theology has based its inferences upon the experience of artists as well as upon the nature of art. Such is particularly the case with the notion of creation. In his *Timaeus*, under the form of a mythical narrative, Plato has presented the world as the work of a divine artist whom he called the Demiurge. We shall have later on to ask ourselves what light this dialogue throws on the nature of artistic production; for our present problem, it will prove more important to consider the notion of creation such as, on the strength of Biblical data, the Christian theologians have understood it.

If we leave aside the history of this religious notion and consider it merely as it became at the very time it reached its point of perfection, this notion points out the act by which a certain being causes other beings to be. Strictly speaking, only one being can thus be the cause of existence for other beings—namely, God, who, because he himself is the pure act of being, is eminently able to impart actual existence. Obviously, no artist can create his works, as God does, from an absolute nothingness of existence. Some material must be at his dis-

---

5 Critics themselves do not like discussing the question of their own attitude toward works of art. It seems hardly possible to consider their position as identical with that of common art lovers. Critics are at their best when they deal with works of art with which they used to be familiar before they began to speak, or to write, as critics. At any rate, to look at a painting *in view of* writing about it must somewhat interfere with the esthetic apprehension of the work in question.

posal before he begins his work; even the forms he creates are the forms of something, and he has seen them in nature, or in the art of his predecessors, before he himself began to create.[6] Moreover, the kind of existence an artist imparts to his works always presupposes his own existence, which, unlike that of God, is a received one. Incidentally, this is the reason why esthetics need not carry its investigations beyond the philosophical level of ontology to the properly theological level of the divine act of existing. The actual existence of the matter to be informed by the art of the painter, as well as that of the painter himself, are two necessary prerequisites for the very possibility of art. The problems that belong to esthetics presuppose the fact that there are works of art, and although esthetics can investigate the mode of being proper to this specific class of artifacts, its inquiry stops at the level of substantial being specified and determined by its form. Actual existence is presupposed as already given, for all its ingredients, from the very beginning of the operation.

This does not mean that actual existence is not at stake in the making of a painting. The actual existence of the painting to be done is the final result that the artist intends to achieve. Since God alone is the pure act of being, no secondary cause,

be it even the art of a creative artist, can conjure up a new being from total non-being. But the artist himself, his art, the matter and the forms he puts to use, all are enjoying an actual existence they have received from the Prime Cause. Artists can impart or communicate to their works the actual existence that is their own. Some pen drawings by Corot are enough to give existence to charming landscapes that seem to be made from nothing, and almost with nothing. An etching done from a pen drawing by Pieter Brueghel succeeds in educing the most complex landscape from the blank surface of a plate. The mere interplay of the lines, ordered as they are by a supremely lucid imagination, even permits him to pretend that the very Journey to Emmaus is included in this creation of his hand. In this sense, the production of plastic works of art truly extends to their very existence. Himself an existent, the painter is an efficient cause of actual existence for other existents.[7]

These notions will have to be reconsidered at a different level in discussing the proper kind of causality a painter exercises with respect to his works. For the present, let it suffice to observe that thus to relate art to metaphysics, and even to theology, is by no means to attempt a deduction of art

---

[6] This point is forcefully developed by Delacroix in his *Journal*, p. 386 (March 1, 1859), particularly: "But not only did these great men create nothing in the proper sense of the word, which means making *something* out of *nothing,* but in order to form their talent, or prevent it from getting rusty, they had to imitate their predecessors and, consciously or unconsciously, to imitate them almost unceasingly." Delacroix himself always had Rubens in mind; Manet could not forget Velázquez during his "Spanish period," and Picasso, perhaps the most inexhaustible source of new forms in our own times, cannot help remembering somebody or something else's style the very moment he is inventing a style of his own.

[7] "To act is nothing else than to communicate that by which the acting being is in act" (Thomas Aquinas, *De potentia,* qu. 2, art. 1, answer). Thomas presently adds to this: "to the extent that it is possible." Now, God, who is the Prime Cause, is the pure act of Being. Consequently, "all the created causes communicate in one single effect, which is actual existence [*esse*], although each one of them has its own effects, by which they differ from one another. For instance, heat makes something to be hot, and an architect causes a house to be [*aedificator facit domum esse*]. Created causes thus agree in this, that they cause being [*conveniunt ergo in hoc quod causant esse*], but they differ in this, that while fire causes fires, an architect causes a house" (qu. 7, art. 2 answer).

from these lofty sciences. On the contrary, when theologians started from the visible world in order to conceive, as best they could, the invisible nature of God, they first borrowed from art the pattern of the most perfect kind of causality given in human experience, and then transcended it in order to make it attributable to God. In their effort to do so, the theologians have unveiled to us the very Idea of what an absolute artistic creation would be: an act in which, because the intellect, the power, the will, and the art of the artist are identically one with his own act of being, the total cause of the total effect is included. Artistic creation is not such an act, but it remains for us the least imperfect image there is of what the theologians call creation. And no wonder, since it is found at the origin of the notion that the theologians have formed of it. Supposing, therefore, that painters can communicate existence to their own works, we must now ascertain the sense in which it is true to say that, because they also produce forms, painters truly produce beings.

6 / SOCIAL PHILOSOPHY

Just as there are universal and objective principles of the individual good, so too there are for the realist such principles of the common or social good. Realists would assert, with Cicero, that the roots of Justice are in Nature or the structure of things and of man. They are opposed to any view that right and justice are founded simply on men's opinions or on convention. And, because there is but a single definition of man, so can there be but a single definition of justice for all men. Virtue, as Aristotle taught, is nature perfected. The common good is similarly the perfection of man's associative nature. The principles of the common good are embodied in law; law is "right reason" and the instrumentality of Justice. The good state, finally, is that state whose actual positive law reflects and embodies the Law of Reason.

NATURE AND JUSTICE

Cicero (106-43)

MARCUS. I shall seek the root of Justice in Nature, under whose guidance our whole discussion must be conducted.

ATTICUS. Quite right. Surely with her as our guide, it will be impossible for us to go astray.

The selection is reprinted by permission of the publishers from the Loeb Classical Library edition, translated by Clinton Walker Keyes, Cicero, *De Re Publica, De Legibus* (Cambridge, Mass.: Harvard University Press, 1928), pp. 319-367 and 379-387, with omissions.

MAR. Do you grant us, then, Pomponius (for I am aware of what Quintus thinks), that it is by the might of the immortal gods, or by their nature, reason, power, mind, will, or any other term which may make my meaning clearer, that all Nature is governed? For if you do not admit it, we must begin our argument with this problem before taking up anything else.

ATT. Surely I will grant it, if you insist upon it. . . .

MAR. I will not make the argument

long. Your admission leads us to this: that animal which we call man, endowed with foresight and quick intelligence, complex, keen, possessing memory, full of reason and prudence, has been given a certain distinguished status by the supreme God who created him; for he is the only one among so many different kinds and varieties of living beings who has a share in reason and thought, while all the rest are deprived of it. But what is more divine, I will not say in man only, but in all heaven and earth, than reason? And reason, when it is full grown and perfected, is rightly called wisdom. Therefore, since there is nothing better than reason, and since it exists both in man and God, the first common possession of man and God is reason. But those who have reason in common must also have right reason in common. And since right reason is Law, we must believe that men have Law also in common with the gods. Further, those who share Law must also share Justice; and those who share these are to be regarded as members of the same commonwealth. If indeed they obey the same authorities and powers, this is true in a far greater degree; but as a matter of fact they do obey this celestial system, the divine mind, and the God of transcendent power. Hence we must now conceive of this whole universe as one commonwealth of which both gods and men are members.

And just as in States distinctions in legal status are made on account of the blood relationships of families, so in the universe the same thing holds true, but on a scale much vaster and more splendid, so that men are grouped with Gods on the basis of blood relationship and descent. For when the nature of man is examined, the theory is usually advanced (and in all probability it is correct) that through constant changes and revolutions in the heavens, a time came which was suitable for sowing the seed of the human race. And when this

seed was scattered and sown over the earth, it was granted the divine gift of the soul. For while the other elements of which man consists were derived from what is mortal, and are therefore fragile and perishable, the soul was generated in us by God. Hence we are justified in saying that there is a blood relationship between ourselves and the celestial beings; or we may call it a common ancestry or origin. Therefore among all the varieties of living beings, there is no creature except man which has any knowledge of God, and among men themselves there is no race either so highly civilized or so savage as not to know that it must believe in a god, even if it does not know in what sort of god it ought to believe. Thus it is clear that man recognizes God because, in a way, he remembers and recognizes the source from which he sprang.

Moreover, virtue exists in man and God alike, but in no other creature besides; virtue, however, is nothing else than Nature perfected and developed to its highest point; therefore there is a likeness between man and God. As this is true, what relationship could be closer or clearer than this one? For this reason, Nature has lavishly yielded such a wealth of things adapted to man's convenience and use that what she produces seems intended as a gift to us, and not brought forth by chance; and this is true, not only of what the fertile earth bountifully bestows in the form of grain and fruit, but also of the animals; for it is clear that some of them have been created to be man's slaves, some to supply him with their products, and others to serve as his food. Moreover innumerable arts have been discovered through the teachings of Nature; for it is by a skilful imitation of her that reason has acquired the necessities of life. Nature has likewise not only equipped man himself with nimbleness of thought, but has also given him the senses, to be, as it were, his attendants and messengers; she has laid bare the obscure and none too [obvious] [1] meanings of a great many things, to serve as the foundations of knowledge, as we may call them; and she has granted us a bodily form which is convenient and well suited to the human mind. For while she has bent the other creatures down toward their food, she has made man alone erect, and has challenged him to look up toward heaven, as being, so to speak, akin to him, and his first home. . . .

The points which are now being briefly touched upon are certainly important; but out of all the material of the philosophers' discussions, surely there comes nothing more valuable than the full realization that we are born for Justice, and that right is based, not upon men's opinions, but upon Nature. This fact will immediately be plain if you once get a clear conception of man's fellowship and union with his fellow-men. For no single thing is so like another, so exactly its counterpart, as all of us are to one another. Nay, if bad habits and false beliefs did not twist the weaker minds and turn them in whatever direction they are inclined, no one would be so like his own self as all men would be like all others. And so, however we may define man, a single definition will apply to all. This is a sufficient proof that there is no difference in kind between man and man; for if there were, one definition could not be applicable to all men; and indeed reason, which alone raises us above the level of the beasts and enables us to draw inferences, to prove and disprove, to discuss and solve problems, and to come to conclusions, is certainly common to us all, and, though varying in what it learns, at least in the capacity to learn it is invariable. For the same things are invariably perceived by the senses, and those things which stimulate the senses stimulate them in the same way in all men; and those

[1] Brackets indicate gaps in Cicero's text. The words within brackets have been supplied by editors of Cicero.

rudimentary beginnings of intelligence to which I have referred, which are imprinted on our minds, are imprinted on all minds alike; and speech, in the mind's interpreter, though differing in the choice of words, agrees in the sentiments expressed. In fact, there is no human being of any race who, if he finds a guide, cannot attain to virtue.

The similarity of the human race is clearly marked in its evil tendencies as well as in its goodness. For pleasure also attracts all men; and even though it is an enticement to vice, yet it has some likeness to what is naturally good. For it delights us by its lightness and agreeableness; and for this reason, by an error of thought, it is embraced as something wholesome. It is through a similar misconception that we shun death as though it were a dissolution of nature, and cling to life because it keeps us in the sphere in which we were born; and that we look upon pain as one of the greatest of evils, not only because of its cruelty, but also because it seems to lead to the destruction of nature. In the same way, on account of the similarity between moral worth and renown, those who are publicly honored are considered happy, while those who do not attain fame are thought miserable. Troubles, joys, desires, and fears haunt the minds of all men without distinction, and even if different men have different beliefs, that does not prove, for example, that it is not the same quality of superstition that besets those races which worship dogs and cats as gods, as that which torments other races. But what nation does not love courtesy, kindliness, gratitude, and remembrance of favors bestowed? What people does not hate and despise the haughty, the wicked, the cruel, and the ungrateful? Inasmuch as these considerations prove to us that the whole human race is bound together in unity, it follows, finally, that knowledge of the principles of right living is what makes men better. . . .

The next point, then, is that we are so

constituted by Nature as to share the sense of Justice with one another and to pass it on to all men. And in this whole discussion I want it understood that what I shall call Nature is [that which is implanted in us by Nature]; that, however, the corruption caused by bad habits is so great that the sparks of fire, so to speak, which Nature has kindled in us are extinguished by this corruption, and the vices which are their opposites spring up and are established. But if the judgments of men were in agreement with Nature, so that, as the poet says, they considered "nothing alien to them which concerns mankind," then Justice would be equally observed by all. For those creatures who have received the gift of reason from Nature have also received right reason, and therefore they have also received the gift of Law, which is right reason applied to command and prohibition. And if they have received Law, they have received Justice also. Now all men have received reason; therefore all men have received Justice. Consequently Socrates was right when he cursed, as he often did, the man who first separated utility from Justice; for this separation, he complained, is the source of all mischief. . . .

Now all this is really a preface to what remains to be said in our discussion, and its purpose is to make it more easily understood that Justice is inherent in Nature. . . .

QUINTUS. You certainly need to say very little more on that head, for from what you have already said, Atticus is convinced, and certainly I am, that Nature is the source of Justice.

ATT. How can I help being convinced, when it has just been proved to us, first, that we have been provided and equipped with what we may call the gifts of the gods; next, that there is only one principle by which men may live with one another, and that this is the same for all, and possessed equally by all; and, finally, that all men are bound together by a certain natural feeling of kindliness and good-will, and also by a partnership in Justice? Now that we have admitted the truth of these conclusions, and rightly, I think, how can we separate Law and Justice from Nature? . . .

MAR. But the most foolish notion of all is the belief that everything is just which is found in the customs or laws of nations. Would that be true, even if these laws had been enacted by tyrants? If the well-known Thirty had desired to enact a set of laws at Athens, or if the Athenians without exception were delighted by the tyrants' laws, that would not entitle such laws to be regarded as just, would it? No more, in my opinion, should that law be considered just which a Roman interrex proposed, to the effect that a dictator might put to death with impunity any citizen he wished, even without a trial. For Justice is one; it binds all human society, and is based on one Law, which is right reason applied to command and prohibition. Whoever knows not this Law, whether it has been recorded in writing anywhere or not, is without Justice.

But if Justice is conformity to written laws and national customs, and if, as the same persons claim, everything is to be tested by the standard of utility, then anyone who thinks it will be profitable to him will, if he is able, disregard and violate the laws. It follows that Justice does not exist at all, if it does not exist in Nature, and if that form of it which is based on utility can be overthrown by that very utility itself. And if Nature is not to be considered the foundation of Justice, that will mean the destruction [of the virtues on which human society depends]. For where then will there be a place for generosity, or love of country, or loyalty, or the inclination to be of service to others or to show gratitude for favors received? For these virtues originate in our natural inclination to love our fellow-men, and this is the foundation of Justice. Otherwise not merely consideration for men but also rites and pious observances in honor of the gods are done away with; for I think that these ought to be maintained, not through fear, but on account of the close relationship which exists between man and God. But if the principles of Justice were founded on the decrees of peoples, the edicts of princes, or the decisions of judges, then Justice would sanction robbery and adultery and forgery of wills, in case these acts were approved by the votes or decrees of the populace. But if so great a power belongs to the decisions and decrees of fools that the laws of Nature can be changed by their votes, then why do they not ordain that what is bad and baneful shall be considered good and salutary? Or, if a law can make Justice out of Injustice, can it not also make good out of bad? But in fact we can perceive the difference between good laws and bad by referring them to no other standard than Nature; indeed, it is not merely Justice and Injustice which are distinguished by Nature, but also and without exception things which are honorable and dishonorable. For since an intelligence common to us all makes things known to us and formulates them in our minds, honorable actions are ascribed by us to virtue, and dishonorable actions to vice; and only a madman would conclude that these judgments are matters of opinion, and not fixed by Nature. For even what we, by a misuse of the term, call the virtue of a tree or of a horse, is not a matter of opinion, but is based on Nature. And if that is true, honorable and dishonorable actions must also be distinguished by Nature. For if virtue in general is to be tested by opinion, then its several parts must also be so tested; who, therefore, would judge a man of prudence and, if I may say so, hard common sense, not by his own character but by some external circumstance? For virtue is reason completely developed; and this certainly is natural; therefore everything honorable is likewise natural. For just as truth and falsehood, the logical and illogical, are judged by themselves and not by anything else, so the steadfast and continuous use of reason in the conduct of life, which is virtue, and also inconstancy, which is vice, [are judged] by their own nature.

[Or, when a farmer judges the quality of a tree by nature,] shall we not use the same standard in regard to the characters of young men? Then shall we judge character by Nature, and judge virtue and vice, which result from character, by some other standard? But if we adopt the same standard for them, must we not refer the honorable and the base to Nature also? Whatever good thing is praiseworthy must have within itself something which deserves praise, for goodness itself is good by reason not of opinion but of Nature. For, if this were not true, men would also be happy by reason of opinion; and what statement could be more absurd than that? Wherefore since both good and evil are judged by Nature and are natural principles, surely honorable and base actions must also be distinguished in a similar way and referred to the standard of Nature. But we are confused by the variety of men's beliefs and by their disagreements, and because this same variation is not found in the senses, we think that Nature has made these accurate, and say that those things about which different people have different opinions and the same people not always identical opinions are unreal. However, this is far from being the case. For our senses are not perverted by parent, nurse, teacher, poet, or the stage, nor led astray by popular feeling; but against our minds all sorts of plots are constantly being laid, either by those whom I have just mentioned, who, taking possession of them while still tender and unformed, color and bend them as they wish, or else by that enemy which lurks deep within us, entwined in our every sense—that counterfeit of good, which is, however, the mother of all evils—pleasure. Corrupted by her allurements, we fail to discern clearly what things are by Nature good, because the same seductiveness and itching does not attend them.

To close now our discussion of this whole subject, the conclusion, which stands clearly before our eyes from what has already been said, is this: Justice and all things honorable are to be sought for their own sake. And indeed all good men love fairness in itself and Justice in itself, and it is unnatural for a good man to make such a mistake as to love what does not deserve love for itself alone. . . .

. . . It is certainly true that, since Law ought to be a reformer of vice and an incentive to virtue, the guiding principles of life may be derived from it. It is therefore true that wisdom is the mother of all good things; and from the Greek expression meaning "the love of wisdom" philosophy has taken its name. And philosophy is the richest, the most bounteous, and the most exalted gift of the immortal gods to humanity. For she alone has taught us, in addition to all other wisdom, that most difficult of all things—to know ourselves. This precept is so important and significant that the credit for it is given, not to any human being, but to the god of Delphi. For he who knows himself will realize, in the first place, that he has a divine element within him, and will think of his own inner nature as a kind of consecrated image of God; and so he will always act and think in a way worthy of so great a gift of the gods, and, when he has examined and thoroughly tested himself, he will understand how nobly equipped by Nature he entered life, and what manifold means he possesses for the attainment and acquisition of wisdom. For from the very first he began to form in his mind and spirit shadowy concepts, as it were, of all sorts, and when these have been illuminated under the guidance of wisdom, he perceives that he will be a good man, and, for that very reason, happy. For when the mind, having attained to a

knowledge and perception of the virtues, has abandoned its subservience to the body and its indulgence of it, has put down pleasure as if it were a taint of dishonor, has escaped from all fear of death or pain, has entered into a partnership of love with its own, recognizing as its own all who are joined to it by Nature; when it has taken up the worship of the gods and pure religion, has sharpened the vision both of the eye and of the mind so that they can choose the good and reject the opposite—a virtue which is called prudence because it foresees —then what greater degree of happiness can be described or imagined? And further, when it has examined the heavens, the earth, the seas, the nature of the universe, and understands whence all these things came and whither they must return, when and how they are destined to perish, what part of them is mortal and transient and what is divine and eternal; and when it almost lays hold of the ruler and governor of the universe, and when it realizes that it is not shut in by [narrow] walls as a resident of some fixed spot, but is a citizen of the whole universe, as it were of a single city—then in the midst of this universal grandeur, and with such a view and comprehension of nature, ye immortal gods, how well it will know itself, according to the precept of the Pythian Apollo! . . .

II

MAR. Once more, then, . . . let us look at the character and nature of Law, for fear that, though it must be the standard to which we refer everything, we may now and then be led astray by an incorrect use of terms, and forget the rational principles on which our laws must be based. . . .

I find that it has been the opinion of the wisest men that Law is not a product of human thought, nor is it any enactment of peoples, but something eternal which rules the whole universe by its wisdom in command and prohibition. Thus they have been accustomed to say that Law is the primal and ultimate mind of God, whose reason directs all things either by compulsion or restraint. Wherefore that Law which the gods have given to the human race has been justly praised; for it is the reason and mind of a wise lawgiver applied to command and prohibition.

QUIN. You have touched upon this subject several times before. But please make the character of this heavenly Law clear to us, so that the waves of habit may not carry us away and sweep us into the common mode of speech on such subjects.

MAR. Ever since we were children, Quintus, we have learned to call, "If one summon another to court," and other rules of the same kind, laws. But we must come to the true understanding of the matter, which is as follows: this and other commands and prohibitions of nations have the power to summon to righteousness and away from wrong-doing; but this power is not merely older than the existence of nations and States, it is coeval with that God who guards and rules heaven and earth. For the divine mind cannot exist without reason, and divine reason cannot but have this power to establish right and wrong. . . . For reason did exist, derived from the Nature of the universe, urging men to right conduct and diverting them from wrong-doing, and this reason did not first become Law when it was written down, but when it first came into existence; and it came into existence simultaneously with the divine mind. Wherefore the true and primal Law, applied to command and prohibition, is the right reason of supreme Jupiter.

QUIN. I agree with you, brother, that what is right and true is also eternal, and does not begin or end with written statutes.

MAR. Therefore, just as that divine mind is the supreme Law, so, when [reason] is perfected in man [that also is Law; and this perfected reason exists] in the mind

of the wise man; but those rules which, in varying forms and for the need of the moment, have been formulated for the guidance of nations, bear the title of laws rather by favor than because they are really such. For every law which really deserves that name is truly praiseworthy, as they prove by approximately the following arguments. It is agreed, of course, that laws were invented for the safety of citizens, the preservation of States, and the tranquillity and happiness of human life, and that those who first put statutes of this kind in force convinced their people that it was their intention to write down and put into effect such rules as, once accepted and adopted, would make possible for them an honorable and happy life; and when such rules were drawn up and put in force, it is clear that men called them "laws." From this point of view it can be readily understood that those who formulated wicked and unjust statutes for nations, thereby breaking their promises and agreements, put into effect anything but "laws." It may thus be clear that in the very definition of the term "law" there inheres the idea and principle of choosing what is just and true. I ask you then, Quintus, according to the custom of the philosophers: if there is a certain thing, the lack of which in a State compels us to consider it no State at all, must we consider this thing a good?

QUIN. One of the greatest goods, certainly.

MAR. And if a State lacks Law, must it for that reason be considered no State at all?

QUIN. It cannot be denied.

MAR. Then Law must necessarily be considered one of the greatest goods.

QUIN. I agree with you entirely.

MAR. What of the many deadly, the many pestilential statutes which nations put in force? These no more deserve to be called laws than the rules a band of robbers might pass in their assembly. For if ignorant and unskilful men have prescribed deadly poisons instead of healing drugs, these cannot possibly be called physicians' prescriptions; neither in a nation can a statute of any sort be called a law, even though the nation, in spite of its being a ruinous regulation, has accepted it. There-

fore Law is the distinction between things just and unjust, made in agreement with that primal and most ancient of all things, Nature; and in conformity to Nature's standard are framed those human laws which inflict punishment upon the wicked but defend and protect the good.

7 / PHILOSOPHY OF SCIENCE

As a philosophy basing itself on a metaphysics of being, realism faces the problem of relating itself to the natural sciences. Both metaphysics and science claim to give us knowledge of the physical order, both claim to be supreme in the sense of not being dependent on other disciplines for their own conclusions. How then are science and metaphysics related? Is there inevitable conflict between them, or can distinctions between them be made so that any apparent conflict is removed?

Professor Maritain, another contemporary Thomist, addresses himself to this problem, seeking to clarify the relations among science or, as he calls it, empiriological physics, philosophy of nature, and metaphysics. The study of nature, he argues, belongs to the first order of abstraction or intellectual consideration. Philosophy of nature or ontological physics deals with mutable being as such and its principles, while empiriological physics deals with a description of phenomena within the order of physical nature. To the second order of abstraction belongs mathematics, the science of quantity. Metaphysics, the science of being as such, is a third abstraction.

Given this analysis, Maritain believes that no conflict can exist among these disciplines. They are ordered hierarchically, with metaphysics at the top; but each has its own problems, its own methods, and, within the proper limits of each, its own validity.

SCIENCE AND NATURE

Jacques Maritain (1882-   )

The conflict between philosophy and science leads to a central problem; that of the philosophy of nature. Ought there to be a philosophy of nature which is distinct at

one and the same time from metaphysics and the special sciences? What are its characteristics, its nature and definition, its spirit? As these questions are of rather a technical order, the aridity of the exposition which they demand will be excused. They are not easy because they reach us charged with historical implications and associations.

The selection is reprinted with the permission of Charles Scribner's Sons and of Geoffrey Bles, Ltd., from Jacques Maritain, *Science and Wisdom*, pp. 34-36, 39, 50-55, and 60-64.

Is not the philosophy of nature what Aristotle called physics? Did not the idea of physics cover, for antiquity, the whole province of the natural sciences? Is not the ruin of the Aristotelian explanations of natural phenomena also the ruin of the whole of Aristotelian physics—and hence of the philosophy of nature? And hence, ought not the place of physics in Aristotle's sense to be occupied still for us today by physics, but by physics as understood in the sense of Einstein, Planck and Louis de Broglie: or more generally by the body of the sciences of the phenomena of nature, called simply Science by the modern world. Such are the connections and liaisons which are involved in the theoretical questions of which I propose to treat.

These questions are fundamental and not easy. We need not hesitate to say that they are of first rate importance for human wisdom. We ought not to neglect the problem of the philosophy of nature. Of all speculative wisdom it is the humblest, the nearest the world of sense, the least perfect. It is not even a form of wisdom in the pure and simple sense of the word, it is wisdom only in the order of mobile and corruptible things. But this is precisely the order most proportioned to our rational nature. This wisdom, which is not even purely and simply wisdom, is the first which is offered in the progressive ascending movement of our thought. And that it why it has such importance for us—precisely because it is at the lowest rung of the ladder of φιλία τῆς σοφίας [the love of wisdom].

In what ways can the real enter within us? There are but two, one natural, the other supernatural: the senses, and the divine Spirit. When we are concerned with the light which descends from heaven it is not metaphysics which is primary, but the highest and purely spiritual wisdom, by which we are enabled to open our soul and being and to receive something which enters into us according to the gift of grace. And

if it is a question of the light which springs from earth, it is likewise not metaphysics which is primary, but an inferior wisdom bound up with sense perception and strictly dependent on experience: because it is through the senses that we are open to things, and something enters us, according to our natural mode of knowing.

Metaphysics lies halfway between. It is not directly open, as the platonists taught, to an intuition of divine things. The intuition with which it deals lies at the summit of the process of visualization or abstraction which begins with the sensible order. It is in itself and formally independent of the philosophy of nature, being superior to it and ruling it. But materially, and *quoad nos,* it presupposes it: not of course in its perfect statement, but at least in its first positions. . . .

Thus it would be quite vain to try to evade the problem of the philosophy of nature. This problem must be regarded squarely and we must try to treat it for its own sake, in point of doctrine. Here the metaphysician of knowledge faces two questions. Should there be a philosophy of nature distinct from the sciences of natural phenomena? (This is the question *an sit.*) And in what exactly does it consist? (This is the question *quid sit.*) A whole volume would be needed to treat them fully. I shall only indicate in the shortest possible way the conclusions I believe we ought to reach.

To reply to the first question we must distinguish—at the first degree of intellectual abstraction, in the order of knowledge of sensible reality—two ways of constructing concepts and of analyzing the real: the analysis we have already called ontological, and the analysis which we have called empiriological, of sensible reality. In the first case we are dealing with an ascending analysis towards intelligible being, in which the sensible plays an indispensable part, but in attendance on intelligible being. In the second case we are dealing with a descending synthesis towards the sensible, towards the observable as such. Not of course that the mind then ceases to have to do with being, which is impossible, but being passes into the service of the sensible, the observable and above all of the measurable, becomes an unknown element assuring the constancy of certain sensible determinations and of certain standards, or assuring the value of certain *entia rationis* with a foundation *in re*.

In one case one seeks a definition by ontological characteristics, by the constituent elements of an intelligible nature or essence—so obscurely that only at times does one grasp this essence. In the other case, one tries to define by possibilities of observation and measurement, by the performance of physical operations: here the permanent possibility of sensible verification and measurement plays for the scientist a part similar to that played by the essence for the philosopher.

This distinction once understood, it is easy to understand that knowledge of the empiriological kind, that is to say, the sciences of natural phenomena, needs to be completed by knowledge of the ontological kind, that is to say, by a philosophy of nature. For these sciences imply, as Meyerson has shown so well, an ontological aspiration and an ontological reference—which they do not satisfy. They aim at being (as real) and they mistrust it (as intelligible) and fall back on sensible phenomena; in such a way that, to constitute themselves in accord with their pure epistemological type, they are in a certain sense obliged to go counter to the inclination of the intellect.

The sciences of phenomena thus bear witness to the fact that nature is knowable and that they only know it in an essentially unsatisfying way. In this measure, therefore, they require to be completed by another knowledge of the same sensible universe, which will be an ontological knowledge—in truth, a philosophy of nature. Not only do we say that the sciences deepen and quicken the desire of the intelligence to pass to deeper and higher truths, just as the philosophy of nature itself quickens the desire of the intelligence to pass to metaphysics, but we say also that inasmuch as they are knowledge ordered to a certain term, the experimental sciences require to be completed, not of course so far as concerns their own proper rule of explanation, or the formal object which *specifies* them, but in regard to the term in which they issue, which is the sensible and the real. In so far as it is mutable and corruptible, the latter is known in an essentially unsatisfying way with the help of the vocabulary which is proper to empiriological knowledge. Thus, this knowledge must be completed by another which exists at the first degree of intellectual abstraction and will grasp the intelligibility of the real which is thus proposed to it.

Moreover, the inverse is equally true. The philosophy of nature must be completed by the experimental sciences. It does not provide for us by itself alone a complete knowledge of the real in which it issues, that is to say, of sensible nature. Because by its very structure, this knowledge of the ontological kind—and on this point ancient philosophers were not clear—must withdraw any claim to explain the detail of phenomena or to exploit the phenomenal wealth of nature. From this point of view one may say that the great modern scientific movement since Galileo has delivered philosophy and ontological knowledge from a whole body of duties which it took upon itself and which in reality did not belong to it. . . .

Let us now turn to the second question. In accord with definitions more rigorous than those we have been using up till now, and in the light of thomist epistemological principles, let us ask ourselves in what the philosophy of nature consists.

The Thomists reply, with Cajetan: [1] it is a form of knowledge whose proper object is that which moves, mutable being as such. Thus its proper object is being, being which is analogous and which imbues all generic and specific diversifications—that is why it is a philosophy—but not being as such, or being in its own intelligible mystery, which is the object of the metaphysician. The object of the philosophy of nature is being taken in the conditions which affect it in the necessitous and divided universe which is the material universe, being in the mystery of its becoming and mutability, of movement in space whereby bodies are in interaction, of substantial generation and corruption—the chief mark of their ontological structure; of the movement of vegetative growth in which is manifested the ascent of matter to the order of living things. But we have need of further precisions. We have already noticed that antiquity did not distinguish, or distinguished very inadequately, the philosophy of nature from the sciences of nature. Warned by the progress of these sciences we must put the accent on this distinction, without however forcing it. What ought we to say on this subject? It seems to me that two points of doctrine need to be stressed. In the first place the philosophy of nature belongs to the same degree of abstractive visualization or intellectual vision as the sciences of nature: and that is why, as I have already mentioned, it is fundamentally different from metaphysics. In the second place, however, it differs from the natural sciences in an essential and specific way. . . .

And so I come to the second of the two points mentioned above. How is the philosophy of nature distinguished from the natural sciences? The considerations we have already discussed show clearly that the philosophy of nature is distinguished from the natural sciences in an essential and specific way.

What is the ultimate principle of the specification of the sciences? Thomist logicians tell us that it is the typical mode according to which the definitions are formed: *modus definiendi.*

If this be so, it is clear that in the generic sphere of intelligibility in the first order of abstraction, the notions and definitions which emerge on the one hand from empiriological analysis, where everything is primarily resolved in the observable, and on the other hand from ontological analysis where everything is primarily resolved in intelligible being, answer to specifically distinct modes of knowledge. The conceptual vocabulary of the philosophy of nature and that of the natural sciences are different in type. Even if they happen to be translated externally by the same words the mental *verbum* signified by one and the same word is formed in each case in a way typically different. The philosophy of nature differs specifically from the natural sciences. Now let us try to reach a more precise definition, on the lines of thomist epistemology. I will spare the reader the apparatus of technical distinctions which are required before beginning, and will only say that as I understand it the philosophy of nature ought to be defined as follows: 1. The appeal of intelligibility *(ratio formalis quae)* to which it answers, is mutability: it deals with mutable being as mutable, *ens sub ratione mobilitatis.* 2. Its objective light is an ontological mode of analysis and conceptualization, a way of abstracting and defining which, while it has an intrinsic reference to sense perception, aims at the intelligible essence. And it is for this reason that it differs specifically from the natural sciences.

Thus the object of natural philosophy does not lie in the detailed phenomena of sensible things but in intelligible being itself *as mutable,* that is to say, as capable of generation and corruption: or again its

[1 The reference is to Cardinal Cajetan (1468-1534), author of many important commentaries on St. Thomas Aquinas. *Ed.*]

object lies in the differences of being which it can decipher (while aiming at intelligible nature but without sacrificing sense data) in the world of ontological mutability.

At this point it is appropriate to describe the spirit and method of natural philosophy. I will touch on one aspect of this question. It goes without saying that natural philosophy ought to make use of facts which are themselves philosophical, that is to say, established and evaluated in the proper light of philosophy. Because a fact can only yield what it contains; and philosophical conclusions can only be drawn from philosophical premises and from facts which have themselves a philosophical value. Ordinary observation, criticized philosophically, can furnish many facts of this kind.

But what ought to be the relationship between the philosophy of nature and scientific facts? Two errors need to be carefully avoided.

The first error consists in expecting philosophical criteria from rough scientific facts. By rough scientific facts I mean scientific facts which have not been philosophically *treated*. As long as they are illuminated only by the light which originally made them discernible in the real and useful to the scientist these facts only interest the scientist, and not the philosopher. The scientist is right if he forbids the philosopher to touch them, and claims them for himself alone. It is an illusion to think that a philosophical discussion can be invalidated by an appeal to scientific facts which have not been examined in the light of philosophy. . . .

The second error would be to reject scientific facts, to try to construct a natural philosophy independent of them, and to maintain a natural philosophy isolated from the sciences. This tendency, it is worth noticing, is inevitable if the philosophy of nature is confounded with metaphysics. In such a case one tries to give to the philosophy of nature the freedom with regard to

detailed scientific fact which is proper to metaphysics.[2] In reality, one is not likely to reach a metaphysic of *sensibilia,* but will run the risk of having a metaphysic of ignorance.

The truth is that the philosopher must make use of scientific facts on condition that they are examined and interpreted philosophically: thanks to which philosophical facts already established may be confirmed, and other philosophical facts may be discovered. By bringing scientific facts into contact with philosophical knowledge already acquired elsewhere and with philosophical first principles, and bringing an objective philosophical light to bear on them, an intelligible content can be deduced from them which can be handled by philosophy.

But here a question may well be asked. If it is true that the philosophy of nature requires to be completed by the sciences and needs for its confirmation or advancement to derive philosophical facts from the material of scientific fact, must it not also accept as a consequence a certain law of aging and renewal? Of course this does not mean substantial change. There is a substantial continuity between the philosophy of nature as it appeared to Aristotle and as it appears to us. But in its passage it has undergone many changes; it has grown old and has been renewed. So that even as a form of knowledge it is much more dependent on time than is metaphysics.

Here we have an indication of the difference in their formal objects and formal

[2] This does not mean that metaphysics can ignore science. But though it needs to keep in contact with the sciences (through the medium of natural philosophy) this contact is not for the sake of the argumentation that is proper to the metaphysician, but rather for his general information; for his knowledge of the world and his scientific imagery which, where dispositive or material causality is concerned, are vital for his thought.

values. A metaphysical treatise, if it be pure (though in fact it always contains allusions to the state of the sciences when it was written, to human opinions and so forth), can cross the centuries. But how long can a treatise on experimental physics or biology last? Twenty years, ten years, two years, the life-span of a horse, of a dog, of the grub of a cockchafer. And a treatise on the philosophy of nature can at the maximum endure a lifetime, and even then it must be periodically revised, supposing it appears in successive editions. This is because it needs to have intimate contact with the phenomenal sciences, and these sciences renew themselves much more rapidly than philosophy.

8 / PHILOSOPHY OF RELIGION

The problem of God as the highest Being is central in realist writings. Plato raised the problem in his dialogues, Aristotle provided the metaphysical concepts for the realist's treatment of it and suggested proofs of God's existence, and St. Anselm and St. Thomas Aquinas presented compact but forceful arguments for God's existence. A number of the preceding selections have raised the question of a Primal Being too; the following selections from St. Anselm and St. Thomas Aquinas contain material of extreme importance in realistic thinking.

The arguments rest upon the realistic analysis of being with its concepts of cause, essence and existence, and actuality and potentiality. St. Anselm's argument, named the ontological argument, attempts to make an inference from the idea of a Perfect Being to the existence of that Being. It presupposes the concept of degrees of being, and finds its inspiration in Platonic sources. (Plato in fact hinted at such an argument.) St. Thomas, however, rejected Anselm's argument; proceeding rather from Aristotelian premises, he argues that proofs must begin with characteristics of the world actually met in human experience and made explicit by metaphysical analysis. The important five arguments for God which he offers begin from such characteristics: motion, causality, contingency, the gradation of things, and order. These, however, are incomplete and unintelligible in themselves and require the intellect to proceed to a conclusion wherein the existence of God is asserted. The five arguments he expounds are rightfully called the classical proofs of God's existence.

THE ONTOLOGICAL ARGUMENT

St. Anselm (1033-1109)

CHAPTER II

Truly there is a God, although the fool hath said in his heart, There is no God.

And so, Lord, do thou, who dost give

The selection is from St. Anselm, *Proslogium* (tr. Sidney Norton Deane) (Chicago: The Open Court Publishing Co., 1903), pp. 7-9.

understanding to faith, give me, so far as thou knowest it to be profitable, to understand that thou art as we believe; and that thou art that which we believe. And, indeed, we believe that thou art a being than which nothing greater can be conceived. Or is there no such nature, since the fool hath said in his heart, there is no God? (Psalms

xiv. 1). But, at any rate, this very fool, when he hears of this being of which I speak—a being than which nothing greater can be conceived—understands what he hears, and what he understands is in his understanding; although he does not understand it to exist.

For, it is one thing for an object to be in the understanding, and another to understand that the object exists. When a painter first conceives of what he will afterwards perform, he has it in his understanding, but he does not yet understand it to be, because he has not yet performed it. But after he has made the painting, he both has it in his understanding, and he understands that it exists, because he has made it.

Hence, even the fool is convinced that something exists in the understanding, at least, than which nothing greater can be conceived. For, when he hears of this, he understands it. And whatever is understood, exists in the understanding. And assuredly that, than which nothing greater can be conceived, cannot exist in the understanding alone. For, suppose it exists in the understanding alone: then it can be conceived to exist in reality; which is greater.

Therefore, if that, than which nothing greater can be conceived, exists in the understanding alone, the very being, than which nothing greater can be conceived, is one, than which a greater can be conceived. But obviously this is impossible. Hence, there is no doubt that there exists a being, than which nothing greater can be conceived, and it exists both in the understanding and in reality.

CHAPTER III

God cannot be conceived not to exist.—God is that, than which nothing greater can be conceived.—That which can be conceived not to exist is not God.

And it assuredly exists so truly, that it cannot be conceived not to exist. For, it is possible to conceive of a being which cannot be conceived not to exist; and this is greater than one which can be conceived not to exist. Hence, if that, than which nothing greater can be conceived, can be conceived not to exist, it is not that, than which nothing greater can be conceived. But this is an irreconcilable contradiction. There is, then, so truly a being than which nothing greater can be conceived to exist, that it cannot even be conceived not to exist; and this being thou art, O Lord, our God.

So truly, therefore, dost thou exist, O Lord, my God, that thou canst not be conceived not to exist; and rightly. For, if a mind could conceive of a being better than thee, the creature would rise above the Creator; and this is most absurd. And, indeed, whatever else there is, except thee alone, can be conceived not to exist. To thee alone, therefore, it belongs to exist more truly than all other beings, and hence in a higher degree than all others. For, whatever else exists does not exist so truly, and hence in a less degree it belongs to it to exist. Why, then, has the fool said in his heart, there is no God (Psalms xiv. 1), since it is so evident, to a rational mind, that thou dost exist in the highest degree of all? Why, except that he is dull and a fool?

FIVE WAYS TO GOD

St. Thomas Aquinas (1225-1274)

FIRST ARTICLE
Whether the existence of God is self-evident?

We proceed thus to the First Article:—

Objection 1. It seems that the Existence of God is self-evident. Those things are said to be self-evident to us the knowledge of which is naturally implanted in us, as we can see in regard to first principles. But the Damascene [1] says that, *the knowledge of God is naturally implanted in all*. Therefore the Existence of God is self-evident.

Obj. 2. Further, those things are said to be self-evident which are known as soon as the terms are known, which the Philosopher says is true of the first principles of demonstration. Thus, when the nature of a whole and of a part is known, it is at once recognized that every whole is greater than its part. But as soon as the signification of the word "God" is understood, it is at once seen that God exists. For by this word is signified that thing than which nothing greater can exist. But that which exists actually and mentally is greater than that which exists only mentally. Therefore, because as soon as the word "God" is understood it exists mentally, it also follows that it exists actually. Therefore the proposition that God exists is self-evident.

Obj. 3. Further, the existence of Truth is self-evident; for whoever denies the existence of Truth concedes that Truth does not exist. Now, if Truth does not exist, then the proposition "Truth does not exist" is true. But if there is anything true, there must be

Truth. God is Truth itself: *I am the way, the truth, and the life* (John xiv. 6). Therefore the proposition that God exists is self-evident.

On the contrary, No one can mentally admit the opposite of what is self-evident; as is clear from the Philosopher, concerning the first principles of demonstration. The opposite of the proposition "God is" can be mentally admitted: *The fool hath said in his heart, There is no God* (Ps. lii. I). Therefore, that God exists is not self-evident.

I answer that, A thing can be self-evident in either of two ways; on the one hand, self-evident in itself, though not to us; on the other, self-evident in itself, and to us. A proposition is self-evident because the predicate is included in the notion of the subject, as "Man is an animal," for animal is contained in the formal idea of man. If, therefore, the essence of the predicate and subject be known to all, the proposition will be self-evident to all; as is clear with regard to the first principles of demonstration, the terms of which are common things that no one is ignorant of, such as being and non-being, whole and part, and such like. If there are some to whom the essence of the predicate and subject are unknown, the proposition will be self-evident in itself, but not to those who do not know the meaning of the predicate and subject of the proposition. Therefore, it happens, as Boethius [2] says, that there are some mental concepts self-evident only to the learned, as that incorporeal substances are not in space. Therefore I say that this proposition, "God exists," of itself is self-evident, for the predicate is the same as the subject; because God is His Own Existence. Forasmuch

The selection is from Question II of Part I of St. Thomas Aquinas, *Summa Theologica* (New York: Benziger Brothers, Inc., 1911), pp. 19-27. Used by permission of the publisher. [1 The reference is to John of Damascus (d. before 754), whose writings include a complete system of theology founded on the teachings of the church fathers and councils. His work was known by St. Thomas. *Ed.*]

[2 The reference is to Boethius (470-525), an important and influential commentator on Aristotle and Cicero. *Ed.*]

as we do not know the Essence of God, the proposition is not self-evident to us; but needs to be proved by such things as are more evident to us, though less evident in their nature—namely, by effects.

Reply Obj. 1. To know that God exists in a general and indefinite way is implanted in us by nature, inasmuch as God is man's beatitude. For man naturally desires happiness, and what is naturally desired by a man must be naturally known to him. This, however, is not to know absolutely that God exists; as to know that someone is approaching is not the same as to know that Peter is approaching, even though it is Peter who is approaching; for many there are who imagine that man's perfect good (which is happiness) consists in riches, and others in pleasures, and others in something else.

Reply Obj. 2. Perhaps not everyone who hears of this word "God" may understand it to signify something than which nothing better can be imagined, seeing that some have believed God to be a body. Yet, granted that everyone understands by this word "God" is signified something than which nothing greater can be imagined, nevertheless, it does not therefore follow that he understands that what the word signifies exists actually, but only that it exists mentally. Nor can it be argued logically that it actually exists, unless it be admitted that there exists something than which nothing greater can be imagined; and this precisely is not admitted by those who hold that God does not exist.

Reply Obj. 3. The existence of truth in a general way is self-evident, but the existence of a Primal Truth is not self-evident to us.

SECOND ARTICLE
Whether it can be demonstrated that God exists?

We proceed thus to the Second Article:—

Objection 1. It seems that the existence of God cannot be demonstrated; for it is an article of Faith that God exists. But what is of Faith cannot be demonstrated, because a demonstration produces knowledge; whereas Faith is of the unseen (Heb. xi. i). Therefore it cannot be demonstrated that God exists.

Obj. 2. Further, the essence is the middle term of demonstration. But we cannot know in what God's essence consists, but solely in what it does not consist; as the Damascene says. Therefore we cannot demonstrate that God exists.

Obj. 3. Further, if the existence of God were demonstrated, this could only be from His effects. But the effects are not proportionate to Him, since He is infinite and His effects are finite; and between the finite and infinite there is no proportion. Therefore, since a cause cannot be demonstrated by an effect not proportionate to it, it seems that the existence of God cannot be demonstrated.

On the contrary, The Apostle says: *The invisible things of God are clearly seen, being understood by the things that are made* (Rom. i. 20). But this would not be unless the existence of God could be demonstrated through the things that are made; for the first thing we must know of anything is, whether it exists.

I answer that, Demonstration can be made in two ways: One is through the cause, and is called *a priori,* and this is to argue from what is prior absolutely. The other is through the effect, and is called a demonstration *a posteriori;* this is to argue from what is prior relatively only to us. When an effect is better known to us than its cause, from the effect we proceed to the knowledge of the cause. From every effect the existence of a proportionate cause can be demonstrated, so long as its effects are better known to us. Since every effect depends upon its cause, if the effect exists, the cause must have preexisted. Hence the existence of God, in so far as it is not self-evident to us, can be demonstrated from those of His effects which are known to us.

Reply Obj. 1. The existence of God and other like truths about God, which can be known by natural reason, are not articles of Faith, but are preambles to the articles; for Faith presupposes natural knowledge, even as grace presupposes nature, and perfection supposes something that can be perfected. Nevertheless, there is nothing to prevent a man, who cannot grasp its proof, accepting, as a matter of Faith, something in itself capable of being known and demonstrated.

Reply Obj. 2. When the existence of a cause is demonstrated from an effect, this effect takes the place of the definition of the cause in proof of the cause's existence. This is especially the case in regard to God, because, in order to prove the existence of anything, it is necessary to accept as a middle term the meaning of the word, and not its essence, for the question of its essence follows on the question of its existence. The names given to God are derived from His effects; consequently, in demonstrating the existence of God from His effects, we may take for the middle term the meaning of the word "God."

Reply Obj. 3. From effects not proportionate to the cause no perfect knowledge of that cause can be obtained. Yet from every effect the existence of the cause can be demonstrated, and so we can demonstrate the existence of God from His effects; though from them we cannot perfectly know God as He is in His own Essence.

THIRD ARTICLE
Whether God exists?

We proceed thus to the Third Article:—

Objection 1. It seems that God does not exist; because if one of two contraries be infinite, the other would be altogether destroyed. But the word "God" means that He is infinite goodness. If, therefore, God existed, there would be no evil discoverable; but there is evil in the world. Therefore God does not exist.

Obj. 2. Further, it is superfluous to suppose that, what can be accounted for by a few principles has been produced by many. But it seems that everything that appears in the world can be accounted for by other principles, supposing God did not exist. For all natural things can be reduced to one principle, which is nature; and all things that happen intentionally can be reduced to one principle, which is human reason, or will. Therefore there is no need to suppose God's existence.

On the contrary, It is said in the person of God: *I am Who am* (Exod. iii. 14).

I answer that, The existence of God can be proved in five ways.

The first and more manifest way is the argument from motion. It is certain and evident to our senses that some things are in motion. Whatever is in motion is moved by another, for nothing can be in motion except it have a potentiality for that towards which it is being moved; whereas a thing moves inasmuch as it is in act. By "motion" we mean nothing else than the reduction of something from a state of potentiality into a state of actuality. Nothing, however, can be reduced from a state of potentiality into a state of actuality, unless by something already in a state of actuality. Thus that which is actually hot as fire, makes wood, which is potentially hot, to be actually hot, and thereby moves and changes it. It is not possible that the same thing should be at once in a state of actuality and potentiality from the same point of view, but only from different points of view. What is actually hot cannot simultaneously be only potentially hot; still, it is simultaneously potentially cold. It is therefore impossible that from the same point of view and in the same way anything should be both moved and mover, or that it should move itself. Therefore, whatever is in motion must be put in motion by another. If that by which it is put in motion be itself put in motion, then this also needs be put in motion by another, and that by another again. This cannot go on to infinity, because then there would be no first mover, and, consequently, no other mover—seeing that subsequent movers only move inasmuch as they are put in motion by the first mover; as the staff only moves because it is put in motion by the hand. Therefore it is necessary to arrive at a First Mover, put in motion by no other; and this everyone understands to be God.

The second way is from the formality of efficient causation. In the world of sense we find there is an order of efficient causation. There is no case known (neither is it, indeed, possible) in which a thing is found to be the efficient cause of itself; for so it would be prior to itself which is impossible. In efficient causes it is not possible to go on to infinity, because in all efficient causes following in order, the first is the cause of the intermediate cause, and the intermediate is the cause of the ultimate cause, whether the intermediate cause be several, or one only. To take away the cause is to take away the effect. Therefore, if there be no first cause among efficient causes, there will be no ultimate cause, nor any intermediate. If in efficient causes it is possible to go on to infinity, there will be no first efficient cause, neither will there be an ultimate effect, nor any intermediate efficient causes; all of which is plainly false. Therefore it is necessary to put forward a First Efficient Cause, to which everyone gives the name of God.

The third way is taken from possibility and necessity, and runs thus. We find in nature things that could either exist or not exist, since they are found to be generated, and then to corrupt; and, consequently, they can exist, and then not exist. It is impossible for these always to exist, for that which can one day cease to exist must at sometime have not existed. Therefore, if everything could cease to exist, then at one time there could have been nothing in existence. If this were true, even now there would be nothing in existence, because that which does not exist only begins to exist by something already existing. Therefore, if at one time nothing was in existence, it would have been impossible for anything to have begun to exist; and thus even now nothing would be in existence—which is absurd. Therefore, not all beings are merely possible, but there must exist something the existence of which is necessary. Every necessary thing either has its necessity caused by another, or not. It is impossible to go on to infinity in necessary things which have their necessity caused by another, as has been already proved in regard to efficient causes. Therefore we cannot but postulate the existence of some being having itself its own necessity, and not receiving it from another, but rather causing in others their necessity. This all men speak of as God.

The fourth way is taken from the gradation to be found in things. Among beings there are some more and some less good, true, noble, and the like. But "more" and "less" are predicated of different things, according as they resemble in their different ways something which is in the degree of "most," as a thing is said to be hotter according as it more nearly resembles that which is hottest; so that there is something which is truest, something best, something noblest, and, consequently, something which is uttermost being; for the truer things are, the more truly they exist. What is most complete in any genus is the cause of all in that genus; as fire, which is the most complete form of heat, is the cause whereby all things are made hot. Therefore there must also be something which is to all beings the cause of their being, goodness, and every other perfection; and this we call God.

The fifth way is taken from the governance of the world; for we see that things which lack intelligence, such as natural bodies, act for some purpose, which fact is evident from their acting always, or nearly always, in the same way, so as to obtain the best result. Hence it is plain that not fortuitously, but designedly, do they achieve their purpose. Whatever lacks intelligence cannot fulfil some purpose, unless it be directed by some being endowed with intelligence and knowledge; as the arrow is shot to its mark by the archer. Therefore some intelligent being exists by whom all natural things are ordained towards a definite purpose; and this being we call God.

Reply Obj. 1. As Augustine says: *Since God is wholly good, He would not allow any evil to exist in His works, unless His omnipotence and goodness were such as to bring good even out of evil.* This is part of the infinite goodness of God, that He should allow evil to exist, and out of it produce good.

Reply Obj. 2. Since nature works out its determinate end under the direction of a higher agent, whatever is done by nature must needs be traced back to God, as to its first cause. So also whatever is done designedly must also be traced back to some higher cause other than human reason or will, for these can suffer change and are defective; whereas things capable of motion and of defect must be traced back to an immovable and self-necessary first principle.

9 / SUMMARY

Classical realism, we have seen, may be called a philosophy of being, in that it places the concept of being and its metaphysical analysis at the center of philosophical concern. Other philosophies, of course, wish to claim this title also; but not all of them, the realist believes, can rightfully do so. This concluding selection presents a realist's conviction that metaphysics is a valid human enterprise, that the first concept of being is its fundamental problem, and that the Aristotelian-Thomistic tradition, among all philosophies, is closest to a true analysis of that concept.

Writing as a philosopher in the contemporary world, Professor Gilson is aware of a variety of criticisms that have been leveled against the speculative metaphysics which lies at the heart of realism. He especially singles out the antimetaphysical position of the German philosopher Immanuel Kant who had argued that metaphysics, in attempting to determine the principles of being that underlie experience, necessarily surpasses the bounds of the valid employment of human reason. Kant's philosophy concludes with the assertion that speculative metaphysics is impossible, and hence it is one of many philosophies which issue in skepticism about metaphysical knowledge. Some of these positions we shall examine later.

Professor Gilson is convinced that these skeptical philosophies either overlook or misuse the first concept of being. There is a fundamental intuition of being that lies at the basis of metaphysical thinking, but the meaning and implications of being have frequently been distorted by philosophers. True and fruitful metaphysical thinking, he concludes, is possible only if the first principle of being is firmly grasped and retained by the metaphysician.

BEING AND REALISM

Étienne Gilson (1884-   )

By his very nature, man is a metaphysical animal. . . . Since man is essentially rational, the constant recurrence of metaphysics in the history of human knowledge must have its explanation in the very structure of reason itself. In other words, the reason why man is a metaphysical animal must lie somewhere in the nature of rationality. Many centuries before Kant, philosophers had stressed the fact that there is more in rational knowledge than we find in sensible experience. The typical attributes of scientific knowledge, that is universality and necessity, are not to be found in sensible reality, and one of the most generally received explanations is that they come to us from our very power of knowing. As Leibniz says, there is nothing in the intellect that has not first been in sense, except the intellect itself. As Kant was the first both to distrust metaphysics and to hold it to the unavoidable, so was he also the first to give a name to human reason's remarkable power to overstep all sensible experience. He called it the *transcendent* use of reason and denounced it as the permanent source of our metaphysical illusions. Let us retain the term suggested by Kant; it will then follow that whether such knowledge be illusory or not, there is, in human reason, a natural aptness, and consequently a natural urge, to transcend the limits of experience and to form transcendental notions by

which the unity of knowledge may be completed. These are metaphysical notions, and the highest of them all is that of the cause of all causes, or first cause, whose discovery has been for centuries the ambition of the metaphysicians. . . . *Metaphysics is the knowledge gathered by a naturally transcendent reason in its search for the first principles, or first causes, of what is given in sensible experience.*

This is, in fact, what metaphysics is, but what about its validity? The Kantian conclusion that metaphysical knowledge is illusory by its own nature was not a spontaneous offspring of human reason. If metaphysical speculation is a shooting at the moon, philosophers have always begun by shooting at it; only after missing it have they said that there was no moon, and that it was a waste of time to shoot at it. Skepticism is defeatism in philosophy, and all defeatisms are born of previous defeats. When one has repeatedly failed in a certain undertaking, one naturally concludes that it was an impossible undertaking. I say naturally, but not logically, for a repeated failure in dealing with a given problem may point to a repeated error in discussing the problem rather than to its intrinsic insolubility.

The question then arises: should the repeated failures of metaphysics be ascribed to metaphysics itself, or to metaphysicians? It is a legitimate question, and one that can be answered in the light of philosophical experience. For indeed that experience itself exhibits a remarkable unity. If our previous analyses are correct, they all point to the

The selection is reprinted with the permission of Charles Scribner's Sons and of Sheed and Ward, Ltd., from Étienne Gilson, *The Unity of Philosophical Experience* copyright 1937 Charles Scribner's Sons, Sheed and Ward, Ltd., pp. 307-316, with omissions.

same conclusion, that metaphysical adventures are doomed to fail when their authors substitute the fundamental concepts of any particular science for those of metaphysics. Theology, logic, physics, biology, psychology, sociology, economics, are fully competent to solve their own problems by their own methods; on the other hand, however, and this must be our . . . conclusion: *as metaphysics aims at transcending all particular knowledge, no particular science is competent either to solve metaphysical problems, or to judge their metaphysical solutions.*

Of course, Kant would object that, so far, his own condemnation of metaphysics still holds good, for he never said that metaphysical problems could be solved in that way; he merely said that they could not be solved at all. True, but it is also true that his condemnation of metaphysics was not the consequence of any personal attempt to reach the foundations of metaphysical knowledge. Kant busied himself with questions about metaphysics, but he had no metaphysical interests of his own. Even during the first part of his career there was always some book between this professor and reality. To him, nature was in the books of Newton, and metaphysics in the books of Wolff.[1] Anybody could read it there; Kant himself had read it, and it boiled down to this, that there are three metaphysical principles or transcendental ideas of pure reason: an immortal soul to unify psychology; freedom to unify the laws of cosmology; and God to unify natural theology. Such, to Kant, was metaphysics; a second-hand knowledge, for which he was no more personally responsible than for the physics of Newton. Before allowing Kant to frighten us away from

metaphysics, we should remember that what he knew about it was mere hearsay.

In fact, what Kant considered as the three principles of metaphysics were not principles, but conclusions. The real principles of metaphysics are the first notions through which all the subsequent metaphysical knowledge has to be gathered. What these first notions are cannot be known unless we begin by bringing forth some metaphysical knowledge; then we can see how it is made and, lastly, we can form an estimate of its value. Now our analysis of the concrete working of various metaphysical minds clearly suggests that the principles of metaphysics are very different from the three transcendental ideas of Kant. The average metaphysician usually overlooks them because, though he aims at the discovery of the ultimate ground of reality as a whole, he attempts to explain the whole by one of its parts. Then he fails and he ascribes his failure to metaphysics, little aware of the fact that now is the proper time for him to metaphysicize, for the most superficial reflection on his failure would take him to the very root of metaphysics.

When Thales [2] said, six centuries before Christ, that everything is water, though he certainly did not prove his thesis, he at least made it clear that reason is naturally able to conceive all that is as being basically one and the same thing, and that such a unification of reality cannot be achieved by reducing the whole to one of its parts. Instead of drawing that conclusion, the successors of Thales inferred from his failure that he had singled out the wrong part. Thus Anaximenes said that it was not water, but air. It still did not work. Then Heraclitus

---

[1 The reference is to Christian Wolff (1697–1754), professor of mathematics at Halle and an outstanding philosopher of the German Enlightenment. *Ed.*]

[2 M. Gilson refers in this paragraph to some of the major pre-Socratic philosophers and their basic doctrines: Thales (6th cen., B.C.), Anaximenes (6th cen., B.C.), Heraclitus (a. 536–470), and Anaximander (6th cen., B.C.). *Ed.*]

said it was fire, and as there were always objections, the Hegel of the time appeared, who said that the common stuff of all things was the *indeterminate,* that is, the initial fusion of all the contraries from which all the rest had been evolved. Anaximander thus completed the first philosophical cycle recorded by the history of Western culture. The description of the later cycles could not take us further, for it is already clear, from a mere inspection of the first, that the human mind must be possessed of a aptitude to conceive all things as the same, but always fails in its endeavor to conceive all things as being the same as one of them. In short, *the failures of the metaphysicians flew from their unguarded use of a principle of unity present in the human mind.*

This new conclusion brings us face to face with the last and truly crucial problem: what is it which the mind is bound to conceive both as belonging to all things and as not belonging to any two things in the same way? Such is the riddle which every man is asked to read on the threshold of metaphysics. It is an easy one, as, after all, was that of the Sphinx; yet many a good man has failed to say the word, and the path to the metaphysical Sphinx is strewn with the corpses of philosophers. The word is—Being. Our mind is so made that it cannot formulate a single proposition without relating it to some being. Absolute nothingness is strictly unthinkable, for we cannot even deny an existence unless we first posit it in the mind as something to be denied. "If any man," says J. Edwards, "thinks that he can conceive well enough how there should be nothing, I will engage, that what he means by nothing, is as much something, as anything that he ever thought of in his life." This, I think, is true. But if it is true that human thought is always about being; that each and every aspect of reality, or even of unreality, is necessarily conceived as being, or defined in reference to being,

it follows that the understanding of being is the first to be attained, the last into which all knowledge is ultimately resolved and the only one to be included in all our apprehensions. What is first, last and always in human knowledge is its first principle, and its constant point of reference. Now if metaphysics is knowledge dealing with the first principles and the first causes themselves, we can safely conclude that *since being is the first principle of all human knowledge, it is a fortiori the first principle of metaphysics.*

The classical objection to this statement is that, from such a vague idea as that of being, no distinct knowledge can be deduced. This is true, but it is not an objection. To describe being as the "principle of knowledge," does not mean that all subsequent knowledge can be analytically deduced from it, but rather that being is the first knowledge through which all subsequent knowledge can be progressively acquired. As soon as it comes into touch with sensible experience the human intellect elicits the immediate intuition of being: X is, or exists; but from the intuition *that* something is, the knowledge of *what* it is, beyond the fact that it is something, cannot possibly be deduced, nor is it the task of the intellect to deduce it. The intellect does not deduce, it intuits, it sees, and, in the light of intellectual intuition, the discursive power of reason slowly builds up from experience a determinate knowledge of concrete reality. Thus, in the light of immediate evidence, the intellect sees that something is, or exists; that what exists is that which it is; that that which is, or exists, cannot be and not be at one and the same time; that a thing either is, or it is not, and no third supposition is conceivable; last, but not least, that being only comes from being, which is the very root of the notion of causality. Reason has not to prove any one of these principles, otherwise they would not be principles, but conclusions; but it is by them that reason proves all the rest. Patiently weaving the threads of concrete knowledge, reason adds to the intellectual evidence of being and of its properties the science of *what* it is. The first principle brings with it, therefore, both the certitude that metaphysics is the science of being as being, and the abstract laws according to which that science has to be constructed. Yet the principle of a certain knowledge is not that knowledge; and the first principle of human knowledge does not bring us a ready-made science of metaphysics, but its principle and its object.

The twofold character of the intellectual intuition of being, to be given in any sensible experience, and yet to transcend all particular experience, is both the origin of metaphysics and the permanent occasion of its failures. If being is included in all my representations, no analysis of reality will ever be complete unless it culminates in a science of being, that is in metaphysics. On the other hand, the same transcendency which makes the first principle applicable to all experience entails at least the possibility of overstepping the limits by which concrete and particular existences are distinguished. This indeed is more than an abstract possibility, it is a temptation, precisely because it is true that the notion of Being applies to all real or possible experience. Yet, if it is also true that everything is what it is, and nothing else, existence belongs to each and every thing in a truly unique manner, as its own existence, which can be shared in by nothing else. Such is the first principle, both universally applicable, and never applicable twice in the same way. When philosophers fail to perceive either its presence or its true nature, their initial error will pervade the whole science of being, and bring about the ruin of philosophy.

When, owing to some fundamental scientific discovery, a metaphysically minded man first grasps the true nature of a whole order of reality, what he is thus grasping for the first time is but a particular determination of being at large. Yet the intuition of being is always there, and if our philosopher fails to discern its meaning, he will fall a victim to its contagious influence. That which is but a particular determination of being, or *a* being, will be invested with the universality of being itself. In other words, a particular essence will be credited with the universality of being, and allowed to exclude all the other aspects of reality. This is precisely what happened to Abailard, to Ockham, to Descartes, to Kant and to Comte. They were truly laboring under a transcendental delusion; Kant himself knew it, but he was wrong in thinking that such an illusion was unavoidable, for it can be avoided; and he was still more wrong in viewing that illusion as the source of metaphysics, for it is not its source but the cause of its destruction; and not only of the destruction of metaphysics, but, for the same reason and at the same time, of the ruin of the very science which has thus been unduly generalized. If every order of reality is defined by its own essence, and every individual is possessed of its own existence, to encompass the universality of being within the essence of this or that being is to destroy the very object of metaphysics; but to ascribe to the essence of this or that being the universality of being itself, is to stretch a particular science beyond its natural limits and to make it a caricature of metaphysics. In short, and this will be our last conclusion: *all the failures of metaphysics should be traced to the fact, that the first principle of human knowledge has been either overlooked or misused by the metaphysicians.*

BIBLIOGRAPHICAL NOTE

Systematic introductions to classical realistic philosophy may be found in such volumes as John Wild, *Introduction to Realistic Philosophy* (New York, 1948) and Jacques Maritain, *An Introduction to Philosophy* (London, 1930). For further intensive study, the student must turn to the basic texts of the great figures in classical realism, Plato, Aristotle, and St. Thomas Aquinas. Their works are available in many editions and compilations. Of value in studying them are such commentaries as A. E. Taylor, *Plato, the Man and His Work*, 4th ed. (New York, 1956); G. M. A. Grube, *Plato's Thought* (Boston, 1958); W. D. Ross, *Aristotle*, 5th ed. (London, 1949); F. C. Copleston, *Aquinas* (Penguin Books, 1955); Jacques Maritain, *Saint Thomas Aquinas* (London, 1933); and Étienne Gilson, *The Christian Philosophy of St. Thomas Aquinas* (New York, 1956). Many works exist on the history of realism, especially of the medieval period; see, for example, Maurice de Wulf, *History of Medieval Philosophy* (New York, 1909) and the interpretive and excellent study by Gilson, *The Spirit of Medieval Philosophy* (New York, 1940). Contemporary work by thinkers of realistic persuasion is found in such volumes as John Wild (ed.), *The Return to Reason* (Chicago, 1953), the Proceedings of the American Catholic Philosophical Association, and the many publications of Maritain and Gilson, who have written on all the major areas of philosophical concern.

II
IDEALISM

BERKELEY / HEGEL / BLANSHARD / ROYCE

BRADLEY / CROCE / BOSANQUET

TENNANT / RASHDALL

URBAN

One of the major philosophic alternatives to realism is idealism. Although there are anticipations of idealism in ancient thought, the flowering of idealism has occurred in the last three centuries. Like realism, idealism is an explicitly metaphysical philosophy, in that it believes that speculative knowledge of reality is both possible and important. Unlike realism, however, which focuses its attention on principles of being like substance and essence, as well as the objective norms grounded in being, idealism bases itself on the centrality of mind and its activity in knowledge, being, and value.

This basic concern suggests an introductory characterization of idealism. As a metaphysics, idealism holds that the real is mind or the mindlike; as an epistemology, it holds that knowledge is a result of mind's creative activity; and in axiology and related disciplines, it holds the mind-dependence of values. In sum, to use a quotation from Professor Urban, the term "idealism" applies to "any theory which maintains that the universe is throughout the work or embodiment of mind."

Although idealists generally accept this description of their position, they do differ in their respective emphases. These differences provide a convenient basis for distinguishing four varieties of idealism. There are, first, mentalists or subjective idealists who, following Bishop Berkeley, deny the reality of material substance, asserting rather that physical objects—"all the choir of heaven and furniture of the earth"—are of such being as mind itself. A second group of idealists are the absolutists, who urge that certain logical concepts like system or universal best characterize reality. A third school seeks to uncover the presuppositions or "transcendental conditions" of experience; in finding them in mind and its activities, they belong to the idealist perspective. Finally, there are philosophers who argue that values are in some sense objective and part of the nature of reality; yet, because value implies mind, they draw the idealist conclusion that reality is in its essence spiritual.

These idealist assertions are expanded and developed in the selections that follow. We shall also trace the implications of the idealist argument in a number of areas of philosophy, just as we have done in the case of realism. Throughout this chapter, however—and here idealism again differs from realism— we shall be dealing with a position that is not so clearly or directly related to "common sense" as realism claims to be. Indeed, the brief characterization of idealism given in this introduction may seem to be presenting a paradoxical philosophy, to say the least. Yet there is a "driving force" in idealism such that many of the best minds of history have been attracted to it as the most adequate expression of the nature of reality. Professor Urban has provided an interpretive summary of this force, and it appears as the concluding selection. As we examine the idealist's solution of some of the same problems that the realist faces, and begin to compare and relate the alternatives, we enter into the dialogue between positions which philosophy most essentially is.

1 / INTRODUCTION

Historically, a major source of idealistic thought is the writings of Bishop George Berkeley, Anglican divine and philosopher; for although much of his argumentation is directed toward the intellectual positions of his day, he nevertheless formulated a basic philosophic vision from which idealists take inspiration even if they revise that formulation severely. Berkeley was motivated to engage in philosophical work by what he considered to be the rising materialism, with its threats to religion, that stemmed from the scientific advances of his day and the philosophical elaborations thereof.

Materialism, the philosophy that holds that only material substance, or matter, is real, seemed to Berkeley to follow from certain philosophical assumptions such as the distinction between primary and secondary qualities. Primary qualities are those qualities of an object such as size and mass that can be measured mathematically; secondary qualities are the *qualia* such as a color or sound that are experienced by a perceiver. Furthermore, it was believed that the former are qualities of the object itself, whereas the latter depend on the perceiver and are relative to him. Matter and primary qualities thus seem to be "objective," whereas mind and secondary qualities seem to be "subjective." The tendency to believe that matter alone is real, and that mind has only a derivative being, follows closely on these distinctions.

Is this tendency, as well as its presuppositions, justified? Berkeley believes not. If we examine experience carefully, we find that an object, say a desk, is only a bundle of qualities: shape, color, weight, and so on. Now what of the supposed independence of primary qualities? Are they not just as much ideas as colors? And are they not, therefore, just as dependent on the perceiver as secondary qualities? To both questions Berkeley answers yes. The desk is a bundle of qualities or ideas, ideas depend for their existence on the perceiver, therefore the desk's existence depends on its being perceived. In his famous formula, *esse* is *percipi,* Berkeley concludes that only perceivers or spirits—one Infinite, many finite—are real. Nature, the realm of objects, exists as God's perceptions; all being, in fact, is ideal.

To such an argument there will be, of course, objections, and Berkeley considers some of these himself. They will bear careful attention for an understanding of the argument itself.

THE REJECTION OF MATTER

George Berkeley (1685-1753)

1. It is evident to any one who takes a survey of the *objects of human knowledge,* that they are either *ideas* actually imprinted on the senses; or else such as are perceived by attending to the passions and operations of the mind; or lastly, *ideas* formed by help of memory and imagination—either compounding, dividing, or barely representing those originally perceived in the aforesaid ways. By sight I have the ideas of light and colors, with their several degrees and variations. By touch I perceive hard and soft, heat and cold, motion and resistance; and of all these more and less either as to quantity or degree. Smelling furnishes me with odors; the palate with tastes; and hearing conveys sounds to the mind in all their variety of tone and composition.

And as several of these are observed to accompany each other, they come to be marked by one name, and so to be reputed as one *thing.* Thus, for example, a certain color, taste, smell, figure and consistence having been observed to go together, are accounted one distinct thing, signified by the name apple; other collections of ideas constitute a stone, a tree, a book, and the like sensible things; which as they are pleasing or disagreeable excite the passions of love, hatred, joy, grief, and so forth.

2. But, besides all that endless variety of ideas or objects of knowledge, there is likewise Something which knows or perceives them; and exercises divers operations, as willing, imagining, remembering, about them. This perceiving, active being is what I call *mind, spirit, soul,* or *myself.* By which words I do not denote any one of my ideas, but a thing entirely distinct from them, wherein they exist, or, which is the same thing, whereby they are perceived; for the existence of an idea consists in being perceived.

The selection follows the text of the second edition of the "Principles of Human Knowledge," in A. C. Fraser (ed.), *The Works of George Berkeley,* 4 vols. (Oxford: Clarendon Press, 1901), Vol. I, pp. 257-279, with omissions.

3. That neither our thoughts, nor passions, nor ideas formed by the imagination, exist without the mind is what everybody will allow. And to me it seems no less evident that the various sensations or ideas imprinted on the Sense, however blended or combined together (that is, whatever objects they compose), cannot exist otherwise than in a mind perceiving them. I think an intuitive knowledge may be obtained of this, by any one that shall attend to what is meant by the term *exist* when applied to sensible things. The table I write on I say exists; that is, I see and feel it: and if I were out of my study I should say it existed; meaning thereby that if I was in my study I might perceive it, or that some other spirit actually does perceive it. There was an odor, that is, it was smelt; there was a sound, that is, it was heard; a color or figure, and it was perceived by sight or touch. This is all that I can understand by these and the like expressions. For as to what is said of the *absolute* existence of unthinking things, without any relation to their being perceived, that is to me perfectly unintelligible. Their *esse* is *percipi;* nor is it possible they should have any existence out of the minds or thinking things which perceive them.

4. It is indeed an opinion strangely prevailing amongst men, that houses, mountains, rivers, and in a word all sensible objects, have an existence, natural or real, distinct from their being perceived by the understanding. But, with how great an assurance and acquiescence soever this Principle may be entertained in the world, yet whoever shall find in his heart to call it in question may, if I mistake not, perceive it to involve a manifest contradiction. For, what are the forementioned objects but the things we perceive by sense? and what do we perceive besides our own ideas or sensations? and is it not plainly repugnant that any one of these, or any combination of them, should exist unperceived?

5. If we thoroughly examine this tenet it will, perhaps, be found at bottom to depend on the doctrine of *abstract ideas*. For can there be a nicer strain of abstraction than to distinguish the existence of sensible objects from their being perceived, so as to conceive them existing unperceived? Light and colors, heat and cold, extension and figures—in a word the things we see and feel—what are they but so many sensations, notions, ideas, or impressions on the sense? and is it possible to separate, even in thought, any of these from perception? For my part, I might as easily divide a thing from itself. I may, indeed, divide in my thoughts, or conceive apart from each other, those things which perhaps I never perceived by sense so divided. Thus, I imagine the trunk of a human body without the limbs, or conceive the smell of a rose without thinking on the rose itself. So far, I will not deny, I can abstract; if that may properly be called *abstraction* which extends only to the conceiving separately such objects as it is possible may really exist or be actually perceived asunder. But my conceiving or imagining power does not extend beyond the possibility of real existence or perception. Hence, as it is impossible for me to see or feel anything without an actual sensation of that thing, so is it impossible for me to conceive in my thoughts any sensible thing or object distinct from the sensation or perception of it.

6. Some truths there are so near and obvious to the mind that a man need only open his eyes to see them. Such I take this important one to be, viz. that all the choir of heaven and furniture of the earth, in a word all those bodies which compose the mighty frame of the world, have not any subsistence without a mind; that their *being* is to be perceived or known; that consequently so long as they are not actually perceived by me, or do not exist in my mind, or that of any other created spirit, they must either have no existence at all, or

else subsist in the mind of some Eternal Spirit: it being perfectly unintelligible, and involving all the absurdity of abstraction, to attribute to any single part of them an existence independent of a spirit. To be convinced of which, the reader need only reflect, and try to separate in his own thoughts the *being* of a sensible thing from its *being perceived.*

7. From what has been said it is evident there is not any other Substance than *Spirit,* or that which perceives. But, for the fuller proof of this point, let it be considered the sensible qualities are color, figure, motion, smell, taste, and such like, that is, the ideas perceived by sense. Now, for an idea to exist in an unperceiving thing is a manifest contradiction; for to have an idea is all one as to perceive: that therefore wherein color, figure, and the like qualities exist must perceive them. Hence it is clear there can be no unthinking substance or *substratum* of those ideas.

8. But, say you, though the ideas themselves do not exist without the mind, yet there may be things like them, whereof they are copies or resemblances; which things exist without the mind, in an unthinking substance. I answer, an idea can be like nothing but an idea; a color or figure can be like nothing but another color or figure. If we look but never so little into our thoughts, we shall find it impossible for us to conceive a likeness except only between our ideas. Again, I ask whether those supposed *originals,* or external things, of which our ideas are the pictures or representations, be themselves perceivable or no? If they are, then *they* are ideas, and we have gained our point: but if you say they are not, I appeal to any one whether it be sense to assert a color is like something which is invisible; hard or soft, like something which is intangible; and so of the rest.

9. Some there are who make a distinction betwixt *primary* and *secondary* qualities. By the former they mean extension, figure, motion, rest, solidity or impenetrability, and number; by the latter they denote all other sensible qualities, as colors, sounds, tastes, and so forth. The ideas we have of these last they acknowledge not to be the resemblances of anything existing without the mind, or unperceived; but they will have our ideas of the *primary qualities* to be patterns or images of things which exist without the mind, in an unthinking substance which they call Matter. By Matter, therefore, we are to understand an inert, senseless substance, in which extension, figure, and motion do actually subsist. But it is evident, from what we have already shewn, that extension, figure, and motion are only ideas existing in the mind, and that an idea can be like nothing but another idea; and that consequently neither they nor their archetypes can exist in an unperceiving substance. Hence, it is plain that the very notion of what is called *Matter* or *corporeal substance,* involves a contradiction in it. . . .

18. But, though it were possible that solid, figured, moveable substances may exist without the mind, corresponding to the ideas we have of bodies, yet how is it possible for us to know this? Either we must know it by Sense or by Reason. As for our senses, by them we have the knowledge only of our sensations, ideas, or those things that are immediately perceived by sense, call them what you will: but they do not inform us that things exist without the mind, or unperceived, like to those which are perceived. This the materialists themselves acknowledge.—It remains therefore that if we have any knowledge at all of external things, it must be by reason inferring their existence from what is immediately perceived by sense. But what reason can induce us to believe the existence of bodies without the mind, from what we perceive, since the very patrons of Matter themselves do not pretend there is any necessary connection betwixt them and our ideas? I say

it is granted on all hands (and what happens in dreams, frenzies, and the like, puts it beyond dispute) that it is possible we might be affected with all the ideas we have now, though no bodies existed without resembling them. Hence it is evident the supposition of external bodies is not necessary for the producing our ideas; since it is granted they are produced sometimes, and might possibly be produced always, in the same order we see them in at present, without their concurrence.

19. But, though we might possibly have all our sensations without them, yet perhaps it may be thought easier to conceive and explain the manner of their production, by supposing external bodies in their likeness rather than otherwise; and so it might be at least probable there are such things as bodies that excite their ideas in our minds. But neither can this be said. For, though we give the materialists their external bodies, they by their own confession are never the nearer knowing how our ideas are produced; since they own themselves unable to comprehend in what manner body can act upon spirit, or how it is possible it should imprint any idea in the mind. Hence it is evident the production of ideas or sensations in our minds, can be no reason why we should suppose Matter or corporeal substances; since that is acknowledged to remain equally inexplicable with or without this supposition. If therefore it were possible for bodies to exist without the mind, yet to hold they do so must needs be a very precarious opinion; since it is to suppose, without any reason at all, that God has created innumerable beings that are entirely useless, and serve to no manner of purpose.

20. In short, if there were external bodies, it is impossible we should ever come to know it; and if there were not, we might have the very same reasons to think there were that we have now. Suppose—what no one can deny possible—an intelligence, without the help of external bodies, to be affected with the same train of sensations or ideas that you are, imprinted in the same order and with like vividness in his mind. I ask whether that intelligence hath not all the reason to believe the existence of Corporeal Substances, represented by his ideas, and exciting them in his mind, that you can possibly have for believing the same thing? Of this there can be no question. Which one consideration were enough to make any reasonable person suspect the strength of whatever arguments he may think himself to have, for the existence of bodies without the mind. . . .

23. But, say you, surely there is nothing easier than for me to imagine trees, for instance, in a park, or books existing in a closet, and nobody by to perceive them. I answer, you may so, there is no difficulty in it. But what is all this, I beseech you, more than framing in your mind certain ideas which you call *books* and *trees,* and at the same time omitting to frame the idea of any one that may perceive them? But do not you yourself perceive or think of them all the while? This therefore is nothing to the purpose: it only shews you have the power of imagining, or forming ideas in your mind; but it does not shew that you can conceive it possible the objects of your thought may exist without the mind. To make out this, it is necessary that you conceive them existing unconceived or unthought of; which is a manifest repugnancy. When we do our utmost to conceive the existence of external bodies, we are all the while only contemplating our own ideas. But the mind, taking no notice of itself, is deluded to think it can and does conceive bodies existing unthought of, or without the mind, though at the same time they are apprehended by, or exist in, itself. A little attention will discover to any one the truth and evidence of what is here said, and make it unnecessary to insist on any other proofs against the existence of *material substance.* . . .

34. Before we proceed any farther it is necessary we spend some time in answering Objections which may probably be made against the Principles we have hitherto laid down. In doing of which, if I seem too prolix to those of quick apprehensions, I desire I may be excused, since all men do not equally apprehend things of this nature; and I am willing to be understood by every one.

First, then, it will be objected that by the foregoing principles all that is real and substantial in nature is banished out of the world, and instead thereof a chimerical scheme of *ideas* takes place. All things that exist exist only in the mind; that is, they are purely notional. What therefore becomes of the sun, moon, and stars? What must we think of houses, rivers, mountains, trees, stones; nay, even of our own bodies? Are all these but so many chimeras and illusions on the fancy?—To all which, and whatever else of the same sort may be objected, I answer, that by the Principles premised we are not deprived of any one thing in nature. Whatever we see, feel, hear, or any wise conceive or understand, remains as secure as ever, and is as real as ever. There is a *rerum natura*, and the distinction between realities and chimeras retains its full force. . . .

35. I do not argue against the existence of any one thing that we can apprehend, either by sense or reflection. That the things I see with my eyes and touch with my hands do exist, really exist, I make not the least question. The only thing whose existence we deny is that which *philosophers* call Matter or corporeal substance. And in doing of this there is no damage done to the rest of mankind, who, I dare say, will never miss it. The Atheist indeed will want the color of an empty name to support his impiety; and the Philosophers may possibly find they have lost a great handle for trifling and disputation.

36. If any man thinks this detracts from the existence or reality of things, he is very far from understanding what hath been premised in the plainest terms I could think of. Take here an abstract of what has been said:—There are spiritual substances, minds, or human souls, which will or excite ideas in themselves at pleasure; but these are faint, weak, and unsteady in respect of others they perceive by sense: which, being impressed upon them according to certain rules or laws of nature, speak themselves the effects of a Mind more powerful and wise than human spirits. These latter are said to have *more reality* in them than the former;—by which is meant that they are more affecting, orderly, and distinct, and that they are not fictions of the mind perceiving them. And in this sense the sun that I see by day is the real sun, and that which I imagine by night is the idea of the former. In the sense here given of *reality*, it is evident that every vegetable, star, mineral, and in general each part of the mundane system, is as much a *real being* by our principles as by any other. Whether others mean anything by the term *reality* different from what I do, I entreat them to look into their own thoughts and see.

37. It will be urged that thus much at least is true, to wit, that we take away all *corporeal substances*. To this my answer is, that if the word *substance* be taken in the vulgar sense, for a *combination* of sensible qualities, such as extension, solidity, weight, and the like—this we cannot be accused of taking away: but if it be taken in a philosophic sense, for the support of accidents or qualities without the mind—then indeed I acknowledge that we take it away, if one may be said to take away that which never had any existence, not even in the imagination.

38. But after all, say you, it sounds very harsh to say we eat and drink ideas, and are clothed with ideas. I acknowledge it does so—the word *idea* not being used in common discourse to signify the several

combinations of sensible qualities which are called *things;* and it is certain that any expression which varies from the familiar use of language will seem harsh and ridiculous. But this doth not concern the truth of the proposition, which in other words is no more than to say, we are fed and clothed with those things which we perceive immediately by our senses. The hardness or softness, the color, taste, warmth, figure, and suchlike qualities, which combined together constitute the several sorts of victuals and apparel, have been shewn to exist only in the mind that perceives them: and this is all that is meant by calling them *ideas;* which word, if it was as ordinarily used as *thing,* would sound no harsher nor more ridiculous than it. I am not for disputing about the propriety, but the truth of the expression. If therefore you agree with me that we eat and drink and are clad with the immediate objects of sense, which cannot exist unperceived or without the mind, I shall readily grant it is more proper or conformable to custom that they should be called *things* rather than *ideas.*

39. If it be demanded why I make use of the word *idea,* and do not rather in compliance with custom call them *things;* I answer, I do it for two reasons:—First, because the term *thing,* in contradistinction to *idea,* is generally supposed to denote somewhat existing without the mind: Secondly, because *thing* hath a more comprehensive signification than *idea,* including spirits, or thinking things, as well as ideas. Since therefore the objects of sense exist only in the mind, and are withal thoughtless and inactive, I chose to mark them by the word *idea;* which implies those properties.

40. But, say what we can, some one perhaps may be apt to reply, he will still believe his senses, and never suffer any arguments, how plausible soever, to prevail over the certainty of them. Be it so; assert the evidence of sense as high as you please, we are willing to do the same. That what I see, hear, and feel doth exist, that is to say, is perceived by me, I no more doubt than I do of my own being. But I do not see how the testimony of sense can be alleged as a proof for the existence of anything which is *not* perceived by sense. We are not for having any man turn skeptic and disbelieve his senses; on the contrary, we give them all the stress and assurance imaginable; nor are there any principles more opposite to Skepticism than those we have laid down, as shall be hereafter clearly shewn.

41. *Secondly,* it will be objected that there is a great difference betwixt real fire for instance, and the idea of fire, betwixt dreaming or imagining oneself burnt, and actually being so. . . . This and the like may be urged in opposition to our tenets.—To all which the answer is evident from what hath been already said; and I shall only add in this place, that if real fire be very different from the idea of fire, so also is the real pain that it occasions very different from the idea of the same pain, and yet nobody will pretend that real pain either is, or can possibly be, in an unperceiving thing, or without the mind, any more than its idea.

The second major historical source of idealism is the philosophy of Hegel, a many-sided, encyclopedic, and at times difficult position. Hegel's emphasis, though idealistic, is rather different from Berkeley's, and hence the term "absolute idealism" is used of it as against Berkeley's subjective idealism or mentalism.

Philosophy, as Hegel understood it, is the attempt to think concretely; that is, to think of experience in all its manifold relations. ("Abstract" thinking is that wherein we drop consideration of some relations in order to concentrate on others.) It is simply an effort to view experience as a whole; and until we have a conception of the whole, our thinking remains partial and inadequate. "The true is the whole" is one of Hegel's basic assertions.

Philosophy leads us, Hegel believes, to posit Reason as the substance and energy of the world. Among the evidences for this belief are the operations of law in nature and the belief in providence in religion. Reason is characterized by Hegel as dialectical; that is, it is unifying of opposites—a mediation—and it is also an unfolding of stages. The three basic stages of this unfolding are Logic, Nature, and Spirit. Only the last is fully concrete. Nature, for example, embodies Reason, but only abstractly and imperfectly. Hence philosophy moves beyond Nature to Spirit, wherein are history and society. Spirit, Hegel holds, is the realm of freedom, the realm of concrete unity, existing in-and-for-itself, which incorporates and mediates all oppositions. World history, viewed by Hegel as the unfolding in time of Spirit, is one of the stages within Spirit. The goal of history, as of all stages of Spirit, is freedom; the means and materials of history are human passions. Within history, Hegel says, concrete freedom is found in the rational State. Beyond the State are other and higher levels of Spirit, however: art, religion, and philosophy, which last is the highest level of Spirit, Reason, and Freedom—that is, the Absolute, in its full and rational totality.

The following selection is from the Introduction to Hegel's philosophy of history. It includes a summary statement of many of the basic points in Hegel's thought as well as his discussion of Reason in history. It is, however, but one of many important sections in Hegel's work that have influenced the course of subsequent idealism.

THE REALITY OF SPIRIT

G. W. F. Hegel (1770-1831)

The only Thought which Philosophy brings with it to the contemplation of History, is the simple conception of *Reason;* that Reason is the Sovereign of the World; that the history of the world, therefore, presents us with a rational process. This conviction and intuition is a hypothesis in the domain of history as such. In that of Philosophy it is no hypothesis. It is there proved by speculative cognition, that Reason—and this term may here suffice us, without investigating the relation sustained by the Universe to the Divine Being—is *Substance,* as well as *Infinite Power;* its own *Infinite Material* underlying all the natural and spiritual life which it originates, as also the *Infinite Form*—that which sets this Material in motion. On the one hand, Reason is the *substance* of the Universe; viz., that by which and in which all reality has its being and subsistence. On the other hand, it is the *Infinite Energy* of the Universe; since Reason is not so powerless as to be capable of producing anything but a mere ideal, a mere intention—having its place outside reality, nobody knows where; something separate and abstract, in the heads of certain human beings. It is *the*

The selection is from Hegel's *Philosophy of History* (tr. J. Sibree) (New York: P. F. Collier & Son, 1902), pp. 52-96, with omissions.

infinite complex of things, their entire Essence and Truth. It is its own material which it commits to its own Active Energy to work up; not needing, as finite action does, the conditions of an external material of given means from which it may obtain its support, and the objects of its activity. It supplies its own nourishment, and is the object of its own operations. While it is exclusively its own basis of existence, and absolute final aim, it is also the energizing power realizing this aim; developing it not only in the phenomena of the Natural, but also of the Spiritual Universe—the History of the World. That this "Idea" or "Reason" is the *True,* the *Eternal,* the absolutely *powerful* essence; that it reveals itself in the World, and that in the World nothing else is revealed but this and its honor and glory—is the thesis which, as we have said, has been proved in Philosophy, and is here regarded as demonstrated. . . .

I will only mention two phases and points of view that concern the generally diffused conviction that Reason has ruled, and is still ruling in the world, and consequently in the world's history; because they give us, at the same time, an opportunity for more closely investigating the question that presents the greatest difficulty, and for indicating a branch of the subject which will have to be enlarged on in the sequel.

I.—One of these points, is that passage in history which informs us that the Greek Anaxagoras was the first to enunciate the doctrine that *nous,* Understanding generally, or Reason, governs the world.[1] It is not intelligence as self-conscious Reason—not a Spirit as such that is meant; and we must clearly distinguish these from each other. The movement of the solar system takes place according to unchangeable laws.

These laws are Reason, implicit in the phenomena in question. But neither the sun nor the planets, which revolve around it according to these laws, can be said to have any consciousness of them.

A thought of this kind—that Nature is an embodiment of Reason; that it is unchangeably subordinate to universal laws, appears nowise striking or strange to us. We are accustomed to such conceptions, and find nothing extraordinary in them. And I have mentioned this extraordinary occurrence, partly to show how history teaches that ideas of this kind, which may seem trivial to us, have not always been in the world; that, on the contrary, such a thought makes an epoch in the annals of human intelligence. Aristotle says of Anaxagoras, as the originator of the thought in question, that he appeared as a sober man among the drunken. Socrates adopted the doctrine from Anaxagoras, and it forthwith became the ruling idea in Philosophy—except in the school of Epicurus,[2] who ascribed all events to chance. "I was delighted with the sentiment"—Plato makes Socrates say—"and hoped I had found a teacher who would show me Nature in harmony with Reason, who would demonstrate in each particlar phenomenon its specific aim, and in the whole, the grand object of the Universe. I would not have surrendered this hope for a great deal. But how very much was I disappointed, when, having zealously applied myself to the writings of Anaxagoras, I found that he adduces only external causes, such as Atmosphere, Ether, Water, and the like." It is evident that the defect which Socrates complains of respecting Anaxagoras's doctrine, does not concern the principle itself, but the shortcoming of the propounder in applying it to Nature in the concrete. Nature is not deduced from that principle: the latter remains in fact a

---

[1 The reference is to the pre-Socratic philosopher, Anaxagoras of Klazomene (a. 430 B.C.), and his doctrine of an eternal, imperishable Reason diffused throughout the universe. *Ed.*]

[2 Some of the ideas of Epicurus and his school are given in Part III in the selection from Lucretius. *Ed.*]

mere abstraction, inasmuch as the former is not comprehended and exhibited as a development of it—an organization produced by and from Reason. I wish, at the very outset, to call your attention to the important difference between a conception, a principle, a truth limited to an *abstract* form and its determinate application, and concrete development. This distinction affects the whole fabric of philosophy; and among other bearings of it there is one to which we shall have to revert at the close of our view of Universal History, in investigating the aspect of political affairs in the most recent period.

We have next to notice the rise of this idea—that Reason directs the World—in connection with a further application of it, well known to us—in the form, viz., of the *religious truth,* that the world is not abandoned to chance and external contingent causes, but that a *Providence* controls it. I stated above, that I would not make a demand on your faith, in regard to the principle announced. Yet I might appeal to your belief in it, *in this religious aspect,* if, as a general rule, the nature of philosophical science allowed it to attach authority to presuppositions. To put it in another shape —this appeal is forbidden, because the science of which we have to treat proposes itself to furnish the proof (not indeed of the abstract *Truth* of the doctrine, but) of its correctness as compared with facts. The truth, then, that a Providence (that of God) presides over the events of the World —consorts with the proposition in question: for *Divine* Providence is Wisdom, endowed with an infinite Power, which realizes its aim, viz., the absolute rational design of the World. Reason is Thought conditioning itself with perfect freedom. . . .

II.—The inquiry into the *essential destiny* of Reason—as far as it is considered in reference to the World—is identical with the question, *what is the ultimate design of the world?* And the expression implies that design is destined to be realized. Two points of consideration suggest themselves: first, the *import* of this design—its abstract definition; and secondly, its *realization.*

It must be observed at the outset, that the phenomenon we investigate—Universal History—belongs to the realm of *Spirit.* The term *"World,"* includes both physical and psychical Nature. Physical Nature also plays its part in the World's History, and attention will have to be paid to the fundamental natural relations thus involved. But Spirit, and the course of its development, is our substantial object. Our task does not require us to contemplate Nature as a Rational System in itself—though in its own proper domain it proves itself such—but simply in its relation to *Spirit.* On the stage on which we are observing it—Universal History—Spirit displays itself in its most concrete reality. Notwithstanding this (or rather for the very purpose of comprehending the *general* principles which this, its form of *concrete reality,* embodies) we must premise some abstract characteristics of the *nature of Spirit.* Such an explanation, however, cannot be given here under any other form than that of bare assertion. The present is not the occasion for unfolding the idea of Spirit speculatively; for whatever has a place in an Introduction, must, as already observed, be taken as simply historical; something assumed as having been explained and proved elsewhere; or whose demonstration awaits the sequel of the Science of History itself.

We have therefore to mention here:
(1.) The abstract characteristics of the nature of Spirit.
(2.) What means Spirit uses in order to realize its Idea.
(3.) Lastly, we must consider the shape which the perfect embodiment of Spirit assumes—the State.

(1.) The nature of Spirit may be understood by a glance at its direct opposite—

Matter. As the essence of Matter is Gravity, so, on the other hand, we may affirm that the substance, the essence of Spirit is Freedom. All will readily assent to the doctrine that Spirit, among other properties, is also endowed with Freedom; but philosophy teaches that all the qualities of Spirit exist only through Freedom; that all are but means for attaining freedom; that all seek and produce this and this alone. It is a result of speculative Philosophy, that Freedom is the sole truth of Spirit. Matter possesses gravity in virtue of its tendency towards a central point. It is essentially composite; consisting of parts that *exclude* each other. It seeks its Unity; and therefore exhibits itself as self-destructive, as verging towards its opposite [an indivisible point]. If it could attain this, it would be Matter no longer, it would have perished. It strives after the realization of its Idea; for in Unity it exists *ideally*. Spirit, on the contrary, may be defined as that which has its center in itself. It has not a unity outside itself, but has already found it; it exists *in* and *with itself*. Matter has its essence out of itself; Spirit is *self-contained existence* (Bei-sich-selbst-seyn). Now this is Freedom, exactly. For if I am dependent, my being is referred to something else which I am not; I cannot exist independently of something external. I am free, on the contrary, when my existence depends upon myself. This self-contained existence of Spirit is none other than self-consciousness—consciousness of one's own being. Two things must be distinguished in consciousness; first, the fact *that I know;* secondly, *what I know*. In *self* consciousness these are merged in one; for Spirit *knows itself*. It involves an appreciation of its own nature, as also an energy enabling it to realize itself; to make itself *actually* that which it is *potentially*. According to this abstract definition it may be said of Universal History, that it is the exhibition of Spirit in the process of working

out the knowledge of that which it is potentially. . . .

The destiny of the spiritual World, and —since this is the *substantial World*, while the physical remains subordinate to it, or, in the language of speculation, has no truth *as against* the spiritual—the *final cause of the World at large,* we allege to be the *consciousness* of its own freedom on the part of Spirit, and *ipso facto*, the *reality* of that freedom. But that this term "Freedom," without further qualification, is an indefinite, and incalculable ambiguous term; and that while that which it represents is the *ne plus ultra* of attainment, it is liable to an infinity of misunderstandings, confusions and errors, and to become the occasion for all imaginable excesses—has never been more clearly known and felt than in modern times. Yet, for the present, we must content ourselves with the term itself without further definition. Attention was also directed to the importance of the infinite difference between a principle in the abstract, and its realization in the concrete. In the process before us, the essential nature of freedom—which involves in it absolute necessity—is to be displayed as coming to a consciousness of itself (for it is in its very nature self-consciousness) and thereby realizing its existence. Itself is its own object of attainment, and the sole aim of Spirit. This result it is, at which the process of the World's History has been continually aiming; and to which the sacrifices that have ever and anon been laid on the vast altar of the earth, through the long lapse of ages, have been offered. This is the only aim that sees itself realized and fulfilled; the only pole of repose amid the ceaseless change of events and conditions, and the sole efficient principle that pervades them. This final aim is God's purpose with the world; but God is the absolutely perfect Being, and can, therefore, will nothing other than himself—his own Will. The Nature of

His Will—that is, His Nature itself—is what we here call the Idea of Freedom; translating the language of Religion into that of Thought. The question, then, which we may next put, is: What means does this principle of Freedom use for its realization? This is the second point we have to consider.

(2.) The question of the *means* by which Freedom develops itself to a World, conducts us to the phenomenon of History itself. Although Freedom is, primarily, an undeveloped idea, the means it uses are external and phenomenal; presenting themselves in History to our sensuous vision. The first glance at History convinces us that the actions of men proceed from their needs, their passions, their characters and talents; and impresses us with the belief that such needs, passions and interests are the sole springs of action—the efficient agents in this scene of activity. Among these may, perhaps, be found aims of a liberal or universal kind—benevolence it may be, or noble patriotism; but such virtues and general views are but insignificant as compared with the World and its doings. We may perhaps see the Ideal of Reason actualized in those who adopt such aims, and within the sphere of their influence; but they bear only a trifling proportion to the mass of the human race; and the extent of that influence is limited accordingly. Passions, private aims, and the satisfaction of selfish desires, are, on the other hand, most effective springs of action. Their power lies in the fact that they respect none of the limitations which justice and morality would impose on them; and that these natural impulses have a more direct influence over man than the artificial and tedious discipline that tends to order and self-restraint, law and morality. When we look at this display of passions, and the consequences of their violence; the Unreason which is associated not only with them, but even (rather we might say *especially*) with

good designs and righteous aims; when we see the evil, the vice, the ruin that has befallen the most flourishing kingdoms which the mind of man ever created; we can scarce avoid being filled with sorrow at this universal taint of corruption; and, since this decay is not the work of mere Nature, but of the Human Will—a moral embitterment —a revolt of the Good Spirit (if it have a place within us) may well be the result of our reflections. Without rhetorical exaggeration, a simply truthful combination of the miseries that have overwhelmed the noblest of nations and polities, and the finest exemplars of private virtue—forms a picture of most fearful aspect, and excites emotions of the profoundest and most hopeless sadness, counterbalanced by no consolatory result. We endure in beholding it a mental torture, allowing no defence or escape but the consideration that what has happened could not be otherwise; that it is a fatality which no intervention could alter. And at last we draw back from the intolerable disgust with which these sorrowful reflections threaten us into the more agreeable environment of our individual life—the Present formed by our private aims and interests. In short we retreat into the selfishness that stands on the quiet shore, and thence enjoys in safety the distant spectacle of "wrecks confusedly hurled." But even regarding History as the slaughter-bench at which the happiness of peoples, the wisdom of States, and the virtue of individuals have been victimized—the question involuntarily arises—to what principle, to what final aim these enormous sacrifices have been offered. From this point the investigation usually proceeds to that which we have made the general commencement of our inquiry. Starting from this we pointed out those phenomena which made up a picture so suggestive of gloomy emotions and thoughtful reflections—as *the very field* which we, for our part, regard as exhibiting only the means for realizing what we assert to be the essential destiny—the absolute aim, or—which comes to the same thing—the true *result* of the World's History. We have all along purposely eschewed "moral reflections" as a method of rising from the scene of historical specialties to the general principles which they embody. Besides, it is not the interest of such sentimentalities really to rise above those depressing emotions; and to solve the enigmas of Providence which the considerations that occasioned them present. It is essential to their character to find a gloomy satisfaction in the empty and fruitless sublimities of that negative result. We return then to the point of view which we have adopted; observing that the successive steps (Momente) of the analysis to which it will lead us, will also evolve the conditions requisite for answering the inquiries suggested by the panorama of sin and suffering that history unfolds. . . .

Philosophy shows that the Idea advances to an infinite antithesis; that, viz., between the Idea in its free, universal form—in which it exists for itself—and the contrasted form of abstract introversion, reflection on itself, which is formal existence-for-self, personality, formal freedom, such as belongs to Spirit only. The universal Idea exists thus as the substantial totality of things on the one side, and as the abstract essence of free volition on the other side. This reflection of the mind on itself is individual self-consciousness—the polar opposite of the Idea in its general form, and therefore existing in absolute Limitation. This polar opposite is consequently limitation, particularization, for the universal absolute being; it is the side of its *definite existence;* the sphere of its formal reality, the sphere of the reverence paid to God.— To comprehend the absolute connection of this antithesis, is the profound task of metaphysics. This Limitation originates all forms of particularity of whatever kind. The formal volition [of which we have spoken] wills itself; desires to make its own personality valid in all that it purposes and does: even the pious individual wishes to be saved and happy. This pole of the antithesis, existing for itself, is—in contrast with the Absolute Universal Being—a special separate existence, taking cognizance of speciality only, and willing that alone. In short it plays its part in the region of mere phenomena. This is the sphere of particular purposes, in effecting which individuals exert themselves on behalf of their individuality—give it full play and objective realization. This is also the sphere of happiness and its opposite. He is happy who finds his condition suited to his special character, will, and fancy, and so enjoys himself in that condition. The History of the World is not the theatre of happiness. Periods of happiness are blank pages in it, for they are periods of harmony—periods when the antithesis is in abeyance. Reflection on self —the Freedom above described—is abstracly defined as the formal element of the activity of the absolute Idea. The realizing *activity* of which we have spoken is the middle term of the Syllogism, one of whose extremes is the Universal essence, the *Idea,* which reposes in the penetralia of Spirit; and the other, the complex of external things—objective matter. That activity is the medium by which the universal latent principle is translated into the domain of objectivity. . . .

(3.) The third point to be analyzed is, therefore—what is the object to be realized by these means; *i.e.* what is the form it assumes in the realm of reality. We have spoken of *means;* but in the carrying out of a subjective, limited aim, we have also to take into consideration the element of a *material,* either already present or which has to be procured. Thus the question would arise: What is the material in which the Ideal of Reason is wrought out? The primary answer would be—Personality itself —human desires—Subjectivity generally. In human knowledge and volition, as its material element, Reason attains positive existence. We have considered subjective volition where it has an object which is the truth and essence of a reality; viz. where it constitutes a great world-historical passion. As a subjective will, occupied with limited passions, it is dependent, and can gratify its desires only within the limits of this dependence. But the subjective will has also a substantial life—a reality—in which it moves in the region of *essential* being and has the essential itself as the object of its existence. This essential being is the union of the *subjective* with the *rational* Will: it is the moral Whole, the *State,* which is that form of reality in which the individual has and enjoys his freedom; but on the condition of his recognizing, believing in and willing that which is common to the Whole. And this must not be understood as if the subjective will of the social unit attained its gratification and enjoyment through that common Will; as if this were a means provided for its benefit; as if the individual, in his relations to other individuals, thus limited his freedom, in order that this universal limitation—the mutual constraint of all—might secure a small space of liberty for each. Rather, we affirm, are Law, Morality, Government, and they alone, the positive reality and completion of Freedom. Freedom of a low and limited order, is mere caprice; which finds its exercise in the sphere of particular and limited desires. . . .

The State is thus the embodiment of rational freedom, realizing and recognizing itself in an objective form. For its objectivity consists in this—that its successive stages are not merely ideal, but are present in an appropriate reality; and that, in their separate and several working, they are absolutely merged in that agency by which the totality—the soul—the individuate unity— is produced, and of which it is the result.

The State is the Idea of Spirit in the external manifestation of human Will and its Freedom. It is to the State, therefore, that change in the aspect of History indissolubly attaches itself; and the successive phases of the Idea manifest themselves in it as distinct political *principles*.

2 / THEORY OF KNOWLEDGE

Two questions in epistemology can be distinguished: that of the criterion of truth, and of the nature of truth. By many idealists they are both answered in the theory of coherence. As a criterion of truth, coherence means that a proposition is to be considered true in terms of its consistent and systematic relationship to other propositions. As a theory of the nature of truth, coherence means that truth itself is a coherent system of propositions—a system such that, as Professor Blanshard writes, no proposition is arbitrary and every proposition is entailed by the others.

In support of his conviction that coherence does define the nature of truth, Professor Blanshard distinguishes the immanent end of thought, systematic vision, from the transcendent end which is fulfillment in an object. But, he argues, these ends must be one: the pursuit of thought's own ideal must at the same time be an apprehension of the real. This involves, then, a metaphysical theory that the immanent end of thought is a clue to the nature of things; in other words, that reality is an ordered, systematic, and intelligible structure, and that truth too is such a structure.

TRUTH AS COHERENCE

Brand Blanshard (1892-   )

1. It has been contended in the last chapter that coherence is in the end our sole criterion of truth. We have now to face the question whether it also gives us the nature of truth. We should be clear at the beginning that these are different questions, and that one may reject coherence as the definition of truth while accepting it as the test. It is conceivable that one thing should be an accurate index of another and still be extremely different from it. There have been philosophers who held that pleasure was an accurate gauge of the amount of good in experience, but that to confuse good with pleasure was a gross blunder. There have been a great many philosophers who held that for every change in consciousness there was a change in the nervous system and that the two corresponded so closely that if we knew the laws connecting them we could infallibly predict one from the other; yet it takes all the hardihood of a behaviorist to say that the two are the same. Similarly it has been held that though coherence supplies an infallible measure of truth, it would be a very grave mistake to identify it with truth.

2. The view that truth *is* coherence rests on a theory of the relation of thought to reality, and since this is the central problem of the theory of knowledge, to begin one's discussion by assuming the answer to it or by trying to make one out of whole cloth would be somewhat ridiculous. But as this was our main problem in the long discussions of Book II, we may be pardoned

here for brevity. First we shall state in *résumé* the relation of thought to reality that we were there driven to accept, and sketch the theory of truth implicit in it. We shall then take up one by one the objections to this theory and ask if they can pass muster.

To think is to seek understanding. And to seek understanding is an activity of mind that is marked off from all other activities by a highly distinctive aim. This aim, as we saw in our chapter on the general nature of understanding, is to achieve systematic vision, so to apprehend what is now unknown to us as to relate it, and relate it necessarily, to what we know already. We think to solve problems; and our method of solving problems is to build a bridge of intelligible relation from the continent of our knowledge to the island we wish to include in it. Sometimes this bridge is causal, as when we try to explain a disease; sometimes teleological, as when we try to fathom the move of an opponent over the chess board; sometimes geometrical, as in Euclid. But it is always systematic; thought in its very nature is the attempt to bring something unknown or imperfectly known into a sub-system of knowledge, and thus also into that larger system that forms the world of accepted beliefs. That is what explanation is. *Why* is it that thought desires this ordered vision? Why should such a vision give satisfaction when it comes? To these questions there is no answer, and if there were, it would be an answer only because it had succeeded in supplying the characteristic satisfaction to this unique desire.

But may it not be that what satisfies thought fails to conform to the real world? Where is the guarantee that when I have brought my ideas into the form my ideal re-

---

The selection is from Brand Blanshard, *The Nature of Thought*, 2 vols. (London: George Allen & Unwin Ltd.; New York: The Macmillan Company, 1939), Vol. II, pp. 260-269. Used by permission of the publishers.

quires, they should be *true?* Here we come round again to the tortured problem of Book II. In our long struggle with the relation of thought to reality we saw that if thought and things are conceived as related only externally, then knowledge is luck; there is no necessity whatever that what satisfies intelligence should coincide with what really is. It may do so, or it may not; on the principle that there are many misses to one bull's-eye, it more probably does not. But if we get rid of the misleading analogies through which this relation has been conceived, of copy and original, stimulus and organism, lantern and screen, and go to thought itself with the question what reference to an object means, we get a different and more hopeful answer. To think of a thing is to get that thing itself in some degree within the mind. To think of a color or an emotion is to have that within us which if it *were developed and completed,* would identify itself with the object. In short, if we accept its own report, thought is related to reality as the partial to the perfect fulfilment of a purpose. The more adequate its grasp the more nearly does it approximate, the more fully does it realize in itself, the nature and relations of its objects.

3. Thought thus appears to have two ends, one immanent, one transcendent. On the one hand it seeks fulfilment in a special kind of satisfaction, the satisfaction of systematic vision. On the other hand it seeks fulfilment in its object. Now it was the chief contention of our second book that these ends are one. Indeed unless they are accepted as one, we could see no alternative to skepticism. If the pursuit of thought's own ideal were merely an elaborate self-indulgence that brought us no nearer to reality, or if the apprehension of reality did not lie in the line of thought's interest, or still more if both of these held at once, the hope of knowledge would be vain. Of course it may really be vain. If anyone cares

to doubt whether the framework of human logic has any bearing on the nature of things, he may be silenced perhaps, but he cannot be conclusively answered. One may point out to him that the doubt itself is framed in accordance with that logic, but he can reply that thus we are taking advantage of his logico-centric predicament; further, that any argument we can offer accords equally well with his hypothesis and with ours, with the view that we are merely flies caught in a logical net and the view that knowledge reveals reality. And what accords equally well with both hypotheses does not support either to the exclusion of the other. But while such doubt is beyond reach by argument, neither is there anything in its favor. It is a mere suspicion which is, and by its nature must remain, without any positive ground; and as such it can hardly be discussed. Such suspicions aside, we can throw into the scale for our theory the impressive fact of the advance of knowledge. It has been the steadfast assumption of science whenever it came to an unsolved problem that there was a key to it to be found, that if things happened thus rather than otherwise they did so for a cause or reason, and that if this were not forthcoming it was never because it was lacking, but always because of a passing blindness in ourselves. Reflection has assumed that pursuit of its own immanent end is not only satisfying but revealing, that so far as the immanent end is achieved we are making progress toward the transcendent end as well. Indeed, that these ends coincide is the assumption of every act of thinking whatever. To think is to raise a question; to raise a question is to seek an explanation; to seek an explanation is to assume that one may be had; so to assume is to take for granted that nature in that region is intelligible. Certainly the story of advancing knowledge unwinds as if self-realization in thought meant also a coming nearer to reality.

4. That these processes are really one is the metaphysical base on which our belief in coherence is founded. If one admits that the pursuit of a coherent system has actually carried us to what everyone would agree to call knowledge, why not take this ideal as a guide that will conduct us farther? What better key can one ask to the structure of the real? Our own conviction is that we should take this immanent end of thought in all seriousness as the clue to the nature of things. We admit that it may prove deceptive, that somewhere thought may end its pilgrimage in frustration and futility before some blank wall of the unintelligible. There are even those who evince their superior insight by taking this as a foregone conclusion and regarding the faith that the real is rational as the wishful thinking of the "tender-minded." Their attitude appears to us a compound made up of one part timidity, in the form of a refusal to hope lest they be disillusioned; one part muddled persuasion that to be skeptical is to be sophisticated; one part honest dullness in failing to estimate rightly the weight of the combined postulate and success of knowledge; one part genuine insight into the possibility of surds in nature. But whatever its motives, it is a view that goes less well with the evidence than the opposite and brighter view. That view is that reality is a system, completely ordered and fully intelligible, with which thought in its advance is more and more identifying itself. We may look at the growth of knowledge, individual or social, either as an attempt by our own minds to return to union with things as they are in their ordered wholeness, or the affirmation through our minds of the ordered whole itself. And if we take this view, our notion of truth is marked out for us. Truth is the approximation of thought to reality. It is thought on its way home. Its measure is the distance thought has travelled, under guidance of its inner compass, toward that intelligible system which unites its ultimate object with its ultimate end. Hence at any given time the degree of truth in our experience as a whole is the degree of system it has achieved. The degree of truth of a particular proposition is to be judged in the first instance by its coherence with experience as a whole, ultimately by its coherence with that further whole, all-comprehensive and fully articulated, in which thought can come to rest.

5. But it is time we defined more explicitly what coherence means. To be sure, no fully satisfactory definition can be given; and as Dr. Ewing says, "it is wrong to tie down the advocates of the coherence theory to a precise definition. What they are doing is to describe an ideal that has never yet been completely clarified but is none the less immanent in all our thinking." Certainly this ideal goes far beyond mere consistency. Fully coherent knowledge would be knowledge in which every judgment entailed, and was entailed by, the rest of the system. Probably we never find in fact a system where there is so much of interdependence. What it means may be clearer if we take a number of familiar systems and arrange them in a series tending to such coherence as a limit. At the bottom would be a junkheap, where we could know every item but one and still be without any clue as to what that remaining item was. Above this would come a stone-pile, for here you could at least infer that what you would find next would be a stone. A machine would be higher again, since from the remaining parts one could deduce not only the general character of a missing part, but also its special form and function. This is a high degree of coherence, but it is very far short of the highest. You could remove the engine from a motor-car while leaving the other parts intact, and replace it with any one of thousands of other engines, but the thought of such an interchange among human heads or hearts shows at once that the interde-

pendence in a machine is far below that of the body. Do we find then in organic bodies the highest conceivable coherence? Clearly not. Though a human hand, as Aristotle said, would hardly be a hand when detached from the body, still it would be something definite enough; and we can conceive systems in which even this something would be gone. Abstract a number from the number series and it would be a mere unrecognizable *x;* similarly, the very thought of a straight line involves the thought of the Euclidean space in which it falls. It is perhaps in such systems as Euclidean geometry that we get the most perfect examples of coherence that have been constructed. If any proposition were lacking, it could be supplied from the rest; if any were altered, the repercussions would be felt through the length and breadth of the system. Yet even such a system as this falls short of ideal system. Its postulates are unproved; they are independent of each other, in the sense that none of them could be derived from any other or even from all the others together; its clear necessity is bought by an abstractness so extreme as to have left out nearly everything that belongs to the character of actual things. A completely satisfactory system would have none of these defects. No proposition would be arbitrary, every proposition would be entailed by the others jointly and even singly,[1] no proposition would stand outside the system. The integration would

be so complete that no part could be seen for what it was without seeing its relation to the whole, and the whole itself could be understood only through the contribution of every part.

6. It may be granted at once that in common life we are satisfied with far less than this. We accept the demonstrations of the geometer as complete, and do not think of reproaching him because he begins with postulates and leaves us at the end with a system that is a skeleton at the best. In physics, in biology, above all in the social sciences, we are satisfied with less still. We test judgments by the amount of coherence which in that particular subject-matter it seems reasonable to expect. We apply, perhaps unconsciously, the advice of Aristotle, and refrain from asking demonstration in the physical sciences, while in mathematics we refuse to accept less. And such facts may be thought to show that we make no actual use of the ideal standard just described. But however much this standard may be relaxed within the limits of a particular science, its influence is evident in the grading of the sciences generally. It is precisely in those sciences that approach most nearly to system as here defined that we achieve the greatest certainty, and precisely in those that are most remote from such system that our doubt is greatest whether we have achieved scientific truth at all. Our immediate exactions shift with the subject-matter; our ultimate standard is unvarying.

7. Now if we accept coherence as the test of truth, does that commit us to any conclusions about the *nature* of truth or reality? I think it does, though more clearly about reality than about truth. It is past belief that the fidelity of our thought to reality should be rightly measured by coherence if reality itself were not coherent. To say that the nature of things may be *in*coherent, but we shall approach the truth about it precisely so far as our thoughts

---

[1] Coherence can be defined without this point, which, as Dr. Ewing remarks (*Idealism*, 231), makes the case harder to establish. In no mathematical system, for example, would anyone dream of trying to deduce all the other propositions from any proposition taken singly. But when we are describing an ideal, such a fact is not decisive, and I follow Joachim in holding that in a perfectly coherent system every proposition would entail all others, if only for the reason that its meaning could never be fully understood without apprehension of the system in its entirety.

become coherent, sounds very much like nonsense. And providing we retained coherence as the test, it would still be nonsense even if truth were conceived as correspondence. On this supposition we should have truth when, our thought having achieved coherence, the correspondence was complete between that thought and its object. But complete correspondence between a coherent thought and an incoherent object seems meaningless. It is hard to see, then, how anyone could consistently take coherence as the test of truth unless he took it also as a character of reality.

8. Does acceptance of coherence as a test commit us not only to a view about the structure of reality but also to a view about the nature of truth? This is a more difficult question. As we saw at the beginning of the chapter, there have been some highly reputable philosophers who have held that the answer to "What is the test of truth?" is "Coherence," while the answer to "What is the nature or meaning of truth?" is "Correspondence." These questions are plainly distinct. Nor does there seem to be any direct path from the acceptance of coherence as the test of truth to its acceptance as the nature of truth. Nevertheless there is an indirect path. If we accept coherence as our test, we must use it everywhere. We must therefore use it to test the suggestion that truth *is* other than coherence. But if we do, we shall find that we must reject the suggestion as leading to *in*coherence. Coherence is a pertinacious concept and, like the well-known camel, if one lets it get its nose under the edge of the tent, it will shortly walk off with the whole.

Suppose that, accepting coherence as the test, one rejects it as the nature of truth in favor of some alternative; and let us assume, for example, that this alternative is correspondence. This, we have said, is incoherent; why? Because if one holds that truth is correspondence, one cannot intelligibly hold either that it is tested by coherence or that there is any dependable test at all. Consider the first point. Suppose that we construe experience into the most coherent picture possible, remembering that among the elements included will be such secondary qualities as colors, odors, and sounds. Would the mere fact that such elements as these are coherently arranged prove that anything precisely corresponding to them exists "out there"? I cannot see that it would, even if we knew that the two arrangements had closely corresponding patterns. If on one side you have a series of elements a, b, c, . . . , and on the other a series of elements α, β, γ . . . , arranged in patterns that correspond, you have no proof as yet that the *natures* of these elements correspond. It is therefore impossible to argue from a high degree of coherence within experience to its correspondence in the same degree with anything outside. And this difficulty is typical. If you place the nature of truth in one sort of character and its test in something quite different, you are pretty certain, sooner or later, to find the two falling apart. In the end, the only test of truth that is not misleading is the special nature or character that is itself constitutive of truth.

Feeling that this is so, the adherents of correspondence sometimes insist that correspondence shall be its own test. But then the second difficulty arises. If truth does consist in correspondence, no test can be sufficient. For in order to know that experience corresponds to fact, we must be able to get at that fact, unadulterated with idea, and compare the two sides with each other. And we have seen in the last chapter that such fact is not accessible. When we try to lay hold of it, what we find in our hands is a judgment which is obviously not itself the indubitable fact we are seeking, and which must be checked by some fact beyond it. To this process there is no end. And even if we did get at the fact directly, rather than through the veil of our ideas, that would be no less fatal to correspondence. This direct seizure of fact presumably gives us truth, but since that truth no longer consists in correspondence of idea with fact, the main theory has been abandoned. In short, if we can know fact only through the medium of our own ideas, the original forever eludes us; if we can get at the facts directly, we have knowledge whose truth is not correspondence. The theory is forced to choose between skepticism and self-contradiction.

Thus the attempt to combine coherence as the test of truth with correspondence as the nature of truth will not pass muster by its own test. The result is *incoherence*. We believe that an application of the test to other theories of truth would lead to a like result. The argument is: assume coherence as the test, and you will be driven by the incoherence of your alternatives to the conclusion that it is also the nature of truth.

3 / METAPHYSICS

One of the major idealist systems was produced by the American thinker Josiah Royce. The following selection is a statement of a central argument Royce developed for his position. Following Berkeley, he first turns to an analysis of experience and concludes that all experience is ideal or mind related. It is but a vast system of ideas that forces itself upon us.

Such an analytic statement ends, however, in a dilemma, for perhaps there lies beyond this system of ideas an unknowable, inscrutable x. Royce therefore turns to the second part of his argument to state his theory of synthetic idealism. Here, through his ingenious "argument from error," he asserts the existence of an inclusive, infinite problem-solver or Self that—even when we are in deepest doubt and uncertainty—possesses in unity our finite ideas and the objects that would make them true. Everything finite is dark and obscure, Royce concludes, but the existence of the Infinite Self is perfectly sure.

REALITY AND IDEALISM

Josiah Royce (1855-1916)

Idealism has two aspects. It is, for the first, a kind of analysis of the world, an analysis which so far has no absolute character about it, but which undertakes, in a fashion that might be acceptable to any skeptic, to examine what you mean by all the things, whatever they are, that you believe in or experience. This idealistic analysis

The selection is from Josiah Royce, *The Spirit of Modern Philosophy* (Boston: Houghton Mifflin Company, 1893), pp. 350-380, with omissions.

consists merely in a pointing out, by various devices, that the world of your knowledge, whatever it contains, is through and through such stuff as ideas are made of, that you never in your life believed in anything definable *but* ideas, that, as Berkeley put it, "this whole choir of heaven and furniture of earth" is nothing for any of us but a system of ideas which govern our belief and our conduct. . . .

The other aspect of idealism is the one which gives us our notion of the absolute

Self. To it the first is only preparatory. This second aspect is the one which from Kant, until the present time, has formed the deeper problem of thought. Whenever the world has become more conscious of its significance, the work of human philosophy will be, not nearly ended (Heaven forbid an end!), but for the first time fairly begun. For then, in critically estimating our passions, we shall have some truer sense of whose passions they are.

I begin with the first and the less significant aspect of idealism. Our world, I say, whatever it may contain, is such stuff as ideas are made of. This preparatory sort of idealism is the one that, as I just suggested, Berkeley made prominent, and, after a fashion familiar. I must state it in my own way, although one in vain seeks to attain novelty in illustrating so frequently described a view.

Here, then, is our so real world of senses, full of light and warmth and sound. If anything could be solid and external, surely, one at first will say, it is this world. Hard facts, not mere ideas, meet us on every hand. Ideas any one can mould as he wishes. Not so facts. In idea socialists can dream out Utopias, disappointed lovers can imagine themselves successful, beggars can ride horses, wanderers can enjoy the fireside at home. In the realm of facts, society organizes itself as it must, rejected lovers stand for the time defeated, beggars are alone with their wishes, oceans roll drearily between home and the wanderer. Yet this world of fact is, after all, not entirely stubborn, not merely hard. The strenuous will can mould facts. We can form our world, in part, according to our ideas. Statesmen influence the social order, lovers woo afresh, wanderers find the way home. . . .

But this bright and beautiful sense-world of ours,—what, amongst these many possible sorts of reality, does that embody? Are the stars and the oceans, the walls and the pictures, real as the maiden's heart is real, —embodying the ideas of somebody, but none the less stubbornly real for that? Or can we make something else of their reality? For, of course, that the stars and the oceans, the walls and the pictures have *some* sort of stubborn reality, just as the minds of our fellows have, our analysis so far does not for an instant think of denying. Our present question is, what sort of reality? Consider, then, in detail, certain aspects of the reality that seems to be exemplified in our sense-world. The sublimity of the sky, the life and majesty of the ocean, the interest of a picture,—to what sort of real facts do these belong? Evidently here we shall have no question. So far as the sense-world is beautiful, is majestic, is sublime, this beauty and dignity exist only for the appreciative observer. If they exist beyond him, they exist only for some other mind, or as the thought and embodied purpose of some universal soul of nature. A man who sees the same world, but who has no eye for the fairness of it, will find all the visible facts, but will catch nothing of their value. At once, then, the sublimity and beauty of the world are thus truths that one who pretends to insight ought to see, and they are truths which have no meaning except for such a beholder's mind, or except as embodying the thought of the mind of the world. So here, at least, is so much of the outer world that is ideal, just as the coin or the jewel or the bank-note or the bond has its value not alone in its physical presence, but in the idea that it symbolizes to a beholder's mind, or to the relatively universal thought of the commercial world. But let us look a little deeper. Surely, if the objects yonder are unideal and outer, odors and tastes and temperatures do not exist in these objects in just the way in which they exist in us. Part of the being of these properties, at least, if not all of it, is ideal and exists for us, or at best is once more the embodiment of the thought or purpose of some world-mind. About tastes you cannot dispute, because they are not only ideal but personal. For the benumbed tongue and palate of diseased bodily conditions, all things are tasteless. As for temperatures, a well-known experiment will show how the same water may seem cold to one hand and warm to the other. But even so, colors and sounds are at least in part ideal. Their causes may have some other sort of reality; but colors themselves are not in the things, since they change with the light that falls on the things, vanish in the dark (whilst the things remained unchanged), and differ for different eyes. And as for sounds, both the pitch and the quality of tones depend for us upon certain interesting peculiarities of our hearing organs, and exist in nature only as voiceless sound-waves trembling through the air. All such sense qualities, then, are ideal. The world yonder may—yes, must—have attributes that give reasons why these qualities are thus felt by us; for so we assume. The world yonder may even be a mind that thus expresses its will to us. But these qualities need not, nay, cannot resemble the ideas that are produced in us, unless, indeed, that is because these qualities have place as ideas in some world-mind. . . .

But now, at this point, the Berkeleyan idealist goes one step further. The real outside world that is still left unexplained and unanalyzed after its beauty, its warmth, its odors, its tastes, its colors, and its tones, have been relegated to the realm of ideal truths, what do you now *mean* by calling it real? No doubt it *is* known as somehow real, but *what* is this reality *known as* being? If you know that this world is still there and outer, as by hypothesis you know, you are bound to say *what* this outer character implies for your thought. And here you have trouble. Is the outer world, as it exists outside of your ideas, or of anybody's ideas, something having shape, filling space, possessing solidity, full of moving things? That would in the first place seem

evident. The sound isn't outside of me, but the sound-waves, you say, are. The colors are ideal facts; but the ether-waves don't need a mind to know them. Warmth is ideal, but the physical fact called heat, this playing to and fro of molecules, is real, and is there apart from any mind. But once more, *is* this so evident? What do I *mean* by the shape of anything, or by the size of anything? Don't I mean just the idea of shape or of size that I am obliged to get under certain circumstances? What is the meaning of any property that I give to the real outer world? How can I express that property except in case I think it in terms of my ideas? As for the sound-waves and the ether-waves, what are they but things ideally conceived to explain the facts of nature? The conceptions have doubtless their truth, but it is an ideal truth. What I mean by saying that the things yonder have shape and size and trembling molecules, and that there is air with sound-waves, and ether with light-waves in it,—what I *mean* by all this is that experience forces upon me, directly or indirectly, a vast system of ideas, which may indeed be founded in truth beyond me, which in fact *must* be founded in such truth if my experience has any sense, but which, like my ideas of color and of warmth, are simply expressions of how the world's order must appear to me, and to anybody constituted like me. . . .

Thus, all the reality that *we* attribute to our world, in so far as *we* know and can tell what we mean thereby, becomes ideal. There is, in fact, a certain system of ideas, forced upon us by experience, which we have to use as the guide of our conduct. This system of ideas we can't change by our wish; it is for us as overwhelming a fact as guilt, or as the bearing of our fellows towards us, but we know it only *as* such a system of ideas. And we call it the world of matter. John Stuart Mill very well expressed the puzzle of the whole thing, as we have now reached the statement of this puzzle, when he called matter a mass of "permanent possibilities of experience" for each of us. Mill's definition has its faults, but is a very fair beginning. You know matter as something that either now gives you this idea or experience, or that would give you some other idea or experience under other circumstances. A fire, while it burns, is for you a permanent possibility of either getting the idea of an agreeable warmth, or of getting the idea of a bad burn, and you treat it accordingly. A precipice amongst mountains is a permanent possibility of your experiencing a fall, or of your getting a feeling of the exciting or of the sublime in mountain scenery. . . . And this acceptance of actual experience, this belief in possible experience, constitutes all that you mean by your faith in the outer world. . . .

What I have desired thus far is merely to give each of you, as it were, the sensation of being an idealist in this first and purely analytical sense of the word idealism. The sum and substance of it all is, you see, this: you know your world in fact as a system of ideas about things, such that from moment to moment you find this system forced upon you by experience. Even matter you know just as a mass of coherent ideas that you cannot help having. Space and time, as you think them, are surely ideas of yours. Now, what more natural than to say that *if* this be so, the real world beyond you must in itself be a system of somebody's ideas? If it is, then you can comprehend what its existence means. If it isn't, then since all you can know of it is ideal, the real world must be utterly unknowable, a bare *x*. Minds I can understand, because I myself am a mind. An existence that has no mental attribute is wholly opaque to me. So far, however, from such a world of ideas, existent beyond me in another mind, seeming to coherent thought essentially *un*real, ideas and minds and their ways, are, on the contrary, the

hardest and stubbornest facts that we can name. *If* the external world is in itself mental, then, be this reality a standard and universal thought, or a mass of little atomic minds constituting the various particles of matter, in any case one can comprehend what it is, and will have at the same time to submit to its stubborn authority as the lover accepts the reality of the maiden's moods. If the world *isn't* such an ideal thing, then indeed all our science, which is through and through concerned with our mental interpretations of things, can neither have objective validity, nor make satisfactory progress towards truth. For a science is concerned with ideas, the world beyond all ideas is a bare *x*.

But with this bare *x*, you will say, this analytical idealism after all leaves me, as with something that, in spite of all my analyses and interpretations, may after all be there beyond me as the real world, which my ideas are vainly striving to reach, but which eternally flees before me. So far, you will say, what idealism teaches is that the real world can only be interpreted by treating it as if it were somebody's thought. So regarded, the idealism of Berkeley and of other such thinkers is very suggestive, yet it doesn't tell us what the true world is, but only that *so much* of the true world as we ever get into our comprehension has to be conceived in ideal terms. . . . Are we not just where we started?

No; there lies now just ahead of us the goal of a synthetic idealistic conception, which will not be content with this mere analysis of the colors and forms of things, and with the mere discovery that all these are for us nothing but ideas. In this second aspect, idealism grows bolder, and fears not the profoundest doubt that may have entered your mind as to whether there is any world at all, or as to whether it is in any fashion knowable. State in full the deepest problem, the hardest question about the world that your thought ever conceived.

In this new form idealism offers you a suggestion that indeed will not wholly answer nor do away with every such problem, but that certainly will set the meaning of it in a new light. What this new light is, I must in conclusion seek to illustrate.

Note the point we have reached. *Either,* as you see, your real world yonder is through and through a world of ideas, an outer mind that you are more or less comprehending through your experience, *or else*, in so far as it is real and outer it is unknowable, and inscrutable *x*, an absolute mystery. The dilemma is perfect. . . . Well, try the darker choice that the dilemma gives you. The world yonder shall be an *x*, an unknowable something, outer, problematic, foreign, opaque. And you,—you shall look upon it and believe in it. Yes, you shall for argument's sake first put on an air of resigned confidence, and say, "I do not only fancy it to be an extra-mental and unknowable something there, an impenetrable *x*, but I know it to be such. I can't help it. I didn't make it unknowable. I regret the fact. But there it is. I have to admit its existence. But I know that I shall never solve the problem of its nature." Ah, its nature is a *problem,* then. But what do you mean by this *"problem"?* Problems are, after a fashion, rather familiar things,— that is, in the world of ideas. There are problems soluble and problems insoluble in that world of ideas. It is a soluble problem if one asks what whole number is the square root of 64. The answer is 8. It is an insoluble problem if one asks me to find what whole number is the square root of 65. There is, namely, no such whole number. . . . Any fair question could be answered by one who knew enough. No fair question has an unknowable answer. But now, *if* your unknowable world out there is a thing of wholly, of absolutely problematic and inscrutable nature, is it so because you don't *yet* know enough about it, or because in its very nature and essence it is an absurd thing, an

x that *would* answer a question, which actually it is nonsense to ask? Surely one must choose the former alternative. The real world may be unknown; it can't be essentially unknowable.

This subtlety is wearisome enough, I know, just here, but I shall not dwell long upon it. Plainly *if* the unknowable world out there is through and through in its nature a really inscrutable problem, this must mean that in nature it resembles such problems as, What is the whole number that is the square root of 65? Or, What two adjacent hills are there that have no valley between them? For in the world of thought such are the *only* insoluble problems. All others either may now be solved, or would be solved if we knew more than we now do. But, once more, *if* this unknowable is only just the real world as now unknown to us, but capable some time of becoming known, then remember that, as we have just seen, only a mind can ever become an object known to a mind. If I know you as external to me, it is only because you are minds. If I can come to know *any* truth, it is only in so far as this truth is essentially mental, is an idea, is a thought, that I can ever come to know it. Hence, if that so-called unknowable, that unknown outer world there, ever could, by any device, come within our ken, then it is already an ideal world. For just that is what our whole idealistic analysis has been proving. Only ideas are knowable. And nothing absolutely unknowable can exist. For the absolutely unknowable, the *x* pure and simple, the Kantian thing in itself, simply cannot be admitted. The notion of it is nonsense. The assertion of it is a contradiction. . . .

Once more, then, to sum up here, *if,* however vast the world of the unknown, only the essentially knowable can exist, and *if* everything knowable is an idea, a mental somewhat, the content of some mind, then once for all we are the world of ideas. Your deepest doubt proves this. Only the nonsense of that inscrutable x, of that Abracadabra, of that Snark, the Unknowable of whose essence you make your real world, prevents you from seeing this.

To return, however, to our dilemma. *Either* idealism, we said, *or* the unknowable. What we have now said is that the absolutely unknowable is essentially an absurdity, a non-existent. For any fair and statable problem admits of an answer. *If* the world exists yonder, its essence is then already capable of being known by some mind. If capable of being known by a mind, this essence is then already essentially ideal and mental. . . .

But with this result we come in presence of a final problem. All this, you say, depends upon my assurance that there is after all a real and therefore an essentially knowable and rational world yonder. Such a world would have to be in essence a mind, or a world of minds. But after all, how does one ever escape from the prison of the inner life? Am I not in all this merely wandering amidst the realm of my own ideas? *My* world, of course, isn't and can't be a mere x, an essentially unknowable thing, just because it *is my* world, and I have an idea of it. But then does not this mean that *my* world is, after all, forever just *my* world, so that I never get to any truth beyond myself? Isn't this result very disheartening? My world is thus a world of ideas, but alas! how do I then ever reach those ideas of the minds beyond me?

The answer is a simple, but in one sense a very problematic one. You, in one sense, namely, never *do* or can get beyond your own ideas, nor ought you to wish to do so, because in truth all those other minds that constitute your outer and real world are in essence one with your own self. This whole world of ideas is essentially *one* world, and so it is essentially the world of one self and *That art Thou.*

The truth and meaning of this deepest proposition of all idealism is now not at all remote from us. The considerations, however, upon which it depends are of the dryest possible sort, as commonplace as they are deep.

Whatever objects you may think about, whether they are objects directly known to you, or objects infinitely far removed, objects in the distant stars, or objects remote in time, or objects near and present,— such objects, then, as a number with fifty places of digits in it, or the mountains on the other side of the moon, or the day of your death, or the character of Cromwell, or the law of gravitation, or a name that you are just now trying to think of and have forgotten, or the meaning of some mood or feeling or idea now in your mind,—all such objects, I insist, stand in a certain constant and curious relation to your mind whenever you are thinking about them,—a relation that we often miss because it is so familiar. What is this relation? Such an object, while you think about it, needn't be, as popular thought often supposes it to be, the *cause* of your thoughts concerning it. Thus, when you think about Cromwell's character, Cromwell's character isn't just now *causing* any ideas in you,—isn't, so to speak, doing anything to you. Cromwell is dead, and after life's fitful fever his character is a very inactive thing. Not as the *cause*, but as the *object* of your thought is Cromwell present to you. Even so, if you choose now to think of the moment of your death, that moment is somewhere off there in the future, and you can make it your object, but it isn't now an active cause of your ideas. The moment of your death has no present physical existence at all, and just now causes nothing. So, too, with the mountains on the other side of the moon. When you make them the object of your thought, they remain indifferent to you. They do not affect you. You never saw them. But all the same you can think about them.

Yet this thinking *about* things is, after all, a very curious relation in which to stand to things. In order to think *about* a thing, it is *not* enough that I should have an idea in me that merely resembles that thing. This last is a very important observation. I repeat, it is *not* enough that I should merely have an idea in me that resembles the thing whereof I think. I have, for instance, in me the idea of a pain. Another man has a pain just like mine. Say we both have toothache; or have both burned our fingertips in the same way. Now my idea of pain is just like the pain in him, but I am not on that account necessarily thinking about *his* pain, merely because what I am thinking about, namely my own pain, resembles his pain. No; to think about an object you must not merely have an idea that resembles the object, but you must *mean* to have your idea resemble that object. Stated in other form, to think of an object you must consciously aim at that object, you must pick out that object, you must already in some measure possess that object enough, namely, to identify it as what you mean. But how can you *mean*, how can you *aim at*, how can you *possess*, how can you *pick out*, how can you *identify* what is not already present in essence to your own hidden self? Here is surely a deep question. When you aim at yonder object, be it the mountains in the moon or the day of your death, you really say, "I, as my real self, as my larger self, as my complete consciousness, already in deepest truth possess that object, have it, own it, identify it. And that, and that alone, makes it possible for me in my transient, my individual, my momentary personality, to mean yonder object, to inquire about it, to be partly aware of it and partly ignorant of it." You can't mean what is utterly foreign to you. You mean an object, you assert about it, you talk about it, yes, you doubt or wonder about it, you admit your private and individual ignorance about it, only in so far as your larger self, your deeper personality, your total of normal consciousness already

has that object. Your momentary and private wonder, ignorance, inquiry, or assertion, about the object, implies, asserts, presupposes, that your total self is in full and immediate possession of the object. This, in fact, is the very nature of that curious relation of a thought to an object which we are now considering. The self that is doubting or asserting, or that is even feeling its private ignorance about an object, and that still, even in consequence of all this, is *meaning,* is *aiming at* such object, is in essence identical with the self for which this object exists in its complete and consciously known truth. . . .

In this way I suggest to you the proof which a rigid analysis of the logic of our most commonplace thought would give for the doctrine that in the world there is but *one* Self, and that it is *his* world which we all alike are truly meaning, whether we talk of one another or of Cromwell's character or of the fixed stars or of the far-off eons of the future. The relation of my thought to its object has, I insist, this curious character, that *unless* the thought and its object are parts of one larger thought, I can't even be *meaning* that object yonder, can't even be in error about it, can't even doubt its existence. You, for instance, are part of one larger self with me, or else I can't even be meaning to address you as outer beings. You are part of one larger self along with the most mysterious or most remote fact of nature, along with the moon, and all the hosts of heaven, along with all truth and all beauty. Else could you not even intend to speak of such objects beyond you. For whatever you speak of you will find that your world is meant by you as just your world. Talk of the unknowable, and it forthwith becomes your unknowable, your problem, whose solution, unless the problem be a mere nonsense question, your larger self must own and be aware of. The deepest problem of life is, "What is this deeper self?" And the only answer is, *It is the self that knows in unity all truth.* This, I insist, is no hypothesis. It is actually the presupposition of your deepest doubt. And that is why I say: Everything finite is more or less obscure, dark, doubtful. Only the Infinite Self, the problem-solver, the complete thinker, the one who knows what we mean even when we are most confused and ignorant, the one who includes us, who has the world present to himself in unity, before whom all past and future truth, all distant and dark truth is clear in one eternal moment, to whom far and forgot is near, who thinks the whole of nature, and in whom are all things, the Logos, the world-possessor,—only his existence, I say, is perfectly sure. . . .

And now, as to the unity of this Self. Can there be many such organic selves, mutually separate unities of moments and of the objects that these moments mean? Nay, were there *many* such, would not their manifoldness be a truth? Their relations, would not these be real? Their distinct places in the world-order, would not these things be objects of possible true or false thoughts? If so, must not there be once more the inclusive real Self for whom these truths were true, these separate selves interrelated, and their variety absorbed in the organism of its rational meaning?

There is, then, at last, but one Self, organically, reflectively, consciously inclusive of all the selves, and so of all truth. I have called this self, Logos, problem-solver, all-knower Consider, then, last of all, his relation to problems. In the previous lecture we doubted many things; we questioned the whole seeming world of the outer order; we wondered as to space and time, as to nature and evolution, as to the beginning and the end of things. Now he who wonders is like him who doubts. Has his wonder any rationality about it? Does he *mean* anything by his doubt? Then the truth that

he means, and about which he wonders, has its real constitution. As wonderer, he in the moment possesses not this solving truth; he appeals to the self who can solve. That self must possess the solution just as surely as the problem has a meaning. The real nature of space and time, the real beginning of things, where matter was at any point of time in the past, what is to become of the world's energy: these are matters of truth, and truth is necessarily present to the Self as in one all-comprehending self-completed moment, beyond which is naught, within which is the world.

The world, then, is such stuff as ideas are made of. Thought possesses all things. But the world isn't unreal. It extends infinitely beyond our private consciousness, because it is the world of an universal mind. What facts it is to contain only experience can inform us. There is no magic that can anticipate the work of science. Absolutely the *only* thing sure from the first about this world, however, is that it is intelligent, rational, orderly, essentially comprehensible, so that all its problems are somewhere solved, all its darkest mysteries are known to the supreme Self. This Self infinitely and reflectively transcends our consciousness, and therefore, since it includes us, it is at the very least a person, and more definitely conscious than we are; for what it possesses is self-reflecting knowledge, and what is knowledge aware of itself, but consciousness? Beyond the seeming wreck and chaos of our finite problems, its eternal insight dwells, therefore, in absolute and supreme majesty. Yet it is not far from every one of us. There is no least or most transient thought that flits through a child's mind, or that troubles with the faintest line of care a maiden's face, and that still does not contain and embody something of this divine Logos.

4 / ETHICS

Idealist ethics has generally centered on an ideal of individual development or personal worth. Values, as T. H. Green wrote, exist "in, of, and for persons"; and the norm of life, as Hegel suggested, is to "be a person and respect others as persons." The theory developed by idealists from premises such as these is usually called—as it is by F. H. Bradley, the author of the following selection—self-realization ethics.

Morality, Bradley holds, is coextensive with the realization of an ideal self. The self to be realized is not, it should be noted carefully, this or that feeling, or a self simply to be pleased. If I wish to achieve my true moral being, I must realize something beyond my present fragmentary being. What should I realize? The first part of Bradley's answer is, "my station and its duties"—that is, my place within the state and society. This is an essential part of the moral life; for man is a social animal, he finds his being only in society, and apart from society he is but an impossible abstraction.

Yet there is a content to this self beyond "my station" in the form of an ideal good that is more than social. Morality for Bradley is ultimately the realization of the self as the *good will*—a will, that is, that realizes an end above particular men, that is superior to them, and that confronts them as a law or obligation. The good will is also a single, "concrete" universal—a universal that is not only above but also in particular details. Finally, the good will remains an ideal, partly perhaps but never fully real.

MORALITY AND SELF-REALIZATION

F. H. Bradley (1846-1924)

It is a moral duty to realize everywhere the best self, which for us in this sphere is an ideal self; and, asking what morality is, we so far must answer, it is coextensive with self-realization in the sense of the realization of the ideal self in and by us. And thus we are led to the enquiry, what is the *content* of this ideal self.

. . . We can at once gather that the good self is the self which realizes (1) a social, (2) a non-social ideal; the self, first, which does, and, second, which does not

directly and immediately involve relation to others. Or from another point of view, what is aimed at is the realization in me (1) of the ideal which is realized in society, of my station and its duties, or (2) of the ideal which is not there fully realized; and this is (a) the perfection of a social and (b) of a non-social self. Or again (it is all the same thing) we may divide into (1) duties to oneself which are not regarded as social duties, (2) duties to oneself which are so regarded, these latter being (a) the duties of my station which I happen to be in, (b) duties beyond that station. Let us further explain.

The content of the good self, we see, has a threefold origin; and (1) the first and

The selection is from Essay VI, "Ideal Morality," in F. H. Bradley, *Ethical Studies* (New York: G. E. Stechert & Co.; London: Henry S. King & Co., 1876), pp. 197-209, with omissions.

most important contribution comes from what we have called my station and its duties, and of this we have spoken already at some length. We saw that the notion of an individual man existing in his own right independent of society was an idle fancy, that a human being is human because he has drawn his being from human society, because he is the individual embodiment of a larger life; and we saw that this larger life, of the family, society, or the nation, was a moral will, an universal the realization of which in his personal will made a man's morality. We have nothing to add here except in passing to call attention to what we lately advanced, viz. that the good man is good throughout all his life and not merely in parts; and further to request the reader to turn to himself and ask himself in what his better self consists. He will find, if we do not mistake, that the greater part of it consists in his loyalty, and according to the spirit, performing his duties and filling his place as the member of a family, society, and the state. He will find that, when he has satisfied the demands of these spheres upon him, he will in the main have covered the claims of what he calls his good self. The basis and foundation of the ideal self is the self which is true to my station and its duties.

But (2) we saw also that, if we investigate our good self, we find something besides, claims beyond what the world expects of us, a will for good beyond what we see to be realized anywhere. The good in my station and its duties was visibly realized in the world, and it was mostly possible to act up to that real ideal; but this good beyond is only an ideal; for it is not wholly realized in the world we see, and, do what we may, we can not find it realized in ourselves. It is what we strive for and in a manner do gain, but never attain to and never possess. And this ideal self (so far as we are concerned with it here) is a social self. The perfect types of zeal and purity, honor

and love, which, figured and presented in our own situation and circumstances, and thereby unconsciously specialized, become the guides of our conduct and law of our being, are social ideals. They directly involve relation to other men, and, if you remove others, you immediately make the practice of these virtues impossible. . . .

But (3) there remains in the good self a further region we have not yet entered on; an ideal, the realization of which is recognized as a moral duty, but which yet in its essence does not involve direct relation to other men. The realization for myself of truth and beauty, the living for the self which in the apprehension, the knowledge, the sight, and the love of them finds its true being, is (all those who know the meaning of the words will bear me out) a moral obligation, which is not felt as such only so far as it is too pleasant.

It is a moral duty for the artist or the enquirer to lead the life of one, and a moral offence when he fails to do so. But on the other hand it is impossible, without violent straining of the facts, to turn these virtues into social virtues or duties to my neighbor. No doubt such virtues do as a rule lead indirectly to the welfare of others, but this is not enough to make them social; their social bearing is indirect, and does not lie in their very essence. The end they aim at is a single end of their own, the content of which does not necessarily involve the good of other men. This we can see from supposing the opposite. If that were true, then it would not be the duty of the enquirer, as such, simply to enquire, or of the artist, as such, simply to produce the best work of art; but each would have to consider ends falling outside his science or art, and would have no right to treat these latter as ends in themselves. "Nor has he," may be the confident answer. I reply that to me this is a question of fact, and to me it is a fact that the moral consciousness recognizes the perfecting of my intellectual or artistic nature by the production of the proper results, as an end in itself and not merely as a means. The pursuit of these ends, apart from what they lead to, is approved as morally desirable, not perhaps by the theory, but, I think, by the instinctive judgment of all persons worth considering; and if, and while, this fact stands, for me at least it is not affected by doctrines which require that it should be otherwise. To say, without society science and art could not have arisen, is true. To say, apart from society the life of an artist or man of science can not be carried on, is also true; but neither truth goes to show that society is the ultimate end, unless by an argument which takes the basis of a result as its final cause, and which would prove the physical and physiological conditions of society to be the end for which it existed. Man is not man at all unless social, but man is not much above the beasts unless more than social. . . .

The field of morality we find is the whole field of life; its claim is as wide as self-realization, and the question raised before now presents itself, Are morality and self-realization the same and not different? This appears at first sight to be the case. The moral end is to realize the self, and all the forms of the realizing of the self are seen to fall within the sphere of morality; and so it seems natural to say that morality is the process of self-realization, and the most moral man is the man who most fully and energetically realizes human nature. Virtue is excellence, and the most excellent is the most virtuous.

If we say this, however, we come into direct collision with the moral consciousness, which clearly distinguishes moral from other excellence, and asserts that the latter is not in itself moral at all; and we find the deliverance of that consciousness in the emphatic maxim that nothing is morally good save a good will. This maxim we shall forthwith take to be true, and so proceed.

Morality then will be the realization of the self as the good will. It is not self-realization from all points of view, though all self-realization can be looked at from this one point of view; for all of it involves will, and, so far as the will is good, so far is the realization moral. Strictly speaking and in the proper sense, morality is self-realization within the sphere of the personal will. We see this plainly in art and science, for there we have moral excellence, and that excellence does not lie in mere skill or mere success, but in single-mindedness and devotion to what seems best as against what we merely happen to like. . . .

The general end is self-realization, the making real of the ideal self; and for morality, in particular, the ideal self is the good will, the identification of my will with the ideal as an universal will. The end for morals is a will, and my will, and an universal will, and one will. Let us briefly refer on these heads to the moral consciousness.

Nothing, we have seen, is good but a good will. The end for morals is not the mere existence of any sort of ideal indifferently, but it is the realization of an ideal will in my will. The end is the ideal willed by me, the willing of the ideal in and by my will, and hence an ideal will. And my will as realizing the ideal is the good will. A will which obeys no law is not moral, a law which is not willed is nothing for morality. Acts, so far as they spring from the good will, are good, and a temper and habits and character are good so far as they are a present good will, result from it and embody it; and what issues from a good character must thus likewise be morally good.

That the good will for morality is my will is obvious enough, and it is no less plain that it is presented as universal. That does not mean that everybody does or has to do what I do, but it means that, if they were I, they must do as I have to do, or else be immoral; it means that my moral will is *not* the mere will of myself as this or that man, but something above it and beyond it. And further, again, the good will is presented as one will; in collisions, going to our moral consciousness, we are told that, if we knew it, there is a right, that the collision is for us, and is not for the good will. We can not bring before us two diverse good wills, or one good will at cross purposes and not in harmony with itself; and we feel sure that, if our will were but one with the universal, then we too should be one with ourselves, with no conflict of desires, but a harmony and system.

Such is the will presented to itself by the moral consciousness, but for the moral consciousness that is ideal and not real. Within the sphere of morality the universal remains but partially realized: it is something that for ever wants to be, and yet is not.

We saw that the will of the social organism might be called an universal will, and a will which was visibly real, as well as ideal; but we saw too that the sphere of my station and its duties did not cover the whole good self; and further, even within

that sphere, and apart from difficulties of progress, for morality in the strict sense ideal and real remain apart. The bad self is not extinguished, and in myself I see an element of will wherein the universal is unrealized, and against which it therefore remains (so far as my morality is concerned) a mere idea, for, even if we assume that society gets no hurt, yet I do not come up to my special type.

For morals then the universal is not realized within my station, and furthermore the moral consciousness does not say that it is realized anywhere at all. The claim of the ideal is to cover the whole field of reality, but our conscience tells us that we will it here, and that there again we do not will it, here it is realized, and there it is not realized, and we can not point to it in ourselves or others and say, Here is the universal incarnate, and fully actual by and as the will of this or that man; and indeed we see that for the ideal self to be in the world as the expressed will of this or that spiritualized animal is quite out of the question.

5 / ESTHETICS

Idealists have produced a variety of esthetic theories, and many of them are extremely important in the history of thought about art. Among these theories is that developed by the Italian philosopher Benedetto Croce. Central to his view is the definition of art as intuition. Intuition he believes to be not some vague feeling or hunch, but rather a realized and formed object. It is not, that is, merely emotion, but rather a total subjective mood wherein *what* is expressed comes into being in the very process of expression. Thus intuition also involves expression, for art is produced only when the spirit creates from the relatively formless materials of experience expressive images. Three further points should be noted. First, for Croce, it is feeling, not thought, which gives art its symbolism. Yet, secondly, art is a kind of knowledge—namely, knowledge of the individual. And last, the unity of art is found in a lyrical content, as embodied in the representation.

ART AS INTUITION

Benedetto Croce (1866-1952)

The question as to what is art,—I will say at once, in the simplest manner, that art is *vision* or *intuition*. The artist produces an image or a phantasm; and he who enjoys art turns his gaze upon the point to which the artist has pointed, looks through the chink which he has opened, and reproduces that image in himself. "Intuition," "vision," "contemplation," "imagination," "fancy," "figurations," "representations," and so on, are words continually recurring, like synonyms, when discoursing upon art, and they all lead the mind to the same conceptual sphere which indicates general agreement.

But this reply, that art is intuition, obtains its force and meaning from all that it implicitly denies and from which it distinguishes art. What negations are implicit in it? I shall indicate the principal, or at least those that are the most important for us at this present moment of our culture.

It denies, above all, that art is a *physical fact:* for example, certain determined colors, or relations of colors; certain definite forms of bodies; certain definite sounds, or relations of sounds; certain phenomena of heat or of electricity—in short, whatsoever be designated as "physical." The inclination toward this error of physicizing art is already present in ordinary thought, and as children who touch the soap-bubble and would wish to touch the rainbow, so the human spirit, admiring beautiful things, hastens spontaneously to trace out the reasons for them in external nature, and proves that it must think, or believes that it should think, certain colors beautiful and certain other colors ugly, certain forms beautiful

and certain other forms ugly. But this attempt has been carried out intentionally and with method on several occasions in the history of thought: from the "canons" which the Greek theoreticians and artists fixed for the beauty of bodies, through the speculations as to the geometrical and numerical relations of figures and sounds, down to the researches of the estheticians of the nineteenth century (Fechner, for example), and to the "communications" presented in our day by the inexpert, at philosophical, psychological, and natural science congresses, concerning the relations of physical phenomena with art. And if it be asked why art cannot be a physical fact, we must reply, in the first place, that physical facts *do not possess reality,* and that art, to which so many devote their whole lives and which fills all with a divine joy, is *supremely real;* thus it cannot be a physical fact, which is something unreal. This sounds at first paradoxical, for nothing seems more solid and secure to the ordinary man than the physical world; but we, in the seat of truth, must not abstain from the good reason and substitute for it one less good, solely because the first should have the appearance of a lie; and besides, in order to surpass what of strange and difficult may be contained in that truth, to become at home with it, we may take into consideration the fact that the demonstration of the unreality of the physical world has not only been proved in an indisputable manner and is admitted by all philosophers (who are not crass materialists and are not involved in the strident contradictions of materialism), but is professed by these same physicists in the spontaneous philosophy which they mingle with their physics, when they conceive physical phenomena as products of principles that are beyond experience, of atoms or of ether,

The selection is from Benedetto Croce, *Breviary of Esthetic,* The Rice Institute Pamphlet, II (1915), pp. 229-237 and 245-250. Quoted by permission of the Rice Institute.

or as the manifestation of an Unknowable: besides, the matter itself of the materialists is a supermaterial principle. Thus physical facts reveal themselves, by their internal logic and by common consent, not as reality, but as a *construction of our intellect for the purposes of science*. Consequently, the question whether art be a physical fact must rationally assume this different signification: that is to say, *whether it be possible to construct art physically*. And this is certainly possible, for we indeed carry it out always, when, turning from the sense of a poem and ceasing to enjoy it, we set ourselves, for example, to count the words of which the poem is composed and to divide them into syllables and letters; or, disregarding the esthetic effect of a statue, we weigh and measure it: a most useful performance for the packers of statues, as is the other for the typographers who have to "compose" pages of poetry; but most useless for the contemplator and student of art, to whom it is neither useful nor licit to allow himself to be "distracted" from his proper object. Thus art is not a physical fact in this second sense, either; which amounts to saying that when we propose to ourselves to penetrate its nature and mode of action, to construct it physically is of no avail.

Another negation is implied in the definition of art as intuition: if it be intuition, and intuition is equivalent to *theory* in the original sense of contemplation, art cannot be a utilitarian act; and since a utilitarian act aims always at obtaining a pleasure and therefore at keeping off a pain, art, considered in its own nature, has nothing to do with the *useful* and with *pleasure* and *pain*, as such. It will be admitted, indeed, without much difficulty, that a pleasure as a pleasure, any sort of pleasure, is not of itself artistic; the pleasure of a drink of water that slakes thirst, or a walk in the open air that stretches our limbs and makes our blood circulate more lightly, or the obtaining of a longed-for post that settles us in practical life, and so on, is not artistic. Finally, the difference between pleasure and art leaps to the eyes in the relations that are developed between ourselves and works of art, because the figure represented may be dear to us and represent the most delightful memories, and at the same time the picture may be ugly; or, on the other hand, the picture may be beautiful and the figure represented hateful to our hearts, or the picture itself, which we approve as beautiful, may also cause us rage and envy, because it is the work of our enemy or rival, for whom it will procure advantage and on whom it will confer new strength: our practical interests, with their relative pleasures and pains, mingle and sometimes become confused with art and disturb, but are never *identified* with, our esthetic interest. At the most it will be affirmed, with a view to maintaining more effectively the definition of art as the pleasurable, that it is not the pleasurable in general, but a *particular* form of the pleasurable. But such a restriction is no longer a defence, it is indeed an abandonment of that thesis; for given that art is a particular form of pleasure, its distinctive character would be supplied, not by the pleasurable, but by what distinguishes that pleasurable from other pleasurables, and it would be desirable to turn the attention to that distinctive element—more than pleasurable or different from pleasurable. Nevertheless, the doctrine that defines art as the pleasurable has a special denomination (hedonistic esthetic), and a long and complicated development in the history of esthetic doctrines: it showed itself in the Graeco-Roman world, prevailed in the eighteenth century, reflowered in the second half of the nineteenth, and still enjoys much favor, being especially well received by beginners in esthetic, who are above all struck by the fact that art causes pleasure. The life of this doctrine has consisted of proposing in turn one or another class of pleasures, or several classes together (the pleasure of the superior senses, the pleasure of play, of consciousness of our own strength, of criticism, etc., etc.), or of adding to it elements differing from the pleasurable, the useful for example (when understood as distinct from the pleasurable), the satisfaction of cognoscitive and moral wants, and the like. And its progress has been caused just by this restlessness, and by its allowing foreign elements to ferment in its bosom, which it introduces through the necessity of somehow bringing itself into agreement with the reality of art, thus attaining to its dissolution as hedonistic doctrine and to the promotion of a new doctrine, or at least to drawing attention to its necessity. And since every error has its element of truth (and that of the physical doctrine has been seen to be the possibility of the physical "construction" of art as of any other fact), the hedonistic doctrine has its eternal element of truth in the placing in relief the hedonistic accompaniment, or pleasure, common to the esthetic activity as to every form of spiritual activity, which it has not at all been intended to deny in absolutely denying the identification of art with the pleasurable, and in distinguishing it from the pleasurable by defining it as intuition.

A third negation, effected by means of the theory of art as intuition, is that art is a *moral act;* that is to say, that form of practical act which, although necessarily uniting with the useful and with pleasure and pain, is not immediately utilitarian and hedonistic, and moves in a superior spiritual sphere. But the intuition, in so far as it is a theoretic act, is opposed to the practical of any sort. And in truth, art, as has been remarked from the earliest times, does not arise as an act of the will; good will, which constitutes the honest man, does not constitute the artist. And since it is not the result of an act of will, so it escapes all moral discrimination, not because a privilege of exemption is accorded to it, but simply be-

cause moral discrimination cannot be applied to art. An artistic image portrays an act morally praiseworthy or blameworthy; but this image, as image, is neither morally praiseworthy nor blameworthy. Not only is there no penal code that can condemn an image to prison or to death, but no moral judgment, uttered by a rational person, can make of it its object: we might just as well judge the square moral or the triangle immoral as the Francesca of Dante immoral or the Cordelia of Shakespeare moral, for these have a purely artistic function, they are like musical notes in the souls of Dante and of Shakespeare. Further, the moralistic theory of art is also represented in the history of esthetic doctrines, though much discredited in the common opinion of our times, not only on account of its intrinsic demerit, but also, in some measure, owing to the moral demerit of certain tendencies of our times, which render possible, owing to psychological dislike, that refutation of it which should be made—and which we here make—solely for logical reasons. The end attributed to art, of directing the good and inspiring horror of evil, of correcting and ameliorating customs, is a derivation of the moralistic doctrine; and so is the demand addressed to artists to collaborate in the education of the lower classes, in the strengthening of the national or bellicose spirit of a people, in the diffusion of the ideals of a modest and laborious life; and so on. These are all things that art cannot do, any more than geometry, which, however, does not lose anything of its importance on account of its inability to do this; and one does not see why art should do so, either. That it cannot do these things was partially perceived by the moralistic estheticians also; who very readily effected a transaction with it, permitting it to provide pleasures that were not moral, provided they were not openly dishonest, or recommending it to employ to a good end the dominion that, owing to its hedonistic power, it possesed over souls, to gild the pill, to sprinkle sweetness upon the rim of the glass containing the bitter draught—in short, to play the courtezan (since it could not get rid of its old and inborn habits), in the service of holy church or of morality: *meretrix ecclesiae.* On other occasions they have sought to avail themselves of it for purposes of instruction, since not only virtue but also science is a difficult thing, and art could remove this difficulty and render pleasant and attractive the entrance into the ocean of science—indeed, lead them through it as through a garden of Armida, gaily and voluptuously, without their being conscious of the lofty protection they had obtained, or of the crisis of renovation which they were preparing for themselves. We cannot now refrain from a smile when we talk of these theories, but should not forget that they were once a serious matter corresponding to a serious effort to understand the nature of art and to elevate the conception of it; and that among those who believed in it (to limit ourselves to Italian literature) were Dante and Tasso, Parini and Alfieri, Manzoni and Mazzini. And the moralistic doctrine of art was and is and will be perpetually beneficial by its very contradictions; it was and will be an effort, however unhappy, to separate art from the merely pleasing, with which it is sometimes confused, and to assign to it a more worthy post: and it, too, has its true side, because, if art be beyond morality, the artist is neither this side of it nor that, but under its empire, in so far as he is a man who cannot withdraw himself from the duties of man, and must look upon art itself—art, which is not and never will be moral—as a mission to be exercized as a priestly office.

Again (and this is the last and perhaps the most important of all the general negations that it suits me to recall in relation to this matter), with the definition of art as intuition, we deny that it has the character of *conceptual knowledge.* Conceptual knowledge, in its true form, which is the philosophical, is always realistic, aiming at establishing reality against unreality, or at lowering unreality by including it in reality as a subordinate moment of reality itself. But intuition means, precisely, indistinction of reality and unreality, the image with its value as mere image, the pure ideality of the image; and opposing the intuitive or sensible knowledge to the conceptual or intelligible, the esthetic to the noetic, it aims at claiming the autonomy of this more simple and elementary form of knowledge, which has been compared to the dream (the dream, and not the sleep) of the theoretic life, in respect to which philosophy would be the waking. And indeed, whoever should ask, when examining a work of art, whether what the artist has expressed be metaphysically and historically true or false, asks a question that is without meaning, and commits an error analogous to his who should bring the airy images of the fancy before the tribunal of morality: without meaning, because the discrimination of true and false always concerns an affirmation of reality, or a judgment, but it cannot fall under the head of an image or of a pure subject, which is not the subject of a judgment, since it is without qualification or predicate. It is useless to object that the individuality of the image cannot subsist without reference to the universal, of which that image is the individuation, because we do not here deny that the universal, as the spirit of God, is everywhere and animates all things with itself, but we deny that the universal is rendered logically explicit and is thought in the intuition. Useless also is the appeal to the principle of the unity of the spirit, which is not broken, but, on the contrary, strengthened by the clear distinction of fancy from thought, because from the distinction comes opposition, and from opposition concrete unity. . . . Certainly art is symbol, all symbol—that is, all significant; but symbol of what? What does it mean?

The intuition is truly artistic, it is truly intuition, and not a chaotic mass of images, only when it has a vital principle that animates it, making it all one with itself; but what is this principle?

The answer to such a question may be said to result from the examination of the greatest ideal strife that has ever taken place in the field of art (and is not confined to the epoch that took its name from it and in which it was predominant): the strife between *romanticism* and *classicism*. Giving the general definition, here convenient, and setting aside minor and accidental determinations, romanticism asks of art, above all, the spontaneous and violent effusion of the affections, of love and hate, of anguish and jubilation, of desperation and elevazion; and is willingly satisfied and pleased with vaporous and indeterminate images, broken and allusive in style, with vague suggestions, with approximate phrases, with powerful and troubled sketches: while classicism loves the peaceful soul, the wise design, figures studied in their characteristics and precise in outline, ponderation, equilibrium, clarity; and resolutely tends toward *representation*, as the other tends toward *feeling*. And whoever puts himself at one or the other point of view finds crowds of reasons for maintaining it and for confuting the opposite point of view; because (say the romantics), What is the use of an art, rich in beautiful images, which, nevertheless, does not speak to the heart? And if it do speak to the heart, what is the use if the images be not beautiful? And the others will say, What is the use of the shock of the passions, if the spirit do not rest upon a beautiful image? And if the image be beautiful, if our taste be satisfied, what matters the absence of those emotions which can all of them be obtained outside art, and which life does not fail to provide, sometimes in greater quantity than we desire?—But when we begin to feel weary of the fruitless defence of both partial views; above all, when we turn away from the ordinary works of art produced by the romantic and classical schools, from works convulsed with passion or coldly decorous, and fix them on the works, not of the disciples, but of the masters, not of the mediocre, but of the supreme, we see the contest disappear in the distance and find ourselves unable to call the great portions of these works, romantic or classic or representative, because they are both classic and romantic, feelings and representations, a vigorous feeling which has become all most brilliant representation. Such, for example, are the works of Hellenic art, and such those of Italian poetry and art: the transcendentalism of the Middle Ages became fixed in the bronze of the Dantesque *terzina;* melancholy and suave fancy, in the transparency of the songs and sonnets of Petrarch; sage experience of life and badinage with the fables of the past, in the limpid *ottava rima* of Ariosto; heroism and the thought of death, in the perfect blank-verse hendecasyllabics of Foscolo; the infinite variety of everything, in the sober and austere songs of Giacomo Leopardi. Finally (be it said in parenthesis and without intending comparison with the other examples adduced), the voluptuous refinements and animal sensuality of international decadentism have received their most perfect expression in the prose and verse of an Italian, D'Annunzio. All these souls were profoundly passionate (all, even the serene Lodovico Ariosto, who was so amorous, so tender, and so often represses his emotion with a smile); their works of art are the eternal flower that springs from their passions.

These expressions and these critical judgments can be theoretically resumed in the formula, that what gives coherence and unity to the intuition is feeling: the intuition is really such because it represents a feeling, and can only appear from and upon that. Not the idea, but the feeling, is what confers upon art the airy lightness of the symbol: an aspiration enclosed in the circle of a representation—that is art; and in it the aspiration alone stands for the representation, and the representation alone for the aspiration. Epic and lyric, or drama and lyric, are scholastic divisions of the indivisible: art is always lyrical—that is, epic and dramatic in feeling. What we admire in genuine works of art is the perfect fanciful form which a state of the soul assumes; and we call this life, unity, solidity of the work of art. . . . A celebrated sentence uttered by an English critic, and become one of the commonplaces of journalism, states that "all the arts tend to the condition of music"; but it would have been more accurate to say that all the arts are music, if it be thus intended to emphasize the genesis of esthetic images in feeling, excluding from their number those mechanically constructed or realistically ponderous. And another not less celebrated utterance of a Swiss semi-philosopher, which has had the like good or bad fortune of becoming trivial, discovers that "every landscape is a state of the soul": which is indisputable, not because the landscape is landscape, but because the landscape is art.

Artistic intuition, then, is always *lyrical* intuition: this latter being a word that is not present as an adjective or definition of the first, but as a synonym, another of the synonyms that can be united to the several that I have mentioned already, and which, all of them, designate the intuition. And if it be sometimes convenient that instead of appearing as a synonym, it should assume the grammatical form of the adjective, that is only to make clear the difference between the intuition-image, or nexus of images (for what is called image is always a nexus of images, since image-atoms do not exist any more than thought-atoms), which constitutes the organism, and, as organism, has its vital principle, which is the organism itself,—between this, which is true and proper intuition, and that false intuition which is a heap of images put together in play or intentionally or for some other practical purpose, the connection of which, being practical, shows itself to be not organic, but mechanic, when considered from the esthetic point of view. But the word *lyric* would be redundant save in this explicative or polemical sense; and art is perfectly defined when it is simply defined as *intuition*.

6 / SOCIAL PHILOSOPHY

The state, many idealists hold, must be distinguished from other forms of human association. It is not simply an artificial arrangement of human beings, based on contractual agreements; rather, it must be viewed as a kind of moral partner of its citizens, guaranteeing to them the external conditions of the good life. It is, in a way, the guardian of the moral world, seeking to mediate conflicts and to maintain a system of rights and duties. Though responsible to its people to use force, its basis is not force but will. In the following selection, these idealistic theses are presented by the important English thinker Bernard Bosanquet.

THEORY OF THE STATE

Bernard Bosanquet (1848-1923)

I wish to present a brief positive account of the theory of the state as I understand it, more particularly with reference to the state in its external relations, and the conditions essential to federations or a world-state.

It seems to me that much misconception is prevalent as to the views which in fact great philosophers have held upon this problem. But I do not wish to raise mere questions in the history of philosophy, but to meet the issue as it seems to me to stand today. The ideas which I express are therefore my own, in the sense that no one else is responsible for the form I give them. But, to the best of my judgment, they represent the Greek tradition as renewed by Hegel and by English thought.

In considering any problem affecting the state I take the primary question to be how self-government is possible. For anything which interferes with the possibility of self-government destroys altogether the conditions of true government. The answer is drawn, I take it, from the conception of the general will, which involves the existence of an actual community, of such a nature as to share an identical mind and feeling. There is no other way of explaining how a free man can put up with compulsion and even welcome it.

Here then we have the universal condition of legitimate outward authority. City-state, Nation-state, Commonwealth, Federation, World-state, it makes no difference. Behind all force there must be a general will, and the general will must represent a communal mind. All other contrivances for government are external and tyrannical.

The selection is from Bernard Bosanquet, *Social and International Ideals* (London: Macmillan and Co., Ltd., 1917), pp. 270-283. Used by permission of the publisher.

1. This is the reason of the unique relation between the state and the individual which is caricatured by critics as state absolutism. Of course the state is not the ultimate end of life. The ultimate end, if we avoid religious phraseology, which would probably furnish the truest expression of it, is surely the best life. I understand by the state the power which, as the organ of a community, has the function of maintaining the external conditions necessary to the best life. These conditions are called rights. They are the claims recognized by the will of a community as the *sine qua non* of the highest obtainable fulfillment of the capacities for the best life possessed by its members.

Now the relation between the state and the individual is the external equivalent of that between the community and the individual. And it is a unique relation, because there is no other body that bears the same relation to the individual's will as that community which is represented by a state in the external world.

This can be said with as much precision as human affairs admit, because there is reason to expect that the community which organizes itself as a state will be for every group the largest body which possesses the unity of experience necessary for constituting a general will. There is, as we shall see, no other body at all comparable with it in intensity of unity. "A national purpose is the most unconquerable and victorious of all things on earth." And the individual's private will, we must bear in mind, is certainly and literally a part of the communal will. There is no other material on which his will can be made. If he rejects the communal will in part, he rejects it on the basis of what it is in him, not from any will of his own which has a different source. This is the ground of the duty of rebellion.

This unique relation between the individual and the community which the state represents—it may be a nation or any other community—is what seems to me to dominate the whole problem. It is further determined when we add the consideration that the state is an organ of action in the external world. In this sphere, which is its special sphere as an organ exercising force, it may really be called absolute, that is, if power extending to life and death and complete disposal of property can be called absolute. This does not mean that it is the whole end of life, nor that it is the only object of loyalty. It means, as I understand it, that, being the special organ of arrangement in the external world, corresponding to that particular community whose will *is* our own will when most highly organized, it has the distinctive function of dictating the final adjustment in matters of external action. This is the only sense in which I have called it absolute, and the ground is obvious and simple. It lies in the tendency of the world of action to bring into collision factors which, apart from action, might never conflict. However purely non-political two associations may be, and however cosmopolitan, if they claim the same funds or the same building they must come before a power which can adjust the difference without appeal. And if such a power were not single in respect of them, obviously there could be no certainty of adjustment without a conflict between the two or more powers which might claim jurisdiction. Cases like that supposed are frequent, of course, with churches.

Thus there are two connected points, which, I think, the critics confuse under the name of absolutism. One is the power of the state as sustainer of all adjustments in the world of external action, on the ground which has just been explained. The other is the unique relation to the individual of such a community as is at present exemplified by his nation-state, because it represents, as nothing else in the world does, that special system of rights and sentiments, the complement of his own being, which the general will of his group has formed a state to maintain.

It is the result, I take it, of these two grounds of unity co-operating, that in times of stress the state, as the organ of the community, will suspend or subject to conditions any form of intercourse between its members and persons or associations within or without its territory, and will require any service that it thinks fit from any of its members. It does, in Mr. Bradley's words, "with the moral approval of all what the explicit theory of scarcely one will morally justify." That it does not exercise such powers to anything like the same degree in ordinary times, and that it recognizes the rights of conscience even in times of stress, flows from the fact that its primary end is the maintenance of rights, and it will override no right by force where an adjustment is possible compatibly with the good life of the whole. And of this possibility it is the sole judge. What it permits, it permits by reason of its end, and no theory can stand which will not justify in principle its habitual action in times of stress.

2. "The state," as I understand the words, is a phrase framed in the normal way, to express that one is dealing with the members of a class strictly according to the connotation of the class-name. If a plural noun is used, there can be no certainty whether we are speaking of the characteristics which belong to the class-members as such, or of circumstances which may occur in each of them for independent reasons. "The state," in a word, is a brief expression for "states *qua* states." I confess that I am a good deal surprised that nearly all recent critics have stumbled, as it seems to me, in this simple matter of interpretation. Would they find the same difficulty in the title of a book on "the heart" or "the steam-engine"? It would be urged, perhaps,

that a heart does not imply other hearts, but that a state does imply other states; but if the thing implies other things its name implies the reference to them.

And, indeed, the whole *raison d'être* of our theory is to show why, and in what sense, there must be states wherever there are groups of human beings, and to explain for what reasons men are distinguished into separate adjacent political bodies instead of forming a single system over the whole earth's surface.

Our theory has told us, for example, that states represent differentiations of the single human spirit (Hegel), whose extent and intensity determine and are determined by territorial limits. They are members, we are told by Plato and Hegel, of an ethical family of nations, so far, at least, as the European world is concerned; they are characterized—it is Mazzini's well-known doctrine—by individual missions or functions which furnish for every state its distinctive contribution to human life. They have a similar task to achieve, each within its territory allotted by history, so Green argues, and the more perfectly each of them attains its proper object of giving free scope to the capacities of all persons living on a certain range of territory, the easier it is for others to do so. Obviously they are co-operating units. This is throughout the essence of the theory.

Now it is not, I think, unfair to point out that my critics, dealing unguardedly with "states" and not with "the state" or with "states *qua* states," have on the whole founded their account of states not upon what they are, so far as states, but just upon what, *qua* states, they are not; upon defects which appear unequally in the several communities, consisting in those evils which the organization of the state exists in order to remove, and does progressively remove in so far as true self-government is attained. Such evils are war, exploitation within or without, class privilege, arbitrary

authority, discontent directing ambitions to foreign conquest and to jealousy of other states, the doctrine that one state's gain is *ipso facto* another's loss.

3. Space and time do not permit me to discuss, what I should be interested in discussing at some length, the continuous relations which extend beyond the frontiers of individual states, their importance compared with that of other continuities which are co-extensive with the area of the states and constituent of them, and why it is necessary to recognize, in spite of the former, separate sovereign political units which undoubtedly, while imperfect, tend to break down at the frontier, in a regrettable way, the continuities which pass beyond it. Broadly speaking, the reason lies, I take it, in the exceptionally intense unity and concreteness of certain group-minds, in which innumerable continuities coincide, while other continuities, which extend beyond the group, nevertheless do not coincide with any marked rival unity.

4. It follows from our theory, as we saw, that the normal relation of states is co-operative. Their influence on each other's structure and culture is mainly a question of wants and materials. The characteristic dealing with them depends after all upon the national mind, as we see in the contrast of Athens and Sparta, the two leading states of one and the same civilization. It is a curious fallacy in the disparagement of the state that the recognition of a debt to foreign culture has been pushed so far as to suggest that nothing great originates in any state because everything is imported from some other.

Further, it follows that the maintenance of this normal relation, or its attainment where unattained, depends on the right discharge by states of their internal function —the maintenance of rights as the conditions of good life. War, as Plato showed, is not of the essence of states, but has its causes in their internal disease and distraction, leading to policies of "expansion." Therefore, in this sense, to begin with, we want more of the state and not less. In order to reinforce the organization of rights by other states, the main thing it has to do is to complete its own. This fundamental truth none of the critics seem to have observed, and to have emphasized it appears to me a very great merit in our philosophy. The fundamental principle is that state *qua* states are—"the state" is—the human mind doing the same work in different localities with different materials. Obviously, in as far as it succeeds, its efforts assist each other.

5. Thus every state as such—that is, "the state"—is "the guardian of a whole moral world," maintaining the peculiar contribution of its community to the total of human life and of human mind. We shall see why this double expression is necessary. And it is very important to observe that this moral world includes a whole distinctive attitude to life and humanity. It is an attitude *of* the community, but *to* the world. Thus you cannot get away from it. All individuals share it, more or less, and every relation of the group, external or internal, is brought to a meeting point within their consciousness, and elicits a response from it.

It is easy to discern how such guardianship on the part of bodies so highly individualized, so deeply conscious of a function and as yet so imperfectly organized, may lead, from time to time, to differences which can only be resolved by force. It is a profound mistake, I am convinced, to direct the moral of the present calamity against the communal sense of a function and a mission; against, in a word, the belief that a community has a conscience. Yet this belief is the root of the doctrine caricatured under the name of state absolutism. It seems to me foolish to take a hostile attitude to a general truth because it displays the root of serious evils. For, indeed, what

displays their root is the only indication of the remedy. The true moral is, surely, not that a community should have no overmastering purpose, no consciousness of a mission and no conscience, but simply that its conscience should as far as possible be enlightened. Enlightened consciences, I venture to assume, cannot bring actions into conflict. But, being internally ill organized, and correspondingly biased and unenlightened, communities enter into conflicts from time to time with their whole heart and soul, just because they *have* consciences and *have* moral worlds to guard. It happens naturally to them as to private persons that they throw their whole sense of right into what is wrong. In order to produce a disastrous collision, we must bear in mind, the aspirations of two communities need not be in conflict at every point. It is like two trains running side by side, where an encroachment of an inch is enough to produce a calamity. Aspirations may be irreconcilable in practice which have a very large factor of agreement. This factor is the ground for hope, which consists in their being, after all, aspirations of communities which possess reason and conscience. Reconciliation of them by harmonious adjustment, though impracticable at certain moments, is never inconceivable.

Now it is surely plain that no power on earth can deal with such a cause of conflict, except something that enables the biased and erroneous factors of the conflicting claims to be eliminated. And this can never be done by external force, but must mainly depend on a better organization of rights by every state at home, with a consequent correction of its ambitions and outlook on the world. A healthy state is not militant.

But the mischief is, that the popular mind, observing that the present trouble has arisen through aspirations in others which we pronounce perverse, is inclined to attribute to a false philosophy the whole conception of national aspirations as representing the conscience of a people and its overmastering sense of duty. Men do not reflect that precisely such aspirations are determining their own group-action at every step. They say, as our critics are saying, that the theory of the unity of a people in the moral consciousness of a pre-eminent duty, and the principle of its expression through an organ supreme in practical life, are absolutism, and ought to be weakened or abandoned. The unique obligation of the private person to the community as incomparably the fullest representative of himself is to be put on a level with isolated abstract obligations arising in the course of this or that special relation, although it is on the communal mind that the task of harmonizing them must ultimately fall. In short, the whole moral status and moral being of the community is to be indefinitely but considerably lowered.

All this seems to me to point exactly the wrong way. We all know, in modern society more especially, that we pay for the existence of great organizing agencies by the possibility of their conflicting. But that does not make us desire to weaken them; it makes us desire to amplify their members' faith in them, and to get them to do their work more completely. The remedy for disorganization is not less organization, but more. All organization, of course, brings a concurrent risk of conflict. You bring claims together, and you find points which for the moment cannot be adjusted. It is a flat contradiction to maintain that the state is morally responsible, and also that it must not face an actual conflict where its conscience is concerned. Even within the community, where obligations to the common will are so high and so determinate, the conscientious objector will follow his conscience to the end, and if we believe him to be sincere we all respect him for it. Why should the community, an individual in a far deeper sense than the citizen, being the nearest approach to a true individual that

exists upon the earth, be expected not to follow its conscience? The clause on which I have just insisted is, as Rousseau pointed out, the fundamental issue. The point to be remembered is that the individual only has his individuality through the social consciousness. The nearer he approaches to being himself the more he approaches identification with the communal mind. This mind can only be expressed as what the individual would be if he possessed in completeness all that his actual consciousness implies regarding group-life. If he sees reason to rebel, it is still as a social duty. It cannot be in virtue of some right of his own, as he would be, *per impossibile,* apart.

No doubt, when there is strife between communities, a wrong is being committed somewhere. But the way to right it is not for the conscientious group to make a rule of yielding on points which it holds fundamental to its function.

Now I think that the critics of our theory speak uncertainly here. Is our fault in saying that the community which asserts itself through the state *is* a moral being, and *has* a conscience, or is not a moral being and has not a conscience? They seem to me in effect to say both at once. But only one can be true.

It is clear, I think, that we are accused of denying the moral responsibility of the community which has the state for its organ. But it can hardly be doubted that we are also accused of putting this moral responsibility much too high. Thus the critics find themselves driven to treat the community which is a state as a mere association of individuals, which cannot possess an organic moral conscience nor general will. Though in one passage disclaiming individualism, the argument breathes its spirit. If you call the state an association, you speak the language of individualism, and still more so, if you speak of individual rights which can be asserted against it, and of the individual judgment as ultimate. To call it an "association" is contrary, I think, both to usage and to truth. The word is, I presume, employed intentionally as paradoxical and aggressive.

It is really, then, the moral being and moral responsibility of the state which we affirm, and which the main attack desires to undermine. The opposite suggestion, that we do not recognize the moral responsibility of the members of a group for its action, is, as we shall see, a mere misconception, derived from the fact that we observe the moral action of a community not to be cap-

able of being criticized by the method of comparison with that of an individual.

The unique position of the state springs, as I said at starting, from the fact that it is molded, as no mere association is, by and for the special task of maintaining in a certain territory the external conditions of good life as a whole. Its territorial area adjusts itself to that unity of communal experience which is most favorable to the maintenance of an organized will, so that it tends to cover the largest area within which, for a certain group, the conditions of such an experience exist.

7 / PHILOSOPHY OF SCIENCE

In its function of critic of experience, idealism includes a distinctive interpretation of science. Such a statement is given in the following selection by F. R. Tennant, author of many books on religion and proponent of a form of pluralistic idealism known as panpsychism.

Two conclusions about science are defended by Tennant: that so-called scientific facts are actually shot full of theory, and that the progress of science has led to a distinction between the ontal and the phenomenal. Concerning the first, Tennant finds that science deals with the repeatable and the common, and does so by abstracting from the unique and individual. Science also has assumed a metaphysics that, at the beginning of science, was simply the assumptions of common sense (and that accounts for Tennant's observation that science itself has never been idealistic), and it has for many people today actually become metaphysics. The second conclusion, however, concerns the ontal and phenomenal, not as two worlds, but the world in itself and as it appears to us. Tennant argues that science came to this distinction and in fact has gone beyond it: science today is neither ontal nor phenomenal but symbolic. It does not reach reality at all. Thus a third conclusion is developed: science is not metaphysics, nor is it equipped to discuss the grounds and validity of metaphysical knowledge.

THE LIMITATIONS OF SCIENCE

F. R. Tennant (1866-   )

The two main conclusions to which I have thus far been led are (1) that, in the facts from which science sets out as if they were of bed-rock nature, there is already an element of suppositional and rationalizing venture, which is justified only by its pragmatic success, and (2) that the forthcomingness of physical science involves that distinction between the ontal and the phenomenal—not between two worlds, but between the real or ontal world and its appearance to our minds—which other theories of knowledge would, in different ways, dispense with. The error inherent in the realism which science initially and uncritically takes over from common sense in no way debars science from being a (phenomenal) version of truth about the ontal, and does not vitiate science, as such; but it becomes a matter of importance when the precise relation of scientific to metaphysical truth is in question. Science, studied in aloofness from what may be called its higher criticism, may foster confidence that critical problems do not exist for it, and so engender superstition or obscurantism.

Diverging for a moment from the metaphysical presuppositions that are intrinsic to science in virtue of its continuity with common sense, I may observe that the truth that our primary scientific facts are partly theory throws light on two eliminations which science makes, thereby constituting itself a kind of knowledge distinguishable from other kinds with which we have been already occupied. Science abstracts from the subjective factors involved in knowing, and regards its objects, though it calls them phenomena, as if they were as independent of all subjects as they are of any one subject. This is a fruitful device, indispensable to science; but, philosophically regarded, it is a fiction. Thus physical science is sharply marked off from psychology, the subject-matter of which science presupposes but ignores, and from philosophy, which cannot wink at this elimination of subjectivity, or treat science as if the elimination had not been made. Again, science abstracts from certain aspects of its objective data. It finds identities for thought by ignoring, as negligible *ad hoc,* what are diversities for sense. In passing from facts to generalizations and laws, science necessarily confines itself to the repeatable and common, which are in some degree abstractions. Hereby science is differentiated from history, though again the historical is presupposed. And in so far as science isolates itself from history in order to pursue its own special business, it may be said to present us with but a diagram or a skeleton of Nature. In other words, science is precluded from supplying a living picture of Nature as manifested in the presentational *continua* of human beings as well as from describing Nature as a sum of interactions between the known constituents of the ultimately real world. Science makes its repeatables out of the historical and unrepeatable by abstraction and by substituting concepts for percepts. The element of art thus introduced into science is as fruitful as it is indispensable; but unfortunately it is also the first step towards a vicious abstractionism which has sometimes been confounded by natural philosophers with the metaphysical method.

As I was observing just now, science sets out with certain metaphysical presuppositions which it took over from common sense. They are revealed by epistemological scrutiny, which is one of the chief functions

The selection is from F. R. Tennant, *Philosophy of the Sciences* (Cambridge: University Press, 1932), pp. 134-143. Used by permission of the publisher.

of philosophy. The plain man who does not exercise this scrutiny is unaware of the tacit assumptions which his common-sense knowledge involves. He is at home in such "knowledge" as he has, and all seems plain in it because his eyes have not been opened to the difficulties with which critical philosophy finds it to be beset. Consequently philosophy seems to him to raise obscurities and to create vain fancies where knowledge had seemed to be clear and sure. Similarly metaphysics is wont to be most vehemently scorned by those whose mentality is most deeply steeped in unsuspected metaphysics, and who are unconscious that they are talking metaphysics of their own while railing at the metaphysics of professionals. One needs to be a philosopher of some standing in order *not* to be a metaphysician. And this explains why scientific thought, issuing in certain doctrines of matter and energy, in conservation-principles, and in a mechanistic world-view, was profoundly metaphysical until it had pursued to some extent that self-examination which it began to undertake about fifty years ago, and the results of which are being expressed by its present representatives.

It will perhaps repay us to recall the changes which have recently taken place in the attitude of science towards metaphysics and philosophy. In the latter half of the nineteenth century some of the chief spokesmen of science sought to commend its unique excellence by disparaging the metaphysics of the more pretentious schools of philosophy. And in this they were not without provocation. For instance, one eminent post-Kantian idealist had declared that "the philosopher performs his task without regard to any experience whatsoever, and absolutely *a priori*"; and another had derided "the blind and thoughtless mode of investigating Nature which has become generally established since the corruption of philosophy by Bacon and of physics by Boyle and Newton." But reac-

tion against extravagances such as these led some physicists, e.g. Tait and Maxwell, to consider themselves to have sacrificed dignity by so much as crossing the borders of metaphysics for war-like purposes, much as the ancient Hebrew regarded himself as rendered unclean by entering a country presided over by other gods than his. In an address contained in his *Scientific Papers* Maxwell alludes to the "den of the metaphysician, strewed with the remains of former explorers, and abhorred by every man of science." "It would indeed be a foolhardy adventure," he tells his audience, to lead them "into those speculations which require, as we know, thousands of years even to shape themselves intelligibly." Nevertheless, Maxwell went on to say, the cultivators of mathematics and physics (such as he was addressing) are led up in their daily work to questions the same in kind with those of metaphysics, but they approach them as trained by a long-continued adjustment of their modes of thought to the facts of external Nature. Maxwell evidently was convinced that the facts of external Nature, as taken over by mathematical physics, are devoid of any metaphysical factors, and that the physico-mathematical modes of thought employed in the scientific explanation of them are adequate to the solution of the quasi-metaphysical problems to which these facts lead up. And these implicit views were explicitly maintained by some of his contemporaries. Not only was it then commonly believed that science was positive knowledge, in the strictest sense, it was also asserted that the scientific method is the sole means of approach to the whole realm of possible knowledge; that there are no reasonably propounded questions that science could not hope to answer, and no problems worth discussing to which its method was inapplicable. Many representatives of science thus sought to identify it with the whole of knowledge and with all that could call itself philosophy. Metaphysics, other than that which consisted in taking physics to be ontology, was deemed impossible, and natural theology was accounted superfluous. From physicists and biologists such views spread to many psychologists and philosophers. Indeed for a time philosophy became as much enslaved to physical science as in the middle ages it had been enslaved to dogmatic theology.

Science has receded from the pretensions into which it rushed, as a giant rejoicing to run his course, when temporarily elated with its own success and its acquired prestige. And it may be observed that the plausibility of those pretensions was due to the prevailing supposition that physical science was independent of, and unrelated to, such departments of knowledge as psychology, theory of knowledge, and history. On the contrary, a philosophy of the sciences must insist that these latter departments of knowledge reveal the presuppositions of physical science, and set the bounds to its scope and functions. Only when its relations to them are appreciated can the true nature of scientific knowledge be apprehended.

To continue the more recent history of the attitude of science, that is to say of its representatives, towards metaphysics, it may next be remarked that contemporaneously with the hostility of Prof. Tait and others to metaphysics, and their endeavor to "sift the truth from the metaphysics" contained in traditional statements concerning physical conceptions such as those of matter and energy, science was claiming, on the strength of the realistic trend in its theory of knowledge, to offer a metaphysical substitute for the metaphysics of pure philosophers. The realities, of which sensible or molar bodies are appearances, were believed to be knowable to science, and indeed to be identical with the *mikra* in terms of which theoretical physics explains macroscopic, or directly observable, phenomena. The physics of this

microscopic order has been developed largely with a view to finding a rigidly mechanical explanation of phenomena which *prima facie* are not mechanical. And it was taken in some quarters to disclose the real which underlies the phenomenal. Thus theoretical physics come to pass for ontology, or metaphysics of the physical world. The reality of the physicist's *mikra*, however, is not a condition of the forthcomingness of molar and empirical facts. It is not even a condition of their explicability, but only of their mechanical explicability. And intelligibility of that particular sort is no precondition of science, as was once commonly believed; it is but a human *desideratum* and a luxury, the craving for which perhaps bespeaks an esthetic element in the constitution of human reason. We can accord to the fruitful theories concerning hypothetical *mikra* the appreciation which is their due without taking figurativeness for literal truth. That Nature behaves *as if* the ether, the electron, the nucleus and revolutions round it and all such microscopic machinery were realities, is largely fact; and that is all that we are entitled by experimental science to assert, and all that such science need demand. That these microscopic entities, which are neither observed nor inferred, mediate metaphysical knowledge, pure and undefiled, is, in the light of the past history and of the present internal inconsistencies of theoretical physics, even more precarious than it is superfluous. Science neither reveals nor presupposes a rigid mechanism of real microscopic entities. Schemes involving thoroughgoing continuity and schemes presupposing radical discreteness are, at the present stage of scientific speculation, as serviceable as they are incompatible. The ultimate elements into which the theoretical physics of today seems to resolve the world are neither ontal nor phenomenal: they constitute a fictional or symbolical descriptive scheme, or rather an incongruous set of schemes, partially applicable, but into all or any of which even inorganic Nature refuses wholly to fit. But it is not necessary at this hour to elaborate indictments against scientific realism, nor even to reproduce the grounds and reasonings on which epistemologists have based them. For the view that microscopic physics yields a metaphysic of Nature is refuted and abandoned by the present generation of physicists. The skepticism with regard to it, which until lately found expression only in a *savant* here and there, has been affirmed by several eminent authorities to have now become a characteristic of scientific mentality. Indeed Sir James Jeans has recently declared that the outstanding achievement of the physics of the twentieth century is not the theory of relativity, or the theory of *quanta*, or the dissection of the atom, but the disclosure that science has not reached ultimate reality. But in the form in which this disclosure had previously been made by certain philosophers it includes the wider assertion that the abstractive method of science never will, because it never can, reach ultimate reality: the very nature of the scientific method of explaining diversity by reducing it to identity, in virtue of which science tends to issue in mathematics, renders this feat intrinsically impossible. In straining out the sensible, the qualitative, or the historical, theoretical science strains out the actual and the real also. It may arrive at valid laws and equations, but not at the realities for which its symbols stand. It may reach the conceptual, or a system of abstract ideas; but an abstract idea is not an ultimate reality: metaphysically it is nothing. If so, the replacement of the

mechanical model, which the science of the nineteenth century favored, by the mathematical symbol will not enable science to pass for an improved metaphysic, nor for metaphysics at all. When Sir James Jeans goes on to say that Nature is written in mathematical language, implying that Nature is pure thought, he would seem to be propounding a doctrine which is further from the truth than scientific realism is.

We may conclude, then, that science of the microscopic order is not genuine metaphysics, or a substitute for ontology. By "metaphysics" I mean ontology, together with the department of epistemology that is concerned with knowledge of the ontal realm. I do not mean *a priori* treatment of cosmological or other problems, though some philosophers would define metaphysics so; for I do not believe that the *a priori* method alone can yield truth as to the actual world. Metaphysics that is not based on science can be but a pastime if the ontal reveals itself only through the phenomenal or the historical, and if the element of "brutality" in the data or the analytica of all knowledge be determinative. But though metaphysics presupposes science, in the order of knowing, science is not ontology. If science claims to be knowledge of the real world it uses the word "real" with the meaning which it bears in ordinary parlance, but not with that which the word bears in ontology. Science presupposes an ontal order—she has never been idealistic—and an order which has a structure enabling reason to find rationality in the phenomenal; but, as to the nature of the ontal, science is agnostic.

8 / PHILOSOPHY OF RELIGION

Idealists who are also theists—that is, who are believers in a personal God—frequently seek to establish the existence of God through the same arguments that lead them to the rejection of matter. This is Hastings Rashdall's position. In the following selection, he reviews the difficulties in materialism and then asserts that the presupposition as well as the goal of thought is a Unity underlying all experience. Such a Unity, however, cannot be conceived except as Mind, for mind can explain matter, but matter cannot explain mind. This means for him that God is personal, that he is indeed the realization of the ideal of personality.

IDEALISM AND GOD

Hastings Rashdall (1858-1924)

I suppose that to nearly everybody who sets himself down to think seriously about the riddle of the Universe there very soon occurs the question whether Materialism may not contain the solution of all difficulties. I think, therefore, our present investigation had better begin with an enquiry whether Materialism can possibly be true. I say "can be true" rather than "is true" because, though dogmatic Materialists are rare, the typical Agnostic is one who is at least inclined to admit the possibility of Materialism even when he does not, at the bottom of his mind, practically assume its truth. The man who is prepared to exclude even this one theory of the Universe from the category of possible but unprovable theories is not, properly speaking, an Agnostic. To know that Materialism at least is not true is to know something, and something very important, about the ultimate nature of things. I shall not attempt here any very precise definition of what is meant by Materialism. Strictly speaking, it ought to mean the view that nothing really exists but matter. But the existence, in some sense or other, of our sensations and thoughts and emotions is so obvious to Common-sense that such a creed can hardly be explicitly maintained: it is a creed which is refuted in the very act of enunciating it. For practical purposes, therefore, Materialism may be said to be the view that the ultimate basis of all existence is matter; and that thought, feeling, emotion—consciousness of every kind—is merely an effect, a by-product or concomitant, of certain material processes.

Now if we are to hold that matter is the only thing which exists, or is the ultimate source of all that exists, we ought to be able to say what matter is. To the unreflecting mind matter seems to be the thing that we know all about. Thought, feeling, will, it may be suggested, are in some sense appearances which (though we can't help having them) might, from the point of view of superior insight, turn out to be mere delusions, or at best entirely unimportant and inconsiderable entities. This attitude of mind has been amusingly satirized by the title of one of Mr. Bradley's philosophical essays—"on the supposed uselessness of the Soul." [1] In this state of mind matter presents itself as the one solid reality—as something undeniable, something perfectly intelligible, something, too, which is preeminently important and respectable; while thinking and feeling and willing, joy and sorrow, hope and aspiration, goodness and badness, if they cannot exactly be got rid of altogether, are, as it were negligible quantities, which must not be allowed to disturb or interfere with the serious business of the Universe.

From this point of view matter is sup-

The selection is from Hastings Rashdall, *Philosophy and Religion* (London: Gerald Duckworth & Co., Ltd., 1910), pp. 5-11, 19-22, 24-26, and 55-56. Used by permission of the publisher.

[1] *Mind*, vol. iv. (N.S.), 1895.

posed to be the one reality with which we are in immediate contact, which we see and touch and taste and handle every hour of our lives. It may, therefore, sound a rather startling paradox to say that matter—matter in the sense of the Materialist—is something which nobody has ever seen, touched, or handled. Yet that is the literal and undeniable fact. Nobody has ever seen or touched or otherwise come in contact with a piece of matter. For in the experience which the plain man calls seeing or touching there is always present another thing. Even if we suppose that he is justified in saying "I touch matter," there is always present the "I" as well as the matter.[2] It is always and inevitably matter $+$ mind that he knows. Nobody ever can get away from this "I," nobody can ever see or feel what matter is like apart from the "I" which knows it. He may, indeed, infer that this matter exists apart from the "I" which knows it. He may infer that it exists, and may even go as far as to assume that, apart from his seeing or touching, or anybody else's seeing or touching, matter possesses all those qualities which it possesses for his own consciousness. But this is inference, and not immediate knowledge. And the validity or reasonableness of the inference may be disputed. How far it is reasonable or legitimate to attribute to matter as it is in itself the qualities which it has for us must depend upon the nature of those qualities. Let us then go on to ask whether the qualities which constitute matter as we know it are qualities which we can reasonably or even intelligibly attribute to a supposed matter-in-itself, to matter considered as something capable of existing by

itself altogether apart from any kind of conscious experience.

In matter, as we know it, there are two elements. There are certain sensations, or certain qualities which we come to know by sensation, and there are certain relations. Now, with regard to the sensations, a very little reflection will, I think, show us that it is absolutely meaningless to say that matter has the qualities implied by these sensations, even when they are not felt, and would still possess them, even supposing it never had been and never would be felt by any one whatever. In a world in which there were no eyes and no minds, what would be the meaning of saying that things were red or blue? In a world in which there were no ears and no minds, there would clearly be no such thing as sound. This is exactly the point at which Locke's analysis stopped. He admitted that the "secondary qualities"—colors, sounds, tastes—of objects were really not in the things themselves but in the mind which perceives them. What existed in the things was merely a power of producing these sensations in us, the quality in the thing being not in the least like the sensations which it produces in us: he admitted that this power of producing a sensation was something different from, and totally unlike, the sensation itself. But when he came to the primary qualities—solidity, shape, magnitude and the like—he supposed that the qualities in the thing were exactly the same as they are for our minds. If all mind were to disappear from the Universe, there would henceforth be no red and blue, no hot and cold; but things would still be big or small, round or square, solid or fluid. Yet, even with these "primary qualities" the reference to mind is really there just as much as in the case of the secondary qualities; only the fact is not quite obvious. And one reason for this is that these primary qualities involve, much more glaringly and unmistakable than the secondary, something which is not *mere*

---

[2] I do not mean of course that in the earliest stages of consciousness this distinction is actually made; but, if there are stages of consciousness in which the "I" is not realized, the idea of matter or even of an "object" or "not-self" existing apart from consciousness must be supposed to be equally absent.

sensation—something which implies thought and not mere sense. What do we mean by solidity, for instance? We mean partly that we get certain sensations from touching the object—sensations of touch and sensations of what is called the muscular sense, sensations of muscular exertion and of pressure resisted. Now, so far as that is what solidity means, it is clear that the quality in question involves as direct a reference to our subjective feelings as the secondary qualities of color and sound. But something more than this is implied in our idea of solidity. We think of external objects as occupying space. And spaciality cannot be analyzed away into mere feelings of ours. The feelings of touch which we derive from an object come to us one after the other. No mental reflection upon sensations which come one after the other in time could ever give us the idea of space, if they were not spacially related from the first. It is of the essence of spaciality that the parts of the object shall be thought of as existing side by side, outside one another. But this side-by-sideness, this outsideness is after all a way in which the things present themselves to a mind. Space is made up of relations; and what is the meaning of relations apart from a mind which relates, or *for* which the things are related? If spaciality were a quality of the thing in itself, it would exist no matter what became of other things. It would be quite possible, therefore, that the top of this table should exist without the bottom: yet everybody surely would admit the meaninglessness of talking about a piece of matter (no matter how small, be it an atom or the smallest electron conceived by the most recent physical speculation) which had a top without a bottom, or a right-hand side without a left. This space-occupying quality which is the most fundamental element in our ordinary conception of matter is wholly made up of the relation of one part of it to another. Now can a relation exist except for a mind? As it

seems to me, the suggestion is meaningless. Relatedness only has a meaning when thought of in connection with a mind which is capable of grasping or holding together both terms of the relation. The relation between point A and point B is not *in* point A or *in* point B taken by themselves. It is all in the "between": "betweenness" from its very nature cannot exist in any one point of space or in several isolated points of space or things in space; it must exist only in some one existent which holds together and connects those points. And nothing, as far as we can understand, can do that except a mind. Apart from mind there can be no relatedness: apart from relatedness no space: apart from space no matter. It follows that apart from mind there can be no matter. . . .

So far I have endeavored to establish the existence of God by a line of thought which also leads to the position that matter has no independent existence apart from conscious mind, that at bottom nothing exists except minds and their experiences. Now I know that this is a line of thought which, to those who are unfamiliar with it, seems so paradoxical and extravagant that, even when a man does not see his way to reply to it, will seldom produce immediate or permanent conviction the first time he becomes acquainted with it. It is for the most part only by a considerable course of habituation, extending over some years, that a man succeeds in thinking himself into the idealistic view of the Universe. And after all, there are many minds—some of them, I must admit, not wanting in philosophical power—who never succeed in accomplishing that feat at all. Therefore, while I feel bound to assert that the clearest and most irrefragable argument for the existence of God is that which is supplied by the idealistic line of thought, I should be sorry to have to admit that a man cannot be a Theist, or that he cannot be a Theist on reasonable grounds, without first being an Idealist. From my own point of view most of the other reasons for believing in the existence of God resolve themselves into idealistic arguments imperfectly thought out. But they may be very good arguments, as far as they go, even when they are not thought out to what seem to me their logical consequences. One of these lines of thought I shall hope to develop in my next lecture; but meanwhile let me attempt to reduce the argument against Materialism to a form in which it will perhaps appeal to Common-sense without much profound metaphysical reflection.

At the level of ordinary common-sense thought there appear to be two kinds of Reality—mind and matter. And yet our experience of the unity of Nature, of the intimate connection between human and animal minds and their organisms (organisms governed by a single intelligible and interconnected system of laws) is such that we can hardly help regarding them as manifestations or products or effects or aspects of some one Reality. There is, almost obviously, some kind of Unity underlying all the diversity of things. Our world does not arise by the coming together of two quite independent Realities—mind and matter—governed by no law or by unconnected and independent systems of law. All things, all phenomena, all events form parts of a single inter-related, intelligible whole: that is the presupposition not only of Philosophy but of Science. Or if any one chooses to say that it *is* a presupposition and so an unwarrantable piece of dogmatism, I will say that it is the hypothesis to which all our knowledge points. It is at all events the one common meeting-point of nearly all serious thinkers. The question remains, "What is the nature of this one Reality?" Now, if this ultimate Reality be not mind, it must be one of two things. It must be matter, or it must be a third thing which is neither mind nor matter, but something quite different from either. Now

many who will not follow the idealistic line of thought the whole way—so far as to recognize that the ultimate Reality is Mind—will at least admit that Idealists have successfully shown the impossibility of supposing that the ultimate Reality can be matter. For all the properties of matter are properties which imply some relation to our sensibility or our thought. Moreover, there is such a complete heterogeneity between consciousness and unconscious matter, considered as something capable of existing without mind, that it seems utterly impossible and unthinkable that mind should be simply the product or attribute of matter. That the ultimate Reality cannot be what we mean by matter has been admitted by the most naturalistic, and, in the ordinary sense, anti-religious thinkers—Spinoza, for instance, and Haeckel, and Herbert Spencer. The question remains, "Which is the easier, the more probable, the more reasonable theory—that the ultimate Reality should be Mind, or that it should be something so utterly unintelligible and inconceivable to us as a *tertium quid*—a mysterious Unknown and Unknowable—which is neither mind nor matter?" For my own part, I see no reason to suppose that our inability to think of anything which is neither matter nor mind but quite unlike either is a mere imperfection of human thought. It seems more reasonable to assume that our inability to think so such a mysterious X is due to there being no such thing. . . .

I do not believe that the human mind is really equal to the task of thinking of a Reality which is one and yet is neither mind nor matter but something which combines the nature of both. Practically, where such a creed is professed, the man either thinks of an unconscious Reality in some way generating or evolving mind, and so falls back into the Materialism which he has verbally disclaimed; or he thinks of a mind produced is something different from itself. This last is of course ordinary Theism in the form in which it is commonly held by those who are not Idealists. From a practical and religious point of view there is nothing to be said against such a view. Still it involves a Dualism, the philosophical difficulties of which I have attempted to suggest to you. I confess that for my own part the only way in which I can conceive of a single ultimate Reality which combines the attributes of what we call mind with those of what we know as matter is by thinking of a Mind conscious of a world or nature which has no existence except in and for the Mind and whatever less complete consciousnesses that may be. I trust that those who have failed to follow my sketch of the arguments which lead to this idealistic conclusion may at least be led by it to see the difficulties either of Materialism or of that kind of agnostic Pantheism which, while admitting in words that the ultimate Reality is not matter, refuses to invest it with the attributes of mind. The argument may be reduced to its simplest form by saying we believe that the ultimate Reality is Mind because mind will explain matter, while matter will not explain mind: while the idea of a Something which is neither in mind nor matter is both unintelligible and gratuitous.

And this line of thought may be supplemented by another. Whatever may be thought of the existence of matter apart from mind, every one will admit that matter possesses no value or worth apart from mind. When we bring into account our moral judgments or judgments of value, we have no difficulty in recognizing mind as the highest or best kind of existence known to us. There is, surely, a certain intrinsic probability in supposing that the Reality from which all being is derived must possess at least as much worth or value as the derived being; and that in thinking of that Reality by the analogy of the highest kind of existence known to us we shall come nearer to a true thought of it than by any other way of thinking possible to us. . . .

If we are justified in thinking of God after the analogy of a human soul—if we are justified in thinking of Him as a self-conscious Being who thinks, feels, and wills, and who is, moreover (if I may a little anticipate the subject of our next lecture) in relation with, capable of loving and being loved by other such beings—then it seems most natural to speak of God's existence as personal. For to be a self-conscious being—conscious of itself and other beings, thinking, willing, feeling, loving—is what we mean by being a person. If any one prefers to speak of God as "super-personal," there is no great objection to so doing, provided that phrase is not made (as it often is) an excuse for really thinking of God after the analogy of some kind of existence lower than that of persons—as a force, an unconscious substance, or merely a name for the totality of things. But for myself, I prefer to say that our own self-consciousness gives us only an ideal of the highest type of existence which it nevertheless very imperfectly satisfies, and therefore I would rather think God is a Person in a far truer, higher, more complete sense than that in which any human being can be a person. God alone fully realizes the ideal of Personality. The essence of Personality is something positive: it signifies to us the highest kind of being within our knowledge—not (as is too often supposed) the mere limitations and restraints which characterize human conscious life as we know it in ourselves. If we are justified in thinking of God after the analogy of the highest existence within our knowledge, we had better call Him a Person. The word is no doubt inadequate to the reality, as is all the language that we can employ about God; but it is at least more adequate than the terms employed by those who scruple to speak of God as a Person. It is at least more adequate and more intelligent than to speak of Him as a force, a substance, a "something not ourselves which makes for righteousness." *Things* do not "make for righteousness"; and in using the term Person we shall at least make it clear that we do not think of Him as a "thing," or a collection of things, or a vague substratum of things, or even a mere totality of minds like our own.

9 / SUMMARY

Idealism, like all philosophic schools, must be defined less in terms of explicitly accepted theses than by a continuity of intention that idealists share. Professor Urban characterizes this continuity as the belief that values and ideals belong to the structure of the universe. Behind this belief he finds three "driving forces" that have led thinkers to accept idealism: this acknowledgment of the reality of the ideal, the belief that the world of sense is not the real world, and the notion that the real is intelligible. This last, Professor Urban believes, is the deepest source of idealism.

THE DRIVING FORCE OF IDEALISM

W. M. Urban (1873-1952)

When one reflects on idealism in the different stages of one's life something like the following usually happens. At first, as a youth, we smile over its silliness; somewhat further on the way we find the idea interesting, clever and forgivable—we discuss it readily and gladly with people who are still, according to their age and development, in an earlier stage. With maturity we are likely to find it meaningful, to annoy ourselves and others with it, but on the whole scarcely worth disproving, and contrary to nature. It is hardly worth the trouble of further thinking because we feel that we have thought often enough about it already. But later, and with more earnest reflection and more extensive knowledge of human life and its interests, idealism acquires a strength which it is difficult to overcome.

This statement, in substance a quotation from Lichtenberg's papers,[1] written in 1853, is still for countless minds as true as when it was first written. It expresses admirably that driving force of idealism which we are now to attempt to understand, and it is for this reason that I have begun my discussion with the quotation. The inherent strength of this belief—the driving force of the idealistic train of thought—is, then, the theme of this chapter. We shall be concerned first of all with idealism as a life form of the human reason, as a way of thinking which, while clothing itself in logical argument, gets its real driving force, as Lichtenberg says, from earnest reflection and fuller knowledge of human life.

But what is this idealism, which many, like Lichtenberg, have found it so difficult to overcome? To this question, as we have already indicated, no single answer can be

The selection is from W. M. Urban, *Beyond Realism and Idealism* (London: George Allen & Unwin, Ltd.; New York: The Macmillan Company, 1949), pp. 38-42 and 67-70. Used by permission of the publishers.

[1 The reference is to Georg Christoph Lichtenberg (1742-1799), German writer whose works were published in the nineteenth century. *Ed.*]

found. Nevertheless, an identity of intention runs throughout the entire series of changes which constitute the history of the notion. It is this continuity of intention . . . which we have now to develop more fully. In presenting the idealistic train of thought the driving force of idealism, we shall allow, in so far as possible, idealism to speak for itself—to express, as it were, its inmost soul, its deepest initiative and its ultimate intentions. We shall, accordingly, avoid all problems of criticism except such self-criticism as idealism has developed from within, or such criticism from without as it has accepted as part or basis of its own constructive belief. On the other hand, criticisms of realism will of necessity enter in, but only in so far as they are part of the idealistic argument.

It is reasonable to suppose that it is the idealists themselves who best know what they really mean and are therefore best able to interpret to us the continuity of intention which underlies all its forms. Despite differences of language, there is little difference among them in essential meaning. Idealism, in this most general sense, has frequently been defined as "any theory which maintains that the universe is throughout the work or embodiment of mind." Since mind is inseparable from value, Dean Inge is, I think, in principle right when he says that "idealism is most satisfactorily defined as interpretation of the world according to a scale of value or, in Plato's phrase, the Idea of the Good." We may agree then with Brightman that "any philosophy may be called idealistic if it embodies the reasoned conviction that ideals and the values they presuppose belong to the very objective structure of the universe." I think he is also right when he insists that this alone is necessary to modern idealism.

These are the attempts of idealists to express the inmost intentions of the position they represent. But apparently non-idealists and realists recognize the truth of this characterization. Thus C. D. Broad writes "By idealism I understand the doctrine that the nature of the universe is such that those characteristics which are highest and most valuable must either be manifested eternally or must be manifested in greater and greater intensity and in wider and wider extent as time goes on." G. E. Moore writes in much the same way. "Idealism in the larger sense," he tells us, "is the metaphysical assertion that the universal is spiritual," and it is because he believes that there is one argument necessary to this belief that he seeks a refutation of idealism by attempting to refute this particular argument.[2]

These statements, we may then assume, represent more or less adequately the deepest spiritual initiatives as well as the ultimate intentions of the entire idealistic train of thought. They embody that *metaphysical* idealism which, as has been already indicated, has been the dominant strain of European philosophy from the beginning. With this metaphysical idealism has, however, always been connected some theory of knowledge with which, it is supposed by its supporters, to be inseparably bound up. It is supposed by some, as for instance Mr. Moore, that there is one argument which is considered necessary to their position by all idealists, "namely, the trivial proposition that *esse est percipi.*" Whether this be true or not—I think it is not—certainly some epistemological position seems involved in idealism "in the larger sense."

This, then, is the idealism which we are to attempt to understand. In order to understand it we must, at the very beginning, dispose of a widespread misconception, which is not only false in itself but makes impossible *ab initio*, any genuine understanding of the persistence or driving force

[2 Professor Urban's references are to a number of recent philosophers. For Moore's position, see Book V below. *Ed.*]

of idealism. It is rather generally assumed—by idealists no less than realists—that realism is the "natural" attitude of man, that idealism appears only as the result of sophistication or a "malicious criticism" of human knowledge, and it is to the "natural man" that appeal is often made. Quite the contrary is really the case. There is a natural idealism and it is only by first examining this natural form that we shall understand either the continuing epistemological intention of idealism or the development of its later more reflective forms.

The "natural man" is both realist and idealist. The world man lives in—and that is the only world that, in the first instance at least, interests the philosopher—is "full of a number of things." It contains the "furniture of earth," but also the "choir of heaven." It contains many physical things but it also contains innumerable objects which are acknowledged by the plain man to exist only on the "mental" plane. Yet there are things which every man feels to be real. Love, empire, fame, justice, God—all belong to a transcendental ideal world. By these he lives, for these he is found willing, not only to live, but in his great moments to suffer and to die. In his great moments of experience these are, in fact, the things which man feels to be most *really real*. All these have their reality not only, nor indeed principally, in their necessity, but still more in their worthiness to be. Hence they partake more of reality than any mere "fact" could do and men, recognizing this, bow to them as the truly real.

This simultaneous acknowledgment of things at once ideal and real is primary, and it is out of this primary acknowledgment that all idealism gets its original driving force. But this is only one side of natural idealism. With it is connected another element which is equally native and original—namely, the feeling that the world of the senses is not the real world—and, as a result of this feeling, the tendency to re-duce things in the mind to ideas. Here various motives are at work in human experience and later in philosophical reflection. There is the relativity of all sense perception and perceptual predicates; the contradictions in our world of common sense objects; and the humanly conditioned character of our world of empirical objects. The point to emphasize here is that these motives arise very early in the experience of the individual and of the race, and once the consciousness of these facts is awakened, the mind is started on a path which inevitably leads to the idealistic train of thought. It is surely a significant moment in the mental history of any individual when he makes the discovery that there are deceptions of the senses and perhaps even more significant when he discovers the deceptions and contradictions of thought. In such a moment there is not only a healthy shock to simple trust, but there enters, long before it can be put into philosophical words, the sense of the phenomenal character and subjective conditions of all the given. From the fact that I see, hear and feel, and with my mind so think the thing, it by no means follows that it is really independent of me and so made. The world of sense is the world of "opinion"; the real world is the world of thought or idea.

In this insight there lies the germ of natural idealism in the second sense. But only the germ. Unless the ground were favorable for its growth the seed would not develop. Idealism would have no chance against the equally primitive and natural "prejudice in favor of the actual" were it not for a third motive without which idealism could never come to flower. This third motive I shall call the ideal of genuine knowledge or the natural notion of intelligibility. The first two motives of natural idealism are both deep-seated and powerful but it is the third, as I believe, which constitutes the driving force of epistemological idealism in its most primitive and most developed forms.

This natural notion of intelligibility is that only that which is akin to mind can really be known, and finds its primitive expression in what we call animism. It is the fashion to carry idealism back to this animism and to speak of the historic idealisms of Plato and Aristotle as "amiable animisms." I shall not dispute the genesis; in fact I shall welcome it as the deepest spring of natural idealism. That man is primarily an animist no one would, I suppose, deny. The real question is the significance of the fact. The naïve mind supposes, to be sure, that animism is a projection into an independent physical world of "mental states" and that it thus constitutes the pathetic fallacy on a huge scale. Quite the contrary is, of course, the case. The direct acceptance of things as having meaning and value is the primary form of consciousness; the bifurcation of "thing" and "meaning"; the separation of the real and the ideal constitutes the secondary, the artificial and the derived. Natural idealism has then its birth in the "mythical" consciousness for which knowledge is always oneness of the knower with the thing known. The idealism of Indian philosophy is at once a supreme expression of natural idealism and a fatal stumbling block in the way of all those who find in "realism" the only natural attitude. Of this idealism, almost racial in character, we must ask How was it ever possible? It is both possible and meaningful if we recognize that Indian thought is permeated by a wholly different ideal of knowledge from that which has characterized Western thought in its later stages—this ideal of knowledge as oneness of the knower with the thing known, native to the human mind as such.

This then is the natural notion of intelligibility—the deepest source of all idealisms. "The direct acceptance of things as having significance and value is," as Creighton has said, "the characteristic mark of idealism as found in the great systems." . . .

In the preceding pages we have tried to let idealism speak for itself and by so doing to make clear the driving force of idealism as it has come down through the ages, and especially as it has expressed itself in the protean forms characteristic of modern thought. The underlying thesis has been that while the forms have changed— changed as dialectically determined by the formulations of realism as they have appeared, and by the logic of its own development—the driving force, the primary epistemological intention, remains the same. This we may describe as the idealistic train of thought, and it is only in the latest and most sophisticated forms of idealism that its true inwardness has become fully self-conscious and the unity and continuity of the entire movement becomes fully understandable.

Part of the driving force of idealism has always been the deep-seated feeling that the postulate of the absolute existence of unthinking things, without any relation to mind, is "repugnant to reason" and, in Berkeley's terms, "perfectly unintelligible." Out of this feeling has arisen the negative aspect of idealistic argument in all stages of the development of idealism, namely, its refutations of realism. A brief consideration of the character of these refutations will make even clearer the nature of the idealistic argument itself.

Strictly speaking, refutations of realism as such did not begin until the modern era. For the idealist naïve forms of realism have always been repugnant to reason, but specific arguments in refutation did not arise until realism itself found self-conscious formulation, as opposed to self-conscious idealism. In this sense Berkeley's criticism of the view "so strangely prevailing among men" constitutes the first specific refutation. It followed two lines, an empirical and a logical, and since his time all refutations have followed more or less this general scheme.

The empirical line of thought takes the form of attempting to show that the proposition that there are objects wholly independent of the knower cannot be empirically verified, and that therefore, "it should not be believed." The second or logical line of argument takes the form of attempting to show that the proposition that there are wholly independent "unthinking things" is in some way logically contradictory, and is therefore repugnant to reason. It is true, of course, that while all refutations follow this general scheme, they vary in important ways according to the form of realism which it is sought to refute. As there is no single form of realism to which all types can be reduced so there is no single refutation which applies to every formulation of realism, but all refutations contain this double appeal to fact and to logic.

Now, as we have already indicated in the introduction and will show more fully in the following chapter, neither of these types of argument really refute. There is no empirical proof or disproof of realism for there are no possible experiences which the disputants might have which are relevant to this solution, one way or another. There is no logical proof or disproof of realism, for there is nothing self-contradictory in the notion of objects wholly independent of the mind. The argument, as we shall see, is neither empirical nor merely logical, but dialectical. . . .

This is, indeed, what all these so-called refutations have always been. The common element in all—from Berkeley to the latest form of logical or axiological idealism—is the supposed demonstration of the impossibility of genuine knowledge if the object of knowledge be conceived of as wholly mind-independent. But it is equally clear that they do not have the slightest force unless some evaluation of knowledge, some "logically unsupported judgment of value," is

presupposed. . . . But in so far as the driving force of idealism is concerned, refutations of realism, in this dialectical sense, are of great significance. Such a refutation is never an *argumentum ad rem,* but an *argumentum ad hominem;* but it is precisely this *argumentum ad hominem* which is so meaningful. Realism itself cannot be refuted, but in the very attempts to refute it is displayed an element in idealism which itself is irrefutable.

It is just this element in idealism which, as Lichtenberg says, makes it so difficult to overcome. The newer forms of idealism serve only to emphasize the force of Lichtenberg's remarks. We may at the beginning find idealism silly, hardly worth disproving because, as we say, it makes no difference to the facts. We may find it difficult to disprove and yet a form of belief which we should scarcely like to accept. Or we may disprove it over and over again (it is the best refuted of all theories) and still find that there remains something that is irrefutable. The fact remains that, "with earnest reflection and more extensive knowledge of human life and its interests, it acquires a force which it is difficult to overcome."

Idealism is, as Ludwig Stein has said, the phoenix of philosophy, and any philosophy reckons ill that leaves it out. The imperishable element in idealism is the curious fact that, in so far as its essence is concerned, whenever we deny it we somehow affirm it. It was for this reason that Royce liked to hear condemnations and refutations of idealism for they served only to bring out more clearly the irrefutable element in idealism.[3] Such criticism is merely a refining fire, and out of the ashes the phoenix of philosophy arises only the stronger.

This is why, as Royce says, "the idealistic movement, although frequently repressed, although often deliberately ignored,

---

[3] *Lectures on Modern Idealism,* p. 240.

has been as constant as the movement of a great river beneath masses of winter ice. Every now and then the ice breaks or melts and the idealistic tendency comes to the light of consciousness. It is irrepressible because it is human. It is true because truth itself is inevitably an ideal which cannot possibly be expressed except in ideal terms. One who has become aware of this universal significance of the idealistic tendency becomes indifferent to the general hostility towards either philosophy or idealism which is so often expressed by the unreflective." [4]

Idealism is irrepressible because it is human, and for that reason it not only continues to express itself in varying forms, but shows itself to contain an element which is irrefutable. It is true because truth itself is inevitably an ideal which cannot possibly be expressed except in ideal terms. It is entirely clear from the immediate context what Royce here means. It is precisely what we have described as the driving force of idealism throughout this entire chapter. As Royce puts it, "the question, how ought I to conceive the real is logically prior to the question what is the real itself?" He quotes Rickert to the effect that the ought is prior to the nature of the real "The proposition I ought to think thus" is prior to the proposition "This is so." In other words, truth being an ideal, always has reference to value. Only an ideal world in this sense is an intelligible world, and in so far as knowledge involves intelligibility, any adequate

theory of knowledge must contain an idealistic element.

This, it seems to me, is the *minimum* of idealism which any meaningful or intelligible theory of knowledge must contain. It is true, as we shall see in the next chapter, that any intelligible theory of knowledge must also contain a realistic *minimum*. It is the very purpose and nature of knowledge to be true to something beyond itself, and unless the content of knowledge is recognized as having a condition in some respect independent of the mind the very significance of knowledge is lost. But this fact by no means excludes the fact that other conditions are necessary to the significance of knowledge, and these conditions we have sought to formulate in the preceding paragraph.

It is these conditions that the various forms of idealism have sought more or less successfully to express—the mentalism of Berkeley, the critical or transcendental idealism of Kant, the logical and axiological forms of later idealism. All these forms are seen to be subordinated to one fundamental epistemological intention of idealism—the intention, namely, which arises out of the recognition of the fact that an ultimate separation of mind and values from reality makes impossible an intelligible theory of knowledge no less than an intelligible theory of life. The excessive claims of certain forms of idealism may be found untenable, and even unnecessary, to the realization of the primary intention of idealism— . . . but this minimum remains.

---

[4] *Op. cit.*, pp. 237 ff.

BIBLIOGRAPHICAL NOTE

Among the best introductory surveys of idealism are two works by Josiah Royce, *Lectures on Modern Idealism* (New Haven, 1923), and, in the relevant chapters, *The Spirit of Modern Philosophy* (New York, 1892). An anthology edited by A. C. Ewing,

The Idealistic Tradition (Glencoe, Illinois, 1957), presents an interesting collection of papers and includes a bibliography that the student may consult for intensive reading in idealism. Among the major idealistic works and authors not included in the preceding selections are: F. H. Bradley, *Appearance and Reality* (London, 1893); A. E. Taylor, *Elements of Metaphysics* (New York, 1909); and, especially for idealistic moral and political philosophy, the works of T. H. Green. An interesting variant of idealism is the position known as personal idealism or personalism. For material on personalism, see Borden Parker Bowne, *Metaphysics* (New York, 1882), and *Personalism* (Boston, 1908), and the recent book by Edgar Sheffield Brightman, *Person and Reality* (New York, 1958). One major philosophical figure, Immanuel Kant, can be classified as idealistic only with great qualification, yet his influence on idealism—as on all of modern philosophy— has been extensive. The student will find his major works, especially the *Critique of Pure Reason*, difficult but rewarding. Another thinker who defies easy classification is Alfred North Whitehead, who developed a variant of idealism called the philosophy of organism or, sometimes, panpsychism. Among his important works are *Science and the Modern World* (New York, 1925) and *Adventures of Ideas* (New York, 1933). Discussions of idealism are found in such books as G. W. Cunningham, *The Idealistic Argument in Recent British and American Philosophy* (New York, 1933), and A. C. Ewing, *Idealism: A Critical Survey* (London, 1934). Finally, the student may find interesting the papers in Clifford Barrett (ed.), *Contemporary Idealism in America* (New York, 1932).

III
NATURALISM

LUCRETIUS / BACON / PEIRCE

ALEXANDER / PERRY

DEWEY / MILL / COHEN

SANTAYANA / NAGEL

The position developed in the selections in this third Part is known as naturalism. Two propositions define the basic orientation of this philosophy: (1) nature is all there is; there is no supernatural being, realm, or entity, and (2) scientific method is the most reliable means of inquiry for men to use in exploring nature. The first statement indicates that naturalism is antithetical to all forms of supernaturalism and that it seeks to understand the various dimensions of experience in the context of nature alone. The second points to a relation between naturalism and science that is of both historical and contemporary importance.

Among the varieties of naturalism, it is possible to distinguish two major emphases. The first, and older, view is known as materialism. Materialism holds that the real is matter or energy, motion, time, and space and that all phenomena can be reduced to these terms. The word "naturalism" is frequently used to denote the second emphasis, which otherwise has no special name. Naturalism cannot always be sharply separated from materialism, although it is generally viewed as a distinct philosophy. For the naturalist, materialism presents too narrow a view of nature, for he finds nature much more complex and varied than an account in terms of matter and motion would seem to show. His aim is rather to describe accurately and fully the variety of levels within nature and to resist the tendency to make severe reductions of these levels to more primitive ones.

The ties between naturalism and science are very important in the rise of contemporary naturalism, even though a link with science has been present from the beginnings of materialism. Arising primarily in the seventeenth century, modern science involved a new methodology for man to follow and offered as well a new promise to man for the control of experience. The method itself has been of as much, and perhaps more, importance than the actual results of science. Yet among the results, too, are special achievements upon which naturalism has based itself. One of these, the theory of evolution, is of unique significance for naturalism, for it provided a theory in terms of which the naturalist could develop a full naturalistic, yet nonreductive account of the higher and more human levels of experience.

No compact definition of naturalism is fully adequate; for just as nature is changing and evolving, so naturalism too is not a fixed, closed system of propositions. Guided by science, it offers only a tentative and cautious statement about the general traits of existence. In proposing its metaphysical visions, naturalism belongs to that group of philosophic schools which finds ultimate generalization an important activity of man. It would separate itself, however, from philosophies that divorce themselves from science to offer what, from its point of view, are unguarded or dogmatic statements about things. It would also be suspicious of the distinction between "appearance and reality." The goal of naturalistic thinking is rather only that vision of man and nature which responsible inquiry will justify.

1 / INTRODUCTION

Materialism in the ancient world found expression in the thought of four major thinkers: Leucippus (a. 450), Democritus (460-360), Epicurus (341-270), and Lucretius. With these men materialism took an atomistic direction, and the proposition that atoms and the void are real is perhaps the basic assertion of the entire school.

The most complete extant statement of ancient materialism is found in the poem by Lucretius, *On the Nature of Things*. Writing under the direct inspiration of Epicurus, Lucretius presents an interesting motivation for turning to philosophy. Mankind's greatest fear, he writes, is the fear of death and of possible punishment in the hereafter. It is therefore necessary to develop a metaphysics in which the mortality of man is so guaranteed that he can pursue without distraction the Epicurean moral ideal of a life free from disturbance in the mind and of pain in the body. These needs are met in the hypothesis of materialistic atomism.

The essential assertions of Lucretius can be briefly summarized. Only atoms and the void are real. They are also both eternal and infinite. Mind, composed of atoms in motion, is corporeal and perishable. Death, being the end of sensation as well as the dissolution of the atomic structure known as man, is consequently of no concern to man. The following selection elaborates upon these theses and includes a number of interesting arguments in their support.

CLASSICAL MATERIALISM

Lucretius (98-54)

I shall proceed to discourse to thee [1] of the whole system of heaven and the gods, and unfold to thee the first principles of all things, from which nature produces, develops, and sustains all, and into which she again resolves them at their dissolution: these, in explaining our subject, we are accustomed to call matter, and the generative bodies of things, and to designate as the seeds of *all* things, and to term them primary bodies, because from them *as* primary all things are derived.

[For the whole nature of the gods must necessarily, of itself, enjoy immortality in absolute repose, separated, and far removed, from our affairs; for, exempt from all pain, exempt from perils, all-sufficient in its own resources, *and* needing nothing from us, it is neither propitiated by services *from the good,* nor affected with anger *against the bad.*] [2]

When the life of men lay foully grovelling before *our* eyes, crushed beneath the weight of a Religion, who displayed her head from the regions of the sky, lowering over mortals with terrible aspect, a man of Greece [3] was the first that dared to raise mortal eyes against *her,* and first to make a stand against *her.* Him neither tales of gods, nor thunderbolts, nor heaven itself with its threatening roar, repressed, but roused the more the active energy of his soul, *so* that he should desire to be the first to break the close bars of nature's portals. Accordingly the vivid force of his intellect prevailed, and proceeded far beyond the flaming battlements of the world, and in mind and thought traversed the whole immensity of space; hence triumphant, he declares to us what can arise *into being,* and what can not; in fine, in what way the powers of all things are limited, and a deeply-fixed boundary assigned to each. By which means Religion, brought down under *our* feet, is bruised in turn; and *his* victory sets us on a level with heaven. . . .

Wilt thou too, overcome by the frightful tales of bards, ever seek to turn away from me? *Surely not;* for doubtless I, even now, could invent for thee many dreams, which might disturb the tenor of thy life, and confound all thy enjoyments with terror. And with reason too *under the present system of belief;* for did men *but* know that there was a fixed limit to their woes, they would be able, in some measure, to defy the religious fictions and menaces of the poets; *but* now, since we must fear eternal punishment at death, there is no mode, no means, of resisting *them.* For men know not what the nature of the soul is; whether it is engendered *with us,* or whether, on the contrary, it is infused into us at our birth, whether it perishes with us, dissolved by death, or whether it haunts the gloomy shades and vast pools of Orcus, or whether, by divine influence, it infuses itself into other animals, as our Ennius [4] sung, who first brought from pleasant Helicon a crown of never-fading leaf, which should be distinguished in fame throughout the Italian tribes of men. . . .

This terror and darkness of the mind,

The selection is from Books I and III of Lucretius' *On the Nature of Things* (tr. John Selby Watson) (London: Henry G. Bohn, 1851).

[1 The poem is addressed to a member of the family of Memmius, possibly the member to whom Cicero wrote letters. *Ed.*]

[2 Brackets have been used by the translator to indicate possibly misplaced lines. *Ed.*]

[3 The reference is to Epicurus, who is greatly praised throughout the poem. *Ed.*]

[4 A Pythagorean who thought that the soul of Homer had passed into himself. *Ed.*]

therefore, it is not the rays of the sun, or the bright shafts of day, that must dispel, but reason and the contemplation of nature; of which our first principle shall hence take its commencement, THAT NOTHING IS EVER DIVINELY GENERATED FROM NOTHING. For thus *it is that* fear restrains all men, because they observe many things effected on the earth and in heaven, of which effects they can by no means see the causes, and *therefore* think that they are wrought by a divine power. For which reasons, when we shall have *clearly* seen that NOTHING CAN BE PRODUCED FROM NOTHING, we shall then have a more accurate perception of that of which we are in search, and *shall understand* whence each individual thing is generated, and how all things are done without the agency of the gods.

For if *things* came forth from nothing, every kind *of thing* might be produced from all things; nothing would require seed. In the first place, men might spring from the sea; the scaly tribe, and birds, *might spring* from the earth; herds, and other cattle, might burst from the sky; the cultivated fields, as well as the deserts, might contain every kind of wild animal, without any settled *law of* production: nor would the same fruits be constant to the *same* trees, but would be changed; *and* all *trees* might bear all *kinds of fruit*. Since, when there should not be generative elements for each *production*, how could a certain parent-producer remain invariable for *all individual* things? But now, because all things are severally produced from certain seeds, *each* is produced, and comes forth into the regions of light, from that spot in which the matter, and first elements of each, subsist. And for this cause all things cannot be produced from all, inasmuch as there are distinct *and peculiar* faculties in certain substances....

Add, too, that nature resolves each thing into its own *constituent* elements, and DOES NOT REDUCE ANY THING TO NOTHING.

For if any thing were perishable in all

its parts, every thing might *then* dissolve, being snatched suddenly from before our eyes; for there would be no need of force to produce a separation of its parts, and break *their* connection. Whereas now, since all things individually consist of eternal seed, nature does not suffer the destruction of any thing to be seen, until such power assail them as to sever them with a blow, or penetrate inwardly through the vacant spaces, and dissolve *the parts*.

Besides, if time utterly destroys whatever things it removes through length of age, consuming all their *constituent* matter, whence does Venus restore to the light of life the race of animals according to their kinds? Whence does the variegated earth nourish and develop them, when restored, affording them sustenance according to their kinds? Whence do pure fountains, and eternal rivers *flowing* from afar, supply the sea? Whence does the ether feed the stars? For infinite time already past, and *length of* days, ought to have consumed all things which are of mortal consistence: but if *those elements*, of which this sum of things consists and is renewed, have existed through that *long* space, and that past duration of time, they are assuredly endowed with an immortal nature. Things therefore cannot return to nothing.

Further, the same force and cause might destroy all things indiscriminately, unless an eternal matter held them more or less bound by mutual connection. For a *mere* touch, indeed, would be a sufficient cause of destruction, supposing that there were no *parts* of eternal consistence, *but all perishable*, the union of which any force might dissolve. But now, because various connections of elements unite together, and matter is eternal, things continue of unimpaired consistence, until some force of sufficient strength be found to assail them, proportioned to the texture of each. No thing, therefore, relapses into nonexistence, but all things at dissolution return to the first principles of matter. . . .

Attend, now, *further:* since I have shown that things cannot be produced from nothing, and also that, when produced, *they cannot* return to nothing, yet, lest haply thou shouldst begin to distrust my words, because the primary particles of things cannot be discerned by the eye, hear, in addition, what substances thou thyself must necessarily confess to exist, although impossible to be seen.

In the first place, the force of the wind, when excited, lashes the sea, agitates the tall ships, and scatters the clouds; at times, sweeping over *the earth* with an impetuous hurricane, it strews the plains with huge trees, and harasses the mountain-tops with forest-rending blasts; so *violently* does the deep chafe with fierce roar and rage with menacing murmur. The winds, then, are invisible bodies, which sweep the sea, the land, the clouds of heaven, and, agitating *them,* carry *them* along with a sudden tornado. Not otherwise do they rush forth, and spread destruction, than *as* when a body of liquid water is borne along in an overwhelming stream, which a vast torrent from the lofty mountains swells with large rain-floods, dashing together fragments of woods and entire groves; nor can the strong bridges sustain the sudden force of the sweeping water, with such overwhelming violence does the river, turbid with copious rain, rush against the *opposing* mounds; it scatters ruin with a mighty uproar, and rolls huge rocks under its waters; it rushes on *triumphant* wheresoever any thing opposes its waves. Thus, therefore, must the blasts of the wind also be borne along; which (when, like a mighty flood, they have bent their force in any direction) drive all things before them, and overthrow them with repeated assaults, and sometimes catch them up in a writhing vortex and rapidly bear them off in a whirling hurricane. Wherefore, I repeat, the winds are sub-

stances, *though* invisible, since in their effects, and modes of *operation,* they are found to rival mighty rivers, which are of manifest bodily substance.

Moreover we perceive various odors of objects, and yet never see them approaching our nostrils. Nor do we behold violent heat, or distinguish cold with our eyes; nor are we in the habit of viewing sounds; all which things, however, must of necessity consist of a corporeal nature, since they have the power of striking the senses: FOR NOTHING, EXCEPT BODILY SUBSTANCE, CAN TOUCH OR BE TOUCHED.

Further, garments, when suspended upon a shore on which waves are broken, grow moist; the same, when spread out in the sun, become dry; yet neither has it been observed how the moisture of the water settled in them, nor, on the other hand, how it escaped under the influence of the heat. The moisture, therefore, is dispersed into minute particles, which our eyes can by no means perceive.

Besides, in the course of many revolutions of the sun, a ring upon the finger is made somewhat thinner by wearing *it;* the fall of the drop from the eaves hollows a stone; the crooked share of the plough, *though* made of iron, imperceptibly decreases in the fields; even the stone pavements of the streets we see worn by the feet of the multitude; and the brazen statues, *which stand* near the gates, show their right hands made smaller by the touch of people frequently saluting them, and passing by. These objects, therefore, after they have been worn, we observe to become diminished; but what particles take their departure on each particular occasion, jealous nature has withheld from us the faculty of seeing.

Lastly, whatever *substances* time and nature add little by little to objects, obliging them to increase gradually, *those substances* no acuteness of vision, *however earnestly* exerted, can perceive; nor, moreover, whatever *substances* waste away through age and decay; nor can you discern what the rocks, which overhang the sea, *and are* eaten by the corroding salt *of the ocean,* lose every time *that they are washed by the waves.* Nature, therefore, carries on her operations by imperceptible particles.

Nor, however, are all things held enclosed by corporeal substance; for there is a VOID in things; *a truth* which it will be useful for you, in reference to many points, to know; and which will prevent you from wandering in doubt, and from perpetually inquiring about the ENTIRE OF THINGS, and from being distrustful of my words. Wherefore, *I say,* there is space INTANGIBLE, EMPTY, and VACANT. If this were not the case, things could by no means be moved; for that which is the quality of body, *namely,* to obstruct and to oppose, would be present *at all times, and would be exerted* against all *bodies;* nothing, therefore, would be able to move forward, since nothing would begin to give way. But now, throughout the sea and land and heights of heaven, we see many things moved before our eyes in various ways *and* by various means, which, if there were no void, would not so much want *their* active motion, *as being* deprived *of it,* as they would, *properly speaking,* never by any means have been produced at all; since matter, crowded together on all sides, would have remained at rest, *and have been unable to act.* . . .

As it is, therefore, all nature of itself has consisted, *and consists,* of two parts; for there are bodily substances, and vacant *space,* in which these *substances* are situate, and in which they are moved in different directions. For the common perception *of all men* shows that there is corporeal consistence; of *the existence of* which, unless the belief shall be first firmly established, there will be no *principle* by reference to which we may succeed, by any means whatever, in settling the mind with argument concerning matters not obvious to sense.

To proceed then, if there were no place, and *no* space which we call vacant, bodies could not be situated any where, nor could at all move any whither in different directions; a fact which we have shown to you a little before.

Besides, there is nothing which you can say is separate from all bodily substance, and distinct from empty space; which would, indeed, be as it were a third kind of nature. For whatsoever shall exist, must *in* itself be something, either of large bulk, or ever so diminutive, provided it be at all; when, if it shall be *sensible to* the touch, however light and delicate, it will increase the number of bodies, and be ranked in the multitude of them; but if it shall be intangible, inasmuch as it cannot hinder in any part any object proceeding to pass through it, it *then,* you may be sure, will be the empty space which we call a vacuum.

Moreover, whatsoever shall exist of itself, will either *do* something, or will be obliged TO SUFFER other things acting upon it, or will *simply* BE, so that other things may exist and be done in it. But nothing can DO or SUFFER without *being possessed of* bodily substance, nor, moreover, afford place *for acting and suffering,* unless *it be* empty and vacant space. No third nature, therefore, *distinct* in itself, besides vacant space and material substance, can possibly be left *undiscovered* in the sum of things; no *third kind of being,* which can at any time fall under *the notice of* our senses, or which any one can find out by the exercise of his reason. . . .

In the first place, since a two-fold nature of two things, *a two-fold nature, or rather two natures* extremely dissimilar, has been found to exist, *namely,* matter, and space in which every thing is done, it must necessarily be that each exists by itself for itself, *independently of the other,* and pure *from admixture;* for wheresoever there is empty space, which we call a vacuum, there there is no matter, *and,* likewise, wheresoever matter maintains itself, there by no means exists empty space. Original substances are therefore solid and without vacuity.

Furthermore, since in things which are produced, *or compounded of matter,* there is *found* empty space, solid matter must exist around it; nor can any thing be proved by just argument to conceal vacuity, and to contain *it* within its body, unless you admit that that which contains *it* is a solid. But that *solid* can be nothing but a combination of matter, *such* as may have the power of keeping a vacuity enclosed. *That* matter, therefore, which consists of solid body, may be eternal, while other *substances, which are only compounds of this matter,* may be dissolved.

In addition, too, if there were no space to be vacant and unoccupied, all *space* would be solid. On the other hand, unless there were certain bodies to fill up completely the *places* which they occupy, all space, which *any where* exists, would be an empty void. Body, therefore, is evidently distinct from empty space, *though each has its place* alternately; since *all space* neither exists entirely full, nor, again, *entirely* empty. There exist, therefore, certain bodies which can *completely fill the places which they occupy,* and distinguish empty space from full.

These bodies, *which thus completely fill space,* can neither be broken in pieces *by* being struck with blows externally, nor, again, can be decomposed *by* being penetrated internally; nor can they be made to yield *if* attempted by any other method; a *principle* which we have demonstrated to you a little above; for neither does it seem possible for any thing to be dashed in pieces without a vacuum, nor to be broken, nor to be divided into two by cutting; nor to admit moisture, nor, moreover, subtle cold, nor penetrating fire, by which *operations and means* all things *compounded* are dissolved. And the more any thing contains empty space within it, the more it yields

when thoroughly tried by these means. If, therefore, the primary atoms are solid and without void, they must of necessity be eternal.

Again, unless there had been eternal matter, all things, before this time, would have been utterly reduced to nothing; and whatsoever *objects* we behold would have been reproduced from nothing. But since I have shown above, that nothing can be produced from nothing, and that that which has been produced *cannot* be resolved into nothing, the primary elements must be of an imperishable substance, into which *primary elements* every body may be dissolved, so that matter may be supplied for the reproduction of things. The primordial elements, therefore, are of pure solidity; nor could they otherwise, preserved, *as they have been,* for ages, repair things, *as they have done,* through *that* infinite space of time *which has elapsed since the commencement of this material system.* . . .

But since I have taught that atoms of matter, entirely solid, pass to-and-fro perpetually, unwasted through *all* time; come now, *and* let us unravel whether there be any limit to their aggregate, or not; also, let us look into that which has been found *to be* vacancy, or the room and space in which things severally are done, *and learn* whether the whole is entirely limited, or extends unbounded and unfathomably profound.

All that exists, therefore, *I affirm,* is bounded in no direction; for, *if it were bounded,* it must have some extremity; but it appears that there cannot be an extremity of any thing, unless there be something beyond, which may limit it; so that there may appear *to be some line* farther than which this faculty of our sense (*i. e. our vision*) cannot extend. Now, since it must be confessed that there is nothing beyond the WHOLE, *the whole* has no extremity; nor does it matter at what part of it you stand, *with a view to being distant from its boundary;* inasmuch as, whatever place any one occupies, he leaves the WHOLE just as much boundless in every direction. . . .

Besides, Nature herself prevents the WHOLE OF THINGS from being able to provide bounds for itself, inasmuch as she compels body to be bounded by *that which is* vacuum, and that which is vacuum to be bounded by body; that so, by *this* alternate *bounding of one by the other,* she may render ALL infinite. Else, moreover, if one or other of these did not bound the other by its simple nature, so that *one of them, the vacuum for instance,* should extend unlimited, neither the sea, nor the land, nor the bright temples of heaven, nor the race of mortals, nor the sacred persons of the gods, could subsist for the small space of an hour. For the body of matter, driven abroad from its union, would be borne dispersed through the mighty void, or rather, in such a case, never having been united, would *never* have produced any thing, since, when *originally* scattered, it could not have been brought together.

For certainly neither the primary elements of things disposed themselves severally in their own order, by *their own* counsel *or* sagacious understanding; nor, assuredly, did they agree among themselves what motions each should produce; but because, being many, and changed in many ways, they are for an infinite *space of time* agitated, being acted upon by forces, throughout the WHOLE, *they thus,* by experiencing movements and combinations of every kind, at length settle into such positions, by which means, *(i. e. positions,)* this SUM *of things,* being produced, exists. And *this sum of things,* when it was once thrown into suitable motions, being also maintained *in that state* through many long years, causes that the rivers recruit the greedy sea with large floods of water, and that the earth, cherished by the heat of the sun, renews *its* productions; also that the race of living creatures flourishes unde-

cayed, and that the gliding fires of heaven live. Which *effects atoms* could by no means produce, unless an abundant supply of matter could arise from the infinite *of space,* whence every thing *that is produced* is accustomed to repair in time the parts lost. . . .

These things if you shall understand, led on by *my* humble effort, (for one *proposition* will appear plain from another,) dark night will not prevent your progress, *or hinder you* from seeing clearly into the last *depths* of nature; so *effectually* will truths kindle light for truths.

And since I have shown of what kind the primordial atoms of all things are, and how, differing in *their* various forms, and actuated by motion from all eternity, they fly *through the void of space* of their own accord; and *since I have also demonstrated* by what means all individual things may be produced from them; the nature of the MIND and of the SOUL now seems, next to these subjects, *proper* to be illustrated in my verses. . . .

I now affirm that the mind and soul are held united with one another, and form of themselves one nature *or substance;* but that *that which* is as it were the head, and *which* rules in the whole body, is the reason, *the thinking or intellectual part* which we call mind and understanding; and this remains seated in the middle portion of the breast. For here dread and terror throb; around these parts joys soothe; here therefore is the understanding and mind. The other part of the soul, *or vital power,* distributed through the whole body, obeys, and is moved according to the will and impulse of the mind. And *this rational or intellectual part* thinks of itself alone, and rejoices for itself, *at times* when nothing *of the kind* moves either *the rest of* the soul or the body. And as when the head or the eye, when pain affects it, is troubled in us, *and as part of us, but* we are not afflicted throughout the whole body, so the mind is sometimes grieved itself *alone,* and is *sometimes* excited with joy, when the other part of the soul, *diffused* through the limbs and joints, is stimulated by no new sensation. But when the mind is more *than ordinarily* shaken by violent terror, we see the whole soul, throughout the *several* members, sympathize with it, and perspirations and paleness, in consequence, arise over the whole body, and the tongue rendered powerless and the voice die away; *while we find* the eyes darkened, the ears ringing, *and* the limbs sinking underneath.

Furthermore, we often see men faint *altogether* from terror of mind; *so that* any one may easily understand from this, that with the mind is united the soul, which, when it has been acted upon by the power of the mind, then influences and affects the body.

This same *course of* reasoning teaches us that the nature *or substance* of the mind and soul is corporeal; for when *this nature or substance* is seen to impel the limbs, to rouse the body from sleep, and to change the countenance, and to guide and turn about the whole man;—of which *effects* we see that none can be produced without touch, and that touch, moreover, *cannot take place* without body;—must we not admit that the mind and soul are of a corporeal nature?

Besides, you see that the mind suffers with the body, and sympathizes for us with the body. *Thus,* if the violent force of a dart, driven into *the body,* the bones and nerves being divided, does not hurt the life *itself,* yet there follows a languor, and a kind of agreeable inclination-to-sink to the ground, and *when we are* on the ground, a perturbation *and giddiness* which is produced in the mind, and sometimes, as it were, an irresolute desire to rise. It therefore necessarily follows that the nature of the mind is corporeal, since it is made to suffer by corporeal weapons and violence. . . .

And now attend. That thou mayest understand that living creatures have minds, and subtle souls, BORN and PERISHABLE, I will proceed to arrange verses worthy of thy life *and virtues, verses* collected during a long time, and prepared with sweet labor. *And* thou, *my friend,* take care to include both of them under one name, *whichsoever of the two I may use;* and, for example, when I proceed to speak of the soul, teaching that it is mortal, suppose that I also speak of the mind; inasmuch as they are one by mutual *combination,* and their substance is united.

In the first place, since I have shown that the *soul, being* subtle, consists of minute particles, and is composed of much smaller atoms than the clear fluid of water, or mist, or smoke; (for it far surpasses *those bodies* in susceptibility-of-motion, and is more readily impelled when acted upon from a slight cause; inasmuch as *both the mind and soul* are moved by the *mere* images of smoke and mist; as when, lulled in sleep, we see high altars exhale with vapor, and carry up smoke; since doubtless these phantasms are produced in us;) now, therefore, *I say,* since, when vessels are broken to pieces, you see water flow about, and *any other* liquid run away; and since, *also,* mist and smoke disperse into the air; *you must* conclude that the soul is likewise scattered abroad, and is dissipated much sooner *than mist and smoke,* and more easily resolved into *its* original elements, when it *has* once *been* withdrawn from the body of a man, *and* has taken its departure. . . .

Death, therefore, is nothing, nor at all concerns us, since the nature *or substance* of the soul is *to be* accounted mortal. And as, in past time, we felt no anxiety, when the Carthaginians gathered on all sides to fight *with our forefathers, and* when all things under the lofty air of heaven, shaken with the dismaying tumult of war, trembled with dread; and *men* were uncertain to the sway of which *power* every thing human, by land and by sea, was to fall; so, when we shall cease to be, when there shall be a separation of the body and soul of which we are conjointly composed, it is certain that to us, who shall not then exist, nothing will by any possibility happen, or excite our feeling, not even if the earth shall be mingled with the sea, and the sea with the heaven.

The close affinity between naturalism and science has already been noted, and in fact there are signs of this relation in Lucretius. But the rise of modern science in the seventeenth century makes this affinity clearer and more important.

Sir Francis Bacon is often referred to as the prophet of modern science. No scientist himself, he nevertheless expressed with vigor and clarity the basic impulse of the new methodology. For Bacon, knowledge, when properly conceived, is power. But in the past, knowledge has been improperly conceived. Human reason, left to itself and unchecked, is prone to a variety of errors. What is needed is a method that will provide such checks; and these Bacon finds in scientific induction and experiment.

THE METHOD OF SCIENCE

Sir Francis Bacon (1561-1626)

1. Man, as the minister and interpreter of nature, does and understands as much as his observations on the order of nature, either with regard to things or the mind, permit him, and neither knows nor is capable of more.

2. The unassisted hand and the understanding left to itself possess but little power. Effects are produced by the means of instruments and helps, which the understanding requires no less than the hand; and as instruments either promote or regulate the motion of the hand, so those that are applied to the mind prompt or protect the understanding.

3. Knowledge and human power are synonymous, since the ignorance of the cause frustrates the effect; for nature is only subdued by submission, and that which in contemplative philosophy corresponds

The selection is from Book I of Bacon's *Novum Organon* (New York: The Colonial Press, 1900).

with the cause in practical science becomes the rule.

19. There are and can exist but two ways of investigating and discovering truth. The one hurries on rapidly from the senses and particulars to the most general axioms, and from them, as principles and their supposed indisputable truth, derives and discovers the intermediate axioms. This is the way now in use. The other constructs its axioms from the senses and particulars, by ascending continually and gradually, till it finally arrives at the most general axioms, which is the true but unattempted way.

26. We are wont, for the sake of distinction, to call that human reasoning which we apply to nature the anticipation of nature (as being rash and premature), and that which is properly deduced from things the interpretation of nature.

36. We have but one simple method of delivering our sentiments, namely, we must bring men to particulars and their regular

series and order, and they must for a while renounce their notions, and begin to form an acquaintance with things.

37. Our method and that of the skeptics agree in some respects at first setting out, but differ most widely, and are completely opposed to each other in their conclusion; for they roundly assert that nothing can be known; we, that but a small part of nature can be known, by the present method; their next step, however, is to destroy the authority of the senses and understanding, whilst we invent and supply them with assistance.

38. The idols and false notions which have already preoccupied the human understanding, and are deeply rooted in it, not only so beset men's minds that they become difficult of access, but even when access is obtained will again meet and trouble us in the instauration of the sciences, unless mankind when forewarned guard themselves with all possible care against them.

39. Four species of idols beset the human mind, to which (for distinction's sake) we have assigned names, calling the first Idols of the Tribe, the second Idols of the Den, the third Idols of the Market, the fourth Idols of the Theatre.

40. The formation of notions and axioms on the foundation of true induction is the only fitting remedy by which we can ward off and expel these idols. It is, however, of great service to point them out; for the doctrine of idols bears the same relation to the interpretation of nature as that of the confutation of sophisms does to common logic.

41. The idols of the tribe are inherent in human nature and the very tribe or race of man; for man's sense is falsely asserted to be the standard of things; on the contrary, all the perceptions both of the senses and the mind bear reference to man and not to the universe, and the human mind resembles those uneven mirrors which impart their own properties to different objects, from which rays are emitted and distort and disfigure them.

42. The idols of the den are those of each individual; for everybody (in addition to the errors common to the race of man) has his own individual den or cavern, which intercepts and corrupts the light of nature, either from his own peculiar and singular disposition, or from his education and intercourse with others, or from his reading, and the authority acquired by those whom he reverences and admires, or from the different impressions produced on the mind, as it happens to be preoccupied and predisposed, or equable and tranquil, and the like; so that the spirit of man (according to its several dispositions), is variable, confused, and, as it were, actuated by chance; and Heraclitus said well that men search for knowledge in lesser worlds, and not in the greater or common world.

43. There are also idols formed by the reciprocal intercourse and society of man with man, which we call idols of the market, from the commerce and association of men with each other; for men converse by means of language, but words are formed at the will of the generality, and there arises from a bad and unapt formation of words a wonderful obstruction to the mind. Nor can the definitions and explanations with which learned men are wont to guard and protect themselves in some instances afford a complete remedy—words still manifestly force the understanding, throw everything into confusion, and lead mankind into vain and innumerable controversies and fallacies.

44. Lastly, There are idols which have crept into men's minds from the various dogmas of peculiar systems of philosophy, and also from the perverted rules of demonstration, and these we denominate idols of the theatre: for we regard all the systems of philosophy hitherto received or imagined, as so many plays brought out and per-

formed, creating fictitious and theatrical worlds. Nor do we speak only of the present systems, or of the philosophy and sects of the ancients, since numerous other plays of a similar nature can be still composed and made to agree with each other, the causes of the most opposite errors being generally the same. Nor, again, do we allude merely to general systems, but also to many elements and axioms of sciences which have become inveterate by tradition, implicit credence, and neglect. We must, however, discuss each species of idols more fully and distinctly in order to guard the human understanding against them.

45. The human understanding, from its peculiar nature, easily supposes a greater degree of order and equality in things than it really finds; and although many things in nature be sui generis and most irregular, will yet invent parallels and conjugates and relatives, where no such thing is. Hence the fiction, that all celestial bodies move in perfect circles, thus rejecting entirely spiral and serpentine lines (except as explanatory terms). Hence also the element of fire is introduced with its peculiar orbit, to keep square with those other three which are objects of our senses. The relative rarity of the elements (as they are called) is arbitrarily made to vary in tenfold progression, with many other dreams of the like nature. Nor is this folly confined to theories, but it is to be met with even in simple notions.

46. The human understanding, when any proposition has been once laid down (either from general admission and belief, or from the pleasure it affords), forces everything else to add fresh support and confirmation; and although most cogent and abundant instances may exist to the contrary, yet either does not observe or despises them, or gets rid of and rejects them by some distinction, with violent and injurious prejudice, rather than sacrifice the authority of its first conclusions. It was

well answered by him [1] who has shown in a temple the votive tablets suspended by such as had escaped to peril of shipwreck, and was pressed as to whether he would then recognize the power of the gods, by an inquiry, But where are the portraits of those who have perished in spite of their vows? All superstition is much the same, whether it be that of astrology, dreams, omens, retributive judgment, or the like, in all of which the deluded believers observe events which are fulfilled, but neglect and pass over their failure, though it be much more common. But this evil insinuates itself still more craftily in philosophy and the sciences, in which a settled maxim vitiates and governs every other circumstance, though the latter be much more worthy of confidence. Besides, even in the absence of that eagerness and want of thought (which we have mentioned), it is the peculiar and perpetual error of the human understanding to be more moved and excited by affirmatives than negatives, whereas it ought duly and regularly to be impartial; nay, in establishing any true axiom the negative instance is the most powerful.

48. The human understanding is active and cannot halt or rest, but even, though without effect, still presses forward. Thus we cannot conceive of any end or external boundary of the world, and it seems necessarily to occur to us that there must be something beyond. Nor can we imagine how eternity has flowed on down to the present day, since the usually received distinction of an infinity, a parte ante and a parte post cannot hold good; for it would thence follow that one infinity is greater than another, and also that infinity is wasting

[1 The reference is to Diagoras of Melos, surnamed the Atheist, who flourished in the Fifth Century B.C. Although religious in his youth, he is said to have become an atheist because a great wrong done to him was left unpunished by the gods. *Ed.*]

away and tending to an end. There is the same difficulty in considering the infinite divisibility of lines arising from the weakness of our minds, which weakness interferes to still greater disadvantage with the discovery of causes; for although the greatest generalities in nature must be positive, just as they are found, and in fact not causable, yet the human understanding, incapable of resting, seeks for something more intelligible. Thus, however, whilst aiming at further progress, it falls back to what is actually less advanced, namely, final causes; for they are clearly more allied to man's own nature, than the system of the universe, and from this source they have wonderfully corrupted philosophy. But he would be an unskilful and shallow philosopher who should seek for causes in the greatest generalities, and not be anxious to discover them in subordinate objects.

49. The human understanding resembles not a dry light, but admits a tincture of the will and passions, which generate their own system accordingly; for man always believes more readily that which he prefers. He, therefore, rejects difficulties for want of patience in investigation; sobriety, because it limits his hope; the depths of nature, from superstition; the light of experiment, from arrogance and pride, lest his mind should appear to be occupied with common and varying objects; paradoxes, from a fear of the opinion of the vulgar; in short, his feelings imbue and corrupt his understanding in innumerable and sometimes imperceptible ways.

50. But by far the greatest impediment and aberration of the human understanding proceeds from the dulness, incompetency, and errors of the senses; since whatever strikes the senses preponderates over everything, however superior, which does not immediately strike them. Hence contemplation mostly ceases with sight, and a very scanty, or perhaps no regard is paid to invisible objects. The entire operation, therefore, of

spirits enclosed in tangible bodies is concealed, and escapes us. All that more delicate change of formation in the parts of coarser substances (vulgarly called alteration, but in fact a change of position in the smallest particles) is equally unknown; and yet, unless the two matters we have mentioned be explored and brought to light, no great effect can be produced in nature. Again, the very nature of common air, and all bodies of less density (of which there are many) is almost unknown; for the senses are weak and erring, nor can instruments be of great use in extending their sphere or acuteness—all the better interpretations of nature are worked out by instances, and fit and apt experiments, where the senses only judge of the experiment, the experiment of nature and the thing itself.

51. The human understanding is, by its own nature, prone to abstraction, and supposes that which is fluctuating to be fixed. But it is better to dissect than abstract nature; such was the method employed by the school of Democritus, which made greater progress in penetrating nature than the rest. It is best to consider matter, its conformation, and the changes of that conformation, its own action, and the law of this action or motion; for forms are a mere fiction of the human mind, unless you will call the laws of action by that name.

52. Such are the idols of the tribe, which arise either from the uniformity of the constitution of man's spirit, or its prejudices, or its limited faculties or restless agitation, or from the interference of the passions, or the incompetency of the senses, or the mode of their impressions.

53. The idols of the den derive their origin from the peculiar nature of each individual's mind and body, and also from education, habit, and accident; and although they be various and manifold, yet we will treat of some that require the greatest cau-

tion, and exert the greatest power in polluting the understanding.

55. The greatest and, perhaps, radical distinction between different men's dispositions for philosophy and the sciences is this, that some are more vigorous and active in observing the differences of things, others in observing their resemblances; for a steady and acute disposition can fix its thoughts, and dwell upon and adhere to a point, through all the refinements of differences, but those that are sublime and discursive recognize and compare even the most delicate and general resemblances; each of them readily falls into excess, by catching either at nice distinctions or shadows of resemblance.

56. Some dispositions evince an unbounded admiration of antiquity, others eagerly embrace novelty, and but few can preserve the just medium, so as neither to tear up what the ancients have correctly laid down, nor to despise the just innovations of the moderns. But this is very prejudicial to the sciences and philosophy, and instead of a correct judgment we have but the factions of the ancients and moderns. Truth is not to be sought in the good fortune of any particular conjecture of time, which is uncertain, but in the light of nature and experience, which is eternal. Such factions, therefore, are to be abjured, and the understanding must not allow them to hurry it on to assent.

58. Let such, therefore, be our precautions in contemplation, that we may ward off and expel the idols of the den, which mostly owe their birth either to some predominant pursuit, or, secondly, to an excess in synthesis and analysis, or, thirdly, to a party zeal in favor of certain ages, or, fourthly, to the extent of narrowness of the subject. In general, he who contemplates nature should suspect whatever particularly takes and fixes his understanding, and should use so much the more caution to preserve it equable and unprejudiced.

59. The idols of the market are the most troublesome of all, those namely which have entwined themselves round the understanding from the associations of words and names. For men imagine that their reason governs words, whilst, in fact, words react upon the understanding; and this has rendered philosophy and the sciences sophistical and inactive. Words are generally formed in a popular sense, and define things by those broad lines which are most obvious to the vulgar mind; but when a more acute understanding, or more diligent observation is anxious to vary those lines, and to adapt them more accurately to nature, words oppose it. Hence the great and solemn disputes of learned men often terminate in controversies about words and names, in regard to which would be better (imitating the caution of mathematicians) to proceed more advisedly in the first instance, and to bring such disputes to a regular issue by definitions. Such definitions, however, cannot remedy the evil in natural and material objects, because they consist themselves of words, and these words produce others; so that we must necessarily have recourse to particular instances, and their regular series and arrangement, as we shall mention when we come to the mode and scheme of determining notions and axioms.

62. The idols of the theatre, or of theories, are numerous, and may, and perhaps will, be still more so. For unless men's minds had been now occupied for many ages in religious and theological considerations, and civil governments (especially monarchies), had been averse to novelties of that nature even in theory (so that men must apply to them with some risk and injury to their own fortunes, and not only without reward, but subject to contumely and envy), there is no doubt that many other sects of philosophers and theorists would have been introduced, like those which formerly flourished in such diversified

abundance amongst the Greeks. For as many imaginary theories of the heavens can be deduced from the phenomena of the sky, so it is even more easy to found many dogmas upon the phenomena of philosophy —and the plot of this our theatre resembles those of the poetical, where the plots which are invented for the stage are more consistent, elegant, and pleasurable than those taken from real history.

In general, men take for the groundwork of their philosophy either too much from a few topics, or too little from many; in either case their philosophy is founded on too narrow a basis of experiment and natural history, and decided on too scanty grounds. For the theoretic philosopher seizes various common circumstances by experiment, without reducing them to certainty or examining and frequently considering them, and relies for the rest upon meditation and the activity of his wit.

There are other philosophers who have diligently and accurately attended to a few experiments, and have thence presumed to deduce and invent systems of philosophy, forming everything to conformity with them.

A third set, from their faith and religious veneration, introduce theology and traditions; the absurdity of some among them having proceeded so far as to seek and derive the sciences from spirits and genii. There are, therefore, three sources of error and three species of false philosophy; the sophistic, empiric, and superstitious.

95. Those who have treated of the sciences have been either empirics or dogmatical. The former like ants only heap up and use their store, the latter like spiders spin out their own webs. The bee, a mean between both, extracts matter from the flowers of the garden and the field, but works and fashions it by its own efforts. The true labor of philosophy resembles hers, for it neither relies entirely nor principally on the powers of the mind, nor yet lays up in the memory the matter afforded by the experiments of natural history and mechanics in its raw state, but changes and works it in the understanding. We have good reason, therefore, to derive hope from a closer and purer alliance of these faculties (the experimental and rational) than has yet been attempted.

99. Again, even in the abundance of mechanical experiments, there is a very great scarcity of those which best inform and assist the understanding. For the mechanic, little solicitous about the investigation of truth, neither directs his attention, nor applies his hand to anything that is not of service to his business. But our hope of further progress in the sciences will then only be well founded, when numerous experiments shall be received and collected into natural history, which, though of no use in themselves, assist materially in the discovery of causes and axioms; which experiments we have termed enlightening, to distinguish them from those which are profitable. They possess this wonderful property and nature, that they never deceive or fail you; for being used only to discover the natural cause of some object, whatever be the result, they equally satisfy your aim by deciding the question.

104. Nor can we suffer the understanding to jump and fly from particulars to remote and most general axioms (such as are termed the principles of arts and things), and thus prove and make out their intermediate axioms according to the supposed unshaken truth of the former. This, however, has always been done to the present time from the natural bent of the understanding, educated too, and accustomed to this very method, by the syllogistic mode of demonstration. But we can then only augur well for the sciences, when the ascent shall proceed by a true scale, and successive steps, without interruption or breach, from particulars to the lesser axioms, thence to the intermediate (rising

one above the other), and lastly, to the most general. For the lowest axioms differ but little from bare experiments; the highest and most general (as they are esteemed at present), are notional, abstract, and of no real weight. The intermediate are true, solid, full of life, and upon them depend the business and fortune of mankind; beyond these are the really general, but not abstract, axioms, which are truly limited by the intermediate.

We must not then add wings, but rather lead and ballast to the understanding, to prevent its jumping or flying, which has not yet been done; but whenever this takes place, we may entertain greater hopes of the sciences.

105. In forming axioms, we must invent a different form of induction from that hitherto in use; not only for the proof and discovery of principles (as they are called), but also of minor, intermediate, and, in short, every kind of axioms. The induction which proceeds by simple enumeration is puerile, leads to uncertain conclusions, and is exposed to danger from one contradictory instance, deciding generally from too small a number of facts, and those only the most obvious. But a really useful induction for the discovery and demonstration of the arts and sciences, should separate nature by proper rejections and exclusions, and then conclude for the affirmative, after collecting a sufficient number of negatives. Now this has not been done, nor even attempted, except perhaps by Plato, who certainly uses this form of induction in some measure, to sift definitions and ideas. But much of what has never yet entered the thoughts of man must necessarily be employed, in order to exhibit a good and legitimate mode of induction or demonstration, so as even to render it essential for us to bestow more pains upon it than have hitherto been bestowed on syllogisms. The assistance of induction is to serve us not only in the discovery of axioms, but also in defining our notions. Much indeed is to be hoped from such an induction as has been described.

2 / THEORY OF KNOWLEDGE

Naturalism not only is interested in historical interpretations of science such as that of Bacon, but it continues both to be concerned with the philosophy of science and to base itself upon scientific method. It is not surprising, therefore, that in his epistemology the naturalist proposes that science is man's only sure path to knowledge. A more recent statement of this position is given in the following selection by the American thinker Charles Sanders Peirce. His interpretation of science is pragmatic, in that he believes that thinking always begins in doubt or felt tensions and aims at consequences that will remove such doubt. Pragmatism means for him that the conceived consequences involved in an idea constitute the meaning of the idea.

Peirce characterizes doubt as a state of irritation that we seek to overcome; and he calls the process of removing doubt and establishing belief "inquiry." Three methods, followed by the great majority of mankind, produce sure belief but not necessarily true belief. He calls them the method of tenacity, of authority, and the a priori method. Only a fourth, the scientific method, presents any distinction of a right and a wrong way, according to Peirce, and thus allows for true as well as sure belief. Science accomplishes this because, unlike the other methods, it involves a new conception—namely, that of Reality.

Although his influence on naturalism has been great, Peirce was not himself a naturalist. In fact, he admired in some ways absolute idealism, believing that although the logic of idealists is bad, their conclusions are essentially right. Yet it is Peirce's work in logic and the philosophy of science rather than in metaphysics that has had the predominant influence.

INQUIRY AND BELIEF

C. S. Peirce (1839-1914)

Few persons care to study logic, because everybody conceives himself to be proficient enough in the art of reasoning already. But I observe that this satisfaction is limited to one's own ratiocination, and does not extend to that of other men.

We come to the full possession of our power of drawing inferences the last of all our faculties, for it is not so much a natural gift as a long and difficult art. The history of its practice would make a grand subject for a book. The medieval schoolmen, following the Romans, made logic the earliest of a boy's studies after grammar, as being very easy. So it was, as they understood it. Its fundamental principle, according to them, was, that all knowledge rests on either authority or reason; but that whatever is deduced by reason depends ultimately on a premise derived from authority. Accordingly, as soon as a boy was perfect in the syllogistic procedure, his intellectual kit of tools was held to be complete.

To Roger Bacon, that remarkable mind who in the middle of the thirteenth century was almost a scientific man, the schoolmen's conception of reasoning appeared only an obstacle to truth. He saw that experience alone teaches anything—a proposition which to us seems easy to understand, be-

cause a distinct conception of experience has been handed down to us from former generations; which to him also seemed perfectly clear, because its difficulties had not yet unfolded themselves. Of all kinds of experience, the best, he thought, was interior illumination, which teaches many things about Nature which the external senses could never discover, such as the transubstantiation of bread.

Four centuries later, the more celebrated Bacon, in the first book of his "Novum Organum," gave his clear account of experience as something which must be opened to verification and re-examination. But, superior as Lord Bacon's conception is to earlier notions, a modern reader who is not in awe of his grandiloquence is chiefly struck by the inadequacy of his view of scientific procedure. That we have only to make some crude experiments, to draw up briefs of the results in certain blank forms, to go through these by rule, checking off everything disproved and setting down the alternatives, and that thus in a few years physical science would be finished up— what an idea! "He wrote on science like a Lord Chancellor," indeed.

The early scientists, Copernicus, Tycho Brahe, Kepler, Galileo and Gilbert, had methods more like those of their modern brethren. Kepler undertook to draw a curve through the places of Mars; and his greatest service to science was in impressing on

The selection is from Peirce's article, "The Fixation of Belief," *The Popular Science Monthly*, 12 (1877-1878), pp. 1-15, with omissions.

men's minds that this was the thing to be done if they wished to improve astronomy; that they were not to content themselves with inquiring whether one system of epicycles was better than another but that they were to sit down by the figures and find out what the curve, in truth, was. He accomplished this by his incomparable energy and courage, blundering along in the most inconceivable way (to us), from one irrational hypothesis to another, until, after trying twenty-two of these, he fell, by the mere exhaustion of his invention, upon the orbit which a mind well furnished with the weapons of modern logic would have tried almost at the outset.

In the same way, every work of science great enough to be remembered for a few generations affords some exemplification of the defective state of the art of reasoning of the time when it was written; and each chief step in science has been a lesson in logic. It was so when Lavoisier and his contemporaries took up the study of Chemistry. The old chemist's maxim had been, "Lege, lege, lege, labora, ora, et relege." Lavoisier's method was not to read and pray, not to dream that some long and complicated chemical process would have a certain effect, to put it into practice with dull patience, after its inevitable failure, to dream that with some modification it would have another result, and to end by publishing the last dream as a fact: his way was to carry his mind into his laboratory, and to make of his alembics and cucurbits instruments of thought, giving a new conception of reasoning as something which was to be done with one's eyes open, by manipulating real things instead of word and fancies. . . .

The object of reasoning is to find out, from the consideration of what we already know, something else which we do not know. Consequently, reasoning is good if it be such as to give a true conclusion from true premises, and not otherwise. Thus, the question of validity is purely one of fact and not of thinking. A being the premises and B being the conclusion, the question is, whether these facts are really so related that if A is B is. If so, the inference is valid; if not, not. It is not in the least the question whether, when the premises are accepted by the mind, we feel an impulse to accept the conclusion also. It is true that we do generally reason correctly by nature. But that is an accident; the true conclusion would remain true if we had no impulse to accept it; and the false one would remain false, though we could not resist the tendency to believe in it. . . .

That which determines us, from given premises, to draw one inference rather than another, is some habit of mind, whether it be constitutional or acquired. The habit is good or otherwise, according as it produces true conclusions from true premises or not; and an inference is regarded as valid or not, without reference to the truth or falsity of its conclusion specially, but according as the habit which determines it is such as to produce true conclusions in general or not. The particular habit of mind which governs this or that inference may be formulated in a proposition whose truth depends on the validity of the inferences which the habit determines; and such a formula is called a *guiding principle* of inference. Suppose, for example, that we observe that a rotating disk of copper quickly comes to rest when placed between the poles of a magnet, and we infer that this will happen with every disk of copper. The guiding principle is, that what is true of one piece of copper is true of another. Such a guiding principle with regard to copper would be much safer than with regard to many other substances —brass, for example. . . .

We generally know when we wish to ask a question and when we wish to pronounce a judgment, for there is a dissimilarity between the sensation of doubting and that of believing.

But this is not all which distinguishes doubt from belief. There is a practical difference. Our beliefs guide our desires and shape our actions. The Assassins, or followers of the Old Man of the Mountain, used to rush into death at his least command, because they believed that obedience to him would insure everlasting felicity. Had they doubted this, they would not have acted as they did. So it is with every belief, according to its degree. The feeling of believing is a more or less sure indication of there being established in our nature some habit which will determine our actions. Doubt never has such an effect.

Nor must we overlook a third point of difference. Doubt is an uneasy and dissatisfied state from which we struggle to free ourselves and pass into the state of belief; while the latter is a calm and satisfactory state which we do not wish to avoid, or to change to a belief in anything else. On the contrary, we cling tenaciously, not merely to believing, but to believing just what we do believe.

Thus, both doubt and belief have positive effects upon us, though very different ones. Belief does not make us act at once, but puts us into such a condition that we shall behave in a certain way, when the occasion arises. Doubt has not the least effect of this sort, but stimulates us to action until it is destroyed. This reminds us of the irritation of a nerve and the reflex action produced thereby; while for the analogue of belief, in the nervous system, we must look to what are called nervous associations—for example, to that habit of the nerves in consequence of which the smell of a peach will make the mouth water.

The irritation of doubt causes a struggle to attain a state of belief. I shall term this struggle *inquiry*, though it must be admitted that this is sometimes not a very apt designation.

The irritation of doubt is the only immediate motive for the struggle to attain belief. It is certainly best for us that our beliefs should be such as may truly guide our actions so as to satisfy our desires; and this reflection will make us reject any belief which does not seem to have been so formed as to insure this result. But it will only do so by creating a doubt in the place of that belief. With the doubt, therefore, the struggle begins, and with the cessation of doubt it ends. Hence, the sole object of inquiry is the settlement of opinion. We may fancy that this is not enough for us, and that we seek not merely an opinion, but a true opinion. But put this fancy to the test, and it proves groundless; for as soon as a firm belief is reached we are entirely satisfied, whether the belief be false or true. And it is clear that nothing out of the sphere of our knowledge can be our object, for nothing which does not affect the mind can be a motive for a mental effort. The most that can be maintained is, that we seek for a belief that we shall *think* to be true. But we think each one of our beliefs to be true, and, indeed, it is mere tautology to say so. . . .

If the settlement of opinion is the sole object of inquiry, and if belief is of the nature of a habit, why should we not attain the desired end, by taking any answer to a question, which we may fancy, and constantly reiterating it to ourselves, dwelling on all which may conduce to that belief, and learning to turn with contempt and hatred from anything which might disturb it? The simple and direct method is really pursued by many men. I remember once being entreated not to read a certain newspaper lest it might change my opinion upon free-trade. "Lest I might be entrapped by its fallacies and misstatements," was the form of expression. "You are not," my friend said, "a special student of political economy. You might, therefore, easily be deceived by fallacious arguments upon the subject. You might, then, if you read this paper, be led to believe in protection. But you admit that free-trade is the true doctrine; and you do not wish to believe what is not true." I have often known this system to be deliberately adopted. Still oftener, the instinctive dislike of an undecided state of mind, exaggerated into a vague dread of doubt, makes men cling spasmodically to the views they already take. The man feels that, if he only holds to his belief without wavering, it will be entirely satisfactory. Nor can it be denied that a steady and immovable faith yields great peace of mind. It may, indeed, give rise to inconveniences, as if a man should resolutely continue to believe that fire would not burn him, or that he would be eternally damned if he received his *ingesta* otherwise than through a stomach-pump. But then the man who adopts this method will not allow that its inconveniences are greater than its advantages. He will say, "I hold steadfastly to the truth and the truth is always wholesome." . . .

But this method of fixing belief, which may be called the method of tenacity, will be unable to hold its ground in practice. The social impulse is against it. The man who adopts it will find that other men think differently from him, and it will be apt to occur to him in some saner moment that their opinions are quite as good as his own, and this will shake his confidence in his belief. This conception, that another man's thought or sentiment may be equivalent to one's own, is a distinctly new step, and a highly important one. It arises from an impulse too strong in man to be suppressed, without danger of destroying the human species. Unless we make ourselves hermits, we shall necessarily influence each other's opinions; so that the problem becomes how to fix belief, not in the individual merely, but in the community.

Let the will of the state act, then, instead of that of the individual. Let an institution be created which shall have for its object to keep correct doctrines before the attention of the people, to reiterate them perpetually, and to teach them to the young; having at the same time power to prevent contrary doctrines from being taught, advocated, or expressed. Let all possible causes of a change of mind be removed from men's apprehensions. Let them be kept ignorant, lest they should learn of some reason to think otherwise than they do. Let their passions be enlisted, so that they may regard private and unusual opinions with hatred and horror. Then, let all men who reject the established belief be terrified into silence. Let the people turn out and tar-and-feather such men, or let inquisitions be made into the manner of thinking of suspected persons, and, when they are found guilty of forbidden beliefs, let them be subjected to some signal punishment. When complete agreement could not otherwise be reached, a general massacre of all who have not thought in a certain way has proved a very effective means of settling opinion in a country. If the power to do this be wanting, let a list of opinions be drawn up, to which no man of the least independence of thought can assent, and let the faithful be required to accept all these propositions, in order to segregate them as radically as possible from the influence of the rest of the world.

This method has, from the earliest times, been one of the chief means of upholding correct theological and political doctrines, and of preserving their universal or catholic character. In Rome, especially, it has been practised from the days of Numa Pompilius to those of Pius Nonus. This is the most perfect example in history; but wherever there is a priesthood—and no religion has been without one—this method has been more or less made use of. Wherever there is an aristocracy, or a guild, or any association of a class of men whose interests depend, or are supposed to depend, on certain propositions, there will be inevitably found some traces of this natural product of social feeling. Cruelties always accompany this system; and when it is consistently carried out, they become atrocities of the most horrible kind in the eyes of any rational man. Nor should this occasion surprise, for the officer of a society does not feel justified in surrendering the interests of that society for the sake of mercy, as he might his own private interests. It is natural, therefore, that sympathy and fellowship should thus produce a most ruthless power.

In judging this method of fixing belief, which may be called the method of authority, we must, in the first place, allow its immeasurable mental and moral superiority to the method of tenacity. Its success is proportionately greater; and, in fact, it has over and over again worked the most majestic results. The mere structures of stone which it has caused to be put together —in Siam, for example, in Egypt, and in Europe—have many of them a sublimity hardly more than rivalled by the greatest works of Nature. And, except the geological epochs, there are no periods of time so vast as those which are measured by some of these organized faiths. If we scrutinize the matter closely, we shall find that there has not been one of their creeds which has remained always the same; yet the change is so slow as to be imperceptible during one person's life, so that individual belief remains sensibly fixed. For the mass of mankind, then, there is perhaps no better method than this. If it is their highest impulse to be intellectual slaves, then slaves they ought to remain.

But no institution can undertake to regulate opinions upon every subject. Only the most important ones can be attended to, and on the rest men's minds must be left to the action of natural causes. This imperfection will be no source of weakness so long as men are in such a state of culture that one opinion does not influence another —that is, so long as they cannot put two

and two together. But in the most priest-ridden states some individuals will be found who are raised above that condition. These men possess a wider sort of social feeling; they see that men in other countries and in other ages have held to very different doctrines from those which they themselves have been brought up to believe; and they cannot help seeing that it is the mere accident of their having been taught as they have, and of their having been surrounded with the manners and associations they have, that has caused them to believe as they do and not far differently. Nor can their candor resist the reflection that there is no reason to rate their own views at a higher value than those of other nations and other centuries; thus giving rise to doubts in their minds.

They will further perceive that such doubts as these must exist in their minds with reference to every belief which seems to be determined by the caprice either of themselves or of those who originated the popular opinions. The willful adherence to a belief, and the arbitrary forcing of it upon others, must, therefore, both be given up. A different new method of settling opinions must be adopted, that shall not only produce an impulse to believe, but shall also decide what proposition it is which is to be believed. Let the action of natural preferences be unimpeded, then, and under their influence let men, conversing together and regarding matters in different lights, gradually develop beliefs in harmony with natural causes. This method resembles that by which conceptions of art have been brought to maturity. The most perfect example of it is to be found in the history of metaphysical philosophy. Systems of this sort have not usually rested upon any observed facts, at least not in any great degree. They have been chiefly adopted because their fundamental propositions seemed "agreeable to reason." This is an apt expression; it does not mean that which agrees with experience, but that which we find ourselves inclined to believe. Plato, for example, finds it agreeable to reason that the distances of the celestial spheres from one another should be proportional to the different lengths of strings which produce harmonious chords. Many philosophers have been led to their main conclusions by considerations like this; but this is the lowest and least developed form which the method takes, for it is clear that another man might find Kepler's theory, that the celestial spheres are proportional to the inscribed and circumscribed spheres of the different regular solids, more agreeable to *his* reason. But the shock of opinions will soon lead men to rest on preferences of a far more universal nature. Take, for example, the doctrine that man only acts selfishly—that is, from the consideration that acting in one way will afford him more pleasure than acting in another. This rests on no fact in the world, but it has had a wide acceptance as being the only reasonable theory.

This method is far more intellectual and respectable from the point of view of reason than either of the others which we have noticed. But its failure has been the most manifest. It makes of inquiry something similar to the development of taste; but taste, unfortunately, is always more or less a matter of fashion, and accordingly metaphysicians have never come to any fixed agreement, but the pendulum has swung backward and forward between a more material and a more spiritual philosophy, from the earliest times to the latest. And so from this, which has been called the *a priori* method, we are driven, in Lord Bacon's phrase, to a true induction. We have examined into this *a priori* method as something which promised to deliver our opinions from their accidental and capricious element. But development, while it is a process which eliminates the effect of some casual circumstances, only magnifies that of others. This method, therefore, does not differ in a very essential way from that of authority. The government may not have lifted its finger to influence my convictions; I may have been left outwardly quite free to choose, we will say, between monogamy and polygamy, and, appealing to my conscience only, I may have concluded that the latter practice is in itself licentious. But when I come to see that the chief obstacle to the spread of Christianity among a people of as high culture as the Hindoos has been a conviction of the immorality of our way of treating women, I cannot help seeing that, though governments do not interfere, sentiments in their development will be very greatly determined by accidental causes. Now, there are some people, among whom I must suppose that my reader is to be found, who, when they see that any belief of theirs is determined by any circumstance extraneous to the facts, will from that moment not merely admit in words that that belief is doubtful, but will experience a real doubt of it, so that it ceases in some degree to be a belief.

To satisfy our doubts, therefore, it is necessary that a method should be found by which our beliefs may be caused by nothing human, but by some external permanency —by something upon which our thinking has no effect. Some mystics imagine that they have such a method in a private inspiration from on high. But that is only a form of the method of tenacity, in which the conception of truth as something public is not yet developed. Our external permanency would not be external, in our sense, if it was restricted in its influence to one individual. It must be something which affects, or might affect, every man. And, though these affections are necessarily as various as are individual conditions, yet the method must be such that the ultimate conclusion of every man shall be the same.

Such is the method of science. Its fundamental hypothesis, restated in more familiar language, is this: There are Real things, whose characters are entirely independent of our opinions about them; those realities affect our senses according to regular laws, and, though our sensations are as different as are our relations to the objects, yet, by taking advantage of the laws of perception, we can ascertain by reasoning how things really are; and any man, if he have sufficient experience and he reason enough about it, will be led to the one True conclusion. The new conception here involved is that of Reality. It may be asked how I know that there are any realities. If this hypothesis is the sole support of my method of inquiry, my method of inquiry must not be used to support my hypothesis. The reply is this: 1. If investigation cannot be regarded as proving that there are Real things, it at least does not lead to a contrary conclusion; but the method and the conception on which it is based remain ever in harmony. No doubts of the method, therefore, necessarily arise from its practice, as is the case with all the others. 2. The feeling which gives rise to any method of fixing belief is a dissatisfaction at two repugnant propositions. But here already is a vague concession that there is some *one* thing to which a proposition should conform. Nobody, therefore, can really doubt that there are realities, for, if he did, doubt would not be a source of dissatisfaction. The hypothesis, therefore, is one which every mind admits. So that the social impulse does not cause men to doubt it. 3. Everybody uses the scientific method about a great many things, and only ceases to use it when he does not know how to apply it. 4. Experience of the method has not led us to doubt it, but, on the contrary, scientific investigation has had the most wonderful triumphs in the way of settling opinion. These afford the explanation of my not doubting the

method or the hypothesis which it supposes; and not having any doubt, nor believing that anybody else whom I could influence has, it would be the merest babble for me to say more about it. If there be anybody with a living doubt upon the subject, let him consider it. . . .

This is the only one of the four methods which presents any distinction of a right and a wrong way. If I adopt the method of tenacity and shut myself out from all influences, whatever I think necessary to doing this is necessary according to that method. So with the method of authority: the state may try to put down heresy by means which, from a scientific point of view, seem very ill-calculated to accomplish its purposes; but the only test *on that method* is what the state thinks, so that it cannot pursue the method wrongly. So with the *a priori* method. The very essence of it is to think as one is inclined to think. All metaphysicians will be sure to do that, however they may be inclined to judge each other to be perversely wrong. The Hegelian system recognizes every natural tendency of thought as logical, although it be certain to be abolished by counter-tendencies. Hegel thinks there is a regular system in the succession of these tendencies, in consequence of which, after drifting one way and the other for a long time, opinion will at last go right. And it is true that metaphysicians get the right ideas at last; Hegel's system of Nature represents tolerably the science of that day; and one may be sure that whatever scientific investigation has put out of doubt will presently receive *a priori* demonstration on the part of the metaphysicians. But with the scientific method the case is different. I may start with known and observed facts to proceed to the unknown; and yet the rules which I follow in doing so may not be such as investigation would approve. The test of whether I am truly following the method is not an immediate appeal to my feelings and purposes, but, on the contrary, itself involves the application of the method. Hence it is that bad reasoning as well as good reasoning is possible; and this fact is the foundation of the practical side of logic.

3 / METAPHYSICS

Naturalists differ in their metaphysical writings and outlooks, depending on whether they tend to speculativeness or caution in their generalizations about nature. The following selection from the work of the British philosopher Samuel Alexander belongs to the more speculative group.

Alexander views nature as a cosmic process within which are critical points where new qualities emerge and where, therefore, new levels of nature develop. To sketch this view quickly: the original matrix of nature is the space-time continuum. From space-time have emerged the levels of primary qualities, secondary qualities, life, and mind. The next level of nature, not yet emerged, and whose characteristic qualities cannot therefore be described, is called deity. Alexander insists that these various levels are true emergents and he holds that there are thus limits to attempts to explain them. In the selection he illustrates his point by reference to the emergence of life from physico-chemical properties. Life, he writes, is resolvable without remainder into these properties, but life is not *merely* such. There is a new property, that of life itself, which has emerged from them. The scientist, then, must be careful not to fall into a "metaphysical mania" by asking unanswerable questions; rather, he must accept the mystery of facts in an attitude not unhappily called "natural piety."

EMERGENCE AND THE LEVELS OF NATURE

Samuel Alexander (1859-1938)

I do not mean by natural piety exactly what Wordsworth [1] meant by it—the rev-erent joy in nature, by which he wished that his days might be bound to each other —though there is enough connection with his interpretation to justify me in using his phrase. The natural piety I am going to speak of is that of the scientific investigator, by which he accepts with loyalty the mysteries which he cannot explain in nature and has no right to try to explain. I may describe it as the habit of knowing when to stop in asking questions of nature. The limits to the right of asking questions are drawn differently for different purposes. They are not the same in science as in ordinary intercourse between men in conversation. I may recall an incident in the life of Dr. Johnson. I was once present, says

The selection is from Alexander's article, "Natural Piety," *The Hibbert Journal,* 20 (1921-1922), pp. 609-621, with omissions. Used by permission of the Editor.
[1 In the fragment beginning "My heart leaps up" and ending

The Child is Father of the man:
And I could wish my days to be
    Bound each to each by natural piety.
He also used the phrase in *The Excursion,* Bk. III, line 266:
Such acquiescence neither doth imply
In me, a meekly-blending spirit soothed
By natural piety; nor a lofty mind
By philosophic discipline prepared
For calm subjection to acknowledged
    law. *Ed.*]

Boswell, when a gentleman (perhaps it was Boswell himself) asked so many (questions), as "What did you do, sir?" "What did you say, sir?" that at last he grew enraged, and said, "I will not be put to the *question*. Don't you consider, sir, that these are not the manners of a gentleman? I will not be baited with *what* and *why*. What is this? What is that? Why is a cow's tail long? Why is a fox's tail bushy?" Boswell adds that the gentleman, who was a good deal out of countenance, said, "Why, sir, you are so good, that I venture to trouble you." JOHNSON.—"Sir, my being so *good* is no reason why you should be so *ill*." The questions which Johnson regarded as typically offensive in conversation about the cow's and the fox's tail might quite legitimately be asked in science, and I fancy, answered by a naturalist without any particular difficulty. There is a mental disease known as the questioning or metaphysical mania, which cannot accept anything, even the most trivial, without demanding explanation. Why do I stand here where I stand? Why is a glass a glass, a chair a chair? How is it that men are only of the size they are? Why not as big as houses? etc. (I quote from William James.) Now the very life of knowledge depends on asking questions. Is it not called inquiry? And its limits are not drawn by considerations of politeness or by shrinking from insanity. But it does recognize that, however far it may push its explanations, the world presents characters which must be accepted reverently as beyond explanation, though they do not pass understanding. And I call this habit af acceptance of nature by the name of natural piety, because simple-minded religion is accustomed to speak of events for which it can find no reason as the will of God. . . .

[The features which can be] traced in human affairs; new creations which lend an unexplained and strange flavor to existing institutions and remodel them; external habits and ways of life retained but their inward meaning transformed; immense complexities of elements, hitherto chaotic, now gathering themselves together and as it were flowering into some undreamed simplicity; these features are found in the nature of which man is but the latest stage. Nature is "stratified," and if we apply to it our customary conceptions of growth and development, we can regard it as a geological formation with a history. But the comparison is still inadequate; for new geological strata are but fresh deposits laid down upon the subjacent ones, not drawing from them their new life. Nature is rather a history of organic growth of species, in which the new type of organism is the outgrowth of the older type, and continues the earlier life into a form at once more complex and more highly simplified. As there is in the animal world or the plant world a hierarchy of forms, so in nature there is a hierarchy of qualities which are characteristics of various levels of development. There are, if I may borrow a metaphor used by Mr. Sellars of Michigan in his recent book,[2] "critical points" in the unfolding of Nature when she gathers up her old resources for a new experiment and breeds a new quality of existence. The earliest of these qualities of being which is familiar to us is that of physical matter, whatever we are to suppose it is that materiality consists in. Other well-marked levels are those of chemical structure and behavior, and life, which is the quality of things which behave physiologically.

I am not concerned to offer a complete enumeration of these levels of existence with their distinguishing qualities. The three qualities mentioned are but a selection. Every attempt at completeness raises questions of difficulty. Certain, however, it is now that mere physical materiality is a

[2 The reference is to the American philosopher Roy Wood Sellars and his book, *Evolutionary Naturalism* (Chicago, 1922). *Ed.*]

highly developed stage, late in the history of the world: that there are forms of sub-material being, and the line between the submaterial and the material is not for me to draw. Neither is it for me to say whether electrons are the lowest existences in the scale. Again, beyond life, some have maintained that mind is itself a new quality which arises out of life, while others treat consciousness merely as a function of all life, and for them consciousness and life are one, and accordingly all the knowing on which we pride ourselves so much is in the end only a special form of vital behavior. There is another debatable question. To me, colors and sounds and tastes and all the sensible characters of material things appear to be resident in things themselves; and colored existence to be a critical point in nature. When a physical body is such that the light which it sends out to our eyes has a determinate wave-length, that body is red. To others, and they are the majority, the color depends upon the possession by the percipient of eyes. These questions I need not raise in this place because they take us away from the central theme into historic problems which have occupied physics and philosophy from the days of Galileo and before. There is still another matter I leave open. Life is without doubt such a critical point in nature. Are the various gradations of life, first of all the difference of plants and animals as a whole, and next the marked differences of kinds among animals and plants themselves, to be regarded likewise? The differences which part a humble amoeba or hydra from the monkey, or even from the lizard or crab, are vast. Are they critical differences? All I need answer is that if they are not, at least the outgrowth of the higher from the lower forms of life helps us mightily to understand the outgrowth at the critical point of the higher level of quality from the lower. Further, if it is right to treat colors as real qualities, not dependent for existence on the physio-logical organs; which are but instruments in that case for apprehending, not for creating them; if this is so, the different kinds of colors—red, green, and the rest—are comparable to the species of animals or plants, and if they do not mark a change of level they mark differences upon that level. All these matters of debate I leave aside, in order to insist on the vital feature of nature that she does exhibit critical changes of quality, which mark new syntheses, that we can but note. We may and must observe with care out of what previous conditions these new creations arise. We cannot tell why they should assume these qualities. We can but accept them as we find them, and this acceptance is natural piety.

These bodies with new qualities, these "creative syntheses," which arise at critical points from a lower level of existence, are therefore no mere mechanical resultants of their lower conditions. If they were they would have merely the quality of their antecedents or components, as the component pulls upon a body along the sides of a parallelogram are equivalent to a resultant pull along the diagonal. Even the chemical combination of sodium and sulphuric acid, though it leads to something new and its process is not purely mechanical, does but issue in a new chemical body, just as the pairing of two living beings may lead to a new variety, but still a variety of living being. They are, therefore, after the usage of the late George Henry Lewes, described as emergents by Mr. Lloyd Morgan, with whom I have for many years shared this conception of things, which he has expounded with a simplicity and lucidity beyond my powers in a chapter of his book, *Instinct and Experience,* and with particular force in the address with which he inaugurated the independent section of Psychology at the recent meeting of the British Association at Edinburgh (1921).

Without attempting to take in the whole

field of nature, I will confine myself here to life, considered as an emergent from the realm of physico-chemical bodies. A living body is, according to this conception, a physico-chemical body of a certain degree and kind of complexity, whose actions may severally be viewed as physical or chemical, but taken in their integration, or entirety (to borrow a word of Lord Haldane's), have the quality of life. Life is therefore resoluble without remainder into physico-chemical processes; but it cannot be treated as *merely* physico-chemical. Certain of its functions may be referred to physical or chemical laws, but it is not these separable processes which constitute life. Life exists only when we have that particular collocation of such physico-chemical actions which we know as living. It is the special co-ordination which conditions the appearance or creation of the new quality of life. We might therefore be disposed to describe the living body indifferently as being a physico-chemical body which is *also* vital, or as being vital and *also* physico-chemical. In reality only the second designation is satisfactory. The first would imply that a certain grouping of such processes remain no more than physical and chemical, that life is not something new but a name for this integration, whereas it is a new quality conditioned by and equivalent to the particular complexity of integration. Given life, we can hope to resolve it into its physico-chemical equivalent. We can even hope to reproduce partially or wholly by artificial means the existence of life. It is well known, for instance, that certain foams or emulsions of oil have exhibited streaming movements like those of living protoplasm. But life has been already attained, and it is our clue to the invention of the necessary machinery. Given mere physical and chemical processes, we can only generate life when we have hit upon the requisite form of integration. Thus life is *also* physico-chemical, because in its separable activities it is

comparable with other physico-chemical processes. But it is not *merely* physico-chemical, because merely physico-chemical processes are not alive, and they do not give us life until the requisite complexity of integration is attained. . . .

The emergence of life with this new collocation of conditions implies that life is continuous with chemical, physical, and mechanical action. To be more explicit, the living body is also physical and chemical. It surrenders no claim to be considered a part of the physical world. But the new quality of life which it possesses is neither chemical nor mechanical, but something new. Thus the parts of the living body have color but life is not colored, and they are material but life itself is not material, but only the body which is alive is material. The lower conditions out of whose collocations life emerges supply a body as it were to a new soul. The specific characters which they possess are not continued into the new soul. The continuity which exists between life and the material does not mean that the material is carried over into life. There would not in that case be continuity between the living body as a new emergent and its predecessors; the living body would be nothing more than an elaborate material mechanism, which would illustrate material action, but could not claim a position of privilege. The characters which *are* continued from the lower level into life are not the specific qualities of the lower level; they are rather those characters which all existence shares in common, such as existence in time and space, intensity, capacity of affecting other existences, all which belong to life as much as to matter. . . .

We are to combine in our thoughts this fundamental unity with the recognition of emergent qualities which can only be accepted but cannot be accounted for. One difficulty in the way of effecting this combination in our thought is the idea that if the world is a determinate growth, each new creation determined by its predecessors on a lower level, the history of the world must be capable of prediction, according to the famous assertion of Laplace.[3] But this conclusion does not follow. Laplace's calculator might foresee that at a certain point a certain complexity might arise, whose actions were capable of measurement and would be those of living things. He could never affirm that this form of action would have the quality of life, unless he lived to see. He might predict ethereal waves but could not predict them to be light; still less that a material body would be material or when touched by light would be red, or even merely look red to a living body with eyes. All known forms of action could be predicted in their measurable characters, but never in their emergent ones. Not even God, if we suppose a God presiding over the birth of the world, in accordance with the conception of the crudest theism, could predict what these emergent qualities would be; he could only accept them like ourselves when the world he made had originated them.

I have chosen as illustrating the attitude of natural piety our acceptance of the emergence of these qualities. They remain for ever a mysterious fact. But they are after all only a part of the mystery which encompasses us and which we have no right to ask to penetrate. They are themselves related to simpler conditions, which it is the object of science to discover. Some persons have even supposed, following the precedent of the early Greek philosophers, and in particular of the chief Pythagorean speaker in Plato's great dialogue, the *Timaeus*, that all these features in the world are but specifications of some ultimate stuff

[3 Pierre Simon Laplace (1749-1827), French mathematician and astronomer who produced a systematized theory of celestial mechanics that would in principle allow mathematical prediction of any event. Once, when asked whether a God was required to complete his explanatory theory, he replied, "I have no need of that hypothesis." *Ed.*]

of which the world is made. If this were true, it might be repugnant to the feelings of some, but natural piety would accept it, as it accepts the law of gravitation, or the law of the progression in the forms of life according to evolution, whatever the law of evolution may turn out to be; or as it would accept, if we are compelled to think so, that the four-dimensional space-time in which we live is bent in the neighborhood of matter. All science attempts to connect the variegated phenomena of the world by expressing them in terms of measurable motions. It seems to take the color and richness from the world of secondary sensible qualities and expresses them in terms of primary qualities which in the end are terms of space and time. It does not, nor does it pretend to remove, the mystery of these qualities, and in all its explanations it does but bring us in face of other mysteries which we must needs accept.

We are thus for ever in presence of miracles; and as old Nathan said, the greatest of all miracles is that the genuine miracles should be so familiar. And here I interpolate a remark, not altogether irrelevant to my subject, upon the uses of great men. The emergence of qualities is the familiar miracle, but great men, and in particular great men of science, are for ever enlarging our mysteries, simplifying them and extending their scope, as when they record the law of attraction, or the idea which lies at the basis of the notion of relativity. And thus with their fresher insight they keep for us our sense of piety to nature alive. Compared with other men they are like the springs of a river. . . .

The mystery of facts, whether these facts are the individual facts of experience or the larger universal facts which are scientific laws, or such facts, more comprehensive still, as may be discovered by a prudent and scientific philosophy, is the last word of knowledge. The reverent temper which accepts them is the mood of natural piety.

4 / ETHICS

Man's moral life, the naturalist holds, is as natural as life itself; it must therefore be understood as natural to him. Ralph Barton Perry attempts to make this formulation in the following selection. When life emerges in nature, it introduces a bias that in turn produces value in an otherwise valueless cosmos. That bias is interest, which produces struggle—the organism seeks to preserve itself and to have its demands satisfied—and the distinction of good and bad. Goodness then is simply the fulfillment of interest, or the satisfaction of desire. Morality, in turn, produces a community of interests or a civilization, for it involves choices so as to mass interests in the struggle of life against a reluctant nature.

ETHICAL NATURALISM

Ralph Barton Perry (1876-1957)

The moral affair of men, a prolonged and complicated historical enterprise, is thrown into historical relief upon the background of a mechanical cosmos. Nature, as interpreted by the inorganic sciences, presents a spectacle of impassivity. It moves, transforms, and radiates, on every scale and in all its gigantic range of temporal and spatial distance, utterly without loss or gain of value. One cannot rightly attribute to such a world even the property of neglect or brutality. Its indifference is absolute.

Such a world is devoid of value because of the elimination of the bias of life. Where no interest is at stake, changes can make no practical difference; where no claims are made, there can be neither fortune nor calamity, neither comedy nor tragedy. There is no object of applause or resentment, if there be nothing in whose behalf such judgments may be urged.

But with the introduction of life, even the least particle of it, the rudest bit of protoplasm that ever made the venture, nature becomes a new system with a new

center. The organism inherits the earth; the mechanisms of nature become its environment, its resources in the struggle to keep for a time body and soul together. The mark of life is partiality for itself. If anything is to become an object of solicitude, it must first announce itself through acting in its own behalf. With life thus instituted there begins the long struggle of interest against inertia and indifference, that war of which civilization itself is only the latest and most triumphant phase.

Nature being thus enlivened, the simpler terms of value now find a meaning. A living thing must suffer calamities or achieve successes; and since its fortunes are *good* or *bad* in the most elementary sense that can be attached to these conceptions, it is worth our while to consider the matter with some care. An *interest*, or unit of life, is essentially an organization which consistently acts for its own preservation. It deals with its environment in such wise as to keep itself intact and bring itself to maturity; appropriating what it needs, and avoiding or destroying what threatens it with injury. The interest so functions as to supply itself with the means whereby it may continue to exist and function. This is the principle of action which may be gen-

Reprinted with the permission of Charles Scribner's Sons from *The Moral Economy* by Ralph Barton Perry, copyright 1909 Charles Scribner's Sons; renewal copyright 1937 Ralph Barton Perry, pp. 9-16, 20, and 22-24.

eralized from its behavior, and through which it may be distinguished within the context of nature. Now the term *interest* being construed in this sense, we may describe goodness as *fulfilment of interest*. The description will perhaps refer more clearly to human life, if for the term *interest* we substitute the term *desire*. Goodness would then consist in the *satisfaction of desire*. In other words, things are good because desired, not desired because good. To say that one desires things because one needs them, or likes them, or admires them, is redundant; in the end one simply desires certain things, that is, one possesses an interest or desire which they fulfil. There are as many varieties of goodness as there are varieties of interest; and to the variety of interest there is no end.

Strictly speaking, goodness belongs to an interest's actual state of fulfilment. This will consist in an activity, exercised by the interest, but employing the environment. With a slight shift of emphasis, goodness in this absolute sense will attach either to interest in so far as nourished by objects, as in the case of hunger appeased, or to objects in so far as assimilated to interest, as in the case of food consumed. It follows that goodness in a relative sense, in the sense of "good for," will attach to whatever *conduces* to good in the absolute sense; that is, actions and objects, such as agriculture and bread, that lead directly or indirectly to the fulfilment of interest. But "good" and "good for," like their opposite "bad" and "bad for," are never sharply distinguishable, because the imagination anticipates the fortunes of interests, and transforms even remote contingencies into actual victory or defeat.

Through their organization into life, the mechanisms of nature thus take on the generic quality of good and evil. They either serve interests or oppose them; and must be employed and assimilated, or avoided and rejected accordingly. Events which once indifferently happened are now objects of hope and fear, or integral parts of success and failure.

But that organization of life which denotes the presence of morality has not yet been defined. The isolated interest extricates itself from mechanism; and, struggling to maintain itself, does, it is true, divide the world into good and bad, according to its uses. But the moral drama opens only when interest meets interest; when the path of one unit of life is crossed by that of another. Every interest is compelled to recognize other interests, on the one hand as parts of its environment, and on the other hand as partners in the general enterprise of life. Thus there is evolved the *moral* idea, or principle of action, according to which *interest allies itself with interest in order to be free-handed and powerful* against the common hereditary enemy, the heavy inertia and the incessant wear of the cosmos. Through morality a plurality of interests becomes an *economy*, or *community of interests*.

I have thus far described the situation as though it were essentially a social one. But while, historically speaking, it is doubtless always social in one of its aspects, the essence of the matter is as truly represented within the group of interests sustained by a single organism, when these, for example, are united in an individual life-purpose. Morality is that procedure in which several interests, whether they involve one or more physical organisms, are so adjusted as to function as one interest, more massive in its support, and more coherent and united in the common task of fulfilment. Interests morally combined are not destroyed or superseded, as are mechanical forces, by their resultant. The power of the higher interest is due to a summing of incentives emanating from the contributing interests; it can perpetuate itself only through keeping these interests alive. The most spectacular instance of this is government, which functions as one, and yet derives its power from an enormous variety of different interests, which it must foster and conserve as the sources of its own life. In all cases the strength of morality must lie in its liberality and breadth.

Morality is simply the forced choice between suicide and abundant life. When interests war against one another they render the project of life, at best a hard adventure, futile and abortive. I hold it to be of prime importance for the understanding of this matter to observe that from the poorest and crudest beginnings, morality is *the massing of interests against a reluctant cosmos*. Life has been attended with discord and mutual destruction, but this is its failure. The first grumbling truce between savage enemies, the first collective enterprise, the first peaceful community, the first restraint on gluttony for the sake of health, the first suppression of ferocity for the sake of a harder blow struck in cold blood,—these were the first victories of morality. They were moral victories in that they organized life into more comprehensive unities, making it a more formidable thing, and securing a more abundant satisfaction. The fact that life thus combined and weighted, was hurled against life, was the lingering weakness, the deficiency which attends upon all partial attainment. The moral triumph lay in the positive access of strength.

Let us now correct our elementary conceptions of value so that they may apply to moral value. The fulfilment of a simple isolated interest is good, but only *the fulfilment of an organization of interests* is morally good. Such goodness appears in the realization of an individual's systematic purpose or in the well-being of a community. That it virtually implies one ultimate good, the fulfilment of the system of all interests, must necessarily follow; although we cannot at present deal adequately with that conclusion.

The quality of moral goodness, like the quality of goodness in the fundamental sense, lies not in the nature of any class of objects, but in any object or activity whatsoever, in so far as this provides a fulfilment of interest or desire. In the case of moral goodness this fulfilment must embrace a group of interests in which each is limited by the others. Its value lies not only in fulfilment, but also in adjustment and harmony. And this value is independent of the special subject-matter of the interests. Moralists have generally agreed that it is impossible to conceive moral goodness exclusively in terms of any special interest, even such as honor, power, or wealth. There is no interest so rare or so humble that its fulfilment is not morally good, provided that fulfilment forms part of the systematic fulfilment of a group of interests. . . .

There is an old and unprofitable quarrel between those who identify, and those who contrast, morality with *nature*. To adjudicate this quarrel, it is necessary to define a point at which nature somehow exceeds herself. Strictly speaking, it is as arbitrary to say that morality, which arose and is immersed in nature, is not natural, as to say that magnetism and electricity are not natural. If nature be defined in terms of the categories of any stage of complexity, all beyond will wear the aspect of a miracle. It would be proper to dismiss the question as only a trivial matter of terminology, did not the discussion of it provide an occasion for alluding to certain confused notions that have obtained wide currency. . . .

If one insists still upon drawing a line between cosmical and moral forces, let it be drawn at the point where there first arises that unstable complex called life. Life does in a sense oppose itself to the balance of nature. To hold itself together, it must play at parry and thrust with the very forces which gave it birth. Once having happened, it so acts as to persist. But it should be remarked that this opposition between the careless and rough course of the cosmos, the insidious forces of dissolution, on the one hand, and the self-preserving care of the organism on the other, is present absolutely from the outset of life.

Vegetable and animal organisms do, it is true, adapt themselves to the environment; but their adaptation is essentially a method of using and modifying the environment in their own favor, precisely as is the case with human action. Therefore Huxley's sharp distinction between natural plant life and man's artificial garden is misleading.

"The tendency of the cosmic process," he says, "is to bring about the adjustment of the forms of plant life to the current conditions; the tendency of the horticultural process is the adjustment of the conditions to the needs of the forms of plant life which the gardener desires to raise." [1]

But this is to ignore the basal fact, which is that plant life in any form is a defiance of current conditions. Art has already begun when natural processes assume a form that feeds itself, reproduces itself, and

[1 Perry refers to the work of the renowned English scientist Thomas Henry Huxley (1825-1895) who devoted himself to a defense of evolutionism. *Ed.*]

grows. The first organisms have only a local footing; they are rooted in the soil, and can turn to their advantage only the conditions characteristic of a time and place. Eventually there evolves a more resourceful unit of life, like the gardener with his cultivated plants, who is capable of inhabiting nature at large. But the method is still the same, that of playing off nature against nature; only it is now done on a larger scale, and in a more aggressive and confident spirit. The need of concession to the demands of locality is reduced, through a concession once and for all to the wider processes of nature. But in relation to its environment, life is never wholly constructive, as it is never wholly passive. Whether it appears in the form of vegetation or civilization, it always involves both an adaptation of nature to itself and of itself to nature.

Morality, then, is natural if life is natural; for it is defined by the same essential principles. It is related to life as a later to an earlier phase of one development. The organization of life answers the self-preservative impulse with which life begins; the deliberate fulfilment of a human purpose is only life grown strong enough through organization to conduct a larger and more adventurous enterprise.

5 / ESTHETICS

Life is more than science, even though science for the naturalist is the most reliable way to knowledge. Among the other dimensions of experience is the esthetic. As with morality, naturalists treat art and the esthetic within nature and experience rather than going beyond them.

The writings of John Dewey provide such a naturalistic interpretation. Dewey defines experience as the interaction of organism and environment, a doing and an undergoing. But experience must be distinguished from *an* experience, for things are not always composed to produce the latter. An experience is had only when the materials experienced led to completion and fulfillment.

A work of art produces such an experience, for its different parts fuse in a unity without losing their own characters, and the unity involves a single pervasive quality. The esthetic experience is thus a total, integrated experience, intrinsically worthwhile, of an emotionally satisfying quality. Dewey points out, however, that art is not alone in producing this quality; thinking, for example, is like art in this respect, differing from art only in its materials.

ART AS EXPERIENCE

John Dewey (1859-1952)

Experience is the result, the sign, and the reward of that interaction of organism and environment which, when it is carried to the full, is a transformation of interaction into participation and communication. Since sense-organs with their connected motor apparatus are the means of this participation, any and every derogation of them, whether practical or theoretical, is at once effect and cause of a narrowed and dulled life-experience. Oppositions of mind and body, soul and matter, spirit and flesh all have their origin, fundamentally, in fear of what life may bring forth. They are marks of contraction and withdrawal. Full recognition, therefore, of the continuity of the organs, needs and basic impulses of the human creature with his animal forbears, implies no necessary reduction of man to the level of the brutes. On the contrary, it makes possible the drawing of a ground-plan of human experience upon which is erected the superstructure of man's marvelous and distinguishing experience. What is distinctive in man makes it possible for him to sink below the level of the beasts. It also makes it possible for him to carry to new and unprecedented heights that unity of sense and impulse, of brain and eye and ear, that is exemplified in animal life, saturating it with the conscious meanings derived from communication and deliberate expression. . . .

Experience occurs continuously, because the interaction of live creature and environing conditions is involved in the very process of living. Under conditions of resistance and conflict, aspects and elements of the self and the world that are implicated in this interaction qualify experience with emotions and ideas so that conscious intent emerges. Oftentimes, however, the experience had is inchoate. Things are experienced but not in such a way that they are composed into *an* experience. There are distraction and dispersion; what we observe and what we think, what we desire and what we get, are at odds with each other. We put our hands to the plow and turn back; we start and then we stop, not because the experience has reached the end for the sake of which it was initiated but because of extraneous interruptions or of inner lethargy.

In contrast with such experience, we have *an* experience when the material experienced runs its course to fulfillment. Then and then only is it integrated within and demarcated in the general stream of experience from other experiences. A piece of work is finished in a way that is satisfactory; a problem receives its solution; a game is played through; a situation, whether that of eating a meal, playing a game of chess, carrying on a conversation, writing a book, or taking part in a political campaign, is so rounded out that its close is a consummation and not a cessation. Such an experience is a whole and carries with it

The selection is from pp. 22-44, with omissions, of *Art as Experience* by John Dewey. Copyright 1934 by John Dewey. Published by Minton, Balch & Co. and George Allen & Unwin, Ltd. Used by permission of G. P. Putnam's Sons and of George Allen & Unwin, Ltd.

its own individualizing quality and self-sufficiency. It is *an* experience.

Philosophers, even empirical philosophers, have spoken for the most part of experience at large. Idiomatic speech, however, refers to experiences each of which is singular, having its own beginning and end. For life is no uniform uninterrupted march or flow. It is a thing of histories, each with its own plot, its own inception and movement toward its close, each having its own particular rhythmic movement; each with its own unrepeated quality pervading it throughout. A flight of stairs, mechanical as it is, proceeds by individualized steps, not by undifferentiated progression, and an inclined plane is at least marked off from other things by abrupt discreteness.

Experience in this vital sense is defined by those situations and episodes that we spontaneously refer to as being "real experiences"; those things of which we say in recalling them, "that *was* an experience." It may have been something of tremendous importance—a quarrel with one who was once an intimate, a catastrophe finally averted by a hair's breadth. Or it may have been something that in comparison was slight—and which perhaps because of its very slightness illustrates all the better what is to be an experience. There is that meal in a Paris restaurant of which one says "that *was* an experience." It stands out as an enduring memorial of what food may be. Then there is that storm one went through in crossing the Atlantic—the storm that seemed in its fury, as it was experienced, to sum up in itself all that a storm can be, complete in itself, standing out because marked out from what went before and what came after.

In such experiences, every successive part flows freely, without seam and without unfilled blanks, into what ensues. At the same time there is no sacrifice of the self-identity of the parts. A river, as distinct from a pond, flows. But its flow gives a definiteness and interest to its successive portions greater than exist in the homogeneous portions of a pond. In an experience, flow is from something to something. As one part leads into another and as one part carries on what went before, each gains distinctness in itself. The enduring whole is diversified by successive phases that are emphases of its varied colors.

Because of continuous merging, there are no holes, mechanical junctions, and dead centers when we have *an* experience. There are pauses, places of rest, but they punctuate and define the quality of movement. They sum up what has been undergone and prevent its dissipation and idle evaporation. Continued acceleration is breathless and prevents parts from gaining distinction. In a work of art, different acts, episodes, occurrences melt and fuse into unity, and yet do not disappear and lose their own character as they do so—just as in a genial conversation there is a continuous interchange and blending, and yet each speaker not only retains his own character but manifests it more clearly than is his wont.

An experience has a unity that gives it its name, that meal, that storm, that rupture of friendship. The existence of this unity is constituted by a single *quality* that pervades the entire experience in spite of the variation of its constituent parts. This unity is neither emotional, practical, nor intellectual, for these terms name distinctions that reflection can make within it. In discourse *about* an experience, we must make use of these adjectives of interpretation. In going over an experience in mind *after* its occurrence, we may find that one property rather than another was sufficiently dominant so that it characterizes the experience as a whole. There are absorbing inquiries and speculations which a scientific man and philosopher will recall as "experiences" in the emphatic sense. In final import they are intellectual. But in their actual occurrence they were emotional as well; they were purposive and volitional. Yet the experience was not a sum of these different characters; they were lost in it as distinctive traits. No thinker can ply his occupation save as he is lured and rewarded by total integral experiences that are intrinsically worth while. Without them he would never know what it is really to think and would be completely at a loss in distinguishing real thought from the spurious article. Thinking goes on in trains of ideas, but the ideas form a train only because they are much more than what an analytic psychology calls ideas. They are phases, emotionally and practically distinguished, of a developing underlying quality; they are its moving variations, not separate and independent like Locke's and Hume's so-called ideas and impressions, but are subtle shadings of a pervading and developing hue. . . .

Hence *an* experience of thinking has its own esthetic quality. It differs from those experiences that are acknowledged to be esthetic, but only in its materials. The material of the fine arts consists of qualities; that of experience having intellectual conclusion are signs or symbols having no intrinsic quality of their own, but standing for things that may in another experience be qualitatively experienced. The difference is enormous. It is one reason why the strictly intellectual art will never be popular as music is popular. Nevertheless, the experience itself has a satisfying emotional quality because it possesses internal integration and fulfillment reached through ordered and organized movement. This artistic structure may be immediately felt. In so far, it is esthetic. What is even more important is that not only is this quality a significant motive in undertaking intellectual inquiry and in keeping it honest, but that no intellectual activity is an integral event (is *an* experience) unless it is rounded out with this quality. Without it, thinking is inconclusive. In short, esthetic cannot be

sharply marked off from intellectual experience since the latter must bear an esthetic stamp to be itself complete.

The same statement holds good of a course of action that is dominantly practical, that is, one that consists of overt doings. It is possible to be efficient in action and yet not have a conscious experience. The activity is too automatic to permit of a sense of what it is about and where it is going. It comes to an end but not to a close or consummation in consciousness. Obstacles are overcome by shrewd skill, but they do not feed experience. There are also those who are wavering in action, uncertain, and inconclusive like the shades in classic literature. Between the poles of aimlessness and mechanical efficiency, there lie those courses of action in which through successive deeds there runs a sense of growing meaning conserved and accumulating toward an end that is felt as accomplishment of a process. . . . There is interest in completing an experience. The experience may be one that is harmful to the world and its consummation undesirable. But it has esthetic quality.

The Greek identification of good conduct with conduct having proportion, grace, and harmony, the *kalon-agathon,* is a more obvious example of distinctive esthetic quality in moral action. One great defect in what passes as morality is its anesthetic quality. Instead of exemplifying wholehearted action, it takes the form of grudging piecemeal concessions to the demands of duty. But illustrations may only obscure the fact that any practical activity will, provided that it is integrated and moves by its own urge to fulfillment, have esthetic quality.

. . . In much of our experience we are not concerned with the connection of one incident with what went before and what comes after. There is no interest that controls attentive rejection or selection of what shall be organized into the developing experience. Things happen, but they are neither definitely included nor decisively excluded; we drift. We yield according to external pressure, or evade and compromise. There are beginnings and cessations, but no genuine initiations and concludings. One thing replaces another, but does not absorb it and carry it on. There is experience, but so slack and discursive that it is not *an* experience. Needless to say, such experiences are anesthetic.

Thus the non-esthetic lies within two limits. At one pole is the loose succession that does not begin at any particular place and that ends—in the sense of ceasing—at no particular place. At the other pole is arrest, constriction, proceeding from parts having only a mechanical connection with one another. There exists so much of one and the other of these two kinds of experience that unconsciously they come to be taken as norms of all experience. Then, when the esthetic appears, it so sharply contrasts with the picture that has been formed of experience, that it is impossible to combine its special qualities with the features of the picture and the esthetic is given an outside place and status. The account that has been given of experience dominantly intellectual and practical is intended to show that there is no such contrast involved in having an experience; that, on the contrary, no experience of whatever sort is a unity unless it has esthetic quality.

The enemies of the esthetic are neither the practical nor the intellectual. They are the humdrum; slackness of loose ends; submission to convention in practice and intellectual procedure. Rigid abstinence, coerced submission, tightness on one side and dissipation, incoherence and aimless indulgence on the other, are deviations in opposite directions from the unity of an experience. Some such considerations perhaps induced Aristotle to invoke the "mean proportional" as the proper designation of what is distinctive of both virtue and the esthetic. He was formally correct. "Mean" and "proportion" are, however, not self-explanatory, nor to be taken over in a prior mathematical sense, but are properties belonging to an experience that has a developing movement toward its own consummation. . . .

I have spoken of the esthetic quality that rounds out an experience into completeness and unity as emotional. The reference may cause difficulty. We are given to thinking of emotions as things as simple and compact as are the words by which we name them. Joy, sorrow, hope, fear, anger, curiosity, are treated as if each in itself were a sort of entity that enters full-made upon the scene, an entity that may last a long time or a short time, but whose duration, whose growth and career, is irrelevant to its nature. In fact emotions are qualities, when they are significant, of a complex experience that moves and changes. I say, when they are *significant,* for otherwise they are but the outbreaks and eruptions of a disturbed infant. All emotions are qualifications of a drama and they change as the drama develops. Persons are sometimes said to fall in love at first sight. But what they fall into is not a thing of that instant. What would love be were it compressed into a moment in which there is no room for cherishing and for solicitude? The intimate nature of emotion is manifested in the experience of one watching a play on the stage or reading a novel. It attends the development of a plot; and a plot requires a stage, a space, wherein to develop and time in which to unfold. Experience is emotional but there are no separate things called emotions in it.

By the same token, emotions are attached to events and objects in their movement. They are not, save in pathological instances, private. And even an "objectless" emotion demands something beyond itself to which to attach itself, and thus it soon generates a delusion in lack of something real. Emotion belongs of a certainty to the self. But it belongs to the self that is concerned in the movement of events toward an issue that is desired or disliked. We jump instantaneously when we are scared, as we blush on the instant when we are ashamed. But fright and shamed modesty are not in this case emotional states. Of themselves they are but automatic reflexes. In order to become emotional they must become parts of an inclusive and enduring situation that involves concern for objects and their issues. The jump of fright becomes emotional fear when there is found or thought to exist a threatening object that must be dealt with or escaped from. The blush becomes the emotion of shame when a person connects, in thought, an action he has performed with an unfavorable reaction to himself of some other person. . . .

There are, therefore, common patterns in various experiences, no matter how unlike they are to one another in the details of their subject matter. There are conditions to be met without which an experience cannot come to be. The outline of the common pattern is set by the fact that every experience is the result of interaction between a live creature and some aspect of the world in which he lives. A man does something; he lifts, let us say, a stone. In consequence he undergoes, suffers, something: the weight, strain, texture of the surface of the thing lifted. The properties thus undergone determine further doing. The stone is too heavy or too angular, not solid enough; or else the properties undergone show it is fit for the use for which it is intended. The process continues until a mutual adaptation of the self and the object emerges and that particular experience comes to a close. What is true of this simple instance is true, as to form, of every experience. The creature operating may be a thinker in his study and the environment with which he interacts may consist of ideas instead of a stone. But interaction of the two constitutes the total experience that is had, and the close which completes it is the institution of a felt harmony.

An experience has pattern and structure, because it is not just doing and undergoing in alternation, but consists of them in relationship. To put one's hand in the fire that consumes it is not necessarily to have an experience. The action and its consequence must be joined in perception. This relationship is what gives meaning; to grasp it is the objective of all intelligence. The scope and content of the relations measure the significant content of an experience.

6 / SOCIAL PHILOSOPHY

A frequent theme in the social writings of naturalists has been the involvement of political freedom with scientific inquiry. The *locus classicus* of this position is the writings of the English thinker, John Stuart Mill. In his work, *On Liberty*, Mill argues in the chapters preceding that from which the selection is taken for the freedom to *form* and to *express* opinions. The reasons justifying these freedoms also lead him to argue for freedom to *act* in terms of one's own opinions.

These reasons are basically two: first, that mankind is not infallible and does not possess all truth, and that freedom of inquiry is useful and valuable for extending human knowledge; and second, that the free development of the individual—mature individuality—requires one to choose and act according to one's own ideas and experiences. Mill warns of the dangers tending to crush individuality and genius, such as the tyranny of public opinion and the despotism of custom; and he urges a degree of nonconformity as important for saving individuality in the modern world.

LIBERTY AND INQUIRY
John Stuart Mill (1806-1873)

Such being the reasons which make it imperative that human beings should be free to form opinions, and to express their opinions without reserve; and such the baneful consequences to the intellectual, and through that to the moral nature of man, unless this liberty is either conceded, or asserted in spite of prohibition; let us next examine whether the same reasons do not require that men should be free to act upon their opinions—to carry these out in their lives, without hindrance, either physical or moral, from their fellow-men, so long as it is at their own risk and peril. This last proviso is of course indispensable. No one pretends that actions should be as free as opinions. On the contrary, even opinions lose their immunity, when the circumstances in which they are expressed are such as to constitute their expression a positive instigation to some mischievous act. An opinion that corn-dealers are starvers of the poor, or that private property is robbery, ought to be unmolested when simply circulated through the press, but may justly incur punishment when delivered orally to an excited mob assembled before the house of a corn-dealer, or when handed about among the same mob in the form of a placard. Acts of whatever kind, which, without justifiable cause, do harm to others, may be, and in the more important cases absolutely require to be, controlled by the unfavorable sentiments, and, when needful, by the active interference of mankind. The liberty of the

individual must be thus far limited; he must not make himself a nuisance to other people. But if he refrains from molesting others in what concerns them, and merely acts according to his own inclination and judgment in things which concern himself, the same reasons which show that opinion should be free, prove also that he should be allowed, without molestation, to carry his opinions into practice at his own cost. That mankind are not infallible; that their truths, for the most part, are only half-truths; that unity of opinion, unless resulting from the fullest and freest comparison of opposite opinions, is not desirable, and diversity not an evil, but a good, until mankind are much more capable than at present of recognizing all sides of the truth, are principles applicable to men's modes of action, not less than to their opinions. As it is useful that while mankind are imperfect there should be different opinions, so is it that there should be different experiments of living; that free scope should be given to varieties of character, short of injury to others; and that the worth of different modes of life should be proved practically, when any one thinks fit to try them. It is desirable, in short, that in things which do not primarily concern others, individuality should assert itself. Where, not the person's own character, but the traditions or customs of other people are the rule of conduct, there is wanting one of the principal ingredients of human happiness, and quite the chief ingredient of individual and social progress.

In maintaining this principle, the great-

The selection is from J. S. Mill, *On Liberty* (New York: Henry Holt & Co., Inc., 1898), pp. 100-132, with omissions.

est difficulty to be encountered does not lie in the appreciation of means towards an acknowledged end, but in the indifference of persons in general to the end itself. If it were felt that the free development of individuality is one of the leading essentials of well-being; that it is not only a co-ordinate element with all that is designated by the terms civilization, instruction, education, culture, but is itself a necessary part and condition of all those things; there would be no danger that liberty should be undervalued, and the adjustment of the boundaries between it and social control would present no extraordinary difficulty. But the evil is, that individual spontaneity is hardly recognized by the common modes of thinking as having any intrinsic worth, or deserving any regard on its own account. The majority, being satisfied with the ways of mankind as they now are (for it is they who make them what they are), cannot comprehend why those ways should not be good enough for everybody; and what is more, spontaneity forms no part of the ideal of the majority of moral and social reformers, but is rather looked on with jealousy, as a troublesome and perhaps rebellious obstruction to the general acceptance of what these reformers, in their own judgment, think would be best for mankind. Few persons, out of Germany, even comprehend the meaning of the doctrine which Wilhelm von Humboldt, so eminent both as a *savant* and as a politician, made the text of a treatise—that "the end of man, or that which is prescribed by the eternal or immutable dictates of reason, and not suggested by vague and transient desires, is the highest and most harmonious development of his powers to a complete and consistent whole"; that, therefore, the object "towards which every human being must ceaselessly direct his efforts, and on which especially those who design to influence their fellowmen must ever keep their eyes, is the individuality of power and development"; that

for this there are two requisites, "freedom, and a variety of situations"; and that from the union of these arise "individual vigor and manifold diversity," which combine themselves in "originality."

Little, however, as people are accustomed to a doctrine like that of von Humboldt, and surprising as it may be to them to find so high a value attached to individuality, the question, one must nevertheless think, can only be one of degree. No one's idea of excellence in conduct is that people should do absolutely nothing but copy one another. No one would assert that people ought not to put into their mode of life, and into the conduct of their concerns, any impress whatever of their own judgment, or of their own individual character. On the other hand, it would be absurd to pretend that people ought to live as if nothing whatever had been known in the world before they came into it; as if experience had as yet done nothing towards showing that one mode of existence, or of conduct, is preferable to another. Nobody denies that people should be so taught and trained in youth, as to know and benefit by the ascertained results of human experience. But it is the privilege and proper condition of a human being, arrived at the maturity of his faculties, to use and interpret experience in his own way. It is for him to find out what part of recorded experience is properly applicable to his own circumstances and character. . . .

He who lets the world, or his own portion of it, choose his plan of life for him, has no need of any other faculty than the apelike one of imitation. He who chooses his plan for himself, employs all his faculties. He must use observation to see, reasoning and judgment to foresee, activity to gather materials for decision, discrimination to decide, and when he has decided, firmness and self-control to hold to his deliberate decision. And these qualities he requires and exercises exactly in proportion as the part of his conduct which he determines according to his own judgment and feelings is a large one. It is possible that he might be guided in some good path, and kept out of harm's way, without any of these things. But what will be his comparative worth as a human being? It really is of importance, not only what men do, but also what manner of men they are that do it. Among the works of man, which human life is rightly employed in perfecting and beautifying, the first in importance surely is man himself. Supposing it were possible to get houses built, corn grown, battles fought, causes tried, and even churches erected and prayers said, by machinery—by automatons in human form—it would be a considerable loss to exchange for these automatons even the men and women who at present inhabit the more civilized parts of the world, and who assuredly are but starved specimens of what nature can and will produce. Human nature is not a machine to be built after a model, and set to do exactly the work prescribed for it, but a tree, which requires to grow and develop itself on all sides, according to the tendency of the inward forces which make it a living thing. . . .

It is not by wearing down into uniformity all that is individual in themselves, but by cultivating it and calling it forth, within the limits imposed by the rights and interests of others, that human beings become a noble and beautiful object of contemplation; and as the works partake the character of those who do them, by the same process human life also becomes rich, diversified, and animating, furnishing more abundant aliment to high thoughts and elevating feelings, and strengthening the tie which binds every individual to the race, by making the race infinitely better worth belonging to. In proportion to the development of his individuality, each person becomes more valuable to himself, and is therefore capable of being more valuable to others. There is a greater fulness of life

about his own existence, and when there is more life in the units there is more in the mass which is composed of them. As much compression as is necessary to prevent the stronger specimens of human nature from encroaching on the rights of others, cannot be dispensed with; but for this there is ample compensation even in the point of view of human development. The means of development which the individual loses by being prevented from gratifying his inclinations to the injury of others, are chiefly obtained at the expense of the development of other people. And even to himself there is a full equivalent in the better development of the social part of his nature, rendered possible by the restraint put upon the selfish part. To be held to rigid rules of justice for the sake of others, develops the feelings and capacities which have the good of others for their object. But to be restrained in things not affecting their good, by their mere displeasure, develops nothing valuable, except such force of character as may unfold itself in resisting the restraint. If acquiesced in, it dulls and blunts the whole nature. To give any fair play to the nature of each, it is essential that different persons should be allowed to lead different lives. In proportion as this latitude has been exercised in any age, has that age been noteworthy to posterity. Even despotism does not produce its worst effects, so long as Individuality exists under it; and whatever crushes individuality is despotism, by whatever name it may be called, and whether it professes to be enforcing the will of God or the injunctions of men.

Having said that Individuality is the same thing with development, and that it is only the cultivation of individuality which produces, or can produce, well-developed human beings, I might here close the argument: for what more or better can be said of any condition of human affairs, than that it brings human beings themselves nearer to the best thing they can be? or what worse can be said of any obstruction to good, than that it prevents this? Doubtless, however, these considerations will not suffice to convince those who most need convincing; and it is necessary further to show, that these developed human beings are of some use to the undeveloped—to point out to those who do not desire liberty, and would not avail themselves of it, that they may be in some intelligible manner rewarded for allowing other people to make use of it without hindrance. . . .

I insist thus emphatically on the importance of genius, and the necessity of allowing it to unfold itself freely both in thought and in practice, being well aware that no one will deny the position in theory, but knowing also that almost every one, in reality, is totally indifferent to it. People think genius a fine thing if it enables a man to write an exciting poem, or paint a picture. But in its true sense, that of originality in thought and action, though no one says that it is not a thing to be admired, nearly all, at heart, think that they can do very well without it. Unhappily this is too natural to be wondered at. Originality is the one thing which unoriginal minds cannot feel the use of. They cannot see what it is to do for them: how should they? If they could see what it would do for them, it would not be originality. The first service which originality has to render them, is that of opening their eyes: which being once fully done, they would have a chance of being themselves original. Meanwhile, recollecting that nothing was ever yet done which some one was not the first to do, and that all good things which exist are the fruits of originality, let them be modest enough to believe that there is something still left for it to accomplish, and assure themselves that they are more in need of originality, the less they are conscious of the want.

In sober truth, whatever homage may be professed, or even paid, to real or supposed mental superiority, the general tendency of things throughout the world is to render mediocrity the ascendant power among mankind. In ancient history, in the Middle Ages, and in a diminishing degree through the long transition from feudality to the present time, the individual was a power in himself; and if he had either great talents or a high social position, he was a considerable power. At present individuals are lost in the crowd. In politics it is almost a triviality to say that public opinion now rules the world. The only power deserving the name is that of masses, and of governments while they make themselves the organ of the tendencies and instincts of masses. This is as true in the moral and social relations of private life as in public transactions. Those whose opinions go by the name of public opinion, are not always the same sort of public: in America, they are the whole white population; in England, chiefly the middle class. But they are always a mass, that is to say, collective mediocrity. And what is a still greater novelty, the mass do not now take their opinions from dignitaries in Church or State, from ostensible leaders, or from books. Their thinking is done for them by men much like themselves, addressing them or speaking in their name, on the spur of the moment, through the newspapers. I am not complaining of all this. I do not assert that anything better is compatible, as a general rule, with the present low state of the human mind. But that does not hinder the government of mediocrity from being mediocre government. No government by a democracy or a numerous aristocracy, either in its political acts or in the opinions, qualities, and tone of mind which it fosters, ever did or could rise above mediocrity, except in so far as the sovereign Many have let themselves be guided (which in their best times they always have done) by the counsels and influence of a more highly gifted and instructed One or Few. The initiation of all wise or noble things, comes and must come from individuals; generally at first from some one individual. The honor and glory of the average man is that he is capable of following that initiative; that he can respond internally to wise and noble things, and be led to them with his eyes open. I am not countenancing the sort of "hero-worship" which applauds the strong man of genius for forcibly seizing on the government of the world and making it do his bidding in spite of itself. All he can claim is, freedom to point out the way. The power of compelling others into it, is not only inconsistent with the freedom and development of all the rest, but corrupting to the strong man himself. It does seem, however, that when the opinions of masses of merely average men are everywhere become or becoming the dominant power, the counterpoise and corrective to that tendency would be, the more and more pronounced individuality of those who stand on the higher eminences of thought. It is in these circumstances most especially, that exceptional individuals, instead of being deterred, should be encouraged in acting differently from the mass. In other times there was no advantage in their doing so, unless they acted not only differently, but better. In this age the mere example of non-conformity, the mere refusal to bend the knee to custom, is itself a service. Precisely because the tyranny of opinion is such as to make eccentricity a reproach, it is desirable, in order to break through that tyranny, that people should be eccentric. Eccentricity has always abounded when and where strength of character has abounded; and the amount of eccentricity in a society has generally been proportional to the amount of genius, mental vigor, and moral courage which it contained. That so few now dare to be eccentric, marks the chief danger of the time. . . .

The despotism of custom is everywhere the standing hindrance to human advancement being in unceasing antagonism to that disposition to aim at something better than customary, which is called, according to circumstances, the spirit of liberty, or that of progress or improvement. The spirit of improvement is not always a spirit of liberty, for it may aim at forcing improvements on an unwilling people; and the spirit of liberty, in so far as it resists such attempts, may ally itself locally and temporarily with the opponents of improvement; but the only unfailing and permanent source of improvement is liberty, since by it there are as many possible independent centers of improvement as there are individuals. The progressive principle, however, in either shape, whether as the love of liberty or of improvement, is antagonistic to the sway of Custom, involving at least emancipation from that yoke; and the contest between the two constitutes the chief interest of the history of mankind. The greater part of the world has, properly speaking, no history, because the despotism of Custom is complete. This is the case over the whole East. Custom is there, in all things, the final appeal; justice and right mean conformity to custom; the argument of custom no one, unless some tyrant intoxicated with power, thinks of resisting. . . . We [in Europe, however] have discarded the fixed costumes of our forefathers; every one must still dress like other people, but the fashion may change once or twice a year. We thus take care that when there is change, it shall be for change's sake, and not from any idea of beauty or convenience; for the same idea of beauty or convenience would not strike all the world at the same moment, and be simultaneously thrown aside by all at another moment. But we are progressive as well as changeable: we continually make new inventions in mechanical things, and keep them until they are again superseded by better; we are eager for improvement in politics, in education, even in morals, though in this last our idea of improvement chiefly consists in persuading or forcing other people to be as good as ourselves. It is not progress that we object to; on the contrary, we flatter ourselves that we are the most progressive people who ever lived. It is individuality that we war against: we should think we had done wonders if we had made ourselves all alike; forgetting that the unlikeness of one person to another is generally the first thing which draws the attention of either to the imperfection of his own type, and the superiority of another, or the possibility, by combining the advantages of both, of producing something better than either. . . .

The combination of all these causes forms so great a mass of influences hostile to Individuality, that it is not easy to see how it can stand its ground. It will do so with increasing difficulty, unless the intelligent part of the public can be made to feel its value—to see that it is good there should be differences, even though not for the better, even though, as it may appear to them, some should be for the worse. If the claims of Individuality are ever to be asserted, the time is now, while much is still wanting to complete the enforced assimulation. It is only in the earlier stages that any stand can be successfully made against the encroachment. The demand that all other people shall resemble ourselves, grows by what it feeds on. If resistance waits till life is reduced *nearly* to one uniform type, all deviations from that type will come to be considered impious, immoral, even monstrous and contrary to nature. Mankind speedily become unable to conceive diversity, when they have been for some time unaccustomed to see it.

7 / PHILOSOPHY OF SCIENCE

Throughout their writings naturalists have stressed the role and importance of scientific thought for their philosophy. Now, with Morris R. Cohen and Ernest Nagel, we must inquire into the fundamental features of that thought for a fuller understanding of science and its method. The selection explains a number of key terms in scientific method such as fact, observation, hypothesis, deduction, evidence, and verification. The ideals of science are seen to be system, self-correction, utility, and truth. Finally, the authors note both the limits and the value of science: limits, for human beings are not omniscient; yet value, for in requiring detachment and disinterestedness science may be seen as "the finest flower and test of a liberal civilization."

THE VALUE OF SCIENCE

M. R. Cohen (1880-1947) and Ernest Nagel (1901-   )

[Earlier in the book,] we asserted that the method of science is free from the limitations and willfulness of the alternative methods for settling doubt which we there rejected. Scientific method, we declared, is the most assured technique man has yet devised for controlling the flux of things and establishing stable beliefs. What are the fundamental features of this method? We have already examined in some detail different constituent parts of it. Let us in this final chapter bring together the more important threads of our discussions.

FACTS AND SCIENTIFIC METHOD. The method of science does not seek to impose the desires and hopes of men upon the flux of things in a capricious manner. It may indeed be employed to satisfy the desires of men. But its successful use depends upon seeking, in a deliberate manner, and irrespective of what men's desires are, to recognize, as well as to take advantage of, the structure which the flux possesses.

1. Consequently, scientific method aims to discover what the facts truly are, and the use of the method must be guided by the discovered facts. But, as we have repeatedly pointed out, what the facts are cannot be discovered without reflection. Knowledge of the facts cannot be equated to the brute immediacy of our sensations. When our skin comes into contact with objects having high temperatures or with liquid air, the immediate experiences may be similar. We cannot, however, conclude without error that the temperatures of the substances touched are the same. Sensory

experience sets the *problem* for knowledge, and just because such experience is immediate and final it must become informed by reflective analysis before knowledge can be said to take place.

2. Every inquiry arises from some felt problem, so that no inquiry can even get under way unless some selection or sifting of the subject matter has taken place. Such selection requires, we have been urging all along, some hypothesis, preconception, prejudice, which guides the research as well as delimits the subject matter of inquiry. Every inquiry is specific in the sense that it has a definite problem to solve, and such solution terminates the inquiry. It is idle to collect "facts" unless there is a problem upon which they are supposed to bear.

3. The ability to formulate problems whose solution may also help solve other problems is a rare gift, requiring extraordinary genius. The problems which meet us in daily life can be solved, if they can be solved at all, by the application of scientific method. But such problems do not, as a rule, raise far-reaching issues. The most striking applications of scientific method are to be found in the various natural and social sciences.

4. The "facts" for which every inquiry reaches out are propositions for whose truth there is considerable evidence. Consequently what the "facts" are must be determined by inquiry, and cannot be determined antecedently to inquiry. Moreover, what we believe to be the facts clearly depends upon the stage of our inquiry. There is therefore no sharp line dividing facts from guesses or hypotheses. During any inquiry the status of a proposition may change from that of hypothesis to that of fact, or from that of fact to that of hypothesis. Every so-called fact, therefore,

The selection is from pp. 391-396 and 399-403 of *An Introduction to Logic and Scientific Method* by Morris R. Cohen and Ernest Nagel; copyright, 1934, by Harcourt, Brace & World, Inc., and Routledge & Kegan Paul, Ltd. Used by permission of the publishers.

may be challenged for the evidence upon which it is asserted to be a fact, even though no such challenge is actually made.

HYPOTHESES AND SCIENTIFIC METHOD. The method of science would be impossible if the hypotheses which are suggested as solutions could not be elaborated to reveal what they imply. The full meaning of a hypothesis is to be discovered in its implications.

1. Hypotheses are suggested to an inquirer by something in the subject matter under investigation, and by his previous knowledge of other subject matters. No rules can be offered for obtaining fruitful hypotheses, any more than rules can be given for discovering significant problems.

2. Hypotheses are required at every stage of an inquiry. It must not be forgotten that what are called general principles or laws (which may have been confirmed in a previous inquiry) can be applied to a present, still unterminated inquiry only with some risk. For they may not in fact be applicable. The general laws of any science function as hypotheses, which guide the inquiry in all its phases.

3. Hypotheses can be regarded as suggestions of possible connections between actual facts or imagined ones. The question of the truth of hypotheses need not, therefore, always be raised. The necessary feature of a hypothesis, from this point of view, is that it should be statable in a determinate form, so that its implications can be discovered by logical means.

4. The number of hypotheses which may occur to an inquirer is without limit, and is a function of the character of his imagination. There is a need, therefore, for a technique to choose between the alternative suggestions, and to make sure that the alternatives are in fact, and not only in appearance, *different* theories. Perhaps the most important and best explored part of such a technique is the technique of formal inference. For this reason, the structure of formal logic has been examined at some length. The object of that examination has been to give the reader an adequate sense of what formal validity means, as well as to provide him with a synoptic view of the power and range of formal logic.

5. It is convenient to have on hand—in storage, so to speak—different hypotheses whose consequences have been carefully explored. It is the task of mathematics to provide and explore alternative hypotheses. Mathematics receives hints concerning what hypotheses to study from the natural sciences; and the natural sciences are indebted to mathematics for suggestions concerning the type of order which their subject matter embodies.

6. The deductive elaboration of hypotheses is not the sole task of scientific method. Since there is a plurality of possible hypotheses, it is the task of inquiry to determine which of the possible explanations or solutions of the problem is in best agreement with the facts. Formal considerations are therefore never sufficient to establish the material truth of any theory.

7. No hypothesis which states a general proposition can be demonstrated as absolutely true. We have seen that all inquiry which deals with matters of fact employs probable inference. The task of such investigations is to select that hypothesis which is the most probable on the factual evidence; and it is the task of further inquiry to find other factual evidence which will increase or decrease the probability of such a theory.

EVIDENCE AND SCIENTIFIC METHOD. Scientific method pursues the road of systematic doubt. It does not doubt *all* things, for this is clearly impossible. But it does question whatever lacks adequate evidence in its support.

1. Science is not satisfied with psychological certitude, for the mere intensity with which a belief is held is no guarantee of its truth. Science demands and looks for

logically adequate grounds for the propositions it advances.

2. No single proposition dealing with matters of fact is beyond every significant doubt. No proposition is so well supported by evidence that other evidence may not increase or decrease its probability. However, while no single proposition is indubitable, the body of knowledge which supports it, and of which it is itself a part, is better grounded than any alternative body of knowledge.

3. Science is thus always ready to abandon a theory when the facts so demand. But the facts must really demand it. It is not unusual for a theory to be modified so that it may be retained in substance even though "facts" contradicted an earlier formulation of it. Scientific procedure is therefore a mixture of a willingness to change, and an obstinacy in holding on to, theories apparently incompatible with facts.

4. The verification of theories is only approximate. Verification simply shows that, within the margin of experimental error, the experiment is *compatible* with the verified hypothesis.

SYSTEM IN THE IDEAL OF SCIENCE. The ideal of science is to achieve a systematic interconnection of facts. Isolated propositions do not constitute a science. Such propositions serve merely as an opportunity to find the logical connection between them and other propositions.

1. "Common sense" is content with a miscellaneous collection of information. As a consequence, the propositions it asserts are frequently vague, the range of their application is unknown, and their mutual compatibility is generally very questionable. The advantages of discovering a system among facts is therefore obvious. A condition for achieving a system is the introduction of accuracy in the assertions made. The limit within which propositions are true is then clearly defined. Moreover, inconsistencies between propositions asserted become eliminated gradually because propositions which are part of a system must support and correct one another. The extent and accuracy of our information is thus increased. In fact, scientific method differs from other methods in the accuracy and number of facts it studies.

2. When, as frequently happens, a science abandons one theory for another, it is a mistake to suppose that science has become "bankrupt" and that it is incapable of discovering the structure of the subject matter it studies. Such changes indicate rather that the science is progressively realizing its ideal. For such changes arise from correcting previous observations or reasoning, and such correction means that we are in possession of more reliable facts.

3. The ideal of system requires that the propositions asserted to be true should be connected without the introduction of further propositions for which the evidence is small or nonexistent. In a system the number of unconnected propositions and the number of propositions for which there is no evidence are at a minimum. Consequently, in a system the requirements of simplicity, as expressed in the principle of Occam's razor,[1] are satisfied in a high degree. For that principle declares that entities should not be multiplied beyond necessity. This may be interpreted as a demand that whatever is capable of proof should be proved. But the ideal of system requires just that.

4. The evidence for propositions which are elements in a system accumulates more rapidly than that for isolated propositions. The evidence for a proposition may come from its own verifying instances, or from the verifying instances of *other* propositions which are connected with the first in a system. It is this systematic character

[1 The reference is to a logical principle stated by the English Franciscan theologian, William of Occam or Ockham (1280-1349). The principle itself is given in the text. *Ed.*]

of scientific theories which gives such high probabilities to the various individual propositions of a science.

THE SELF-CORRECTIVE NATURE OF SCIENTIFIC METHOD. Science does not desire to obtain conviction for its propositions in *any* manner and at *any* price. Propositions must be supported by logically acceptable evidence, which must be weighed carefully and tested by the well-known canons of necessary and probable inference. It follows that the *method* of science is more stable, and more important to men of science, than any particular result achieved by its means.

1. In virtue of its method, the enterprise of science is a self-corrective process. It appeals to no special revelation or authority whose deliverances are indubitable and final. It claims no infallibility, but relies upon the methods of developing and testing hypotheses for assured conclusions. The canons of inquiry are themselves discovered in the process of reflection, and may themselves become modified in the course of study. The method makes possible the noting and correction of errors by continued application of itself.

2. General propositions can be established only by the method of repeated sampling. Consequently, the propositions which a science puts forward for study are either confirmed in all possible experiments or modified in accordance with the evidence. It is this self-corrective nature of the method which allows us to challenge any proposition, but which also assures us that the theories which science accepts are more probable than any alternative theories. By not claiming more certainty than the evidence warrants, scientific method succeeds in obtaining more logical certainty than any other method yet devised.

3. In the process of gathering and weighing evidence, there is a continuous appeal from facts to theories or principles, and from principles to facts. For there is nothing intrinsically indubitable, there are

no absolutely first principles, in the sense of principles which are self-evident or which must be known prior to everything else.

4. The method of science is thus essentially circular. We obtain evidence for principles by appealing to empirical material, to what is alleged to be "fact"; and we select, analyze, and interpret empirical material on the basis of principles. In virtue of such give and take between facts and principles, every thing that is dubitable falls under careful scrutiny at one time or another. . . .

THE LIMITS AND THE VALUE OF SCIENTIFIC METHOD. The desire for knowledge for its own sake is more widespread than is generally recognized by anti-intellectualists. It has its roots in the animal curiosity which shows itself in the cosmological questions of children and in the gossip of adults. No ulterior utilitarian motive makes people want to know about the private lives of their neighbors, the great, or the notorious. There is also a certain zest which makes people engage in various intellectual games or exercises in which one is required to find out something. But while the desire to know is wide, it is seldom strong enough to overcome the more powerful organic desires, and few indeed have both the inclination and the ability to face the arduous difficulties of scientific method in more than one special field. The desire to know is not often strong enough to sustain critical inquiry. Men generally are interested in the results, in the story or romance of science, not in the technical methods whereby these results are obtained and their truth continually is tested and qualified. Our first impulse is to accept the plausible as true and to reject the uncongenial as false. We have not the time, inclination, or energy to investigate everything. Indeed, the call to do so is often felt as irksome and joy-killing. And when we are asked to treat our cherished beliefs as mere hypotheses, we rebel as violently as when those dear to us are insulted. This provides the ground for various movements that are hostile to rational scientific procedure (though their promoters do not often admit that it is science to which they are hostile).

Mystics, intuitionists, authoritarians, voluntarists, and fictionalists are all trying to undermine respect for the rational methods of science. These attacks have always met with wide acclaim and are bound to continue to do so, for they strike a responsive note in human nature. Unfortunately they do not offer any reliable alternative method for obtaining verifiable knowledge. The great French writer Pascal opposed to logic the spirit of subtlety or finesse *(esprit géometrique* and *esprit de finesse)* and urged that the heart has its reasons as well as the mind, reasons that cannot be accurately formulated but which subtle spirits apprehend none the less. Men as diverse as James Russell Lowell and George Santayana are agreed that:

The soul is oracular still,

and

It is wisdom to trust the heart . . .
To trust the soul's invincible surmise.

Now it is true that in the absence of omniscience we must trust our soul's surmise; and great men are those whose surmises or intuitions are deep or penetrating. It is only by acting on our surmise that we can procure the evidence in its favor. But only havoc can result from confusing a surmise with a proposition for which there is already evidence. Are all the reasons of the heart sound? Do all oracles tell the truth? The sad history of human experience is distinctly discouraging to any such claim. Mystic intuition may give men absolute subjective certainty, but can give no proof that contrary intuitions are erroneous. It is obvious that when authorities conflict we must weigh the evidence in their favor logically if we are to

make a rational choice. Certainly, when a truth is questioned it is no answer to say, "I am convinced," or, "I prefer to rely on this rather than on another authority." The view that physical science is no guide to proof, but is a mere fiction, fails to explain why it has enabled us to anticipate phenomena of nature and to control them. These attacks on scientific method receive a certain color of plausibility because of some indefensible claims made by uncritical enthusiasts. But it is of the essence of scientific method to limit its own pretension. Recognizing that we do not know everything, it does not claim the ability to solve all of our practical problems. It is an error to suppose, as is often done, that science denies the truth of all unverified propositions. For that which is unverified today may be verified tomorrow. We may get at truth by guessing or in other ways. Scientific method, however, is concerned with verification. Admittedly the wisdom of those engaged in this process has not been popularly ranked as high as that of the sage, the prophet, or the poet. Admittedly, also, we know of no way of supplying creative intelligence to those who lack it. Scientists, like all other human beings, may get into ruts and apply their techniques regardless of varying circumstances. There will always be formal procedures which are fruitless. Definitions and formal distinctions may be a sharpening of tools without the wit to use them properly, and statistical information may conform to the highest technical standards and yet be irrelevant and inconclusive. Nevertheless, scientific method is the only way to increase the general body of tested and verified truth and to eliminate arbitrary opinion. It is well to clarify our ideas by asking for the precise meaning of our words, and to try to check our favorite ideas by applying them to accurately formulated propositions. . . .

In general the chief social condition of scientific method is a widespread desire for truth that is strong enough to withstand the powerful forces which make us cling tenaciously to old views or else embrace every novelty because it is a change. Those who are engaged in scientific work need not only leisure for reflection and material for their experiments, but also a community that respects the pursuit of truth and allows freedom for the expression of intellectual doubt as to its most sacred or established institutions. Fear of offending established dogmas has been an obstacle to the growth of astronomy and geology and other physical sciences; and the fear of offending patriotic or respected sentiment is perhaps one of the strongest hindrances to scholarly history and social science. On the other hand, when a community indiscriminately acclaims every new doctrine the love of truth becomes subordinated to the desire for novel formulations.

On the whole it may be said that the safety of science depends on there being men who care more for the justice of their methods than for any results obtained by their use. For this reason it is unfortunate when scientific research in the social field is largely in the hands of those not in a favorable position to oppose established or popular opinion.

We may put it the other way by saying that the physical sciences can be more liberal because we are sure that foolish opinions will be readily eliminated by the shock of facts. In the social field, however, no one can tell what harm may come of foolish ideas before the foolishness is finally, if ever, demonstrated. None of the precautions of scientific method can prevent human life from being an adventure, and no scientific investigator knows whether he will reach his goal. But scientific method does enable large numbers to walk with surer step. By analyzing the possibilities of any step or plan, it becomes possible to anticipate the future and adjust ourselves to it in advance. Scientific method thus minimizes the shock of novelty and the uncertainty of life. It enables us to frame policies of action and of moral judgment fit for a wider outlook than those of immediate physical stimulus or organic response.

Scientific method is the only effective way of strengthening the love of truth. It develops the intellectual courage to face difficulties and to overcome illusions that are pleasant temporarily but destructive ultimately. It settles differences without any external force by appealing to our common rational nature. The way of science, even if it is up a steep mountain, is open to all. Hence, while sectarian and partisan faiths are based on personal choice or temperament and divide men, scientific procedure unites men in something nobly devoid of all pettiness. Because it requires detachment, disinterestedness, it is the finest flower and test of a liberal civilization.

8 / PHILOSOPHY OF RELIGION

Religion, like art and morality, is understood by the naturalist within the contexts of experience and nature. He makes no reference to the supernatural in his treatments of these subjects, for his basic metaphysical orientation disallows such reference. Though it may seem strange to treat religion without the supernatural, there are nevertheless many sensitive and discerning studies of religion by naturalists. Among them is that by George Santayana.

The selection is taken from Santayana's five-volume work, *The Life of Reason.* Reason for him is the seat of all ultimate values. Historical religions,

Santayana observes, have also pursued ultimate value, although unlike reason, they have been unsuccessful in that pursuit. The cause of this failure lies in the fact that religion pursues truth through the imagination. Hence it is allied to poetry; and, as with poetry, we must therefore judge religions as better or worse depending on the moral plane to which they lift their adherents, but never as true or false.

REASON AND RELIGION

George Santayana (1863-1952)

Experience has repeatedly confirmed that well-known maxim of Bacon's, that "a little philosophy inclineth man's mind to atheism, but depth in philosophy bringeth men's minds about to religion." In every age the most comprehensive thinkers have found in the religion of their time and country something they could accept, interpreting and illustrating that religion so as to give it depth and universal application. Even the heretics and atheists, if they have had profundity, turn out after a while to be forerunners of some new orthodoxy. What they rebel against is a religion alien to their nature; they are atheists only by accident, and relatively to a convention which inwardly offends them, but they yearn mightily in their own souls after the religious acceptance of a world interpreted in their own fashion. So it appears in the end that their atheism and loud protestation were in fact the hastier part of their thought, since what emboldened them to deny the poor world's faith was that they were too impatient to understand it. Indeed, the enlightenment common to young wits and worm-eaten old satirists, who plume themselves on detecting the scientific ineptitude of religion—something which the

The selection is reprinted with the permission of Charles Scribner's Sons from *The Life of Reason: Reason in Religion* by George Santayana, copyright 1905 Charles Scribner's Sons; renewal copyright 1933 George Santayana; and with the permission of Constable and Company, Ltd., pp. 3-14.

blindest half see—is not nearly enlightened enough: it points to notorious facts incompatible with religious tenets literally taken, but it leaves unexplored the habits of thought from which those tenets sprang, their original meaning, and their true function. Such studies would bring the skeptic face to face with the mystery and pathos of mortal existence. They would make him understand why religion is so profoundly moving and in a sense so profoundly just. There must needs be something humane and necessary in an influence that has become the most general sanction of virtue, the chief occasion for art and philosophy, and the source, perhaps, of the best human happiness. If nothing, as Hooker said, is "so malapert as a splenetic religion," a sour irreligion is almost as perverse.

At the same time, when Bacon penned the sage epigram we have quoted he forgot to add that the God to whom depth in philosophy brings back men's minds is far from being the same from whom a little philosophy estranges them. It would be pitiful indeed if mature reflection bred no better conceptions than those which have drifted down the muddy stream of time, where tradition and passion have jumbled everything together. Traditional conceptions, when they are felicitous, may be adopted by the poet, but they must be purified by the moralist and disintegrated by the philosopher. Each religion, so dear to those whose life it sanctifies, and fulfilling so necessary a function in the society that has adopted it, necessarily contradicts every other religion, and probably contradicts itself. What religion a man shall have is a historical accident, quite as much as what language he shall speak. In the rare circumstances where a choice is possible, he may, with some difficulty, make an exchange; but even then he is only adopting a new convention which may be more agreeable to his personal temper but which is essentially as arbitrary as the old.

The attempt to speak without speaking any particular language is not more hopeless than the attempt to have a religion that shall be no religion in particular. A courier's or a dargoman's speech may indeed be often unusual and drawn from disparate sources, not without some mixture of personal originality; but that private jargon will have a meaning only because of its analogy to one or more conventional languages and its obvious derivation from them. So travellers from one religion to another, people who have lost their spiritual nationality, may often retain a neutral and confused residuum of belief, which they may egregiously regard as the essence of all religion, so little may they remember the graciousness and naturalness of that ancestral accent which a perfect religion should have. Yet a moment's probing of the conceptions surviving in such minds will show them to be nothing but vestiges of old beliefs, creases which thought, even if emptied of all dogmatic tenets, has not been able to smooth away at its first unfolding. Later generations, if they have any religion at all, will be found either to revert to ancient authority, or to attach themselves spontaneously to something wholly novel and immensely positive, to some faith promulgated by a fresh genius and passionately embraced by a converted people. Thus every living and healthy religion has a marked idiosyncrasy. Its power consists in its special and surprising message and in the bias

which that revelation gives to life. The vistas it opens and the mysteries it propounds are another world to live in; and another world to live in—whether we expect ever to pass wholly into it or no— is what we mean by having a religion.

What relation, then, does this great business of the soul, which we call religion, bear to the Life of Reason? That the relation between the two is close seems clear from several circumstances. The Life of Reason is the seat of all ultimate values. Now the history of mankind will show us that whenever spirits at once lofty and intense have seemed to attain the highest joys, they have envisaged and attained them in religion. Religion would therefore seem to be a vehicle or a factor in rational life, since the ends of rational life are attained by it. Moreover, the Life of Reason is an ideal to which everything in the world should be subordinated; it establishes lines of moral cleavage everywhere and makes right eternally different from wrong. Religion does the same thing. It makes absolute moral decisions. It sanctions, unifies, and transforms ethics. Religion thus exercises a function of the Life of Reason. And a further function which is common to both is that of emancipating man from his personal limitations. In different ways religions promise to transfer the soul to better conditions. A supernaturally favored kingdom is to be established for posterity upon earth, or for all the faithful in heaven, or the soul is to be freed by repeated purgations from all taint and sorrow, or it is to be lost in the absolute, or it is to become an influence and an object of adoration in the places it once haunted or wherever the activities it once loved may be carried on by future generations of its kindred. Now reason in its ways lays before us all these possibilities: it points to common objects, political and intellectual, in which an individual may lose what is mortal and accidental in himself and immortalize what is rational and human; it teaches us how sweet and fortunate death may be to those whose spirit can still live in their country and in their ideas; it reveals the radiating effects of action and the eternal objects of thought.

Yet the difference in tone and language must strike us, so soon as it is philosophy that speaks. That change should remind us that even if the function of religion and that of reason coincide, this function is performed in the two cases by very different organs. Religions are many, reason one. Religion consists of conscious ideas, hopes, enthusiasms, and objects of worship; it operates by grace and flourishes by prayer. Reason, on the other hand, is a mere principle or potential order, on which, indeed, we may come to reflect, but which exists in us ideally only, without variation or stress of any kind. We conform or do not conform to it; it does not urge or chide us, nor call for any emotions on our part other than those naturally aroused by the various objects which it unfolds in their true nature and proportion. Religion brings some order into life by weighing it with new materials. Reason adds to the natural materials only the perfect order which it introduces into them. Rationality is nothing but a form, an ideal constitution which experience may more or less embody. Religion is a part of experience itself, a mass of sentiments and ideas. The one is an inviolate principle, the other a changing and struggling force. And yet this struggling and changing force of religion seems to direct man toward something eternal. It seems to make for an ultimate harmony within the soul and for an ultimate harmony between the soul and all the soul depends upon. So that religion, in its intent, is a more conscious and direct pursuit of the Life of Reason than is society, science, or art. For these approach and fill out the ideal life tentatively and piecemeal, hardly regarding the goal or caring for the ultimate justification of their

instinctive aims. Religion also has an instinctive and blind side, and bubbles up in all manner of chance practices and intuitions; soon, however, it feels its way toward the heart of things, and, from whatever quarter it may come, veers in the direction of the ultimate.

Nevertheless, we must confess that this religious pursuit of the Life of Reason has been singularly abortive. Those within the pale of each religion may prevail upon themselves to express satisfaction with its results, thanks to a fond partiality in reading the past and generous draughts of hope for the future; but any one regarding the various religions at once and comparing their achievements with what reason requires, must feel how terrible is the disappointment which they have one and all prepared for mankind. Their chief anxiety has been to offer imaginary remedies for mortal ills, some of which are incurable essentially, while others might have been really cured by well-directed effort. The Greek oracles, for instance, pretended to heal our natural ignorance, which has its appropriate though difficult cure, while the Christian vision of heaven pretended to be an antidote to our natural death, the inevitable correlate of birth and of a changing and conditioned existence. By methods of this sort little can be done for the real betterment of life. To confuse intelligence and dislocate sentiment by gratuitous fictions is a short-sighted way of pursuing happiness. Nature is soon avenged. An unhealthy exaltation and a one-sided morality have to be followed by regrettable reactions. When these come, the real rewards of life may seem vain to a relaxed vitality, and the very name of virtue may irritate young spirits untrained in any natural excellence. Thus religion too often debauches the morality it comes to sanction, and impedes the science it ought to fulfil.

What is the secret of this ineptitude? Why does religion, so near to rationality in its purpose, fall so far short of it in its texture and in its results? The answer is easy: Religion pursues rationality through the imagination. When it explains events or assigns causes, it is an imaginative substitute for science. When it gives precepts, insinuates ideals, or remolds aspiration, it is an imaginative substitute for wisdom—I mean for the deliberate and impartial pursuit of all good. The conditions and the aims of life are both represented in religion poetically, but this poetry tends to arrogate to itself literal truth and moral authority, neither of which it possesses. Hence the depth and importance of religion become intelligible no less than its contradictions and practical disasters. Its object is the same as that of reason, but its method is to proceed by intuition and by unchecked poetical conceits. These are repeated and vulgarized in proportion to their original fineness and significance, till they pass for reports of objective truth and come to constitute a world of faith, superposed upon the world of experience and regarded as materially enveloping it, if not in space at least in time and in existence. The only truth of religion comes from its interpretation of life, from its symbolic rendering of that moral experience which it springs out of and which it seeks to elucidate. Its falsehood comes from the insidious misunderstanding which clings to it, to the effect that these poetic conceptions are not merely representations of experience as it is or should be, but are rather information about experience or reality elsewhere—an experience and reality which, strangely enough, supply just the defects betrayed by reality and experience here.

Thus religion has the same original relation to life that poetry has; only poetry, which never pretends to literal validity, adds a pure value to existence, the value of a liberal imaginative exercise. The poetic value of religion would initially be greater than that of poetry itself, because religion deals with higher and more practical themes, with sides of life which are in greater need of some imaginative touch and ideal interpretation than are those pleasant or pompous things which ordinary poetry dwells upon. But this initial advantage is neutralized in part by the abuse to which religion is subject, whenever its symbolic rightness is taken for scientific truth. Like poetry, it improves the world only by imagining it improved, but not content with making this addition to the mind's furniture—an addition which might be useful and ennobling—it thinks to confer a more radical benefit by persuading mankind that, in spite of appearances, the world is really such as that rather arbitrary idealization has painted it. This spurious satisfaction is naturally the prelude to many a disappointment, and the soul has infinite trouble to emerge again from the artificial problems and sentiments into which it is thus plunged. The value of religion becomes equivocal. Religion remains an imaginative achievement, a symbolic representation of moral reality which may have a most important function in vitalizing the mind and in transmitting, by way of parables, the lessons of experience. But it becomes at the same time a continuous incidental deception; and this deception, in proportion as it is strenuously denied to be such, can work indefinite harm in the world and in the conscience.

On the whole, however, religion should not be conceived as having taken the place of anything better, but rather as having come to relieve situations which, but for its presence, would have been infinitely worse. In the thick of active life, or in the monotony of practical slavery, there is more need to stimulate fancy than to control it. Natural instinct is not much disturbed in the human brain by what may happen in that thin superstratum of ideas which commonly overlays it. We must not blame religion for preventing the development of a moral and natural science which at any rate would seldom have appeared; we must rather thank it for the sensibility, the reverence, the speculative insight which it has introduced into the world.

We may therefore proceed to analyze the significance and the function which religion has had at its different stages, and, without disguising or in the least condoning its confusion with literal truth, we may allow ourselves to enter as sympathetically as possible into its various conceptions and emotions. They have made up the inner life of many sages, and of all those who without great genius or learning have lived steadfastly in the spirit. The feeling of reverence should itself be treated with reverence, although not at a sacrifice of truth, with which alone, in the end, reverence is compatible. Nor have we any reason to be intolerant of the partialities and contradictions which religions display. Were we dealing with a science, such contradictions would have to be instantly solved and removed; but when we are concerned with the poetic interpretation of experience, contradiction means only variety, and variety means spontaneity, wealth of resource, and a nearer approach to total adequacy.

If we hope to gain any understanding of these matters we must begin by taking them out of that heated and fanatical atmosphere in which the Hebrew tradition has enveloped them. The Jews had no philosophy, and when their national traditions came to be theoretically explicated and justified, they were made to issue in a puerile scholasticism and a rabid intolerance. The question of monotheism, for instance, was a terrible question to the Jews. Idolatry did not consist in worshipping a god who, not being ideal, might be unworthy of worship, but rather in recognizing other gods than the one worshipped in Jerusalem. To the Greeks, on the contrary, whose philosophy was enlightened and ingenuous, monotheism and polytheism seemed perfectly innocent and compatible. To say God or the gods was only to use different expressions for the same influence, now viewed in its abstract unity and correlation with all existence, now viewed in its various manifestations in moral life, in nature, or in history. So that what in Plato, Aristotle, and the Stoics meets us at every step—the combination of monotheism with polytheism—is no contradiction, but merely an intelligent variation of phrase to indicate various aspects or functions in physical and moral things. When religion appears to us in this light its contradictions and controversies lose all their bitterness. Each doctrine will simply represent the moral plane on which they live who have devised or adopted it. Religions will thus be better or worse, never true or false. We shall be able to lend ourselves to each in turn, and seek to draw from it the secret of its inspiration.

9 / SUMMARY

Naturalism, we have seen, is a speculative vision of man and the cosmos grounded, the naturalist believes, on methods of responsible inquiry. Professor Ernest Nagel provides an important summary statement of this vision in the following selection. He finds two theses central to naturalism: the primacy of organized matter, and the plurality of things and events. Man's career and destiny must, therefore, be seen as taking place within nature. Professor Nagel also examines two objections to naturalism: first, that in relying on the methods of science, naturalism has "stacked the cards" in its favor; second, in committing itself to science, naturalism rests on a faith similar to religious faith. He finds these objections unwarranted; and he concludes his reconsideration of naturalism by stating that among the possible philosophies open to men's belief, naturalism is best supported by the evidence.

NATURALISM RECONSIDERED

Ernest Nagel (1901-   )

The past quarter century has been for philosophy in many parts of the world a period of acute self-questioning, engendered in no small measure by developments in scientific and logical thought, and in part no doubt by fundamental changes in the social order. In any event, there has come about a general loss of confidence in the competence of philosophy to provide by way of a distinctive intellectual method a basic ground-plan of the cosmos, or for that matter to contribute to knowledge of any primary subject matter except by becoming a specialized positive science and subjecting itself to the discipline of empirical inquiry. Although the abysses of human ignorance are undeniably profound, it has also become apparent that ignorance, like actual knowledge, is of many special and heterogeneous things; and we have come to think, like the fox and unlike the hedgehog of whom Mr. Isaiah Berlin has recently reminded us,[1] that there are a great many things which are already known or remain to be discovered, but that there is no one "big thing" which,

The selection is from Ernest Nagel, "Naturalism Reconsidered," *Proceedings of the American Philosophical Association,* 28 (1954-55), pp. 5-17, with omissions. Reprinted in Nagel, *Logic Without Metaphysics,* Copyright 1956 by The Free Press, a corporation. Used by permission of the American Philosophical Association, The Free Press, and the author. [1 This reference is to the use by Sir Isaiah Berlin in his book, *The Hedgehog and the Fox* (London, 1953), of a line from the Greek poet Archilochus: "The fox knows many things, but the hedgehog knows one big thing." *Ed.*]

if known, would make everything else coherent and unlock the mystery of creation. In consequence, many of us have ceased to emulate the great system-builders in the history of philosophy. In partial imitation of the strategy of modern science, and in the hope of achieving responsibly held conclusions about matters concerning which we could acquire genuine competence, we have tended to become specialists in our professional activities. We have come to direct our best energies to the resolution of limited problems and puzzles that emerge in the analysis of scientific and ordinary discourse, in the evaluation of claims to knowledge, in the interpretation of validation of ethical and esthetic judgments, and in the assessment of types of human experience. I hope I shall not be regarded as offensive in stating my impression that the majority of the best minds among us have turned away from the conception of the philosopher as the spectator of all time and existence, and have concentrated on restricted but manageable questions, with almost deliberate unconcern for the bearing of their often minute investigations upon an inclusive view of nature and man. . . .

On the other hand, philosophers like other men conduct their lives within the framework of certain comprehensive if not always explicit assumptions about the world they inhabit. These assumptions color evaluations of major ideals and proposed policies. I also suspect that the directions taken by analyses of specific intellectual problems are frequently if subtly controlled by the expressed or tacit beliefs philosophers hold concerning the over-all nature of things, by their views on human destiny, and by their conceptions of the scope of human reason. But conversely, resolutions of special problems made plausible by recent philosophical analysis, as well as by the findings of various positive sciences, seem to me to support certain broad generalizations about the cosmos and to disconform others. It is clearly desirable that such basic intellectual commitments, which are at once the matrix and the outcome of inquiries into specific problems, be made as explicit as possible. A philosopher who is a reflective man by profession, certainly owes it to himself to articulate, if only occasionally, what sort of world he thinks he inhabits, and to make clear to himself where approximately lies the center of his convictions.

The discharge of the important obligation which is mine this evening, seems to me an appropriate occasion for stating as simply and as succinctly as I can the substance of those intellectual commitments I like to call "naturalism." The label itself is of no importance, but I use it partly because of its historical associations, and partly because it is a reminder that the doctrines for which it is a name are neither new nor untried. With Santayana, I prefer not to accept in philosophic debate what I do not believe when I am not arguing; and naturalism as I construe it merely formulates what centuries of human experience have repeatedly confirmed. At any rate, naturalism seems to me a sound generalized account of the world encountered in practice and in critical reflection, and a just perspective upon the human scene. I wish to state briefly and hence with little supporting argument what I take to be its major tenets, and to defend it against some recent criticisms.

Claims to knowledge cannot ultimately be divorced from an evaluation of the intellectual methods used to support those claims. It is nevertheless unfortunate that in recent years naturalists in philosophy have so frequently permitted their allegiance to a dependable method of inquiry to obscure their substantive views on things in general. For it is the inclusive intellectual image of nature and man which naturalism supplies that sets it off from other comprehensive philosophies. In my conception of it, at any rate, naturalism embraces a generalized account of the cosmic scheme and of man's place in it, as well as a logic of inquiry.

I hasten to add, however, that naturalism does not offer a theory of nature in the sense that Newtonian mechanics, for example, provides a theory of motion. Naturalism does not, like the latter, specify a set of substantive principles with the help of which the detailed course of concrete happenings can be explained or understood. Moreover, the principles affirmed by naturalism are not proposed as competitors or underpinnings for any of the special theories which the positive sciences assert. Nor, finally, does naturalism offer its general view of nature and man as the product of some special philosophical mode of knowing. The account of things proposed by naturalism is a distillation from knowledge acquired in the usual way in daily encounters with the world or in specialized scientific inquiry. Naturalism articulates features of the world which, because they have become so obvious, are rarely mentioned in discussions of special subject matter, but which distinguish our actual world from other conceivable worlds. The major affirmations of naturalism are accordingly meager in content; but the principles affirmed are nevertheless effective guides in responsible criticism and evaluation.

Two theses seem to me central to naturalism as I conceive it. The first is the existential and causal primacy of organized matter in the executive order of nature. This is the assumption that the occurrence of events, qualities and processes, and the characteristic behaviors of various individuals, are contingent on the organization of spatio-temporally located bodies, whose internal structures and external relations determine and limit the appearance and disappearance of everything that happens. That this is so, is one of the best-tested conclusions of experience. We are frequently ignorant of the special conditions under which things come into being or pass away; but we have also found repeatedly that when we look closely, we eventually ascertain at least the approximate and gross conditions under which events occur, and we discover that those conditions invariably consist of some more or less complex organization of material substances. Naturalism does not maintain that only what is material exists, since many things noted in experience, for example, modes of action, relations of meaning, dreams, joys, plans, aspirations, are not as such material bodies or organizations of material bodies. What naturalism does assert as a truth about nature is that though *forms* of behavior or *functions* of material systems are indefeasibly parts of nature, forms and functions are not themselves agents in their own realization or in the realization of anything else. In the conception of nature's processes which naturalism affirms, there is no place for the operation of disembodied forces, no place for an immaterial spirit directing the course of events, no place for the survival of personality after the corruption of the body which exhibits it.

The second major contention of naturalism is that the manifest plurality and variety of things, of their qualities and their functions, are an irreducible feature of the cosmos, not a deceptive appearance cloaking some more homogeneous "ultimate reality" or transempirical substance, and that the sequential orders in which events occur or the manifold relations of dependence in which things exist are *contingent* connec-tions, not the embodiments of a fixed and unified pattern of logically necessary links. The existential primacy of organized matter does not make illusory either the relatively permanent or the comparatively transient characters and forms which special configurations of bodies may possess. In particular, although the continued existence of the human scene is precarious and is dependent on a balance of forces that doubtless will not endure indefinitely, and even though its distinctive traits are not pervasive throughout space, it is nonetheless as much a part of the "ultimate" furniture of the world, and is as genuine a sample of what "really" exists, as are atoms and stars. There undoubtedly occur integrated systems of bodies, such as biological organisms, which have the capacity because of their material organization to maintain themselves and the direction of their characteristic activities. But there is no positive evidence, and much negative evidence, for the supposition that all existential structures are teleological systems in this sense, or for the view that whatever occurs is a phase in a unitary, teleologically organized, and all-inclusive process or system. . . . In brief, if naturalism is true, irreducible variety and logical contingency are fundamental traits of the world we actually inhabit. The orders and connections of things are all accessible to rational inquiry; but these orders and connections are not all derivable by deductive methods from any set of premises that deductive reason can certify.

It is in this framework of general ideas that naturalism envisages the career and destiny of man. Naturalism views the emergence and the continuance of human society as dependent on physical and physiological conditions that have not always obtained, and that will not permanently endure. But it does not in consequence regard man and his works as intrusions into nature, any more than it construes as intrusions the presence of heavenly bodies or of terrestrial protozoa. The stars are no more foreign to the cosmos than are men, even if the conditions for the existence of both stars and men are realized only occasionally or only in a few regions. Indeed, the conception of human life as a war with nature, as a struggle with an implacable foe that has doomed man to extinction, is but an inverted theology, with a malicious Devil in the seat of Omnipotence. It is a conception that is immodest as well as anthropomorphic in the importance it imputes to man in the scheme of things.

On the other hand, the affirmation that nature is man's "home" as much as it is the "home" of anything else, and the denial that cosmic forces are *intent* on destroying the human scene, do not warrant the interpretation that every sector of nature is explicable in terms of traits known to characterize only human individuals and human actions. Man undoubtedly possesses characteristics which are shared by everything that exists; but he also manifests traits and capacities that appear to be distinctive of him. Is anything gained but confusion when all forms of dependence between things, whether animate or inanimate, and all types of behaviors they display, are subsumed under distinctions that have an identifiable content only in reference to the human psyche? Measured by the illumination they bring, there is nothing to differentiate the thesis that human traits are nothing but the properties of bodies which can be formulated exclusively in the language of current physical theory, from the view that every change and every mode of operation, in whatever sector of the cosmos it may be encountered, is simply an illustration of some category pertinent to the description of human behavior. . . .

Human nature and history, in short, are *human* nature and history, not the history and nature of anything else, however much knowledge of other things contributes to a just appraisal of what man is. In particular,

the adequacy of proposed ideals for human life must be judged, not in terms of their causes and origins, but in reference to how the pursuit and possible realization of ideals contribute to the organization and release of *human* energies. Men are animated by many springs of action, no one of which is intrinsically good or evil; and a moral ideal is the imagined satisfaction of some complex of impulses, desires, and needs. When ideals are handled responsibly, they therefore function as hypotheses for achieving a balanced exercise of human powers. Moral ideals are not self-certifying, any more than are the theories of the physical sciences; and evidence drawn from experienced satisfactions is required to validate them, however difficult may be the process of sifting and weighing the available data. Moral problems arise from a conflict of specific impulses and interests. They cannot, however, be effectively resolved by invoking standards derived from the study of non-human nature, or of what is allegedly beyond nature. If moral problems can be resolved at all, they can be resolved only in the light of specific human capacities, historical circumstance and acquired skills, and the opportunities (revealed by an imagination disciplined by knowledge) for altering the physical and social environment and for redirecting habitual behaviors. Moreover, since human virtues are in part the products of the society in which human powers are matured, a naturalistic moral theory is at the same time a critique of civilization, that is, a critique of the institutions that channel human energies, so as to exhibit the possibilities and limitations of various forms and arrangements of society for bringing enduring satisfactions to individual human careers.

These are the central tenets of what I take to be philosophical naturalism. They are tenets which are supported by compelling empirical evidence, rather than by dicta based on dogmatic preference. In my view of it, naturalism does not dismiss every other different conception of the scheme of things as logically impossible; and it does not rule out all alternatives to itself on a priori grounds. It is possible, I think, to conceive without logical inconsistency a world in which disembodied forces are dynamic agents, or in which whatever happens is a manifestation of an unfolding logical pattern. In such possible worlds it would be an error to be a naturalist. But philosophy is not identical with pure mathematics, and its ultimate concern is with the actual world, even though philosophy must take cognizance of the fact that the actual world contains creatures who can envisage possible worlds and who employ different logical procedures for deciding which hypothetical world is the actual one. It is partly for this reason that contemporary naturalists devote so much attention to methods of evaluating evidence. When naturalists give their allegiance to the method of intelligence commonly designated as the method of modern empirical science, they do so because that method appears to be the most assured way of achieving reliable knowledge.

As judged by that method, the evidence in my opinion is at present conclusive for the truth of naturalism, and it is tempting to suppose that no one familiar with the evidence can fail to acknowledge that philosophy. Indeed, some commentators there are who assert that all philosophies are at bottom only expressions in different idioms of the same conceptions about the nature of things, so that the strife of philosophic systems is mainly a conflict over essentially linguistic matters. Yet many thinkers for whom I have a profound respect explicitly reject naturalism, and their espousal of contrary views seems to me incompatible with the irenic claim that we really are in agreement on fundamentals.

Although I do not have the time this evening to consider systematically the criticisms currently made of naturalism, I do wish to examine briefly two repeatedly voiced objections which, if valid, would in my opinion seriously jeopardize the integrity and adequacy of naturalism as a philosophy. Stated summarily, the first objection is that in relying exclusively on the logico-empirical method of modern science for establishing cognitive claims, naturalists are in effect stacking the cards in their own favor, since thereby all alternative philosophies are antecedently disqualified. It is maintained, for example, that naturalism rejects any hypothesis about transempirical causes or time-transcending spiritual substances as factors in the order of things, not because such hypotheses are actually shown to be false, but simply because the logic of proof adopted dismisses as irrelevant any evidence which might establish them.

This criticism does not seem to me to have merit: the logico-empirical method of evaluating cognitive claims to which naturalists subscribe does not eliminate by fiat any hypothesis about existence for which evidence can be procured, that is, evidence that in the last resort can be obtained through sensory or introspective observation. Thus, anyone who asserts a hypothesis postulating a transempirical ground for all existence, presumably seeks to understand in terms of that ground the actual occurrences in nature, and to account thereby for what actually happens as distinct from what is merely imagined to happen. There must therefore be some connection between the postulated character of the hypothetical transempirical ground, and the empirically observable traits in the world around us; for otherwise the hypothesis is otiose, and not relevant to the spatio-temporal processes of nature. This does not mean, as some critics of naturalism suppose the latter to maintain, that the hypothetical transempirical ground must be characterized exclusively in terms of the observable properties of the world, any more than that the sub-microscopic particles and processes which current physical theory postulates must be logical constructions out of the observable traits of macroscopic objects. But it does mean that unless the hypothesis implies, even if only by a circuitous route, some statements about empirical data, it is not adequate to the task for which it is proposed. If naturalists reject hypotheses about transempirical substances, they do not do so arbitrarily. They reject such hypotheses either because their relevance to the going concerns of nature is not established, or because, though their relevance is not in question, the actual evidence does not support them.

Nor does naturalism dismiss as unimportant and without consideration experiences such as of the holy, of divine illumination, or of mystical ecstasy, experiences which are of the greatest moment in the lives of many men, and which are often taken to signify the presence and operation of some purely spiritual reality. Such experiences have dimensions of meaning for those who have undergone them, that are admittedly not on par with the import of more common experiences like those of physical hunger, general well-being, or feelings of remorse and guilt. Yet such experiences are nonetheless events among other events; and though they may be evidence for something, their sheer occurrence does not certify *what* they are evidence for, any more than the sheer occurrence of dreams, hopes, and delusions authenticates the actual existence of their ostensible objects. In particular, whether the experience labelled as an experience of divine illumination is evidence for the existence of a divinity, is a question to be settled by inquiry, not by dogmatic affirmations or denials. . . .

There is, however, a further objection to naturalism, to the effect that in committing itself to the logic of scientific proof, it is quite analogous to religious belief in resting on unsupported and indemonstrable faith. For that logic allegedly involves assump-

tions like the uniformity of nature or similar principles which transcend experience, cannot be justified empirically, and yet provide the premises that constitute the ultimate warrant for the conclusions of empirical inquiry. But if naturalism is thus based on unprovable articles of faith, on what cogent grounds can it reject a different conception of the true order of governance of events which rests on a different faith?

I cannot here deal adequately with the complex issues raised by this objection. Its point is not satisfactorily turned by claiming, as some have done, that instead of being articles of faith, the alleged indemonstrable postulates of scientific method are simply rules of the scientific game which *define* what in that game is to be understood by the words "knowledge" and "evidence." As I see it, however, the objection has force only for those whose ideal of reason is demonstration, and who therefore refuse to dignify anything as genuine knowledge unless it is demonstrable from self-luminous and self-evident premises. But if, as I also think, that ideal is not universally appropriate, and if, furthermore, a *wholesale* justification for knowledge and its methods is an unreasonable demand and a misplaced effort, the objection appears as quite pointless. . . .

It is almost painful to have to make a point of the elementary fact that whatever may happen to be the range of special interests and sensibilities of individual naturalists, there is no incompatibility, whether logical or psychological, between maintaining that warranted knowledge is secured only through the use of a definite logical method, and recognizing that the world can be experienced in many other ways than by knowing it. It is a matter of record that outstanding exponents of naturalism, in our own time as well as in the past, have exhibited an unequaled and tender sensitivity to the esthetic and moral dimensions of human experience; and they have been not only movingly eloquent celebrants of the role of moral idealism and of intellectual and esthetic contemplation in human life, but also vigorous defenders of the distinctive character of these values against facile attempts to reduce them to something else.

It seems to me singularly inept, moreover, to indict naturalism as a philosophy without a sense for the tragic aspects of life. For unlike many world-views, naturalism offers no cosmic consolation for the unmerited defeats and undeserved sufferings which all men experience in one form or another. It has never sought to conceal its view of human destiny as an episode between two oblivions. To be sure, naturalism is not a philosophy of despair. For one facet in its radical pluralism is the truth that a human good is nonetheless a good, despite its transitory existence. There doubtless are foolish optimists among those professing naturalism, though naturalism has no monopoly in this respect, and it is from other quarters that one usually receives glad tidings of a universal nostrum. But in any event, neither the pluralism so central to naturalism, nor its cultivation of scientific reason, is compatible with any dogmatic assumption to the effect that men can be liberated from *all* the sorrows and evils to which they are now heirs, through the eventual advances of science and the institution of appropriate physical and social innovations. Indeed, why suppose that a philosophy which is wedded to the use of the sober logic of scientific intelligence, should thereby be committed to the dogma that there are no irremediable evils? On the contrary, human reason is potent only against evils that are *remediable*. At the same time, since it is impossible to decide responsibly, *antecedent* to inquiry, *which* of the many human ills can be mitigated if not eradicated by extending the operations of scientific reason into human affairs, naturalism is not a philosophy of *general* renunciation, even though it recognizes that it is the better part of wisdom to be equally resigned to what, in the light of available evidence, cannot be avoided. Human reason is not an omnipotent instrument for the achievement of human goods; but it is the only instrument we do possess, and it is not a contemptible one. Although naturalism is acutely sensitive to the actual limitations of rational effort, those limitations do not warrant a romantic philosophy of general despair, and they do not blind naturalism to the possibilities implicit in the exercise of disciplined reason for realizing human excellence.

BIBLIOGRAPHICAL NOTE

A broad historical survey of materialism is given in F. H. Lange's *History of Materialism* (New York, 1926), although naturalists have frequently given their own interpretive views of that history for themselves; see, for example, Santayana's essay on Lucretius in *Three Philosophical Poets* (Cambridge, 1910). A great number of volumes trace the rise of modern science, including its philosophical assumptions, from the seventeenth century to the present. Among the most valuable of these works are Herbert Butterfield's *The Origins of Modern Science* (New York, 1951) and A. R. Hall, *The Scientific Revolution* (Boston, 1954). The varieties of naturalism, including those of a pragmatic temper, are represented in such works as Samuel Alexander, *Space, Time and Deity*, 2 vols. (London, 1920); John Dewey's many books, including especially *Experience and Nature* (Chicago, 1925); J. B. Pratt, *Naturalism* (New Haven, 1939); the writings of Santayana; and F. J. E. Woodbridge, *Nature and Mind*

(New York, 1937). Two of these thinkers, Dewey and Santayana, are included in the series of volumes, The Library of Living Philosophers, edited by P. A. Schilpp. Two anthologies may also be of interest to the student: R. W. Sellars, V. J. McGill, and M. Farber (eds.), *Philosophy for the Future* (New York, 1949), and Y. H. Krikorian (ed.), *Naturalism and the Human Spirit* (New York, 1944).

IV
POSITIVISM

HUME / RUSSELL / POINCARÉ
PEARSON / STEVENSON
RICHARDS / POPPER / CARNAP
AYER / FEIGL

The term "positivism" was first associated with the doctrines of the eccentric French thinker Auguste Comte (1798-1857). By it he meant that the highest form of knowledge is simple description of sensory experience. He based this view on an evolutionary "law of three stages," which he believed he had discovered in 1822. The three stages are the *theological*, where spiritual, anthropomorphic beings are appealed to to explain natural phenomena; the *metaphysical*, where these beings are depersonalized and become forces and essences; and the *positive*, where explanation of phenomena proceeds by scientific description.[1] Although this law is Comte's discovery, the basic ideas of positivism are found in numerous thinkers; and actually, contemporary positivists rely very little on Comte's thought in the development of their philosophies.

Like naturalism, positivism holds that science alone provides reliable knowledge of nature; indeed, in some ways it goes farther than naturalism in its emphasis on science. But it differs from naturalism in two fundamental ways: its analysis of science is based more on logic than on the psychological categories of doubt and belief; and it is more explicitly—even at times vehemently—antimetaphysical.

Central to the positivisit's analysis of knowledge is the distinction be-

---

[1] The student may find this view developed in Comte's book, *The Positive Philosophy* (tr. Harriet Martineau) (New York: Calvin Blanchard, 1855).

tween analytic and synthetic propositions. Analytic propositions are those whose truth value depends on the terms occurring in them, as, "No bachelors are married"; synthetic propositions are those that refer to facts and whose truth depends on a relation to them, as, "There is gold in Siberia." The positivist believes that the former group, made up of propositions that contain no factual content, really consists only of tautologies. With them, truth and falsehood can be determined by logical and linguistic analysis. The second group, containing all propositions having factual meaning, belongs entirely to the sciences; and there are no factual propositions, the positivist holds, except scientific ones.

This division itself rules out metaphysical statements as cognitive or meaningful. Yet there is another positivistic doctrine, derived from an analysis of the "meaning of factual meaning," that is even more explicitly antimetaphysical. This is the verifiability theory of meaning. Many attempts have been made to formulate the theory accurately; in essence, they all seek to define the meaning of an empirical concept by reference to the sensory observations that will verify or disconfirm it. When a proposition involves such reference, it is meaningful and open to scientific inquiry; when it does not, it is (unless it is a logical truth) only a pseudo statement, noncognitive and nonsense.

A third positivist doctrine follows from the preceding ideas. All statements are divided into three groups: cognitive, such as those of logic and science; directive, which includes the uses of language for purposes of action; and emotive, the use of language to express emotion. It is in these latter two groups that positivists put many of the propositions of traditional philosophy, including ethical, metaphysical, and theological statements.

The student may well ask after reading these three theses, What then is the task of philosophy? The positivist replies that philosophy is not a separate, identifiable body of statements, but rather an activity of analysis. He eschews speculation and the attempt to find ultimate meanings, and concentrates rather on the analysis, first, of key terms in scientific inquiry, and second, of discourse generally. Philosophy, guided by the analytic-synthetic distinction and the verification principle, is thus analysis, and its object of study is primarily language.

The original positivism of Comte and some of his nineteenth-century followers is identifiable by its concern with science. Contemporary positivism is in many ways much more sophisticated, for it utilizes the recent developments in logic in conducting its analyses. It is for this reason frequently called logical positivism. It has also, because of its stress on scientific inquiry, been termed logical empiricism. These different names, however, all refer to the same distinctive position in contemporary philosophy.

1 / INTRODUCTION

The writings of the British philosopher David Hume are a major source of some of the ideas just outlined. In the following selection, Hume makes the distinction between analytic and synthetic propositions, or, as he calls them, relations of ideas and matters of fact. The truth or falsehood of the former, he observes, can be determined "by the mere operation of thought." But what of the second group? Hume sees no self-contradiction in the statement, "The sun will not rise tomorrow," hard as it may be to believe it. How then do we come to accept this belief? Hume answers, through experience.

The next question to ask concerns the basis of reasonings from experience. Hume finds this basis to be the principle of causality, for it is this principle which allows the distinct events of experience to be tied together in some meaningful way. What kind of principle is it? It is not a priori, for every effect is distinct from its cause, and no reasoning can take one from a cause to its precise effect. Is the principle then derived from experience? To ask this question, however, is to become involved in a logical circle: experience is based and depends on the causal principle; hence experience cannot be utilized to warrant it.

Hume therefore concludes in a metaphysically skeptical position. Metaphysical propositions like causality rest on no rational grounds whatsoever. If we use such ideas (and for Hume we do), their only ground can be the psychological principle of custom or habit.

KNOWLEDGE AND CAUSALITY

David Hume (1711-1776)

All the objects of human reason or inquiry may naturally be divided into two kinds, to wit, *Relations of Ideas,* and *Matters of Fact.* Of the first kind are the sciences of Geometry, Algebra, and Arithmetic, and, in short, every affirmation which is either intuitively or demonstratively certain. *That the square of the hypotenuse is equal to the square of the two sides,* is a proposition which expresses a relation between these figures. *That three times five is equal to the half of thirty,* expresses a relation between these numbers. Propositions of this kind are discoverable by the mere operation of thought, without dependence on what is anywhere existent in the universe. Though there never were a circle or triangle in nature, the truths demonstrated by Euclid would for ever retain their certainty and evidence.

Matters of fact, which are the second objects of human reason, are not ascertained in the same manner; nor is our evidence of their truth, however great, of a like nature with the foregoing. The contrary of every matter of fact is still possible; because it can never imply a contradiction, and is conceived by the mind with the same facility and distinctness, as if ever so conformable to reality. *That the sun will not rise tomorrow* is no less intelligible a propo-

The selection is from Hume's *An Inquiry Concerning the Human Understanding,* in *The Philosophical Works of David Hume,* 4 vols. (Boston: Little, Brown and Co., 1854), Vol. IV, pp. 30-54, with omissions.

sition, and implies no more contradiction, than the affirmation, *that it will rise*. We should in vain, therefore, attempt to demonstrate its falsehood. Were it demonstratively false, it would imply a contradiction, and could never be distinctly conceived by the mind.

It may therefore be a subject worthy of curiosity, to inquire what is the nature of that evidence, which assures us of any real existence and matter of fact, beyond the present testimony of our senses, or the records of our memory. This part of philosophy, it is observable, had been little cultivated either by the ancients or moderns; and therefore our doubts and errors, in the prosecution of so important an inquiry, may be the more excusable, while we march through such difficult paths without any guide or direction. They may even prove useful, by exciting curiosity, and destroying that implicit faith and security which is the bane of all reasoning and free inquiry. The discovery of defects in the common philosopher, if any such there be, will not, I presume, be a discouragement, but rather an incitement, as is usual, to attempt something more full and satisfactory than has yet been proposed to the public.

All reasonings concerning matter of fact seem to be founded on the relation of *Cause and Effect*. By means of that relation alone we can go beyond the evidence of our memory and senses. If you were to ask a man why he believes any matter of fact which is absent, for instance, that his friend is in the country, or in France, he would give you a reason, and this reason would be some other fact: as a letter received from him, or the knowledge of his former resolutions and promises. A man, finding a watch or any other machine in a desert island, would conclude that there had once been men in that island. All our reasonings concerning fact are of the same nature. And here it is constantly supposed, that there is

a connection between the present fact and that which is inferred from it. Were there nothing to bind them together, the inference would be entirely precarious. The hearing of an articulate voice and rational discourse in the dark, assures us of the presence of some person: why? because these are the effects of the human make and fabric, and closely connected with it. If we anatomize all the other reasonings of this nature, we shall find that they are founded on the relation of cause and effect, and that this relation is either near or remote, direct or collateral. Heat and light are collateral effects of fire, and the one effect may justly be inferred from the other.

If we would satisfy ourselves, therefore, concerning the nature of that evidence which assures us of matters of fact, we must inquire how we arrive at the knowledge of cause and effect.

I shall venture to affirm, as a general proposition which admits of no exception, that the knowledge of this relation is not, in any instance, attained by reasonings *a priori;* but arises entirely from experience, when we find, that any particular objects are constantly conjoined with each other. Let an object be presented to a man of ever so strong natural reason and abilities; if that object be entirely new to him, he will not be able, by the most accurate examination of its sensible qualities, to discover any of its causes or effects. Adam, though his rational faculties be supposed, at the very first, entirely perfect, could not have inferred from the fluidity and transparency of water that it would suffocate him; or from the light and warmth of fire that it would consume him. No object ever discovers, by the qualities which appear to the senses, either the causes which produced it, or the effects which will arise from it; nor can our reason, unassisted by experience, ever draw any inference concerning real existence and matter of fact.

This proposition, *that causes and effects*

are discoverable, not by reason, but by experience, will readily be admitted with regard to such objects as we remember to have once been altogether unknown to us; since we must be conscious of the utter inability which we then lay under of foretelling what would arise from them. Present two smooth pieces of marble to a man who has no tincture of natural philosophy; he will never discover that they will adhere together in such a manner as to require great force to separate them in a direct line, while they make so small a resistance to a lateral pressure. Such events as bear little analogy to the common course of nature, are also readily confessed to be known only by experience; nor does any man imagine that the explosion of gunpowder, or the attraction of a loadstone, could ever be discovered by arguments *a priori.* In like manner, when an effect is supposed to depend upon an intricate machinery or secret structure of parts, we make no difficulty in attributing all our knowledge of it to experience. Who will assert that he can give the ultimate reason, why milk or bread is proper nourishment for a man, not for a lion or tiger?

But the same truth may not appear at first sight to have the same evidence with regard to events, which have become familiar to us from our first appearance in the world, which bear a close analogy to the whole course of nature, and which are supposed to depend on the simple qualities of objects, without any secret structure of parts. We are apt to imagine, that we could discover these effects by the mere operation of our reason without experience. We fancy, that we were brought on a sudden into this world, we could at first have inferred, that one billiard-ball would communicate motion to another upon impulse; and that we needed not to have waited for the event, in order to pronounce with certainty concerning it. Such is the influence of custom, that where it is strongest, it not only covers our natural ignorance, but even conceals itself, and seems not to take place, merely because it is found in the highest degree.

But to convince us, that all the laws of nature, and all the operations of bodies, without exception, are known only by experience, the following reflections may perhaps suffice. Were any object presented to us, and were we required to pronounce concerning the effect which will result from it, without consulting past observation; after what manner, I beseech you, must the mind proceed in this operation? It must invent or imagine some event which it ascribes to the object as its effect; and it is plain that this invention must be entirely arbitrary. The mind can never possibly find the effect in the supposed cause, by the most accurate scrutiny and examination. For the effect is totally different from the cause, and consequently can never be discovered in it. Motion in the second billiard-ball is a quite distinct event from motion in the first; nor is there any thing in the one to suggest the smallest hint of the other. A stone or piece of metal raised into the air, and left without any support, immediately falls: but to consider the matter *a priori,* is there anything we discover in this situation which can beget the idea of a downward, rather than an upward, or any other motion, in the stone or metal?

And as the first imagination or invention of a particular effect, in all natural operations, is arbitrary, where we consult not experience; so must we also esteem the supposed tie or connection between the cause and effect which binds them together, and renders it impossible, that any other effect could result from the operation of that cause. When I see, for instance, a billiard-ball moving in a straight line towards another; even suppose motion in the second ball should by accident be suggested to me as the result of their contact or impulse; may I not conceive that a hundred different events might as well follow from that cause?

May not both these balls remain at absolute rest? May not the first ball return in a straight line, or leap off from the second in any line or direction? All these suppositions are consistent and conceivable. Why then should we give the preference to one, which is no more consistent or conceivable than the rest? All our reasonings *a priori* will never be able to show us any foundation for this preference.

In a word, then, every effect is a distinct event from its cause. It could not, therefore, be discovered in the cause; and the first invention or conception of it, *a priori*, must be entirely arbitrary. And even after it is suggested, the conjunction of it with the cause must appear equally arbitrary; since there are always many other effects, which, to reason, must seem fully as consistent and natural. In vain, therefore, should we pretend to determine any single event, or infer any cause or effect, without the assistance of observation and experience. . . .

But we have not yet attained any tolerable satisfaction with regard to the question first proposed. Each solution still gives rise to a new question as difficult as the foregoing, and leads us on to further inquiries. When it is asked, *What is the nature of all our reasonings concerning matter of fact?* the proper answer seems to be, that they are founded on the relation of cause and effect. When again it is asked, *What is the foundation of all our reasonings and conclusions concerning that relation?* it may be replied in one word, *experience*. But if we still carry on our sifting humor, and ask, *What is the foundation of all conclusions from experience?* this implies a new question, which may be of more difficult solution and explication. Philosophers that give themselves airs of superior wisdom and sufficiency, have a hard task when they encounter persons of inquisitive dispositions, who push them from every corner to which they retreat, and who are sure at last to bring them to some dangerous dilemma.

The best expedient to prevent this confusion, is to be modest in our pretensions, and even to discover the difficulty ourselves before it is objected to us. By this means we may make a kind of merit of our very ignorance.

I shall content myself in this section with an easy task, and shall pretend only to give a negative answer to the question here proposed. I say then, that even after we have experience of the operations of cause and effect, our conclusions from that experience are *not* founded on reasoning, or any process of the understanding. This answer we must endeavor both to explain and to defend.

It must certainly be allowed, that nature has kept us at a great distance from all her secrets, and has afforded us only the knowledge of a few superficial qualities of objects; while she conceals from us those powers and principles on which the influence of those objects entirely depends. Our senses inform us of the color, weight, and consistence of bread; but neither sense nor reason can ever inform us of those qualities which fit it for the nourishment and support of a human body. Sight or feeling conveys an idea of the actual motion of bodies, but as to that wonderful force or power which would carry on a moving body for ever in a continued change of place, and which bodies never lose but by communicating it to others; of this we cannot form the most distant conception. But notwithstanding this ignorance of natural powers and principles, we always presume when we see like sensible qualities, that they have like secret powers, and expect that effects similar to those which we have experienced will follow from them. If a body of like color and consistence with that bread which we have formerly eat, be presented to us, we make no scruple of repeating the experiment, and foresee, with certainty, like nourishment and support. Now, this is a process of the mind or thought, of which I would willingly know the foundation. It is allowed on all hands, that there is no known connection between the sensible qualities and the secret powers; and consequently, that the mind is not led to form such a conclusion concerning their constant and regular conjunction, by anything which it knows of their nature. As to past *Experience,* it can be allowed to give *direct* and *certain* information of those precise objects only, and that precise period of time which fell under its cognizance: but why this experience should be extended to future times, and to other objects, which, for aught we know, may be only in appearance similar, this is the main question on which I would insist. . . .

If we be, therefore, engaged by arguments to put trust in past experience, and make it the standard of our future judgment, these arguments must be probable only, or such as regard matter of fact and real existence, according to the division above mentioned. But that there is no argument of this kind, must appear, if our explication of that species of reasoning be admitted as solid and satisfactory. We have said that all arguments concerning existence are founded on the relation of cause and effect; that our knowledge of that relation is derived entirely from experience; and that all our experimental conclusions proceed upon the supposition, that the future will be conformable to the past. To endeavor, therefore, the proof of this last supposition by probable arguments, or arguments regarding existence, must be evidently going in a circle, and taking that for granted which is the very point in question. . . .

When a man says, *I have found, in all past instances, such sensible qualities, conjoined with such secret powers*; and when he says, *similar sensible qualities will always be conjoined with similar secret powers;* he is not guilty of a tautology, nor are these propositions in any respect the same. You say that the one proposition is an inference

from the other: but you must confess that the inference is not intuitive, neither is it demonstrative. Of what nature is it then? To say it is experimental, is begging the question. For all inferences from experience suppose, as their foundation, that the future will resemble the past, and that similar powers will be conjoined with similar sensible qualities. If there be any suspicion that the course of nature may change, and that the past may be no rule for the future, all experience becomes useless, and can give rise to no inference or conclusion. It is impossible, therefore, that any arguments from experience can prove this resemblance of the past to the future: since all these arguments are founded on the supposition of that resemblance. Let the course of things be allowed hitherto ever so regular, that alone, without some new argument or inference, proves not that for the future it will continue so. In vain do you pretend to have learned the nature of bodies from your past experience. Their secret nature, and consequently all their effects and influence, may change, without any change in their sensible qualities. This happens sometimes, and with regard to some objects: why may it not happen always, and with regard to all objects? What logic, what process of argument secures you against this supposition? My practice, you say, refutes my doubts. But you mistake the purport of my question. As an agent, I am quite satisfied in the point; but as a philosopher, who has some share of curiosity, I will not say skepticism, I want to learn the foundation of this inference. No reading, no inquiry has yet been able to remove my difficulty, or give me satisfaction in a matter of such importance. Can I do better than propose the difficulty to the public, even though, perhaps, I have small hopes of obtaining a solution? We shall at least, by this means, be sensible of our ignorance, if we do not augment our knowledge. . . .

Suppose a person, though endowed with

the strongest facilities of reason and reflection, to be brought on a sudden into this world; he would, indeed, immediately observe a continual succession of objects, and one event following another; but he would not be able to discover any thing further. He would not at first, by any reasoning, be able to reach the idea of cause and effect; since the particular powers, by which all natural operations are performed, never appear to the senses; nor is it reasonable to conclude, merely because one event in one instance precedes another, that therefore the one is the cause, the other the effect. Their conjunction may be arbitrary and casual. There may be no reason to infer the existence of one, from the appearance of the other: and, in a word, such a person without more experience, could never employ his conjecture or reasoning concerning any matter of fact, or be assured of any thing beyond what was immediately present to his memory and senses.

Suppose again, that he has acquired more experience, and has lived so long in the world as to have observed similar objects or events to be constantly conjoined together; what is the consequence of this experience? He immediately infers the existence of one object from the appearance of the other: yet he has not, by all his experience, acquired any idea or knowledge of the secret power, by which the one object produces the other; nor is it, by any process of reasoning, he is engaged to draw this inference; but still he finds himself determined to draw it; and though he should be convinced that his understanding has no part in the operation, he would nevertheless continue in the same course of thinking. There is some other principle which determines him to form such a conclusion.

This principle is *Custom* or *Habit*. For wherever the repetition of any particular act or operation produces a propensity to renew the same act or operation, without being impelled by any reasoning or process

of the understanding, we always say, that this propensity is the effect of *Custom*. By employing that word, we pretend not to have given the ultimate reason of such a propensity. We only point out a principle of human nature, which is universally acknowledged, and which is well known by its effects. Perhaps we can push our inquiries no further, or pretend to give the cause of this cause; but must rest contented with it as the ultimate principle, which we can assign, of all our conclusions from experience. It is sufficient satisfaction, that we can go so far without repining at the narrowness of our faculties; because they will carry us no further. And, it is certain, we here advance a very intelligible proposition at least, if not a true one, when we assert, that after the constant conjunction of two objects, heat and flame, for instance, weight and solidity, we are determined by custom alone to expect the one from the appearance of the other. This hypothesis seems even the only one which explains the difficulty, why we draw from a thousand instances, an inference which we are not able to draw from one instance, that is in no respect different from them. Reason is incapable of any such variation. The conclusions which it draws from considering one circle, are the same which it would form upon surveying all the circles in the universe. But no man, having seen only one body move after being impelled by another, could infer, that every other body will move after a like impulse. All inferences from experience, therefore, are effects of custom, not of reasoning. . . .

What then is the conclusion of the whole matter? A simple one; though, it must be confessed, pretty remote from the common theories of philosophy. All belief of matter of fact or real existence is derived merely from some present object to the memory or senses, and a customary conjunction between that and some other object; or, in other words, having found, in many instances, that any two kinds of objects, flame and heat, snow and cold, have always been conjoined together: if flame or snow be presented anew to the senses, the mind is carried by custom to expect heat or cold, and to *believe* that such a quality does exist, and will discover itself upon a nearer approach. This belief is the necessary result of placing the mind in such circumstances. It is an op-eration of the soul, when we are so situated, as unavoidable as to feel the passion of love, when we receive benefits; or hatred, when we meet with injuries. All these operations are a species of natural instincts, which no reasoning or process of the thought and understanding is able either to produce or to prevent.

With the development of modern logic in the last one hundred years, philosophers have been given new and powerful tools for analysis. In the following selection, the eminent British philosopher Bertrand Russell discusses these developments—developments to which he himself made major contributions. He distinguishes the form of a proposition from its content, and he believes that it is the task of philosophy to isolate and study logical form. He also observes that many of the errors of traditional philosophy arose from flaws in logical theory, and that while the old logic put thought in fetters, the new logic gives it wings.

Russell also provides a brief sketch of the philosophical position that he thinks the new logic involves. Much if not most of this theory, called "logical atomism," would now be rejected by positivists (and Russell would disassociate himself from much of positivism), but it is of great historical interest. The world, according to this position, consists of many things with many qualities and relations. A thing with its quality or relation is called a fact; and facts may be either molecular,—that is, composed of other facts—or atomic—that is, only the thing and its quality. An atomic proposition expresses an atomic fact, and whether it is to be asserted can only be determined empirically. If, however, all atomic facts were known, it would be possible to determine by inference alone all truths of whatever form.

LOGIC AND PHILOSOPHY

Bertrand Russell (1872-   )

Logic, in the Middle Ages, and down to the present day in teaching, meant no more than a scholastic collection of technical terms and rules of syllogistic inference. Aristotle had spoken, and it was the part of humbler men merely to repeat the lesson after him. The trivial nonsense embodied

The selection is from Bertrand Russell, "Logic As the Essence of Philosophy," Chapter II of *Our Knowledge of the External World* (Chicago: The Open Court Publishing Co., 1914), pp. 33-59, with omissions. Used by permission of The Open Court Publishing Company.

in this tradition is still set in examinations, and defended by eminent authorities as an excellent "propædeutic," *i.e.* a training in those habits of solemn humbug which are so great a help in later life. But it is not this that I mean to praise in saying that all philosophy is logic. Ever since the beginning of the seventeenth century, all vigorous minds that have concerned themselves with inference have abandoned the medieval tradition, and in one way or other have widened the scope of logic. . . .

The modern development of mathematical logic dates from Boole's *Laws of Thought* (1854). But in him and his successors, before Peano and Frege, the only thing really achieved, apart from certain details, was the invention of a mathematical symbolism for deducing consequences from the premisses which the newer methods shared with those of Aristotle. This subject has considerable interest as an independent branch of mathematics, but it has very little to do with real logic. The first serious advance in real logic since the time of the Greeks was made independently by Peano and Frege—both mathematicians. They both arrived at their logical results by an analysis of mathematics. Traditional logic regarded the two propositions, "Socrates is mortal" and "All men are mortal," as being of the same form; Peano and Frege showed that they are utterly different in form. The philosophical importance of logic may be illustrated by the fact that this confusion—which is still committed by most writers—obscured not only the whole study of the forms of judgment and inference, but also the relations of things to their qualities, of concrete existence to abstract concepts, and of the world of sense to the world of Platonic ideas. Peano and Frege, who pointed out the error, did so for technical reasons, and applied their logic mainly to technical developments; but the philosophical importance of the advance which they made is impossible to exaggerate.

Mathematical logic, even in its most modern form, is not *directly* of philosophical importance except in its beginnings. After the beginnings, it belongs rather to mathematics than to philosophy. Of its beginnings, which are the only part of it that can properly be called *philosophical* logic, I shall speak shortly. But even the later developments, though not directly philosophical, will be found of great indirect use in philosophizing. They enable us to deal easily with more abstract conceptions than merely verbal reasoning can enumerate; they suggest fruitful hypotheses which otherwise could hardly be thought of; and they enable us to see quickly what is the smallest store of materials with which a given logical or scientific edifice can be constructed. . . .

In every proposition and in every inference there is, besides the particular subject matter concerned, a certain *form*, a way in which the constituents of the proposition or inference are put together. If I say, "Socrates is mortal," "Jones is angry," "The sun is hot," there is something in common in these three cases, something indicated by the word "is." What is in common is the *form* of the proposition, not an actual constituent. If I say a number of things about Socrates—that he was an Athenian, that he married Xantippe, that he drank the hemlock—there is a common constituent, namely Socrates, in all the propositions I enunciate, but they have diverse forms. If, on the other hand, I take any one of these propositions and replace its constituents, one at a time, by other constituents, the form remains constant, but no constituent remains. Take (say) the series of propositions, "Socrates drank the hemlock," "Coleridge drank the hemlock," "Coleridge drank opium," "Coleridge ate opium." The form remains unchanged throughout this series, but all the constituents are altered. Thus form is not another constituent, but is the way the constituents are put together. It is forms, in this sense, that are the proper object of philosophical logic.

It is obvious that the knowledge of logical forms is something quite different from knowledge of existing things. The form of "Socrates drank the hemlock" is not an existing thing like Socrates or the hemlock, nor does it even have that close relation to existing things that drinking has. It is something altogether more abstract and remote. We might understand all the separate words of a sentence without understanding the sentence: if a sentence is long and complicated, this is apt to happen. In such a case we have knowledge of the constituents, but not of the form. We may also have knowledge of the form without having knowledge of the constituents. If I say, "Rorarius drank the hemlock," those among you who have never heard of Rorarius (supposing there are any) will understand the form, without having knowledge of all the constituents. In order to understand a sentence, it is necessary to have knowledge both of the constituents and of the particular instance of the form. It is in this way that a sentence conveys information, since it tells us that certain known objects are related according to a certain known form. Thus some kind of knowledge of logical forms, though with most people it is not explicit, is involved in all understanding of discourse. It is the business of philosophical logic to extract this knowledge from its concrete integuments, and to render it explicit and pure.

In all inference, form alone is essential: the particular subject matter is irrelevant except as securing the truth of the premisses. This is one reason for the great importance of logical form. When I say, "Socrates was a man, all men are mortal, therefore Socrates was mortal," the connection of premisses and conclusion does not in any way depend upon its being Socrates and man and mortality that I am mentioning. The general form of the inference may be expressed in some such words as, "If a thing has a certain property, and whatever has this property has a certain other property, then the thing in question also has that other property." Here no particular things or properties are mentioned: the proposition is absolutely general. All inferences, when stated fully, are instances of propositions having this kind of generality. If they seem to depend upon the subject matter otherwise than as regards the truth of the premises, that is because the premises have not been all explicitly stated. In logic, it is a waste of time to deal with inferences concerning particular cases: we deal throughout with completely general and purely formal implications, leaving it to other sciences to discover when the hypotheses are verified and when they are not.

But the forms of propositions giving rise to inferences are not the simplest forms: they are always hypothetical, stating that if one proposition is true, then so is another. Before considering inference, therefore, logic must consider those simpler forms which inference presupposes. Here the traditional logic failed completely: it believed that there was only one form of simple proposition (*i.e.* of proposition not stating a relation between two or more other propositions), namely, the form which ascribes a predicate to a subject. This is the appropriate form in assigning the qualities of a given thing—we may say "this thing is round, and red, and so on." Grammar favors this form, but philosophically it is so far from universal that it is not even very common. If we say "this thing is bigger than that," we are not assigning a mere quality of "this," but a relation of "this" and "that." We might express the same fact by saying "that thing is smaller than this," where grammatically the subject is changed. Thus propositions stating that two things have a certain relation have a different form from subject-predicate propositions, and the failure to perceive this difference or to allow for it has been the source of many errors in traditional metaphysics. . . .

The existing world consists of many things with many qualities and relations. A complete description of the existing world would require not only a catalogue of the things, but also a mention of all their qualities and relations. We should have to know not only this, that, and the other thing, but also which was red, which yellow, which was earlier than which, which was between which two others, and so on. When I speak of a "fact," I do not mean one of the simple things in the world; I mean that a certain thing has a certain quality, or that certain things have a certain relation. Thus, for example, I should not call Napoleon a fact, but I should call it a fact that he was ambitious, or that he married Josephine. Now a fact, in this sense, is never simple, but always has two or more constituents. When it simply assigns a quality to a thing, it has only two constituents, the thing and the quality. When it consists of a relation between two things, it has three constituents, the things and the relation. When it consists of a relation between three things, it has four constituents, and so on. The constituents of facts, in the sense in which we are using the word "fact," are not other facts, but are things and qualities or relations. When we say that there are relations of more than two terms, we mean that there are single facts consisting of a single relation and more than two things. I do not mean that one relation of two terms may hold between A and B, and also between A and C, as, for example, a man is the son of his father and also the son of his mother. This constitutes two distinct facts: if we choose to treat it as one fact, it is a fact which has facts for its constituents. But the facts I am speaking of have no facts among their constituents, but only things and relations. For example, when A is jealous of B on account of C, there is only one fact, involving three people; there are not two instances of jealousy, but only one. It is in such cases that I speak of a relation of three terms, where the simplest possible fact in which the relation occurs is one involving three things in addition to the relation. And the same applies to relations of four terms or five or any other number. All such relations must be admitted in our inventory of the logical forms of facts: two facts involving the same number of things have the same form, and two which involve different numbers of things have different forms.

Given any fact, there is an assertion which expresses the fact. The fact itself is objective, and independent of our thought or opinion about it; but the assertion is something which involves thought, and may be either true or false. An assertion may be positive or negative: we may assert that Charles I was executed, or that he did *not* die in his bed. A negative assertion may be said to be a *denial*. Given a form of words which must be either true or false, such as "Charles I died in his bed," we may either assert or deny this form of words: in the one case we have a positive assertion, in the other a negative one. A form of words which must be either true or false I shall call a *proposition*. Thus a proposition is the same as what may be significantly asserted or denied. A proposition which expresses what we have called a fact, *i.e.* which, when asserted, asserts that a certain thing has a certain quality, or that certain things have a certain relation, will be called an atomic proposition, because, as we shall see immediately, there are other propositions into which atomic propositions enter in a way analogous to that in which atoms enter into molecules. Atomic propositions, although, like facts, they may have any one of an infinite number of forms, are only one kind of propositions. All other kinds are more complicated. In order to preserve the parallelism in language as regards facts and propositions, we shall give the name "atomic facts" to the facts we have hitherto been considering. Thus atomic facts are what determine whether atomic propositions are to be asserted or denied.

Whether an atomic proposition, such as "this is red," or "this is before that," is to be asserted or denied can only be known empirically. Perhaps one atomic fact may sometimes be capable of being inferred from another, though this seems very doubtful; but in any case it cannot be inferred from premises no one of which is an atomic fact. It follows that, if atomic facts are to be known at all, some at least must be known without inference. The atomic facts which we come to know in this way are the facts of sense-perception; at any rate, the facts of sense-perception are those which we most obviously and certainly come to know in this way. If we knew all atomic facts, and also knew that there were none except those we knew, we should, theoretically, be able to infer all truths of whatever form. Thus logic would then supply us with the whole of the apparatus required. But in the first acquisition of knowledge concerning atomic facts, logic is useless. In pure logic, no atomic fact is ever mentioned: we confine ourselves wholly to forms, without asking ourselves what objects can fill the forms. Thus pure logic is independent of atomic facts; but conversely, they are, in a sense, independent of logic. Pure logic and atomic facts are the two poles, the wholly *a priori* and the wholly empirical. . . .

When we were discussing atomic facts, we saw that we should be able, theoretically, to infer all other truths by logic if we knew all atomic facts and also knew that there were no other atomic facts besides those we knew. The knowledge that there are no other atomic facts is positive general knowledge; it is the knowledge that "all atomic facts are known to me," or at least "all atomic facts are in this collection"—however the collection may be given. It is easy to see that general propositions, such as "all men are mortal," cannot be known by inference from atomic facts alone. If we could know each individual man, and know that he was mortal, that would not enable us to know that all men are mortal, unless we *knew* that those were all the men there are, which is a general proposition. If we knew every other existing thing throughout the universe, and knew that each separate thing was not an immortal man, that would not give us our result unless we *knew* that we had explored the whole universe,

i.e. unless we knew "all things belong to this collection of things I have examined." Thus general truths cannot be inferred from particular truths alone, but must, if they are to be known, be either self-evident, or inferred from premisses of which at least one is a general truth. But all *empirical* evidence is of *particular* truths. Hence, if there is any knowledge of general truths at all, there must be *some* knowledge of general truths which is independent of empirical evidence, *i.e.* does not depend upon the data of sense. . . .

A proposition such as, "If Socrates is a man, and all men are mortal, then Socrates is mortal," is true in virtue of its *form* alone. Its truth, in this hypothetical form, does not depend upon whether Socrates actually is a man, nor upon whether in fact all men are mortal; thus it is equally true when we substitute other terms for Socrates and *man* and *mortal*. The general truth of which it is an instance is purely formal, and belongs to logic. Since it does not mention any particular thing, or even any particular quality or relation, it is wholly independent of the accidental facts of the existent world, and can be known, theoretically, without any experience of particular things or their qualities and relations.

Logic, we may say, consists of two parts. The first part investigates what propositions are and what forms they may have; this part enumerates the different kinds of atomic propositions, of molecular propositions, of general propositions, and so on. The second part consists of certain supremely general propositions, which assert the truth of all propositions of certain forms. This second part merges into pure mathematics, whose propositions all turn out, on analysis, to be such general formal truths. The first part, which merely enumerates forms, is the more difficult, and philosophically the more important; and it is the recent progress in this first part, more than anything else, that has rendered a truly scientific discussion of many philosophical problems possible. . . .

Modern logic, as I hope is now evident, has the effect of enlarging our abstract imagination, and providing an infinite number of possible hypotheses to be applied in the analysis of any complex fact. In this respect it is the exact opposite of the logic practiced by the classical tradition. In that logic, hypotheses which seem *prima facie* possible are professedly proved impossible, and it is decreed in advance that reality must have a certain special character. In modern logic, on the contrary, while the *prima facie* hypotheses as a rule remain admissible, others, which only logic would

have suggested, are added to our stock, and are very often found to be indispensable if a right analysis of the facts is to be obtained. The old logic put thought in fetters, while the new logic gives it wings. It has, in my opinion, introduced the same kind of advance into philosophy as Galileo introduced into physics, making it possible at last to see what kinds of problems may be capable of solution, and what kinds must be abandoned as beyond human powers. And where a solution appears possible, the new logic provides a method which enables us to obtain results that do not merely embody personal idiosyncrasies, but must command the assent of all who are competent to form an opinion.

2 / THEORY OF KNOWLEDGE

"Experiment is the sole source of truth." This theme, analyzed and expressed in a variety of ways, is the distinctive mark of positivistic epistemology. Henri Poincaré, physicist and philosopher, goes on to observe that it is experiment alone that can reveal the novel and achieve certainty.

A good experiment, Poincaré writes, is one that enables the scientist to predict future experience and to achieve generalizations about experience. These goals are made more attainable by mathematical techniques that can direct generalization and so increase the productivity of science. Generalization, however, raises the questions of the unity of nature and simplicity of explanation. The former question, Poincaré believes, involves no difficulty; the latter does, for scientific explanation proceeds by resolving the complex into the simple and elementary. But how can the scientist know that he has achieved the truly elementary phenomenon? This problem, Poincaré concludes, can also only be resolved by experiment.

TRUTH AND EXPERIMENT

Henri Poincaré (1854-1912)

THE ROLE OF EXPERIMENT AND GENERALIZATION. Experiment is the sole source

The selection is from Henri Poincaré, *Science and Hypothesis* (tr. J. Larmor) (New York: The Walter Scott Publishing Co., Ltd., 1905), pp. 140-159, with omissions.

of truth. It alone can teach us something new; it alone can give us certainty. These are two points that cannot be questioned. But then, if experiment is everything, what place is left for mathematical physics? What can experimental physics do with such an auxiliary—an auxiliary, moreover, which seems useless, and even may be dangerous?

However, mathematical physics exists. It has rendered undeniable service, and that is a fact which has to be explained. It is not sufficient merely to observe; we must use our observations, and for that purpose we must generalize. This is what has always been done, only as the recollection of past errors has made man more and more circumspect, he has observed more and more and generalized less and less. Every age has scoffed at its predecessor, accusing it of having generalized too boldly and too naïvely. Descartes used to commiserate the Ionians. Descartes in his turn makes us smile, and no doubt some day our children will laugh at us. Is there no way of getting at once to the gist of the matter, and thereby escaping the raillery which we foresee? Cannot we be content with experiment alone? No, that is impossible; that would be a complete misunderstanding of the true character of science. The man of science must work with method. Science is built up of facts, as a house is built of stones; but an accumulation of facts is no more a science than a heap of stones is a house. Most important of all, the man of science must exhibit foresight. Carlyle has written somewhere something after this fashion. "Nothing but facts are of importance. John Lackland passed by here. Here is something that is admirable. Here is a reality for which I would give all the theories in the world." Carlyle was a compatriot of Bacon, and, like him, he wished to proclaim his worship of *the God of Things as they are.*

But Bacon would not have said that. That is the language of the historian. The physicist would most likely have said: "John Lackland passed by here. It is all the same to me, for he will not pass this way again."

We all know that there are good and bad experiments. The latter accumulate in vain. Whether there are a hundred or a thousand, one single piece of work by a real master—by a Pasteur, for example—will be sufficient to sweep them into oblivion. Bacon would have thoroughly understood that, for he invented the phrase *experimentum crucis;* but Carlyle would not have understood it. A fact is a fact. A student has read such and such a number on his thermometer. He has taken no precautions. It does not matter; he has read it, and if it is only the fact which counts, this is a reality that is as much entitled to be called a reality as the peregrinations of King John Lackland. What, then, is a good experiment? It is that which teaches us something more than an isolated fact. It is that which enables us to predict, and to generalize. Without generalization, prediction is impossible. The circumstances under which one has operated will never again be reproduced simultaneously. The fact observed will never be repeated. All that can be affirmed is that under analogous circumstances an analogous fact will be produced. To predict it, we must therefore invoke the aid of analogy—that is to say, even at this stage, we must generalize. However timid we may be, there must be interpolation. Experiment only gives us a certain number of isolated points. They must be connected by a continuous line, and this is a true generalization. But more is done. The curve thus traced will pass between and near the points observed; it will not pass through the points themselves. Thus we are not restricted to generalizing our experiment, we correct it; and the physicist who would abstain from these corrections, and really content himself with experiment pure and simple, would be compelled to enunciate very extraordinary laws indeed. Detached facts cannot therefore satisfy us, and that is why our science must be ordered, or, better still, generalized.

It is often said that experiments should be made without preconceived ideas. That is impossible. Not only would it make every experiment fruitless, but even if we wished to do so, it could not be done. Every man has his own conception of the world, and this he cannot so easily lay aside. We must, for example, use language, and our language is necessarily steeped in preconceived ideas. Only they are unconscious preconceived ideas, which are a thousand times the most dangerous of all. Shall we say, that if we cause others to intervene of which we are fully conscious, that we shall only aggravate the evil? I do not think so. I am inclined to think that they will serve as ample counterpoises—I was almost going to say antidotes. They will generally disagree, they will enter into conflict one with another, and *ipso facto,* they will force us to look at things under different aspects. This is enough to free us. He is no longer a slave who can choose his master.

Thus, by generalization, every fact observed enables us to predict a large number of others; only, we ought not to forget that the first alone is certain, and that all the others are merely probable. However solidly founded a prediction may appear to us, we are never *absolutely* sure that experiment will not prove it to be baseless if we set to work to verify it. But the probability of its accuracy is often so great that practically we may be content with it. It is far better to predict without certainty, than never to have predicted at all. We should never, therefore, disdain to verify when the opportunity presents itself. But every experiment is long and difficult, and the laborers are few, and the number of facts which we require to predict is enormous; and besides this mass, the number of direct verifications that we can make will never be more than a negligible quantity. Of this little that we can directly attain we must choose the best. Every experiment must enable us to make a maximum number of predictions having the highest possible degree of probability. The problem is, so to speak, to increase the output of the scientific machine. I may be permitted to compare science to a library which

must go on increasing indefinitely; the librarian has limited funds for his purchases, and he must, therefore, strain every nerve not to waste them. Experimental physics has to make the purchases, and experimental physics alone can enrich the library. As for mathematical physics, her duty is to draw up the catalogue. If the catalogue is well done the library is none the richer for it; but the reader will be enabled to utilize its riches; and also by showing the librarian the gaps in his collection, it will help him to make a judicious use of his funds, which is all the more important, inasmuch as those funds are entirely inadequate. That is the role of mathematical physics. It must direct generalization, so as to increase what I called just now the output of science. By what means it does this, and how it may do it without danger, is what we have now to examine.

THE UNITY OF NATURE. Let us first of all observe that every generalization supposes in a certain measure a belief in the unity and simplicity of Nature. As far as the unity is concerned, there can be no difficulty. If the different parts of the universe were not as the organs of the same body, they would not react one upon the other; they would mutually ignore each other, and we in particular should only know one part. We need not, therefore, ask if Nature is one, but how she is one.

As for the second point, that is not so clear. It is not certain that Nature is simple. Can we without danger act as if she were?

There was a time when the simplicity of Mariotte's law was an argument in favor of its accuracy: when Fresnel himself, after having said in a conversation with Laplace that Nature cares naught for analytical difficulties, was compelled to explain his words so as not to give offence to current opinion. Nowadays, ideas have changed considerably; but those who do not believe that natural laws must be simple, are still often obliged to act as if they did believe it. They cannot entirely dispense with this necessity without making all generalization, and therefore all science, impossible. It is clear that any fact can be generalized in an infinite number of ways, and it is a question of choice. The choice can only be guided by considerations of simplicity. Let us take the most ordinary case, that of interpolation. We draw a continuous line as regularly as possible between the points given by observation. Why do we avoid angular points and inflections that are too sharp? Why do we not make our curve describe the most capricious zigzags? It is because we know beforehand, or think we know, that the law we have to express cannot be so complicated as all that. The mass of Jupiter may be deduced either from the movements of his satellites, or from the perturbations of the major planets, or from those of the minor planets. If we take the mean of the determinations obtained by these three methods, we find three numbers very close together, but not quite identical. This result might be interpreted by supposing that the gravitation constant is not the same in the three cases; the observations would be certainly much better represented. Why do we reject this interpretation? Not because it is absurd, but because it is uselessly complicated. We shall only accept it when we are forced to, and it is not imposed upon us yet. To sum up, in most cases every law is held to be simple until the contrary is proved. . . .

No doubt, if our means of investigation became more and more penetrating, we should discover the simple beneath the complex, and then the complex from the simple, and then again the simple beneath the complex, and so on, without ever being able to predict what the last term will be. We must stop somewhere, and for science to be possible we must stop where we have found simplicity. That is the only ground on which we can erect the edifice of our generalizations. But, this simplicity being only ap-

parent, will the ground be solid enough? That is what we have now to discover.

For this purpose let us see what part is played in our generalizations by the belief in simplicity. We have verified a simple law in a considerable number of particular cases. We refuse to admit that this coincidence, so often repeated, is a result of mere chance, and we conclude that the law must be true in the general case.

Kepler remarks that the positions of a planet observed by Tycho are all on the same ellipse. Not for one moment does he think that, by a singular freak of chance, Tycho had never looked at the heavens except at the very moment when the path of the planet happened to cut that ellipse. What does it matter then if the simplicity be real or if it hide a complex truth? Whether it be due to the influence of great numbers which reduces individual differences to a level, or to the greatness or the smallness of certain quantities which allow of certain terms to be neglected—in no case is it due to chance. This simplicity, real or apparent, has always a cause. We shall therefore always be able to reason in the same fashion, and if a simple law has been observed in several particular cases, we may legitimately suppose that it still will be true in analogous cases. To refuse to admit this would be to attribute an inadmissible role to chance. However, there is a difference. If the simplicity were real and profound it would bear the test of the increasing precision of our methods of measurement. If, then, we believe Nature to be profoundly simple, we must conclude that it is an approximate and not a rigorous simplicity. This is what was formerly done, but it is what we have no longer the right to do. The simplicity of Kepler's laws, for instance, is only apparent; but that does not prevent them from being applied to almost all systems analogous to the solar system, though that prevents them from being rigorously exact.

ROLE OF HYPOTHESIS. Every generalization is a hypothesis. Hypothesis therefore plays a necessary role, which no one has ever contested. Only, it should always be as soon as possible submitted to verification. It goes without saying that, if it cannot stand this test, it must be abandoned without any hesitation. This is, indeed, what is generally done; but sometimes with a certain impatience. Ah well! this impatience is not justified. The physicist who has just given up one of his hypotheses should, on the contrary, rejoice, for he found an unexpected opportunity of discovery. His hypothesis, I imagine, had not been lightly adopted. It took into account all the known factors which seem capable of intervention in the phenomenon. If it is not verified, it is because there is something unexpected and extraordinary about it, because we are on the point of finding something unknown and new. Has the hypothesis thus rejected been sterile? Far from it. It may be even said that it has rendered more service than a true hypothesis. Not only has it been the occasion of a decisive experiment, but if this experiment had been made by chance, without the hypothesis, no conclusion could have been drawn; nothing extraordinary would have been seen; and only one fact the more would have been catalogued, without deducing from it the remotest consequence.

Now, under what conditions is the use of hypothesis without danger? The proposal to submit all to experiment is not sufficient. Some hypotheses are dangerous—first and foremost those which are tacit and unconscious. And since we make them without knowing them, we cannot get rid of them. Here again, there is a service that mathematical physics may render us. By the precision which it its characteristic, we are compelled to formulate all the hypotheses that we would unhesitatingly make without its aid. Let us also notice that it is important not to multiply hypotheses indefinitely. If we construct a theory based upon multiple hypotheses, and if experiment condemns it, which of the premises must be changed? It is impossible to tell. Conversely, if the experiment succeeds, must we suppose that it has verified all these hypotheses at once? Can several unknowns be determined from a single equation?

We must also take care to distinguish between the different kinds of hypotheses. First of all, there are those which are quite natural and necessary. It is difficult not to suppose that the influence of very distant bodies is quite negligible, that small movements obey a linear law, and that effect is a continuous function of its cause. I will say as much for the conditions imposed by symmetry. All these hypotheses affirm, so to speak, the common basis of all the theories of mathematical physics. They are the last that should be abandoned. There is a second category of hypotheses which I shall qualify as indifferent. In most questions the analyst assumes, at the beginning of his calculations, either that matter is continuous, or the reverse, that it is formed of atoms. In either case, his results would have been the same. On the atomic supposition he has a little more difficulty in obtaining them—that is all. If, then, experiment confirms his conclusions, will he suppose that he has proved, for example, the real existence of atoms? . . .

These indifferent hypotheses are never dangerous provided their characters are not misunderstood. They may be useful, either as artifices for calculation, or to assist our understanding by concrete images, to fix the ideas, as we say. They need not therefore be rejected. The hypotheses of the third category are real generalizations. They must be confirmed or invalidated by experiment. Whether verified or condemned, they will always be fruitful; but, for the reasons I have given, they will only be so if they are not too numerous.

ORIGIN OF MATHEMATICAL PHYSICS. Let us go further and study more closely the conditions which have assisted the development of mathematical physics. We recognize at the outset that the efforts of men of science have always tended to resolve the complex phenomenon given directly by experiment into a very large number of elementary phenomena, and that in three different ways.

First, with respect to time. Instead of embracing in its entirety the progressive development of a phenomenon, we simply try to connect each moment with the one immediately preceding. We admit that the present state of the world only depends on the immediate past, without being directly influenced, so to speak, by the recollection of a more distant past. Thanks to this postulate, instead of studying directly the whole succession of phenomena, we may confine ourselves to writing down its *differential equation;* for the laws of Kepler we substitute the law of Newton.

Next, we try to decompose the phenomena in space. What experiment gives us is a confused aggregate of facts spread over a scene of considerable extent. We must try to deduce the elementary phenomenon, which will still be localized in a very small region of space. . . .

When we have discovered in which direction to seek for the elementary phenomena, by what means may we reach it? . . . Evidently the best means of reaching the elementary phenomenon would be experiment. It would be necessary by experimental artifices to dissociate the complex system which nature offers for our investigations and carefully to study the elements as dissociated as possible; for example, natural white light would be decomposed into monochromatic lights by the aid of the prism, and into polarized lights by the aid of the polarizer. Unfortunately, that is neither always possible nor always sufficient, and sometimes the mind must run ahead of experiment. I shall only give one example which has always struck me rather forcibly. If I decompose white light, I shall be able

to isolate a portion of the spectrum, but however small it may be, it will always be a certain width. In the same way the natural lights which are called *monochromatic* gives us a very fine ray, but a ray which is not, however, infinitely fine. It might be supposed that in the experimental study of the properties of these natural lights, by operating with finer and finer rays, and passing on at last to the limit, so to speak, we should eventually obtain the properties of a rigorously monochromatic light. That would not be accurate. I assume that two rays emanate from the same source, that they are first polarized in planes at right angles, that they are then brought back again to the same plane of polarization, and that we try to obtain interference. If the light were *rigorously* monochromatic, there would be interference; but with our nearly monochromatic lights, there will be no interference, and that, however narrow the ray may be. For it to be otherwise, the ray would have to be several million times finer than the finest known rays.

Here then we should be led astray by proceeding to the limit. The mind has to run ahead of the experiment, and if it has done so with success, it is because it has allowed itself to be guided by the instinct of simplicity. The knowledge of the elementary fact enables us to state the problem in the form of an equation. It only remains to deduce from it by combination the observable and verifiable complex fact. That is what we call *integration,* and it is the province of the mathematician. It might be asked, why in physical science generalization so readily takes the mathematical form. The reason is now easy to see. It is not only because we have to express numerical laws; it is because the observable phenomenon is due to the superposition of a large number of elementary phenomena which are *all similar to each other;* and in this way differential equations are quite naturally introduced. It is not enough that each elementary phenomenon should obey simple laws: all those that we have to combine must obey the same law; then only is the intervention of mathematics of any use. Mathematics teaches us, in fact, to combine like with like. Its object is to divine the result of a combination without having to reconstruct that combination element by element. If we have to repeat the same operation several times, mathematics enables us to avoid this repetition by telling the result beforehand by a kind of induction. This I have explained before in the chapter on mathematical reasoning. But for that purpose all these operations must be similar; in the contrary case we must evidently make up our minds to working them out in full one after the other, and mathematics will be useless. It is therefore, thanks to the approximate homogeneity of the matter studied by physicists, that mathematical physics came into existence. In the natural sciences the following conditions are no longer to be found:— homogeneity, relative independence of remote parts, simplicity of the elementary fact; and that is why the student of natural science is compelled to have recourse to other modes of generalization.

3 / METAPHYSICS

Positivism rests on the claim that science has an unlimited field of inquiry, that all facts are scientific facts, and that a complete interpretation of the universe is the goal of scientific activity. Karl Pearson, English mathematician and scientist, develops this claim in the following selection. The formal validity of a scientific conception, he writes, is determined by its self-consistency and by its deducibility from the perceptions of a normal human being. The material of science is coextensive with the universe in the sense that all things are open to scientific inquiry.

These assertions lead Pearson to hold that no discipline is exempt from scientific controls, even though it may claim a knowledge superior to science. In particular he discusses metaphysics, which he compares to poetry as an imaginative activity. Yet the metaphysician is really more dangerous than the poet because he makes truth claims for his visions. Pearson believes that the metaphysician is a sinister member of the community, and he concludes by stating that science rather than philosophy offers the better training for modern citizenship.

THE REJECTION OF METAPHYSICS

Karl Pearson (1857-1936)

The reader may perhaps feel that I am laying stress upon *method* at the expense of material content. Now this is the peculiarity of scientific method, that when once it has become a habit of mind, that mind converts *all* facts whatsoever into science. The field of science is unlimited; its material is endless, every group of natural phenomena, every phase of social life, every stage of past or present development is material for

The selection is from Karl Pearson, *The Grammar of Science* (London: Adam and Charles Black, 1900), pp. 12-14, 53-55, and 14-19.

science. *The unity of all science consists alone in its method, not in its material.* The man who classifies facts of any kind whatever, who sees their mutual relation and describes their sequences, is applying the scientific method and is a man of science. The facts may belong to the past history of mankind, to the social statistics of our great cities, to the atmosphere of the most distant stars, to the digestive organs of a worm, or to the life of a scarcely visible bacillus. It is not the facts themselves which form science, but the method in which they are dealt with. The material of science is coextensive with the whole physical universe, not only that universe as it now exists, but with its past history and the past history of all life therein. When every fact, every present or past phenomenon of that universe, every phase of present or past life therein, has been examined, classified, and co-ordinated with the rest, then the mission of science will be completed. What is this but saying that the task of science can never end till man ceases to be, till history is no longer made, and development itself ceases?

It might be supposed that science has made such strides in the last two centuries, and notably in the last fifty years, that we might look forward to a day when its work would be practically accomplished. At the beginning of this century it was possible for an Alexander von Humboldt to take a survey of the entire domain of then extant science. Such a survey would be impossible for any scientist now, even if gifted with more than Humboldt's powers. Scarcely any specialist of today is really master of all the work which has been done in his own comparatively small field. Facts and their classification have been accumulating at such a rate, that nobody seems to have leisure to recognize the relations of sub-groups to the whole. It is as if individual workers in both Europe and America were bringing their stones to one great building and piling them on and cementing them together without

regard to any general plan or to their individual neighbor's work; only where some one has placed a great corner-stone, is it regarded, and the building then rises on this firmer foundation more rapidly than at other points, till it reaches a height at which it is stopped for want of side support. Yet this great structure, the proportions of which are beyond the ken of any individual man, possesses a symmetry and unity of its own, notwithstanding its haphazard mode of construction. This symmetry and unity lie in scientific method. The smallest group of facts, if properly classified and logically dealt with, will form a stone which has its proper place in the great building of knowledge, wholly independent of the individual workman who has shaped it. Even when two men work unwittingly at the same stone they will but modify and correct each other's angles. In the face of all this enormous progress of modern science, when in all civilized lands men are applying the scientific method to natural, historical, and mental facts, we have yet to admit that the goal of science is and must be infinitely distant.

For we must note that when from a sufficient if partial classification of facts a simple principle has been discovered which describes the relationship and sequences of any group, then this principle or law itself generally leads to the discovery of a still wider range of hitherto unregarded phenomena in the same or associated fields. Every great advance of science opens our eyes to facts which we had failed before to observe, and makes new demands on our powers of interpretation. This extension of the material of science into regions where our great-grandfathers could see nothing at all, or where they would have declared human knowledge impossible, is one of the most remarkable features of modern progress. Where they interpreted the motion of the planets of our own system, we discuss the chemical constitution of stars, many of which did not exist for them, for their telescopes could not reach them. Where they discovered the circulation of the blood, we see the physical conflict of living poisons within the blood, whose battles would have been absurdities for them. Where they found void and probably demonstrated to their own satisfaction that there was void, we conceive great systems in rapid motion capable of carrying energy through brick walls as light passes through glass. Great as the advance of scientific knowledge has been, it has not been greater than the growth of the material to be dealt with. The goal of science is clear—it is nothing short of the complete interpretation of the universe. But the goal is an ideal one—it marks the *direction* in which we move and strive, but never a stage we shall actually reach. The universe grows ever larger as we learn to understand more of our own corner of it. . . .

In order that a conception may have scientific validity, it must be self-consistent, and deducible from the perceptions of the normal human being. For instance, a centaur is not a self-consistent conception; as soon as our knowledge of human and equine anatomy became sufficiently developed, the centaur became an unthinkable thing—a self-negating idea. As the man-horse is seen to be a compound of sense-impressions, which are irreconcilable anatomically, so the man-god, whose cruder type is Hercules, is also seen to be a chimera, a self-contradictory conception, as soon as we have clearly defined the physical and mental characteristics of man. But even if an individual mind has reached a conception, which at any rate for that mind is perfectly self-consistent, it does not follow that such a conception must have scientific validity, except as far as science may be concerned with the analysis of that individual mind. When a person conceives that one color—green—suffices to describe the flowers and leaves of a rose-tree in my garden, I know that his conception

may, after all, be self-consistent, it may be in perfect harmony with his sense-impressions. I merely assert that his perceptive faculty is *abnormal,* and hold him to be color-blind. I may study the individual abnormality scientifically, but his conception has no scientific validity, for it is not deducible from the perceptions of the normal human being. Here indeed we have to proceed very cautiously if we are to determine what self-consistent conceptions have scientific validity. Above all, we must note that a conception does not cease to be valid because it has not been deduced by the majority of normal human beings from their perceptions. The conception that a new individual will originate from the union of a male and female cell may never have actually been deduced by a majority of normal human beings from their perceptions. But if any normal human being be trained in the proper methods of observation, and be placed in the right circumstances for investigating, he will draw from his perceptions this conception and not its negation. It is in this sense, therefore, that we are to understand the assertion that a conception to have scientific validity must be *deducible* from the perceptions of the normal human being.

The preceding paragraph shows us how important it is that the observations and experiments of science should be repeated as often and by as many observers as possible, in order to ensure that we are dealing with what has validity for all normal human beings, and not with the result of an abnormal perceptive faculty. It is not only, however, in experiments or observations which can be repeated easily, but still more in those which it is very difficult or impossible to repeat, that a great weight of responsibility lies upon the recorder and the public which is called upon to accept his results. An event may have occurred in the presence of a limited number of observers. That the event itself cannot recur, and that it is totally out of accord with our customary experience, are not in themselves sufficient grounds for disregarding it scientifically. Yet what an onus is laid on the individual observers to test whether their perceptive faculties were normal on the occasion, and whether their conceptions of what took place were justified by their perceptions! Still greater onus is laid on men at large to criticize and probe the evidence given by such observers, to question whether they were men trained to observe, and calm and collected at the time of the reported event. Were they not, perhaps, in an exalted state of mind, biassed by preconceptions or hindered by the physical surroundings from clear perception? In short, were or were not their perceptive faculties in a normal condition, and were or were not the circumstances such that normal perception was possible? It can scarcely be questioned that when the truth or falsehood of an event or observation may have important bearings on conduct, over-doubt is more socially valuable than over-credulity. In an age like our own, which is essentially an age of scientific inquiry, the prevalence of doubt and criticism ought not to be regarded with despair or as a sign of decadence. It is one of the safeguards of progress;—*la critique est la vie de la science* [criticism is the life of science], I must again repeat. One of the most fatal (and not so impossible) features for science would be the institution of a scientific hierarchy which would brand as heretical all doubt as to its conclusions, all criticism of its results. . . .

Now I want to draw the reader's attention to two results which flow from the above considerations, namely: that the material of science is coextensive with the whole life, physical and mental, of the universe, and furthermore that the limits to our perception of the universe are only apparent, not real. It is no exaggeration to say that the universe was not the same for our

great-grandfathers as it is for us, and that in all probability it will be utterly different for our great-grandchildren. The universe is a variable quantity, which depends upon the keenness and structure of our organs of sense, and upon the fineness of our powers and instruments of observation. We shall see more clearly the important bearing of this latter remark when we come to discuss more closely in another chapter how the universe is largely the construction of each individual mind. For the present we must briefly consider the former remark, which defines the unlimited scope of science. To say that there are certain fields—for example, *metaphysics*—from which science is excluded, wherein its methods have no application, is merely to say that the rules of methodical observation and the laws of logical thought do not apply to the facts, if any, which lie within such fields. These fields, if indeed such exist, must lie outside any intelligible definition which can be given of the word *knowledge*. If there are facts, and sequences to be observed among those facts, then we have all the requisites of scientific classification and knowledge. If there are no facts, or no sequences to be observed among them, then the possibility of *all* knowledge disappears. The greatest assumption of everyday life—the inference which the metaphysicians tell us is wholly beyond science—namely, that other beings have consciousness as well as ourselves, seems to have just as much or as little *scientific* validity as the statement that an earth-grown apple would fall to the ground if carried to the planet of another star. Both are beyond the range of experimental demonstration, but to assume uniformity in the characteristics of brain "matter" under certain conditions seems as scientific as to assume uniformity in the characteristics of stellar "matter." Both are only working hypotheses and valuable in so far as they simplify our description of the universe. Yet the distinction between science and metaphysics is often insisted upon, and not unadvisedly, by the devotees of both. If we take any group of physical or biological facts—say, for example, electrical phenomena or the development of the ovum—we shall find that, though physicists or biologists may differ to some extent in their measurements or in their hypotheses, yet in the fundamental principles and sequences the professors of each individual science are in practical agreement among themselves. A similar if not yet so complete agreement is rapidly springing up in both mental and social science, where the facts are more difficult to classify and the bias of individual opinion is much stronger. Our more thorough classification, however, of the facts of human development, our more accurate knowledge of the early history of human societies, of primitive customs, laws, and religions, our application of the principle of natural selection to man and his communities, are converting anthropology, folklore, sociology, and psychology into true sciences. We begin to see indisputable sequences in groups of both mental and social facts. The causes which favor the growth or decay of human societies become more obvious and more the subject of scientific investigation. Mental and social facts are thus not beyond the range of scientific treatment, but their classification has not been so complete, nor for obvious reasons so unprejudiced, as those of physical or biological phenomena.

The case is quite different with metaphysics and those other supposed branches of human knowledge which claim exemption from scientific control. Either they are based on an accurate classification of facts, or they are not. But if their classification of facts were accurate, the application of the scientific method ought to lead their professors to a practically identical system. Now one of the idiosyncrasies of metaphysicians lies in this: that each metaphysician has his own system, which to a large extent excludes that of his predecessors and colleagues.

Hence we must conclude that metaphysics are built either on air or on quicksands—either they start from no foundation in facts at all, or the superstructure has been raised before a basis has been found in the accurate classification of facts. I want to lay special stress on this point. There is no short cut to truth, no way to gain a knowledge of the universe except through the gateway of scientific method. The hard and stony path of classifying facts and reasoning upon them is the only way to ascertain truth. It is the reason and not the imagination which must ultimately be appealed to. The poet may give us in sublime language an account of the origin and purport of the universe, but in the end it will not satisfy our esthetic judgment, our idea of harmony and beauty, like the few facts which the scientist may venture to tell us in the same field. The one will agree with all our experiences past and present, the other is sure, sooner or later, to contradict our observation because it propounds a dogma, where we are yet far from knowing the whole truth. Our esthetic judgment demands harmony between the representation and the represented, and in this sense science is often more artistic than modern art.

The poet is a valued member of the community, for he is known to be a poet; his value will increase as he grows to recognize the deeper insight into nature with which modern science provides him. The metaphysician is a poet, often a very great one, but unfortunately he is not known to be a poet, because he strives to clothe his poetry in the language of reason, and hence it follows that he is liable to be a dangerous member of the community. The danger at the present time that metaphysical dogmas may check scientific research is, perhaps, not very great. The day has gone by when the Hegelian philosophy threatened to strangle infant science in Germany;—that it begins to languish at Oxford is a proof that it is practically dead in the country of its birth. The day has gone by when philosophical or theological dogmas of any kind can throw back for generations the progress of scientific investigation. There is no restriction now on research in any field, or on the publication of the truth when it has been reached. But there is nevertheless a danger which we cannot afford to disregard, a danger which retards the spread of scientific knowledge among the unenlightened, and which flatters obscurantism by discrediting the scientific method. There is a certain school of thought which finds the laborious process by which science reaches truth too irksome; the temperament of this school is such that it demands a short and easy cut to knowledge, where knowledge can only be gained, if at all, by the long and patient toiling of many groups of workers, perhaps through several centuries. There are various fields at the present day wherein mankind is ignorant, and the honest course for us is simply to confess our ignorance. This ignorance may arise from the want of any proper classification of facts, or because supposed facts are themselves inconsistent, unreal creations of untrained minds. But because this ignorance is frankly admitted by science, an attempt is made to fence off these fields as ground which science cannot profitably till, to shut them up as a preserve whereon science has no business to trespass. Wherever science has succeeded in ascertaining the truth, there, according to the school we have referred to, are the "legitimate problems of science." Wherever science is yet ignorant, there, we are told, its method is inapplicable; there some other relation than cause and effect (than the same sequence recurring with the like grouping of phenomena), some new but undefined relationship rules. In these fields, we are told, problems become philosophical and can only be treated by the method of philosophy. The philosophical method is opposed to the scientific method; and here, I think, the danger I have referred to arises. We have defined the scientific method to consist in the orderly classification of facts followed by the recognition of their relationship and recurring sequences. The scientific judgment is the judgment based upon this recognition and free from personal bias. If this were the philosophical method there would be no need of further discussion, but as we are told the subject matter of philosophy is not the "legitimate problem of science," the two methods are presumably not identical. Indeed the philosophical method seems based upon an analysis which does not start with the classification of facts, but reaches its judgments by some obscure process of internal cogitation. It is therefore dangerously liable to the influence of individual bias; it results, as experience shows us, in an endless number of competing and contradictory systems. It is because the so-called philosophical method does not, when different individuals approach the same range of facts, lead, like the scientific, to practical unanimity of judgment, that science, rather than philosophy, offers the better training for modern citizenship.

4 / ETHICS

In the following selection, Professor Charles L. Stevenson turns to the problem of value, particularly ethical value. He describes his task as a philosopher to be analysis and clarification of ethical questions such as, "Is X good?" and he lays down certain conditions to be met by his analysis. It must account for ethical disagreement, show the connection between ethical judgments and action, and be so stated that goodness is not verifiable by science (as he says, "ethics is not psychology").

Two uses of language must be distinguished: a descriptive use that expresses belief, and a dynamical use that is related to interests, attitudes, and emotions. Ethical judgments belong to the second group, for their major use is to suggest, to create an influence on the hearer of the judgment. To speak or ask about the goodness of anything, then, is to ask about its influence relative to human interests. Incidentally, it is because of this emphasis on influence rather than the description found in traditional interest theories that Stevenson rejects them. The language of ethics, therefore, is one of persuasion; and ethical disagreements are disagreements in attitude, not in belief. Stevenson's subtle analysis reflects the positivist position, but it also looks forward to the view of philosophy we shall consider in the next part.

ETHICS AS EMOTIVE

Charles L. Stevenson (1908-   )

Ethical questions first arise in the form "Is so and so good?" or "Is this alternative better than that?" These questions are difficult partly because we don't quite know what we are seeking. We are asking, "Is there a needle in that haystack?" without even knowing just what a needle is. So the first thing to do is to examine the questions themselves. We must try to make them clearer, either by defining the terms in which they are expressed, or by any other method that is available.

The present paper is concerned wholly with this preliminary step of making ethical questions clear. In order to help answer the question "Is X good?" we must *substitute* for it a question which is free from ambiguity and confusion.

It is obvious that in substituting a clearer question we must not introduce some utterly different kind of question. It won't do (to take an extreme instance of a prevalent fallacy) to substitute for "Is X

good?" the question "Is X pink with yellow trimmings?" and then point out how easy the question really is. This would beg the original question, not help answer it. On the other hand, we must not expect the substituted question to be strictly "identical" with the original one. The original question may embody hypostatization, anthropomorphism, vagueness, and all the other ills to which our ordinary discourse is subject. If our substituted question is to be clearer, it must remove these ills. The questions will be identical only in the sense that a child is identical with the man he later becomes. Hence we must not demand that the substitution strike us, on immediate introspection, as making no change in meaning.

Just how, then, must the substituted question be related to the original? Let us assume (inaccurately) that it must result from replacing "good" by some set of terms which define it. The question then resolves itself to this: How must the defined meaning of "good" be related to its original meaning?

I answer that it must be *relevant*. A defined meaning will be called "relevant" to

The selection is from C. L. Stevenson, "The Emotive Meaning of Ethical Terms," *Mind*, 46 (1937), pp. 14-16 and 18-30, with omissions. Used by permission of the Editor and the author.

the original meaning under these circumstances: Those who have understood the definition must be able to say all that they then want to say by using the term in the defined way. They must never have occasion to use the term in the old, unclear sense. (If a person did have to go on using the word in the old sense, then to this extent his meaning would not be clarified, and the philosophical task would not be completed.) It frequently happens that a word is used so confusedly and ambiguously that we must give it *several* defined meanings, rather than one. In this case only the whole set of defined meanings will be called "relevant," and any one of them will be called "partially relevant." This is not a rigorous treatment of *relevance*, by any means; but it will serve for the present purposes.

Let us now turn to our particular task—that of giving a relevant definition of "good.". . .

There are certain requirements, however, with which this "vital" sense has been expected to comply—requirements which appeal strongly to our common sense. It will be helpful to summarize these. . . .

In the first place, we must be able sensibly to *disagree* about whether something is "good." This condition rules out Hobbes's definition. For consider the following argument: "This is good." "That isn't so; it's not good." As translated by Hobbes, this becomes: "I desire this." "That isn't so, for *I* don't." The speakers are not contradicting one another, and think they are, only because of an elementary confusion in the use of pronouns. The definition, "good" means *desired by my community,* is also excluded, for how could people from different communities disagree?

In the second place, "goodness" must have, so to speak, a magnetism. A person who recognizes X to be "good" must *ipso facto* acquire a stronger tendency to act in its favor than he otherwise would have had.

This rules out the Humian type of definition. For according to Hume, to recognize that something is "good" is simply to recognize that the majority approve of it. Clearly, a man may see that the majority approve of X without having, himself, a stronger tendency to favor it. This requirement excludes any attempt to define "good" in terms of the interest of people *other* than the speaker.

In the third place, the "goodness" of anything must not be verifiable solely by use of the scientific method. "Ethics must not be psychology." This restriction rules out all of the traditional interest theories, without exception. . . .

Let us now turn to my own analysis of ethical judgments. First let me present my position dogmatically, showing to what extent I vary from tradition.

I believe that the three requirements, given above, are perfectly sensible; that there is some *one* sense of "good" which satisfies all three requirements; and that no traditional interest theory satisfies them all. But this does not imply that "good" must be explained in terms of a Platonic Idea, or of a Categorical Imperative, or of an unique, unanalyzable property. On the contrary, the three requirements can be met by a *kind* of interest theory. *But we must give up a presupposition which all the traditional interest theories have made.*

Traditional interest theories hold that ethical statements are *descriptive* of the existing state of interest—that they simply *give information* about interests. (More accurately, ethical judgments are said to describe what the state of interests is, was, or will be, or to indicate what the state of interests *would* be under specified circumstances.) It is this emphasis on description, on information, which leads to their incomplete relevance. Doubtless there is always *some* element of description in ethical judgments, but this is by no means all. Their major use is not to indicate facts, but to *create an influence*. Instead of merely describing people's interests, they *change* or *intensify* them. They *recommend* an interest in an object, rather than state that the interest already exists. . . .

Thus ethical terms are *instruments* used in the complicated interplay and readjustment of human interests. This can be seen plainly from more general observations. People from widely separated communities have different moral attitudes. Why? To a great extent because they have been subject to different social influences. Now clearly this influence doesn't operate through sticks and stones alone; words play a great part. People praise one another, to encourage certain inclinations, and blame one another, to discourage others. Those of forceful personalities issue commands which weaker people, for complicated instinctive reasons, find it difficult to disobey, quite apart from fears of consequences. Further influence is brought to bear by writers and orators. Thus social influence is exerted, to an enormous extent, by means that have nothing to do with physical force or material reward. The ethical terms facilitate such influence. Being suited for use in *suggestion*, they are a means by which men's attitudes may be led this way or that. The reason, then, that we find a greater similarity in the moral attitudes of one community than in those of different communities is largely this: ethical judgments propagate themselves. One man says "This is good"; this may influence the approval of another person, who then makes the same ethical judgment, which in turn influences another person, and so on. In the end, by a process of mutual influence, people take up more or less the same attitudes. Between people of widely separated communities, of course, the influence is less strong; hence different communities have different attitudes.

These remarks will serve to give a general idea of my point of view. We must now go into more detail. There are several questions which must be answered: How does an ethical sentence acquire its power of influencing people—why is it suited to suggestion? Again, what has this influence to do with the *meaning* of ethical terms? And finally, do these considerations really lead us to a sense of "good" which meets the requirements mentioned in the preceding section?

Let us deal first with the question about *meaning*. This is far from an easy question, so we must enter into a preliminary inquiry about meaning in general. Although a seeming digression, this will prove indipensable.

Broadly speaking, there are two different *purposes* which lead us to use language. On the one hand we use words (as in science) to record, clarify, and communicate *beliefs*. On the other hand we use words to give vent to our feelings (interjections), or to create moods (poetry), or to incite people to actions or attitudes (oratory).

The first use of words I shall call "descriptive"; the second, "dynamic." Note that the distinction depends solely upon the *purpose* of the *speaker*.

When a person say "Hydrogen is the lightest known gas," his purpose *may* be simply to lead the hearer to believe this, or to believe that the speaker believes it. In that case the words are used descriptively. When a person cuts himself and says "Damn," his purpose is not ordinarily to record, clarify, or communicate any belief. The word is used dynamically. The two ways of using words, however, are by no means mutually exclusive. This is obvious from the fact that our purposes are often complex. Thus when one says "I want you to close the door," part of his purpose, ordinarily, is to lead the hearer to believe that he has this want. To that extent the words are used descriptively. But the major part of one's purpose is to lead the hearer to *satisfy* the want. To that extent the words are used dynamically. . . .

We must now proceed to an important

question: What has the dynamic use of words to do with their *meaning?* One thing is clear—we must not define "meaning" in a way that would make meaning vary with dynamic usage. If we did, we should have no use for the term. All that we could say about such "meaning" would be that it is very complicated, and subject to constant change. So we must certainly distinguish between the dynamic use of words and their meaning. . . .

There will be a kind of meaning, however, in the sense above defined, which has an intimate relation to dynamic usage. I refer to "emotive" meaning (in a sense roughly like that employed by Ogden and Richards).[1] The emotive meaning of a word is a tendency of a word, arising through the history of its usage, to produce (result from) *affective* responses in people. It is the immediate aura of feeling which hovers about a word. Such tendencies to produce affective responses cling to words very tenaciously. It would be difficult, for instance, to express merriment by using the interjection "alas." Because of the persistence of such affective tendencies (among other reasons) it becomes feasible to classify them as "meanings."

Just *what* is the relation between emotive meaning and the dynamic use of words? Let us take an example. Suppose that a man is talking with a group of people which includes Miss Jones, age 59. He refers to her, without thinking, as an "old maid." Now even if his purposes are perfectly innocent —even if he is using the words purely descriptively—Miss Jones won't think so. She will think he is encouraging the others to have contempt for her, and will draw in her skirts, defensively. The man might have done better if instead of saying "old maid" he had said "elderly spinster." The latter words could have been put to the

same descriptive use, and would not so readily have caused suspicions about the dynamic use.

"Old maid" and "elderly spinster" differ, to be sure, only in emotive meaning. From the example it will be clear that certain words, because of their emotive meaning, are suited to a certain kind of dynamic use—so well suited, in fact, that the hearer is likely to be misled when we use them in any other way. The more pronounced a word's emotive meaning is, the less likely people are to use it purely descriptively. Some words are suited to encourage people, some to discourage them, some to quiet them, and so on.

Even in these cases, of course, the dynamic purposes are not to be identified with any sort of meaning; for the emotive meaning accompanies a word much more persistently than do the dynamic purposes. But there is an important contingent relation between emotive meaning and dynamic purpose: the former assists the latter. Hence if we define emotively laden terms in a way that neglects their emotive meaning, we are likely to be confusing. *We lead people to think that the terms defined are used dynamically less often than they are.*

Let us now apply these remarks in defining "good." This word may be used morally or non-morally. I shall deal with the non-moral usage almost entirely, but only because it is simpler. The main points of the analysis will apply equally well to either usage.

As a preliminary definition, let us take an inaccurate approximation. It may be more misleading than helpful, but will do to begin with. Roughly, then, the sentence "X is good" means *We like* X. ("We" includes the hearer or hearers.)

At first glance this definition sounds absurd. If used, we should expect to find the following sort of conversation: A. "This is good." B. "But I *don't* like it. What led you to believe that I did?" The unnatural-

---

[1] See *The Meaning of Meaning,* by C. K. Ogden and I. A. Richards.

ness of B's reply, judged by ordinary word-usage, would seem to cast doubt on the revelance of my definition.

B's unnaturalness, however, lies simply in this: he is assuming that "We like it" (as would occur implicitly in the use of "good") is being used descriptively. This won't do. When "We like it" is to take the place of "This is good," the former sentence must be used not purely descriptively, but dynamically. More specifically, it must be used to promote a very subtle (and for the non-moral sense in question, a very easily resisted) kind of *suggestion*. To the extent that "we" refers to the hearer, it must have the dynamic use, essential to suggestion, of leading the hearer to *make* true what is said, rather than merely to believe it. And to the extent that "we" refers to the speaker, the sentence must have not only the descriptive use of indicating belief about the speaker's interest, but the quasi-interjectory, dynamic function of giving direct expression to the interest. (This immediate expression of feelings assists in the process of suggestion. It is difficult to disapprove in the face of another's enthusiasm.)

For an example of a case where "We like this" is used in the dynamic way that "This is good" is used, consider the case of a mother who says to her several children, "One thing is certain, *we all like to be neat.*" If she really believed this, she wouldn't bother to say so. But she is not using the words descriptively. She is *encouraging* the children to like neatness. By telling them that they like neatness, she will lead them to *make* her statement true, so to speak. If, instead of saying "We all like to be neat" in this way, she had said "It's a good thing to be neat," the effect would have been approximately the same.

But these remarks are still misleading. Even when "We like it" is used for suggestion, it isn't quite like "This is good." The latter is more subtle. With such a sentence as "This is a good book," for ex-

ample, it would be practically impossible to use instead "We like this book." When the latter is used, it must be accompanied by so exaggerated an intonation, to prevent its becoming confused with a descriptive statement, that the force of suggestion becomes stronger, and ludicrously more overt, than when "good" is used.

The definition is inadequate, further, in that the definiens has been restricted to dynamic usage. Having said that dynamic usage was different from meaning, I should not have to mention it in giving the *meaning* of "good."

It is in connection with this last point that we must return to emotive meaning. The word "good" has a pleasing emotive meaning which fits it especially for the dynamic use of suggesting favorable interest. But the sentence "We like it" has no such emotive meaning. Hence my definition has neglected emotive meaning entirely. Now to neglect emotive meaning is likely to lead to endless confusions, as we shall presently see; so I have sought to make up for the inadequacy of the definition by letting the restriction about dynamic usage take the place of emotive meaning. What I should do, of course, is to find a definiens whose emotive meaning, like that of "good," simply does *lead* to dynamic usage.

Why didn't I do this? I answer that it isn't possible, if the definition is to afford us increased clarity. No two words, in the first place, have quite the same emotive meaning. The most we can hope for is a rough approximation. But if we seek for such an approximation for "good," we shall find nothing more than synonyms, such as "desirable" or "valuable"; and these are profitless because they do not clear up the connection between "good" and favorable interest. If we reject such synonyms, in favor of non-ethical terms, we shall be highly misleading. For instance: "This is good" has something like the meaning of "I *do* like this; do so as well." But this is certainly not accurate. For the imperative makes an appeal to the conscious efforts of the hearer. Of course he can't like something just by trying. He must be led to like it through suggestion. Hence an ethical sentence differs from an imperative in that it enables one to make changes in a much more subtle, less fully conscious way. Note that the ethical sentence centers the hearer's attention not on his interest, but on the object of interests, and thereby facilitates suggestion. Because of its subtlety, moreover, an ethical sentence readily permits counter-suggestion, and leads to the give and take situation which is so characteristic of arguments about values.

Strictly speaking, then, it is impossible to define "good" in terms of favorable interest if emotive meaning is not to be distorted. Yet it is possible to say that "This is good" is *about* the favorable interest of the speaker and the hearer or hearers, and that it has a pleasing emotive meaning which fits the words for use in suggestion. This is a rough description of meaning, not a definition. But it serves the same clarifying function that a definition ordinarily does; and that, after all, is enough.

A word must be added about the moral use of "good." This differs from the above in that it is about a different kind of interest. Instead of being about what the hearer and speaker *like*, it is about a stronger sort of approval. When a person *likes* something, he is pleased when it prospers, and disappointed when it doesn't. When a person *morally approves* of something, he experiences a rich feeling of security when it prospers, and is indignant, or "shocked" when it doesn't. These are rough and inaccurate examples of the many factors which one would have to mention in distinguishing the two kinds of interest. In the moral usage, as well as in the non-moral, "good" has an emotive meaning which adapts it to suggestion.

And now, are these considerations of any

importance? Why do I stress emotive meanings in this fashion? Does the omission of them really lead people into errors? I think, indeed, that the errors resulting from such omissions are enormous. In order to see this, however, we must return to the restrictions, mentioned in [the beginning], with which the "vital" sense of "good" has been expected to comply.

The first restriction, it will be remembered, had to do with disagreement. Now there is clearly some sense in which people disagree on ethical points; but we must not rashly assume that all disagreement is modelled after the sort that occurs in the natural sciences. We must distinguish between "disagreement in belief" (typical of the sciences) and "disagreement in interest." Disagreement in belief occurs when A believes p and B disbelieves it. Disagreement in interest occurs when A has a favorable interest in X, when B has an unfavorable one in it, and when neither is content to let the other's interest remain unchanged.

Let me give an example of disagreement in interest. A. "Let's go to a cinema tonight." B. "I don't want to do that. Let's go to the symphony." A continues to insist on the cinema, B on the symphony. This is disagreement in a perfectly conventional sense. They can't agree on where they want to go, and each is trying to redirect the other's interest. (Note that imperatives are used in the example.)

It is disagreement in *interest* which takes place in ethics. When C says "This is good," and D says "No, it's bad," we have a case of suggestion and counter-suggestion. Each man is trying to redirect the other's interest. There obviously need be no domineering, since each may be willing to give ear to the other's influence; but each is trying to move the other none the less. It is in this sense that they disagree. Those who argue that certain interest theories make no provision for disagreement have been misled, I believe, simply because the traditional theories, in leaving out emotive meaning, give the impression that ethical judgments are used descriptively only; and of course when judgments are used purely descriptively, the only disagreement that can arise is disagreement *in belief*. Such disagreement may be disagreement in belief *about* interests; but this is not the same as disagreement *in* interest. My definition doesn't provide for disagreement in belief about interests, any more than does Hobbes's; but that is no matter, for there is no reason to believe, at least on common-sense grounds, that this kind of disagreement exists. There is only disagreement *in* interest. (We shall see in a moment that disagreement in interest does not remove ethics from sober argument—that this kind of disagreement may often be resolved through empirical means.)

The second restriction, about "magnetism," or the connection between goodness and actions, requires only a word. This rules out *only* those interest theories which do *not* include the interest of the speaker, in defining "good." My account does include the speaker's interest; hence is immune.

The third restriction, about the empirical method, may be met in a way that springs naturally from the above account of disagreement. Let us put the question in this way: When two people disagree over an ethical matter, can they completely resolve the disagreement through empirical considerations, assuming that each applies the empirical method exhaustively, consistently, and without error?

I answer that sometimes they can, and sometimes they cannot; and that at any rate, even when they can, the relation between empirical knowledge and ethical judgments is quite different from the one which traditional interest theories seem to imply.

This can best be seen from an analogy. Let's return to the example where A and B couldn't agree on a cinema or a symphony. The example differed from an ethical argument in that imperatives were used, rather than ethical judgments; but was analogous to the extent that each person was endeavoring to modify the other's interest. Now how would these people argue the case, assuming that they were too intelligent just to shout at one another?

Clearly, they would give "reasons" to support their imperatives. A might say, "But you know, Garbo is at the Bijou." His hope is that B, who admires Garbo, will acquire a desire to go to the cinema when he knows what play will be there. B may counter, "But Toscanini is guest conductor tonight, in an all-Beethoven programme." And so on. Each supports his imperative ("*Let's* do so and so") by reasons which may be empirically established.

To generalize from this: disagreement in interest may be rooted in disagreement in belief. That is to say, people who disagree in interest would often cease to do so if they knew the precise nature and consequences of the object of their interest. To this extent disagreement in interest may be resolved by securing agreement in belief, which in turn may be secured empirically.

This generalization holds for ethics. If A and B, instead of using imperatives, had said, respectively, "It would be *better* to go to the cinema," and "It would be better to go to the symphony," the reasons which they would advance would be roughly the same. They would each give a more thorough account of the object of interest, with the purpose of completing the redirection of interest which was begun by the suggestive force of the ethical sentence. On the whole, of course, the suggestive force of the ethical statement merely exerts enough pressure to start such trains of reasons, since the reasons are much more essential in resolving disagreement in interest than the persuasive effect of the ethical judgment itself.

Thus the empirical method is relevant to ethics simply because our knowledge of the world is a determining factor to our interests. But note that empirical facts are not inductive grounds from which the ethical judgment problematically follows. (This is what traditional interest theories imply.) If someone said "Close the door," and added the reason "We'll catch cold," the latter would scarcely be called an inductive ground of the former. Now imperatives are related to the reasons which support them in the same way that ethical judgments are related to reasons.

Is the empirical method *sufficient* for attaining ethical agreement? Clearly not. For empirical knowledge resolves disagreement in interest only to the extent that such disagreement is rooted in disagreement in belief. Not all disagreement in interest is of this sort. For instance: A is of a sympathetic nature, and B isn't. They are arguing about whether a public dole would be good. Suppose that they discovered all the consequences of the dole. Isn't it possible, even so, that A will say that it's good, and B that it's bad? The disagreement in interest may arise not from limited factual knowledge, but simply from A's sympathy and B's coldness. Or again, suppose, in the above argument, that A was poor and unemployed, and that B was rich. Here again the disagreement might not be due to different factual knowledge. It would be due to the different social positions of the men, together with their predominant self-interest.

When ethical disagreement is not rooted in disagreement in belief, is there *any* method by which it may be settled? If one means by "method" a *rational* method, then there is no method. But in any case there is a "way." Let's consider the above example, again, where disagreement was due to A's sympathy and B's coldness. Must

they end by saying, "Well, it's just a matter of our having different temperaments"? Not necessarily. A, for instance, may try to *change* the temperament of his opponent. He may pour out his enthusiasms in such a moving way—present the sufferings of the poor with such appeal—that he will lead his opponent to see life through different eyes. He may build up, by the contagion of his feelings, an influence which will modify B's temperament, and create in him a sympathy for the poor which didn't previously exist. This is often the only way to obtain ethical agreement, if there is any way at all. It is persuasive, not empirical or rational; but that is no reason for neglecting it. There is no reason to scorn it, either, for it is only by such means that our personalities are able to grow, through our contact with others.

The point I wish to stress, however, is simply that the empirical method is instrumental to ethical agreement only to the extent that disagreement in interest is rooted in disagreement in belief. There is little reason to believe that all disagreement is of this sort. Hence the empirical method is not sufficient for ethics. In any case, ethics is not psychology, since psychology doesn't endeavor to *direct* our interests; it discovers facts about the ways in which interests are or can be directed, but that's quite another matter.

To summarize this section: my analysis of ethical judgments meets the three requirements for the "vital" sense of "good" that were mentioned in [the beginning]. The traditional interest theories fail to meet these requirements simply because they neglect emotive meaning. This neglect leads them to neglect dynamic usage, and the sort of disagreement that results from such usage, together with the method of resolving the disagreement. I may add that my analysis answers Moore's objection about the open question. Whatever scientifically knowable properties a thing may have, it *is* always open to question whether a thing having these (enumerated) qualities is good. For to ask whether it is good is to ask for *influence*. And whatever I may know about an object, I can still ask, quite pertinently, to be influenced with regard to my interest in it.

5 / ESTHETICS

For the positivist, the language of value is emotive, never cognitive. In discussing the language of poetry, I. A. Richards distinguishes the pseudo-statement from statements proper. The latter are always scientific, and hence always subject to verification. Pseudo-statements, however, though frequently having the form of scientific statements, serve only to organize or release human attitudes, not to make true descriptive judgments. Poetry, in dealing in pseudo-statements, is not in the business of making true statements, and it tends toward the ridiculous if it tries. In fact, if the pseudo-statement—in poetry or any other "emotive" activity—is confused with the scientific, we revert to a primitive and magical view of the world.

ART AND BELIEF

I. A. Richards (1893-   )

The business of the poet . . . is to give order and coherence, and so freedom, to a body of experience. To do so through words which act as its skeleton, as a structure by which the impulses which make up the experience are adjusted to one another and act together. The means by which words do this are many and varied. To work them out is a problem for linguistic psychology, that embarrassed young heir to philosophy. What little can be done shows already that most critical dogmas of the past are either false or nonsense. A little knowledge is not here a danger, but clears the air in a remarkable way.

Roughly and inadequately, even in the dim light of present knowledge, we can say that words work in the poem in two main fashions. As sensory stimuli and as (in the *widest* sense) symbols. We must refrain from considering the sensory side of the poem, remarking only that it is *not* in the least independent of the other side, and that it has for definite reasons prior importance in most poetry. We must confine ourselves to the other function of words in the poem, or rather, omitting much that is of secondary relevance, to one form of that function, let me call it *pseudo-statement*.

It will be admitted—by those who distinguish between scientific statement, where truth is ultimately a matter of verification as this is understood in the laboratory, and emotive utterance, where "truth" is primarily acceptability *by* some attitude, and more remotely is the acceptability *of* this attitude itself—that it is *not* the poet's business to make scientific statements. Yet poetry has constantly the air of making statements, and important ones; which is

The selection is from I. A. Richards, *Science and Poetry*, rev. ed. (London: Kegan Paul, Trench, Trubner and Co., Ltd., 1935), pp. 61-74 and 92-94. Used by permission of the executors of the estate of Mr. C. K. Ogden, and the author.

one reason why some mathematicians cannot read it. They find the alleged statements to be *false*. It will be agreed that their approach to poetry and their expectations from it are mistaken. But what exactly is the other, the right, the poetic, approach and how does it differ from the mathematical?

The poetic approach evidently limits the framework of possible consequences into which the pseudo-statement is taken. For the scientific approach this framework is unlimited. Any and every consequence is relevant. If any of the consequences of a statement conflicts with acknowledged fact then so much the worse for the statement. Not so with the psuedo-statement when poetically approached. The problem is— just how does the limitation work? One tempting account is in terms of a supposed universe of discourse, a world of make-believe, of imagination, of recognized fictions common to the poet and his readers. A pseudo-statement which fits into this system of assumptions would be regarded as "poetically true"; one which does not, as "poetically false." This attempt to treat "poetic truth" - on the model of general "coherence theories" is very natural for certain schools of logicians but is inadequate, on the wrong lines from the outset. To mention two objections, out of many; there is no means of discovering what the "universe of discourse" is on any occasion, and the kind of coherence which must hold within it, supposing it to be discoverable, is not an affair of logical relations. Attempt to define the system of propositions into which

O Rose, thou art sick!

must fit, and the logical relations which must hold between them if it is to be "poetically true"; the absurdity of the theory becomes evident.

We must look further. In the poetic approach the relevant consequences are not logical or to be arrived at by a partial relaxation of logic. Except occasionally and by accident logic does not enter at all. They are the consequences which arise through our emotional organization. The acceptance which a pseudo-statement receives is entirely governed by its effects upon our feelings and attitudes. Logic only comes in, if at all, in subordination, as a servant to our emotional response. It is an unruly servant, however, as poets and readers are constantly discovering. A pseudo-statement is "true" if it suits and serves some attitude or links together attitudes which on other grounds are desirable. This kind of "truth" is so opposed to scientific "truth" that it is a pity to use so similar a word, but at present it is difficult to avoid the malpractice.[1]

This brief analysis may be sufficient to indicate the fundamental disparity and opposition between pseudo-statements as they occur in poetry and statements as they occur in science. A pseudo-statement is a form of words which is justified entirely by its effect in releasing or organizing our impulses and attitudes (due regard being had for the better or worse organizations of these *inter se*); a statement, on the other hand, is justified by its truth, that is, its correspondence, in a highly technical sense, with the fact to which it points.

Statements true and false alike do, of course, constantly touch off attitudes and action. Our daily practical existence is largely guided by them. On the whole true statements are of more service to us than false ones. None the less we do not and, at present, cannot order our emotions and attitudes by true statements alone. Nor is there any probability that we ever shall

---

[1] A pseudo-statement, as I use the term, is not necessarily false in any sense. It is merely a form of words whose scientific truth or falsity is irrelevant to the purpose in hand.

"Logic" in this paragraph is, of course, being used in a limited and conventional, or popular, sense.

contrive to do so. This is one of the great new dangers to which civilization is exposed. Countless pseudo-statements—about God, about the universe, about human nature, the relations of mind to mind, about the soul, its rank and destiny—pseudo-statements which are pivotal points in the organization of the mind, vital to its well-being, have suddenly become, for sincere, honest and informed minds, impossible to believe as for centuries they have been believed.[2] The accustomed incidences of the modes of believing are changed irrecoverably; and the knowledge which has displaced them is not of a kind upon which an equally fine organization of the mind can be based.

This is the contemporary situation. The remedy, since there is no prospect of our gaining adequate knowledge, and since indeed it is fairly clear that scientific knowledge cannot meet this need, is to cut our pseudo-statements free from that kind of belief which is appropriate to verified statements. So released they will be changed, of course, but they can still be the main instruments by which we order our attitudes to one another and to the world. This is not a desperate remedy, for, as poetry conclusively shows, even the most important among our attitudes can be aroused and

---

[2] See Appendix. For the mind I am considering here the question "Do I believe *x?*" is no longer the same. Not only the "What" that is to be believed but the "How" of the believing has changed—through the segregation of science and its clarification of the techniques of proof. This is the danger; and the remedy suggested is a further differentiation of the "Hows." To these differences correspond differences in the senses of "is so" and "being" where, as is commonly the case, "is so" and "being" assert believings. As we admit this, the world that "is" divides into worlds incommensurable in respect of so called "degrees of reality." Yet, and this is all-important, these worlds have an order, with regard to one another, which is the order of the mind; and interference between them imperils sanity.

maintained without any believing of a factual or verifiable order entering in at all. We need no such beliefs, and indeed we must have none, if we are to read *King Lear*. Pseudo-statements to which we attach no belief and statements proper, such as science provides, cannot conflict. It is only when we introduce inappropriate kinds of believing into poetry that danger arises. To do so is from this point of view a profanation of poetry.

Yet an important branch of criticism which has attracted the best talents from prehistoric times until today consists of the endeavor to persuade men that the functions of science and poetry are identical, or that the one is a "higher form" of the other, or that they conflict and we must choose between them.

The root of this persistent endeavor has still to be mentioned; it is the same as that from which the Magical View of the world arose. If we give to a pseudo-statement the kind of unqualified acceptance which belongs by right only to certified scientific statements—and those judgments of the routine of perception and action from which science derives—, if we can contrive to do this, the impulses and attitudes with which we respond to it gain a notable stability and vigor. Briefly, if we can contrive to believe poetry, then the world *seems*, while we do so, to be transfigured. It used to be comparatively easy to do this, and the habit has become well established. With the extension of science and the neutralization of nature it has become difficult as well as dangerous. Yet it is still alluring; it has many analogies with drug-taking. Hence the endeavors of the critics referred to. Various subterfuges have been devised along the lines of regarding Poetic Truth as figurative, symbolic; or as more immediate, as a truth of Intuition transcending common knowledge; or as a higher form of the same truth that science yields. Such attempts to use poetry as a denial or as a corrective of science are very common. One point can be made against them all: they are never worked out in detail. There is no equivalent of Mill's *Logic* expounding any of them. The language in which they are framed is usually a blend of obsolete psychology and emotive exclamations.

The long-established and much-encouraged habit of giving to emotive utterances—whether pseudo-statements simple, or looser and larger wholes taken as saying something figuratively—the kind of assent which we give to unescapable facts, has for most people debilitated a wide range of their responses. A few scientists, caught young and brought up in the laboratory, are free from it; but then, as a rule, they pay no *serious* attention to poetry. For most men the recognition of the neutrality of nature brings about—through this habit—a divorce from poetry. They are so used to having their responses propped up by beliefs, however vague, that when these shadowy supports are removed they are no longer able to respond. Their attitudes to so many things have been forced in the past, over-encouraged. And when the world-picture ceases to assist there is a collapse. Over whole tracts of natural emotional response we are today like a bed of dahlias whose sticks have been removed. And this effect of the neutralization of nature is perhaps only in its beginnings. However, human nature has a prodigious resilience. Love poetry seems able to out-play psycho-analysis.

A sense of desolation, of uncertainty, of futility, of the groundlessness of aspirations, of the vanity of endeavor, and a thirst for a life-giving water which seems suddenly to have failed, are the signs in consciousness of this necessary reorganization of our lives.[3] Our attitudes and impulses are being compelled to become self-supporting; they are being driven back upon their biological justification, made once again sufficient to themselves. And the only impulses which seem strong enough to continue unflagging are commonly so crude that, to more finely developed individuals they hardly seem worth having. Such people cannot live by warmth, food, fighting, drink, and sex alone. Those who are least affected by the change are those who are emotionally least removed from the animals. As we shall see at the close of this essay, even a considerable poet may attempt to find relief by a reversion to primitive mentality.

It is important to diagnose the disease correctly and to put the blame in the right quarter. Usually it is some alleged "materialism" of science which is denounced. This mistake is due partly to clumsy thinking, but chiefly to relics of the Magical View. For even if the Universe were "spiritual" all through (whatever that assertion might mean; all such assertions are probably nonsense), that would not make it any more

---

[3] My debt to *The Waste Land* here will be evident. The original footnote seems to have puzzled Mr. Eliot and some other readers. Well it might! In saying, though, that he

"had effected a complete severance between his poetry and all beliefs" I was referring not to the poet's own history, but to the technical detachment of the poetry. And the way in which he then seemed to me to have "realized what might otherwise have remained a speculative possibility" was by finding a new order through the contemplation and exhibition of disorder.

"Yes! Very funny this terrible thing is. A man that is born falls into a dream like a man who falls into the sea. If he tries to climb out into the air as inexperienced people endeavor to do, he drowns—*nicht wahr?* . . . No! I tell you! The way is to the destructive element submit yourself, and with the exertions of your hands and feet in the water make the deep, deep sea keep you up. So if you ask me how to be? In the destructive element immerse . . . that was the way." *Lord Jim*, p. 216. Mr. Eliot's later verse has sometimes shown still less "dread of the unknown depths." That, at least, seems in part to explain to me why *Ash Wednesday* is better poetry than even the best sections of *The Waste Land*.

accordant to human attitudes. It is not what the universe is made of but how it works, the law it follows, which makes verifiable knowledge of it incapable of spurring on our emotional responses, and further, the nature of knowledge itself makes it inadequate. The contact with things which we therein establish is too sketchy and indirect to help us. We are beginning to know too much about the bond which unites the mind to its object in knowledge [4] for that old dream of a perfect knowledge which would guarantee perfect life to retain its sanction. What was thought to be pure knowledge, we see now to have been shot through with hope and desire, with fear and wonder; and these intrusive elements indeed gave it all its power to support our lives. In knowledge, in the "How?" of events, we can find hints by which to take advantage of circumstances in our favor and avoid mischances. But we cannot get from it a *raison d'être* or a justification of more than a relatively lowly kind of life.

The justification, on the reverse, of any attitude lies, not in the object, but in itself, in its serviceableness to the whole personality. Upon its place in the whole system of attitudes, which is the personality, all its worth depends. This is as true for the subtle, finely compounded attitudes of the civilized individual as for the simpler attitudes of the child.

In brief, the imaginative life is its own justification; and this fact must be faced, although sometimes—by a lover, for example—it may be very difficult to accept. When it is faced, it is apparent that all the attitudes to other human beings and to the world in all its aspects, which have been serviceable to humanity, remain as they were, as valuable as ever. Hesitation felt in admitting this is a measure of the strength of the evil habit I have been describing. But many of these attitudes, valuable as ever, are, now that they are being set free, more difficult to maintain, because we still hunger after a basis in belief.

APPENDIX [5]

Two chief words seem likely occasions of misunderstanding in the above; and they have in fact misled some readers. One is *Nature,* the other is *Belief.*

Nature is evidently as variable a word as can be used. Its senses range from the mere inclusive THAT, in which we live and of which we are a part, to whatever would correspond to the most detailed and interconnected account we could attain of this. Or we omit ourselves (and other minds) and make Nature *either* what influences us (in which case we should not forget our metabolism), *or* an object we apprehend (in which case there are as many Natures as there are types of aprehension we care to distinguish). And what is "natural" to one culture is strange and artificial to another. (See *Mencius on the Mind,* chap. III.) More deceptively, the view here being inseparable from the eye, and this being a matter of habitual speculation, we may talk, as we think, the same language and yet put very different things into Nature; and what we then find will not be unconnected with what we have put in. I have attempted some further discussion of these questions in Chapters VI and VII of *Coleridge on Imagination.*

---

[4] Verifiable scientific knowledge, of course. Shift the sense of "knowledge" to include hope and desire and fear as well as reference, and what I am saying would no longer be true. But then the relevant sense of "true" would have changed too. Its sanction would no longer be verifiability.

[5 This appendix, added in the second edition, was directed by Mr. Richards toward certain misunderstandings which arose among readers of the first edition. He has treated the subjects of this entire selection further in such works as *Speculative Instruments* (Chicago, 1955) and *How to Read a Page* (New York, 1942). *Ed.*]

Belief. Two "beliefs" may differ from one another: (1) In their objects (2) In their statements or expressions (3) In their modes (4) In their grounds (5) In their occasions (6) In their connections with other "beliefs" (7) In their links with possible action (8) And in other ways. Our chief evidence usually for the beliefs of other people (and often for our own) must be some statement or other expression. But very different beliefs may fittingly receive the same expression. Most words used in stating any speculative opinion are as ambiguous as "Belief"; and yet by such words belief-objects must be distinguished.

But in the case of "belief" there is an additional difficulty. Neither it nor its partial synonyms suggest the great variety of the attitudes (3) that are commonly covered (and confused) by the term. They are often treated as though they were mere variations in degree. Of what? Of belief, it would be said. But this no better than the parallel trick of treating all varieties of love as a mere more or less only further differentiated by their objects. Such crude oversimplifications distort the structure of the mind and, although favorite suasive devises with some well-intentioned preachers, are disastrous.

There is an ample field here awaiting a type of dispassionate inquiry which it has seldom received. A world threatened with ever more and more leisure should not be too impatient of important and explorable subtleties.

Meanwhile, as with "Nature," misunderstanding should neither provoke nor surprise. I should not be much less at my reader's mercy if I were to add notes doubling the length of this little book. On so vast a matter, even the largest book could contain no more than a sketch of how things have seemed to be sometimes to the writer.

6 / SOCIAL PHILOSOPHY

In holding that all factual questions are scientific, the positivist frequently meets with the objection that some areas of experience are not amenable to scientific treatment. This opinion, as applied to society, is called by Professor Popper "historicism." Believing that scientific techniques of observation, experiment, and generalization are inapplicable to society because of the changing conditions of historical existence, the historicist may either deny all knowledge in this area, or he may resort to a metaphysical justification of his social beliefs. Popper attacks historicism by showing that its arguments against the use of scientific method in the social studies are inconclusive; and while recognizing the special difficulties of using the methods of science in the study of society, he nevertheless believes that in this study, as in the investigation of nature, science alone provides reliable belief.

THE ERROR OF HISTORICISM

Karl Popper (1902-   )

In strong opposition to methodological naturalism in the field of sociology, historicism claims that some of the characteristic methods of physics cannot be applied to the social sciences, owing to the profound differences between sociology and physics. Physical laws, or the "laws of nature," it tells us, are valid anywhere and always; for the physical world is ruled by a system of physical uniformities invariable throughout space and time. Sociological laws, however, or the laws of social life, differ in different places and periods. Although historicism admits that there are plenty of typical social conditions whose regular recurrence can be observed, it denies that the regularities detectable in social life have the character of the immutable regularities of the physical world. For they depend upon history, and upon differences in culture. They depend on a particular *historical situation*. Thus one should not, for example, speak without further qualification of the laws of economics, but only of the economic laws of the feudal period, or of the early industrial period, and so on; always mentioning the historical period in which the laws in question are assumed to have prevailed.

Historicism asserts that the historical relativity of social laws makes most of the methods of physics inapplicable to sociology. Typical historicist arguments on which this view is based concern generalization, experiment, the complexity of social phenomena, the difficulties of exact prediction, and the significance of methodological essentialism. I will treat these arguments in turn.

The possibility of generalization and its success in the physical sciences rests, according to historicism, on the general uniformity of nature: upon the observation—perhaps better described as an assumption—that in similar circumstances similar things will happen. This principle, which is taken to be valid throughout space and time, is said to underlie the method of physics.

Historicism insists that this principle is necessarily useless in sociology. Similar circumstances only arise within a single historical period. They never persist from one period to another. Hence there is no long-run uniformity in society on which long-term generalizations could be based— that is, if we disregard trivial regularities such as the truism that human beings always live in groups, or that the supply of certain things is limited and the supply of others, like air, unlimited, and that only the former can have any market or exchange value.

A method which ignores this limitation and attempts a generalization of social uniformities will, according to historicism, implicitly assume that the regularities in question are everlasting; so that a methodologically naïve view—the view that the method of generalization can be taken over from physics by the social sciences—will produce a false and dangerously misleading sociological theory. It will be a theory denying that society develops; or that it ever changes significantly; or that social developments, if there are any, can affect the basic regularities of social life.

Historicists often emphasize that behind such mistaken theories there is usually an apologetic purpose; and indeed, the assumption of unchanging sociological laws can easily be misused for such ends. It may appear, first, as the argument that unpleasant or undesirable things must be accepted since they are determined by invariable laws of nature. For example, the

The selection is from Karl R. Popper, *The Poverty of Historicism* (Boston: The Beacon Press, 1957), pp. 5-9 and 93-97. Used by permission of the publisher.

"inexorable laws" of economics have been invoked to demonstrate the futility of statutory interference with the wage bargain. A second apologetic misuse of the assumption of persistence is the fostering of a general feeling of inevitability, and thus of a readiness to endure the inevitable calmly and without protest. What is now will be for ever, and attempts to influence the march of events, or even to evaluate it, are ridiculous: one does not argue against the laws of nature, and attempts to overthrow them can only lead to disaster.

These, says the historicist, are the conservative, apologetic, and even fatalistic arguments which are the necessary corollaries of the demand that a naturalist method should be adopted in sociology.

The historicist opposes them by maintaining that social uniformities differ widely from those of the natural sciences. They change from one historical period to another, and *human* activity is the force that changes them. For social uniformities are not laws of nature, but man-made; and although they may be said to depend on human nature, they do so because human nature has the power to alter and, perhaps, to control them. Therefore things can be bettered or worsened: active reform need not be futile.

These tendencies of historicism appeal to those who feel a call to be active; to interfere, especially with human affairs, refusing to accept the existing state of things as inevitable. The tendency towards activity and against complacency of any kind may be called *"activism."*. . . I may here quote the well-known exhortation of a famous historicist, Marx, which strikingly expresses the "activist" attitude: "The philosophers have only *interpreted* the world in various ways; the point however is to *change it.*"

Physics uses the method of experiment; that is, it introduces artificial controls, artificial isolation, and thereby ensures the reproduction of similar conditions, and the consequent production of certain effects. This method is obviously based on the idea that where circumstances are similar, similar things will happen. The historicist claims that this method is not applicable in sociology. Nor would it be useful, he argues, even if it were applicable. For, as similar conditions occur only within the limits of a single period, the outcome of any experiment would be a very limited significance. Moreover, artificial isolation would eliminate precisely those factors in sociology which are most important. Robinson Crusoe and his isolated individual economy can never be a valuable model of an economy whose problems arise precisely from the economic interaction of individuals and groups.

It is further argued that no really valuable experiments are possible. Large-scale experiments in sociology are never experiments in the physical sense. They are not made to advance knowledge as such, but to achieve political success. They are not performed in a laboratory detached from the outside world; rather, their very performance changes the conditions of society. They can never be repeated under precisely similar conditions since the conditions were changed by their first performance. . . .

The historicist contends that the experimental method cannot be applied to the social sciences because we cannot, in the social field, reproduce at will precisely similar experimental conditions. This brings us a little closer to the heart of the historicist position. I admit that there may be something in this contention: no doubt there are some differences here between physical and sociological methods. Nevertheless, I assert that the historicist contention rests upon a gross misunderstanding of the experimental methods of physics.

Let us first consider these methods. Every experimental physicist knows that very dissimilar things may happen under what appear to be precisely similar conditions. Two wires may at first sight look exactly alike, but if the one is exchanged for the other in a piece of electrical apparatus, the resulting difference may be very great. Upon closer inspection (say, through a microscope), we may perhaps find that they were not as similar as they first appeared. But often it is very hard indeed to detect a difference in the conditions of the two experiments that lead to different results. Long research, experimental as well as theoretical, may be needed in order to find what kind of similarity is relevant, and what degree of similarity sufficient. This research may have to be carried out before we are able to secure similar conditions for our experiments, and before we even know what "similar conditions" means in this case. And yet, *the method of experiment is applied all the time.*

Thus we can say that the question of what are to be described as "similar conditions" depends on the kind of experiment, and can be answered only by using experiments. It is impossible to decide *a priori* about any observed difference or similarity, however striking, whether or not it will be relevant for the purpose of reproducing an experiment. So we must allow the experimental method to take care of itself. Precisely analogous considerations hold for the much debated problem of the artificial *isolation* of experiments from disturbing influences. Clearly, we cannot isolate a piece of apparatus against *all* influences; for example, we cannot know *a priori* whether the influence of the position of the planets or of the moon upon a physical experiment is considerable or negligible. What kind of artificial isolation, if any, is needed, we can learn only from the result of experiments, or from theories which, in turn, are tested by experiments.

In the light of such considerations, the historicist argument that social experiments are fatally hampered by the variability of social conditions, and especially by the changes which are due to historical develop-

ments, loses its force. The striking differences with which the historicist is so much preoccupied, that is to say, the differences between the conditions prevalent in various historical periods, need not create any difficulties peculiar to social science. It may be admitted that if we were suddenly transported into another historical period, we should probably find that many of our social expectations, formed on the basis of piecemeal experiments made in our society, are disappointed. In other words, experiments may lead to unforeseen results. But it would be *experiments* which led us to discover the change in social conditions; experiments would teach us that certain social conditions vary with the *historical period;* just as experiments have taught the physicist that the temperature of boiling water may vary with *the geographical position.*[1] In other words, the doctrine of the difference between historical periods, far from making social experiments impossible, is merely an expression of the assumption that, if shifted into another period, we should continue to make our piecemeal experiments, but with surprising or disappointing results. In fact, if we know anything about different attitudes in different historical periods, then it is from experiments, carried out in our imagination. Historians find difficulties in interpreting certain records, or they discover facts showing that some of their predecessors had misinterpreted some historical evidence. These difficulties of historical interpretation are our only evidence of the kind of historical change the historicist has in mind; yet they are nothing but discrepancies between the expected and the actual results of our thought experiments.

---

[1] In both cases—historical periods and geographical positions—we may find, using theories tested by experiments, that any reference to temporal or spatial locations can be replaced by some *general* description of certain prevailing relevant conditions, such as the state of education, or the altitude.

It is these surprises and disappointments which, by the method of trial and error, have led to improvements in our ability to interpret strange social conditions. And what in the case of historical interpretation we achieve by thought-experiment has been achieved by anthropologists in practical field work. Those modern investigators who have succeeded in adjusting their expectations to conditions which are perhaps no less remote than those of the Stone Age, owe their success to piecemeal experiments.

Some historicists doubt the possibility of such successful adjustments; and they even defend their doctrine of the futility of social experiments by the argument that, if shifted to remote historical periods, far too many of our social experiments would lead to disappointment. They assert that we should be able to adjust our habits of thought, and especially our habits of analyzing social events, to these bewildering conditions. Such fears seem to me part of the historicist hysteria—the obsession with the importance of social change; but I must admit that it would be difficult to dispel those fears on *a priori* grounds. After all, the ability to adjust oneself to a new environment varies from person to person, and there seems to be no reason why we should expect of a historicist (who holds such defeatist views) that he will be able to adapt his mind successfully to changes in the social environment. Also, matters will depend on the character of the new environment. The possibility that a social investigator may find himself being eaten before he succeeds in adjusting himself, by trial and error, to cannibal habits, cannot be excluded any more than the possibility that, in some "planned" society, his investigations may end in a concentration camp. Yet analogous

remarks hold for the realm of physics. There are many places in which physical conditions prevail which offer to the physicist little chance of adjusting himself by trial and error.

To sum up, there does not seem any basis for the plausible historicist assertion that the variability of historical conditions renders the experimental method inapplicable to the problems of society, or for the assertion that, in this point, the study of society is fundamentally different from the study of nature. It is quite a different matter if we admit that, in practice, it is often very difficult for the social scientist to choose and to vary his experimental conditions at will. The physicist is in a better position although he too is sometimes faced by similar difficulties. Thus the possibilities of carrying out experiments in varying gravitational fields, or under extreme temperature conditions, are very limited. But we must not forget that many possibilities which are open to the physicist today were impracticable not long ago, not because of physical but because of social difficulties, i.e. because we were not prepared to risk the money needed for research. It is a fact, however, that very many physical investigations can now be carried out under experimental conditions which leave little to be desired, while the social scientist is in a very different position. Many experiments which would be most desirable will remain dreams for a long time to come, in spite of the fact that they are not of a Utopian but of a piecemeal character. In practice, he must rely too often on experiments carried out mentally, and on an analysis of political measures carried out under conditions, and in a manner, which leave much to be desired from the scientific point of view.

7 / PHILOSOPHY OF SCIENCE

Traditionally, the various branches of knowledge have been separated into departments and divisions, usually with some of them considered "higher," others "lower." For many positivists, however, not only are all facts scientific, but science itself is a unity in the sense that all empirical statements can be expressed in a single language, all states of affairs are of one kind, and all of them are known by the same method. This thesis of the unity of science is defended by Professor Carnap in the following selection.

Two of the traditional divisions of knowledge are eliminated immediately. Philosophy, Carnap writes, enunciates no propositions of its own, but is simply the activity of clarifying the concepts of science. The statements of mathematics and logic are only analytic, and hence have no content. This leaves only synthetic statements which belong to science. But does science form a unity? To defend the thesis that it does, Carnap notes that science is a set of statements based on direct experience, verified by experiment, and expressed in "protocol" statements. These statements are composed into an often elaborate system, though there is always a reference within the system to their physical determinations. This view Carnap calls methodological positivism or physicalism; to preserve it, he introduces the distinctions of material and formal modes of speech. The material mode speaks of objects, but is in danger of considering pseudo-questions about them. The formal mode considers linguistic forms, and preserves the physicalist thesis. The conclusion Professor Carnap reaches is that, because there is but a single language of science, there is really only one science—namely, physics.

THE UNITY OF SCIENCE

Rudolf Carnap (1891-   )

1. THE HETEROGENEITY OF SCIENCE

Science in its traditional form constitutes no unity, and is separated into philosophy and the technical sciences. The latter are classified again as formal sciences (logic and mathematics) and empirical sciences. It is usual to subdivide the last class further and to understand that it includes, in addition to the "natural" sciences, psychology

The selection is from Rudolf Carnap, *The Unity of Science* (tr. M. Black) (London: Kegan Paul, Trench, Trubner and Co., 1934), pp. 31-40, 42-45, and 93-101. Used by permission of the executors of the estate of Mr. C. K. Ogden and of the author.

and the *Geisteswissenschaften* (social sciences and humanities) generally.

The basis of these various divisions is not merely convenience; rather is the opinion generally accepted that the various sciences named are fundamentally distinct in respect of subject matter, sources of knowledge and technique. Opposed to this opinion is the thesis defended in this paper that science is a unity, that all empirical statements can be expressed in a single language, all states of affairs are of one kind and are known by the same method.

Very little will be said here concerning the nature of philosophy and the formal sciences. The author's views on this point have already been sufficiently explained by others on several occasions. Detailed attention will however be given to the question of the unity of the empirical sciences.

It is to modern developments in logic and particularly in the logical analysis of language that we owe our present insight into the nature of logic, philosophy and mathematics. Analysis of language has ultimately shown that philosophy cannot be a distinct system of statements, equal or superior in rank to the empirical sciences. For the activity of philosophy consists rather in clarifying the notions and statements of science. In this way does cleavage of the field of knowledge into philosophy and empirical science disappear; all statements are statements of the one science. Scientific research may be concerned with the empirical *content* of theorems, by experiment, observation, by the classification and organization of empirical material; or again it may be concerned with establishing the *form* of scientific statements, either without regard for content (formal logic) or else with a view to establishing logical connections between certain specific concepts (theory of knowledge considered as applied logic).

Statements in logic and mathematics are tautologies, analytic propositions, certified on account of their form alone. They have no content, that is to say, assert nothing as to the occurrence or non-occurrence of some state of affairs. If to the statement: *"The (thing) A is black"* we add *"or A is blue,"* the supplemented statement still conveys some information though less than at first. If, however, we replace the supplementary phrase previously chosen by "or A is not black" the compound statement no longer conveys any information at all. It is a tautology, i.e., is verified by *all* circumstances. From such a statement no knowledge of the properties of the thing A can be derived. Theorems in *logic* and *mathematics* have, nevertheless, in spite of tautologous character and lack of content, considerable im-

portance for science by virtue of their use in transforming statements having content. For the present thesis it is important to emphasize that logic and mathematics are sciences having no proper subject matter analogous to the material of the empirical sciences. Postulation of "formal" or "ideal" objects to be set against the "real" objects of empirical sciences is unnecessary in the theory here briefly sketched.

Statements having content, i.e., statements, as is usually said, expressing some state of affairs, belong to the field of *empirical sciences*. Our *chief question* is whether these statements, or to speak more conventionally, whether the states of affairs expressed by such statements are divided into several mutually irreducible kinds. The traditional answer is in the affirmative; and it has been usual to make the chief distinctions between the subject matters of natural science, history, the social sciences, etc. *(Geisteswissenschaften)*, and psychology.

On the basis of observations and experiments, the *natural sciences* describe the spatio-temporal events in the system which we call "Nature." From the individual accounts thus obtained arise general formulae, so-called "laws of nature" (the process of "induction"). These in turn make it possible to obtain new specific statements, e. g., predictions (the process of "deduction").

History, and the social sciences also use the method of observing material events. The usual view maintains, however, that observation in such fields is merely a subordinate method, the proper method being "understanding," empathy ("Einfühlung") projection of oneself into historical monuments and events in order to grasp their "essence." The further question arises, so it is maintained, in all sciences dealing with culture in the widest sense as well as in specifically normative disciplines such as ethics, of comprehending "values," of establishing "norms." The usual view therefore is that the subject matter of such branches of knowledge, the *Geisteswissenschaften* as Germans say, whether they are significant forms or systems of values, are of a nature fundamentally different from the subject matter of natural science and cannot be understood by the methods of natural science.

As to the nature of *psychology* widely divergent views are prevalent. Experiments are made, measurements often taken of factors capable of quantitative determination. Many psychologists therefore include their science among the natural sciences, but while doing so accentuate the difference between their respective subject matters. Psychology, they say, deals with the "mental," with the phenomena of consciousness, perhaps also of unconsciousness, while other natural sciences treat of the "physical." Other psychologists, again, lay the emphasis on the relation between their science and the moral sciences. In psychology also, they say, knowledge is gained by "understanding" and empathy. The difference consists in the fact that psychology does not deal with works of art and institutions, as ethics and sociology do, but with the regularities to be found in the phenomena of consciousness. These various conceptions yet agree in the answer they furnish to the questions which we wish to discuss. Psychology is a science with its own fundamentally distinct and isolated subject matter.

We shall not need to discuss in further detail at this point divergent views of the relations between the various sciences. It is sufficient to remember that it is usual to speak of fundamentally distinct kinds of objects; it matters little for our purpose whether the distinction is made in the manner described above (e. g., "ideal" and "real" objects; physical, mental objects; "values") or in some other. All such accepted views are contrary to the *thesis of the unity of science*.

2. LANGUAGES [1]

In formulating the thesis of the unity of science as the assertion that objects are of a single kind, that states of affairs are of a single kind, we are using the ordinary fashion of speech in terms of "objects" by "states of affairs." The correct formulation replaces "objects" by "words" and "states of affairs" by "statements," for a philosophical, i. e., a logical, investigation must be an analysis of language. Since the terminology of the analysis of language is unfamiliar we propose to use the more usual mode of speech (which we will call *"material"*) side by side with the correct manner of speaking (which we will call the *"formal"*). The first speaks of "objects," "states of affairs," of the "sense," "content" or "meaning" of words, while the second refers only to linguistic forms.

In order to characterize a definite *language* it is necessary to give its *vocabulary* and *syntax*, i. e., the words which occur in it and the rules in accordance with which (1) sentences can be formed from those words and (2) such sentences can be transformed into other sentences, either of the same or of another language (the so-called rules of inference and rules for translation). But is it not also necessary in order to understand the "sense" of the sentences, to indicate the "meaning" of the words? No; the demand

[1 In giving his permission for the use of his material, Professor Carnap made the following remarks on this section:

The formal theory of language here indicated was afterwards elaborated in the book *Logical syntax of language* (German 1934, English translation 1937). The thesis that the logical analysis of language must be purely formal and hence syntactical, was later recognized as too narrow. It was broadened through the development of semantics as a theory of truth and meaning (*Introduction to semantics,* 1942; the changes in the views concerning the nature of logical analysis and of philosophy are specified in Section 39 of this book). (1960). *Ed.*]

thereby made in the material mode is satisfied by specifying the formal rules which constitute its syntax. For the "meaning" of a word is given either by translation or by definition. A translation is a rule for transforming a word from one language to another, (e. g., "cheval" = "horse"); a definition is a rule for mutual transformation of words in the same language. This is true both of so-called nominal definitions (e. g., "Elephant" = animal with such and such distinguishing characteristics) and also, a fact usually forgotten, for so-called ostensive definitions (e. g., "Elephant" = animal of the same kind as the animal in this or that position in space-time); both definitions are translations of words.

At the expense of some accuracy we may also characterize a language in a manner other than in the formal mode above and, using the more "intuitive" material mode, say a language is such that its statements describe such and such (here would follow a list of the objects named in the language). The alternative formulation is permissible provided the writer and the reader are clear that the material mode is only a more vivid translation of the previous description in the formal mode. If this is forgotten the danger may arise of being diverted by the material mode of speech into considering pseudo-questions concerning the essence or reality of the objects mentioned in the definition of a language. Nearly all philosophers and even many positivists have taken the wrong turning and gone astray in this way. . . .

3. PROTOCOL LANGUAGE

Science is a system of statements based on direct experience, and controlled by experimental verification. Verification in science is not, however, of single statements but of the entire system or a sub-system of such statements. Verification is based upon "protocol statements," a term whose mean-

ing will be made clearer in the course of further discussion. This term is understood to include statements belonging to the basic protocol or direct record of a scientist's (say a physicist's or psychologist's) experience. Implied in this notion is a simplification of actual scientific procedure as if all experiences, perceptions, and feelings, thoughts, etc., in everyday life as well as in the laboratory, were first recorded in writing as "protocol" to provide the raw material for a subsequent organization. A "primitive" protocol will be understood to exclude all statements obtained indirectly by induction or otherwise and postulates therefore a sharp (theoretical) distinction between the raw material of scientific investigation and its organization. In practice, the laboratory record of a physicist may have approximately the following form: "Apparatus set up as follows: . . . . ; arrangement of switches: . . . . ; pointer readings of various instruments at various times: . . . . ; sparking discharge takes place at 500 volts." Such a set of statements is not a primitive protocol in view of the occurrence of statements

deduced with the help of other statements from the protocol.

which describe states of affairs not directly observed.

A primitive protocol would perhaps run as follows: "Arrangement of experiment: at such and such positions are objects of such and such kinds (e. g. "copper wire"; the statement should be restricted perhaps to "a thin, long, brown body" leaving the characteristics denoted by "copper" to be deduced from previous protocols in which the same body has occurred): here now pointer 5, simultaneously spark an explosion, then smell of ozone there." Owing to the great clumsiness of primitive protocols it is necessary in practice to include terms of derivative application in the protocol itself. This is true of the physicist's protocol and true in far greater measure of the protocols made by biologists, psychologists and anthropologists. In spite of this fact, questions of the justification of any scientific statement, i. e., of its origin in protocol statements, involve reference back to the primitive protocol.

From now onwards "protocol statements" will be used as an abbreviation for "statements belonging to the primitive protocol"; the language to which such statements belong will be called the *"protocol-language."* (Sometimes also termed "language of direct experience" or "phenomenal language"; the neutral term "primary language" is less objectionable.) In the present state of research it is not possible to characterize this language with greater precision, i. e., to specify its vocabulary, syntactical forms and rules. This is, however, unnecessary for the subsequent arguments of this paper. . . .

7. UNIFIED SCIENCE IN PHYSICAL LANGUAGE

Our view that protocols constitute the basis of the entire scientific edifice might be termed *methodical positivism;* and more specifically as *methodical solipsism,* inasmuch as every subject can use only his own protocol as a basis. (It is true, S_1 can utilize also the protocol of S_2; and this procedure is considerably simplified by embedding both protocol languages into the physical language. However, this utilization is an indirect one; S_1 describes in his protocol the experience of observing a written document of a specified wording.) Similarly, the thesis that the physical language is the universal language might be denoted as *methodical materialism*. The adjective "methodical" is intended to express the fact that we are referring to a thesis which speaks simply of the logical possibility of certain linguistic transformations and derivations and not at all of the "reality" or "appearance" (the "existence" or the "non-existence") of the "given," the "mental" or the "physical." Pseudo-statements of this kind occasionally occur in classical formulations of positivism and materialism. They will be eliminated directly they are recognized as metaphysical admixtures; this is in the spirit of the founders of these movements who were the enemies of all metaphysics. Such admixtures can be formulated only in the material mode and by eliminating them we obtain methodical positivism and methodical materialism in the sense defined. When the two views are so purified they are, as we have seen, in perfect harmony, whereas positivism and materialism in their historic dress have often been regarded as incompatibles.

Our approach has often been termed "positivist"; it might equally well be termed "materialist." No objection can be made to such a title provided that the distinction between the older form of materialism and methodical materialism—the same theory in a purified form—is not neglected. Nevertheless, for the sake of clarity we would prefer the name of *"physicalism."* For our theory is that the physical language is the universal language and can therefore serve as the basic language of science.[2]

[2 Professor Carnap remarks as follows on "physicalism":

The thesis of *physicalism,* asserting the universal character of the physical language, is still maintained today in its essentials. But the details of its formulation have undergone some modifications. The present conception of physicalism, especially in its application to psychology, and the arguments for it, are represented in the two articles by Herbert Feigl: (1) "Physicalism, Unity of Science and the Foundations of Psychology," in P. A. Schilpp (ed.), *The Philosophy of Rudolf Carnap,* forthcoming; see also my reply to Feigl in the same volume; (2) "The 'Mental' and the 'Physical,'" in Vol. II of *Minnesota Studies in Philosophy of Science,* 1958.

The most important modification concerns the relation between the terms of the scientific vocabularies of physics and the other

The physicalist thesis should not be misunderstood to assert that the terminology used by physicists can be applied in every department of science. It is convenient, of course, for each department to have a special terminology adapted to its distinct subject matter. All our thesis asserts is that immediately these terminologies are arranged in the form of a system of definitions they must ultimately refer back to physical terms. For the sake of precision we might supplement or replace the term "physical language" by the term *"physicalistic language"*; denoting by the latter the universal language which contains not only physical terms (in the narrow sense) but also all the various special terminologies (of biology, psychology, sociology, etc.) understood as reduced by definitions to their basis in physical terms.

If we have a single language for the whole of science the cleavage between different departments disappears. Hence the thesis of physicalism leads to the thesis of the *unity of science*. Not the physicalist language alone but any universal language would effect a unification of science but no such language other than the physicalist is known. The possibility of setting up such a language must not, however, be excluded. Its construction would involve the determi-

nation of its vocabulary and of its syntax, including rules for transformations inside the language and for inferring protocol statements. Moreover, in accordance with our previous discussion, every statement P of this language in order to have any sense must allow protocol statements to be inferred according to stated rules. In that case it would be possible, in view of the inferential connection between physical language and protocol language, to construct a statement P_1 of the physical language in such a way that all those statements of the protocol language could be inferred from it which could be inferred from P. The two propositions P and P_1 of the two different systematic languages would then be so related that in every case where P was true P_1 would also be true, and conversely. Hence P could be translated into P_1, and conversely.

In general,

every statement in the new language could be translated into a statement of the physical language and conversely.

every statement in the new language could be interpreted as having the same sense as a statement of the physical language, i. e., every statement of the new language would refer to physical facts, to spatio-temporal events.

Hence, every systematic language of this kind can be translated into the physical language and can be interpreted as a portion of the physical language in an altered dress.

Because the physical language is thus the basic language of science *the whole of science becomes physics*. That is not to be understood as if it were already certain that the present system of physical laws is sufficient to explain all phenomena. It means

---

branches of empirical science, including psychology, on the one hand, and, on the other, the terms of the thing language (e. g., "hard," "hot," etc.). The present paper asserts that the former terms are *definable* on the basis of the latter. I soon recognized that this was an oversimplification. In the article "Testability and Meaning" (*Philosophy of Science*, 3 and 4, 1936-37, later published separately) reducibility through a kind of conditional definition took the place of explicit definability. In recent years the relation, now described as that between theoretical terms and terms for observables, has been made still more flexible (see "The methodological character of theoretical concepts," in H. Feigl and M. Scriven (eds.), *Minnesota Studies*, Vol. I, 1956). (1960). *Ed.*]

every scientific statement can be interpreted, in principle, as a physical statement, i. e., it can be brought into such a form that it correlates a certain numerical value (or interval, or probability distribution of values) of a co-efficient of state to a set of values of position coordinates (or into the form of a complex of such statements).

An explanation, i. e., the deduction of a scientific statement consists of deducing it from a law of the same form as physical laws, i. e., from a general formula for inferring singular statements of the kind specified.

every scientific fact can be interpreted as a physical fact, i. e., as a quantitatively determinable property of a spatio-temporal position (or as a complex of such properties).

Every scientific explanation of fact occurs by means of a law, i. e., by means of a formula which expresses the fact that situations or events or specified kinds in any spatio-temporal region are accompanied by specified events in associated regions related in specified fashion.

It is specifically for *explaining* statements (or facts) by means of laws that a unitary language is essential. It is theoretically always possible inside the total system of physics

to find an explanation for every singular statement, i. e., a law by means of which this statement (or a corresponding probability statement) can be inferred from other propositions based on the protocol.

to find an explanation for every single fact, i. e., a law in accordance with which this fact is implied (with some degree of probability) by the existence of other, known, facts.

For our discussion, it is of no importance

whether these laws take the form of unique determinations as assumed in classical physics (determinism), or, alternatively, as assumed in present-day physics, determine the probability of certain value distributions of parameters (statistical laws of quantum mechanics).

In contrast to the universality of physics cases arise in every partial language which can be expressed in that language but are fundamentally incapable of explanation in that language alone,

e. g., in psychology where no explanatory law can be formulated of a statement of the kind "Mr. A is now seeing a red circle" since the explanation must deduce this statement from statements such as "A red sphere is lying before Mr. A" and "Mr. A has his eyes open," etc.

e. g., a psychological event such as a perception can be described but not explained; for such an event is conditioned not only by other mental events but also by physical and physiological events.

The *prediction* of an unknown is similar to the explanation of a known statement or event, viz. derivation with the help of laws. Hence partial languages are not sufficient for predication and a unitary language is necessary. If our thesis that there is a unitary language were false, the practical application of science to most regions would be crippled. The thorough applicability of science is ensured only by the fact that physical language supplies the basis for unified science.

The thesis of *the unity of science* has nothing to say against the practical separation of various regions for the purposes of division of labor. It is directed only against the usual view that in spite of the many relations between the various regions they themselves are fundamentally distinct in subject matter and methods of investigation. In our view these differences of the various regions rest only upon the uses of different definitions, i. e., of different linguistic forms in various regions, while

the statements and words

the facts and objects

of the various branches of science are fundamentally of the same kind. For all branches are part of the unified science, of physics.

8 / PHILOSOPHY OF RELIGION

We have still to see application made of positivistic theses to the problems of religion. This is done with boldness and clarity in the following selection by A. J. Ayer. Having disposed of metaphysics, he proceeds to show that religious knowledge is in a similar manner to be dismissed. Consider the existence of God. This proposition cannot be proved demonstratively because the argument would rest on an empirical premise, and no empirical premise is certain. Nor can God's existence be shown even as a matter of probability; for if one took his existence as an empirical hypothesis, it would mean that other experiential propositions could be deduced from it—which is not the case. Finally, the argument from religious experience or mysticism is invalid because the mystic does not render the object of his experience intelligible; and failing this, the argument for God can be neither meaningful nor verifiable.

In sum, if God is a metaphysical term, then to say that he exists is neither true nor false, but nonsense. The same generalization applies to other religious terms like soul and immortality. Such a position, in making religious assertions meaningless (rather than taking them as false), is neither agnostic nor atheistic, but positivistic.

VERIFICATION AND RELIGION

A. J. Ayer (1910-   )

This mention of God brings us to the question of the possibility of religious knowledge. We shall see that this possibility has already been ruled out by our treatment of metaphysics. But, as this is a point of considerable interest, we may be permitted to discuss it at some length.

It is now generally admitted, at any rate

The selection is from A. J. Ayer, pp. 114-120 of *Language, Truth and Logic* (London: Victor Gollancz, Ltd.; New York: Dover Publications, Inc., 1949). Reprinted by permission of Victor Gollancz, Ltd., and of Dover Publications, Inc., New York 14, New York.

by philosophers, that the existence of a being having the attributes which define the god of any non-animistic religion cannot be demonstratively proved. To see that this is so, we have only to ask ourselves what are the premises from which the existence of such a god could be deduced. If the conclusion that a god exists is to be demonstratively certain, then these premises must be certain; for, as the conclusion of a deductive argument is already contained in the premises, any uncertainty there may be about the truth of the premises is necessarily shared by it. But we know that no empirical proposition can ever be anything more than probable. It is only *a priori* propositions that are logically certain. But we cannot deduce the existence of a god from an *a priori* proposition. For we know that the reason why *a priori* propositions are certain is that they are tautologies. And from a set of tautologies nothing but a further tautology can be validly deduced. It follows that there is no possibility of demonstrating the existence of a god.

What is not so generally recognized is that there can be no way of proving that the existence of a god, such as the God of Christianity, is even probable. Yet this also is easily shown. For if the existence of such a god were probable, then the proposition that he existed would be an empirical hypothesis. And in that case it would be possible to deduce from it, and other empirical hypotheses, certain experiential propositions which were not deducible from those other hypotheses alone. But in fact this is not possible. It is sometimes claimed, indeed, that the existence of a certain sort of regularity in nature constitutes sufficient evidence for the existence of a god. But if the sentence "God exists" entails no more than that certain types of phenomena occur in certain sequences, then to assert the existence of a god will be simply equivalent to asserting that there is the requisite regularity in nature; and no religious man would admit that this was all he intended to assert in asserting the existence of a god. He would say that in talking about God, he was talking about a transcendent being who might be known through certain empirical manifestations, but certainly could not be defined in terms of those manifestations. But in that case the term "god" is a metaphysical term. And if "god" is a metaphysical term, then it cannot be even probable that a god exists. For to say that "God exists" is to make a metaphysical utterance which cannot be either true or false. And by the same criterion, no sentence which

purports to describe the nature of a transcendent god can possess any literal significance.

It is important not to confuse this view of religious assertions with the view that is adopted by atheists, or agnostics.[1] For it is characteristic of an agnostic to hold that the existence of a god is a possibility in which there is no good reason either to believe or disbelieve; and it is characteristic of an atheist to hold that it is at least probable that no god exists. And our view that all utterances about the nature of God are nonsensical, so far from being identical with, or even lending any support to, either of these familiar contentions, is actually incompatible with them. For if the assertion that there is a god is nonsensical, then the atheist's assertion that there is no god is equally nonsensical, since it is only a significant proposition that can be significantly contradicted. As for the agnostic, although he refrains from saying either that there is or that there is not a god, he does not deny that the question whether a transcendent god exists is a genuine question. He does not deny that the two sentences "There is a transcendent god" and "There is no transcendent god" express propositions one of which is actually true and the other false. All he says is that we have no means of telling which of them is true, and therefore ought not to commit ourselves to either. But we have seen that the sentences in question do not express propositions at all. And this means that agnosticism also is ruled out.

Thus we offer the theist the same comfort as we gave to the moralist. His assertions cannot possibly be valid, but they cannot be invalid either. As he says nothing at all about the world, he cannot justly be accused of saying anything false, or anything for which he has insufficient grounds. It is only when the theist claims that in

---

[1] This point was suggested to me by Professor H. H. Price.

asserting the existence of a transcendent god he is expressing a genuine proposition that we are entitled to disagree with him.

It is to be remarked that in cases where deities are identified with natural objects, assertions concerning them may be allowed to be significant. If, for example, a man tells me that the occurrence of thunder is alone both necessary and sufficient to establish the truth of the proposition that Jehovah is angry, I may conclude that, in his usage of words, the sentence "Jehovah is angry" is equivalent to "It is thundering." But in sophisticated religions, though they may be to some extent based on men's awe of natural process which they cannot sufficiently understand, the "person" who is supposed to control the empirical world is not himself located in it; he is held to be superior to the empirical world, and so outside it; and he is endowed with superempirical attributes. But the notion of a person whose essential attributes are nonempirical is not an intelligible notion at all. We may have a word which is used as if it named this "person," but, unless the sentences in which it occurs express propositions which are empirically verifiable, it cannot be said to symbolize anything. And this is the case with regard to the word "god," in the usage in which it is intended to refer to a transcendent object. The mere existence of the noun is enough to foster the illusion that there is a real, or at any rate a possible entity corresponding to it. It is only when we enquire what God's attributes are that we discover that "God," in this usage, is not a genuine name.

It is common to find belief in a transcendent god conjoined with belief in an after-life. But, in the form which it usually takes, the content of this belief is not a genuine hypothesis. To say that men do not ever die, or that the state of death is merely a state of prolonged insensibility, is indeed to express a significant proposition, though all the available evidence goes to show that

it is false. But to say that there is something imperceptible inside a man, which is his soul or his real self, **and** that it goes on living after he is dead, is to make a metaphysical assertion which has no more factual content than the assertion that there is a transcendent god.

It is worth mentioning that, according to the account which we have given of religious assertions, there is no logical ground for antagonism between religion and natural science. As far as the question of truth or falsehood is concerned, there is no opposition between the natural scientist and the theist who believes in a transcendent god. For since the religious utterances of the theist are not genuine propositions at all, they cannot stand in any logical relation to the propositions of science. Such antagonism as there is between religion and science appears to consist in the fact that science takes away one of the motives which make men religious. For it is acknowledged that one of the ultimate sources of religious feeling lies in the inability of men to determine their own destiny; and science tends to destroy the feeling of awe with which men regard an alien world, by making them believe that they can understand and anticipate the course of natural phenomena, and even to some extent control it. The fact that it has recently become fashionable for physicists themselves to be sympathetic towards religion is a point in favor of this hypothesis. For this sympathy towards religion marks the physicists' own lack of confidence in the validity of their hypotheses, which is a reaction on their part from the anti-religious dogmatism of nineteenth-century scientists, and a natural outcome of the crisis through which physics has just passed.

It is not within the scope of this enquiry to enter more deeply into the causes of religious feeling, or to discuss the probability of the continuance of religious belief. We are concerned only to answer those questions which arise out of our discussion of the possibility of religious knowledge. The point which we wish to establish is that there cannot be any transcendent truths of religion. For the sentences which the theist uses to express such "truths" are not literally significant.

An interesting feature of this conclusion is that it accords with what many theists are accustomed to say themselves. For we are often told that the nature of God is a mystery which transcends the human understanding. But to say that something transcends the human understanding is to say that it is unintelligible. And what is unintelligible cannot significantly be described. Again, we are told that God is not an object of reason but an object of faith. This may be nothing more than an admission that the existence of God must be taken on trust, since it cannot be proved. But it may also be an assertion that God is the object of a purely mystical intuition, and cannot therefore be defined in terms which are intelligible to the reason. And I think there are many theists who would assert this. But if one allows that it is impossible to define God in intelligible terms, then one is allowing that it is impossible for a sentence both to be significant and to be about God. If a mystic admits that the object of his vision is something which cannot be described, then he must also admit that he is bound to talk nonsense when he describes it.

For his part, the mystic may protest that his intuition does reveal truths to him, even though he cannot explain to others what these truths are; and that we who do not possess this faculty of intuition can have no ground for denying that it is a cognitive faculty. For we can hardly maintain *a priori* that there are no ways of discovering true propositions except those which we ourselves employ. The answer is that we set no limit to the number of ways in which one may come to formulate a true proposition.

We do not in any way deny that a synthetic truth may be discovered by purely intuitive methods as well as by the rational method of induction. But we do say that every synthetic proposition, however it may have been arrived at, must be subject to the test of actual experience. We do not deny *a priori* that the mystic is able to discover truths by his own special methods. We wait to hear what are the propositions which embody his discoveries, in order to see whether they are verified or confuted by our empirical observations. But the mystic, so far from producing propositions which are empirically verified, is unable to produce any intelligible propositions at all. And therefore we say that his intuition has not revealed to him any facts. It is no use his saying that he has apprehended facts but is unable to express them. For we know that if he really had acquired any information, he would be able to express it. He would be able to indicate in some way or other how the genuineness of his discovery might be empirically determined. The fact that he cannot reveal what he "knows," or even himself devise an empirical test to validate his "knowledge," shows that his state of mystical intuition is not a genuinely cognitive state. So that in describing his vision the mystic does not give us any information about the external world; he merely gives us direct information about the condition of his own mind.

These considerations dispose of the argument from religious experience, which many philosophers still regard as a valid argument in favor of the existence of a god. They say that it is logically possible for men to be immediately acquainted with God, as they are immediately acquainted with a sense-content, and that there is no reason why one should be prepared to believe a man when he says that he is seeing a yellow patch, and refuse to believe him when he says that he is seeing God. The answer to this is that if the man who asserts that he is seeing God is merely asserting that he is experiencing a peculiar kind of sense-content, then we do not for a moment deny that his assertion may be true. But, ordinarily, the man who says that he is seeing God is saying not merely that he is experiencing a religious emotion, but also that there exists a transcendent being who is the object of this emotion; just as the man who says that he sees a yellow patch is ordinarily saying not merely that his visual sense-field contains a yellow sense-content, but also that there exists a yellow object to which the sense-content belongs. And it is not irrational to be prepared to believe a man when he asserts the existence of a yellow object, and to refuse to believe him when he asserts the existence of a transcendent god. For whereas the sentence "There exists here a yellow-colored material thing" expresses a genuine synthetic proposition which could be empirically verified, the sentence "There exists a transcendent god" has, as we have seen, no literal significance.

We conclude, therefore, that the argument from religious experience is altogether fallacious. The fact that people have religious experiences is interesting from the psychological point of view, but it does not in any way imply that there is such a thing as religious knowledge, any more than our having moral experiences implies that there is such a thing as moral knowledge. The theist, like the moralist, may believe that his experiences are cognitive experiences, but, unless he can formulate his "knowledge" in propositions that are empirically verifiable, we may be sure that he is deceiving himself. It follows that those philosophers who fill their books with assertions that they intuitively "know" this or that moral or religious "truth" are merely providing material for the psychoanalyst. For no act of intuition can be said to reveal a truth about any matter of fact unless it issues in verifiable propositions. And all such propositions are to be incorporated in the system of empirical propositions which constitutes science.

9 / SUMMARY

Much of positivism may appear to the student to be only negative and destructive, for it seems to be restrictive in its application of the word "knowledge" and to rule out as nonsense many of the questions that human beings have considered to be of supreme importance. Professor Feigl addresses himself to this sentiment in the following selection, noting that the philosophy for which he speaks is not negativism, but positivism. It is positive because, in eliminating verbal magic and pseudo-problems, it frees thought for the steady advance of science. In his summary restatement of the verification principle, he observes that positivism merely holds that if there are differences, they must make a difference—if there is meaning, it must make for meaningfulness. To eliminate meaninglessness and metaphysical baggage is positivism's valued contribution to science.

THE MEANING OF POSITIVISM

Herbert Feigl (1902-   )

POSITIVISM, NOT NEGATIVISM. Probably the most decisive division among philosophical attitudes is the one between the worldly and the other-worldly types of thought. Profound differences in personality and temperament express themselves in the ever changing forms these two kinds of outlook assume. Very likely there is here an irreconciliable divergence. It goes deeper than disagreement in doctrine; at bottom it is a difference in basic aim and interest. Countless frustrated discussions and controversies since antiquity testify that logical argument and empirical evidence are unable to resolve the conflict. In the last analysis this is so because the very issue of the jurisdictive power of the appeal to logic and experience (and with it the question of just what empirical evidence can establish) is at stake.

It seems likely that this situation in philosophy will continue as long as human nature in its relations to its cultural environment remains what it has been for the last three or four thousand years. The tough-minded and the tender-minded, as William James described them so brilliantly, are perennial types, perennially antagonistic. There will always be those who find this world of ours, as cruel and deplorable as it may be in some respects, an exciting, fascinating place to live in, to explore, to adjust to, and to improve. And there will always be those who look upon the universe of experience and nature as an unimportant or secondary thing in comparison with something more fundamental and more significant. This tendency of thought may express itself

The selection is from Herbert Feigl, "Logical Empiricism," in Dagobert D. Runes (ed.), *Twentieth-Century Philosophy* (New York: Philosophical Library, Inc., 1943), pp. 373-377, 381-384, and 386-387. Used by permission of the author and the publisher.

theologically or metaphysically. It may lead to a faith in extra-mundane existence, or it may in various attenuated fashions assert merely the supremacy of some rational or intuitive principles.

Empiricism, Skepticism, Naturalism, Positivism, and Pragmatism are typical thought movements of the worldly, tough-minded variety. Respect for the facts of experience, open-mindedness, an experimental trial-and-error attitude, and the capacity for working within the frame of an incomplete, unfinished world view distinguish them from the more impatient, imaginative, and often aprioristic thinkers in the tender-minded camp. Among the latter are speculative metaphysicians, intuitionists, rationalists, and absolute idealists. An amusing anecdote concerning two celebrated contemporary philosophers has become widely known. One considers the other muddleheaded and the other thinks the one simpleminded. This fairly epitomizes the history of philosophy, that grandiose "tragicomedy of wisdom." Plato and Protagoras, St. Thomas and William of Ockham, Spinoza and Hobbes, Leibniz and Locke, Kant and Hume, Hegel and Comte, Royce and James, Whitehead and Russell are in many regards, though of course not in every feature, outstanding examples of that basic difference.

Inasmuch as this divergence of attitudes establishes a continuum of positions between extremes, there is also among the tough-minded thinkers a gradation of shades from a nominalistic, pan-scientific radicalism to a more liberal, flexible form of empiricism. Typical among the radicals is the use of the phrase "nothing but." We are familiar with this expression from earlier doctrines, such as *materialism:* "Organisms are nothing but machines." "Mind is nothing but matter." "The history of ideas is only an epiphenomenon of the economic processes." We also know it from *phenomenalism:* "Matter is nothing but clusters of sensations." Or from *nominalism:* "Universals are mere words." Or from *ethical skepticism* and *relativism:* "Good and evil are no more than projections of our likes and dislikes."

One of the great merits of logical empiricism lies in the fact that it is conscious of the danger of these reductive fallacies. It may not always have been able to avoid them. A young and aggressive movement in its zeal to purge thought of confusions and superfluous entities, naturally brandishes more destructive weapons than it requires for its genuinely constructive endeavor. But that is a socio-psychological accident which in time will become less important. The future of empiricism will depend on its ability to avoid both the *reductive* fallacies of a narrowminded positivism—stigmatized as *negativism*—as well as the *seductive* fallacies of metaphysics. Full maturity of thought will be attained when neither aggressive destruction nor fantastic construction, both equally infantile, characterize the philosophic intellect. The alternative left between a philosophy of the "Nothing But" and a philosophy of the "Something More" is a philosophy of the "What is What." Thus an attitude of *reconstruction* is emerging: an attitude which recognizes that analysis is vastly different from destruction or reduction to absurdity, an attitude that is favorable to the integration of our knowledge, as long as that integration is carried on in the truly scientific spirit of caution and open-mindedness. The reconstructive attitude demands that we describe the world in a way that does not impoverish it by artificial reductions, and it thus requires that we make important distinctions wherever there is an objective need for them. But, on the other hand, the empiricist will with equal decision reject wishful thinking of all sorts, the read-

ing into experience of features which are incapable of test and the multiplication of entities beyond necessity.

It would be puerile optimism to hope that out of such revision and reform should grow a generally accepted philosophy to end all philosophies. But what may seem questionable as an historical prediction may yet be justifiable as a working attitude in a living enterprise. The spirit of enlightenment, the spirit of Galileo, of Hume, and of the French Encyclopedists is fully alive again in the contemporary encyclopedists of a unified science. These modern logical empiricists hope to have freed themselves from the naïveté and dogmatism of the various nineteenth century materialists and monists. They are conscious of their philosophy's role as a turning point in the history of critical thought. Nevertheless, they do not claim originality, for they are aware that the empirical and analytic trend in philosophy is no less persistent than the speculative and intuitive approach, though it is admittedly less spectacular and popular. The tradition they now represent has centered its chief inquiries around the two humble questions, "What do you mean?" and "How do you know?" The systematic pursuit of meaning by the Socratic method and the searching scrutiny of the foundations of knowledge are thus again declared the genuine task of philosophy, a task which differs from the quest for truth as carried on by science and yet is most intimately related to it.

Neither the construction of a world view nor a vision of a way of living is the primary aim. If through the progress of knowledge and through social, political, and educational reform one or the other objective is pursued, philosophy in its critical and clarifying capacity may aid or guide such developments. But it cannot, by mere reflective analysis, *prescribe or produce* them. Quackish and dilettantish projects in both directions have always been abundant and cheap in the market of ideas. The main contribution that philosophical reconstruction can make in this regard lies in the direction of an education toward maturer ways of thinking, thinking which possesses the virtues characteristic of science: clarity and consistency, testability and adequacy, precision and objectivity. Immature attitudes are associated with attempts to explain experience in ways which lack the distinguishing marks of science. Certain of these pre-scientific modes of explanation, like the magical, the animistic, and the mythological, are nearly defunct; others, like the theological and the metaphysical, still prevail.

Throughout its history, philosophy has been the particular stronghold of verbal magic. By purely verbal means it has tried to explain things which only science could explain or which cannot be explained at all. In the process it creates its own perplexities, and at its worst it attempts the "solution" of these pseudo-problems—problems arising only out of linguistic confusion—by means of pseudo-techniques—more verbal magic. Analysis teaches us that all this is altogether unnecessary. Thus, if a little levity be permitted, we may define philosophy as the disease of which it should be the cure. . . .

THE CRITERION OF FACTUAL MEANING AND THE CRITIQUE OF METAPHYSICS. The most important, the most widely debated, and, unfortunately, the most frequently misunderstood regulative principle used by Logical Empiricism is the criterion of factual meaningfulness. The purpose of this criterion is to delimit the type of expression which has possible reference to fact from the other types which do not have this kind of significance: the emotive, the logico-mathematical, the purely formal, and—if there should be such—the completely non-significant.

If it is the ostensive steps that connect a purely formal array of signs (e. g. words) with something outside of language, no sign or combination of signs can have factual meaning without this reference to experience. Furthermore, if a sentence is considered true when it corresponds to an existing state of affairs, a sentence is factually meaningful only if we are in principle capable of recognizing such states of affairs as would either validate or invalidate the sentence. If we cannot possibly conceive of what would have to be the case in order to confirm or disconfirm an assertion we would not be able to distinguish between its truth and its falsity. In that case we would simply not know what we are talking about. C. S. Peirce's pragmatic maxim, formulated in his epoch-making essay, *How to make our ideas clear,* has essentially the same import. We may paraphrase it crudely: A difference that is to be a difference (i. e., more than merely a verbal or an emotive one) must *make* a difference. Or, a little more precisely: If and only if assertion and denial of a sentence imply a difference capable of observational (experiential, operational, or experimental) test, does this sentence have factual meaning. Another useful formulation is Ayer's: "It is the mark of a genuine factual proposition . . . that some experiential propositions can be deduced from it in conjunction with certain other premises without being deducible from these other premises alone." This is simply empiricism brought up to date. The psychologistic formulations, an example of which may be found in Hume (ideas must have their basis and origin in impressions), are replaced by logical ones. The most helpful exposition of these concepts for physical scientists was given by P. W. Bridgman. Realizing the close relationship between knowledge and action, or as Dewey would put it, the place of meaning in the context of inquiry, he asks by what procedures we decide the validity of our assertions. Thus Bridgman maintains that concepts and assertions are meaningless if no operations can be specified that define the former and test the latter. . . .

Thus in a general classification of sentences and expressions we distinguish today: (1) Logically true sentences, also called analytic sentences. (2) Logically false sentences, also called contradictions. These sentences are true or false, respectively, by virtue of their form. Even if descriptive empirical terms are contained in them they functon only "vacuously," and their factual reference is irrelevant to the validity of the sentence. (3) Factually true and (4) factually false sentences whose validity depends upon their correspondence to observed fact. In the majority of instances this correspondence or non-correspondence is only incompletely and indirectly indicated by whatever is immediately observable. Therefore these sentences are usually not *known* to be true or false but are considered to be confirmed or disconfirmed to an extent which may vary considerably with the accumulation of favorable or unfavorable evidence. (5) Emotive expressions without cognitive meaning and the emotive components of otherwise cognitive expressions. Pictorial, figurative, and metaphorical expressions, exclamations, interjections, words of praise or blame, appeals, suggestions, requests, imperatives, commands, questions, and prayers belong to this category. Even in definitions we recognize a motivational element: the resolution or invitation to use a term in a certain way.

In the light of the preceding distinctions, we may say that an expression is devoid of empirical meaning (i. e., of factual reference) or, briefly, is *factually meaningless,* if it belongs to any one or several of the following five groups: (a) Expressions violating the syntactical formation-rules of a given language; (b) Analytic sentences; (c) Contradictory sentences; (d) Sentences containing extra-logical terms for which no experiential or operational definitions can be provided; (e) Sentences whose confirm-

ability, i. e., even indirect and incomplete testability-in-principle, is logically excluded by the assumptions of the system of which they are a part. . . .

To the empiricist one of the most gratifying trends in the history of science is the gradual liberation of theory from metaphysical bondage. The ideas of absolute space, time, and substance, of numbers as real entities, of the cause-effect relation as an intrinsic necessity, of vital forces and entelechies, and of all manner of obscure faculties and mythical powers have gradually disappeared from respectable science as it was seen that they were either ad hoc explanations or samples of verbal legerdemain or both. One incident in this process of growing epistemological sophistication must suffice for illustration. When after many experiments (Fizeau, Michelson-Morley, de Sitter, Toruton-Noble) physicists realized that it was hopeless to look for effects of the universal ether upon moving bodies, some of them were nevertheless not ready to give up the ether hypothesis. H. A. Lorentz, certainly one of the greatest physicists, pardoned the ether of its undiscoverability by postulating an ingenious set of assumptions, which jointly guaranteed that whatever effects might be produced by the ether, such effects would be exactly cancelled by other counter-effects. Einstein very soon afterwards realized that by this token the stationary-ether hypothesis had become not only scientifically superfluous but strictly meaningless as well. An essentially similar situation prevailed long before in the Newton-Leibniz controversy regarding absolute space and time in which Leibniz used arguments very much like those of the modern pragmatists and positivists.

A word of warning should not be amiss here. The danger of a fallaciously reductive use of the meaning-criterion is great, especially in the hands of young iconoclasts. It is only too tempting to push a very difficult problem aside and by stigmatizing it as meaningless to discourage further investigation. If, for example, some of the extremely tough-minded psychologists relegate questions such as those concerning the instincts, the unconscious, or the relative roles of constitution and environment to the limbo of metaphysics, then they cut with Ockham's razor far into the flesh of knowledge instead of merely shaving away the metaphysical whiskers. No meaningful problem is in principle insoluble, but there is no doubt that the human race will leave a great many problems unsolved.

BIBLIOGRAPHICAL NOTE

For earlier statements of positivism, see the works of Auguste Comte, especially *A General View of Positivism*, English translation (London, 1908), as well as the writings of Lévy-Bruhl, E. Littre, Ernst Mach, and H. Poincaré. A survey of recent positivism is given in V. Kraft, *The Vienna Circle* (New York, 1953). Introductory textbooks of positivistic persuasion include Richard von Misis, *Positivism: A Study in Human Understanding* (Cambridge, 1951); Arthur Pap, *Elements of Analytic Philosophy* (New York, 1949); and Hans Reichenbach, *The Rise of Scientific Philosophy* (Berkeley, 1951). A. J. Ayer's *Language, Truth and Logic*, 2d ed. (London, 1949), is an influential and readable book. More advanced treatments of philosophical problems are found in the writings of such thinkers as Rudolf Carnap, Otto Neurath, and Moritz Schlick. Their important papers, together with others of equal interest, are collected in such anthologies and compilations as H. Feigl and W. Sellars (eds.), *Readings in Philosophical Analysis* (New York, 1949); H. Feigl and M. Brodbeck (eds.), *Readings in the Philosophy of Science* (New York, 1953); *International Encyclopedia of Unified Science;* and *Minnesota Studies in the Philosophy of Science*. Deserving of special mention is A. J. Ayer's *Logical Positivism* (Glencoe, Illinois, 1959), a broad anthology with excellent bibliographical material. R. L. Hawkins, *Positivism in the United States* (Cambridge, 1938), may be of special interest to the student. Critical studies include J. K. Weinberg, *An Examination of Logical Positivism* (New York, 1936), and C. E. M. Joad, *A Critique of Logical Positivism* (London, 1950).

V

ANALYTIC PHILOSOPHY

MOORE / RYLE / WITTGENSTEIN

WISDOM / WEITZ

WELDON / WAISMANN

Philosophy, we have seen, has been variously defined, and its proper task and subject matter have been variously characterized. In what is called analytic philosophy or, frequently, linguistic analysis, we find a rather different philosophy, and one most difficult to describe in brief compass. Not so much a philosophy definable in terms of commonly accepted theses, it is rather a school or position through its temper of mind and its approach to problems.

Analytic philosophy owes much to positivism, from which it in part developed. Analytic thought would agree with positivism in the latter's emphasis on analysis as against speculation; that therefore philosophy is not a body of propositions but an activity; and that the object of its analytic concern is language.

Opposed to these agreements, however, are certain crucial differences. First, linguistic philosophers generally reject the verification principle. They find it either a kind of metaphysical proposition—and they reject all metaphysics—or highly reductive in viewing meaning solely in reference to sense-experience. To use a slogan of this philosophy, "the meaning is the use," not verification. Secondly, analysts reject a rigid interpretation of the analytic-synthetic distinction. Within certain types of discourse, to be sure, this distinction can be maintained; but in actual and living languages, it does not hold. Thirdly, the analysts reject any simple classification of uses of language and insist rather that sentences perform an indefinitely large number of tasks. To use a second slogan, "every statement has its own logic"; that is, the uses and functions of words are richer and more varied than a rigid classification would imply.

But why this exclusive concern with analysis and ordinary language? And what is analysis? The answer to the first question rests on the observation that language can give rise to puzzlement because some expressions, as Professor Gilbert Ryle has written, are "systematically misleading." [1] Consider an illustration: the statement, "Mr. Baldwin is a politician," is not misleading, for it states a fact in a straightforward way. The statement, "Mr. Baldwin is objective," however, though similar in structure, does not exhibit the form of the fact and is misleading without analysis. Traditional philosophy, the analyst holds, has been particularly susceptible to error because of such expressions. He therefore is concerned with language because certain expressions are misleading and give rise to puzzles; and what he deals with is not problems or theories but puzzlement.

This type of analysis aims, not at ontology or the traits of experience, but rather at clearing up linguistic confusion, preventing the misuse and misconception of language, and exposing absurd theories. The selections that follow define and articulate, as well as show applications of, this philosophical approach. To conclude with Professor Ryle, "we can often succeed in stating [a] fact in a new form of words which does exhibit what the other failed to exhibit. And I am for the present inclined to believe that this is what philosophical analysis is, and that this is the sole and whole function of philosophy."

1 / INTRODUCTION

Much of philosophy, linguistic philosophers believe, has been an attack on common sense and the ordinary, everyday language that expresses common sense. In the following selection, the eminent British philosopher G. E. Moore defends common sense against its attackers. There are, he writes, a number of propositions that both he and a great number of people have known to be true with certainty; and he takes them as true in their ordinary sense. Knowing the *truth* of such propositions, however, is not the same as knowing their correct *analysis,* which is not only a different but often a very difficult thing. Moore observes that in saying this he is reversing what is the position of most philosophers; that is, that they have no doubt about the analysis of concepts, but they would reject their truth.

For Moore to say that he knows the truth of these propositions means that he is vindicating common-sense knowledge. Common-sense judgments, he holds, are never *systematically* in error but only inadvertently so. Moore's general technique in refuting philosophical statements, then, is simply to show that they go against ordinary language. Ordinary language is correct language. If a philoso-

[1] See his article, "Systematically Misleading Expressions," *Proceedings of the Aristotelian Society,* 1931-32.

pher says, for example, that a man does not see a tree when he looks at it, he falls into great absurdity. He implies, according to Moore, that a person can use an expression to describe something—the expression, namely, that is used for such a description—and yet be using incorrect language.

Moore's influence upon contemporary philosophy has been tremendous. It has been said of him that he was the first philosopher to sense that any philosophical statement which violates ordinary language is false. His own philosophical activity was one of defending ordinary language against its philosophical violators.

PHILOSOPHY AND COMMON SENSE

G. E. Moore (1873-1958)

In what follows I have merely tried to state, one by one, some of the most important points in which my philosophical position differs from positions which have been taken up by *some* other philosophers. It may be that the points which I have had room to mention are not really the most important, and possibly some of them may be points as to which no philosopher has ever really differed from me. But, to the best of my belief, each is a point as to which many have really differed; although (in most cases, at all events) each is also a point as to which many have agreed with me.

I. The first point is a point which embraces a great many other points. And it is one which I cannot state as clearly as I wish to state it, except at some length. The method I am going to use for stating it is this. I am going to begin by enunciating, under the heading (1), a whole long list of propositions, which may seem, at first sight, such obvious truisms as not to be worth stating: they are, in fact, a set of propositions, every one of which (in my own opin-

The selection is from G. E. Moore, "A Defence of Common Sense," in J. H. Muirhead (ed.), *Contemporary British Philosophy*, Second Series (London: George Allen and Unwin, Ltd.; New York: The Macmillan Company, 1925), pp. 193-199, 216-217, and 222-223. Used by permission of the publishers.

ion) I *know*, with certainty, to be true. I shall, next, under the heading (2), state a single proposition which makes an assertion about a whole set of *classes* of propositions—each class being defined, as the class consisting of all propositions which resemble *one* of the propositions in (1) in a certain respect. (2), therefore, is a proposition which could not be stated, until the list of propositions in (1), or some similar list, had already been given. (2) is itself a proposition which may seem such an obvious truism as not to be worth stating: and it is also a proposition which (in my own opinion) I *know*, with certainty, to be true. But, nevertheless, it is, to the best of my belief, a proposition with regard to which many philosophers have, for different reasons, differed from me; even if they have not directly denied (2) itself, they have held views incompatible with it. My first point, then, may be said to be that (2), together with all its implications, some of which I shall expressly mention, is true.

(1) I begin, then, with my list of truisms, every one of which (in my own opinion) I *know*, with certainty, to be true. The propositions to be included in this list are the following:—

There exists at present a living human body, which is *my* body. This body was born at a certain time in the past, and has existed continuously ever since, though not without undergoing changes: it was, for instance, much smaller when it was born, and for some time afterwards, than it is now. Ever since it was born, it has been either in contact with or not far from the surface of the earth; and, at every moment since it was born, there have also existed many other things, having shape and size in three dimensions (in the same familiar sense in which it has), from which it has been *at various distances* (in the familiar sense in which it is now at a distance both from that mantel-piece and from that book-case, and at a greater distance from the book-case than it is from the mantel-piece); also there have (very often, at all events) existed some other things of this kind with which it was *in contact* (in the familiar sense in which it is now in contact with the pen I am holding in my right hand and with some of the clothes I am wearing). Among the things which have, in this sense, formed part of its environment (i.e. have been either in contact with it, or at *some* distance from it, however *great*) there have, at every moment since its birth, been large numbers of other living human bodies, each of which has, like it, (*a*) at some time been born, (*b*) continued to exist for some time after birth, (*c*) been, at every moment of its life after birth, either in contact with or not far from the surface of the earth; and many of these bodies have already died and ceased to exist. But the earth had existed also for many years before my body was born; and for many of these years, also, large numbers of human bodies had, at every moment, been alive upon it; and many of these bodies had died and ceased to exist before it was born. Finally (to come to a different class of propositions), I am a human being, and I have, at different times since my body was born, had many different experiences, of each of many different kinds: e.g. I have often perceived both my own body and other things which formed part of its en-

vironment, including other human bodies; I have not only perceived things of this kind, but have also observed facts about them, such as, for instance, the fact which I am now observing, that that mantel-piece is at present nearer to my body than that book-case; I have been aware of other facts, which I was not at the time observing, such as, for instance, the fact, of which I am now aware, that my body existed yesterday and was then also for some time nearer to that mantel-piece than to that book-case; I have had expectations with regard to the future, and many beliefs of other kinds, both true and false; I have thought of imaginary things, and persons and incidents, in the reality of which I did not believe; I have had dreams; and I have had feelings of many different kinds. And, just as my body has the body of a human being, namely myself, who has, during its life-time, had many experiences of each of these (and other) different kinds; so, in the case of very many of the other human bodies which have lived upon the earth, each has been the body of a different human being, who has, during the life-time of that body, had many different experiences of each of these (and other) different kinds.

(2) I now come to the single truism which, as will be seen, could not be stated except by reference to the whole list of truisms, just given in (1). This truism also (in my own opinion) I *know*, with certainty, to be true; and it is as follows:—

In the case of *very many* (I do not say *all*) of the human beings belonging to the class (which includes myself) defined in the following way, i.e. as human beings who have had human bodies, that were born and lived for some time upon the earth, and who have, during the life-time of those bodies, had many different experiences of each of the kinds mentioned in (1), it is true that each has frequently, during the life of his body, known, with regard to *him*self or *his* body, and with regard to some time earlier than any of the times at which I wrote down the propositions in (1), a proposition *corresponding* to each of the propositions in (1), in the sense that it asserts with regard to *him*self or *his* body and the earlier time in question (namely, in each case, the time at which he knew it), just what the corresponding proposition in (1) asserts with regard to *me* or *my* body and the time at which I wrote that proposition down.

In other words what (2) asserts is only (what seems an obvious enough truism) that each of *us* (meaning by "us," very many human beings of the class defined) has frequently *known,* with regard to *him*self or *his* body and the time at which he knew it, everything which, in writing down my list of propositions in (1), I was claiming to know about *my*self or *my* body and the time at which I wrote that proposition down. I.e. just as *I* knew (when I wrote it down) "There exists at present a living human body which is my body," so each of us has frequently known with regard to himself and some other time the different but corresponding proposition, which *he* could *then* have properly expressed by, "There exists *at present* a human body which is *my* body"; just as *I* know "Many human bodies other than mine have before now lived on the earth," so each of us has frequently known the different but corresponding proposition "Many human bodies other than *mine* have before *now* lived on the earth"; just as *I* know "Many human beings other than myself have before now perceived, and dreamed, and felt," so each of *us* has frequently known the different but corresponding proposition "Many human beings other than *myself* have before *now* perceived, and dreamed, and felt"; and so on, in the case of *each* of the propositions enumerated in (1).

I hope there is no difficulty in understanding, so far, what this proposition (2) asserts. I have tried to make clear by examples what I mean by "propositions *corresponding* to each of the propositions in (1)." And what (2) asserts is merely that each of us has frequently known to be true a proposition *corresponding* (in that sense) to each of the propositions in (1)— a *different* corresponding proposition, of course, at each of the times at which he knew such a proposition to be true.

But there remain two points, which, in view of the way in which some philosophers have used the English language, ought, I think, to be expressly mentioned, if I am to make quite clear exactly how much I am asserting in asserting (2).

The first point is this. Some philosophers seem to have thought it legitimate to use the word "true" in such a sense, that a proposition which is partially false may nevertheless also be true; and some of these, therefore, would perhaps *say* that propositions like those enumerated in (1) are, in their view, true, when all the time they believe that every such proposition is partially false. I wish, therefore, to make it quite plain that I am not using "true" in any such sense. I am using it in such a sense (and I think this is the ordinary usage) that if a proposition is partially false, it follows that it is *not* true, though, of course, it may be *partially* true. I am maintaining, in short, that all the propositions in (1), and also many propositions corresponding to each of these, are *wholly* true; I am asserting this in asserting (2). And hence any philosopher, who does in fact believe, with regard to any or all of these classes of propositions, that every proposition of the class in question is partially false, is, in fact, disagreeing with me and holding a view incompatible with (2), even though he may think himself justified in *saying* that he believes some propositions belonging to all of these classes to be "true."

And the second point is this. Some philosophers seem to have thought it legitimate to use such expressions as, e.g., "The earth has existed for many years past," as if they expressed something which they really believe, when in fact they believe that every proposition, which such an expression would *ordinarily* be understood to express, is, at least partially, false; and all they really believe is that there is some *other* set of propositions, related in a certain way to those which such expressions do actually express, which, unlike these, really are true. That is to say, they use the expression "The earth has existed for many years past" to express, not what it would ordinarily be understood to express, but the proposition that some proposition, related to this in a certain way, is true; when all the time they believe that the proposition, which this expression would ordinarily be understood to express, is, at least partially, false. I wish, therefore, to make it quite plain that I was not using the expressions I used in (1) in any such subtle sense. I meant by each of them precisely what every reader, in reading them, will have understood me to mean. And any philosopher, therefore, who holds that any of these expressions, if understood in this popular manner, expresses a proposition which embodies some popular error, is disagreeing with me and holding a view incompatible with (2), even though he may hold that there is some *other,* true, proposition which the expression in question might be legitimately used to express.

In what I have just said, I have assumed that there is some meaning which is *the* ordinary or popular meaning of such expressions as "The earth has existed for many years past." And this, I am afraid, is an assumption which some philosophers are capable of disputing. They seem to think that the question "Do you believe that the earth has existed for many years past?" is not a plain question, such as should be met either by a plain "Yes" or "No," or by a plain "I can't make up my mind," but is the sort of question which can be properly met by: "It all depends on what you mean by 'the earth' and 'exists' and 'years': if

you mean so and so, and so and so, and so and so, then I do; but if you mean so and so, and so and so, and so and so, or so and so, and so and so, and so and so, or so and so, and so and so, and so and so, then I don't, or at least I think it is extremely doubtful." It seems to me that such a view is as profoundly mistaken as any view can be. Such an expression as "The earth has existed for many years past" is the very type of an unambiguous expression, the meaning of which we all understand. Any one who takes a contrary view must, I suppose, be confusing the question whether we understand its meaning (which we all certainly do) with the entirely different question whether we *know what it means,* in the sense that we are able to *give a correct analysis* of its meaning. The question what is the correct analysis of *the* proposition meant *on any occasion* (for, of course, as I insisted in defining (2), a different proposition is meant at every different time at which the expression is used) by "The earth has existed for many years past" is, it seems to me, a profoundly difficult question, and one to which, as I shall presently urge, no one knows the answer. But to hold that we do not know what, in certain respects, is the analysis of what we understand by such an expression, is an entirely different thing from holding that we do not understand the expression. It is obvious that we cannot even raise the question how what we do understand by it is to be analyzed, unless we do understand it. So soon, therefore, as we know that a person who uses such an expression, is using it in its ordinary sense, we understand his meaning. So that in explaining that I was using the expressions used in (1) in their ordinary sense (those of them which have an ordinary sense, which is not the case with quite all of them), I have done all that is required to make my meaning clear. . . .

IV. I now come to a point of a very different order.

As I have explained under I., I am not

at all skeptical as to the *truth* of such propositions as "The earth has existed for many years past," "Many human bodies have each lived for many years upon it," i.e. propositions which assert the existence of material things: on the contrary, I hold that we all know, with certainty, many such propositions to be true. But I am very skeptical as to what, in certain respects, the correct *analysis* of such propositions is. And this is a matter as to which I think I differ from many philosophers. Many seem to hold that there is no doubt at all as to their *analysis,* nor, therefore, as to the analysis of the proposition "Material things have existed," in certain respects in which I hold that the analysis of the propositions in question is extremely doubtful; and some of them, as we have seen, while holding that there is no doubt as to their *analysis,* seem to have doubted whether any such propositions are *true.* I, on the other hand, while holding that there is no doubt whatever that many such propositions are wholly true, hold also that no philosopher, hitherto, has succeeded in suggesting an analysis of them, as regards certain important points, which comes anywhere near to being certainly true.

It seems to me quite evident that the question how propositions of the type I have just given are to be analyzed, depends on the question how propositions of another and simpler type are to be analyzed. I know, at present, that I am perceiving a human hand, a pen, a sheet of paper, etc.; and it seems to me that I cannot know how the proposition "Material things exist" is to be analyzed, until I know how, in certain respects, these simpler propositions are to be analyzed. But even these are not simple enough. It seems to me quite evident that my knowledge that I am now perceiving a human hand is a deduction from a pair of propositions simpler still—propositions which I can only express in the form "I am perceiving *this*" and "*This* is a human hand." It is the analysis of propositions of

the latter kind, which seems to me to present such great difficulties; while nevertheless the whole question as to the *nature* of material things obviously depends upon their analysis. It seems to me a surprising thing that so few philosophers, while saying a great deal as to what material things *are* and as to what it is to perceive them, have attempted to give a clear account as to what precisely they suppose themselves to *know* (or to *judge,* in case they have held that we don't *know* any such propositions to be true, or even that no such propositions *are* true) when they know or judge such things as "This is a hand," "That is the sun," "This is a dog," etc. etc. etc.

Two things only seem to me to be quite certain about the analysis of such propositions (and even with regard to these I am afraid some philosophers would differ from me) namely that whenever I know, or judge, such a proposition to be true, (1) there is always some *sense-datum* about which the proposition in question is a proposition— some sense-datum which is *a* subject (and, in a certain sense, the principal or ultimate subject) of the proposition in question, and (2) that, nevertheless, *what* I am knowing or judging to be true about this sense-datum is not (in general) that it is *itself* a hand, or a dog, or the sun, etc. etc., as the case may be. . . .

V. Just as I hold that the proposition "there are and have been material things" is quite certainly true, but that the question how this proposition is to be analyzed is one to which no answer that has been hitherto given is anywhere near certainly true; so I hold that the proposition "There are and have been many Selves" is quite certainly true, but that here again all the analyses of this proposition that have been suggested by philosophers are highly doubtful.

That I am now perceiving many different sense-data, and that I have at many times in the past perceived many different sense-data, I know for certain—that is to say, I know that there are mental facts of class (β), connected in a way which it is proper to express by saying that they are all of them facts about *me;* but how this kind of connection is to be analyzed, I do not know for certain, nor do I think that any other philosopher knows with any approach to certainty. Just as in the case of the proposition "This is part of the surface of a human hand," there are several extremely different views as to its analysis, each of which seems to me *possible,* but none nearly certain, so also in the case of the proposition "This, that and that sense-

datum are all at present being perceived by *me,*" and still more so in the case of the proposition "*I* am now perceiving this sense-datum, and *I* have in the past perceived sense-data of these other kinds." Of the *truth* of these propositions there seems to me to be no doubt, but as to what is the correct analysis of them there seems to me to be the gravest doubt. . . . Many philosophers, on the other hand, seem to me to have assumed that there is little or no doubt as to the correct analysis of such propositions; and many of these, just reversing my position, have also held that the propositions themselves are not true.

To explain the elucidation and analysis practiced by linguistic philosophers, the following review article by Professor Ryle is included in this introduction. Ryle is discussing the work of Ludwig Wittgenstein, who, with Moore, is a major influence on contemporary philosophy. Wittgenstein's influence is really twofold. In his earlier book, *Tractatus Logico-Philosophicus,* he developed a number of ideas—including the view of logical truths as tautologies and of meaning as certain complexes of words—that contributed to the development of logical positivism. In a second, posthumous book, *Philosophical Investigations,* Wittgenstein breaks with positivism in two important respects: he now defines meaning as the rules for the employment of an expression; and, related to this, language is seen to have an indefinite variety of uses.

In both of these works—though with differences, of course—the task of philosophy is seen as meaning-elucidation. Analysis must disclose the logical architecture or structure that may be concealed in the ordinary uses of language. This elucidation prevents us from falling into philosophical quandaries and puzzlement.

PHILOSOPHICAL ELUCIDATION

Gilbert Ryle (1900-   )

What of the philosopher?

He had no formal training in philosophy. His ferments came from his own insides. I

do not know just what shape his initial perplexities about mathematics took. Anyhow he consulted Frege [1] and Russell, and studied their logico-mathematical writings; the central problems of his *Tractatus,*

The selection is from Gilbert Ryle's review article on Wittgenstein published in *Scientific American,* 197 (Sept., 1957), pp. 251-259. Used by permission of the publisher of *Scientific American.*

[1 The reference is to F. L. G. Frege (1848-1925), regarded by many as the greatest logician of the nineteenth century. *Ed.*]

though not the same as theirs, were clearly reactions to their doctrines.

Frege and Russell tried to show that all pure mathematics derives from the completely general truths of formal logic, i.e., that these truths stand to arithmetical truths as Euclid's axioms to his theorems. But what was the point of trying to demonstrate this continuity between logic and arithmetic? Surely the truths of mathematics are as well established as anyone could demand, so what is gained, except for tidiness, by underpinning them with an ulterior foundation?

At that time reflective mathematicians were in trouble. Their science seemed all limbs and no body. The very vigor of these branches was generating cross-purposes between them. The notion of number itself seemed to take as many shapes as there were branches of the science of number. Mathematics felt like a caravanserai, not a house.

Its external relations with other sciences also were precarious. John Stuart Mill had likened the truths of mathematics to those of the natural sciences: they are generalizations from experience, susceptible of overthrow by unexpected exceptions. It would be much more surprising to find an exception to $7 + 5 = 12$ than to find a black swan, but only much more. Which is absurd. For another thing, many thinkers, when asked, "Of what entities is mathematics the science?" were giving a psychological answer. The physical world contains countless sorts of things, but it does not contain numbers. There are nine planets, and the earth has one moon. But you cannot see 9 or 1. So, if numbers are not physical things, what else is there for them to be, save ideas in our minds or thoughts or something of the sort? But then arithmetic ought to make allowances for the differences between what goes on in lunatic and in sane minds; in visualizers' and in nonvisualizers' minds, and so on. Which is absurd.

Because mathematics needed, internally, coordination between its members and, externally, autonomy from the inductive sciences, especially psychology, its affiliation to logic felt like a rescue operation. Mathematics could be saved from internal discord and from external pressures by becoming part of the unchallengeable science of logic.

But what sort of science is this? What sort of truths are the truths of logic? What sorts of information does logic give us about what sorts of entities? That is, I think, the central problem of Wittgenstein's *Tractatus logico-philosophicus*.

The truths and falsehoods of the natural sciences are truths and falsehoods about what exists and happens in the world. Their truth or falsehood depends upon what is the case with things in the world. But the truths of logic give us no information about the world. "Either it is raining or it is not raining" exemplifies a logical truism, but it tells us nothing about the weather. It is true whatever the weather. "Socrates is mortal" gives us important information or misinformation about Socrates, but "*If* all men are mortal and Socrates is a man, *then* he is mortal" gives us an applied logical truth, which is true whether or not he is mortal.

The truths of the natural sciences are factual truths, while those of logic are purely formal. Their truth is neutral between the world as it is and as it might have been. This formal nature of logical truths shows itself in another way. The truism "Either it is raining or it is not" remains true if for "raining" we substitute "snowing," "freezing" or anything you please. For any proposition whatsoever, either it or its negative is true. The force of "either . . . , or not . . ." is indifferent to the material fillings of the clauses that it links, so long as the clauses are the same. Hence truths of logic can be expressed most cleanly if we algebraize away all material elements like "Socrates," "mortal," and "it is raining." This leaves, for example, "For any *p*, either *p* or not-*p*."

Thus logic is unconcerned with the actual truth or falsity of the factual statements which can be draped on its skeletons. Nonetheless logic is essentially concerned with the truth-or-falsity of these statements, since it has to work out how the truth or falsity of one *would* follow, if another *were* true or *were* false. That Jack went up the hill would have to be true *if* Jack and Jill went up the hill; and from the falsity of "Jack went up the hill" would follow the falsity of "Jack and Jill went up the hill."

Well then, why should we not answer the original problem by saying that the subject matter of logic consists of truths-or-falsehoods, and that it has to discover in them their formal properties which secure that one would be true if another were true? But then what sorts of entities are truths-or-falsehoods, and what sorts of properties are these formal properties?

When I say "It is raining," my words convey something to you. You understand them even though you do not know that it is raining. They make sense, even if it is not raining. So the actual state of the weather is one thing; the truth-or-falsehood that it is raining is something else. In getting the meaning of my words, you are getting not what the state of the weather is, but what-it-is-being-represented-as-being. But what enables expressions to represent things as they are, or as they are not? What enables a complex of symbols to *mean* something *vis à vis* some actual matter of fact? Consider a simple map representing, truly or falsely, the relative positions and distances of three towns: A, B and C. The dot "A" is one inch higher on the page than the dot "B," and this is two inches higher than the dot "C." This map might tell you that the town A is north of B, which is north of C, and that B is 20 miles from C and 10

from A. How does it do this? By an understood code by which lettered dots stand for towns, the top of the page for north and an inch for 10 miles. It is the way in which the dots are situated on the page that says how the towns are related to one another on the ground. In this case the map, if true, is in certain respects photographically like the corresponding stretch of ground. But with a different code the same dots might represent or misrepresent the heights of three peaks, or the degrees below boiling point of three saucepans. Representation can, but need not, be photographic. The notes played by the musician are not *like* the black marks on his score, yet the arrangement of the latter, by a complex code, may faithfully represent the arrangement of the former.

The "codes" which enable different arrangements of words to represent different states of affairs are enormously complicated, and they vary among different tongues. In English, if you wish to say that Brutus killed Caesar you must put "Brutus" before the verb and "Caesar" after it. Not so in Latin, which achieves the same result by different word terminations. But without applying some syntatical rule or other you cannot say anything, not even anything false. Symbol-structures can represent and misrepresent the structures of actual states of affairs because, though the representing structure is not usually *like* the represented structure, they are still structurally analogous to one another. A sentence has a meaning if its syntax *could* be the structural analogue of an actual state of affairs, even though, when false, it actually has no such factual counterpart. Caesar did not kill Brutus, but "Caesar killed Brutus" makes sense, since there is, so to speak, room in reality, though unfilled room, for this uncommitted murder.

Not all complexes of words or dots or gestures convey truths or falsehoods. An unorganized jumble of words or dots makes no sense. Even a sequence of words with an orthodox grammar can make nonsense. Lewis Carroll concocted many such sentences; for example, "The Cheshire cat vanished leaving only her grin behind her." Sometimes serious thinkers inadvertently construct senseless sentences. Early geometricians seriously held that Euclidean points are round. A truth-or-falsehood, then, is an organized complex of symbols representing, by analogy of structure, a counterpart actual-or-possible state of affairs. It is, for example, a sentence "in its projective relation to the world." To find out whether it is actually true or actually false we have to match it against its should-be counterpart state of affairs in the world.

Already we can see how Wittgenstein's account of what it is to make sense, that is, to be true-or-false, led to the famous principle of verifiability, by which the logical positivists ostracized as nonsensical the pronouncements of metaphysicians, theologians and moralists. Observation and experiment are our ways of matching the propositions of, say, astronomy against the stellar facts. Where observation and experiment are excluded, our pretended truths-or-falsehoods have no anchorage in facts and so say nothing. They are nothing but disguised gibberish.

What of the truths of logic, the status of which it had been Wittgenstein's main task to fix? Are these also disguised gibberish? Or are they salved by being classed with the most general truths of natural science? Wittgenstein steers between this Scylla and this Charybdis.

An everyday "either-or" statement, like "Either Jack climbed the hill or Jill did," leaves it open which climbed the hill; but it still rules out something that might have been the case, namely, the climbing of the hill by neither of them. But if we ask of an "either-or" truism of logic, like " 'Either Jack climbed the hill or he did not'; what is ruled out by *this* assertion?" we see that the only thing ruled out is Jack's neither climbing nor not climbing the hill. And this is not something which might have been but just happens not to be the case. An ordinary factual assertion gives the "yes" or the "no" answer to a question; it invites us to select the one and to forswear the other. But a truth of logic gives us nothing forswearable to forswear, and so nothing selectable to select. It is factually empty, or "tautological."

It does not, however, follow that the truths of logic are of no use simply because they are uninformative. They serve to show up, by contrast with their own absolute hospitality, the ways in which ordinary statements convey, by their relative shut-doored-ness, positive information or misinformation.

The truths of logic, then, are not nonsensical, though they are empty of information or misinformation. Their business is to *show* us, by evaporation of content, how our ordinary thoughts and assertions are organized.

I pass over Wittgenstein's accounts of the connections and differences between logic and mathematics and between logic and mechanics, important though these are for showing up, by contrast, the positive nature of logic. But I must not pass over his account of the relations between logic and philosophy. For, as his title *Tractatus logico-philosophicus* hints, his book was secondarily concerned to fix the status of philosophy. What sorts of things can philosophers tell us—philosophers as distinct from logicians and from scientists? Are the truths of philosophy factual or formal truths?

Earlier philosophers, if they tried at all to place philosophy, had tended to treat it either as psychology or as non-empirical cosmology. But Russell and others realized that philosophy was neither a natural science nor yet a supernatural science. Russell had emphasized the close connection between logic and philosophy by treating all seriously philosophical questions as problems for "logical analysis," as if logic supplied the lines of latitude and longitude, while philosophy had to fill in the geographical detail.

In partly the same way Wittgenstein, having separated off all philosophical from any scientific questions, describes the positive function of philosophy as "elucidatory." Its function is to disclose that logical architecture of our ordinary and scientific thoughts which our vernaculars conceal but which the designed symbolism of logic would expose. But now there breaks out a seemingly disastrous difference between logic and philosophy. The formulae of logic, though they tell us nothing, still show us, so to speak, at their limit the positive force of the "ors," "ands," "alls" and so forth on which our ordinary truths and falsehoods are built. But philosophical pronouncements are in a worse state, since their elucidatory mission is to *tell* us what sort of sense or nonsense belongs to the propositions of the sciences and of daily life; and this is not the sort of thing that can conceivably be told. The meanings, that is, the truths or falsehoods that we express, cannot then be lifted out of their expressions. We can talk sense, but we cannot talk sense about the sense that we talk.

Consider again my map in which the situations of three dots on the page told you, truly or falsely, the situations of three towns. Now I ask you to draw another map which is to tell me not about things on the ground, but about the information or misinformation conveyed by the first map. It is to tell me whether the first map is accurate or inaccurate, and especially it is to tell me the cartographical code by which the three original dots represent the compass bearings and distances of the towns. You will promptly protest that you cannot make a map of what another map says or of how it says it. What an ordinary map

alleges about the earth's surface is not another bit of that surface and so a second map could not map it. The significance-conditions which an ordinary map exemplifies are not *stated* by these or any other maps.

Similarly, we normally know when a sentence expresses a truth-or-falsehood, and when it is nonsensical. We read the composition of an actual-or-possible state of affairs out of the composition of the sentence. But we are debarred from *stating* this correlation. Attempts to state it would be attempts to stand outside the significance-conditions of statements. They would therefore break these conditions, and so be nonsense.

Philosophical elucidation advances only over the ruins of its attempted articulations. The sort of clarity that we seek we achieve in becoming conscious of what makes us stammer. Critics quickly pointed out that Wittgenstein managed to say many important and understandable things. So perhaps the language of maps has limitations from which the language of words is exempt; and perhaps the notion of sense is wider than the notion of truth-or-falsehood to empirical fact.

Wittgenstein left many manuscripts which are now in process of being published. The first book to be so published was his *Philosophical Investigations*. This has the German text faced by a quite good English translation. . . .

How does the later differ from the earlier Wittgenstein? First, his central problem is different. He is no longer exercised about the status of logic. It is philosophy now that is pestering him for justice. Next he had in the *Tractatus* been scanning the notions of sense and nonsense through the perforated screen of logic. Through its apertures he could see only elementary atoms of truth and falsehood being combined into molecular truths and falsehoods by the operations of "and," "or" and "not." The only discernible differences between sayables were in their degrees and patterns of compositeness. All their other differences had been algebraized away. But now he forsakes this screen. He examines those differences between sayables which will not reduce to degrees of compositeness. Where he had examined the algebraized skeletons of statements in which only the logical constants were left functioning, now he watches the functioning of the live expressions with which we say real things. One thing that he quickly remarks is this. Not all sayables are truths or falsehoods. The logician attends only to assertable premises and conclusions. But not all saying is asserting. There is questioning, advising, entreating, ordering, reassuring, rebuking, joking, warning, commiserating, promising, deploring, praising, parodying. We talk a lot to infants and dogs, but we do not make statements to them.

In the *Tractatus* we were told, in effect, that only those sentences made positive sense which could be the premises or conclusions of a bit of natural science. In the *Philosophical Investigations* the door is opened to anything that anyone might say. We are home, again, in the country of real discourse.

The central notion of sense or meaning has correspondingly thawed. In the *Tractatus* truths-or-falsehoods seemed to be icicles of printer's ink; and their coordination with states of affairs in the real world resembled the congruence between the structures of two crystals. But sentences are normally things said, not written, by one person to another. So now Wittgenstein constantly discusses such questions as "How do children, in real life, actually learn to understand this or that expression?" and "How would we teach a savage to count, or tell the time?" Talking sense and following the sense talked by others are things that we have learned how to do; so the notion of sense comes out of the fog if we constantly ask just what we must have learned, and just how we must have learned it in order to be able to communicate. Most of Part I of the *Philosophical Investigations* is concerned with questions about sense, understanding, grasping, mastering, interpreting, etc.

One device that Wittgenstein constantly uses is that of exploring imaginary situations in which people have to think up and teach ways of communicating. A builder, for example, wants his inarticulate assistant to pass him bricks and slabs. How would he teach him to distinguish between the orders "Brick" and "Slab"? How would he teach him to bring *two* or *five* bricks, that is, to understand number-words? Wittgenstein calls these imaginary lingo-creations "language-games." This is unfortunate because many readers think he implies that talking is a sort of *playing*. In fact the central idea behind the label "language-game" is the notion of *rules*. Learning to communicate is like learning to play chess or tennis in this respect, that in both we have to master written or unwritten rules—and there are many different, but interlocking, sorts of rules to be learned in both. The chess player has had to learn what moves are allowed, what moves in what situations would be tactical mistakes, and even what moves in what situations would be unsporting. A crude generalization of Wittgenstein's new account of sense or meaning is that the meaning of an expression is the rules for the employment of that expression; that is, the rules licensing or banning its coemployment with other expressions, those governing its effective employment in normal and abnormal communication-situations, and so on. The dynamic notion of rules to be mastered has replaced the notion of an imposed structural congruence.

With his new notion of meaning, Wittgenstein is in a position to say new things about the philosopher's task of meaning-elucidation. But in the main he avoids trying to give any general account of what sort of task this is, or why and when it needs to be done, though there are passages in which he does enigmatically give such an account. Rather, especially in Part II of *Philosophical Investigations,* he tries to demonstrate in examples what philosophical quandaries are like, how to get out of them and what sideslips of thought get us into them. He is trying to teach us methods of operation, rather than give us the answer to a question in an examination.

I do not think that anybody could read the *Philosophical Investigations* without feeling that its author had his finger on the pulse of the activity of philosophizing. We can doubt whether his hinted diagnosis will do; not that he has located, by touch, that peculiar and important intellectual commotion—philosophical puzzlement.

2 / THEORY OF KNOWLEDGE

The proper object of philosophy being language, it is necessary to get some understanding of it. To do this, Wittgenstein writes of "language-games," by which expression he wishes to call attention to the fact that speaking a language is part of an activity or of a form of life. In order to know more of language, however, Wittgenstein asks that we look closely at the actual uses of language. These uses are found to be greatly varied, so much so that no reduction of them to a set classification of uses is possible. Only "family resemblances," not a common essence, exist among them.

Not only do the uses of language have no single structure, but, in the same way, meanings have no fixed, single structure or boundary. Rather, they can be known and determined solely by a study of the ordinary meanings of a language. To put it another way, Wittgenstein holds that "an expression has meaning only in the stream of life." The meaning of a word, that is, is its use in the language.

Philosophy, Wittgenstein holds, cannot interfere with the actual use of language. It can rather "only put things before us" in the sense of putting words, sometimes torn by the philosopher from their place in ordinary language, back into their everyday use. Therefore philosophy, Wittgenstein concludes, is not a set of theses but rather more like the treatment of an illness, aiming to remove the disease of puzzlement.

LANGUAGE AND MEANING

Ludwig Wittgenstein (1889-1951)

1. *"Cum ipsi (majors homines) appella-
bant rem aliquam, et cum secundum eam
vocem corpus ad aliquid movebant, vide-
bam, et tenebam hoc ab eis vocari rem illam,
quod sonabant, cum eam vellent ostendere.
Hoc autem eos velle ex motu corporis
aperiebatur: tamquam verbis naturalibus
omnium gentium, quae fiunt voltu et nutu
oculorum, ceterorumque membrorum actu,
et sonitu vocis indicante affectionem animi
in petendis, habendis, rejiciendis, fugien-
disve rebus. Ita verba in variis sententiis
locis suis posita, et crebro audita, quarum
rerum signa essent, paulatim colligebam,
measque jam voluntates, edomito in eis
signis ore, per haec enuntiabam." (Augustine,* Confessions, *I. 8.)* [1]

The selection includes various sections from
Part I of *Philosophical Investigations* (tr.
G. E. M. Anscombe) (Oxford: Basil Blackwell & Mott, Ltd.; New York: The Macmillan Company, 1953). Used by permission
of the publishers.

Wittgenstein expressed the wish that his
German text always be available to his
readers. His publisher, Basil Blackwell of
Oxford, in granting permission to use this
material, wishes it to be noted that this text,
with an English translation, is available in
the full edition.

[1] "When they (my elders) named some object,
and accordingly moved towards something,
I saw this and I grasped that the thing was
called by the sound they uttered when they
meant to point it out. Their intention was
shewn by their bodily movements, as it were
the natural language of all peoples: the expression of the face, the play of the eyes, the
movement of other parts of the body, and the
tone of voice which expresses our state of
mind in seeking, having, rejecting, or avoiding something. Thus, as I heard words repeatedly used in their proper places in various
sentences, I gradually learnt to understand
what objects they signified; and after I had
trained my mouth to form these signs, I
used them to express my own desires."

These words, it seems to me, give us a
particular picture of the essence of human
language. It is this: the individual words
in language name objects—sentences are
combinations of such names.—In this picture of language we find the roots of the
following idea: Every word has a meaning.
This meaning is correlated with the word.
It is the object for which the word stands.

Augustine does not speak of there being
any difference between kinds of word. If
you describe the learning of language in
this way you are, I believe, thinking
primarily of nouns like "table," "chair,"
"bread," and of people's names, and only
secondarily of the names of certain actions
and properties; and of the remaining kinds
of word as something that will take care
of itself.

Now think of the following use of language: I send someone shopping. I give
him a slip marked "five red apples." He
takes the slip to the shopkeeper, who opens
the drawer marked "apples"; then he looks
up the word "red" in a table and finds a
color sample opposite it; then he says the
series of cardinal numbers—I assume that
he knows them by heart—up to the word
"five" and for each number he takes an
apple of the same color as the sample out
of the drawer.—It is in this and similar
ways that one operates with words.—"But
how does he know where and how he is to
look up the word 'red' and what he is to
do with the word 'five'?"—Well, I assume
that he *acts* as I have described. Explanations come to an end somewhere.—But what
is the meaning of the word "five"?—No
such thing was in question here, only how
the word "five" is used.

2. That philosophical concept of meaning has its place in a primitive idea of the
way language functions. But one can also

say that it is the idea of a language more primitive than ours.

Let us imagine a language for which the description given by Augustine is right. The language is meant to serve for communication between a builder A and an assistant B. A is building with buildingstones: there are blocks, pillars, slabs and beams. B has to pass the stones, and that in the order in which A needs them. For this purpose they use a language consisting of the words "block," "pillar," "slab," "beam." A calls them out;—B brings the stone which he has learned to bring at such-and-such a call. —Conceive this as a complete primitive language.

3. Augustine, we might say, does describe a system of communication; only not everything that we call language is this system. And one has to say this in many cases where the question arises "Is this an appropriate description or not?" The answer is: "Yes, it is appropriate, but only for this narrowly circumscribed region, not for the whole of what you were claiming to describe."

It is as if someone were to say: "A game consists in moving objects about on a surface according to certain rules . . ."—and we replied: You seem to be thinking of board games, but there are others. You can make your definition correct by expressly restricting it to those games.

8. Let us now look at an expansion of language (2). Besides the four words "block," "pillar," etc., let it contain a series of words used as the shopkeeper in (1) used the numerals (it can be the series of letters of the alphabet); further, let there be two words, which may as well be "there" and "this" (because this roughly indicates their purpose), that are used in connection with a pointing gesture; and finally a number of color samples. A gives an order like: "d—slab—there." At the same time he shews the assistant a color sample, and when he says "there" he points to a place on the building

site. From the stock of slabs B takes one for each letter of the alphabet up to "d," of the same color as the sample, and brings them to the place indicated by A.—On other occasions A gives the order "this—there." At "this" he points to a building stone. And so on.

9. When a child learns this language, it has to learn the series of "numerals" a, b, c, . . . by heart. And it has to learn their use.— Will this training include ostensive teaching of the words?—Well, people will, for example, point to slabs and count: "a, b, c slabs." —Something more like the ostensive teaching of the words "block," "pillar," etc. would be the ostensive teaching of numerals that serve not to count but to refer to groups of objects that can be taken in at a glance. Children do learn the use of the first five or six cardinal numerals in this way.

Are "there" and "this" also taught ostensively?—Imagine how one might perhaps teach their use. One will point to places and things—but in this case the pointing occurs in the *use* of the words too and not merely in learning the use.—

10. Now what do the words of this language *signify?*—What is supposed to shew what they signify, if not the kind of use they have? And we have already described that. So we are asking for the expression "This word signifies *this*" to be made a part of the description. In other words the description ought to take the form: "The word . . . signifies. . . ."

Of course, one can reduce the description of the use of the word "slab" to the statement that this word signifies this object. This will be done when, for example, it is merely a matter of removing the mistaken idea that the word "slab" refers to the shape of building-stone that we in fact call a "block"—but the kind of *"referring"* this is, that is to say the use of these words for the rest, is already known.

Equally one can say that the signs "a," "b," etc. signify numbers; when for example this removes the mistaken idea that "a," "b," "c," play the part actually played in language by "block," "slab," "pillar." And one can also say that "c" means this number and not that one; when for example this serves to explain that the letters are to be used in the order a, b, c, d, etc. and not in the order a, b, d, c.

But assimilating the descriptions of the uses of words in this way cannot make the uses themselves any more like one another. For, as we see, they are absolutely unlike.

11. Think of the tools in a tool-box: there is a hammer, pliers, a saw, a screw-driver, a rule, a glue-pot, glue, nails and screws.—The functions of words are as diverse as the functions of these objects. (And in both cases there are similarities.)

Of course, what confuses us is the uniform appearance of words when we hear them spoken or meet them in script and print. For their *application* is not presented to us so clearly. Especially not, when we are doing philosophy!

12. It is like looking into the cabin of a locomotive. We see handles all looking more or less alike. (Naturally, since they are all supposed to be handled.) But one is the handle of a crank which can be moved continuously (it regulates the opening of a valve); another is the handle of a switch, which has only two effective positions, it is either off or on; a third is the handle of a brake-lever, the harder one pulls on it, the harder it brakes; a fourth, the handle of a pump: it has an effect only so long as it is moved to and fro.

19. It is easy to imagine a language consisting only of orders and reports in battle. —Or a language consisting only of questions and expressions for answering yes and no. And innumerable others.—And to imagine a language means to imagine a form of life. . . .

20. But now it looks as if when someone says "Bring me a slab" he could mean this expression as *one* long word corresponding

to the single word "Slab!"—Then can one mean it sometimes as one word and sometimes as four? And how does one usually mean it?—I think we shall be inclined to say: we mean the sentence as *four* words when we use it in contrast with other sentences such as *"Hand* me a slab," "Bring *him* a slab," "Bring *two* slabs," etc.; that is, in contrast with sentences containing the separate words of our command in other combinations.—But what does using one sentence in contrast with others consist in? Do the others, perhaps, hover before one's mind? *All* of them? And *while* one is saying the one sentence, or before, or afterwards? —No. Even if such an explanation rather tempts us, we need only think for a moment of what actually happens in order to see that we are going astray here. We say that we use the command in contrast with other sentences because *our language* contains the possibility of those other sentences. Someone who did not understand our language, a foreigner, who had fairly often heard someone giving the order: "Bring me a slab!" might believe that this whole series of sounds was one word corresponding perhaps to the word for "building-stone" in his language. If he himself had then given this order perhaps he would have pronounced it differently, and we should say: he pronounces it so oddly because he takes it for a *single* word.—But then, is there not also something different going on in him when he pronounces it,—something corresponding to the fact that he conceives the sentence as a *single* word?—Either the same thing may go on in him, or something different. For what goes on in you when you give such an order? Are you conscious of its consisting of four words *while* you are uttering it? Of course you have a *mastery* of this language —which contains those other sentences as well—but is this having a mastery something that *happens* while you are uttering the sentence?—And I have admitted that the foreigner will probably pronounce a sentence differently if he conceives it differently; but what we call his wrong conception *need* not lie in anything that accompanies the utterance of the command.

The sentence is "elliptical," not because it leaves out something that we think when we utter it, but because it is shortened—in comparison with a particular paradigm of our grammar.—Of course one might object here: "You grant that the shortened and the unshortened sentence have the same sense.—What is this sense, then? Isn't there a verbal expression for this sense?"—But doesn't the fact that sentences have the same sense consist in their having the same *use?*—(In Russian one says "Stone red" instead of "the stone is red"; do they feel the copula to be missing in the sense, or attach it in *thought?*)

23. But how many kinds of sentence are there? Say assertion, question, and command?—There are *countless* kinds: countless different kinds of use of what we call "symbols," "words," "sentences." And this multiplicity is not something fixed, given once for all; but new types of language, new language-games, as we may say, come into existence, and others become obsolete and get forgotten. (We can get a *rough picture* of this from the changes in mathematics.)

Here the term "language-*game*" is meant to bring into prominence the fact that the *speaking* of language is part of an activity, or of a form of life.

Review the multiplicity of language-games in the following examples, and in others:

Giving orders, and obeying them—

Describing the appearance of an object, or giving its measurements—

Constructing an object from a description (a drawing)—

Reporting an event—

Speculating about an event—

Forming and testing a hypothesis—

Presenting the results of an experiment in tables and diagrams—

Making up a story; and reading it—

Play-acting—

Singing catches—

Guessing riddles—

Making a joke; telling it—

Solving a problem in practical arithmetic—

Translating from one language into another—

Asking, thanking, cursing, greeting, praying.

—It is interesting to compare the multiplicity of the tools in language and of the ways they are used, the multiplicity of kinds of word and sentence, with what logicians have said about the structure of language. (Including the author of the *Tractatus Logico-Philosophicus*.)

43. For a *large* class of cases—though not for all—in which we employ the word "meaning" it can be defined thus: the meaning of a word is its use in the language.

And the *meaning* of a name is sometimes explained by pointing to its *bearer*.

65. Here we come up against the great question that lies behind all these considerations.—For someone might object against me: "You take the easy way out! You talk about all sorts of language-games, but have nowhere said what the essence of a language-game, and hence of language, is: what is common to all these activities, and what makes them into language or parts of language. So you let yourself off the very part of the investigation that once gave you yourself most headache, the part about the *general form of propositions* and of language."

And this is true.—Instead of producing something common to all that we call language, I am saying that these phenomena have no one thing in common which makes us use the same word for all,—but that they are *related* to one another in many different ways. And it is because of this relationship, or these relationships, that we call them all "language." I will try to explain this.

66. Consider for example the proceedings that we call "games." I mean board-games, card-games, ball-games, Olympic games, and so on. What is common to them all?—Don't say: "There *must* be something common, or they would not be called 'games' "—but *look and see* whether there is anything common to all.—For if you look at them you will not see something that is common to *all*, but similarities, relationships, and a whole series of them at that. To repeat: don't think, but look!—Look for example at board-games, with their multifarious relationships. Now pass to card-games; here you find many correspondences with the first group, but many common features drop out, and others appear. When we pass next to ball-games, much that is common is retained, but much is lost.—Are they all "amusing"? Compare chess with noughts and crosses. Or is there always winning and losing, or competition between players? Think of patience. In ball games there is winning and losing; but when a child throws his ball at the wall and catches again, this feature has disappeared. Look at the parts played by skill and luck; and at the difference between skill in chess and skill in tennis. Think now of games like ring-a-ring-of-roses; here is the element of amusement, but how many other characteristic features have disappeared! And we can go through the many, many other groups of games in the same way; can see how similarities crop up and disappear.

And the result of this examination is: we see a complicated network of similarities overlapping and criss-crossing: sometimes overall similarities, sometimes similarities of detail.

67. I can think of no better expression to characterize these similarities than "family resemblances"; for the various resemblances between members of a family: build, features, color of eyes, gait, temperament, etc. etc. overlap and criss-cross in the same way.—And I shall say: "games" form a family.

And for instance the kinds of number form a family in the same way. Why do we call something a "number"? Well, perhaps because it has a—direct—relationship with several things that have hitherto been called number; and this can be said to give it an indirect relationship to other things we call the same name. And we extend our concept of number as in spinning a thread we twist fibre on fibre. And the strength of the thread does not reside in the fact that some one fibre runs through its whole length, but in the overlapping of many fibres.

But if someone wished to say: "There is something common to all these constructions—namely the disjunction of all their common properties"—I should reply: Now you are only playing with words. One might as well say: "Something runs through the whole thread—namely the continuous overlapping of those fibres."

108. We see that what we call "sentence" and "language" have not the formal unity that I imagined, but are families of structures more or less related to one another.—But what becomes of logic now? Its rigor seems to be giving way here.—But in that case doesn't logic altogether disappear?—For how can it lose its rigor? Of course not by our bargaining any of its rigor out of it.—The *preconceived idea* of crystalline purity can only be removed by turning our whole examination round. (One might say: the axis of reference of our examination must be rotated, but about the fixed point of our real need.)

The philosophy of logic speaks of sentences and words in exactly the sense in which we speak of them in ordinary life when we say e. g. "Here is a Chinese sentence," or "No, that only looks like writing; it is actually just an ornament" and so on.

We are talking about the spatial and temporal phenomenon of language, not about some non-spatial, non-temporal phantasm. [Note in margin: Only it is possible to be interested in a phenomenon in a variety of ways.] But we talk about it as we do about the pieces in chess when we are stating the rules of the game, not describing their physical properties.

The question "What is a word really?" is analogous to "What is a piece in chess?"

109. It was true to say that our considerations could not be scientific ones. It was not of any possible interest to us to find out empirically "that, contrary to our preconceived ideas, it is possible to think such-and-such"—whatever that may mean. (The conception of thought as a gaseous medium.) And we may not advance any kind of theory. There must not be anything hypothetical in our considerations. We must do away with all *explanation,* and description alone must take its place. And this description gets its light, that is to say its purpose—from the philosophical problems. These are, of course, not empirical problems; they are solved, rather, by looking into the workings of our language, and that in such a way as to make us recognize those workings: *in despite of* an urge to misunderstand them. The problems are solved, not by giving new information, but by arranging what we have always known. Philosophy is a battle against the bewitchment of our intelligence by means of language.

116. When philosophers use a word—"knowledge," "being," "object," "I," "proposition," "name"—and try to grasp the *essence* of the thing, one must always ask oneself: is the word ever actually used in this way in the language-game which is its original home?—

What *we* do is to bring words back from their metaphysical to their everyday use.

123. A philosophical problem has the form: "I don't know my way about."

124. Philosophy may in no way interfere with the actual use of language; it can in the end only describe it.

For it cannot give it any foundation either.

It leaves everything as it is.

It also leaves mathematics as it is, and no mathematical discovery can advance it. A "leading problem of mathematical logic" is for us a problem of mathematics like any other.

125. It is the business of philosophy, not to resolve a contradiction by means of a mathematical or logico-mathematical discovery, but to make it possible for us to get a clear view of the state of mathematics that troubles us: the state of affairs *before* the contradiction is resolved. (And this does not mean that one is side-stepping a difficulty.)

The fundamental fact here is that we lay down rules, a technique, for a game, and that then when we follow the rules, things do not turn out as we had assumed. That we are therefore as it were entangled in our own rules.

This entanglement in our rules is what we want to understand (i. e. get a clear view of).

It throws light on our concept of *meaning* something. For in those cases things turn out otherwise than we had meant, foreseen. That is just what we say when, for example, a contradiction appears: "I didn't mean it like that."

The civil status of a contradiction, or its status in civil life: there is the philosophical problem.

126. Philosophy simply puts everything before us, and neither explains nor deduces anything.—Since everything lies open to view there is nothing to explain. For what is hidden, for example, is of no interest to us.

One might also give the name "philosophy" to what is possible *before* all new discoveries and inventions.

127. The work of the philosopher consists in assembling reminders for a particular purpose.

128. If one tried to advance *theses* in philosophy, it would never be possible to question them, because everyone would agree to them.

255. The philosopher's treatment of a question is like the treatment of an illness.

3 / METAPHYSICS

The writer of the following selection, John Wisdom, has produced several papers of great importance to the analytic movement. He views philosophy as less like trying to discover elusive facts than getting out of a maze. Puzzlement leads to the asking of philosophical questions, but these are really requests for a ruling on the use of sentences where ordinary language gives no clear answer. Philosophical statements, then, are verbal recommendations made in response to such questions. Yet they are more than this, for they clarify and give us a better understanding of the language we use. "Philosophical theories are illuminating . . . when they suggest or draw attention to a terminology which reveals likenesses and differences which are concealed by ordinary language." They may be likened to a net that catches some similarities but allows others to slip away. Thus "philosophical theories exhibit both linguistic confusion and linguistic penetration."

This view of philosophy is utilized by Wisdom as he turns to the problems of metaphysics and the verification principle. He finds that the verification principle, so often used against metaphysics, is actually a metaphysical principle itself; for it is a recommendation about meaning, designed to be illuminating. (The opposite principle is called by Wisdom the Idiosyncrasy Platitude: namely, every statement has its own sort of meaning.) Like all metaphysics, the principle is concerned with "reduplication questions"; are X facts to be identified with Y facts? It is this question which leads the metaphysician to his metaphysical statements. So identified, however, metaphysics must not be identified with crude falsehoods or nonsense; it is, rather, suggestions of how language might be used to reveal the hidden in the actual use of language.

METAPHYSICS AND VERIFICATION

John Wisdom (1904-   )

"The meaning of a statement is the method of its verification." Some philosophers bring out this principle with confi-

The selection is from John Wisdom, "Metaphysics and Verification," *Mind,* 46 (1937), pp. 452-498, with omissions. Reprinted in *Philosophy and Psychoanalysis* (Oxford: Basil Blackwell; New York: Philosophical Library, 1953). Used by permission of the author, the Editor of *Mind,* and the publishers.

dence and satisfaction, others are utterly opposed to it and cannot understand how anyone can be so wrong-headed as to insist upon what so little reflection shows to be so palpably untrue. This conflict is of the greatest importance in philosophy today, and it is easy to see why. The Verification Principle is the generalization of a very large class of metaphysical theories, namely all naturalistic, empirical, positivistic theories. While its opposite, which I venture to call the Idiosyncrasy Platitude, is the generalization of all common-sense, realist, transcendental theories. The verification principle is the generalization of such theories as: A cherry is nothing but sensations and possibilities of more; A mind is nothing but a pattern of behavior; There are no such things as numbers only numerals, and the laws of logic and mathematics are really rules of grammar; Beauty is nothing but the features in respect of which a thing is beautiful, and the feelings these arouse. According to the idiosyncrasy platitude every sort of statement has its own sort of meaning, and when philosophers ask "What is the analysis of X-propositions?" the answer is that they are ultimate, that "everything is what it is and not another thing" (Butler, quoted by Moore on the title-page of *Principia Ethica*). This principle is the generalization of theories such as: Ethical propositions involve value predicates and are ultimate; Psychological propositions are not reducible to physiological propositions, they are ultimate; Mathematical propositions are necessary synthetic propositions—an ultimate sort of proposition; Statements about nations are not to be reduced to statements about individuals, they are about a certain sort of concrete universal.

There are not other answers to these metaphysical questions. Consequently most or all metaphysical conflict finds expression in "Shall we or shall we not accept the principle that the meaning of a statement is the method of its verification?" and sometimes "Is the verification principle true?" I do not at all wish to suggest that we cannot get on with metaphysical questions without first dealing with this question. On the contrary if I were forced to consider either first the verification principle and then other metaphysical theories or first the other theories and then the principle, I should much prefer the latter plan. In fact an intermediate plan

is best—first an examination of easier metaphysical and nearly metaphysical questions, then a mention of the verification principle, then an attack upon the more difficult theories, then a more thorough investigation of the verification principle, then a return to the theories. . . .[1]

But now suppose someone were to ask "Is the verification principle true?" What would you do? I myself should at once ask for the question to be put in the wider, less answer-fixing form "Shall we accept the verification principle?" For I believe the other form misleads us as to the general nature of the question asked. I believe that this is of the utmost importance because I believe that once its general nature is apparent the question "Is it true or not?" vanishes into insignificance while its important metaphysical merits and demerits will have become apparent in the process. . . .

Well, shall we accept the verification principle? What is it to accept it? When people bring out with a dashing air the words "The meaning of a statement is really simply the method of its verification," like

---

[1] On the whole the process of thought has been from the more specific theories to the more general, from the doctrine that analytic propositions are verbal to the doctrine that all necessary propositions are verbal, and from this and such theories as those mentioned above to the verification principle, rather than deductively downwards from it. I admit that in the writings of those supporters of the principle who are positivists (I have in mind such writings as those of Ayer and Schlick) there is to be found ground for Dr. Ewing's accusation that the procedure has been from the principle to the specific theories. Such a procedure, once the verification principle has been recommended by the specific cases, is perfectly satisfactory in a way I shall try to explain. But when the verification principle is regarded as an equation and the "deductions" treated as deductions (calculations) then such a procedure leads to what it has led to—insistence and contra-insistence without end—dead-lock.

one who says "The value of a thing is really simply its power in exchange," [2] in what sort of way are they using words? What is the general nature of their theory?

The answer is "It is a metaphysical theory." True, it is a peculiar metaphysical theory as appears from the fact that we are inclined to say: It is not so much a metaphysical theory as a recipe for framing metaphysical theories; It is not a metaphysical theory, it is a mnemonic device for getting from metaphysical theories which have been illuminating in easy metaphysical difficulties to theories which shall work in harder cases, a mnemonic device reminding us how to meet objections to positivistic theories; It is a recommendation to so use "mean" that S means the same as S' provided they are verified in the same way, where this recommendation is not for the purpose of metaphysically illuminating the use of "meaning" but for another metaphysical purpose, namely the illumination of the use of expressions which on the recommended use of "meaning" will be said to mean the same. It is this "altruism" which makes the verification principle a peculiar metaphysical theory. But it is the *likeness* of the verification principle to metaphysical theories which I now want to emphasize and explain. It is like not only to such theories as "A mind is really simply a pattern of behavior," "Goodness is a matter of causing approval," but also to such theories as "We never really know that what we see is real and not a dream," "We never really know what is going on in another's person's mind," "Nothing is really the same from moment to moment," "All words are vague." It is to emphasize this likeness that I call the verification principle a metaphysical theory. I should be prepared to argue that there is nothing incorrect in calling it this.

---

[2] Indeed one might put the verification principle in the form "the meaning of symbols is really simply their power in prediction."

But that is neither here nor there. What we are concerned with is its metaphysical nature. And to illuminate this I say that it is a sort of metaphysical theory; and for our purpose it does not matter whether it is a sort of metaphysical theory (*a*) in the way that a hackney is a sort of horse, or (*b*) in the way that a motor cycle is, because it is a sort of tireless horse on wheels. If (*a*) my statement is correct; if (*b*) it is not. But this correctness is of no importance. For I make the statement to draw attention to certain likenesses, and whether they suffice or no for the proper application of "metaphysical" does not affect their existence. I say that the verification principle is a metaphysical principle because I want (1) to draw the attention of those who accept it to the deplorably old-fashioned clothes in which it presents itself. Indeed it resembles not only positivistic theories but also the worst transcendental theories by appearing in the disguise either of a scientific discovery removing popular illusion, or of a logical equation (incorrect) from which deductions may be made. No wonder our conservative friends cannot accept it. I want (2) to draw the attention of those who reject it to the fact that because they are taken in by its disguise they fail to recognize the merits which like other metaphysical theories it conceals. Both those who accept it and those who reject it do not realize what they are doing because they do not notice that it is disguised. But metaphysics reveals the hidden, plucks the mask of appearance from the face of reality—and we shall now see what a metaphysical theory really is and thus the general nature of the verification principle.

To say that the verification principle is a sort of metaphysical theory would be already extremely illuminating if we had already an adequate grasp of the ultimate nature of metaphysical theories, but lacking this we must go on. It is possible to go on in either of the two following ways: We may examine the nature of the verification principle and thus throw light on the nature of other metaphysical theories, or we may examine the nature of other metaphysical theories and thus throw light on the nature of the verification principle. Let us adopt the latter plan and work from the specific to the general. Then applying our results in a direct examination of the verification principle we shall obtain a review of the whole of metaphysics because the verification principle is the generalization of one set of answers to metaphysical questions while its opposite is the generalization of the opposing answers. . . .

Let us now take an example from another class of metaphysical questions. These arise, not from the "queerness" of the form of the class of propositions which is felt to be queer, but because of the queerness of the category of what they are about. These are apt to present themselves in the form "What is X?" "What are X's?" where "X" is a name for the puzzling category, or a name for a species of that category. We have for example, "What are characteristics? What are numbers? What are abstract, necessary propositions about?" and we have "What are chairs and tables? What are material things?" "What is a nation? Is it something over and above the individuals of that nation?" "What is Time?"

Suppose we offer an answer to the last on the lines suggested by Moore. We say, "Well, when we speak about time, what are we talking about? Such facts as this—that lunch is over, supper to come, that Smith's anger is past and so on. Let us call such facts 'temporal facts.' Then 'Time is unreal,' can be translated into the concrete (Moore's phrase) by 'There are no temporal facts.'" When we read this, we draw a breath of relief. This is the stuff. With this translation into the concrete, we get "the cash value" (Broad), the predictive power, of the statement "Time is unreal." What a contrast to the answer "Time is an abstract entity, super-sensible, having a sort of existence all its own." For the latter answer only tells us that time is not brown or yellow, not big or little, not to be found in the bathroom, and like Space only different. Such an answer only emphasizes what ordinary language suggests that, besides the facts that lunch is over and his anger past, there is the fact that Time is real. True, Moore did not *find* a definition, but he showed how it was a mere accident of language that we could not provide a definition and thus remove an uneasy feeling about Time, just as we did when we had the uneasy feeling that though the class of all men is not to be identified with its members, yet there were not in addition to the facts about men, *e. g.,* that men exist, that all are mortal, facts about the class of men, *e. g.,* that it exists, has members, has members which are mortal.

We may say here that Moore meets a philosophical request, even, if you like, a metaphysical request, not indeed by finding but by creating an analytic definition.

I do not wish to deny this any more than I wish to deny that Russell did the same with his definition of number.[3] They both translated sentences which trouble us into others which do not.

But of course there will be people dissatisfied with this answer. They fall into two very different classes: In the first place, some will say "What is meant by 'Time is real' is different from what is meant by 'Either lunch is over, or my supper yet to come, or his anger is past, or something of that sort (i. e., and so on).' What I have in mind when I say 'Time is unreal,' is very different from what I have in mind if I say 'Either lunch is over or etc.'" And yet these same people, some of them, will not be

[3 Russell's definition is: "The number of a class is the class of all those classes that are similar to it." It is discussed in Chapter II of his *Introduction to Mathematical Philosophy* (London, 1919). *Ed.*]

METAPHYSICS *297*

satisfied by any definition which does not put "Time is unreal" in terms of individual events. So they reject every definition either on the ground that it is incorrect or on the ground that it is not sufficiently profound. The nature of this difficulty in metaphysics and the light it throws upon its nature will appear later.

In the second place, there are people who will say that even the definition in terms of individual events or temporal facts is not sufficiently profound; they ask that the definition should be taken further. And if we say "By temporal facts we mean such facts as 'Smith's anger is past' and so on" they complain (*a*) against the "specimen" fact as again involving time, or (*b*) against the phrase "and so on." It is soon clear that there is nothing to be done for them with regard to (*a*). We may try saying "His anger is past" means "He was angry and is not." But it is a hopeless game. The reply will be that "He was angry" involves Time again. And of course it involves it if any sentence using a verb with a tense involves Time. And it is now apparent that this is how the metaphysician uses "involves Time." He cannot translate sentences which work like the ones with tenses into sentences involving only a timeless "is" such as "Red is a color." But this is what he wants. Nothing short of it will do, nothing else will be a reduction of temporal facts to non-temporal. No new language will help. Suppose we invent a new language with no time-indicating words such as "was," "will be" and no time-indicating endings such as "ed." Now the new sentences, if they are to provide translations, must do the work the old did; so there must be differences between those which correspond to the old "was"-sentences and those which correspond to the old "will be"-sentences. We might put them in different colored inks (compare Ramsey's writing negatives as positives upside down). But then the new sentences

would surely again express temporal propositions.

I am well aware that there is nothing novel in the conclusion that temporal propositions are unanalyzable, and that this unanalyzability is not a matter of our being unable to do or find the analysis but of the nature of the facts. Prof. Broad supports far more fully and carefully than I have done this very conclusion about temporal facts. . . .

In general: The metaphysically-minded person feels that the actual world is made up solely of positive, specific, determinate, concrete, contingent, individual, sensory facts, and that the appearance of a penumbra of fictional, negative, general, indeterminate, abstract, necessary, super-individual, physical facts is somehow only an appearance due to a lack of penetration upon our part. And he feels that there are not, in addition to the ways of knowing the non-penumbral facts, additional ways of knowing employed for ascertaining the penumbral facts. At the same time the penumbral do not seem to be identical with the non-penumbral and thus *do* seem to call for extra ways of knowing.

Now this feeling of taking the same reality twice over (McTaggart), this feeling of superfluous entities (Russell), this feeling of metaphysical double vision has been removed in certain cases by definition. . . . We can imagine someone wondering how we know that when (1) there are two white goats and four black in a field then (2) there are six goats in the field or there exists a class *goats-in-that-field* which has six members. Definition removes these troubles. Take the last case. When we saw that the two sentences meant the same or that the meaning of the one included the meaning of the other, then the appearance of plurality was explained by the plurality of sentences, while the assurance of identity was justified in the single meaning made true by a single fact. And with the disappearance of the ontological puzzle the epistemological puzzle vanished also. No wonder the definition model fascinated.

But unfortunately, as we have seen, there are cases where definitions cannot be found, where no ingenuity reveals non-penumbral sentences which we can feel sure mean the same as the penumbrals. And yet we cannot feel that the facts which make the penumbral true are anything but the positive, concrete etc. non-penumbral facts which make up the actual world. Indeed there are cases where we know that there are no non-penumbral sentences which mean the same in the ordinary use of "mean the same" as the penumbral, while yet some of us feel that there is no differencee between the facts which make those penumbral sentences true and those which make the non-penumbral sentences true. Some people come down on one side of the fence, some on the other. Thus Broad argues from the fact that the question "Fido behaves in all respects intelligently, but is he intelligent?" is not silly like "Smith is rich, but is he wealthy?" to the conclusion that the question is synthetic like "I have given Smith 2 ounces of arsenic, but will it kill him?" That is, he concludes that the sentences "Fido behaves in all respects intelligently" and "Fido is intelligent" do not mean the same, do not stand for the same proposition, do not stand for the same fact. To do this is to represent the question "Smith still breathes, and he nods, smiles, and talks as usual, but does he really think and feel?" as like the question "Smoke still comes from the chimneys, the lights go on in the evenings, but have the inhabitants fled?" Has Smith's soul left his body but arranged with the nervous system that appearances shall be kept up in its absence? Has his *rha* flown? And yet we feel that the question is *not* like this—yet surely it must be, for Broad's premisses are true and there is no logical slip. . . .

To sum up: The metaphysician is concerned with certain fundamental ontological and epistemological reduplication questions: Are X facts to be identified with Y facts? How do we get from knowledge of the latter to knowledge of the former?

Usually, even as questions of logic, there is no right or wrong answer to these questions. I should be inclined to say this in every case where the question is in the form in which reduplication is most intolerable, namely, "Are X facts nothing but Y facts or are they something over and above Y facts?" Sometimes in the form in which reduplication is less intolerable, namely, "Do X sentences mean the same as Y sentences" (taken as a question of logic) there is a correct answer "No."

But in either case the metaphysical dispute is resolved by explaining what induces each disputant to say what he does. This is done as follows: 1. Explain the nature of the question or request; (*a*) Negatively—remove the wrong idea that it is a question of fact whether natural *or logical;* (*b*) Positively—give the right idea by showing how, as in other disputes of this unanswerable sort, the questions are really requests for a description of (1) those features of the use of the expressions involved in the questions which incline one to answer "Yes," and of (2) those features of their use which incline one to answer "No." In the case of ontological questions such as "Are X facts to be identified with Y facts?" "Do X sentences mean the same as Y sentences?" "Does the sentence S stand for the same fact as the sentence S'?" the expressions involved are, of course, (*a*) the expressions "X facts," "Y facts," "X sentences," "Y sentences," "The sentence S" and so on, and (*b*) the *connectives* "stand for the same fact," "mean the same" and so on. In the case of epistemological questions, expressions such as "know," "rational," take the place of the connectives.

2. Second there is the work of providing the descriptions that are really wanted.

Fortunately when the nature of the questions has been explained, then the nature of the "answers," "theories" and "reasons" which they have been "offering" and "advancing" becomes clear to the disputants. And then it becomes clear how much of the work of providing the descriptions has been already done, though under the disguise of a logical dispute. Thus the metaphysical paradoxes appear no longer as crude falsehoods about how language is actually used, but as penetrating suggestions as to how it might be used so as to reveal what, by the actual use of language, is hidden. And metaphysical platitudes appear as timely reminders of what is revealed by the actual use of language and would be hidden by the new. To take an example which we have ourselves come upon: Some have said "Analytic propositions are verbal," others have said "They are not," and, in supporting these "views," they have between them done all that is primarily asked for by one who asks "Are analytic propositions verbal or are they not?"

Thus it appears how it is that, to give metaphysicians what they want, we have to do little more than remove the spectacles through which they look at their own work. Then they see how those hidden identities and diversities which lead to the "insoluble" reduction questions about forms, categories and predicates, have already been revealed, though in a hidden way.

4 / ETHICS

Ethics for Moore is the general inquiry into what is good. Such an inquiry takes the form of searching for the meaning, the definition, or the analysis of good. To ask how good is to be defined is not to ask a verbal question, but rather to be concerned with the idea or object that the word is used to stand for. Analysis proceeds by resolving complex notions into simpler ones. Such resolution, however, must finally end in the simple which is itself unanalyzable; or, put another way, there are certain ultimate terms by reference to which any definable thing is defined but which are themselves indefinable. The nature of the simple cannot be made known by definition.

How is good to be defined? Moore's position is that good is a simple property of things, and therefore it cannot be defined. It is like yellow, another simple notion. All that can be said is that good is a simple, unique, indefinable property of things—but, for Moore, this is saying a great deal. Failure to recognize this concept of the word has led some philosophers to make the mistake of believing that in naming other properties like pleasure or object of desire they were defining good. This mistake Moore calls the "naturalistic fallacy." The definition of good cannot be given by referring to natural properties because it cannot be given at all.

THE INDEFINABILITY OF GOOD

G. E. Moore (1873-1958)

1. It is very easy to point out some among our every-day judgments, with the truth of which Ethics is undoubtedly concerned. Whenever we say, "So and so is a good man," or "That fellow is a villain"; whenever we ask, "What ought I to do?" or "Is it wrong for me to do like this?"; whenever we hazard such remarks as "Temperance is a virtue and drunkenness a vice"— it is undoubtedly the business of Ethics to discuss such questions and such statements; to argue what is the true answer when we ask what it is right to do, and to give reasons for thinking that our statements about the character of persons or the morality of actions are true or false. In the vast majority of cases, where we make statements involving any of the terms "virtue," "vice," "duty," "right," "ought," "good," "bad," we are making ethical judgments; and if we wish to discuss their truth, we shall be discussing a point of Ethics. . . .

2. . . . Accordingly, we find that many ethical philosophers are disposed to accept as an adequate definition of "Ethics" the statement that it deals with the question what is good or bad in human conduct. They hold that its enquiries are properly confined to "conduct" or to "practice"; they hold that the name "practical philosophy" covers all the matter with which it has to do. Now, without discussing the proper meaning of the word (for verbal questions are properly left to the writers of dictionaries and other persons interested in literature; philosophy, as we shall see, has no concern with them), I may say that I intend to use "Ethics" to cover more than this— a usage, for which there is, I think, quite sufficient authority. I am using it to cover

The selection is from G. E. Moore, *Principia Ethica* (Cambridge: University Press, 1903), pp. 1-17, with omissions.

an enquiry for which, at all events, there is no other word: the general enquiry into what is good.

Ethics is undoubtedly concerned with the question what good conduct is; but, being concerned with this, it obviously does not start at the beginning, unless it is prepared to tell us what is good as well as what is conduct. For "good conduct" is a complex notion: all conduct is not good; for some is certainly bad and some may be indifferent. And on the other hand, other things, beside conduct, may be good; and if they are so, then, "good" denotes some property, that is common to them and conduct; and if we examine good conduct alone of all good things, then we shall be in danger of mistaking for this property, some property which is not shared by those other things: and thus we shall have made a mistake about Ethics even in this limited sense; for we shall not know what good conduct really is. This is a mistake which many writers have actually made, from limiting their enquiry to conduct. And hence I shall try to avoid it by considering first what is good in general; hoping, that if we can arrive at any certainty about this, it will be much easier to settle the question of good conduct: for we all know pretty well what "conduct" is. This, then, is our first question: What is good? and What is bad? and to the discussion of this question (or these questions) I give the name of Ethics, since that science must, at all events, include it.

3. But this is a question which may have many meanings. If, for example, each of us were to say "I am doing good now" or "I had a good dinner yesterday," these statements would each of them be some sort of answer to our question, although perhaps a false one. So, too, when A asks B what

school he ought to send his son to, B's answer will certainly be an ethical judgment. And similarly all distribution of praise or blame to any personage or thing that has existed, now exists, or will exist, does give some answer to the question "What is good?" In all such cases some particular thing is judged to be good or bad: the question "What?" is answered by "This." But this is not the sense in which a scientific Ethics asks the question. Not one, of all the many million answers of this kind, which must be true, can form a part of an ethical system; although that science must contain reasons and principles sufficient for deciding on the truth of all of them. There are far too many persons, things and events in the world, past, present, or to come, for a discussion of their individual merits to be embraced in any science. Ethics, therefore, does not deal at all with facts of this nature, facts that are unique, individual, absolutely particular; facts with which such studies as history, geography, astronomy, are compelled, in part at least, to deal. And, for this reason, it is not the business of the ethical philosopher to give personal advice or exhortation.

4. But there is another meaning which may be given to the question "What is good?" "Books are good" would be an answer to it, though an answer obviously false; for some books are very bad indeed. And ethical judgments of this kind do indeed belong to Ethics; though I shall not deal with many of them. Such is the judgment "Pleasure is good"—a judgment, of which Ethics should discuss the truth, although it is not nearly as important as that other judgment, with which we shall be much occupied presently—"Pleasure *alone* is good." It is judgments of this sort, which are made in such books on Ethics as contain a list of "virtues"—in Aristotle's "Ethics" for example. But it is judgments of precisely the same kind, which form the

substance of what is commonly supposed to be a study different from Ethics, and one much less respectable—the study of Casuistry. We may be told that Casuistry differs from Ethics, in that it is much more detailed and particular, Ethics much more general. But it is most important to notice that Casuistry does not deal with anything that is absolutely particular—particular in the only sense in which a perfectly precise line can be drawn between it and what is general. It is not particular in the sense just noticed, the sense in which this book is a particular book, and A's friend's advice particular advice. Casuistry may indeed be *more* particular and Ethics *more* general; but that means that they differ only in degree and not in kind. And this is universally true of "particular" and "general," when used in this common, but inaccurate, sense. So far as Ethics allows itself to give lists of virtues or even to name constituents of the Ideal, it is indistinguishable from Casuistry. . . . Casuistry forms, therefore, part of the ideal of ethical science: Ethics cannot be complete without it. The defects of Casuistry are not defects of principle; no objection can be taken to its aim and object. It has failed only because it is far too difficult a subject to be treated adequately in our present state of knowledge. The casuist has been unable to distinguish, in the cases which he treats, those elements upon which their value depends. Hence he often thinks two cases to be alike in respect of value, when in reality they are alike only in some other respect. It is to mistakes of this kind that the pernicious influence of such investigations has been due. For Casuistry is the goal of ethical investigation. It cannot be safely attempted at the beginning of our studies, but only at the end.

5. But our question "What is good?" may have still another meaning. We may, in the third place, mean to ask, not what thing or things are good, but how "good"

is to be defined. This is an enquiry which belongs only to Ethics, not to Casuistry; and this is the enquiry which will occupy us first.

It is an enquiry to which most special attention should be directed; since this question, how "good" is to be defined, is the most fundamental question in all Ethics. That which is meant by "good" is, in fact, except its converse "bad," the *only* simple object of thought which is peculiar to Ethics. Its definition is, therefore, the most essential point in the definition of Ethics; and moreover a mistake with regard to it entails a far larger number of erroneous ethical judgments than any other. Unless this first question be fully understood, and its true answer clearly recognized, the rest of Ethics is as good as useless from the point of view of systematic knowledge. True ethical judgments, of the two kinds last dealt with, may indeed be made by those who do not know the answer to this question as well as by those who do; and it goes without saying that the two classes of people may lead equally good lives. But it is extremely unlikely that the *most general* ethical judgments will be equally valid, in the absence of a true answer to this question: I shall presently try to shew that the gravest errors have been largely due to beliefs in a false answer. And, in any case, it is impossible that, till the answer to this question be known, any one should know *what is the evidence* for any ethical judgment whatsoever. But the main object of Ethics, as a systematic science, is to give correct *reasons* for thinking that this or that is good; and, unless this question be answered, such reasons cannot be given. Even, therefore, apart from the fact that a false answer leads to false conclusions, the present enquiry is a most necessary and important part of the science of Ethics.

6. What, then, is good? How is good to be defined? Now, it may be thought that this is a verbal question. A definition does indeed often mean the expressing of one word's meaning in other words. But this is not the sort of definition I am asking for. Such a definition can never be of ultimate importance in any study except lexicography. If I wanted that kind of definition I should have to consider in the first place how people generally used the word "good"; but my business is not with its proper usage, as established by custom. I should, indeed, be foolish, if I tried to use it for something which it did not usually denote: if, for instance, I were to announce that, whenever I used the word "good," I must be understood to be thinking of that object which is usually denoted by the word "table." I shall, therefore, use the word in the sense in which I think it is ordinarily used; but at the same time I am not anxious to discuss whether I am right in thinking that it is so used. My business is solely with that object or idea, which I hold, rightly or wrongly, that the word is generally used to stand for. What I want to discover is the nature of that object or idea, and about this I am extremely anxious to arrive at an agreement.

But, if we understand the question in this sense, my answer to it may seem a very disappointing one. If I am asked "What is good?" my answer is that good is good, and that is the end of the matter. Or if I am asked "How is good to be defined?" my answer is that it cannot be defined, and that is all I have to say about it. But disappointing as these answers may appear, they are of the very last importance. To readers who are familiar with philosophic terminology, I can express their importance by saying that they amount to this: That propositions about the good are all of them synthetic and never analytic; and that is plainly no trivial matter. And the same thing may be expressed more popularly, by saying that, if I am right, then nobody can foist upon us such an axiom as that "Pleasure is the only good" or that "The good is the desired" on the pretence that this is "the very meaning of the word."

7. Let us, then, consider this position. My point is that "good" is a simple notion, just as "yellow" is a simple notion; that, just as you cannot, by any manner of means, explain to any one who does not already know it, what yellow is, so you cannot explain what good is. Definitions of the kind that I was asking for, definitions which describe the real nature of the object or notion denoted by a word, and which do not merely tell us what the word is used to mean, are only possible when the object or notion in question is something complex. You can give a definition of a horse, because a horse has many different properties and qualities, all of which you can enumerate. But when you have enumerated them all, when you have reduced a horse to his simplest terms, then you can no longer define those terms. They are simply something which you think of or perceive, and to any one who cannot think of or perceive them, you can never, by any definition, make their nature known. It may perhaps be objected to this that we are able to describe to others, objects which they have never seen or thought of. We can, for instance, make a man understand what a chimaera is, although he has never heard of one or seen one. You can tell him that it is an animal with a lioness's head and body, with a goat's head growing from the middle of its back, and with a snake in place of a tail. But here the object which you are describing is a complex object; it is entirely composed of parts, with which we are all perfectly familiar—a snake, a goat, a lioness; and we know, too, the manner in which those parts are to be put together, because we know what is meant by the middle of a lioness's back, and where her tail is wont to grow. And so it is with all objects, not previously known, which we are able to define: they are all complex;

all composed of parts, which may themselves, in the first instance, be capable of similar definition, but which must in the end be reducible to simplest parts, which can no longer be defined. But yellow and good, we say, are not complex: they are notions of that simple kind, out of which definitions are composed and with which the power of further defining ceases. . . .

9. But I am afraid I have still not removed the chief difficulty which may prevent acceptance of the proposition that good is indefinable. I do not mean to say that *the* good, that which is good, is thus indefinable; if I did think so, I should not be writing on Ethics, for my main object is to help towards discovering that definition. It is just because I think there will be less risk of error in our search for a definition of "the good," that I am now insisting that *good* is indefinable. I must try to explain the difference between these two. I suppose it may be granted that "good" is an adjective. Well "the good," "that which is good," must therefore be the substantive to which the adjective "good" will apply: it must be the whole of that to which the adjective will apply, and the adjective must *always* truly apply to it. But if it is that to which the adjective will apply, it must be something different from that adjective itself; and the whole of that something different, whatever it is, will be our definition of *the* good. Now it may be that this something will have other adjectives, beside "good," that will apply to it. It may be full of pleasure, for example; it may be intelligent: and if these two adjectives are really part of its definition, then it will certainly be true, that pleasure and intelligence are good. And many people appear to think that, if we say "Pleasure and intelligence are good," or if we say "Only pleasure and intelligence are good," we are defining "good." Well, I cannot deny that propositions of this nature may sometimes be called definitions; I do not know

well enough how the word is generally used to decide upon this point. I only wish it to be understood that that is not what I mean when I say there is no possible definition of good, and that I shall not mean this if I use the word again. I do most fully believe that some true proposition of the form "Intelligence is good and intelligence alone is good" can be found; if none could be found, our definition of *the* good would be impossible. As it is, I believe *the* good to be definable; and yet I still say that good itself is indefinable.

10. "Good," then, if we mean by it that quality which we assert to belong to a thing, when we say that the thing is good, is incapable of any definition, in the most important sense of that word. The most important sense of "definition" is that in which a definition states what are the parts which invariably compose a certain whole; and in this sense "good" has no definition because it is simple and has no parts. It is one of those innumerable objects of thought which are themselves incapable of definition, because they are the ultimate terms by reference to which whatever *is* capable of definition must be defined. That there must be an indefinite number of such terms is obvious, on reflection; since we cannot define anything except by an analysis, which, when carried as far as it will go, refers us to something, which is simply different from anything else, and which by that ultimate difference explains the peculiarity of the whole which we are defining: for every whole contains some parts which are common to other wholes also. There is, therefore, no intrinsic difficulty in the contention that "good" denotes a simple and indefinable quality. There are many other instances of such qualities.

Consider yellow, for example. We may try to define it, by describing its physical equivalent; we may state what kind of light-vibrations must stimulate the normal eye, in order that we may perceive it. But a moment's reflection is sufficient to shew that those light-vibrations are not themselves what we mean by yellow. *They* are not what we perceive. Indeed we should never have been able to discover their existence, unless we had first been struck by the patent difference of quality between the different colors. The most we can be entitled to say of those vibrations is that they are what corresponds in space to the yellow which we actually perceive.

Yet a mistake of this simple kind has commonly been made about "good." It may be true that all things which are good are *also* something else, just as it is true that all things which are yellow produce a certain kind of vibration in the light. And it is a fact, that Ethics aims at discovering what are those other properties belonging to all things which are good. But far too many philosophers have thought that when they named those other properties they were actually defining good; that these properties, in fact, were simply not "other," but absolutely and entirely the same with goodness. This view I propose to call the "naturalistic fallacy" and of it I shall now endeavor to dispose.

11. Let us consider what it is such philosophers say. And first it is to be noticed that they do not agree among themselves. They not only say that they are right as to what good is, but they endeavor to prove that other people who say that it is something else, are wrong. One, for instance, will affirm that good is pleasure, another, perhaps, that good is that which is desired; and each of these will argue eagerly to prove that the other is wrong. But how is that possible? One of them says that good is nothing but the object of desire, and at the same time tries to prove that it is not pleasure. But from his first assertion, that good just means the object of desire, one of two things must follow as regards his proof:

(1) He may be trying to prove that the

object of desire is not pleasure. But, if this be all, where is his Ethics? The position he is maintaining is merely a psychological one. Desire is something which occurs in our minds, and pleasure is something else which so occurs; and our would-be ethical philosopher is merely holding that the latter is not the object of the former. But what has that to do with the question in dispute? His opponent held the ethical proposition that pleasure was the good, and although he should prove a million times over the psychological proposition that pleasure is not the object of desire, he is no nearer proving his opponent to be wrong. . . .

(2) The other alternative will scarcely be more welcome. It is that the discussion is after all a verbal one. When A says "Good means pleasant" and B says "Good means desired," they may merely wish to assert that most people have used the word for what is pleasant and for what is desired respectively. And this is quite an interesting subject for discussion: only it is not a whit more an ethical discussion than the last was. Nor do I think that any exponent of naturalistic Ethics would be willing to allow that this was all he meant. They are all so anxious to persuade us that what they call the good is what we really ought to do. "Do, pray, act so, because the word 'good' is generally used to denote actions of this nature": such, on this view, would be the substance of their teaching. And in so far as they tell us how we ought to act, their teaching is truly ethical, as they mean it to be. But how perfectly absurd is the reason they would give for it! "You are to do this, because most people use a certain word to denote conduct such as this." "You are to say the thing which is not, because most people call it lying." That is an argument just as good!—My dear sirs, what we want to know from you as ethical teachers, is not how people use a word; it is not even, what kind of actions they approve, which the use of this word "good" may

certainly imply: what we want to know is simply what *is* good. We may indeed agree that what most people do think good, is actually so; we shall at all events be glad to know their opinions: but when we say their opinions about what *is* good, we do mean what we say; we do not care whether they call that thing which they mean "horse" or "table" or "chair," "gut" or "bon" or "ἀγαθός"; we want to know what it is that they so call. When they say "Pleasure is good," we cannot believe that they merely mean "Pleasure is pleasure" and nothing more than that.

12. Suppose a man says "I am pleased"; and suppose that is not a lie or a mistake but the truth. Well, if it is true, what does that mean? It means that his mind, a certain definite mind, distinguished by certain definite marks from all others, has at this moment a certain definite feeling called pleasure. "Pleased" *means* nothing but having pleasure, and though we may be more pleased or less pleased, and even, we may admit for the present, have one or another kind of pleasure; yet in so far as it is pleasure we have, whether there be more or less of it, and whether it be of one kind or another, what we have is one definite thing, absolutely indefinable, some one thing that is the same in all the various degrees and in all the various kinds of it that there may be. We may be able to say how it is related to other things: that, for example, it is in the mind, that it causes desire, that we are conscious of it, etc., etc. We can, I say, describe its relations to other things, but define it we can *not*. And if anybody tried to define pleasure for us as being any other natural object; if anybody were to say, for instance, that pleasure *means* the sensation of red, and were to proceed to deduce from that that pleasure is a color, we should be entitled to laugh at him and to distrust his future statements about pleasure. Well, that would be the same fallacy which I have called the naturalistic fallacy. . . .

13. . . . But whoever will attentively consider with himself what is actually before his mind when he asks the question "Is pleasure (or whatever it may be) after all good?" can easily satisfy himself that he is not merely wondering whether pleasure is pleasant. And if he will try this experiment with each suggested definition in succession, he may become expert enough to recognize that in every case he has before his mind a unique object, with regard to the connection of which with any other object, a distinct question may be asked. Every one does in fact understand the question "Is this good?" When he thinks of it, his state of mind is different from what it would be, were he asked "Is this pleasant, or desired, or approved?" It has a distinct meaning for him, even though he may not recognize in what respect it is distinct. Whenever he thinks of "intrinsic value," or "intrinsic worth," or says that a thing "ought to exist," he has before his mind the unique object—the unique property of things—which I mean by "good." Everybody is constantly aware of this notion, although he may never become aware at all that it is different from other notions of which he is also aware. But, for correct ethical reasoning, it is extremely important that he should become aware of this fact; and, as soon as the nature of the problem is clearly understood, there should be little difficulty in advancing so far in analysis.

5 / ESTHETICS

Is esthetic theory, in the sense of stating a true definition of art, possible? Writing under the direct influence of Wittgenstein, Professor Weitz answers, No. Theory is never possible in esthetics, and it is wrong in principle. To understand this denial, it must be remembered from Wittgenstein that how we view our concepts is exceedingly important. More specifically, we must begin, not with the question, "What is art?" but rather with, "What sort of concept is 'art'?" The latter question generates an inquiry elucidating the concept; and like all elucidation, it gives the relation between the use of the concept and the conditions under which it can be correctly employed.

Professor Weitz likens his treatment of "art" to Wittgenstein's analysis of games. If we look at what we call art, we find only resemblances rather than common properties. This means that "art" has an "open texture" in that it has no fixed boundary of application and the conditions for its application are never final. When we use and apply "art," we do so on the basis of a decision.

Esthetic theory must, therefore, elucidate the concept of art by describing the conditions for its employment. In doing this, it may learn from traditional esthetic theories. It must not fail to recognize, however, that they are only recommendations to us to attend to certain features of art.

THEORY AND ART

Morris Weitz (1916-   )

Theory has been central in esthetics and is still the preoccupation of the philosophy of art. Its main avowed concern remains the determination of the nature of art which can be formulated into a definition of it. It construes definition as the statement of the necessary and sufficient properties of what is being defined, where the statement purports to be a true or false claim about the essence of art, what characterizes and distinguishes it from everything else. Each of the great theories of art—Formalism, Voluntarism, Emotionalism, Intellectualism, Intuitionism, Organicism—converges on the attempt to state the defining properties of art. Each claims that it is the true theory because it has formulated correctly into a real definition the nature of art; and that the others are false because they have left out some necessary or sufficient property. Many theorists contend that their enterprise is no mere intellectual exercise but an absolute necessity for any understanding of art and our proper evaluation of it. Unless we know what art is, they say, what are its necessary and sufficient properties, we cannot begin to respond to it adequately or to say why one work is good or better than another. Esthetic theory, thus, is important not only in itself but for the foundations of both appreciation and criticism. Philosophers, critics, and even artists who have written on art, agree that what is primary in esthetics is a theory about the nature of art.

Is esthetic theory, in the sense of a true definition or set of necessary and sufficient

properties of art, possible? If nothing else does, the history of esthetics itself should give one enormous pause here. For, in spite of the many theories, we seem no nearer our goal today than we were in Plato's time. Each age, each art-movement, each philosophy of art, tries over and over again to establish the stated ideal only to be succeeded by a new or revised theory, rooted, at least in part, in the repudiation of preceding ones. Even today, almost everyone interested in esthetic matters is still deeply wedded to the hope that the correct theory of art is forthcoming. We need only examine the numerous new books on art in which new definitions are proffered; or, in our own country especially, the basic textbooks and anthologies to recognize how strong the priority of a theory of art is.

In this essay I want to plead for the rejection of this problem. I want to show that theory—in the requisite classical sense —is *never* forthcoming in esthetics, and that we would do much better as philosophers to supplant the question, "What is the nature of art?" by other questions, the answers to which will provide us with all the understanding of the arts there can be. I want to show that the inadequacies of the theories are not primarily occasioned by any legitimate difficulty such e.g., as the vast complexity of art, which might be corrected by further probing and research. Their basic inadequacies reside instead in a fundamental misconception of art. Esthetic theory —all of it—is wrong in principle in thinking that a correct theory is possible because it radically misconstrues the logic of the concept of art. Its main contention that "art" is amenable to real or any kind of true definition is false. Its attempt to discover the necessary and sufficient properties of art is logically misbegotten for the very

The selection is from Morris Weitz, "The Role of Theory in Aesthetics," *Journal of Aesthetics and Art Criticism*, 15 (1956), pp. 27-28 and 30-35. Used by permission of the Editor.

simple reason that such a set and, consequently, such a formula about it, is never forthcoming. Art, as the logic of the concept shows, has no set of necessary and sufficient properties, hence a theory of it is logically impossible and not merely factually difficult. Esthetic theory tries to define what cannot be defined in its requisite sense. But in recommending the repudiation of esthetic theory I shall not argue from this, as too many others have done, that its logical confusions render it meaningless or worthless. On the contrary, I wish to reassess its role and its contribution primarily in order to show that it is of the greatest importance to our understanding of the arts. . . .

The problem with which we must begin is not "What is art?," but "What sort of concept is 'art'?" Indeed, the root problem of philosophy itself is to explain the relation between the employment of certain kinds of concepts and the conditions under which they can be correctly applied. If I may paraphrase Wittgenstein, we must not ask, What is the nature of any philosophical x? or even, according to the semanticist, What does "x" mean?—a transformation that leads to the disastrous interpretation of "art" as a name for some specifiable class of objects; but rather, What is the use or employment of "x"? What does "x" do in the language? This, I take it, is the initial question, the begin-all if not the end-all of any philosophical problem and solution. Thus, in esthetics, our first problem is the elucidation of the actual employment of the concept of art, to give a logical description of the actual functioning of the concept, including a description of the conditions under which we correctly use it or its correlates.

My model in this type of logical description or philosophy derives from Wittgenstein. It is also he who, in his refutation of philosophical theorizing in the sense of constructing definitions of philosophical entities, has furnished contemporary esthetics

with a starting point for any future progress. In his new work, *Philosophical Investigations*, Wittgenstein raises as an illustrative question, What is a game? The traditional philosophical, theoretical answer would be in terms of some exhaustive set of properties common to all games. To this Wittgenstein says, let us consider what we call "games": "I mean board-games, card-games, ball-games, Olympic games, and so on. What is common to them all— Don't say: 'there *must* be something common, or they would not be called "games"' but *look and see* whether there is anything common to all.—For if you look at them you will not see something that is common to *all*, but similarities, relationships, and a whole series of them at that . . ."

Card games are like board games in some respects but not in others. Not all games are amusing, nor is there always winning or losing or competition. Some games resemble others in some respects—that is all. What we find are no necessary and sufficient properties, only "a complicated network of similarities overlapping and crisscrossing," such that we can say of games that they form a family with family resemblances and no common trait. If one asks what a game is, we pick out sample games, describe these, and add, "This and *similar things* are called 'games.'" This is all we need to say and indeed all any of us knows about games. Knowing what a game is is not knowing some real definition or theory but being able to recognize and explain games and to decide which among imaginary and new examples would or would not be called "games."

The problem of the nature of art is like that of the nature of games, at least in these respects: If we actually look and see what it is that we call "art," we will also find no common properties—only strands of similarities. Knowing what art is is not apprehending some manifest or latent essence but being able to recognize, describe, and explain those things we call "art" in virtue of these similarities.

But the basic resemblance between these concepts is their open texture. In elucidating them, certain (paradigm) cases can be given, about which there can be no question as to their being correctly described as "art" or "game," but no exhaustive set of cases can be given. I can list some cases and some conditions under which I can apply correctly the concept of art but I cannot list all of them, for the all-important reason that unforeseeable or novel conditions are always forthcoming or envisageable.

A concept is open if its conditions of application are emendable and corrigible; i.e., if a situation or case can be imagined or secured which would call for some sort of *decision* on our part to extend the use of the concept to cover this, or to close the concept and invent a new one to deal with the new case and its new property. If necessary and sufficient conditions for the application of a concept can be stated, the concept is a closed one. But this can happen only in logic or mathematics where concepts are constructed and completely defined. It cannot occur with empirically-descriptive and normative concepts unless we arbitrarily close them by stipulating the ranges of their uses.

I can illustrate this open character of "art" best by examples drawn from its subconcepts. Consider questions like "Is Dos Passos' *U. S. A.* a novel?" "Is V. Woolf's *To the Lighthouse* a novel?" "Is Joyce's *Finnegan's Wake* a novel?" On the traditional view, these are construed as factual problems to be answered yes or no in accordance with the presence or absence of defining properties. But certainly this is not how any of these questions is answered. Once it arises, as it has many times in the development of the novel from Richardson to Joyce (e.g., "Is Gide's *The School for Wives* a novel or a diary?"), what is at stake is no

factual analysis concerning necessary and sufficient properties but a decision as to whether the work under examination is similar in certain respects to other works, already called "novels," and consequently warrants the extension of the concept to cover the new case. The new work is narrative, fictional, contains character delineation and dialogue but (say) it has no regular time-sequence in the plot or is interspersed with actual newspaper reports. It is like recognized novels, A, B, C . . . , in some respects but not like them in others. But then neither were B and C like A in some respects when it was decided to extend the concept applied to A to B and C. Because work N + 1 (the brand new work) is like A, B, C . . . N in certain respects—has strands of similarity to them—the concept is extended and a new phase of the novel engendered. "Is N 1 a novel?" then, is no factual, but rather a decision problem, where the verdict turns on whether or not we enlarge our set of conditions for applying the concept.

What is true of the novel is, I think, true of every sub-concept of art: "tragedy," "comedy," "painting," "opera," etc., of "art" itself. No "Is X a novel, painting, opera, work of art, etc.?" question allows of a definitive answer in the sense of a factual yes or no report. "Is this *collage* a painting or not?" does not rest on any set of necessary and sufficient properties of painting but on whether we decide—as we did!—to extend "painting" to cover this case.

"Art," itself, is an open concept. New conditions (cases) have constantly arisen and will undoubtedly constantly arise; new art forms, new movements will emerge, which will demand decisions on the part of those interested, usually professional critics, as to whether the concept should be extended or not. Estheticians may lay down similarity conditions but never necessary and sufficient ones for the correct application of the concept. With "art" its conditions of application can never be exhaustively enumerated since new cases can always be envisaged or created by artists, or even nature, which would call for a decision on someone's part to extend or to close the old or to invent a new concept. (E.g., "It's not a sculpture, it's a mobile.")

What I am arguing, then, is that the very expansive, adventurous character of art, its ever-present changes and novel creations, makes it logically impossible to ensure any set of defining properties. We can, of course, choose to close the concept. But to do this with "art" or "tragedy" or "portraiture," etc., is ludicrous since it forecloses on the very conditions of creativity in the arts.

Of course there are legitimate and serviceable closed concepts in art. But these are always those whose boundaries of conditions have been drawn for a *special* purpose. Consider the difference, for example, between "tragedy" and "(extant) Greek tragedy." The first is open and must remain so to allow for the possibility of new conditions, e.g., a play in which the hero is not noble or fallen or in which there is no hero but other elements that are like those of plays we already call "tragedy." The second is closed. The plays it can be applied to, the conditions under which it can be correctly used are all in, once the boundary, "Greek," is drawn. Here the critic can work out a theory or real definition in which he lists the common properties at least of the extant Greek tragedies. Aristotle's definition, false as it is as a theory of all the plays of Aeschylus, Sophocles, and Euripides, since it does not cover some of them, properly called "tragedies," can be interpreted as a real (albeit incorrect) definition of this closed concept; although it can also be, as it unfortunately has been, conceived as a purported real definition of "tragedy," in which case it suffers from the logical mistake of

trying to define what cannot be defined—of trying to squeeze what is an open concept into an honorific formula for a closed concept.

What is supremely important, if the critic is not to become muddled, is to get absolutely clear about the way in which he conceives his concepts; otherwise he goes from the problem of trying to define "tragedy," etc., to an arbitrary closing of the concept in terms of certain preferred conditions or characteristics which he sums up in some linguistic recommendation that he mistakenly thinks is a real definition of the open concept. Thus, many critics and estheticians ask, "What is tragedy?," choose a class of samples for which they may give a true account of its common properties, and then go on to construe this account of the chosen closed class as a true definition or theory of the whole open class of tragedy. This, I think, is the logical mechanism of most of the so-called theories of the subconcepts of art: "tragedy," "comedy," "novel," etc. In effect, this whole procedure, subtly deceptive as it is, amounts to a transformation of correct criteria for *recognizing* members of certain legitimately closed classes of works of art into recommended criteria for *evaluating* any putative member of the class.

The primary task of esthetics is not to seek a theory but to elucidate the concept of art. Specifically, it is to describe the conditions under which we employ the concept correctly. Definition, reconstruction, patterns of analysis are out of place here since they distort and add nothing to our understanding of art. What, then, is the logic of "X is a work of art"?

As we actually use the concept, "Art" is both descriptive (like "chair") and evaluative (like "good"); i.e., we sometimes say, "This is a work of art," to describe something and we sometimes say it to evaluate something. Neither use surprises anyone.

What, first, is the logic of "X is a work

of art," when it is a descriptive utterance? What are the conditions under which we would be making such an utterance correctly? There are no necessary and sufficient conditions but there are the strands of similarity conditions, i.e., bundles of properties, none of which need be present but most of which are, when we describe things as works of art. I shall call these the "criteria of recognition" of works of art. All of these have served as the defining criteria of the individual traditional theories of art; so we are already familiar with them. Thus, mostly, when we describe something as a work of art, we do so under the conditions of there being present some sort of artifact, made by human skill, ingenuity, and imagination, which embodies in its sensuous, public medium—stone, wood, sounds, words, etc.—certain distinguishable elements and relations. Special theorists would add conditions like satisfaction of wishes, objectification or expression of emotion, some act of empathy, and so on; but these latter conditions seem to be quite adventitious, present to some but not to other spectators when things are described as works of art. "X is a work of art and contains *no* emotion, expression, act of empathy, satisfaction, etc.," is perfectly good sense and may frequently be true. "X is a work of art and . . . was made by no one," or . . . "exists only in the mind and not in any publicly observable thing," or . . . "was made by accident when he spilled the paint on the canvas," in each case of which a normal condition is denied, are also sensible and capable of being true in certain circumstances. None of the criteria of recognition is a defining one, either necessary or sufficient, because we can sometimes assert of something that it is a work of art and go on to deny any one of these conditions, even the one which has traditionally been taken to be basic, namely, that of being an artifact: Consider, "This piece of driftwood is a lovely piece of sculpture." Thus, to say

of anything that it is a work of art is to commit oneself to the presence of *some* of these conditions. One would scarcely describe X as a work of art if X were not an artifact, or a collection of elements sensuously presented in a medium, or a product of human skill, and so on. If none of the conditions were present, if there were no criteria present for recognizing something as a work of art, we would not describe it as one. But, even so, no one of these or any collection of them is either necessary or sufficient.

The elucidation of the descriptive use of "Art" creates little difficulty. But the elucidation of the evaluative use does. For many, especially theorists, "This is a work of art" does more than describe; it also praises. Its conditions of utterance, therefore, include certain preferred properties or characteristics of art. I shall call these "criteria of evaluation." Consider a typical example of this evaluative use, the view according to which to say of something that it is a work of art is to imply that it is a *successful* harmonization of elements. Many of the honorific definitions of art and its sub-concepts are of this form. What is at stake here is that "Art" is construed as an evaluative term which is either identified with its criterion or justified in terms of it. "Art" is defined in terms of its evaluative property, e.g., successful harmonization. On such a view, to say "X is a work of art" is (1) to say something which is taken *to mean* "X is a successful harmonization" (e.g., "Art *is* significant form") or (2) to say something praiseworthy *on the basis* of its successful harmonization. Theorists are never clear whether it is (1) or (2) which is being put forward. Most of them, concerned as they are with this evaluative use, formulate (2), i.e., that feature of art that *makes* it art in the praise-sense, and then go on to state (1), i.e., the definition of "Art" in terms of its art-making feature. And this is clearly to confuse the conditions under which we say something evaluatively with the meaning of what we say. "This is a work of art," said evaluatively, cannot mean "This is a successful harmonization of elements"—except by stipulation—but at most is said in virtue of the art-making property, which is taken as a (the) criterion of "Art," when "Art" is employed to assess. "This is a work of art," used evaluatively, serves to praise and not to affirm the reason why it is said.

The evaluative use of "Art," although distinct from the conditions of its use, relates in a very intimate way to these conditions. For, in every instance of "This is a work of art" (used to praise), what happens is that the criterion of evaluation (e.g., successful harmonization) for the employment of the concept of art is converted into a criterion of recognition. This is why, on its evaluative use, "This is a work of art" implies "This has P," where "P" is some chosen art-making property. Thus, if one chooses to employ "Art" evaluatively, as many do, so that "This is a work of art and not (esthetically) good" makes no sense, he uses "Art" in such a way that he refuses to *call* anything a work of art unless it embodies his criterion of excellence.

There is nothing wrong with the evaluative use; in fact, there is good reason for using "Art" to praise. But what cannot be maintained is that theories of the evaluative use of "Art" are true and real definitions of the necessary and sufficient properties of art. Instead they are honorific definitions, pure and simple, in which "Art" has been redefined in terms of chosen criteria.

But what makes them—these honorific definitions—so supremely valuable is not their disguised linguistic recommendations; rather it is the *debates* over the reasons for changing the criteria of the concept of art which are built into the definitions. In each of the great theories of art, whether correctly understood as honorific definitions or incorrectly accepted as real definitions,

what is of the utmost importance are the reasons proffered in the argument for the respective theory, that is, the reasons given for the chosen or preferred criterion of excellence and evaluation. It is this perennial debate over these criteria of evaluation which makes the history of esthetic theory the important study it is. The value of each of the theories resides in its attempt to state and to justify certain criteria which are either neglected or distorted by previous theories. Look at the Bell-Fry theory again. Of course, "Art is significant form" cannot be accepted as a true, real definition of art; and most certainly it actually functions in their esthetics as a redefinition of art in terms of the chosen condition of significant form. But what gives it its esthetic importance is what lies behind the formula: In an age in which literary and representational elements have become paramount in painting, *return* to the plastic ones since these are indigenous to painting. Thus, the role of the theory is not to define anything but to use the definitional form, almost epigrammatically, to pin-point a crucial recommendation to turn our attention once again to the plastic elements in painting.

Once we, as philosophers, understand this distinction between the formula and what lies behind it, it behooves us to deal generously with the traditional theories of art; because incorporated in every one of them is a debate over and argument for emphasizing or centering upon some particular feature of art which has been neglected or perverted. If we take the esthetic theories literally, as we have seen, they all fail; but if we reconstrue them, in terms of their function and point, as serious and argued-for recommendations to concentrate on certain criteria of excellence in art, we shall see that esthetic theory is far from worthless. Indeed, it becomes as central as anything in esthetics, in our understanding of art, for it teaches us what to look for and how to look at it in art. What is central and must be articulated in all the theories are their debates over the reasons for excellence in art —debates over emotional depth, profound truths, natural beauty, exactitude, freshness of treatment, and so on, as criteria of evaluation—the whole of which converges on the perennial problem of what makes a work of art good. To understand the role of esthetic theory is not to conceive it as definition, logically doomed to failure, but to read it as summaries of seriously made recommendations to attend in certain ways to certain features of art.

6 / SOCIAL PHILOSOPHY

Another area in which the puzzlement leading to metaphysical or absurd theories easily arises is social thought. Professor Weldon finds that the chief reason for this puzzlement is the commonly held but erroneous belief that words "have" meanings corresponding to objects; a subsequent further error is in believing that by the analysis of words one can come to know objects. Words do not have meanings, however; rather, they have uses. Or, to put it another way, to know the meaning of a term is to know how to use it. Thus accepting Wittgenstein's view of meaning, Weldon explores political concepts like state and democracy. His study, as do the preceding selections, covers the rules and conditions for the application of such concepts. Once these relations are seen, no reference in political theory to transcendent meanings or principles is necessary.

THE VOCABULARY OF POLITICS

T. D. Weldon (1896-   )

The central doctrine taken for granted by all classical [political] theorists is . . . that words have meanings in the same sort of sense as that in which children have parents. Thus, if little Willie was deposited in a telephone booth at an early age, nobody may know who his parents are, but it is certain that he had parents, and it is possible to start an enquiry with a view to discovering their identity. This may well be wholly or partially unsuccessful. The evidence may be lost or the detectives may not be clever enough to discover it or to see the

relevance of it. Nevertheless this is the kind of enquiry we know well enough how to conduct, and so it is reasonable to suppose that, if words and especially nouns always have meanings, we should, if we are pertinacious and fairly clever, usually be able to unearth those meanings.

But why should this supposition have been made? To answer this would require an extensive enquiry into anthropology since the supposition was by no means confined to the Greeks but was very widely spread. It is common knowledge that in the early stages of civilization names tended to have magical significance. One acquired power over a person by ferreting out his true name, earthly and heavenly names were different, Lohengrin and other heroes

The selection is from T. D. Weldon, *The Vocabulary of Politics* (Harmondsworth: Penguin Books, Ltd., 1953), pp. 17-20, 46-50, and 97-101. Used by permission of the publisher.

were forbidden to disclose their names, and the true names of gods were not to be spoken except by priests as part of a ritual. In this sort of atmosphere (and early Greek philosophy was very closely connected with religious mysticism) it is natural enough to ask for the true name of a person or a thing, and it is not difficult to reverse the order of the enquiry. One may know a name or a title, but not the person to whom it refers.

Whatever may have been the psychological origin of this type of belief, it is now clear that it was erroneous. Admittedly it was valuable as a starting point since it directed attention to the importance of language as an object of study and so gave logical analysis a beginning. It was dangerously misleading because it led insensibly to the further assumption that the analysis of words and logical forms could by itself provide information about matter of fact. Thinking by itself without any observation or consideration of instances seemed capable of finding out the true meanings of words, and this process in some indefinable way was held to give information as to the nature and relations of the things to which words referred. The application of this to political enquiries is almost painfully evident. It is that we must begin by asking for the meanings of "justice," "freedom," "authority," and similar words, and that, when we have discovered what these meanings are, we shall be qualified to pronounce on whether Communism is to be praised or condemned.

The enquiry, however, is doomed to sterility because words do not have meanings in the required sense at all; they simply have uses. There is nothing divine or magical about "justice" or "freedom"; they are only part of the verbal apparatus we make use of for describing and criticizing certain types of human conduct. They are not the names of Ideas or archetypes of which honest transactions and fearless letters to the newspapers are more or less

imperfect copies or expressions, for they are not the names of anything. To know their meaning is to know how to use them correctly, that is, in such a way as to be generally intelligible, in ordinary and technical discourse, and there is nothing more lurking behind them which you might discover if only you had some special qualifications as a member of the philosophical C.I.D. This is a very dogmatic statement. I shall do something to elucidate and to justify it in what follows, but those who rightly feel the need for further discussion must pursue the question in books on logic.

This radical misunderstanding as to the meanings of words has given rise to a whole family of philosophical illusions which make up the greater part of what is known as "metaphysics." . . .

The confident and uncritical way in which "the State" is used by many modern writers suggests that "State" is the same sort of word as "water," "mountain," or "sun." It is easy to see that this is a mistake. There is no reason to doubt that when Cicero wrote *"aqua," "mons,"* or *"sol,"* he was referring to things indistinguishable for practical purposes from those to which we refer by "water," "mountain," and "sun." But "State" is not in the same way equivalent to *"res publica"* or *"civitas."* Human institutions, as we have noted in considering "own" and "owe," change more rapidly and radically than physical objects.

"State" as might be expected on historical grounds is not even a very old word in English. It dates, as far as the usage in which we are interested is concerned, only from the middle of the sixteenth century. It then sometimes stands for what we now call "the Government" or "the rulers," the modern Marxist use as will appear later, and sometimes, less precisely, it is roughly equivalent to "commonwealth" or "polity." In the second of these uses it inherits a good many associations, some of them mystical or supernatural from the Greek *"Polis"* and

"Politeia" as well as from the Roman *"Res publica"* and the medieval "Empire" and "Monarchy." It is only in the seventeenth and eighteenth centuries that it acquires technical or semi-technical status as a legal and political term.

These are elementary points, but it is wise to bear them in mind since much of the apparent obscurity and real confusion involved in questions about the State occur only because they are neglected in the search for real meanings.

Today, however, we all know how to use "the State" in ordinary speech. The U.S.S.R. is certainly a State. So is Switzerland. Surrey is certainly not a State. Nor is U.N.O. But there are cases in which we are liable to become uncertain. Is Liechtenstein a State? or New York? There is nothing mystifying about this uncertainty, and we know how to remove it. International lawyers have created a technical usage for "State" and have elaborated tests for deciding whether a particular association belongs to this class. "Is Liechtenstein a State?" is just like "Is the whale a fish?" The correct answer in both cases is to be found in books of reference. What then does it mean to say "I don't think Liechtenstein is really a State" or "I don't think the whale is really a fish"? I may mean either of two things. (1) That it does not satisfy the tests. The definition says that the term "State" or "fish" should be used if and only if certain tests are passed. In the case of "State" the lawyers say these are independence, geographical definition, some standards of organization and so on, and it may be that Liechtenstein fails to pass some of them. In the case of "fish" the biologists say they are coldness of blood and so on, and the whale does fail to pass some of these. Provided the technical terms are devised with reasonable skill and care, there is no difficulty in this sort of case. If they are not, what is needed is a conference of experts or a recognized court of some kind to settle the matter. (2)

Verbal usage may not be in dispute, but I may be suggesting that it is inconvenient or misleading. I may agree that Liechtenstein passes the test but consider that it differs from the U.S.S.R. in such important ways that it is confusing to locate both of them in the same class. This is the same sort of thing as to say "A tortoise isn't really an insect, even though it may be classified in that way by the Railway Company." "State" then has a vague but convenient ordinary use and a precise, technical, legal use. Has it any other use which can be called philosophical? I do not think it has. With some reservation which will appear when the idealist theory of the State is under discussion it seems to me that all the relevant phenomena can be fully described without further complication.

There are, however, two points which need to be cleared up if this account is to be acceptable. First there are what I have called the mystical overtones. It is undeniable that from the days of Greece onwards States have tended to be personified. Their names have often been linked with those of deities and their rulers have been credited with divine or semi-divine sanctity and power. It remained for some writers in the nineteenth and twentieth centuries to deify the State itself, that is to pretend that "Britain" or "Gross-Deutschland" is the name of a kind of supernatural person with superhuman attributes. This pretense was dangerously misleading and in so far as it is still an ingredient in the popular use of "the State" it should be abandoned in the same way that the magical ingredients in "life," "force," and "matter" have now been abandoned. Even as metaphors they are unsafe and we are much better off without them.

The second point is more important. It is often argued that "State" is not merely a term standing for one type of association but also that this one type of association is unique and not at all like cricket clubs, trade unions, or even Churches. Many reasons have been advanced for maintaining this, but only three of them have sufficient plausibility to deserve attention. The first is that of involuntary membership. It is argued that if I do not like my cricket club or my trade union or even my Church, I can resign from it and join a different one. But I cannot escape from my State in this way. There seems to me to be very little in this. At most there is a difference of degree, and even this is difficult to establish at all firmly. Resigning from any institution involves some inconvenience. This is usually minimal in cricket clubs and very considerable in trade unions. In the case of Churches it has sometimes been lethal. But to say that one cannot escape from one's State is simply untrue. Normally emigration is possible, though it is sometimes so difficult as to be practically out of the question. But there is always suicide, and it is not in these days so very uncommon.

The second argument which is also unconvincing is that the State is concerned with the whole of our lives whereas other associations concern only part of them. But even if this is true, does it matter? It is not true except in a rather trivial sense. In modern times we tend to be bothered a good deal by State regulations. People do sometimes shoot themselves to avoid filling in any more forms for the Ministry of Agriculture. They are not, however, a very substantial minority and most of us are little worried by the omnipresence of the State. It is equally trivial to say that the State makes culture or "the good life" possible. Perhaps it is more important in this respect than other types of association, but this is highly dubitable. It looks plausible only if "State" is defined so widely as to embrace all types of association. Finally it may be maintained that the State is qualitatively different or of a different order from other types of association since it determines their legality and therefore makes it possible for

them to exist at all. This has force only if we fail to distinguish between legal and factual existence. There is a sense in which the Roman Catholic Church or the Communist Party could be abolished in this country by legislation, but there is another and much more important one in which they could not. The legal non-existence of the Communist Party in Tsarist Russia did not prevent the Bolshevist Revolution of 1917.

In fact I think these poor reasons are adduced because of an unconscious addiction to the mystical residue. It is felt that "State" ought to designate something different in kind from cricket clubs and trade unions. Hence an effort is made to show that Britain and the rest really do have something which other types of association do not have. The attempt seems to me to be unnecessary and unsuccessful.

It is sometimes suggested however that while "State" is the word for one association among others, "Society" or "the Community" stand for something different. It is in this something that we find wholes which are more than the sums of their parts (whatever that is supposed to mean) superpersons, transcendent unities, and so on. There really is a difference between "State" and "Society," but it is not philosophically important and not at all what the exponents of Social Solidarity would like it to be. "Society" is used to stand for something less organized than an association. We talk more here of customs, habits, and traditions and less of rights, laws, and obligations. The position is not yet formalized and the relations between individuals are not clearly defined. But there is no hard and fast line to be drawn, as is indicated by the fact that in ordinary speech "association" and "society" are interchangeable words. It is perhaps convenient to make a technical distinction of this kind between less and more highly organized groups of people, but there seems to be nothing more to it than that.

We do not need the fiction of a social contract to explain the transition from society to State. . . .

The metaphysical foundations of democracy then are roughly these: (1) human beings as such ought to be respected because they are endowed with Reason; (2) they are bound only by laws of their own making, and to be bound by such laws is to be free; (3) Reason provides them with a test by which they can satisfy themselves of the appropriateness or otherwise of proposed or actual laws; (4) the test is whether these laws would be acceptable to a community of completely rational beings. I do not suggest that democratic writers and thinkers have all been as metaphysical as that, but I believe that their proofs will not work unless these or very similar premises are accepted.

What we really want to know however is what is the use of all this. Suppose we could accept the premises and the reasonings, should we be any better off? I think that we should not. The objection to this sort of argument is not merely that it depends for its force on the fallacious assumptions considered in Chapter 2,[1] but that the conclusions to which it leads are either vacuous or highly disputable and not at all self-evident. The position is not that the statements which go to make up the fundamental principles of democracy are false or that the basic rules of democratic legislation are bad. It is that we are mistaken in supposing that what we have to do with here are statements or rules at all. Admittedly "All men are created free and equal" looks like a statement and "Men are always to be treated as ends and never as means" looks like the formulation of a rule. It is natural to suppose therefore that we have here fundamental rules from which others can

[1 Weldon here refers to errors arising from the misuse of language, some of which are discussed in the preceding part of the selection. *Ed.*]

be deduced. If this were so "foundations" would be a suitable word for describing them. But it is not so. Nothing follows from these high abstractions, or if you like anything does. They are not concerned with actual people but with "real" or metaphysical ones. By themselves they tell us nothing whatever about how to deal with prisoners of war, criminals, or taxi-drivers. We can derive no actual law from them and appraise no actual law by means of them. That is what I mean by saying that as foundations they are useless. They do not and cannot do what they purport to do, that is, serve as axioms from which practical conclusions can be derived.

Their function is quite a different one. They are much more like the model Bye-Laws which are issued by the Home Office to guide subordinate legislative bodies, or like forms which require to be filled in before they give any information. It is easy to see that this is in fact the way in which they work. Take for example the well-known clause in the XIVth Amendment to the Constitution of the United States, "nor shall any State deprive any person of life, liberty, or property, without due process of law, nor deny to any person within its jurisdiction the equal protection of its laws." This looks like, and is often taken as being, the statement of a fundamental democratic principle. But what exactly does it mean? As it stands the answer is "Nothing." It is a formula which has no application until the variables which it contains are replaced by actual values. We do not even know what kind of values it will accept. When it was passed nobody supposed that it protected legal persons as well as actual ones. It was not intended to make the world safe for big corporations nor need it have done so. But the Supreme Court ruled that it did, i. e., that the names of corporations could be used to fill one of the blanks.

So these basic principles do not, as their formulators hoped they would, make arbitrariness impossible. They simply transfer it from the monarch to whatever body is empowered to interpret them. And "interpret" means "decide how the blanks can be filled in." There are not two types of law, namely fundamental law and derived or positive law, of which the second is a copy, reflection, or expression of the first. The mistake which is made by those who have supposed that there are may be illustrated in this way.

There are rules of Association Football, Rugby Football, Northern League, American Football, Seven-a-side, and perhaps of other kinds of football as well. It would be possible to take all these and construct a sort of schema or form which would cover all of them if the blanks in it were suitably filled up. One might even verbalize the result, though it would be rather awkward to do, and say "Football is played by two sides, each consisting of a specified number of players on a field of limited dimensions" and so on. The result might be described as the fundamental rules of football, but this would not be a happy description, since you could not discover the laws of any actual game by reasoning from it. You would however gain some information about the use of the word "football," and be able say with confidence when taken to watch a game of cricket "They are not playing football." That is about as much as can be done with the fundamental principles of democracy. A great many very dubious proceedings can easily be reconciled with them by means of suitable definitions. But there does come a point at which one can say with considerable confidence "I don't think *that* régime could be described as democratic in the ordinary meaning of the term."

It must be repeated however that by no means all writers about democracy have made this mistake. Many have recognized that it is right to obey the law on nearly all occasions and wrong to torture people in concentration camps. And they have avoided asking the further and mistaken questions "Why is it wrong?" "What makes it wrong?" It is only when these questions are asked and no straightforward factual answers to them are discoverable that the plunge into democratic metaphysics is taken and found in the end to be of no assistance. It is pointless to invent an axiom that men ought always to be treated as ends in themselves in order to demonstrate the truth of "It was wicked to send people to Belsen or Buchenwald," for this is not the sort of statement which requires or admits of demonstration.

Yet when all is said and done it may fairly be claimed that the metaphysics of democracy unlike those of the rival ideologies has done a great deal more good than harm. Although it proves nothing, the belief that it does prove something has at least tended to encourage humane rather than brutal conduct. It is true that human beings are very important, but they are not important because they are possessed of Reason or because God created them or because of anything else. "Because" is out of place in this context. The chief reason why philosophers have tried so hard to insert it is that they have been alarmed by a demon called "Subjectivism" and have sought to exorcise it in this way; but . . . this demon is illusory, and if he were not he could not be disposed of by any metaphysical argument about foundations. Unfortunately the alternative foundations of politics which will now be considered, though they are theoretically as valueless, have been practically far more deleterious than any variety of the democratic mythology has ever been.

It may be said that these criticisms of democratic foundations are out of date. They are relevant to the theories of the eighteenth and early nineteenth centuries, but nobody nowadays talks about the rights of man or the supremacy of Reason. In modern terminology the foundations of democracy are representative government, universal suffrage, social equality, and, of course, the Rule of Law. The precise meaning of such claims as this is not very clear. They may perhaps be regarded as the formulation of tests by which we can decide whether the term "democracy" is being correctly used or not, and if this is the case they are only of linguistic interest. But if more than this is meant, the arguments already advanced against the earlier state-

ments of democratic foundations still apply to them. They are either vacuous or, if they are made specific by being given a definite context (England or the U.S.S.R. in 1953), their rationality or advisability is a matter of discussion and controversy in which empirical arguments are highly relevant. There is then nothing sacrosanct about them and it is inappropriate to describe them as foundations.

7 / PHILOSOPHY OF SCIENCE

A frequent puzzle to the young student of science is how the scientific world about which he is learning is related to the everyday world of his experience. Often this puzzle leads him to make a distinction between the two worlds, one real, the other appearance. The removal of the puzzle is Professor Ryle's concern in the following selection. He warns us first about the words "science" and "world," in a sense deflating them and cautioning us in our use of them. He then proceeds to elucidate and clarify the logical pattern that gives rise to the problem of "two worlds," doing so through an extended analogy between science and an auditor's balance sheet. The auditor, Ryle says, gives information by exhibiting relations among things, not by giving a rival description of them. So too, the scientist does not give a rival description of things such as would make his world real and the everyday world appearance. Rather, the scientist, the poet, and the theologian produce compatible pictures of the same "world"—even though they have different businesses to perform—and they do not give conflicting answers to the same questions. This point, Ryle concludes, is likely to be forgotten if we fail to note the "smothering" effect of words like depict, describe, and explain.

SCIENCE AND ORDINARY LANGUAGE

Gilbert Ryle (1900-   )

We often worry ourselves about the relations between what we call "the world of science" and "the world of real life" or "the world of common sense." Sometimes we are even encouraged to worry about the rela-

The selection is from Gilbert Ryle, *Dilemmas,* Chapter V, "The World of Science and the Everyday World" (Cambridge: University Press, 1954), pp. 68-81, with omissions. Used by permission of the publisher.

tions between "the desk of physics" and the desk on which we write.

When we are in a certain intellectual mood, we seem to find clashes between the things that scientists tell us about our furniture, clothes and limbs and the things that we tell about them. We are apt to express these felt rivalries by saying that the world whose parts and members are described by scientists is different from the world whose parts and members we describe ourselves, and yet, since there can be only one world, one of these seeming worlds must be a dummy-world. Moreover, as no one nowadays is hardy enough to say "Bo" to science, it must be the world that we ourselves describe which is the dummy-world. . . .

As a preface to the serious part of the argument I want to deflate two over-inflated ideas, from which derives not the cogency but some of the persuasiveness of the argument for the irreconcilability of the world of science with the everyday world. One is the idea of *science*, the other that of *world*.

(*a*) There is no such animal as "Science." There are scores of sciences. Most of these sciences are such that acquaintance-ship with them or, what is even more captivating, hearsay knowledge about them has not the slightest tendency to make us contrast their world with the everyday world. Philology is a science, but not even popularizations of its discoveries would make anyone feel that the world of philology cannot be accommodated by the world of familiar people, things and happenings. Let philologists discover everything discoverable about the structures and origins of the expressions that we use; yet their discoveries have no tendency to make us write off as mere dummies the expressions that we use and that philologists also use. The sole dividedness of mind that is induced in us by learning any of the lessons of philology is akin to that which we sometimes experience when told, say, that our old, familiar paper-weight was once an axe-head used by a prehistoric warrior. Something utterly ordinary becomes also, just for the moment, charged with history. A mere paper-weight becomes also, just for the moment, a death-dealing weapon. But that is all.

Nor do most of the other sciences give us the feeling that we live our daily lives in a bubble-world. Botanists, entomologists, meteorologists, and geologists do not seem to threaten the walls, floors and ceilings of our common dwelling-place. On the contrary, they seem to increase the quantity and improve the arrangement of its furniture. Nor even, as might be supposed, do all branches of physical science engender in us the idea that our everyday world is a dummy-world. The discoveries and theories of astronomers and astro-physicists may make us feel that the earth is very small, but only by making us feel that the heavens are very big. The gnawing suspicion that both the terrestrial and the super-terrestrial alike are merely painted stage-canvas is not begotten by even hearsay knowledge of the physics of the immense. It is not begotten, either, by hearsay knowledge of the physics of the middle-sized. The theory of the pendulum, the cannon-ball, the water-pump, the fulcrum, the balloon and the steam-engine does not by itself drive us to vote between the everyday world and the so-called world of science. Even the comparatively minute can be accommodated by us without theoretical heart-searchings in our everyday world. Pollen-grains, frost-crystals and bacteria, though revealed only through the microscope, do not by themselves make us doubt whether middle-sized and immense things may not belong where rainbows and mirages or even dreams belong. We always knew that there were things too small to be seen with the naked eye; the magnifying-glass and the microscope have surprised us not by establishing their existence but by disclosing their variety and, in some cases, their importance.

No, there are, I think, two branches of science which, especially when in collusion with one another, produce what I may describe as the "poison-pen effect," the effect of half-persuading us that our best friends are really our worst enemies. One is the physical theory of the ultimate elements of matter; the other is that one wing of human physiology which investigates the mechanism and functioning of our organs of perception. I do not think it makes much difference to the issue whether these ultimate elements of matter are described as the Greek atomists described them or as the twentieth-century nuclear physicist describes them. Nor do I think that it makes much difference whether we consider old-fashioned guesses or recent conclusive discoveries about the mechanism of perception. The upsetting moral drawn by Epicurus, Galileo, Sydenham and Locke is precisely that drawn by Eddington, Sherrington and Russell. The fact that this upsetting moral was once drawn from a piece of speculation and is now drawn from well-established scientific theory makes no difference. The moral drawn is not a piece of good science now, and it was not a piece of bad science then.

So the so-called world of science which, we gather, has the title to replace our everyday world is, I suggest, the world not of science in general but of atomic and subatomic physics in particular, enhanced by some slightly incongruous appendages borrowed from one branch of neuro-physiology.

(*b*) The other idea which needs prefatory deflation is that of *world*. When we hear that there is a grave disparity between our everyday world and the world of science or, a little more specifically, the world of one wing of physical science, it is difficult for us to shake off the impression that there are some physicists who by dint of their experiments, calculations and theorizing have qualified themselves to tell us everything that is really important about the cosmos, whatever that may be. Where theologians used to be the people to tell us about the creation and management of the cosmos, now these physicists are the experts —for all that in the articles and books that they write for their colleagues and pupils the word "world" seldom occurs, and the grand word "cosmos," I hope, never occurs. There is some risk of a purely verbal mud-dle here. We know that a lot of people are interested in poultry and would not be surprised to find in existence a periodical called "The Poultry World." Here the word "world" is not used as theologians use it. It is a collective noun used to label together all matters pertaining to poultry-keeping. It could be paraphrased by "field" or "sphere of interest" or "province." In this use there could be no question of a vendetta between the poultry world and the Christian world, since, while "world" could be paraphrased by "cosmos" in the phrase "Christian world," it could not be so paraphrased in the other.

It is obviously quite innocuous to speak of the physicist's world, if we do so in the way in which we speak of the poultry-keeper's world or the entertainment world. We could correspondingly speak of the bacteriologist's world and the marine zoologist's world. In this use there is no connotation of cosmic authority, for the word "world" in this use does not mean "*the* world" or "the cosmos." On the contrary, it means the *department* of interests which physicists' interests constitute.

But this is not the whole story. For while there are hosts of interests, scientific, political, artistic, etc., from which the interests peculiar to physicists are distinguished, while, that is, there are hosts of provinces of interest, which are different from without being rivals of the physicist's province, there remains an important respect in which the subject matters of fundamental physical theory do comprehend or cover the subject matters of all the other natural sciences. The specimens collected by the marine biologist, though of no special interest to the physical theorist, are still, in an indirect way, specimens of what he is specially interested in. So too are the objects studied by the geologist, the mycologist and the philatelist. There is nothing that any natural scientist studies of which the truths of physics are not true; and from this it is tempting to infer that the physicist is therefore talking about everything, and so that he is, after all, talking about the cosmos. So, after all, the cosmos must be described only in his terms, and can only be misdescribed in the terms of any of these other more special sciences or, more glaringly, in theological terms, or most glaringly of all, in the terms of everyday conversation. . . .

I am now going to try to bring out the underlying logical pattern of the view that the truths of physical theory leave no room for the truths of daily life, and this I do by means of a long-drawn out analogy with which I hope you will bear for some little time. An undergraduate member of a college is one day permitted to inspect the college accounts and to discuss them with the auditor. He hears that these accounts show how the college has fared during the year. "You will find," he is told, "that all the activities of the college are represented in these columns. Undergraduates are taught, and here are the tuition-fees that they pay. Their instructors teach, and here are the stipends that they receive. Games are played, and here are the figures; so much for rent of the ground, so much for the wages of the groundsman, and so on. Even your entertainments are recorded; here is what was paid out to the butchers, grocers and fruiterers, here are the kitchen-charges, and here is what you paid in your college battels." At first the undergraduate is merely mildly interested. He allows that these columns give him a different sort of view of the life of the college from the patchwork-quilt of views that he had previously acquired from his own experiences of working in the library, playing football, dining with his friends, and the rest. But then under the influence of the auditor's grave and sober voice he suddenly begins to wonder. Here everything in the life of the college is systematically marshalled and couched in terms which, though colorless, are precise, impersonal and susceptible of conclusive checking. To every plus there corresponds an equal and opposite minus; the entries are classified; the origins and destinations of all payments are indicated. Moreover, a general conclusion is reached; the financial position of the college is exhibited and compared with its position in previous years. So is not this expert's way, perhaps, the right way in which to think of the life of the college, and the other muddled and emotionally charged ways to which he had been used the wrong ways?

At first in discomfort he wriggles and suggests "May not these accounts give us just one part of the life of the college? The chimney-sweep and the inspector of electricity-meters see their little corners of the activities of the college; but no one supposes that what they have to tell is more than a petty fragment of the whole story. Perhaps you, the auditor, are like them and see only a small part of what is going on." But the auditor rejects this suggestion. "No," he says, "here are the payments to the chimney-sweep at so much per chimney swept, and here are the payments to the Electricity Board at so much a unit. Everybody's part in the college life, including my own, is down here in figures. There is nothing departmental in the college accounts. Everything is covered. What is more, the whole system of accountancy is uniform for all colleges and is, at least in general pattern, uniform for all businesses, government departments and town councils. No speculations or hypotheses are admitted; our results are lifted above the horizons of opinion and prejudice by the sublime Principle of Double Entry. These accounts tell the objective truth about the entire life of the whole college; the stories that you tell about it to your brothers and sisters are only picturesque travesties of the audited facts. They are only dreams. Here are the realities." What is the undergraduate to reply? He cannot question the accuracy, comprehensiveness or exhaustiveness of the accounts. He cannot complain that they cover five or six sides of college life, but do not cover the other sixteen sides. All the sides that he can think of are indeed duly covered.

Perhaps he is acute enough to suspect that there has been some subtle trick played by this word "covered." The tuition he had received last term from the lecturer in Anglo-Saxon was indeed covered, yet the accounts were silent about what had been taught and the auditor betrayed no inquisitiveness about what progress the student had made. He, too, the undergraduate himself, had been covered in scores of sections of the accounts, as a recipient of an Exhibition, as a pupil of the lecturer in Anglo-Saxon and so on. He had been covered, but not characterized or mischaracterized. Nothing was said about him that would not have fitted a much taller Exhibitioner or a much less enthusiastic student of Anglo-Saxon. Nothing had been said about him personally at all. He has not been described, though he has been financially accounted for.

Take a special case. In one way the auditor is very much interested in the books that the librarian buys for the college library. They must be scrupulously accounted for, the price paid for each must be entered, the fact of the actual receipt of the book must be recorded. But in another way the auditor need not be at all interested in these books, since he need not have any idea what the books contain or whether anybody reads them. For him the book is merely what is indicated by the price mark on its jacket. For him the differences between one book and another are differences in shillings. The figures in the section devoted to library accounts do indeed cover every one of the actual books bought; yet nothing in these figures would have been different had these books been different in subject matter, language, style and binding, so long as their prices were the same. The accounts tell neither lies nor the truth about the contents of any of the books. In the reviewer's sense of "describe," they do not describe any of the books, though they scrupulously cover all of the books.

Which, now, is the real and which the bubble-book, the book read by the undergraduate or the book whose price is entered in the library-accounts? Clearly there is no answer. There are not two books, nor yet one real book, side by side with another bubble-book—the latter, queerly, being the one that is useful for examinations. There is just a book available for students, and an entry in the accounts specifying what the college paid for it. There could have been no such entry had there not been the book. There could not be a library stocked with mere book-prices; though also there could not be a well-conducted college which had a library full of books but required no library accounts to be kept.

The library used by the student is the same library as that accounted for by the accountant. What the student finds in the library is what the accountant tells the pounds, shillings and pence of. I am suggesting, you see, that it is in partially the same way that the world of the philologist, the marine-biologist, the astronomer and the housewife is the same world as that of the physicist; and what the pedestrian and the bacteriologist find in the world is what the physicist tells him about in his double-entry notation.

I do not want to press the analogy beyond a certain point. I am not arguing that a scientific theory is in all or many respects like a balance-sheet, but only that it is like a balance-sheet in one important respect, namely that the formulae of the one and the financial entries of the other are constitutionally speechless about certain sorts of matters, just because they are *ex officio* explicit about other, but connected matters. Everything that the student says about the books in the library may be true, and everything that the accountant says about them may be true. The student's information about the books is greatly unlike the accountant's, and neither is it deducible from the accountant's information, nor vice versa. Yet the student's information is covered, in an important way, by the accounts, although these are constitutionally speechless about the literary and scholarly qualities of books which are just what interest the student. The appearance of a vendetta between the different ways of describing the library is as delusive an appearance as was the appearance of a vendetta between my way of talking about my brother and the economist's way of talking about anybody's brother.[1] For though the accountant is, in some very general sense, telling the college about the books in the library, he is not, in the reviewer's sense of the word, describing or, of course, misdescribing these books at all. He is exhibiting the arithmetical relations holding during the financial year between the total bills paid to the booksellers for books and, somewhat indirectly, the total bills paid to the college for the use of those books. That there are such bills to record and, consequently, such arithmetical relations between their totals, itself logically presupposes that there are books in the library, actually bought from booksellers and actually available for reading by students. It logically presupposes that there are things of which the student's descriptions are either true or false, though these descriptions cannot be read out of the library accounts. Not only can the full history of the life of the college during the year accommodate both of these kinds of information about the books, but it could not include a page for either kind without having a page for the other. It is not a question of two rival libraries, or of two rival descriptions of one library, but of two different but

complementary ways of giving information of very different sorts about the one library. . . .

I hope that this protracted analogy has satisfied you at least that there is a genuine logical door open for us; that at least there is no general logical objection to saying that physical theory, while it covers the things that the more special sciences explore and the ordinary observer describes, still does not put up a rival description of them; and even that for it to be true in its way, there must be descriptions of these other kinds which are true in their quite different way or ways. It need not be a matter of rival worlds of which one has to be a bubble-world, nor yet a matter of different sectors or provinces of one world, such that what is true of one sector is false of the other.

In the way in which a landscape-painter paints a good or bad picture of a range of hills, the geologist does not paint a rival picture, good or bad, of those hills, though what he tells us the geology of are the same hills that the painter depicts or misdepicts. The painter is not doing bad geology and the geologist is not doing good or bad landscape painting. In the way in which the joiner tells us what a piece of furniture is like and gets his description right or wrong (no matter whether he is talking about its color, the wood it is made of, its style, carpentry or period), the nuclear physicist does not proffer a competing description, right or wrong, though what he tells us the nuclear physics of covers what the joiner describes. They are not giving conflicting answers to the same questions or to the same sort of question, though the physicist's questions are, in a rather artificial sense of "about," what the joiner gives his information about. The physicist does not mention the furniture; what he does mention are, so to speak, bills for such goods as, *inter alia,* bits of furniture.

Part of this point is sometimes expressed in this way. As the painter in oils on one

[1 Discussed earlier in the chapter. *Ed.*]

side of the mountain and the painter in water-colors on the other side of the mountain produce very different pictures, which may still be excellent pictures of the same mountain, so the nuclear physicist, the theologian, the historian, the lyric poet and the man in the street produce very different, yet compatible and even complementary pictures of one and the same "world." But this analogy is perilous. It is risky enough to say that the accountant and the reviewer both give descriptions of the same book, since in the natural sense of "describe" in which the reviewer does describe or misdescribe the book, the accountant does neither. But it is far riskier to characterize the physicist, the theologian, the historian, the poet and the man in the street as all alike producing "pictures," whether of the same object or of different objects. The highly concrete word "picture" smothers the enormous differences between the businesses of the scientist, historian, poet and theologian even worse than the relatively abstract word "description" smothers the big differences between the businesses of the accountant and the reviewer. It is just these smothered

differences which need to be brought out into the open. If the seeming feuds between science and theology or between fundamental physics and common knowledge are to be dissolved at all, their dissolution can come not from making the polite compromise that both parties are really artists of a sort working from different points of view and with different sketching materials, but only from drawing uncompromising contrasts between their businesses. To satisfy the tobacconist and the tennis-coach that there need be no professional antagonisms between them, it is not necessary or expedient to pretend that they are really fellow-workers in some joint but unobvious missionary enterprise. It is better policy to remind them how different and independent their trades actually are. Indeed, this smothering effect of using notions like *depicting, describing, explaining,* and others to cover highly disparate things reinforces other tendencies to assimilate the dissimilar and unsuspiciously to impute just those parities of reasoning, the unreality of which engenders dilemmas.

8 / PHILOSOPHY OF RELIGION

Concern for the logic of statements in all their variety naturally leads the analyst to religious statements. In the following selection the central problem is the logic of belief in divinity. Professor Wisdom begins by observing that the existence of God is not an experimental or experiential issue in the way it was in the past, for we now find explanations of nature in science. But the issue is more complicated than this. The reasonableness of religious belief is, to be sure, a question of whether there are supporting facts in nature; yet the question is partly scientific and partly metaphysical (in Wisdom's sense of a recommendation based · on attitude). Consider the problem through an analogous question, "Do flowers feel?" We would interpret the question, are flowers mindlike enough for us to apply to them the concept "feel"? Similarly, is nature "divinelike" enough for us to apply to it or use the concept "divinity"? These questions can be answered only by a decision about the application of the concepts.

Yet the religious decision is a difficult one to describe. Wisdom offers still another analogy, comparing it to a decision in law, where there may be agreement about the facts but disagreement about their significance. Disagreements about decisions have their own sort of logic: they are neither deductions nor inductions, nor are they arbitrary and irrational. The religious decision, reflecting as it does an attitude toward nature and life, expresses a connection, based on feelings, between nature and higher beings in the universe.

TALK ABOUT GOD

John Wisdom (1904-   )

1. *The existence of God is not an experimental issue in the way it was.* An atheist or agnostic might say to a theist "You still think there are spirits in the trees, nymphs in the streams, a God of the world." He might say this because he noticed the theist in time of drought pray for rain and make a sacrifice and in the morning look for rain. But disagreement about whether there are gods is now less of this experimental or betting sort than it used to be. This is due in part, if not wholly, to our better knowledge of why things happen as they do.

It is true that even in these days it is seldom that one who believes in God has no hopes or fears which an atheist has not. Few believers now expect prayer to still the waves, but some think it makes a difference to people and not merely in ways the atheist would admit. Of course with people, as opposed to waves and machines, one never knows what they won't do next, so that expecting prayer to make a difference to them is not so definite a thing as believing in its mechanical efficacy. Still, just as primitive people pray in a business-like way for rain so some people still pray for others with a real feeling of doing something to help. However, in spite of this persistence of an experimental element in some theistic

belief, it remains true that Elijah's method on Mount Carmel of settling the matter of what god or gods exist would be far less appropriate today than it was then.

2. *Belief in gods is not merely a matter of expectation of a world to come.* Someone may say "The fact that a theist no more than an atheist expects prayer to bring down fire from heaven or cure the sick does not mean that there is no difference between them as to the facts, it does not mean that the theist has no expectations different from the atheist's. For very often those who believe in God believe in another world and believe that God is there and that we shall go to that world when we die."

This is true, but I do not want to consider here expectations as to what one will see and feel after death nor what sort of reasons these logically unique expectations could have. So I want to consider those theists who do not believe in a future life, or rather, I want to consider the differences between atheists and theists in so far as these differences are not a matter of belief in a future life.

3. *What are these differences? And is it that theists are superstitious or that atheists are blind?* A child may wish to sit a while with his father and he may, when he has done what his father dislikes, fear punishment and feel distress at causing vexation, and while his father is alive he may feel sure of help when danger threatens and feel that there is sympathy for him when disaster has come. When his father is dead

---

The selection is from John Wisdom's article, "Gods," in Anthony Flew (ed.), *Essays on Logic and Language* (Oxford: Basil Blackwell and Mott, Ltd., 1951), pp. 187-206, with omissions. Used by permission of the publisher.

he will no longer expect punishment or help. Maybe for a moment an old fear will come or a cry for help escape him, but he will at once remember that this is no good now. He may feel that his father is no more until perhaps someone says to him that his father is still alive though he lives now in another world and one so far away that there is no hope of seeing him or hearing his voice again. The child may be told that nevertheless his father can see him and hear all he says. When he has been told this the child will still fear no punishment nor expect any sign of his father, but now, even more than he did when his father was alive, he will feel that his father sees him all the time and will dread distressing him and when he has done something wrong he will feel separated from his father until he has felt sorry for what he has done. Maybe when he himself comes to die he will be like a man who expects to find a friend in the strange country where he is going. But even when this is so, it is by no means all of what makes the difference between a child who believes that his father lives still in another world and one who does not.

Likewise one who believes in God may face death differently from one who does not, but there is another difference between them besides this. This other difference may still be described as belief in another world, only this belief is not a matter of expecting one thing rather than another here or hereafter, it is not a matter of a world to come but of a world that now is, though beyond our senses. . . .

4. *The question "Is belief in gods reasonable?" has more than one source.* It is clear now that in order to grasp fully the logic of belief in divine minds we need to examine the logic of belief in animal and human minds. But we cannot do that here and so for the purposes of this discussion about divine minds let us acknowledge the reasonableness of our belief in human minds without troubling ourselves about its logic.

The question of the reasonableness of belief in divine minds then becomes a matter of whether there are facts in nature which support claims about divine minds in the way facts in nature support our claims about human minds.

In this way we resolve the force behind the problem of the existence of gods into two components, one metaphysical and the same which prompts the question "Is there *ever any* behavior which gives reason to believe in *any* sort of mind?" and one which finds expression in "Are there other mind-patterns in nature beside the human and animal patterns which we can all easily detect, and are these other mind-patterns super-human?"

Such over-determination of a question syndrome is common. Thus, the puzzling questions "Do dogs think?" "Do animals feel?" are partly metaphysical puzzles and partly scientific questions. They are not purely metaphysical; for the reports of scientists about the poor performances of cats in cages and old ladies' stories about the remarkable performances of their pets are not irrelevant. But nor are these questions purely scientific; for the stories never settle them and therefore they have other sources. One other source is the metaphysical source we have already noticed, namely, the difficulty about getting behind an animal's behavior to its mind, whether it is a non-human animal or a human one.

But there's a third component in the force behind these questions, these disputes have a third source, and it is one which is important in the dispute which finds expression in the words "I believe in God," "I do not." This source comes out well if we consider the question "Do flowers feel?" Like the questions about dogs and animals this question about flowers comes partly from the difficulty we sometimes feel over inference from *any* behavior to thought or feeling and partly from ignorance as to what behavior is to be found. But these questions, as opposed to a like question about human beings, come also from hesitation as to whether the behavior in question is *enough* mind-like, that is, is it enough similar to or superior to human behavior to be called "mind-proving"? Likewise, even when we are satisfied that human behavior shows mind and even when we have learned whatever mind-suggesting things there are in nature which are not explained by human and animal minds, we may still ask "But are these things sufficiently striking to be called a mind-pattern? Can we fairly call them manifestations of a divine being?"

"The question," someone may say, "has then become merely a matter of the application of a name. And 'What's in a name?'"

5. *But the line between a question of fact and a question or decision as to the application of a name is not so simple as this way of putting things suggests.* The question "What's in a name?" is engaging because we are inclined to answer both "Nothing" and "Very much." And this "Very much" has more than one source. We might have tried to comfort Heloise by saying "It isn't that Abelard no longer loves you, for this man isn't Abelard"; we might have said to poor Mr. Tebrick in Mr. Garnet's *Lady into Fox* "But this is no longer Silvia." But if Mr. Tebrick replied "Ah, but it is!" this might come not at all from observing facts about the fox which we have not observed, but from noticing facts about the fox which we had missed, although we had in a sense observed all that Mr. Tebrick had observed. It is possible to have before one's eyes all the items of a pattern and still to miss the pattern. . . .

The line between using a name because of how we feel and because of what we have noticed isn't sharp. "A difference as to the facts," "a discovery," "a revelation," these phrases cover many things. Discoveries have been made not only by Christopher Columbus and Pasteur, but also by Tolstoy and Dostoievsky and Freud. Things are revealed to us not only by the scientists with miscroscopes, but also by the poets, the prophets, and the painters. What is so isn't merely a matter of "the facts." For sometimes when there is agreement as to the facts there is still argument as to whether defendent did or did not "exercise reasonable care," was or was not "negligent."

And though we shall need to emphasize how much "There is a God" evinces an attitude to the familiar [1] we shall find in the end that it also evinces some recognition of patterns in time easily missed and that, therefore, difference as to there being any gods is in part a difference as to what is so and therefore as to the facts, though not in the simple ways which first occurred to us.

6. *Let us now approach these same points by a different road.*

6.1. *How it is that an explanatory hypothesis, such as the existence of God, may start by being experimental and gradually become something quite different can be seen from the following story:*

Two people return to their long neglected garden and find among the weeds a few of the old plants surprisingly vigorous. One says to the other "It must be that a gardener has been coming and doing something about these plants." Upon inquiry they find that no neighbor has ever seen anyone at work in their garden. The first man says to the other "He must have worked while people slept." The other says "No, someone would have heard him and besides, anybody who cared about the plants would have kept down these weeds." The first man says "Look at the way these are arranged. There is purpose and a feeling for beauty here. I believe that someone

[1] "Persuasive Definitions," *Mind,* July, 1938, by Charles Leslie Stevenson, should be read here.

329 PHILOSOPHY OF RELIGION

comes, someone invisible to mortal eyes. I believe that the more carefully we look the more we shall find confirmation of this." They examine the garden ever so carefully and sometimes they come on new things suggesting that a gardener comes and sometimes they come on new things suggesting the contrary and even that a malicious person has been at work. Besides examining the garden carefully they also study what happens to gardens left without attention. Each learns all the other learns about this and about the garden. Consequently, when after all this, one says "I still believe a gardener comes" while the other says "I don't" their different words now reflect no difference as to what they have found in the garden, no difference as to what they would find in the garden if they looked further and no difference about how fast untended gardens fall into disorder. At this stage, in this context, the gardener hypothesis has ceased to be experimental, the difference between one who accepts and one who rejects it is now not a matter of the one expecting something the other does not expect. What is the difference between them? The one says "A gardener comes unseen and unheard. He is manifested only in his works with which we are all familiar," the other says "There is no gardener" and with this difference in what they say about the gardener goes a difference in how they feel towards the garden, in spite of the fact that neither expects anything of it which the other does not expect.

But is this the whole difference between them—that the one calls the garden by one name and feels one way towards it, while the other calls it by another name and feels in another way towards it? And if this is what the difference has become then is it any longer appropriate to ask "Which is right?" or "Which is reasonable?"

And yet surely such questions *are* appropriate when one person says to another "You still think the world's a garden and not a wilderness, and that the gardener has not forsaken it" or "You still think there are nymphs of the streams, a presence in the hills, a spirit of the world." Perhaps when a man sings "God's in His heaven" we need not take this as more than an expression of how he feels. But when Bishop Gore or Dr. Joad writes about belief in God and young men read them in order to settle their religious doubts the impression is not simply that of persons choosing exclamations with which to face nature and the "changes and chances of this mortal life." The disputants speak as if they are concerned with a matter of scientific fact, or of trans-sensual, trans-scientific and metaphysical fact, but still of fact and still a matter about which reasons for and against may be offered, although no scientific reasons in the sense of field surveys for fossils or experiments on delinquents are to the point.

6.2. *Now can an interjection have a logic?* Can the manifestation of an attitude in the utterance of a word, in the application of a name, have a logic? When all the facts are known how can there still be a question of fact? How can there still be a question? Surely as Hume says ". . . after every circumstance, every relation is known, the understanding has no further room to operate"?[2]

6.3. When the madness of these questions leaves us for a moment *we can all easily recollect disputes which though they cannot be settled by experiment are yet disputes in which one party may be right and the other wrong* and in which both parties may offer reasons and the one better reasons than the other. *This may happen in pure and applied mathematics and logic.* Two accountants or two engineers provided with the same data may reach different results and this difference is resolved not by collecting further data but by going over the calculations again. Such differences indeed

---

[2] Hume, *An Enquiry concerning the Principles of Morals.* Appendix I.

share with differences as to what will win a race, the honor of being among the most "settlable" disputes in the language.

6.4. *But it won't do to describe the theistic issue as one settlable by such calculation,* or as one about what can be deduced in this *vertical* fashion from the facts we know. No doubt dispute about God has sometimes, perhaps especially in medieval times, been carried on in this fashion. But nowadays it is not and we must look for some other analogy, some other case in which a dispute is settled but not by experiment.

6.5. *In courts of law* it sometimes happens that opposing counsel are agreed as to the facts and are not trying to settle a question of further fact, are not trying to settle whether the man who admittedly had quarrelled with the deceased did or did not murder him, but are concerned with whether Mr. A who admittedly handed his long-trusted clerk signed blank cheques did or did not exercise reasonable care, whether a ledger is or is not a document, whether a certain body was or was not a public authority.

In such cases we notice that the process of argument is not a *chain* of demonstrative reasoning. It is a presenting and re-presenting of those features of the case which *severally co-operate* in favor of the conclusion, in favor of saying what the reasoner wishes said, in favor of calling the situation by the name by which he wishes to call it. The reasons are like the legs of a chair, not the links of a chain. Consequently although the discussion is *a priori* and the steps are not a matter of experience, the procedure resembles scientific argument in that the reasoning is not *vertically* extensive but *horizontally* extensive —it is a matter of the cumulative effect of several independent premises, not of the repeated transformation of one or two. And because the premises are severally inconclusive the process of deciding the issue

becomes a matter of weighing the cumulative effect of one group of severally inconclusive items against the cumulative effect of another group of severally inconclusive items, and thus lends itself to description in terms of conflicting "probabilities." This encourages the feeling that the issue is one of fact—that it is a matter of guessing from the premises at a further fact, at what is to come. But this is a muddle. *The dispute does not cease to be* a priori *because it is a matter of the cumulative effect of severally inconclusive premises.* The logic of the dispute is not that of a chain of deductive reasoning as in a mathematic calculation. But nor is it a matter of collecting from several inconclusive items of information an expectation as to something further, as when a doctor from a patient's symptoms guesses at what is wrong, or a detective from many clues guesses the criminal. It has its own sort of logic and its own sort of end—the solution of the question at issue is a decision, a ruling by the judge. But it is not an arbitrary decision though the rational connections are neither quite like those in vertical deductions nor like those in inductions in which from many signs we guess at what is to come; and though the decision manifests itself in the application of a name it is no more merely the application of a name than is the pinning on of a medal merely the pinning on of a bit of metal. Whether a lion with stripes is a tiger or a lion is, if you like, merely a matter of the application of a name. Whether Mr. So-and-So of whose conduct we have so complete a record did or did not exercise reasonable care is not merely a matter of the application of a name or, if we choose to say it is, then we must remember that with this name a game is lost and won and a game with very heavy stakes. With the judges' choice of a name for the facts goes an attitude, and the declaration, the ruling, is an exclamation evincing that attitude. But *it is an exclama-*

tion which not only has a purpose but also has a logic, a logic surprisingly like that of "futile," "deplorable," "graceful," "grand," "divine.". . .

6.7. *And if we say as we did at the beginning that when a difference as to the existence of a God is not one as to future happenings then it is not experimental and therefore not as to the facts, we must not forthwith assume that there is no right and wrong about it,* no rationality or irrationality, no appropriateness or inappropriateness, no procedure which tends to settle it, *nor even that this procedure is in no sense a discovery of new facts.* After all even in science this is not so. Our two gardeners even when they had reached the stage when neither expected any experimental result which the other did not, might yet have continued the dispute, each presenting and representing the features of the garden favoring his hypothesis, that is, fitting his model for describing the accepted fact; each emphasizing the pattern he wishes to emphasize. True, in science, there is seldom or never a pure instance of this sort of dispute, for nearly always with difference of hypothesis goes some difference of expectation as to the facts. But scientists argue about rival hypotheses with a vigor which is not exactly proportioned to difference in expectations of experimental results.

The difference as to whether a God exists involves our feelings more than most scientific disputes and in this respect is more like a difference as to whether there is beauty in a thing.

7. *The connecting technique.* Let us consider again the technique used in revealing or proving beauty, in removing a blindness, in inducing an attitude which is lacking, in reducing a reaction that is inappropriate. Besides running over in a special way the features of the picture, tracing the rhythms, making sure that this and that are not only seen but noticed, and their relation to each other—besides all this—

there are other things we can do to justify our attitude and alter that of the man who cannot see. For features of the picture may be brought out by setting beside it other pictures; just as the merits of an argument may be brought out, proved, by setting beside it other arguments, in which striking but irrelevant features of the original are changed and relevant features emphasized; just as the merits and demerits of a line of action may be brought out by setting beside it other actions. . . .

Imagine that a man picks up some flowers that lie half withered on a table and gently puts them in water. Another man says to him "You believe flowers feel." He says this although he knows that the man who helps the flowers doesn't expect anything of them which he himself doesn't expect; for he himself expects the flowers to be "refreshed" and to be easily hurt, injured, I mean, by rough handling, while the man who puts them in water does not expect them to whisper "Thank you." The Skeptic says "You believe flowers feel" because something about the way the other man lifts the flowers and puts them in water suggests an attitude to the flowers which he feels inappropriate although perhaps he would not feel it inappropriate to butterflies. He feels that this attitude to flowers is somewhat crazy *just as it is sometimes felt that a lover's attitude is somewhat crazy even when this is not a matter of his having false hopes about how the person he is in love with will act.* It is often said in such cases that reasoning is useless. But the very person who says this feels that the lover's attitude is crazy, is inappropriate like some dreads and hatreds, such as some horrors of enclosed places. And often one who says "It is useless to reason" proceeds at once to reason with the lover, nor is this reasoning always quite without effect. We may draw the lover's attention to certain things done by her he is in love with and trace for him a path to these from things done by others at other times which have disgusted and infuriated him. And by this means we may weaken his admiration and confidence, make him feel it unjustified and arouse his suspicion and contempt and make him feel our suspicion and contempt reasonable. It is possible, of course, that he has already noticed the analogies, the connections, we point out and that he has accepted them—that is, he has not denied them nor passed them off. He has recognized them and they have altered his attitude, altered his love, but he still loves. We then feel that perhaps it is we who are blind and cannot see what he can see.

8. *Connecting and disconnecting.* But before we confess ourselves thus inadequate there are other fires his admiration must pass through. For when a man has an attitude which it seems to us he should not have or lacks one which it seems to us he should have then, not only do we suspect that he is not influenced by connections which we feel should influence him and draw his attention to these, but also we suspect he is influenced by connections which should not influence him and draw his attention to these. It may, for a moment, seem strange that we should draw his attention to connections which we feel should not influence him, and which, since they do influence him, he has in a sense already noticed. But we do—such is our confidence in "the light of reason."

Sometimes the power of these connections comes mainly from a man's mismanagement of the language he is using. This is what happens in the Monte Carlo fallacy, where by mismanaging the laws of chance a man passes from noticing that a certain color or number has not turned up for a long while to an improper confidence that now it soon will turn up. In such cases our showing up of the false connections is a process we call "explaining a fallacy in reasoning." To remove fallacies in reasoning we urge a man to call a spade a spade, ask him what he means by "the State" and

having pointed out ambiguities and vaguenesses ask him to reconsider the steps in his argument.

9. *Unspoken connections. Usually, however, wrongheadedness or wrongheartedness in a situation, blindness to what is there or seeing what is not, does not arise merely from mismanagement of language but is more due to connections which are not mishandled in language, for the reason that they are not put into language at all.* And often these misconnections too, weaken in the light of reason, if only we can guess where they lie and turn it on them. In so far as these connections are not presented in language the process of removing their power is not a process of correcting the mismanagement of language. But it is still akin to such a process; for though it is not a process of setting out fairly what has been set out unfairly, it is a process of setting out fairly what has not been set out at all. And we must remember that the line between connections ill-presented or half-presented in language and connections operative but not presented in language, or only hinted at, is not a sharp one.

Whether or not we call the process of showing up these connections "reasoning to remove bad unconscious reasoning" or not, it is certain that in order to settle in ourselves what weight we shall attach to someone's confidence or attitude we not only ask him for his reasons but also look for unconscious reasons both good and bad; that is, for reasons which he can't put into words, isn't explicitly aware of, is hardly aware of, isn't aware of at all—perhaps it's long experience which he *doesn't* recall which lets him know a squall is coming, perhaps it's old experience which he *can't* recall which makes the cake in the tea mean so much and makes Odette so fascinating.[3]

---

[3] Proust, *Swann's Way*, Vol. I, p. 58, Vol. II. Phoenix Edition.

I am well aware of the distinction between the question "What reasons are there for the belief that S is P?" and the question "What are the sources of beliefs that S is P?" There are cases where investigation of the rationality of a claim which certain persons make is done with very little inquiry into why they say what they do, into the causes of their beliefs. This is so when we have very definite ideas about what is really logically relevant to their claim and what is not. Offered a mathematical theorem we ask for the proof; offered the generalization that parental discord causes crime we ask for the correlation co-efficients. But even in this last case, if we fancy that only the figures are reasons we underestimate the complexity of the logic of our conclusion; and yet it is difficult to describe the other features of the evidence which have weight and there is apt to be disagreement about the weight they should have. In criticizing other conclusions and especially conclusions which are largely the expression of an attitude, we have not only to ascertain what reasons there are for them but also to decide what things are reasons and how much. This latter process of sifting reasons from causes is part of the critical process for every belief, but in some spheres it has been done pretty fully already. In these spheres we don't need to examine the actual processes to belief and distil from them a logic. But in other spheres this remains to be done. Even in science or on the stock exchange or in ordinary life we sometimes hesitate to condemn a belief or a hunch merely because those who believe it cannot offer the sort of reasons we had hoped for. . . .

10. *Now what happens, what should happen, when we inquire in this way into the reasonableness, the propriety of belief in gods?* The answer is: A double and opposite-phased change. Wordsworth writes:

. . . And I have felt
A presence that disturbs me with the joy

Of elevated thoughts; a sense sublime
Of something far more deeply interfused,
Whose dwelling is the light of setting suns,
And the round ocean and the living air,
And the blue sky, and in the mind of man:
A motion and a spirit, that impels
All thinking things, all objects of all thought,
And rolls through all things . . . [4]

We most of us know this feeling. But is it well placed like the feeling that here is first-rate work, which we sometimes rightly have even before we have fully grasped the picture we are looking at or the book we are reading? Or is it misplaced like the feeling in a house that has long been empty that someone secretly lives there still? Wordsworth's feeling *is* the feeling that the world is haunted, that something watches in the hills and manages the stars. The child feels that the stone tripped him when he stumbled, that the bough struck him when it flew back in his face. He has to learn that the wind isn't buffeting him, that there is not a devil in it, that he was wrong, that his attitude was inappropriate. And as he learns that the wind wasn't hindering him so he also learns it wasn't helping him. But we know how, though he learns, his attitude lingers. It is plain that Wordsworth's feeling is of this family.

Belief in gods, it is true, is often very different from belief that stones are spiteful, the sun kindly. For the gods appear in human form and from the waves and control these things and by so doing reward and punish us. But varied as are the stories of the gods they have a family likeness and we have only to recall them to feel sure of the other main sources which co-operate with animism to produce them.

What are the stories of the gods? What are our feelings when we believe in God? They are feelings of awe before power, dread of the thunderbolts of Zeus, confidence in the everlasting arms, unease beneath the all-seeing eye. They are feelings of guilt and

---

[4] *Tintern Abbey.*

inescapable vengeance, of smothered hate and of a security we can hardly do without. We have only to remind ourselves of these feelings and the stories of the gods and goddesses and heroes in which these feelings find expression, to be reminded of how we felt as children to our parents and the big people of our childhood. . . .

But here a new aspect of the matter may strike us.[5] For the very facts which make us feel that now we can recognize systems of super-human, sub-human, elusive, beings for what they are—the persistent projections of infantile phantasies—include facts which make these systems less fantastic. What are these facts? They are patterns in human reactions which are well described by saying that we are as if there were hidden within us powers, persons, not ourselves and stronger than ourselves. That this is so may perhaps be said to have been common knowledge yielded by ordinary observation of people,[6] but we did not know the degree in which this is so until recent

study of extraordinary cases in extraordinary conditions had revealed it. I refer, of course, to the study of multiple personalities and the wider studies of psychoanalysts. Even when the results of this work are reported to us that is not the same as tracing the patterns in the details of the cases on which the results are based; and even that is not the same as taking part in the studies oneself. One thing not sufficiently realized is that some of the things shut within us are not bad but good. . . .

Many have tried to find ways of salvation. The reports they bring back are always incomplete and apt to mislead even when they are not in words but in music or paint. But they are by no means useless; and not the worst of them are those which speak of oneness with God. But in so far as we become one with Him He becomes one with us. St. John says he is in us as we love one another.

This love, I suppose, is not benevolence but something that comes of the oneness with one another of which Christ spoke.[7] Sometimes it momentarily gains strength.[8] Hate and the Devil do too. And what is oneness without otherness?

---

[5] This different aspect of the matter and the connection between God, the heavenly Father, and "the good father" of the psycho-analysts, was put into my head by some remarks of Dr. Susan Isaacs.

[6] Consider Tolstoy and Dostoievsky—I do not mean, of course, that their observation was ordinary.

[7] *St. John*, xvi: 21.

[8] "The Harvesters" in *The Golden Age*, Kenneth Graham.

9 / SUMMARY

In order to gain understanding of the work of linguistic philosophy it is important to keep its conception of philosophy clearly in mind. The following summary by Professor Waismann provides an opportunity to review that conception. Philosophy, he writes, begins in puzzlement, in wonder. Before attempting to answer our questions, however, we must find sense for them. The error of traditional philosophy is that it failed to do this. Finding sense for them means calling to mind the uses and rules of language. But this in turn leads, not to the solution of problems, but to their *dis*solution. Is this only a negative view of philosophy? No, Professor Waismann concludes: philosophizing leads men to new horizons of thought—to new similarities and to new questions.

ANALYSIS AND PHILOSOPHY

Friedrich Waismann (1896-   )

From Plato to Schopenhauer philosophers are agreed that the source of their philosophizing is wonder. What gives rise to it is nothing recondite and rare but precisely those things which stare us in the face: memory, motion, general ideas. (Plato: What does "horse" mean? A single particular horse? No, for it may refer to *any* horse; *all* the horses, the total class? No, for we may speak of this or that horse. But if it means neither a single horse nor all horses, what *does* it mean?) The idealist is shaken in just the same way when he comes to reflect that he has, in Schopenhauer's words, "no knowledge of the sun but only of an eye that sees a sun, and no knowledge of the earth but only of a hand that feels an earth." Can it be, then, that nothing whatever is known to us except our own consciousness?

In looking at such questions, it seems as if the mind's eye were growing dim and as if everything, even that which ought to be absolutely clear, was becoming oddly puzzling and unlike its usual self. To bring out what seems to be peculiar to these questions one might say that they are not so much questions as tokens of a profound uneasiness of mind. Try for a moment to put yourself into the frame of mind of which Augustine was possessed when he asked: How is it possible to measure time? Time consists of past, present and future. The past can't be measured, it is gone; the future can't be measured, it is not yet here; and the present can't be measured, it

has no extension. Augustine knew of course how time is measured and this was not his concern. What puzzled him was how it is *possible* to measure time, seeing that the past hour cannot be lifted out and placed alongside the present hour for comparison. Or look at it this way: what is measured is in the past, the measuring in the present: how can that be?

The philosopher as he ponders over some such problem has the appearance of a man who is deeply disquieted. He seems to be straining to grasp something which is beyond his powers. The words in which such a question presents itself do not quite bring out into the open the real point— which may, perhaps more aptly, be described as the recoil from the incomprehensible. If, on a straight railway journey, you suddenly come in sight of the very station you have just left behind, there will be terror, accompanied perhaps by slight giddiness. That is exactly how the philosopher feels when he says to himself, "Of course time can be measured; but how *can* it?" It is as though, up to now, he had been passing heedlessly over the difficulties, and now, all of a sudden, he notices them and asks himself in alarm, "But how can that be?" That is a sort of question which we only ask when it is the very facts themselves which confound us, when something about them strikes us as preposterous. . . .

We all have our moments when something quite ordinary suddenly strikes us as queer—for instance, when time appears to us as a curious thing. Not that we are often in this frame of mind; but on some occasions, when we look at things in a certain way, unexpectedly they seem to change as though by magic: they stare at us with a puzzling expression, and we begin to wonder

The selection is from F. Waismann, "How I See Philosophy," in H. D. Lewis (ed.), *Contemporary British Philosophy*, Third Series (London: George Allen & Unwin, Ltd.; New York: The Macmillan Company, 1956), pp. 449-451, 453-458, and 461-467, with omissions. Used by permission of the publishers.

whether they can possibly be the things we have known all our lives.

"Time flows" we say—a natural and innocent expression, and yet one pregnant with danger. It flows "equably," in Newton's phrase, at an even rate. What can this mean? When something moves, it moves with a definite speed (and speed means: rate of change in time). To ask with what speed time moves, i.e. to ask how quickly time changes in time, is to ask the unaskable. It also flows, again in Newton's phrase, "without relation to anything external." How are we to figure that? Does time flow on irrespective of what happens in the world? Would it flow on even if everything in heaven and on earth came to a sudden standstill as Schopenhauer believed? For if this were not so, he said, time would have to stop with the stopping of the clock and move with the clock's movement. How odd: time flows at the same rate and yet without speed; and perhaps even without anything to occur in it? . . .

But isn't the answer to this that what mystifies us lies in the *noun* form "the time"? Having a notion embodied in the form of a noun almost irresistibly makes us turn round to look for what it is "the name of." We are trying to catch the shadows cast by the opacities of speech. A wrong analogy absorbed into the forms of our language produces mental discomfort; (and the feeling of discomfort, when it refers to language, is a profound one). "All sounds, all colors . . . evoke indefinite and yet precise emotions, or, as I prefer to think, call down among us certain disembodied powers whose footsteps over our hearts we call emotions" (W. B. Yeats).

Yet the answer is a prosaic one: don't ask what time is but how the *word* "time" is being used. Easier said than done; for if the philosopher rectifies the use of language, ordinary language has "the advantage of being in possession of declensions,"

to speak with Lichtenberg, and thus renews its spell over him, luring him on into the shadow chase. It is perhaps only when we turn to languages of a widely different grammatical structure that the way towards such possibilities of interpretation is entirely barred. "It is highly probable that philosophers within the domain of the Ural-Altaic languages (where the subject-concept is least developed) will look differently 'into the world' and be found on paths of thought different from those of the Indo-Europeans or Mussulman's" (Nietzsche).

It may be well at this point to remind ourselves that the words "question" and "answer," "problem" and "solution" are not always used in their most trite sense. It is quite obvious that we often have to do something very different to find the way out of a difficulty. A problem of politics is solved by adopting a certain line of action, the problems of novelists perhaps by the invention of devices for presenting the inmost thoughts and feelings of their characters; there is the painter's problem of how to suggest depth or movement on the canvas, the stylistic problem of expressing things not yet current, not yet turned into cliché; there are a thousand questions of technology which are answered, not by the discovery of some truth, but by a practical achievement; and there is of course the "social question." In philosophy, the real problem is not to find the answer to a given question but to find a sense for it. . . .

Many are the types of bewilderment: there is the obsessional doubt—can I ever know that other people have experiences, that they see, hear and feel as I do? Can I be sure that memory does not always deceive me? Are there really material objects and not only sense-impressions "of" them? There is the doubtlike uneasiness—what sort of being is possessed by numbers? There is the anxiety-doubt—are we really free? This doubt has taken many different forms one of which I shall single out for discussion—the question, namely, whether the law of excluded middle, when it refers to statements in the future tense, forces us into a sort of logical Predestination. A typical argument is this. If it is true now that I shall do a certain thing tomorrow, say, jump into the Thames, then no matter how fiercely I resist, strike out with hands and feet like a madman, when the day comes I cannot help jumping into the water; whereas, if this prediction is false now, then whatever efforts I may make, however many times I may nerve and brace myself, look down at the water and say to myself, "One, two, three—," it is impossible for me to spring. Yet that the prediction is either true or false is itself a necessary truth, asserted by the law of excluded middle. From this the startling consequence seems to follow that it is already now decided what I shall do tomorrow, that indeed the entire future is somehow fixed, logically preordained. Whatever I do and whichever way I decide, I am merely moving along lines clearly marked in advance which lead me towards my appointed lot. We are all, in fact, marionettes. If we are not prepared to swallow *that,* then—and there is a glimmer of hope in the "then"—there is an alternative open to us. We need only renounce the law of excluded middle for statements of this kind, and with it the validity of ordinary logic, and all will be well. Descriptions of what will happen are, at present, neither true nor false. (This sort of argument was actually propounded by Lukasiewicz in favor of a three-valued logic with "possible" as a third truth-value alongside "true" and "false.")

The way out is clear enough. The asker of the question has fallen into the error of so many philosophers: of giving an answer before stopping to consider the question. For is he clear what he is asking? He seems to suppose that a statement referring to an event in the future is at present undecided, neither true nor false, but that when the event happens the proposition enters into a sort of new state, that of being true. But how are we to figure the change from "undecided" to "true"? Is it sudden or gradual? At what moment does the statement "it will rain tomorrow" begin to be true? When the first drop falls to the ground? And supposing that it will not rain, when will the statement begin to be false? Just at the end of the day, at 12 P.M. sharp? Supposing that the event *has* happened, that the statement *is* true, will it remain so for ever? If so, in what way? Does it remain uninterruptedly true, at every moment of day and night? Even if there were no one about to give it any thought? Or is it true only at the moment when it is being thought of? In that case, how long does it remain true? For the duration of the thought? We wouldn't know how to answer these questions; this is due not to any particular ignorance or stupidity on our part but to the fact that something has gone wrong with the way the words "true" and "false" are applied here. . . .

Now it begins to look a bit less paradoxical to say that when a philosopher wants to dispose of a question the one thing he must not do is: to give an answer. A philosophic question is not solved: it *dissolves.* And in what does the "dissolving" consist? In making the meaning of the words used in putting the question so clear to ourselves that we are released from the spell it casts on us. Confusion was removed by calling to mind the use of language or, so far as the use *can* be distilled into rules, the rules: it therefore *was* a confusion about the use of language, or a confusion about rules. It is here that philosophy and grammar meet. . . .

What, only criticism and no meat? The philosopher a fog dispeller? If that were all he was capable of I would be sorry for him and leave him to his devices. Fortunately, this is not so. For one thing, a philosophic question, if pursued far enough, may lead to something positive—for instance, to a more profound understanding of language. Take the skeptical doubts as to material objects, other minds, etc. The first reaction is perhaps to say: these doubts are idle. Ordinarily, when I doubt whether I shall finish this article, after a time my doubt comes to an end. I cannot go on doubting for ever. It's the destiny of doubt to die. But the doubts raised by the skeptic never die. Are they doubts? Are they pseudo-questions? They appear so only when judged by the twin standards of common sense and common speech. The real trouble lies deeper: it arises from the skeptic casting doubt on the very facts which underlie the use of language, those permanent features of experience which make concept formation possible, which in fact are precipitated in the use of our most common words. Suppose that you see an object in front of you quite clearly, say, a pipe, and when you are going to pick it up it melts into thin air, then you may feel, "Lord, I'm going mad" or something of the sort (unless the whole situation is such that you have reason to suspect that it was some clever trick). But what, the skeptic may press now, if such experiences were quite frequent? Would you be prepared to *dis*solve the connection between different sense experiences which form the hard core of our idea of a solid object, to *un*do what language has done—to part with the category of thing-hood? And would you then be living in a phenomenalist's paradise with color patches and the other paraphernalia of the sense-datum theory, in a disobjected, desubstantialized world? To say in such circumstances, "Look, it's just tabling now" would be a joke (for even in the weakened verb forms "tabling," "chairing" an element of the thing-category lingers on). That is why the skeptic struggles to express himself in a

language which is not fit for this purpose. He expresses himself misleadingly when he says that he doubts such-and-such *facts:* his doubts cut so deep that they affect the fabric of language itself. For what he doubts is already embodied in the very forms of speech, e.g. in what is condensed in the use of thing-words. The moment he tries to penetrate those deep-sunken layers, he undermines the language in which he ventilates his qualms—with the result that he seems to be talking nonsense. He is not. But in order to make his doubts fully expressible, language would first have to go into the melting-pot. (We can get a glimmering of what is needed from modern science where all the long-established categories—thinghood, causality, position—had to be revolutionized. This required nothing less than the construction of some new language, not the expression of new facts with the old one.)

If we look at the matter in this way the attitude of the skeptic is seen in a new light. He considers possibilities which lie far outside the domain of our current experience. If his doubts are taken seriously, they turn into observations which cast a new and searching light on the subsoil of language, showing what possibilities are open to our thought (though not to ordinary language), and what paths might have been pursued if the texture of our experience were different from what it is. These problems are not spurious: they make us aware of the vast background in which any current experiences are embedded, and to which language has adapted itself; thus they bring out the unmeasured sum of experience stored up in the use of our words and syntactical forms. . . .

A whole chapter might be written on the fate of questions, their curious adventures and transformations—how they change into others and in the process remain, and yet do not remain, the same. The original question may split and multiply almost like a character in a dream play. To mention just a few examples: can logic be characterized completely in a formal way, i.e. without bringing in any extraneous ideas such as the use of language and all that goes with it? Can arithmetic be characterized in any such way, entirely "from within"? Or will any interpretation include some *Erdenrest* of the empiric? These questions have given rise to extensive research on mathematical interpretation of formal systems. The query how far logical intuition is correct has got ramified into a bunch of questions pertaining to the theory of logical types, the axiom of choice, etc., indeed to a far more fundamental issue, namely, whether ordinary logic itself is "right" as contrasted with the system of inferences evolved by the intuitionists. Or again, are there undecidable questions in mathematics, not in the restricted sense of Gödel, but undecidable in an absolute sense? Are there natural limits to generalization? It is interesting to watch how from a question of this sort, not too precise, somewhat blurred, new and better defined questions detach themselves, the parent question—in Frege's case philosophic *par excellence* [1]—giving rise to a scientist's progeny. . . .

The question is the first groping step of the mind in its journeyings that lead towards new horizons. The genius of the philosopher shows itself nowhere more strikingly than in the new kind of question he brings into the world. What distinguishes him and gives him his place is the passion of questioning. That his questions are at times not so clear is perhaps of not so much moment as one makes of it. There is nothing like clear thinking to protect one from making discoveries. It is all very well to talk

[1 The reference is to the logician Frege's work that—as Waismann points out elsewhere—resulted from philosophic wonder about the nature of arithmetical truths and led to the development of modern logic. *Ed.*]

of clarity, but when it becomes on obsession it is liable to nip the living thought in the bud. This, I am afraid, is one of the deplorable results of Logical Positivism, not foreseen by its founders, but only too striking in some of its followers. Look at these people, gripped by a clarity neurosis, haunted by fear, tongue-tied, asking themselves continually, "Oh dear, now does this make perfectly good sense?" Imagine the pioneers of science, Kepler, Newton, the discoverers of non-Euclidean geometry, of field physics, the unconscious, matter waves or heaven knows what, imagine them asking themselves this question at every step—this would have been the surest means of sapping any creative power. No great discoverer has acted in accordance with the motto, "Everything that can be said can be said clearly." And some of the greatest discoveries have even emerged from a sort of primordial fog. (Something to be said for the fog. For my part, I've always suspected that clarity is the last refuge of those who have nothing to say.) . . .

But here a new problem presents itself: How do we know what will satisfy a given question? More generally: How does the answer fit the question? Questions of the current sort ("What is the right time?") show already by their form what sort of answer to expect. They are, so to speak, cheques with a blank to be filled; yet not always so: Augustine's question, "How is it possible to measure time?" or Kant's question, "How is geometry possible?" do not trace out the form of the answer. There is no *obvious* link between question and answer, any more than there is in the case of asking "What is a point?" When Hilbert's idea—that the axioms of geometry jointly provide the "implicit definition" of the basic terms—was first propounded it came totally unexpected; no one had ever thought of that before; on the contrary, many people had an uneasy feeling as if this were a way of evading the issue rather than an answer, amongst them no less a man than Frege. He thought the problem still unsolved. . . .

Frege behaves not so very unlike a man mystified by the question, "What is time?" We may suggest converting the latter into the question how the word "time" is being used (which would bring him down to earth). But aren't we cheating him? We seem to be holding out the answer to *one* question, but not to that one which he was asking. He may suspect that we are trying to fob him off with the second best we have in store, his original question still remaining an enigma. Similarly Frege: he considered it a scandal that the questions "What is a point?" "What is a number?" were still unanswered.

In either of these cases, the aim of a discussion, in the absence of a proof, can only be to change the asker's attitude. We may, for instance, scrutinize similar, or partially similar, cases, point out that the form of the answer is not always that of the question; by going patiently over such cases, the vast background of analogies against which the question is seen will slowly change. The turning up of a wide field of language loosens the position of certain standards which are so ingrained that we do not see them for what they are; and if we do this in an effective manner, a mind like Frege's will be released from the obsession of seeking strainingly for an answer to fit the mould. Arguments are used in such a discussion, not as proofs though but rather as means to make him see things he had not noticed before: e.g. to dispel wrong analogies, to stress similarities with other cases and in this way to bring about something like a shift of perspective. However, there is no way of proving him wrong or bullying him into mental acceptance of the proposal: when all is said and done the decision is his.

BIBLIOGRAPHICAL NOTE

Introductory historical surveys of analytic or linguistic philosophy, including frequently its relations to positivism, are given in the following volumes: A. J. Ayer *et al.*, *The Revolution in Philosophy* (London, 1956); D. F. Pears (ed.), *The Nature of Metaphysics* (London, 1957); J. Passmore, *A Hundred Years of Philosophy* (London, 1957); J. O. Urmson, *Philosophical Analysis* (Oxford, 1956); and G. J. Warnock, *English Philosophy Since 1900* (London, 1958). Among the books that are considered classics for this position are G. E. Moore's *Philosophical Studies* (London, 1922); L. Wittgenstein, *Tractatus Logico-Philosophicus* (London, 1922), which greatly influenced positivism, his *Philosophical Investigations* (New York, 1953) and *The Blue and Brown Books* (New York, 1958), which are clearly expressive of analytic principles and which, though not published until recently, were known to many European philosophers; Gilbert Ryle, *The Concept of Mind* (London, 1949); and John Wisdom, *Other Minds* (Oxford, 1952) and *Philosophy and Psycho-Analysis* (Oxford, 1953), both collections of journal articles. Anthologies of important discussions from an analytic point of view are: A. G. N. Flew (ed.), *Logic and Language,* First Series (Oxford, 1951), Second Series (Oxford, 1953); M. Macdonald (ed.), *Philosophy and Analysis* (Oxford, 1954); and C. A. Mace (ed.), *British Philosophy in the Mid-Century* (London, 1957). Much of the important material within this position, however, is found in philosophical journals. A bibliography of many of these articles is given by J. O. Urmson, "Bibliography of Analytic Philosophy," *Revue Internationale de Philosophie*, 7 (1953).

VI

EXISTENTIALISM

PASCAL / KIERKEGAARD / HEIDEGGER

SARTRE / NIETZSCHE / ORTEGA Y GASSET

JASPERS / TILLICH / HEINEMANN

The term "existentialism" is commonly used to refer to a contemporary type of thinking that emphasizes human existence and the qualities of being that are peculiar to it rather than to nature or the physical world. So characterized, existentialism is sometimes seen as simply a new name for an ancient philosophical tradition. Taken only as a revival of ancient thought, however, it loses what in fact are its distinctive features.

"Emphasis on human existence" is the beginning of a definition of existentialism, but actually it is too vague for use in reference to the modern movement; for existentialism's concern about man grows out of specifically modern conditions and concludes in a quite unique position. Among these conditions are the loss of the individual in mass culture and technology, the consequent alienation of the human person from himself as well as from his productions, and the loss of meaning in life through divisions within the human spirit. The result of these conditions is frequently called the "existential experience." Recorded by many artists and writers as well as philosophers, it is, in sum, an experience of the decomposition of our phenomenal world—first, of all rational concepts, next of objects, then of time and history, until finally all coherence is gone—to the point where one faces only Nothing and experiences only despair. Sometimes also called an experience of crisis, it has arisen in times of social and personal catastrophe in our century.

Whatever the conditions that produce it, however, existentialism is not simply a philosophy of despair. A second expression, "the existentialist attitude," indicates that the existential experience results in an important philosophical alternative. This attitude is directed toward human existence. Other philosophies also study man; but they view him in terms of some concept or essence derived from reason. The existentialist opposes such traditional conceptualism and its abstract, general concept of existence, for he believes that *what* man is can only be determined from *how* he is; that is, man's essence is to be found only in his concrete existence. The desire to know the meaning of the individual man in a more radical way than other philosophers have sought leads the existentialist to hold that the starting point of philosophy is the concrete situation of man in the world.

Much of existentialist writing aims at describing the whole of human life—not just reason but emotional and conative states as well. Reason and rational structure are not equivalent to human life; feeling, passion, and decision are equally if not more important clues to man's being. Yet existentialism is not simply phenomenology, great as is its reliance on descriptive techniques. It also desires to know the reality of human existence and, for some existentialists, to produce a general theory of being. The phenomenological interest is directed toward an ontological goal, though the latter can be achieved only through the former.

This ontological interest links existentialism with certain aspects of traditional philosophy, though it would agree to some extent with positivism and analysis in their distrust of philosophic rationalism. But it has in turn its doubts about them. In particular, existentialism takes issue with efforts to make philosophy another technology, for this would destroy philosophy; it doubts that science or reason can interpret the whole universe; and it is suspicious of the "disinterestedness" of modern "objective" thought. Its closer tie is with classical philosophy, which was occupied with the problems of human existence, although, as this introductory sketch has indicated, existentialism's approach to them is unique.

1 / INTRODUCTION

Although the number of thinkers in the history of ideas who reflected the existentialist position is small, one—the French mathematician and philosopher Blaise Pascal—surely belongs within the stream of existentialism. Caught in the religious strifes of his day, at the same time being a contributor to the rising mathematical science of his century, he was extremely sensitive to the human condition with its frailty, uncertainty, and despair. His *Pensées* provides a good introduction to existentialism.

Two aspects of his thought are reflected in the following selection. There is first the phenomenological or descriptive approach to individual existence. Many of the recurring themes of existentialist thought are found here: the problem of knowing oneself concretely, the distrust of science and reason for existential concerns, the uncertainties of existence, the nothingness of man's being, the elusiveness of finality, the reality of temporality and change, and man's corruption—his untruth—as revealed in disguise, falsehood, and hypocrisy. The second aspect is ontological. Pascal offers a view of man as spirit, yet a spirit in nature. Hence man is a riddle, a paradox: as spirit, his reality is found in his passion for the Eternal; as natural, his being is an insignificant speck between two infinites.

THE DISCOVERY OF FINITUDE

Blaise Pascal (1623-1662)

One must know oneself. If this does not serve to discover truth, it at least serves as a rule of life, and there is nothing better.

Physical science will not console me for the ignorance of morality in the time of affliction. But the science of ethics will always console me for the ignorance of the physical sciences.

Man's disproportion. This is where our intuitive knowledge leads us. If it be not true, there is no truth in man; and if it be, he finds therein a great reason for humiliation, because he must abase himself in one way or another. And since he cannot exist without such knowledge, I wish that before entering on deeper researches into nature he would consider her seriously and at leisure, that he would examine himself also, and knowing what proportion there is. Let man then contemplate the whole realm of nature in her full and exalted majesty, and turn his eyes from the low objects which hem him round; let him observe that brilliant light set like an eternal lamp to illumine the universe, let the earth appear to him a point in comparison with the vast circle described by that sun, and let him see with amazement that even this vast

circle is itself but a fine point in regard to that described by the stars revolving in the firmament. If our view be arrested there, let imagination pass beyond, and it will sooner exhaust the power of thinking than nature that of giving scope for thought. The whole visible world is but an imperceptible speck in the ample bosom of nature. No idea approaches it. We may swell our conceptions beyond all imaginable space, yet bring forth only atoms in comparison with the reality of things. It is an infinite sphere, the center of which is every where, the circumference no where. It is, in short, the greatest sensible mark of the almighty power of God, that imagination loses itself in that thought.

Then, returning to himself, let man consider his own being compared with all that is; let him regard himself as wandering in this remote province of nature; and from the little dungeon in which he finds himself lodged, I mean the universe, let him learn to set a true value on the earth, on its kingdoms, its cities, and on himself.

What is a man in the infinite? But to show him another prodigy no less astonishing, let him examine the most delicate things he knows. Let him take a mite which in its minute body presents him with parts incomparably more minute; limbs with their joints, veins in the limbs, blood in the veins, humors in the blood, drops in

Selected and arranged from C. Kegan Paul (tr.), *The Thoughts of Blaise Pascal* (London: Kegan Paul, Trench and Co., 1888), pp. 19-87.

the humors, vapors in the drops; let him, again dividing these last, exhaust his power of thought; let the last point at which he arrives be that of which we speak, and he will perhaps think that here is the extremest diminutive in nature. Then I will open before him therein a new abyss. I will paint for him not only the visible universe, but all that he can conceive of nature's immensity in the enclosure of this diminished atom. Let him therein see an infinity of universes of which each has its firmament, its planets, its earth, in the same proportion as in the visible world; in each earth animals, and at the last the mites, in which he will come upon all that was in the first, and still find in these others the same without end and without cessation; let him lose himself in wonders as astonishing in their minuteness as the others in their immensity; for who will not be amazed at seeing that our body, which before was imperceptible in the universe, itself imperceptible in the bosom of the whole, is now a colossus, a world, a whole, in regard to the nothingness to which we cannot attain.

Whoso takes this survey of himself will be terrified at the thought that he is upheld in the material being, given him by nature, between these two abysses of the infinite and nothing, he will tremble at the sight of these marvels; and I think that as his curiosity changes into wonder, he will be more disposed to contemplate them in silence than to search into them with presumption.

For after all what is man in nature? A nothing in regard to the infinite, a whole in regard to nothing, a mean between nothing and the whole; infinitely removed from understanding either extreme. The end of things and their beginnings are invincibly hidden from him in impenetrable secrecy, he is equally incapable of seeing the nothing whence he was taken, and the infinite in which he is engulfed.

What shall he do then, but discern somewhat of the middle of things in an eternal despair of knowing either their beginning or their end? All things arise from nothing, and tend towards the infinite. Who can follow their marvellous course? The author of these wonders can understand them, and none but he.

Of these two infinites in nature, the infinitely great and the infinitely little, man can more easily conceive the great.

Because they have not considered these infinities, men have rashly plunged into the research of nature, as though they bore some proportion to her.

It is strange that they have wished to understand the origin of all that is, and thence to attain to the knowledge of the whole, with a presumption as infinite as their object. For there is no doubt that such a design cannot be formed without presumption or without a capacity as infinite as nature.

If we are well informed, we understand that nature having graven her own image and that of her author on all things, they are almost all partakers of her double infinity. Thus we see that all the sciences are infinite in the extent of their researches, for none can doubt that geometry, for instance, has an infinite infinity of problems to propose. They are also infinite in the number and in the nicety of their premises, for it is evident that those which are finally proposed are not self-supporting, but are based on others, which again having others as their support have no finality.

But we make some apparently final to the reason, just as in regard to material things we call that an indivisible point beyond which our senses can no longer perceive anything, though by its nature this also is infinitely divisible.

Of these two scientific infinities, that of greatness is the most obvious to the senses, and therefore a few persons have made pretensions to universal knowledge. "I will discourse of the all," said Democritus.

But beyond the fact that it is a small

thing to speak of it simply, without proving and knowing, it is nevertheless impossible to do so, the infinite multitude of things being so hidden, that all we can express by word or thought is but an invisible trace of them. Hence it is plain how foolish, vain, and ignorant is that title of some books: *De omni scibili.*

But the infinitely little is far less evident. Philosophers have much more frequently asserted they have attained it, yet in that very point they have all stumbled. This has given occasion to such common titles as *The Origin of Creation, The Principles of Philosophy,* and the like, as presumptuous in fact though not in appearance as that dazzling one, *De omni scibili.*

We naturally think that we can more easily reach the center of things than embrace their circumference. The visible bulk of the world visibly exceeds us, but as we exceed little things, we think ourselves more capable of possessing them. Yet we need no less capacity to attain the nothing than the whole. Infinite capacity is needed for both, and it seems to me that whoever shall have understood the ultimate principles of existence might also attain to the knowledge of the infinite. The one depends on the other, and one leads to the other. Extremes meet and reunite by virtue of their distance, to find each other in God, and in God alone.

Let us then know our limits; we are something, but we are not all. What existence we have conceals from us the knowledge of first principles which spring from the nothing, while the pettiness of that existence hides from us the sight of the infinite.

In the order of intelligible things our intelligence holds the same position as our body holds in the vast extent of nature.

Restricted in every way, this middle -state between two extremes is common to all our weaknesses.

Our senses can perceive no extreme. Too much noise deafens us, excess of light blinds

us, too great distance or nearness equally interfere with our vision, prolixity or brevity equally obscure a discourse, too much truth overwhelms us. I know even those who cannot understand that if four be taken from nothing nothing remains. First principles are too plain for us, superfluous pleasure troubles us. Too many concords are unpleasing in music, and too many benefits annoy, we wish to have wherewithal to overpay our debt. *Beneficia eo usque læta sunt dum videntur exsolvi posse; ubi multum antevenere, pro gratia odium redditur* ["Benefits are pleasing so long as they appear able to be repaid; but when they are excessive in number, then enmity is returned instead of favor"].

We feel neither extreme heat nor extreme cold. Qualities in excess are inimical to us and not apparent to the senses, we do not feel but are passive under them. The weakness of youth and age equally hinder the mind, as also too much and too little teaching . . .

In a word, all extremes are for us as though they were not; and we are not, in regard to them: they escape us, or we them.

This is our true state; this is what renders us incapable both of certain knowledge and of absolute ignorance. We sail on a vast expanse, ever uncertain, ever drifting, hurried from one to the other goal. If we think to attach ourselves firmly to any point, it totters and fails us; if we follow, it eludes our grasp, and flies us, vanishing for ever. Nothing stays for us. This is our natural condition, yet always the most contrary to our inclination; we burn with desire to find a steadfast place and an ultimate fixed basis whereon we may build a tower to reach the infinite. But our whole foundation breaks up, and earth opens to the abysses.

We may not then look for certainty or stability. Our reason is always deceived by changing shows, **nothing can fix the finite** between the two infinites, which at once enclose and fly from it.

If this be once well understood I think that we shall rest, each in the state wherein nature has placed him. This element which falls to us as our lot being always distant from either extreme, it matters not that a man should have a trifle more knowledge of the universe. If he has it, he but begins a little higher. He is always infinitely distant from the end, and the duration of our life is infinitely removed from eternity, even if it last ten years longer.

In regard to these infinites all finites are equal, and I see not why we should fix our imagination on one more than on another. The only comparison which we can make of ourselves to the finite troubles us.

Were man to begin with the study of himself, he would see how incapable he is of proceeding further. How can a part know the whole? But he may perhaps aspire to know at least the parts with which he has proportionate relation. But the parts of the world are so linked and related, that I think it impossible to know one without another, or without the whole.

Man, for instance, is related to all that he knows. He needs place wherein to abide, time through which to exist, motion in order to live; he needs constituent elements, warmth and food to nourish him, air to breathe. He sees light, he feels bodies, he contracts an alliance with all that is.

To know man then it is necessary to understand how it comes that he needs air to breathe, and to know the air we must understand how it has relation to the life of man, etc.

Flame cannot exist without air, therefore to know one, we must know the other.

All that exists then is both cause and effect, dependent and supporting, mediate and immediate, and all is held together by a natural though imperceptible bond, which unites things most distant and most different. I hold it impossible to know the parts without knowing the whole, or to know the whole without knowing the parts in detail.

I hold it impossible to know one alone without all the others, that is to say impossible purely and absolutely.

The eternity of things in themselves or in God must also confound our brief duration. The fixed and constant immobility of Nature in comparison with the continual changes which take place in us must have the same effect.

And what completes our inability to know things is that they are in their essence simple, whereas we are composed of two opposite natures differing in kind, soul and body. For it is impossible that our reasoning part should be other than spiritual; and should any allege that we are simply material, this would far more exclude us from the knowledge of things, since it is an inconceivable paradox to affirm that matter can know itself, and it is not possible for us to know how it should know itself.

So, were we simply material, we could know nothing whatever, and if we are composed of spirit and matter we cannot perfectly know what is simple, whether it be spiritual or material. For how should we know matter distinctly, since our being, which acts on this knowledge, is partly spiritual, and how should we know spiritual substances clearly since we have a body which weights us, and drags us down to earth.

Moreover what completes our inability is the simplicity of things compared with our double and complex nature. To dispute this point were an invincible absurdity, for it is as absurd as impious to deny that man is composed of two parts, differing in their nature, soul and body. This renders us unable to know all things; for if this complexity be denied, and it be asserted that we are entirely material, it is plain that matter is incapable of knowing matter. Nothing is more impossible than this.

Let us conceive then that this mixture

of spirit and clay throws us out of proportion . . .

Hence it comes that almost all philosophers have confounded different ideas, and speak of material things in spiritual phrase, and of spiritual things in material phrase. For they say boldly that bodies have a tendency to fall, that they seek after their center, that they fly from destruction, that they fear a void, that they have inclinations, sympathies, antipathies; and all of these are spiritual qualities. Again, in speaking of spirits, they conceive of them as in a given spot, or as moving from place to place; qualities which belong to matter alone.

Instead of receiving the ideas of these things simply, we color them with our own qualities, and stamp with our complex being all the simple things which we contemplate.

Who would not think, when we declare that all that is consists of mind and matter, that we really understood this combination? Yet it is the one thing we least understand. Man is to himself the most marvellous object in Nature, for he cannot conceive what matter is, still less what is mind, and less than all how a material body should be united to a mind. This is the crown of all his difficulties, yet it is his very being: *Modus quo corporibus adhæret spiritus comprehendi ab homine non potest et hoc tamen homo est* ["The manner by which the mind clings to bodies cannot be comprehended by man and yet this is man"].

The nature of man is his whole nature, *omne animal*.

There is nothing we cannot make natural, nothing natural we cannot lose.

Of Self-love.—The nature of self-love and of this human "I" is to love self only, and consider self only. But what can it do? It cannot prevent the object it loves from being full of faults and miseries; man would fain be great and sees that he is little, would fain be happy, and sees that he is miserable, would fain be perfect, and sees that he is full of imperfections, would fain be the object of the love and esteem of men, and sees that his faults merit only their aversion and contempt. The embarrassment wherein he finds himself produces in him the most unjust and criminal passion imaginable, for he conceives a mortal hatred against that truth which blames him and convinces him of his faults. Desiring to annihilate it, yet unable to destroy it in its essence, he destroys it as much as he can in his own knowledge, and in that of others; that is to say, he devotes all his care to the concealment of his faults, both from others and from himself, and he can neither bear that others should show them to him, nor that they should see them.

It is no doubt an evil to be full of faults, but it is a greater evil to be full of them, yet unwilling to recognize them, because that is to add the further fault of a voluntary illusion. We do not like others to deceive us, we do not think it just in them to require more esteem from us than they deserve; it is therefore unjust that we should deceive them, desiring more esteem from them than we deserve.

Thus if they discover no more imperfections and vices in us than we really have, it is plain they do us no wrong, since it is not they who cause them; but rather they do us a service, since they help us to deliver ourselves from an evil, the ignorance of these imperfections. We ought not to be troubled that they know our faults and despise us, since it is but just they should know us as we are, and despise us if we are despicable.

Such are the sentiments which would arise in a heart full of equity and justice. What should we say then of our own heart, finding in it an wholly contrary disposition? For is it not true that we hate truth, and those who tell it us, and that we would wish them to have an erroneously favorable opinion of us, and to esteem us other than indeed we are?

One proof of this fills me with dismay. The Catholic religion does not oblige us to tell out our sins indiscriminately to all, it allows us to remain hidden from men in general, but she excepts one alone, to whom she commands us to open the very depths of our heart, and to show ourselves to him as we are. There is but this one man in the world whom she orders us to undeceive; she binds him to an inviolable secrecy, so that this knowledge is to him as though it were not. We can imagine nothing more charitable and more tender. Yet such is the corruption of man, that he finds even this law harsh, and it is one of the main reasons which has set a large portion of Europe in revolt against the Church.

How unjust and unreasonable is the human heart which finds it hard to be obliged to do in regard to one man what in some degree it were just to do to all men. For is it just that we should deceive them?

There are different degrees in this dislike to the truth, but it may be said that all have it in some degree, for it is inseparable from self-love. This false delicacy causes those who must needs reprove others to choose so many windings and modifications in order to avoid shocking them. They must needs lessen our faults, seem to excuse them, mix praises with their blame, give evidences of affection and esteem. Yet this medicine is always bitter to self-love, which takes as little as it can, always with disgust, often with a secret anger against those who administer it.

Hence it happens, that if any desire our love, they avoid doing us a service which they know to be disagreeable; they treat us as we would wish to be treated: we hate the truth, and they hide it from us; we wish to be flattered, they flatter us; we love to be deceived, they deceive us.

Thus each degree of good fortune which raises us in the world removes us further from truth, because we fear most to wound those whose affection is most useful, and whose dislike is most dangerous. A prince may be the by-word of all Europe, yet he alone know nothing of it. I am not surprised; to speak the truth is useful to whom it is spoken, but disadvantageous to those who speak it, since it makes them hated. Now those who live with princes love their own interests more than that of the prince they serve, and thus they take care not to benefit him so as to do themselves a disservice.

This misfortune is, no doubt, greater and more common in the higher classes, but lesser men are not exempt from it, since there is always an interest in making men love us. Thus human life is but a perpetual illusion, an interchange of deceit and flattery. No one speaks of us in our presence as in our absence. The society of men is founded on this universal deceit: few friendships would last if every man knew what his friend said of him behind his back, though he then spoke in sincerity and without passion.

Man is then only disguise, falsehood, and hypocrisy, both in himself and with regard to others. He will not be told the truth, he avoids telling it to others, and all these tendencies, so far removed from justice and reason, have their natural roots in his heart.

Contraries. Man is naturally credulous and incredulous, timid and rash.

Description of man: dependency, desire of independence, bodily needs.

The condition of man; inconstancy, weariness, unrest.

Our nature consists in motion; perfect rest is death.

Weariness. Nothing is so insufferable to man as to be completely at rest, without passions, without business, without diversion, without study. He then feels his nothingness, his forlornness, his insufficiency, his dependence, his weakness, his emptiness. There will immediately arise from the depth of his heart weariness, gloom, sadness, fretfulness, vexation, despair.

Contradiction. To despise existence, to die for nothing, to hate our existence.

We run carelessly to the precipice, after we have put something before us to prevent us seeing it.

When I consider the short duration of my life, swallowed up in the eternity before and after, the little space which I fill, and even can see, engulfed in the infinite immensity of spaces whereof I know nothing and which know nothing of me, I am terrified, and wonder that I am here rather than there, for there is no reason why here rather than there, or now rather than then. Who has set me here? By whose order and design have this place and time been destined for me? *Memoria hospitis unius diei praetereuntis* ["Memory of a guest passing by for a day"].

Important as Pascal is, it is nevertheless necessary to place the real origin of existentialism in the writings of another thinker, Soren Kierkegaard. Kierkegaard's central idea is how one may become a Christian, and much of his writing defends Christianity against false values. His day and age, he believes, has forgotten what it means to be a Christian, or even what it means to *be.* Hence he is led to introduce into Western thought—many believe for the first time—the categories of "individual" and "existence."

By existence Kierkegaard means the striving of a person to fulfill himself. That men must strive points to a tension within their very being. In describing and analyzing the experience of despair, Kierkegaard finds this tension to be a result of the fact that man is a spiritual being, that he is a synthesis of the temporal and eternal, the finite and infinite.

Man is a synthesis, but simply as synthesis he is not a self. Despair arises because man is a synthesis, and ultimately it is despair over this synthesis— that is, over the self itself. Despair reveals that, simply as given, the self with all finite things is meaningless. The recognition of the self's meaninglessness, however, reveals an ultimate meaning by positing the infinite and the eternal. Hence despair also reveals that men are spiritual beings and that they exist before God. Since true selfhood can be attained only when the self is related to the Power that constitutes the synthesis (even though men may try to find substitutes for God in pleasure or duty), despair posits the necessity of genuine endeavor through decision. Only decision or faith can bring meaning into human personality, and the achievement of meaning is the achievement of "subjective truth."

EXISTENCE AND DESPAIR

Soren Kierkegaard (1813-1855)

Man is spirit. But what is spirit? Spirit is the self. But what is the self? The self is a relation which relates itself to its own self, or it is that in the relation [which accounts for it] that the relation relates itself to its own self; the self is not the relation but [consists in the fact] that the relation relates itself to its own self. Man is a synthesis of the infinite and the finite, of the temporal and the eternal, of freedom and necessity, in short it is a synthesis. A synthesis is a relation between two factors. So regarded, man is not yet a self.

In the relation between two, the relation is the third term as a negative unity, and the two relate themselves to the relation, and in the relation to the relation; such a relation is that between soul and body, when man is regarded as soul. If on the contrary the relation relates itself to its own self, the relation is then the positive third term, and this is the self.

Such a relation which relates itself to its own self (that is to say, a self) must either have constituted itself or have been constituted by another.

If this relation which relates itself to its own self is constituted by another, the relation doubtless is the third term, but this relation (the third term) is in turn a relation relating itself to that which constituted the whole relation.

Such a derived, constituted, relation is the human self, a relation which relates itself to its own self, and in relating itself to its own self relates itself to another.

Hence it is that there can be two forms of despair properly so called. If the human self had constituted itself, there could be a question only of one form, that of not willing to be one's own self, of willing to get rid of oneself, but there would be no question of despairingly willing to be oneself. This formula [i.e. that the self is constituted by another] is the expression for the total dependence of the relation (the self namely), the expression for the fact that the self cannot of itself attain and remain in equilibrium and rest by itself, but only by relating itself to that Power which constituted the whole relation. Indeed, so far is it from being true that this second form of despair (despair at willing to be one's own self) denotes only a particular kind of despair, that on the contrary all despair can in the last analysis be reduced to this. . . .

This then is the formula which describes the condition of the self when despair is completely eradicated: by relating itself to its own self and by willing to be itself the self is grounded transparently in the Power which posited it.

Is despair an advantage or a drawback? Regarded in a purely dialectical way it is both. If one were to stick to the abstract notion of despair, without thinking of any concrete despairer, one might say that it is an immense advantage. The possibility of this sickness is man's advantage over the beast, and this advantage distinguishes him far more essentially than the erect posture, for it implies the infinite erectness or loftiness of being spirit. The possibility of this sickness is man's advantage over the beast; to be sharply observant of the sickness constitutes the Christian's advantage over the natural man; to be healed of this sickness is the Christian's bliss.

The selection is from Soren Kierkegaard, *Fear and Trembling; The Sickness Unto Death* (tr. Walter Lowrie) (Garden City: Doubleday & Co., Inc., 1954), pp. 146-161, with omissions. Copyright, 1941, 1954, by Princeton University Press. Used by permission of Princeton University Press.

So then it is an infinite advantage to be able to despair; and yet it is not only the greatest misfortune and misery to be in despair; no, it is perdition. Ordinarily there is no such relation between possibility and actuality; if it is an advantage to be able to be this or that, it is a still greater advantage to be such a thing. That is to say, being is related to the ability to be as an ascent. In the case of despair, on the contrary, being is related to the ability to be as a fall. Infinite as is the advantage of the possibility, just so great is the measure of the fall. So in the case of despair the ascent consists in not being in despair. Yet this statement is open to misunderstanding. The thing of not being in despair is not like not being lame, blind, etc. In case the not being in despair means neither more nor less than not being this, then it is precisely to be it. The thing of not being in despair must mean the annihilation of the possibility of being this; if it is to be true that a man is not in despair, one must annihilate the possibility every instant. Such is not ordinarily the relation between possibility and actuality. Although thinkers say that actuality is the annihilated possibility, yet this is not entirely true; it is the fulfilled, the effective possibility. Here, on the contrary, the actuality (not being in despair), which in its very form is a negation, is the impotent, annihilated possibility; ordinarily, actuality in comparison with possibility is a confirmation, here it is a negation.

Despair is the disrelationship in a relation which relates itself to itself. But the synthesis is not the disrelationship, it is merely the possibility, or, in the synthesis is latent the possibility of the disrelationship. If the synthesis were the disrelationship, there would be no such thing as despair, for despair would then be something inherent in human nature as such, that is, it would not be despair, it would be something that befell a man, something he suffered passively, like an illness into which a man falls,

or like death which is the lot of all. No, this thing of despairing is inherent in man himself; but if he were not a synthesis, he could not despair, neither could he despair if the synthesis were not originally from God's hand in the right relationship.

Whence then comes despair? From the relation wherein the synthesis relates itself to itself, in that God who made man a relationship lets this go as it were out of His hand, that is, in the fact that the relation relates itself to itself. And herein, in the fact that the relation is spirit, is the self, consists the responsibility under which all despair lies, and so lies every instant it exists, however much and however ingeniously the despairer, deceiving himself and others, may talk of his despair as a misfortune which has befallen him, with a confusion of things different, as in the case of vertigo aforementioned, with which, though it is qualitatively different, despair has much in common, since vertigo is under the rubric soul what despair is under the rubric spirit, and is pregnant with analogies to despair. . . .

The concept of the sickness unto death must be understood, however, in a peculiar sense. Literally it means a sickness the end and outcome of which is death. Thus one speaks of a mortal sickness as synonymous with a sickness unto death. In this sense despair cannot be called the sickness unto death. But in the Christian understanding of it death itself is a transition unto life. In view of this, there is from the Christian standpoint no earthly, bodily sickness unto death. For death is doubtless the last phase of the sickness, but death is not the last thing. If in the strictest sense we are to speak of a sickness unto death, it must be one in which the last thing is death, and death the last thing. And this precisely is despair.

Yet in another and still more definite sense despair is the sickness unto death.

It is indeed very far from being true that, literally understood, one dies of this sickness, or that this sickness ends with bodily death. On the contrary, the torment of despair is precisely this, not to be able to die. So it has much in common with the situation of the moribund when he lies and struggles with death, and cannot die. So to be sick *unto* death is, not to be able to die—yet not as though there were hope of life; no, the hopelessness in this case is that even the last hope, death, is not available. When death is the greatest danger, one hopes for life; but when one becomes acquainted with an even more dreadful danger, one hopes for death. So when the danger is so great that death has become one's hope, despair is the disconsolateness of not being able to die. . . .

A despairing man is in despair over *something*. So it seems for an instant, but only for an instant; that same instant the true despair manifests itself, or despair manifests itself in its true character. For in the fact that he despaired of *something*, he really despaired of himself, and now would be rid of himself. Thus when the ambitious man whose watchword was "Either Caesar or nothing" does not become Caesar, he is in despair thereat. But this signifies something else, namely, that precisely because he did not become Caesar he now cannot endure to be himself. So properly he is not in despair over the fact that he did not become Caesar, but he is in despair over himself for the fact that he did not become Caesar. This self which, had he become Caesar, would have been to him a sheer delight (though in another sense equally in despair), this self is now absoluetly intolerable to him. In a profounder sense it is not the fact that he did not become Caesar which is intolerable to him, but the self which did not become Caesar is the thing that is intolerable; or, more correctly, what is intolerable to him is that he cannot get rid of himself. If he had become Caesar he

would have been rid of himself in desperation, but now that he did not become Caesar he cannot in desperation get rid of himself. Essentially he is equally in despair in either case, for he does not possess himself, he is not himself. By becoming Caesar he would not after all have become himself but have got rid of himself, and by not becoming Caesar he falls into despair over the fact that he cannot get rid of himself. Hence it is a superficial view (which presumably has never seen a person in despair, not even one's own self) when it is said of a man in despair, "He is consuming himself." For precisely this it is he despairs of, and to his torment it is precisely this he cannot do, since by despair fire has entered into something that cannot burn, or cannot burn up, that is, into the self.

So to despair over something is not yet properly despair. It is the beginning, or it is as when the physician says of a sickness that it has not yet declared itself. The next step is the declared despair, despair over oneself. A young girl is in despair over love, and so she despairs over her lover, because he died, or because he was unfaithful to her. This is not a declared despair; no, she is in despair over herself. This self of hers, which, if it had become "his" beloved, she would have been rid of in the most blissful way, or would have lost, this self is now a torment to her when it has to be a self without "him"; this self which would have been to her her riches (though in another sense equally in despair) has now become to her a loathsome void, since "he" is dead, or it has become to her an abhorrence, since it reminds her of the fact that she was betrayed. Try it now, say to such a girl, "Thou art consuming thyself," and thou shalt hear her reply, "Oh, no, the torment is precisely this, that I cannot do it."

To despair over oneself, in despair to will to be rid of oneself, is the formula for all despair, and hence the second form of despair (in despair at willing to be oneself) can be followed back to the first (in despair at not willing to be oneself), just as in the foregoing we resolved the first into the second. . . . A despairing man wants despairingly to be himself. But if he despairingly wants to be himself, he will not want to get rid of himself. Yes, so it seems; but if one inspects more closely, one perceives that after all the contradiction is the same. That self which he despairingly wills to be is a self which he is not (for to will to be that self which one truly is, is indeed the opposite of despair); what he really wills is to tear his self away from the Power which constituted it. But notwithstanding all his despair, this he is unable to do, not withstanding all the efforts of despair, that Power is the stronger, and it compells him to be the self he does not will to be. But for all that he wills to be rid of himself, to be rid of the self which he is, in order to be the self he himself has chanced to choose. To be *self* as he wills to be would be his delight (though in another sense it would be equally in despair), but to be compelled to be *self* as he does not will to be is his torment, namely, that he cannot get rid of himself.

Socrates proved the immortality of the soul from the fact that the sickness of the soul (sin) does not consume it as sickness of the body consumes the body. So also we can demonstrate the eternal in man from the fact that despair cannot consume his self, that this precisely is the torment of contradiction in despair. If there were nothing eternal in a man, he could not despair; but if despair could consume his self, there would still be no despair.

Thus it is that despair, this sickness in the self, is the sickness unto death. The despairing man is mortally ill. In an entirely different sense than can appropriately be said of any disease, we may say that the sickness has attacked the noblest part; and yet the man cannot die. Death is not the last phase of the sickness, but death is continually the last. To be delivered from this sickness by death is an impossibility, for the sickness and its torment . . . and death consist in not being able to die.

This is the situation in despair. And however thoroughly it eludes the attention of the despairer, and however thoroughly the despairer may succeed (as in the case of that kind of despair which is characterized by unawareness of being in despair) in losing himself entirely, and losing himself in such a way that it is not noticed in the least—eternity nevertheless will make it manifest that his situation was despair, and it will so nail him to himself that the torment nevertheless remains that he cannot get rid of himself, and it becomes manifest that he was deluded in thinking that he succeeded. And thus it is eternity must act, because to have a self, to be a self, is the greatest concession made to man, but at the same time it is eternity's demand upon him.

Just as the physician might say that there lives perhaps not one single man who is in perfect health, so one might say perhaps that there lives not one single man who after all is not to some extent in despair, in whose inmost parts there does not dwell a disquietude, a perturbation, a discord, an anxious dread of an unknown something, or of a something he does not even dare to make acquaintance with, dread of a possibility of life, or dread of himself, so that, after all, as physicians speak of a man going about with a disease in him, this man is going about and carrying a sickness of the spirit, which only rarely and in glimpses, by and with a dread which to him is inexplicable, gives evidence of its presence within. At any rate there has lived no one and there lives no one outside of Christendom who is not in despair, and no one in Christendom, unless he be a true Christian, and if he is not quite that, he is somewhat in despair after all.

This view will doubtless seem to many a

paradox, an exaggeration, and a gloomy and depressing view at that. Yet it is nothing of the sort. It is not gloomy; on the contrary, it seeks to throw light upon a subject which ordinarily is left in obscurity. It is not depressing; on the contrary it is uplifting, since it views every man in the aspect of the highest demand made upon him, that he be spirit. Nor is it a paradox; on the contrary, it is a fundamental apprehension consistently carried through, and hence it is no exaggeration. . . .

Not only is despair far more dialectical than an illness, but all its symptoms are dialectical, and for this reason the superficial view is so readily deceived in determining whether despair is present or not. For not to be in despair may mean to be in despair, and it may also mean to be delivered from being in despair. A sense of security and tranquillity may mean that one is in despair, precisely this security, this tranquility, may be despair; and it may mean that one has overcome despair and gained peace. In this respect despair is unlike bodily sickness; for not to be sick cannot possibly mean to be sick; but not to be despairing may mean precisely to be despairing. It is not true of despair, as it is of bodily sickness, that the feeling of indisposition is the sickness. By no means. The feeling of indisposition is again dialectical. Never to have been sensible of this indisposition is precisely to be in despair.

This points to the fact, and has its ground therein, that man, regarded as spirit, is always in a critical condition—and if one is to talk of despair, one must conceive of man as spirit. In relation to sickness we talk of a crisis, but not in relation to health. And why not? Because bodily health is an "immediate" qualification, and only becomes dialectical in sickness, when one can speak of the crisis. But spiritually, or when man is regarded as spirit, both health and sickness are critical. There is no

such thing as "immediate" health of the spirit. . . .

Therefore it is as far as possible from being true that the vulgar view is right in assuming that despair is a rarity; on the contrary, it is quite universal. It is as far as possible from being true that the vulgar view is right in assuming that everyone who does not think or feel that he is in despair is not so at all, and that only he is in despair who says that he is. On the contrary, one who without affectation says that he is in despair is after all a little bit nearer, a dialectical step nearer to being cured than all those who are not regarded and do not regard themselves as being in despair. But precisely this is the common situation (as the physician of souls will doubtless concede), that the majority of men live without being thoroughly conscious that they are spiritual beings—and to this is referable all the security, contentment with life, etc., etc., which precisely is despair. Those, on the other hand, who say that they are in despair are generally such as have a nature so much more profound that they must become conscious of themselves as spirit, or such as by the hard vicissitudes of life and its dreadful decisions have been helped to become conscious of themselves as spirit—either one or the other, for rare is the man who truly is free from despair.

Ah, so much is said about human want and misery—I seek to understand it, I have also had some acquaintance with it at close range; so much is said about wasted lives—but only that man's life is wasted who lived on, so deceived by the joys of life or by its sorrows that he never became eternally and decisively conscious of himself as spirit, as self, or (what is the same thing) never became aware and in the deepest sense received an impression of the fact that there is a God, and that he, he himself, his self, exists before this God, which gain of infinity is never attained except through despair. And, oh, this misery, that so many live on and are defrauded of this most blessed of all thoughts; this misery, that people employ themselves about everything else, or, as for the masses of men, that people employ them about everything else, utilize them to generate the power for the theater of life, but never remind them of their blessedness; that they heap them in a mass and defraud them, instead of splitting them apart so that they might gain the highest thing, the only thing worth living for, and enough to live in for an eternity—it seems to me that I could weep for an eternity over the fact that such misery exists! And, oh, to my thinking this is one expression the more of the dreadfulness of this most dreadful sickness and misery, namely, its hiddenness—not only that he who suffers from it may wish to hide it and may be able to do so, to the effect that it can so dwell in a man that no one, no one whatever discovers it; no, rather that it can be so hidden in a man that he himself does not know it! And, oh, when the hour-glass has run out, the hour-glass of time, when the noise of worldliness is silenced, and the restless or the ineffectual busyness comes to an end, when everything is still about thee as it is in eternity— whether thou wast man or woman, rich or poor, dependent or independent, fortunate or unfortunate, whether thou didst bear the spendor of the crown in a lofty station, or didst bear only the labor and heat of the day in an inconspicuous lot; whether thy name shall be remembered as long as the world stands (and so was remembered as long as the world stood), or without a name thou didst cohere as nameless with the countless multitude; whether the glory which surrounded thee surpassed all human description, or the judgment passed upon thee was the most severe and dishonoring human judgment can pass—eternity asks of thee and of every individual among these million millions only one question, whether thou hast lived in despair or not, whether thou wast in despair in such a way that thou didst not know thou wast in despair, or in such a way that thou didst hiddenly carry this sickness in thine inward parts as thy gnawing secret, carry it under thy heart as the fruit of a sinful love, or in such a way that thou, a horror to others, didst rave in despair. And if so, if thou hast lived in despair (whether for the rest thou didst win or lose), then for thee all is lost, eternity knows thee not, it never knew thee, or (even more dreadful) it knows thee as thou art known, it puts thee under arrest by thyself in despair.

2 / THEORY OF KNOWLEDGE

The writer of the next selection, Martin Heidegger, has disclaimed the title "existentialist" because the question that concerns him is not human existence but Being in its totality and as such. Yet he continues to be classified with the existentialists because of his approach to the question of Being. He believes this question can be answered only by beginning with the being we can examine—namely, "the being which we ourselves are." Thus we see that, as in the other schools we have examined, existentialism includes a diversity of interests and problems.

In the following essay Heidegger discusses the problem of truth. Traditional definitions of truth center on the idea of correspondence or representation of ideas and objects. But such definitions are primarily of propositional truth, and they also involve difficulties over "representation." Heidegger asks, what can representation mean except: letting something *be* an object to us? If this is done, statements about the object will "right" themselves—and truth is rightness.

For a thing to be revealed and rightness to be possible, there must be freedom. "The essence of truth is freedom," and truth is not, then, originally in the proposition. Freedom is an ex-posing of the nature of what is; truth is a revealing of what is.

But human beings, Heidegger believes, live essentially in error, for the what-is—even and especially of themselves—is not revealed, is not open. Hence their existence is unauthentic and compulsive. To achieve authentic existence, men must live in freedom and truth.

THE ESSENCE OF TRUTH

Martin Heidegger (1889-   )

What do we ordinarily understand by "truth"? This exalted but at the same time overworked and almost exhausted word "truth" means: that which makes something true into a truth. What is "something true"? We say, for example: "It is a true pleasure to collaborate in the accomplishment of this task." We mean, it is a pure, real joy. The True is the Real. In the same way we speak of "true coin" as distinct from false. False coin is not really what it seems. It is only a "seeming" and therefore unreal. The unreal stands for the opposite of the real. But counterfeit coin too is something real. Hence we say more precisely: "Real coin is genuine coin." Yet both are "real," the counterfeit coin in circulation no less than the genuine. Therefore the truth of the genuine coin cannot be verified by its reality. The question returns: What do "genuine" and "true" mean here? Genuine coin is that real thing whose reality agrees with *(in der Uebereinstimmung steht mit)* what we always and in advance

The selection is from Martin Heidegger, "On the Essence of Truth," in Werner Brock (tr.), *Existence and Being* (Chicago: Henry Regnery Co.; London: Vision Press, Ltd., 1949), pp. 321-350, with omissions. Used by permission of the publishers.

"really" mean by "coin." Conversely, where we suspect false coin we say: "There is something not quite right here" *(Hier stimmt etwas nicht)*. On the other hand we say of something that is "as it should be": "It's right" *(es stimmt)*. The *thing (Sache)* is right.

We call "true" not only a real pleasure, genuine coin and all actualities of that sort, we also and principally call "true" or "false" our statements concerning such actualities as are themselves true or false in their kind, which may be thus or thus in their reality. A statement is true when what it means and says agrees with the thing of which it speaks. Here too we say: "It's right." Though now it is not the *thing* that is right but the *proposition (Satz)*.

The True, then, be it a true thing or a true proposition, is that which is right, which corresponds *(das Stimmende)*. Being true and truth here mean correspondence, and that in a double sense: firstly the correspondence of a thing with the idea of it as conceived in advance *(dem über sie Vorgemeinten)*, and secondly the correspondence of that which is intended by the statement with the thing itself.

The dual aspect of this correspondence

is brought out very clearly by the traditional definition of truth: *veritas est adaequatio rei et intellectus*. Which can be
taken to mean: truth is the approximation of thing (object) to perception. But
it can also mean: truth is the approximation of perception to thing (object). Admittedly the above definition is usually
employed only in the formula: *veritas est
adaequatio intellectus ad rem*. Yet truth so
understood, i.e. *propositional* truth, is only
possible on the basis of *objective* truth, the
adaequatio rei ad intellectum. Both conceptions of the nature of *veritas* always imply
"putting oneself right by" *(sich richten
nach)* something and thus conceive truth
as *rightness (Richtigkeit)*. . . .

We speak of "agreement" in different
senses. We say, for example, seeing two
half-crowns lying on the table, that they
agree with one another, are like one another.
Both agree in identity of appearance. They
have this in common and are therefore in
this respect alike. Further, we speak of
agreement when we say of one of these
half-crowns: this coin is round. Here the
statement "agrees" with the subject or
thing. The relationship now obtains not between thing and thing, but between statement and thing. But in what do statement
and thing agree, seeing that the referents
are obviously different in appearance? The
coin is of metal. The statement is in no
sense material. The coin is round. The statement has absolutely nothing spatial about
it. With the coin you can buy something.
The statement about it can never be legal
tender. But despite the disparity between
the two, the above statement agrees with
and is true of the coin. And, according to
the accepted idea of truth, this agreement
is supposed to be an approximation *(An-
gleichung)*. How can something completely
unlike—the statement—approximate to the
coin? It would have to *become* the coin and
present itself entirely in that form. No state-

ment can do that. The moment it succeeded
in doing so the statement, as statement,
could no longer agree with the thing. In any
approximation the statement has to remain,
indeed it has first to become, what it is.
In what does its nature, so entirely different
from any other thing, consist? How can the
statement, precisely by insisting on its own
nature, approximate to something else, to
the thing?

"Approximation" in this instance cannot
mean a material likeness between two
things unlike in kind. The nature of the
approximation is rather determined by the
kind of relationship obtaining between
statement and thing. So long as this "relationship" remains indeterminate and its
nature unfathomed, all argument as to the
possibility or impossibility, the kind and
degree of approximation, leads nowhere.

The statement about the coin relates
"itself" to this thing by representing it and
saying of the thing represented "how it is,"
"what it is like," in whatever respect is
important at that moment. The representative statement has its say about the thing
represented, stating it to be *such as* it is.
This "such-as" *(so-wie)* applies to the representation and what it represents. "Representation" means here, if we disregard all
"psychological" and "theory of consciousness" preconceptions, *letting something take
up a position opposite to us, as an object*.
The thing so opposed must, such being its
position, come across the open towards us
and at the same time stand fast in itself
as the thing and manifest itself as a constant. This manifestation of the thing in
making a move towards us is accomplished
in the open, within the realm of the Overt
(das Offene), the overt character *(Offenheit)* of which is not initially created by
the representation but is only entered into
and taken over each time as an area of
relationships *(Bezugsbereich)*. The relation
between representative statement and thing
serves to implement that condition *(Ver-*

hältnis) which originally started to vibrate, and now continues to vibrate, as *behavior (Verhalten)*. But all behavior is characterized by the fact that, obtaining as ıt does in the open, it must always relate to something manifest *as such (ein Offenbares als einsolches)*. What is thus, and solely in this narrow sense, made manifest was experienced in the early stages of Western thought as "that which is present" and has long been termed "that which is" *(das Seiende)*.

All behavior is "overt" (lit. "stands open": *offen-ständig)* to what-is, and all "overt" relationship is behavior. Man's "overtness" varies with the nature of what-is and the mode of behavior. All working and carrying out of tasks, all transaction and calculation, sustains itself in the open, an overt region within which what-is can expressly take up its stand *as* and *how* it is *what* it is, and thus become capable of expression. This can only occur when what-is represents itself *(selbst vorstellig wird)* with the representative statement, so that the statement submits to a directive enjoining it to express what-is "such-as" or just as it is. By following this directive the statement "rights itself" *(sich richtet nach)* by what-is. Directing itself in this way the statement is right (true). And what is thus stated is rightness (truth).

The statement derives its rightness from the overtness of behavior, for it is only through this that anything manifest can become the criterion for the approximation implicit in the representative statement. Overt behavior must apply this criterion to itself. Which means: it must be for a start something of a criterion for all representation. This is implicit in the overtness of behavior. But if rightness (truth) of statement is only made possible by the overt character of behavior, then it follows that the thing that makes rightness possible in the first place must have a more original claim to be regarded as the essence of truth.

Thus the traditional practice of attributing truth exclusively to the statement as its sole and essential place of origin, falls to the ground. Truth does not possess its original seat in the proposition. At the same time the question arises: on what basis does it become inwardly possible for overt behavior to postulate a criterion—a possibility which alone invests propositional rightness with sufficient status to achieve, in any measure, the essence of truth?

Whence does the representative statement receive its command to "right itself" by the object and thus to be in accord with rightness? Why does this accord *(Stimmen)* at the same time determine *(bestimmen)* the nature of truth? How, in fact, can there be such a thing at all as approximation to a pre-established criterion, or a directive enjoining such an accord? Only because this postulate *(Vorgeben)* has already freed itself *(sich freigegeben hat)* and become open to a manifestation operating in this openness—a manifestation which is binding on all representation whatsoever. This "freeing" for the sake of submitting to a binding criterion is only possible as freedom to reveal something already overt *(zum Offenbaren eines Offenen)*. Being free in this way points to the hitherto uncomprehended nature of freedom. The overt character of behavior in the sense that it makes rightness a possibility, is grounded in freedom. *The essence of truth is freedom. . . .*

But to turn truth into freedom—is that not to abandon truth to the caprice of man? Can truth be more basically undetermined than by being delivered up to the whim of this wavering reed? The thing that has forced itself time and again on our sound judgment during the course of this exposition so far, now becomes all the more evident: truth is brought down to the subjective level of the human subject. Even if this subject can attain to some kind of objectivity, it still remains human in its subjectivity and subject to human control.

Admittedly, guile and dissimulation, lies and deception, fraud and pretense, in short, all manner of untruth, are ascribed to man. But untruth is the opposite of truth, for which reason it is, as the very negation of truth, its "dis-essence" rightly kept at a remove from the field of enquiry into the pure essence of truth. This human origin of untruth merely confirms by contrast the essential nature of truth "as such" which holds sway "over" man and which metaphysics regard as something imperishable and eternal, something that can never be founded on the transitoriness and fragility of humankind. How then can the essence of truth possibly have a stable basis in human freedom?

Resistance to the proposition that the essence of truth is freedom is rooted in prejudices, the most obstinate of which contends that freedom is a property of man and that the nature of freedom neither needs nor allows of further questioning. As for man, we all know what *he* is.

The indication, however, of the essential connection between truth *as rightness,* and freedom, shatters these preconceived notions, provided of course that we are prepared to change our way of thinking. Consideration of the natural affinity between truth and freedom induces us to pursue the question as to the nature of man in one of its aspects—an aspect vouched for by our experience of a hidden ground in man's nature and being, so that we are transported in advance into the original living realm of truth. But at this point it also becomes evident that freedom is the basis of the inner possibility of rightness only because it receives its own essence from that thing of earlier origin: the uniquely essential truth.

Freedom was initially defined as freedom for the revelation of something already overt. How are we to think of the essence of freedom so conceived? The Manifest *(das Offenbare),* to which a representative statement approximates in its rightness, is that which obviously "is" all the time and has some manifest form of behavior. The freedom to reveal something overt lets whatever "is" at the moment *be* what it is. Freedom reveals itself as the "letting-be" of what-is.

We usually talk of "letting be" when, for instance, we stand off from some undertaking we have planned. "We let it be" means: not touching it again, not having anything more to do with it. "Letting be" here has the negative sense of disregarding something, renouncing something, of indifference and even neglect.

The phrase we are now using, namely the "letting-be" of what-is, does not, however, refer to indifference and neglect, but to the very opposite of them. To let something be *(Seinlassen)* is in fact to have something to do with it *(sich einlassen auf).* This is not to be taken merely in the sense of pursuing, conserving, cultivating and planning some actuality casually met with or sought out. To let what-is *be* what it is means participating in something overt and its overtness, in which everything that "is" takes up its position and which entails such overtness. Western thought at its outset conceived this overtness as τὰ ἀληϑέα, the Unconcealed. If we translate ἀλήϑεια by "unconcealment" or "revealment" instead of truth, the translation is not only more "literal" but it also requires us to revise our ordinary idea of truth in the sense of propositional correctitude and trace it back to that still uncomprehended quality: the revealedness *(Entborgenheit)* and revelation *(Entbergung)* of what-is. Participation in the revealed nature of what-is does not stop there, it develops into a retirement before it so that what-is may reveal itself as *what* and *how* it is, and the approximation which represents it in the statement may take it for a criterion. In this manner "letting-be" exposes itself *(setzt sich aus)* to what-is-as-such and brings all behavior into the open *(versetzt ins Offene)*. "Letting-be", i.e. freedom, is in its own self "ex-posing" *(aus-setzend)* and "ex-sistent" *(ek-sistent)*.

The nature of freedom, seen from the point of view of the nature of truth, now shows itself as an "exposition" into the revealed nature of what-is.

Freedom is not what common sense is content to let pass under that name: the random ability to do as we please, to go this way or that in our choice. Freedom is not license in what we do or do not do. Nor, on the other hand, is freedom a mere readiness to do something requisite and necessary—and thus in a sense "actual" *(Seiendes)*. Over and above all this ("negative" and "positive" freedom) freedom is a participation in the revealment of what-is-as-such *(das Seiende als ein solches)*. The revelation of this is itself guaranteed in that ex-sistent participation whereby the overtness of the overt *(die Offenheit des Offenen)*, i.e. the "There" *(Da)* of it, *is* what it is.

In this Da-sein there is preserved for mankind that long unfathomed and essential basis on which man is able to ex-sist. "Existence" in this case does not signify *existentia* in the sense of the "occurrence" *(Vorkommen)* and "being" *(Dasein)*, i.e. "presence" *(Vorhandensein)* of an "existent" *(eines Seienden)*. Nor does "existence" mean, "existentially" speaking, man's moral preoccupation with himself—a preoccupation arising out of his psycho-physical constitution. Ex-sistence, grounded in truth as freedom, is nothing less than exposition into the revealed nature of what-is-as-such. Still unfathomed and not even conscious of the need for any deeper fathoming of its essence, the ex-sistence of historical man begins at that moment when the first thinker to ask himself about the revealed

nature of what-is, poses the question: What is what-is? With this question unconcealment and revealment are experienced for the first time. . . .

But if ex-sistent *Da-sein*, understood as the letting-be of what-is, sets man free for his "freedom" which confronts him, then and only then, with a choice between actual possibilities and which imposes actual necessities upon him, then freedom is not governed by human inclination. Man does not "possess" freedom as a property, it is the contrary that is true: freedom, or ex-sistent, revelatory *Da-sein* possesses man and moreover in so original a manner that it alone confers upon him that relationship with what-is-in-totality which is the basis and distinctive characteristic of his history. Only ex-sistent man is historical. "Nature" has no history.

Freedom, so understood as the letting-be of what-is, fulfils and perfects the nature of truth in the sense that truth is the unconcealment and revealment of what-is. "Truth" is not the mark of some correct proposition made by a human "subject" in respect of an "object" and which then—in precisely what sphere we do not know—counts as "true"; truth is rather the revelation of what-is, a revelation through which something "overt" comes into force. All human behavior is an exposition into that overtness. Hence man *is* in virtue of his ex-sistence.

Because all modes of human behavior *(Verhalten)* are, each in its own way, overt and always relate to that which they must *(wozu es sich verhält)*, it follows that the restraint *(Verhaltenheit)* of "letting things be," i.e. freedom, must necessarily have given man an inner directive to approximate his ideas (representions: *Vorstellen*) to what-is at any moment. Man ex-sists, and this now means: historical man has his history and all its possibilities guaranteed him in the revelation of what-is-in-totality. The manner in which the original nature of truth operates *(west)* gives rise to the rare and simple decisions of history.

But because truth is in essence freedom, historical man, though he lets things be, cannot really let what-is be just *what* it is and *as* it is. What-is is then covered up and distorted. Illusion comes into its own. The essential negation of truth, its "dis-essence" *(Unwesen)*, makes its appearance. But because ex-sistent freedom, being the essence of truth, is not a property of man (it being rather the case that man only ex-sists as the property of this freedom and so becomes capable of history), it follows that the dis-essence of truth cannot, in its turn, simply arise *a posteriori* from the mere incapacity and negligence of man. On the contrary, untruth must derive from the essence of truth. Only because truth and untruth are not *in essence* indifferent to one another, can a true proposition contrast so sharply with its correspondingly untrue proposition. Our quest for the nature of truth only extends into the original realm of interrogation when, having gained a preliminary insight into the complete essence of truth, we now include a consideration of untruth in the revelation of "essence." The enquiry into the dis-essence of truth is not a subsequent filling of the gap; it is the decisive step towards any adequate posing of the question as to the nature of truth. Yet, how are we to conceive truth's dis-essence as part of its essence? If the essence of truth is not fully displayed in the rightness of a statement, then neither can untruth be equated with the wrongness of an opinion. . . .

Man errs. He does not merely fall into error, he lives in error always because, by ex-sisting, he in-sists and is thus already in error. The error in which he lives is not just something that runs along beside him like a ditch, something he occasionally falls into. No, error is part of the inner structure of *Da-sein*, in which historical man is in-

volved. Error is the theatre for that variable mode of being *(Wende)* where in-sistent ex-sistence, turning and turning about, perpetually forgets and mistakes itself. The dissimulation of what-is concealed in totality comes into force through the revelation of what-is at any moment, and this revelation, because it is a forgetting of the dissimulation; leads to error.

Error is the essential counter-essence *(das wesentliche Gegenwesen)* of the original essence of truth. It opens out as the manifest theatre for all counter-play to essential truth. Error is the open ground, the basis of Wrong *(Irrtum)*. Wrong is not just the isolated mistake, it is the empire, the whole history of all the complicated and intricate ways of erring.

All modes of behavior have, according to their overtness and correlation to what-is-in-totality, each their way of erring. Wrong ranges from the commonest mistake, oversight, miscalculation to going astray and getting utterly lost when it comes to adopting important attitudes and making essential decisions. What we ordinarily understand by "wrong" and moreover, according to the teachings of philosophy— namely the wrongness *(Unrichtigheit)* of a judgment and the falseness of perception, is only one, and that the most superficial, way of erring. The error in which historical man must always walk, which makes his road erratic *(irrig)* is essentially one with the manifest character of what-is. Error dominates man through and through by leading him astray. But, by this self-same aberration *(Beirrung)*, error collaborates in the possibility which man has (and can always extract from his ex-sistence) of *not allowing* himself to be led astray, of himself experiencing error and thus not overlooking the mystery of *Da-sein*.

Because man's in-sistent ex-sistence leads to error, and because error always oppresses in one way or another and out of this oppression becomes capable of commanding the mystery, albeit forgotten, it follows that man in his *Da-sein* is *especially* subject to the rule of mystery and his own affliction. Between them, *he lives in an extremity of compulsion.* The total essence of truth, which contains in its own self its "dis-essence," keeps *Da-sein* ever turning this way and that but always into misery. *Da-sein* is, in fact, a turning to misery, a turning into need. From man's *Da-sein* and from this alone comes the revelation of necessity and, as a result, the possibility of turning this necessity into something *needed,* something unavoidable. . . .

The present essay leads the question concerning the nature of truth beyond the accustomed confines of our fundamental ideas and helps us to consider whether this question of the essence of truth is not at the same time necessarily the question of the truth of essence. Philosophy, however, conceives "essence" as Being. By tracing the inner possibility of a statement's "rightness" back to the ex-sistent freedom of "letting-be" as the very basis of that statement, and by suggesting that the essential core of this basis is to be found in dissimulation and error, we may have indicated that the nature of truth is not just the empty, "general" character of some "abstract" commonplace, but something that is unique in history (itself unique): the self-dissimulation of the unveiling of the "meaning" of what we call "Being," which we have long been accustomed to think of only as "what-is-in-totality."

3 / METAPHYSICS

Existentialists show a unity of philosophical concern in their belief that man's nature or essence can be found only in his concrete, lived experience. In the lecture from which the following selection is taken, the French philosopher Jean-Paul Sartre develops this belief in terms of the statement, "existence precedes essence." There has been much discussion of this view, and there is disagreement over it even among existentialists. The lecture itself shows signs of being a public lecture rather than a careful essay (Jaspers, for example, is mistakenly referred to as a Catholic). Yet Sartre's statement remains a brilliant and incisive summary of his fundamental position.

To say that existence precedes essence means that man first appears and only later defines himself in his experience. There being no antecedent essence to which he must conform, man is both free and responsible for the definition he produces. In his freedom, man exists outside and beyond himself or his essence, and this in fact is existence. Sartre's version of existentialism is an effort to draw all the consequences of an atheistic position; though men experience anguish, forlornness, and despair in their existing, Sartre says that even if God existed, nothing would change.

ESSENCE AND EXISTENCE

Jean-Paul Sartre (1905-   )

Most people who use the word [existentialism] would be rather embarrassed if they had to explain it, since, now that the word is all the rage, even the work of a musician or painter is being called existentialist. A gossip columnist in *Clartés* signs himself *The Existentialist*, so that by this time the word has been so stretched and has taken on so broad a meaning, that it no longer means anything at all. It seems that for want of an advance-guard doctrine analogous to surrealism, the kind of people who are eager for scandal and flurry turn to this philosophy which in other respects does not at all serve their purposes in this sphere.

Actually, it is the least scandalous, the most austere of doctrines. It is intended strictly for specialists and philosophers. Yet it can be defined easily. What complicates matters is that there are two kinds of existentialist; first, those who are Christian, among whom I would include Jaspers and Gabriel Marcel, both Catholic; and on the other hand the atheistic existentialists, among whom I class Heidegger, and then the French existentialists and myself. What they have in common is that they think that existence precedes essence, or, if you prefer, that subjectivity must be the starting point.

Just what does that mean? Let us consider some object that is manufactured, for example, a book or a paper-cutter: here is an object which has been made by an artisan whose inspiration came from a concept. He referred to the concept of what a paper-cutter is and likewise to a known method of production, which is part of the concept, something which is, by and large, a routine. Thus, the paper-cutter is at once an object produced in a certain way and, on the other hand, one having a specific use; and one can not postulate a man who produces a paper-cutter but does not know what it is used for. Therefore, let us say that, for the paper-cutter, essence—that is, the ensemble of both the production routines and the properties which enable it to be both produced and defined—precedes existence. Thus, the presence of the paper-cutter or book in front of me is determined. Therefore, we have here a technical view of the world whereby it can be said that production precedes existence.

When we conceive God as the Creator, He is generally thought of as a superior sort of artisan. Whatever doctrine we may be considering, whether one like that of Descartes or that of Leibnitz, we always grant that will more or less follows understanding or, at the very least, accompanies it, and that when God creates He knows exactly what He is creating. Thus, the concept of man in the mind of God is comparable to the concept of paper-cutter in the mind of the manufacturer, and, following certain techniques and a conception, God produces man, just as the artisan, following a definition and a technique, makes a paper-cutter. Thus, the individual man is the realization of a certain concept in the divine intelligence.

In the eighteenth century, the atheism of the *philosophes* discarded the idea of God, but not so much for the notion that essence precedes existence. To a certain extent, this idea is found everywhere; we find it in Diderot, in Voltaire, and even in Kant. Man has a human nature; this hu-

The selection is from Jean-Paul Sartre, "Existentialism," in *Existentialism and Human Emotions* (tr. Bernard Frechtman) (New York: Philosophical Library, 1957), pp. 12-51, with omissions. Used by permission of the publisher.

man nature, which is the concept of the human, is found in all men, which means that each man is a particular example of a universal concept, man. In Kant, the result of this universality is that the wild-man, the natural man, as well as the bourgeois, are circumscribed by the same definition and have the same basic qualities. Thus, here too the essence of man precedes the historical existence that we find in nature.

Atheistic existentialism, which I represent, is more coherent. It states that if God does not exist, there is at least one being in whom existence precedes essence, a being who exists before he can be defined by any concept, and that this being is man, or, as Heidegger says, human reality. What is meant here by saying that existence precedes essence? It means that, first of all, man exists, turns up, appears on the scene, and, only afterwards, defines himself. If man, as the existentialist conceives him, is indefinable, it is because at first he is nothing. Only afterward will be he be something, and he himself will have made what he will be. Thus, there is no human nature, since there is no God to conceive it. Not only is man what he conceives himself to be, but he is also only what he wills himself to be after this thrust toward existence.

Man is nothing else but what he makes of himself. Such is the first principle of existentialism. It is also what is called subjectivity, the name we are labeled with when charges are brought against us. But what do we mean by this, if not that man has a greater dignity than a stone or table? For we mean that man first exists, that is, that man first of all is the being who hurls himself toward a future and who is conscious of imagining himself as being in the future. Man is at the start a plan which is aware of itself, rather than a patch of moss, a piece of garbage, or a cauliflower; nothing exists prior to this plan; there is nothing in heaven; man will be what he will have planned to be. Not what he will want

to be. Because by the word "will" we generally mean a conscious decision, which is subsequent to what we have already made of ourselves. I may want to belong to a political party, write a book, get married; but all that is only a manifestation of an earlier, more spontaneous choice that is called "will." But if existence really does precede essence, man is responsible for what he is. Thus, existentialism's first move is to make every man aware of what he is and to make the full responsibility of his existence rest on him. And when we say that a man is responsible for himself, we do not only mean that he is responsible for his own individuality, but that he is responsible for all men.

The word subjectivism has two meanings, and our opponents play on the two. Subjectivism means, on the one hand, that an individual chooses and makes himself; and, on the other, that it is impossible for man to transcend human subjectivity. The second of these is the essential meaning of existentialism. When we say that man chooses his own self, we mean that every one of us does likewise; but we also mean by that that in making this choice he also chooses all men. In fact, in creating the man that we want to be, there is not a single one of our acts which does not at the same time create an image of man as we think he ought to be. To choose to be this or that is to affirm at the same time the value of what we choose, because we can never choose evil. We always choose the good, and nothing can be good for us without being good for all.

If, on the other hand, existence precedes essence, and if we grant that we exist and fashion our image at one and the same time, the image is valid for everybody and for our whole age. Thus, our responsibility is much greater than we might have supposed, because it involves all mankind. If I am a workingman and choose to join a Christian trade-union rather than be a communist, and if by being a member I want to show that the best thing for man is resignation, that the kingdom of man is not of this world, I am not only involving my own case—I want to be resigned for everyone. As a result, my action has involved all humanity. To take a more individual matter, if I want to marry, to have children; even if this marriage depends solely on my own circumstances or passion or wish, I am involving all humanity in monogamy and not merely myself. Therefore, I am responsible for myself and for everyone else. I am creating a certain image of man of my own choosing. In choosing myself, I choose man.

This helps us understand what the actual content is of such rather grandiloquent words as anguish, forlornness, despair. As you will see, it's all quite simple.

First, what is meant by anguish? The existentialists say at once that man is anguish. What that means is this: the man who involves himself and who realizes that he is not only the person he chooses to be, but also a lawmaker who is, at the same time, choosing all mankind as well as himself, can not help escape the feeling of his total and deep responsibility. Of course, there are many people who are not anxious; but we claim that they are hiding their anxiety, that they are fleeing from it. Certainly, many people believe that when they do something, they themselves are the only ones involved, and when someone says to them, "What if everyone acted that way?" they shrug their shoulders and answer, "Everyone doesn't act that way." But really, one should always ask himself, "What would happen if everybody looked at things that way?" There is no escaping this disturbing thought except by a kind of double-dealing. A man who lies and makes excuses for himself by saying "not everybody does that," is someone with an uneasy conscience, because the act of lying implies that a universal value is conferred upon the lie.

Anguish is evident even when it conceals itself. This is the anguish that Kierkegaard called the anguish of Abraham. You know the story: an angel has ordered Abraham to sacrifice his son; if it really were an angel who has come and said, "You are Abraham, you shall sacrifice your son," everything would be all right. But everyone might first wonder, "Is it really an angel, and am I really Abraham? What proof do I have?"

There was a madwoman who had hallucinations; someone used to speak to her on the telephone and give her orders. Her doctor asked her, "Who is it who talks to you?" She answered, "He says it's God." What proof did she really have that it was God? If an angel comes to me, what proof is there that it's an angel? And if I hear voices, what proof is there that they come from heaven and not from hell, or from the subconscious, or a pathological condition? What proves that they are addressed to me? What proof is there that I have been appointed to impose my choice and my conception of man on humanity? I'll never find any proof or sign to convince me of that. If a voice addresses me, it is always for me to decide that this is the angel's voice; if I consider that such an act is a good one, it is I who will choose to say that it is good rather than bad.

Now, I'm not being singled out as an Abraham, and yet at every moment I'm obliged to perform exemplary acts. For every man, everything happens as if all mankind had its eyes fixed on him and were guiding itself by what he does. And every man ought to say to himself, "Am I really the kind of man who has the right to act in such a way that humanity might guide itself by my actions?" And if he does not say that to himself, he is masking his anguish. . . .

When we speak of forlornness, a term Heidegger was fond of, we mean only that God does not exist and that we have to face all the consequences of this. The existentialist is strongly opposed to a certain kind of secular ethics which would like to abolish God with the least possible expense. About 1880, some French teachers tried to set up a secular ethics which went something like this: God is a useless and costly hypothesis; we are discarding it; but, meanwhile, in order for there to be an ethics, a society, a civilization, it is essential that certain values be taken seriously and that they be considered as having an *a priori* existence. It must be obligatory, *a priori*, to be honest, not to lie, not to beat your wife, to have children, etc., etc. So we're going to try a little device which will make it possible to show that values exist all the same, inscribed in a heaven of ideas, though otherwise God does not exist. In other words—and this, I believe, is the tendency of everything called reformism in France—nothing will be changed if God does not exist. We shall find ourselves with the same norms of honesty, progress, and humanism, and we shall have made of God an outdated hypothesis which will peacefully die off by itself.

The existentialist, on the contrary, thinks it very distressing that God does not exist, because all possibility of finding values in a heaven of ideas disappears along with Him; there can no longer be an *a priori* Good, since there is no infinite and perfect consciousness to think it. Nowhere is it written that the Good exists, that we must be honest, that we must not lie; because the fact is we are on a plane where there are only men. Dostoievsky said, "If God didn't exist, everything would be possible." That is the very starting point of existentialism. Indeed, everything is permissible if God does not exist, and as a result man is forlorn, because neither within him nor without does he find anything to cling to. He can't start making excuses for himself.

If existence really does precede essence, there is no explaining things away by reference to a fixed and given human nature. In other words, there is no determinism, man is free, man is freedom. On the other hand, if God does not exist, we find no values or commands to turn to which legitimize our conduct. So, in the bright realm of values, we have no excuse behind us, nor justification before us. We are alone, with no excuses.

That is the idea I shall try to convey when I say that man is condemned to be free. Condemned, because he did not create himself, yet, in other respects is free; because, once thrown into the world, he is responsible for everything he does. The existentialist does not believe in the power of passion. He will never agree that a sweeping passion is a ravaging torrent which fatally leads a man to certain acts and is therefore an excuse. He thinks that man is responsible for his passion.

The existentialist does not think that man is going to help himself by finding in the world some omen by which to orient himself. Because he thinks that man will interpret the omen to suit himself. Therefore, he thinks that man, with no support and no aid, is condemned every moment to invent man. Ponge, in a very fine article, has said, "Man is the future of man." That's exactly it. But if it is taken to mean that this future is recorded in heaven, that God sees it, then it is false, because it would really no longer be a future. If it is taken to mean that, whatever a man may be, there is a future to be forged, a virgin future before him, then this remark is sound. But then we are forlorn. . . .

As for despair, the term has a very simple meaning. It means that we shall confine ourselves to reckoning only with what depends upon our will, or on the ensemble of probabilities which make our action possible. When we want something, we always have to reckon with probabilities. I may be counting on the arrival of a friend. The friend is coming by rail or street-car; this supposes that the train will arrive on schedule, or that the street-car will not jump the track. I am left in the realm of possibility; but possibilities are to be reckoned with only to the point where my action comports with the ensemble of these possibilities, and no further. The moment the possibilities I am considering are not rigorously involved by my action, I ought to disengage myself from them, because no God, no scheme, can adapt the world and its possibilities to my will. When Descartes said, "Conquer yourself rather than the world," he meant essentially the same thing. . . .

At heart, what existentialism shows is the connection between the absolute character of free involvement, by virtue of which every man realizes himself in realizing a type of mankind, an involvement always comprehensible in any age whatsoever and by any person whosoever, and the relativeness of the cultural ensemble which may result from such a choice; it must be stressed that the relativity of Cartesianism and the absolute character of Cartesian involvement go together. In this sense, you may, if you like, say that each of us performs an absolute act in breathing, eating, sleeping, or behaving in any way whatever. There is no difference between being free, like a configuration, like an existence which chooses its essence, and being absolute. There is no difference between being an absolute temporarily localized, that is, localized in history, and being universally comprehensible. . . .

Man is constantly outside of himself; in projecting himself, in losing himself outside of himself, he makes for man's existing; and, on the other hand, it is by pursuing transcendent goals that he is able to exist; man, being this state of passing-beyond, and seizing upon things only as they bear upon this passing-beyond, is at the heart, at the center of this passing-beyond. There is no universe other than a human universe, the universe of human subjectivity. This connection between transcendency, as a constituent element of man—not in the sense that God is transcendent, but in the sense of passing beyond—and subjectivity, in the sense that man is not closed in on himself but is always present in a human universe, is what we call existentialism humanism. Humanism, because we remind man that there is no law-maker other than himself, and that in his forlornness he will decide by himself; because we point out that man will fulfill himself as man, not in turning toward himself, but in seeking outside of himself a goal which is just this liberation, just this particular fulfillment.

From these few reflections it is evident that nothing is more unjust than the objections that have been raised against us. Existentialism is nothing else than an attempt to draw all the consequences of a coherent atheistic position. It isn't trying to plunge man into despair at all. But if one calls every attitude of unbelief despair, like the Christians, then the word is not being used in its original sense. Existentialism isn't so atheistic that it wears itself out showing that God doesn't exist. Rather, it declares that even if God did exist, that would change nothing. There you've got our point of view. Not that we believe that God exists, but we think that the problem of His existence is not the issue. In this sense existentialism is optimistic, a doctrine of action, and it is plain dishonesty for Christians to make no distinction between their own despair and ours and then to call us despairing.

4 / ETHICS

The "existential experience" with its loss of meaning and its general nihilism is present in the ethical as well as in all other dimensions of experience. One of the greatest diagnosticians of this nihilism is Friedrich Nietzsche, a thinker whose influence on present existentialism was tremendous. Nietzsche saw Western culture with its science, technology, mass society, and nationalism as tending to create a complete fear of individuality and an absence of meaning and value. He expresses this observation poignantly in his statement, "God is dead, and we have killed him." No belief in an objective moral order, that is, is possible in modern society because of the very activities and institutions that it has produced. But how, then, are meaning and ethical value to be achieved? Nietzsche's answer is, only by the deliberate, creative willing of value by strong personalities. These creators he called *Uebermenschen.*

The following selections expand these themes of existentialist as well as ethical interest. Nietzsche's style is aphoristic but very moving. The individual, the value of honesty or subjective truth, master or creative morality, men who by rejecting the conventional, the dishonest, the mass, and all that subdues individual existence prepare for the *Uebermenschen:* such ideas are clearly developments of the existential experience, and they place Nietzsche within the existentialist position.

A NEW ETHICS

Friedrich Nietzsche (1844-1900)

[*The will to truth.*] The Will to Truth, which is to tempt us to many a hazardous enterprise, the famous Truthfulness of which all philosophers have hitherto spoken with respect, what questions has this Will to Truth not laid before us! What strange, perplexing, questionable questions! It is already a long story; yet it seems as if it

were hardly commenced. Is it any wonder if we at last grow distrustful, lose patience, and turn impatiently away? That this Sphinx teaches us at last to ask questions ourselves? *Who* is it really that puts questions to us here? *What* really is this "Will to Truth" in us? In fact we made a long halt at the question as to the origin of this Will—until at last we came to an absolute standstill before a yet more fundamental question. We inquired about the *value* of this Will. Granted that we want the truth: *why not rather* untruth? And uncertainty? Even ignorance? The problem of the value of truth presented itself before us—or was it we who presented ourselves before the problem? Which of us is the Œdipus here? Which the Sphinx? It would seem to be a rendezvous of questions and notes of inter-

The selection, except the last two sections, is from Friedrich Nietzsche, *Beyond Good and Evil* (tr. Helen Zimmern) (London: George Allen & Unwin, Ltd.; New York: The Macmillan Company, 1907), pp. 5-6, 227-232, and 8-9. Used by permission of George Allen & Unwin, Ltd. The next to last paragraph is from *The Dawn of Day* (tr. Johanna Volz) (New York: The Macmillan Company, 1903), p. 170. The last paragraph has been translated from *Die fröhliche Wissenschaft* (Leipzig: C. G. Naumann, 1900), pp. 214-215.

rogation. And could it be believed that it at last seems to us as if the problem had never been propounded before, as if we were the first to discern it, get a sight of it, and *risk raising* it. For there is risk in raising it; perhaps there is no greater risk. . . .

[*Master and slave morality.*] In a tour through the many finer and coarser moralities which have hitherto prevailed or still prevail on the earth, I found certain traits recurring regularly together, and connected with one another, until finally two primary types revealed themselves to me, and a radical distinction was brought to light. There is *master-morality* and *slave-morality;*—I would at once add, however, that in all higher and mixed civilizations, there are also attempts at the reconciliation of the two moralities; but one finds still oftener the confusion and mutual misunderstanding of them, indeed, sometimes their close juxtaposition—even in the same man, within one soul. The distinctions of moral values have either originated in a ruling caste, pleasantly conscious of being different from the ruled— or among the ruled class, the slaves and dependents of all sorts. In the first case, when it is the rulers who determine the conception "good," it is the exalted, proud disposition which is regarded as the distinguishing feature, and that which determines the order of rank. The noble type of man separates from himself the beings in whom the opposite of this exalted, proud disposition displays itself: he despises them. Let it at once be noted that in this first kind of morality the antithesis "good" and "bad" means practically the same as "noble" and "despicable";—the antithesis "good" and *"evil"* is of a different origin. The cowardly, the timid, the insignificant, and those thinking merely of narrow utility are despised; moreover, also, the distrustful, with their constrained glances, the self-abasing, the dog-like kind of men who let themselves be abused, the mendicant flatterers, and above

all the liars:—it is a fundamental belief of all aristocrats that the common people are untruthful. "We truthful ones"—the nobility in ancient Greece called themselves. It is obvious that everywhere the designations of moral value were at first applied to *men,* and were only derivatively and at a later period applied to *actions;* it is a gross mistake, therefore, when historians of morals start with questions like, "Why have sympathetic actions been praised?" The noble type of man regards *himself* as a determiner of values; he does not require to be approved of; he passes the judgment: "What is injurious to me is injurious in itself"; he knows that it is he himself only who confers honor on things; he is a *creator of values.* He honors whatever he recognizes in himself: such morality is self-glorification. In the foreground there is the feeling of plenitude, of power, which seeks to overflow, the happiness of high tension, the consciousness of a wealth which would fain give and bestow:—the noble man also helps the unfortunate, but not—or scarcely—out of pity, but rather from an impulse generated by the superabundance of power. The noble man honors in himself the powerful one, him also who has power over himself, who knows how to speak and how to keep silence, who takes pleasure in subjecting himself to severity and hardness, and has reverence for all that is severe and hard. "Wotan placed a hard heart in my breast," says an old Scandinavian Saga: it is thus rightly expressed from the soul of a proud Viking. Such a type of man is even proud of *not* being made for sympathy; the hero of the Saga therefore adds warningly: "He who has not a hard heart when young, will never have one." The noble and brave who think thus are the furthest removed from the morality which sees precisely in sympathy, or in acting for the good of others, or in *désintéressement,* the characteristic of the moral; faith in oneself, pride in oneself, a radical enmity and irony towards "selflessness," belong as definitely to noble morality, as do a careless scorn and precaution in presence of sympathy and the "warm heart."—It is the powerful who *know* how to honor, it is their art, their domain for invention. The profound reverence for age and for tradition—all law rests on this double reverence,—the belief and prejudice in favor of ancestors and unfavorable to newcomers, is typical in the morality of the powerful; and if, reversely, men of "modern ideas" believe almost instinctively in "progress" and the "future," and are more and more lacking in respect for old age, the ignoble origin of these "ideas" has complacently betrayed itself thereby. A morality of the ruling class, however, is more especially foreign and irritating to present-day taste in the sternness of its principle that one has duties only to one's equals; that one may act towards beings of a lower rank, towards all that is foreign, just as seems good to one, or "as the heart desires," and in any case "beyond good and evil": it is here that sympathy and similar sentiments can have a place. The ability and obligation to exercise prolonged gratitude and prolonged revenge—both only within the circle of equals,—artfulness in retaliation, *raffinement* of the idea in friendship a certain necessity to have enemies (as outlets for the emotions of envy, quarrelsomeness, arrogance—in fact, in order to be a good *friend*): all these are typical characteristics of the noble morality, which, as has been pointed out, is not the morality of "modern ideas," and is therefore at present difficult to realize, and also to unearth and disclose.—It is otherwise with the second type of morality, *slave-morality*. Supposing that the abused, the oppressed, the suffering, the unemancipated, the weary, and those uncertain of themselves, should moralize, what will be the common element in their moral estimates? Probably a pessimistic suspicion with regard to the entire situation of man will find expression, perhaps a condemnation of man,

together with his situation. The slave has an unfavorable eye for the virtues of the powerful; he has a skepticism and distrust, a *refinement* of distrust of everything "good" that is there honored—he would fain persuade himself that the very happiness there is not genuine. On the other hand, *those* qualities which serve to alleviate the existence of sufferers are brought into prominence and flooded with light; it is here that sympathy, the kind, helping hand, the warm heart, patience, diligence, humility, and friendliness attain to honor; for here these are the most useful qualities, and almost the only means of supporting the burden of existence. Slave-morality is essentially the morality of utility. Here is the seat of the origin of the famous antithesis "good" and *"evil"*:—power and dangerousness are assumed to reside in the evil, a certain dreadfulness, subtlety, and strength, which do not admit of being despised. According to slave-morality, therefore, the "evil" man arouses fear; according to master-morality, it is precisely the "good" man who arouses fear and seeks to arouse it, while the bad man is regarded as the despicable being. The contrast attains its maximum when, in accordance with the logical consequences of slave-morality, a shade of depreciation—it may be slight and well-intentioned—at last attaches itself to the "good" man of this morality; because, according to the servile mode of thought, the good man must in any case be the *safe* man: he is good-natured, easily deceived, perhaps a little stupid, *un bonhomme*. Everywhere that slave-morality gains the ascendency, language shows a tendency to approximate the significations of the words "good" and "stupid."—At last fundamental difference: the desire for *freedom,* the instinct for happiness and the refinements of the feeling of liberty belong as necessarily to slave-morals and morality, as artifice and enthusiasm in reverence and devotion are the regular symptoms of an aristocratic mode of thinking and estimating.—

Hence we can understand without further detail why love *as a passion*—it is our European specialty—must absolutely be of noble origin; as is well known, its invention is due to the Provençal poet-cavaliers, those brilliant ingenious men of the *"gai saber"* to whom Europe owes so much, and almost owes itself.

[*Beyond good and evil.*] The falseness of an opinion is not for us any objection to it: it is here, perhaps, that our new language sounds most strangely. The question is, how far an opinion is life-furthering, life-preserving, species-preserving, perhaps species-rearing; and we are fundamentally inclined to maintain that the falsest opinions (to which the synthetic judgments *a priori* belong), are the most indispensable to us; that without a recognition of logical fictions, without a comparison of reality with the purely *imagined* world of the absolute and immutable, without a constant counterfeiting of the world by means of numbers, man could not live—that the renunciation of false opinions would be a renunciation of life, a negation of life. *To recognize untruth as a* condition of life: that is certainly to impugn the traditional ideas of value in a dangerous manner, and a philosophy which ventures to do so, has thereby alone placed itself beyond good and evil.

The panegyrists of work.—In the glorification of work, in the incessant chatter about the "blessings of work," I discover the same secret thought as in the praise of the benevolent, impersonal actions, namely, the dread of the individual. At the sight of work—which always implies that severe toil from morning till night—we really feel that such work is the best police, that it keeps everybody in bounds, and effectually checks the development of reason, of covetousness, of a desire after independence. For it consumes an enormous amount of nervous force, withdrawing it from reflection, brooding, dreaming, care, love, hatred; it always dangles a small object before the eye, affording easy and regular gratifications. Thus a society in which hard work is constantly being performed will enjoy greater security, and security is now worshipped as the supreme deity. And now! Oh horror! the very "workman" has grown dangerous! the world is swarming with "dangerous individuals"! And in their train follows the danger of all dangers—the individual.

Pioneering men.—I welcome all signs that a more manly, warlike age is about to begin which, above all, will again bring honor to valor! For it shall prepare the way for a higher age and gather the strength which this higher age will someday need—that age, which shall bear heroism into knowledge and *wage wars* for the sake of ideas and their consequences. For this there is now needed many pioneering valorous men, who cannot spring up out of nothing—any more than out of the sand and filth of our present civilization and its metropolitanism: men who understand how to be silent, solitary, resolute, content and steadfast in imperceptible activity: men who then with inner inclination seek after that which is to be *overcome* in them: men in whom cheerfulness, patience, unpretentiousness, and contempt for all great vanities are just as much part of them as magnanimity in victory and forbearance toward the small vanities of the vanquished: men with a keen and free judgment on all victors and on the share of chance in every victory and fame: men with their own festivals, workdays, times of mourning, accustomed and sure in command and likewise ready, where necessary, to obey, in one as in the other equally proud, equally serving their own cause: men in greater danger, more fruitful men, happier men! For, believe me!—the secret of the greatest fruitfulness and the greatest enjoyment of being is: *to live dangerously!* Build your cities on the slopes of Vesuvius!

Send your ships into unmapped seas! Live
at war with your peers and with yourselves.
Be robbers and conquerors, as long as you
cannot be rulers and owners, you lovers of
knowledge! The time is soon past when it
will be enough for you to live hidden like
timid deer in the woods. Finally the pursuit
of knowledge will stretch out for its due:—
it will want to *rule* and *possess,* and you
along with it.

5 / ESTHETICS

Esthetic values, like moral values, are never simply *given* for the existentialist. Rather, they come into being only by a creative decision and act of
some creator. In the following selection, Sartre writes that the *esthetic* object, as
distinct from the physical thing we call a book or a painting, is present only to a
realizing consciousness that has become imaginative. But imaginative conscious-
nesss negates the world and grasps or contemplates an *unreality.* Hence the
esthetic object, as a product of imagination, is itself an unreality. In turn, beauty
is a value only in reference to the imaginary: the real is never beautiful. Beauty,
therefore, is a negation of the world.

ART AS UNREALITY

Jean-Paul Sartre (1905-   )

The following comments will be concerned essentially with the existential type
of the work of art. And we can at once formulate the law that the work of art is an
unreality.

This appeared to us clearly from the
moment we took for our example, in an entirely different connection, the portrait of
Charles VIII. We understood at the very
outset that this Charles VIII was an object.
But this, obviously, is not the same object
as is the painting, the canvas, which are the
real objects of the painting. As long as we
observe the canvas and the frame for themselves the esthetic object "Charles VIII"
will not appear. It is not that it is hidden by

The selection is from Jean-Paul Sartre, *The
Psychology of Imagination* (tr. Bernard
Frechtman) (New York: Philosophical Library, Inc.; London: John F. Rider, 1948),
pp. 273-282. Used by permission of the Philosophical Library and The Hutchinson
Group.

the picture, but because it cannot present
itself to a realizing consciousness. It will
appear at the moment when consciousness,
undergoing a radical change in which the
world is negated, will itself become imaginative. The situation here is like that of the
cubes which can be seen at will to be five or
six in number. It will not do to say that
when they are seen as five it is because at
that time the aspect of the drawing in which
they are six is *concealed.* The intentional act
that apprehends them as five is sufficient
unto itself, it is complete and *exclusive* of
the act which grasps them as six. And so it
is with the apprehension of Charles VIII
as an image which is depicted on the picture. This Charles VIII on the canvas is
necessarily the correlative of the intentional
act of an imaginative consciousness. And
since this Charles VIII, who is an unreality
so long he is grasped on the canvas, is precisely the object of our esthetic apprecia-
tions (it is he who "moves" us, who is

"painted with intelligence, power, and grace," etc.), we are led to recognize that, in a picture, the esthetic object is something *unreal*. This is of great enough importance once we remind ourselves of the way in which we ordinarily confuse the real and the imaginary in a work of art. We often hear it said, in fact, that the artist first has an idea in the form of an image which he then *realizes* on canvas. This mistaken notion arises from the fact that the painter can, in fact, begin with a mental image which is, as such, incommunicable, and from the fact that at the end of his labors he presents the public with an object which anyone can observe. This leads us to believe that there occurred a transition from the imaginary to the real. But this is in no way true. That which is real, we must not fail to note, are the results of the brush strokes, the stickiness of the canvas, its grain, the polish spread over the colors. But all this does not constitute the object of esthetic appreciation. What is "beautiful" is something which cannot be experienced as a perception and which, by its very nature, is out of the world. We have just shown that it cannot be *brightened,* for instance, by projecting a light beam on the canvas: it is the canvas that is brightened and not the painting. The fact of the matter is that the painter did not *realize* his mental image at all: he has simply constructed a material analogue of such a kind that everyone can grasp the image provided he looks at the analogue. But the image thus provided with an external analogue remains an image. There is no realization of the imaginary, nor can we speak of its *objectification*. Each stroke of the brush was not made *for itself* nor even for the constructing of a coherent real whole (in the sense in which it can be said that a certain lever in a machine was conceived in the interest of the whole and not for itself). It was given together with an unreal synthetic whole and the aim of the artist was to construct a whole of *real* colors which en-

able this unreal to manifest itself. The painting should then be conceived as a material thing *visited* from time to time (every time that the spectator assumes the imaginative attitude) by an unreal which is precisely the *painted object*. What deceives us here is the real and sensuous pleasure which certain real colors on the canvas give us. Some reds of Matisse, for instance, produce a sensuous enjoyment in those who see them. But we must understand that this sensuous enjoyment, if thought of in isolation—for instance, if aroused by a color in nature—has nothing of the esthetic. It is purely and simply a pleasure of sense. But when the red of the painting is grasped, it is grasped, in spite of everything, as a part of an unreal whole and it is in this whole that it is beautiful. For instance it is the red of a rug by a table. There is, in fact, no such thing as pure color. Even if the artist is concerned solely with the sensory relationships between forms and colors, he chooses for that very reason a rug in order to increase the sensory value of the red: tactile elements, for instance, must be intended through the red, it is a *fleecy* red, because the rug is of a fleecy material. Without this "fleeciness" of the color something would be lost. And surely the rug is painted there *for the red* it justifies and not the red for the rug. If Matisse chose a rug rather than a sheet of dry and glossy paper it is because of the voluptuous mixture of the color, the density and the tactile quality of the wool. Consequently the red can be truly enjoyed only in grasping it as the *red of the rug*, and therefore unreal. And he would have lost his strongest contrast with the green of the wall if the green were not rigid and cold, because it is the green of a wall tapestry. It is therefore in the unreal that the relationship of colors and forms takes on its real meaning. And even when drawn objects have their usual meaning reduced to a minimum, as in the painting of the cubists, the painting is at least not flat.

The forms we see are certainly not the forms of a rug, a table, nor anything else we see in the world. They nevertheless do have a density, a material, a depth, they bear a relationship of perspective towards each other. They are *things*. And it is precisely in the measure in which they are things that they are unreal. Cubism has introduced the fashion of claiming that a painting should not *represent* or *imitate* reality but should constitute an object in itself. As an esthetic doctrine such a program is perfectly defensible and we owe many masterpieces to it. But it needs to be understood. To maintain that the painting, although altogether devoid of meaning, nevertheless is a *real* object, would be a grave mistake. It is certainly not an object of nature. The real object no longer functions as an analogue of a bouquet of flowers or a glade. But when I "contemplate" it, I nevertheless am not in a realistic attitude. The painting is still an *analogue*. Only what manifests itself through it is an unreal collection of *new things*, of objects I have never seen or ever will see, but which are not less unreal because of it, objects which do not exist *in the painting*, nor anywhere in the world, but which manifest themselves by means of the canvas, and which have gotten hold of it by some sort of possession. And it is the configuration of these unreal objects that I designate as *beautiful*. The esthetic enjoyment is real but it is not grasped for itself, as if produced by a real color: it is but a manner of apprehending the unreal object and, far from being directed on the real painting, it serves to constitute the imaginary object through the real canvas. This is the source of the celebrated disinterestedness of esthetic experience. This is why Kant was able to say that it does not matter whether the object of beauty, when experienced as beautiful, is or is not objectively real; why Schopenhauer was able to speak of a sort of suspension of the Will. This does not come from some mysterious way of apprehending the real, which we are able to use occasionally. What happens is that the esthetic object is constituted and apprehended by an imaginative consciousness which posits it as unreal.

What we have just shown regarding painting is readily applied to the art of fiction, poetry and drama, as well. It is self-evident that the novelist, the poet and the dramatist construct an unreal object by means of verbal analogues; it is also self-evident that the actor who plays Hamlet makes use of himself, of his whole body, as an analogue of the imaginary person. Even the famous dispute about the paradox of the comedian is enlightened by the view here presented. It is well known that certain amateurs proclaim that the actor *does not believe* in the character he portrays. Others, leaning on many witnesses, claim that the actor becomes identified in some way with the character he is enacting. To us these two views are not exclusive of each oher; if by "belief" is meant actually real it is obvious that the actor does not actually consider himself to be Hamlet. But this does not mean that he does not "mobilize" all his powers to make Hamlet real. He uses all his feelings, all his strength, all his gestures as analogues of the feelings and conduct of Hamlet. But by this very fact he takes the reality away from them. *He lives completely in an unreal way*. And it matters little that he is *actually* weeping in enacting the role. These tears . . . he himself experiences—and so does the audience—as the tears of Hamlet, that is as the analogue of unreal tears. The transformation that occurs here is like that we discussed in the dream: the actor is completely caught up, inspired, by the unreal. It is not the character who becomes real in the actor, it is the actor who *becomes unreal* in his character.[1]

---

[1] It is in this sense that a beginner in the theatre can say that stage-fright served her to represent the timidity of Ophelia. If it did so, it is because she suddenly turned it into an unreality, that is, that she ceased to apprehend it for itself and that she grasped it as *analogue* for the timidity of Ophelia.

But are there not some arts whose objects seem to escape unreality by their very nature? A melody, for instance, refers to nothing but itself. Is a cathedral anything more than a mass of *real* stone which dominates the surrounding house tops? But let us look at this matter more closely. I listen to a symphony orchestra, for instance, playing the Beethoven Seventh Symphony. Let us disregard exceptional cases—which are besides on the margin of esthetic contemplation—as when I go mainly "to hear Toscanini" interpret Beethoven in his own way. As a general rule what draws me to the concert is the desire "to hear the Seventh Symphony." Of course I have some objection to hearing an amateur orchestra, and prefer this or that well-known musical organization. But this is due to my desire to hear the symphony "played perfectly," because the symphony will then be *perfectly itself.* The shortcomings of a poor orchestra which plays "too fast" or "too slow," "in the wrong tempo," etc., seem to me to rob, to "betray" the work it is playing. At most the orchestra effaces itself before the work it performs, and, provided I have reasons to trust the performers and their conductor, I am confronted by the symphony itself. This everyone will grant me. But now, what is the Seventh Symphony itself? Obviously it is a *thing,* that is something which is before me, which endures, which lasts. Naturally there is no need to show that that thing is a synthetic whole, which does not consist of tones but of a thematic configuration. But is that "thing" real or unreal? Let us first bear in mind that I am listening to the Seventh Symphony. For me that "Seventh Symphony" does not exist in time, I do not grasp it as a dated event, as an artistic manifestation which is unrolling itself in the Châtelet auditorium on the 17th of November, 1938. If I hear Furtwaengler tomorrow or eight days later conduct another orchestra performing the same symphony, I am in the presence of the same symphony once more. Only it is being played either better or worse. Let us now see *how* I hear the symphony: some persons shut their eyes. In this case they detach themselves from the *visual* and dated event of this particular interpretation: they give themselves up to the pure sounds. Others watch the orchestra or the back of the conductor. But they do not see what they are looking at. This is what Revault d'Allonnes calls reflection with auxiliary fascination. The auditorium, the conductor and even the orchestra have disappeared. I am therefore confronted by the Seventh Symphony, but on the express condition of understanding *nothing about it,* that I do not think of the event as an actuality and dated, and on condition that I listen to the succession of themes as an absolute succession and not as a real succession which is unfolding itself, for instance, on the occasion when Peter paid a visit to this or that friend. In the degree to which I hear the symphony it is *not here,* between these walls, at the tip of the violin bows. Nor is it "in the past" as if I thought: this is the work that matured in the mind of Beethoven on such a date. It is completely beyond the real. It has its own time, that is, it possesses an inner time, which runs from the first tone of the allegro to the last tone of the finale, but this time is not a succession of a preceding time which it continues and which happened "before" the beginning of the allegro; nor is it followed by a time which will come "after" the finale. The Seventh Symphony is in no way *in time.* It is therefore in no way real. It occurs *by itself,* but as absent, as being out of reach. I cannot act upon it, change a single note of it, or slow down its movement. But it depends on the real for its appearance: that the conductor does not faint away, that a fire in the hall does not put an end to the performance. From this we cannot conclude that *the* Seventh Symphony has come to an end. No, we only think that the *performance* of the symphony has ceased. Does this not show clearly that the performance of the symphony is its *analogue?*

It can manifest itself only through analogues which are dated and which unroll in our time. But to experience it on these analogues the imaginative reduction must be functioning, that is, the real sounds must be apprehended as analogues. It therefore occurs as a perpetual elsewhere, a perpetual absence. We must not picture it (as does Spandrell in *Point Counterpoint* by Huxley—as so many platonisms) as existing in another world, in an intelligible heaven. It is not only outside of time and space—as are essences, for instance—it is outside of the real, outside of existence. I do not hear it actually, I listen to it in the imaginary. Here we find the explanation for the considerable difficulty we always experience in passing from the world of the theatre or of music into that of our daily affairs. There is in fact no passing from one world into the other, but only a passing from the imaginative attitude to that of reality. Esthetic contemplation is an induced dream and the passing into the real is an actual waking up. We often speak of the "deception" experienced on returning to reality. But this does not explain that this discomfort also exists, for instance, after having witnessed a realistic and cruel play, in which case reality should be experienced as comforting. This discomfort is simply that of the dreamer on awakening; an entranced consciousness, engulfed in the imaginary, is suddenly freed by the sudden ending of the play, of the symphony, and comes suddenly in contact with existence. Nothing more is needed to arouse the nauseating disgust that characterizes the consciousness of reality.

From these few observations we can already conclude that the real is never beautiful. Beauty is a value applicable only to the imaginary and which means the negation of the world in its essential structure. This is why it is stupid to confuse the moral with the esthetic. The values of the Good presume being-in-the-world, they concern action in the real and are subject from the outset to the basic absurdity of existence. To say that we "assume" an esthetic attitude to life is to constantly confuse the real and the imaginary. It does happen, however, that we do assume the attitude of esthetic contemplation towards real events or objects. But in such cases everyone of us can feel in himself a sort of recoil in relation to the object contemplated which slips into nothingness so that, from this moment on, it is no longer *perceived;* it functions as an *analogue* of itself, that is, that an unreal image of what it is appears to us through its actual presence. This image can be purely and simply the object "itself" neutralized, annihilated, as when I contemplate a beautiful woman or death at a bull fight; it can also be the imperfect and confused appearance of *what it could be* through what it is, as when the painter grasps the harmony of two colors as being greater, more vivid, *through* the real blots he finds on a wall. The object at once appears to be *in back of* itself, becomes *untouchable,* it is beyond our reach; and hence arises a sort of sad disinterest in it. It is in this sense that we may say that great beauty in a woman kills the desire for her. In fact we cannot at the same time place ourselves on the plane of the esthetic when this unreal "herself" which we admire appears and on the realistic plane of physical possession. To desire her we must forget she is beautiful, because desire is a plunge into the heart of existence, into what is most contingent and most absurd. Esthetic contemplation of *real* objects is of the same structure as paramnesia, in which the real object functions as analogue of itself in the past. But in one of the cases there is a negating and in the other a placing a thing in the past. Paramnesia differs from the esthetic attitude as memory differs from imagination.

6 / SOCIAL PHILOSOPHY

With the loss of meaning in modern life has gone the loss of social values; and with their disappearance comes a threat to the individual and his existence from the forces of society. The important Spanish thinker Ortega y Gasset finds a peculiar contradiction in contemporary life. On the one hand, our technological culture opens to men more possibilities for action than has any previous society; on the other, modern man seems completely satisfied with himself as he is. This "mass-man" as Ortega y Gasset terms him, must be distinguished from "excellent-man." By imposing discipline upon himself, the latter seeks to live the noble life, the life of effort and creativity.

Human life is such that it must be dedicated to something, must express nobility through dedication to ends. But in our day human beings are lost and wandering for lack of commitments. Mass-man is lost because of his inertia. Society needs nobility, Ortega y Gasset concludes, and nobility posits a true concept of obedience: dedication, creativity, and acceptance of the ruler's leadership.

MASS-MAN AND SOCIETY

José Ortega y Gasset (1883-1955)

To start with, we are what our world invites us to be, and the basic features of our soul are impressed upon it by the form of its surroundings as in a mould. Naturally, for our life is no other than our relations with the world around. The general aspect which it presents to us will form the general aspect of our own life. It is for this reason that I stress so much the observation that the world into which the masses of today have been born displays features radically new to history. Whereas in past times life for the average man meant finding all around him difficulties, dangers, want, limitations of his destiny, dependence, the new world appears as a sphere of practically limitless possibilities, safe, and independent of anyone. Based on this primary and lasting impression, the mind of every contemporary man will be formed, just as previous minds were formed on the opposite impression. For that basic impression becomes an interior voice which ceaselessly utters certain words in the depths of each individual, and tenaciously suggests to him a definition of life which is, at the same time, a moral imperative. And if the traditional sentiment whispered: "To live is to feel oneself limited, and therefore to have to count with that which limits us," the newest voice shouts: "To live is to meet with no limitation whatever and, consequently, to abandon oneself calmly to one's self. Practically nothing is impossible, nothing is dangerous, and, in principle, nobody is superior to anybody." This basic experience completely modifies the traditional, persistent structure of the mass-man. For the latter always felt himself, by his nature, confronted with ma-

The selection is reprinted from José Ortega y Gasset, *The Revolt of the Masses* (New York: W. W. Norton & Company, Inc.; London: George Allen & Unwin, Ltd., 1932), pp. 61-67 and 140-145. Copyright, 1932, by W. W. Norton & Company, Inc., and George Allen & Unwin, Ltd.; copyright, 1960, by Teresa Carey. Used by permission of W. W. Norton & Company, Inc., and George Allen & Unwin, Ltd.

terial limitations and higher social powers. Such, in his eyes, was life. If he succeeded in improving his situation, if he climbed the social ladder, he attributed this to a piece of fortune which was favorable to him in particular. And if not to this, then to an enormous effort, of which he knew well what it had cost him. In both cases it was a question of an exception to the general character of life and the world; an exception which, as such, was due to some very special cause.

But the modern mass finds complete freedom as its natural, established condition, without any special cause for it. Nothing from outside incites it to recognize limits to itself and, consequently, to refer at all times to other authorities higher than itself. Until lately, the Chinese peasant believed that the welfare of his existence depended on the private virtues which the Emperor was pleased to possess. Therefore, his life was constantly related to this supreme authority on which it depended. *But the man we are now analyzing accustoms himself not to appeal from his own to any authority outside him.* He is satisfied with being exactly as he is. Ingenuously, without any need of being vain, as the most natural thing in the world, he will tend to consider and affirm as good everything he finds within himself: opinions, appetites, preferences, tastes. Why not, if, as we have seen, nothing and nobody force him to realize that he is a second-class man, subject to many limitations, incapable of creating or conserving that very organization which gives his life the fullness and contentedness on which he bases this assertion of his personality?

The mass-man would never have accepted authority external to himself had not his surroundings violently forced him to do so. As today, his surroundings do not so force him, the everlasting mass-man, true to his character, ceases to appeal to other authority and feels himself lord of his own existence. On the contrary the select man, the excellent man is urged, by interior

necessity, to appeal from himself to some standard beyond himself, superior to himself, whose service he freely accepts. Let us recall that at the start we distinguished the excellent man from the common man by saying that the former is the one who makes great demands on himself, and the latter the one who makes no demands on himself, but contents himself with what he is, and is delighted with himself.[1] Contrary to what is usually thought, it is the man of excellence, and not the common man who lives in essential servitude. Life has no savor for him unless he makes it consist in service to something transcendental. Hence he does not look upon the necessity of serving as an oppression. When, by chance, such necessity is lacking, he grows restless and invents some new standard, more difficult, more exigent, with which to coerce himself. This is life lived as a discipline—the noble life. Nobility is defined by the demands it makes on us—by obligations, not by rights. *Noblesse oblige.* "To live as one likes is plebeian; the noble man aspires to order and law" (Goethe). The privileges of nobility are not in their origin concessions or favors; on the contrary, they are conquests. And their maintenance supposes, in principle, that the privileged individual is capable of reconquering them, at any moment, if it were necessary, and anyone were to dispute them. Private rights or *privileges* are not, then, passive possession and mere enjoyment, but they represent the standard attained by personal effort. On the other hand, common rights, such as those "of the man and the citizen," are passive property, pure usufruct and benefit, the generous gift

---

[1] That man is intellectually of the mass who, in face of any problem, is satisfied with thinking the first thing he finds in his head. On the contrary, the excellent man is he who contemns what he finds in his mind without previous effort, and only accepts as worthy of him what is still far above him and what requires a further effort in order to be reached.

of fate which every man finds before him, and which answers to no effort whatever, unless it be that of breathing and avoiding insanity. I would say, then, that an impersonal right is held, a personal one is upheld.

It is annoying to see the degeneration suffered in ordinary speech by a word so inspiring as "nobility." For, by coming to mean for many people hereditary "noble blood," it is changed into something similar to common rights, into a static, passive quality which is received and transmitted like something inert. But the strict sense, the *etymon* of the word nobility is essentially dynamic. Noble means the "well known," that is, known by everyone, famous, he who has made himself known by excelling the anonymous mass. It implies an unusual effort as the cause of his fame. Noble, then, is equivalent to effortful, excellent. The nobility or frame of the son is pure benefit. The son is known because the father made himself famous. He is known by reflection, and in fact, hereditary nobility has an indirect character, it is mirrored light, lunar nobility, something derived from the dead. The only thing left to it of living, authentic, dynamic is the impulse it stirs in the descendant to maintain the level of effort reached by the ancestor. Always, even in this altered sense, *noblesse oblige*. The original noble lays an obligation on himself, the noble heir receives the obligation with his inheritance. But in any case there is a certain contradiction in the passing-on of nobility from the first noble to his successors. The Chinese, more logical, invert the order of transmission; it is not the father who ennobles the son, but the son who, by acquiring noble rank, communicates it to his forbears, by his personal efforts bringing fame to his humble stock. Hence, when granting degrees of nobility, they are graduated by the number of previous generations which are honored; there are those who ennoble only their fathers, and those who stretch back their fame to

the fifth or tenth grandparent. The ancestors live by reason of the actual man, whose nobility is effective, active—in a word: *is*, not *was*.[2]

"Nobility" does not appear as a formal expression until the Roman Empire, and then precisely in opposition to the hereditary nobles, then in decadence.

For me, then, nobility is synonymous with a life of effort, ever set on excelling oneself, in passing beyond what one is to what one sets up as a duty and an obligation. In this way the noble life stands opposed to the common or inert life, which reclines statically upon itself, condemned to perpetual immobility, unless an external force compels it to come out of itself. Hence we apply the term mass to this kind of man—not so much because of his multitude as because of his inertia.

As one advances in life, one realizes more and more that the majority of men—and of women—are incapable of any other effort than that strictly imposed on them as a reaction to external compulsion. And for that reason, the few individuals we have come across who are capable of a spontaneous and joyous effort stand out isolated, monumentalised, so to speak, in our experience. These are the select men, the nobles, the only ones who are active and not merely reactive, for whom life is a perpetual striving, an incessant course of training. Training = *askesis*. These are the ascetics. This apparent digression should not cause surprise. In order to define the actual massman, who is as much "mass" as ever, but who wishes to supplant the "excellent," it has been necessary to contrast him with the two pure forms which are mingled in

---

[2] As in the foregoing it is only a matter of bringing the word "nobility" back to its original sense which excludes inheritance, this is not the place to study the fact that a "nobility of blood" makes its appearance so often in history. This question, then, is left untouched.

him: the normal mass and the genuine noble or man of effort.

Now we can advance more rapidly, because we are now in possession of what, to my thinking, is the key—the psychological equation—of the human type dominant today. All that follows is a consequence, a corollary, of that root-structure, which may be summed up thus: the world as organized by the XIXth Century, when automatically producing a new man, has infused into him formidable appetites and powerful means of every kind for satisfying them. These include the economic, the physical (hygiene, average health higher than any preceding age), the civil and the technical (by which I mean the enormous quantity of partial knowledge and practical efficiency possessed by the average man today and lacking to him in the past). After having supplied him with all these powers, the XIXth Century has abandoned him to himself, and the average man, following his natural disposition, has withdrawn into himself. Hence, we are in presence of a mass stronger than that of any preceding period, but differing from the traditional type in that it remains, hermetically enclosed within itself, incapable of submitting to anything or anybody, believing itself self-sufficient—in a word, indocile. If things go on as they are at present, it will be every day more noticeable in Europe—and by reflection, throughout the whole world—that the masses are incapable of submitting to direction of any kind. In the difficult times that are at hand for our continent, it is possible that, under a sudden affliction, they may for a moment have the good will to accept, in certain specially urgent matters, the direction of the superior minorities.

But even that good will will result in failure. For the basic texture of their soul is wrought of hermetism and indocility; they are from birth deficient in the faculty of giving attention to what is outside themselves, be it fact or person. They will wish to follow someone, and they will be unable. They will want to listen, and will discover they are deaf.

On the other hand, it is illusory to imagine that the mass-man of today, however superior his vital level may be compared with that of other times, will be able to control, by himself, the process of civilization. I say process, and not progress. The simple process of preserving our present civilization is supremely complex, and demands incalculably subtle powers. Ill-fitted to direct it is this average man who has learned to use much of the machinery of civilization, but who is characterized by root-ignorance of the very principles of that civilization.

I reiterate to the reader who has patiently followed me up to this point, the importance of not giving to the facts enunciated a primarily political significance. On the contrary, political activities, of all those in public life the most efficient and the most visible, are the final product of others more intimate, more impalpable. Hence, political indocility would not be so grave did it not proceed from a deeper, more decisive intellectual indocility. In consequence, until we have analyzed this latter, the thesis of this essay will not stand out in its final clarity. . . .

The function of commanding and obeying is the decisive one in every society. As long as there is any doubt as to who commands and who obeys, all the rest will be imperfect and ineffective. Even the very consciences of men, apart from special exceptions, will be disturbed and falsified. If man were a solitary being, finding himself only on occasion thrown into association with others, he might come out intact from such disturbances, brought about by the displacements and crises of the ruling Power. But as he is social in his most intimate texture, his personal character is transformed by changes which strictly speaking only immediately affect the collectivity. Hence it is, that if an individual be taken apart and analyzed, it is possible without further data to deduce how his country's conscience is organized in the matter of command and obedience.

It would be interesting and even useful to submit to this test the individual character of the average Spaniard. However, the operation would be an unpleasant one, and though useful, depressing, so I avoid it. But it would make clear the enormous dose of personal demoralization, of degradation, which is produced in the average man of our country by the fact that Spain is a nation which has lived for centuries with a false conscience in the matter of commanding and obeying. This degradation is nothing else than the acceptance, as a normal, constituted condition, of an irregularity, of something which, though accepted, is still regarded as not right. As it is impossible to change into healthy normality what is of its essence unhealthy and abnormal, the individual decides to adapt himself to the thing that is wrong, making himself a part of the crime or irregularity. It is a mechanism similar to that indicated by the popular saying, "One lie makes a hundred." All countries have passed through periods when someone who should not rule has made the attempt to rule over them, but a strong instinct forced them at once to concentrate their energies and to crush that irregular claim to exercise power. They rejected the passing irregularity and thus reconstituted their morale as a people. But the Spaniard has done just the opposite; instead of resisting a form of authority which his innermost conscience repudiated, he has preferred to falsify all the rest of his being in order to bring it into line with that initial unreality. As long as this continues in our country it is vain to hope for anything from the men of our race. There can be no elastic vigor for the difficult task of retaining a worthy position in history in a society whose State, whose authority, is of its very nature a fraud.

There is, then, nothing strange in the fact that a slight doubt, a simple hesitation as to who rules in the world, should be sufficient to bring about a commencement of demoralization in everyone, both in his public and his private life.

Human life, by its very nature, has to be dedicated to something, an enterprise glorious or humble, a destiny illustrious or trivial. We are faced with a condition, strange but inexorable, involved in our very existence. On the one hand, to live is something which each one does of himself and for himself. On the other hand, if that life of mine, which only concerns myself, is not directed by me towards something, it will be disjointed, lacking in tension and in "form." In these years we are witnessing the gigantic spectacle of innumerable human lives wandering about lost in their own labyrinths, through not having anything to which to give themselves. All imperatives, all commands, are in a state of suspension. The situation might seem to be an ideal one, since every existence is left entirely free to do just as it pleases—to look after itself. The same with every nation. Europe has slackened its pressure on the world. But the result has been contrary to what might have been expected. Given over to itself, every life has been left empty, with nothing to do. And as it has to be filled with something, it invents frivolities for itself, gives itself to false occupations which impose nothing intimate, sincere. Today it is one thing, tomorrow another, opposite to the first. Life is lost at finding itself all alone. Mere egoism is a labyrinth. This is quite understandable. Really to live is to be directed towards something, to progress towards a goal. The goal is not my motion, not my life, it is the something to which I put my life and which consequently is outside it, beyond it. If I decide to walk alone inside my own existence, egotistically, I make no progress. I arrive nowhere. I keep turning round and round in the one spot. That is the labyrinth, the road that leads nowhere, which loses itself, through being a mere turning round within itself. Since the war the European has shut himself up within himself, has been left without projects either for himself or for others. Hence we are continuing historically as we were ten years ago.

Command is not exercised in the void. It implies a pressure exercised on others. But it does not imply this alone. If it were only this, it would be mere violence. We must not forget that command has a double effect —someone is commanded, and he is commanded to do something. And in the long run what he is ordered to do is to take his share in an enterprise, in a historic destiny. Hence there is no empire without a programme of life; more precisely, without a programme of imperial life. As the line of Schiller says: "When kings build, the carters have work to do." It will not do, then, to adopt the trivial notion which thinks it sees in the activity of great nations—as of great men—a merely egoistic inspiration. It is not as easy as you imagine to be pure egoist, and none such have ever succeeded. The apparent egoism of great nations and of great men is the inevitable sternness with which anyone who has his life fixed on some undertaking must bear himself. When we are really going to do something and have dedicated ourselves to a purpose, we cannot be expected to be ready at hand to look after every passer-by and to lend ourselves to every chance display of altruism. One of the things that most delight travellers in Spain is that if they ask someone in the street where such a building or square is, the man asked will often turn aside from his own path and generously sacrifice himself to the stranger, conducting him to the point he is interested in. I am not going to deny that there may be in this disposition of the worthy Spaniard some element of

generosity, and I rejoice that the foreigner so interprets his conduct. But I have never, when hearing or reading of this, been able to repress a suspicion: "Was my countryman, when thus questioned, really going anywhere?" Because it might very well be, in many cases, that the Spaniard is going nowhere, has no purpose or mission, but rather goes out into life to see if others' lives can fill his own a little. In many instances I know quite well that my countrymen go out to the street to see if they will come across some stranger to accompany on his way.

It is serious enough that this doubt as to the rule over the world, hitherto held by Europe, should have demoralized the other nations, except those who by reason of their youth are still in their pre-history. But it is still more serious that this marking-time should reach the point of entirely demoralizing the European himself. I do not say this because I am a European or something of the sort. I am not saying, "If the European is not to rule in the immediate future, I am not interested in the life of the world." Europe's loss of command would not worry me if there were in existence another group of countries capable of taking its place in power and in the direction of the planet. I should not even ask so much. I should be content that no one rule, were it not that this would bring in its train the volatilization of all the virtues and qualities of European man.

Well, this is what would inevitably happen. If the European grows accustomed not to rule, a generation and a half will be sufficient to bring the old continent, and the whole world along with it, into moral inertia, intellectual sterility, universal barbarism. It is only the illusion of rule, and the discipline of responsibility which it entails, that can keep Western minds in tension. Science, art, technique, and all the rest live on the tonic atmosphere created by the consciousness of authority. If this is lacking, the European will gradually become degraded. Minds will no longer have that radical faith in themselves which impels them, energetic, daring, tenacious, towards the capture of great new ideas in every order of life. The European will inevitably become a day-to-day man. Incapable of creative, specialized effort, he will be always falling back on yesterday, on custom, on routine. He will turn into a commonplace, conventional, empty creature, like the Greeks of the decadence and those of the Byzantine epoch.

A creative life implies a regime of strict mental health, of high conduct, of constant stimulus, which keep active the consciousness of man's dignity. A creative life is energetic life, and this is only possible in one or other of these two situations: either being the one who rules, or finding oneself placed in a world which is ruled by someone in whom we recognize full right to such a function: either I rule or I obey. By obedience I do not mean mere submission —this is degradation—but on the contrary, respect for the ruler and acceptance of his leadership, solidarity with him, an enthusiastic enrolment under his banner.

7 / PHILOSOPHY OF SCIENCE

Existentialists rather generally hold that reason, concepts, and science do not grasp the whole of life, and that they may even be instruments that destroy existence and individuality. This theme is explored by Karl Jaspers in the following selection. In former ages, Jaspers observes, philosophy was itself considered a science. Today this view is no longer possible. The name "science" can belong properly only to the sciences. But they need to be purified: all that is pseudoscience and partial science needs to be removed from them. In turn, purified science demands a new and purified philosophy: new, for it must be developed within the new conditions produced by modern science; and purified, for it must grant a full recognition to scientific activity and conclusions. Such recognition, however, indicates that science does not encompass all truth, and that philosophy points beyond scientific objects to the individual in his inward action and freedom. Thus philosophy is the act of becoming conscious of our genuine being.

PURITY IN SCIENCE AND PHILOSOPHY

Karl Jaspers (1883-   )

Philosophy has from its very beginnings looked upon itself as science, indeed as science par excellence. To achieve the highest and most certain knowledge is the goal that has always animated its devotees.

The selection is from Karl Jaspers, "Philosophy and Science," (tr. Ralph Manheim), in *Partisan Review,* 16 (1949), pp. 871 and 878-882. Copyright 1949 by *Partisan Review.* Used by permission of the Editors and the author.

How its scientific character came to be questioned can be understood only in the light of the development of the specifically modern sciences. These sciences made their greatest strides in the nineteenth century, largely outside philosophy, often in opposition to philosophy, and finally in an atmosphere of indifference to it. If philosophy was still expected to be a science, it was in a different sense than before; it was now expected to be a science in the same sense as those modern sciences that convince by virtue of their accomplishments. If it were unable to do so, it was argued, it had become pointless and might just as well die out.

Some decades ago the opinion was widespread that philosophy had had its place up to the moment when all the sciences had become independent of it, the original universal science. Now that all possible fields of research have been marked off, the days of philosophy are over. Now that we know how science obtains its universal validity, it has become evident that philosophy cannot stand up against judgment by these criteria. It deals in empty ideas because it sets up undemonstrable hypotheses, it disregards experience, it seduces by illusions, it takes possession of energies needed for genuine investigation and squanders them in empty talk about the whole. . . .

At a time when confusion prevails regarding the meaning of science, three tasks are imperative. . . .

First, the idea that total philosophical knowledge is scientific knowledge must be exposed as false. The sciences themselves critically explode this false total knowledge. It is here that the opposition to philosophy has its root, and in this respect contempt of it is justifiable.

Second, the sciences must be made pure. This can be accomplished through constant struggle and awareness in the course of our scientific activity itself. By and large, the need for basic clarity concerning science and its limits is readily admitted even by those who sin against such clarity in practice. But the essential is to achieve this purity within the specific sciences. This must be done largely through the critical work of the scientists themselves. But the philosopher who wishes to test the truth-meaning of scientific knowledge, to auscultate it, so

to speak, must participate in the actual work of these scientists.

Third, a pure philosophy must be worked out in the new conditions that have been created by the modern sciences. This is indispensable for the sake of the sciences themselves. For philosophy is always alive in the sciences and so inseparable from them that the purity of both can be achieved only jointly. The rejection of philosophy usually leads to the unwitting development of a bad philosophy. The concrete work of the scientist is guided by his conscious or unconscious philosophy, and this philosophy cannot be the object of scientific method.

For example: It is impossible to prove scientifically that there should be such a thing as science. Or: The choice of an object of science that is made from among an infinite number of existing objects on the basis of this object itself is a choice that cannot be justified scientifically. Or: The ideas that guide us are tested in the systematic process of investigation, but they themselves do not become an object of direct investigation.

Science left to itself as mere science becomes homeless. The intellect is a whore, said Nicholas of Cusa, for it can prostitute itself to anything. Science is a whore, said Lenin, for it sells itself to any class interest. For Nicholas of Cusa it is Reason, and ultimately the knowledge of God, that gives meaning, certainty, and truth to intellectual knowledge; for Lenin, it is the classless society that promotes pure science. Be that as it may, awareness of all this is the business of philosophical reflection. Philosophy is inherent in the actual sciences themselves; it is their inner meaning that provides the scientist with sustenance and guides his methodical work. He who consolidates this guidance through reflection and becomes conscious of it has reached the stage of explicit philosophizing. If this guidance fails, science falls into gratuitous convention, meaningless correctness, aimless busy-ness, and spineless servitude.

A pure science requires a pure philosophy.

But how can philosophy be pure? Has it not always striven to be science? Our answer is: It is "science" but science of such a sort that in the sense of modern scientific inquiry it is both less and more than science.

Philosophy can be called science in so far as it presupposes the sciences. There is no tenable philosophy outside the sciences. Although conscious of its distinct character, philosophy is inseparable from science. It refuses to transgress against universally binding insight. Anyone who philosophizes must be familiar with scientific method.

Any philosopher who is not trained in a scientific discipline and who fails to keep his scientific interests constantly alive will inevitably bungle and stumble and mistake uncritical rough drafts for definitive knowledge. Unless an idea is submitted to the coldly dispassionate test of scientific inquiry, it is rapidly consumed in the fire of emotions and passions, or else it withers into a dry and narrow fanaticism.

Moreover, anyone who philosophizes strives for scientific knowledge, for it is the only way to genuine nonknowledge, it is as though the most magnificent insights could be achieved only through man's quest for the limit at which cognition runs aground, not seemingly and temporarily but genuinely and definitively, not with a sense of loss and despair but with a sense of genuine internal evidence. Only definitive knowledge can make definitive nonknowledge possible; it alone can achieve the authentic failure which opens up a vista, not merely upon the discoverable existent but upon being itself.

In accomplishing the great task of dispelling all magical conceptions, modern science enters upon the path that leads to the intuition of the true depth, the authentic mystery, which becomes present only through the most resolute knowledge in the consummation of nonknowledge.

Consequently philosophy turns against those who despise the sciences, against the sham prophets who deprecate scientific inquiry, who mistake the errors of science for science itself, and who would even hold science, "modern science," responsible for the evils and the inhumanity of our era.

Rejecting superstitious belief in science as well as contempt of science, philosophy grants its unconditional recognition to modern science. In its eyes science is a marvellous thing which can be relied upon more than anything else, the most significant achievement of man in his history, an achievement that is the source of great dangers but of even greater opportunities and that from now on must be regarded as a prerequisite of all human dignity. Without science, the philosopher knows, his own pursuits eventuate in nothing.

These pursuits can continue to be called scientific because philosophy proceeds methodically and because it is conscious of its methods. But these methods differ from those of science in that they have no object of inquiry. Any specific object is the object of a particular science. Were I to say that the object of philosophy is the whole, the world, being, philosophical critique would answer that such terms do not denote genuine objects. The methods of philosophy are methods of transcending the object. To philosophize is to transcend. But since our thinking is inseparable from objects, the history of philosophy is an account of how the progress of human thought has succeeded in transcending the objects of philosophy. These objects, the great creations of philosophy, function as road signs, indicating the direction of philosophical transcending. Thus there is no substitute for the profound discourse of the metaphysician, which speaks to us from the centuries; to assimilate it from its source in the history of philosophy is not only to know something that once was but to make it come to life.

The mass of sham philosophical knowledge taught in the schools originates in the hypostatization of entities that have served for a time as the signpost of philosophy but are always being transcended by it. Such hypostatized entities are nothing but the *capita mortua,* the ossuaries of the great metaphysical systems. To imagine that they confer knowledge is a philosophical perversion. In philosophizing we must not fall under the spell of the object that we use as a means of transcendence. We must remain masters of our thoughts and not be subjugated by them.

Yet in this intellectual transcendence, which is proper to philosophy and which is analogous to scientific forms, philosophy is less than science. For it does not gain any tangible results or any intellectually binding insight. There is no overlooking the simple fact that while scientific cognition is identical throughout the world, philosophy, despite its claim to universality, is not actually universal in any shape or form. This fact is the outward characteristic of the peculiar nature of philosophical truth. Although scientific truth is universally valid, it remains relative to method and assumptions; philosophical truth is absolute for him who conquers it in historical actuality, but its statements are not universally valid. Scientific truth is one and the same for all —philosophical truth wears multiple historical cloaks; each of these is the manifestation of a unique reality, each has its justification, but they are not identically transmissible.

The one philosophy is the *philosophia perennis* around which all philosophies revolve, which no one possesses, in which every genuine philosopher shares, and which nevertheless can never achieve the form of an intellectual edifice valid for all and exclusively true.

Thus philosophy is not only less but also more than science, namely, as the source of a truth that is inaccessible to scientifically binding knowledge. It is this philosophy that is meant in such definitions as: To philosophize is to learn how to die or to rise to godhead—or to know being *qua* being. The meaning of such definitions is: Philosophical thought is inward action; it appeals to freedom; it is a summons to transcendence. Or the same thing can be formulated differently: Philosophy is the act of becoming conscious of genuine being —or is the thinking of a faith in man that must be infinitely elucidated—or is the way of man's self-assertion through thinking.

But none of these propositions is properly speaking a definition. There is no definition of philosophy, because philosophy cannot be determined by something outside it. There is no genus above philosophy, under which it can be subsumed as a species. Philosophy defines itself, relates itself directly to godhead, and does not justify itself by any kind of utility. It grows out of the primal source in which man is given to himself.

To sum up: The sciences do not encompass all of the truth but only the exact knowledge that is binding to the intellect and universally valid. Truth has a greater scope, and part of it can reveal itself only to philosophical reason. Throughout the centuries since the early Middle Ages, philosophical works have been written under the title "On the Truth"; today the same task still remains urgent, i.e., to gain insight into the essence of truth in its full scope under the present conditions of scientific knowledge and historical experience.

The foregoing considerations also apply to the relation between science and philosophy. Only if the two are strictly distinguished can the inseparable connection between them remain pure and truthful.

8 / PHILOSOPHY OF RELIGION

As a general position, existentialism includes both atheists and theists, and the latter in some variety. The religious value has always been central in man's experience; and a philosophy of concrete experience will explore it avidly.

There is some doubt about applying the technical term "existentialist" to the writer of the following selection, Paul Tillich, for he rejects many of the formulations of other existentialists. Yet if the term is used broadly, he may be included here, for he approaches the problems of religion through concrete experience and its ontology rather than through arguments from nature, or arguments at all. Professor Tillich is here defining and characterizing the concept of faith. Faith, he writes, is the state of being ultimately concerned. It is an act of the total personality and lies at the very center of the self. Man is driven toward faith by the sense of the infinite, which he both possesses and yearns for. Faith is about the unconditioned and ultimate. Idolatrous faith such as worship of the self or the state is about something neither unconditional or ultimate. It inevitably ends in "existential disappointment." Only the faith of theism can bring existential fulfillment.

THE NATURE OF FAITH

Paul Tillich (1886-   )

1. FAITH AS ULTIMATE CONCERN. Faith is the state of being ultimately concerned: the dynamics of faith are the dynamics of man's ultimate concern. Man, like every living being, is concerned about many things, above all about those which condition his very existence, such as food and shelter. But man, in contrast to other living beings, has spiritual concerns—cognitive, esthetic, social, political. Some of them are urgent, often extremely urgent, and each of them as well as the vital concerns can claim ultimacy for a human life or the life of a social group. If it claims ultimacy it demands the total surrender of him who accepts this claim, and it promises total fulfillment even

if all other claims have to be subjected to it or rejected in its name. If a national group makes life and growth of the nation its ultimate concern, it demands that all other concerns, economic well-being, health and life, family, esthetic and cognitive truth, justice and humanity, be sacrificed. The extreme nationalisms of our century are laboratories for the study of what ultimate concern means in all aspects of human existence, including the smallest concern of one's daily life. Everything is centered in the only god, the nation—a god who certainly proves to be a demon, but who shows clearly the unconditional character of an ultimate concern.

But it is not only the unconditional demand made by that which is one's ultimate concern, it is also the promise of ultimate fulfillment which is accepted in the act of faith. The content of this promise is not necessarily defined. It can be expressed in

The selection is from Paul Tillich, *Dynamics of Faith* (New York: Harper & Brothers; London: George Allen & Unwin, Ltd.), pp. 1-12. Copyright © 1957 by Paul Tillich. Reprinted by permission of Harper & Brothers and George Allen & Unwin, Ltd.

indefinite symbols or in concrete symbols which cannot be taken literally, like the "greatness" of one's nation in which one participates even if one has died for it, or the conquest of mankind by the "saving race," etc. In each of these cases it is "ultimate fulfillment" that is promised, and it is exclusion from such fufillment which is threatened if the unconditional demand is not obeyed.

An example—and more than an example —is the faith manifest in the religion of the Old Testament. It also has the character of ultimate concern in demand, threat and promise. The content of this concern is not the nation—although Jewish nationalism has sometimes tried to distort it into that —but the content is the God of justice, who, because he represents justice for everybody and every nation, is called the universal God, the God of the universe. He is the ultimate concern of every pious Jew, and therefore in his name the great commandment is given: "You shall love the Lord your God with all your heart, and with all your soul, and with all your might" (Deut. 6:5). This is what ultimate concern means and from these words the term "ultimate concern" is derived. They state unambiguously the character of genuine faith, the demand of total surrender to the subject of ultimate concern. The Old Testament is full of commands which make the nature of this surrender concrete, and it is full of promises and threats in relation to it. Here also are the promises of symbolic indefiniteness, although they center around fulfillment of the national and individual life, and the threat is the exclusion from such fulfillment through national extinction and individual catastrophe. Faith, for the men of the Old Testament, is the state of being ultimately and unconditionally concerned about Jahweh and about what he represents in demand, threat and promise.

Another example—almost a counter-example, yet nevertheless equally revealing— is the ultimate concern with "success" and with social standing and economic power. It is the god of many people in the highly competitive Western culture and it does what every ultimate concern must do: it demands unconditional surrender to its laws even if the price is the sacrifice of genuine human relations, personal conviction, and creative *eros*. Its threat is social and economic defeat, and its promise—indefinite as all such promises—the fulfillment of one's being. It is the breakdown of this kind of faith which characterizes and makes religiously important most contemporary literature. Not false calculations but a misplaced faith is revealed in novels like *Point of No Return*. When fulfilled, the promise of this faith proves to be empty.

Faith is the state of being ultimately concerned. The content matters infinitely for the life of the believer, but it does not matter for the formal definition of faith. And this is the first step we have to make in order to understand the dynamics of faith.

2. FAITH AS A CENTERED ACT. Faith as ultimate concern is an act of the total personality. It happens in the center of the personal life and includes all its elements. Faith is the most centered act of the human mind. It is not a movement of a special section or a special function of man's total being. They all are united in the act of faith. But faith is not the sum total of their impacts. It transcends every special impact as well as the totality of them and it has itself a decisive impact on each of them.

Since faith is an act of the personality as a whole, it participates in the dynamics of personal life. These dynamics have been described in many ways, especially in the recent developments of analytic psychology. Thinking in polarities, their tensions and their possible conflicts, is a common characteristic of most of them. This makes the psychology of personality highly dynamic and requires a dynamic theory of faith as the most personal of all personal acts. The first and decisive polarity in analytic psychology is that between the so-called unconscious and the conscious. Faith as an act of the total personality is not imaginable without the participation of the unconscious elements in the personality structure. They are always present and decide largely about the content of faith. But, on the other hand, faith is a conscious act and the unconscious elements participate in the creation of faith only if they are taken into the personal center which transcends each of them. If this does not happen, if unconscious forces determine the mental status without a centered act, faith does not occur, and compulsions take its place. For faith is a matter of freedom. Freedom is nothing more than the possibility of centered personal acts. The frequent discussion in which faith and freedom are contrasted could be helped by the insight that faith is a free, namely, centered act of the personality. In this respect freedom and faith are identical.

Also important for the understanding of faith is the polarity between what Freud and his school call ego and superego. The concept of the superego is quite ambiguous. On the one hand, it is the basis of all cultural life because it restricts the uninhibited actualization of the always-driving libido; on the other hand, it cuts off man's vital forces, and produces disgust about the whole system of cultural restrictions, and brings about a neurotic state of mind. From this point of view, the symbols of faith are considered to be expressions of the superego or, more concretely, to be an expression of the father image which gives content to the superego. Responsible for this inadequate theory of the superego is Freud's naturalistic negation of norms and principles. If the superego is not established through valid principles, it becomes a suppressive tyrant. But real faith, even if it uses the father image for its expression, transforms this image into a principle of truth and justice to be defended even against the "father."

Faith and culture can be affirmed only if the superego represents the norms and principles of reality.

This leads to the question of how faith as a personal, centered act is related to the rational structure of man's personality which is manifest in his meaningful language, in his ability to know the true and to do the good, in his sense of beauty and justice. All this, and not only his possibility to analyze, to calculate and to argue, makes him a rational being. But in spite of this larger concept of reason we must deny that man's essential nature is identical with the rational character of his mind. Man is able to decide for or against reason, he is able to create beyond reason or to destroy below reason. This power is the power of his self, the center of self-relatedness in which all elements of his being are united. Faith is not an act of any of his rational functions, as it is not an act of the unconscious, but it is an act in which both the rational and the nonrational elements of his being are transcended.

Faith as the embracing and centered act of the personality is "ecstatic." It transcends both the drives of the nonrational unconscious and the structures of the rational conscious. It transcends them, but it does not destroy them. The ecstatic character of faith does not exclude its rational character although it is not identical with it, and it includes nonrational strivings without being identical with them. In the ecstasy of faith there is an awareness of truth and of ethical value; there are also past loves and hates, conflicts and reunions, individual and collective influences. "Ecstasy" means "standing outside of oneself"—without ceasing to be oneself—with all the elements which are united in the personal center.

A further polarity in these elements, relevant for the understanding of faith, is the tension between the cognitive function of man's personal life, on the one hand, and emotion and will, on the other hand. In a later discussion I will try to show that many distortions of the meaning of faith are rooted in the attempt to subsume faith to the one or the other of these functions. At this point it must be stated as sharply and insistently as possible that in every act of faith there is cognitive affirmation, not as the result of an independent process of inquiry but as an inseparable element in a total act of acceptance and surrender. This also excludes the idea that faith is the result of an independent act of "will to believe." There is certainly affirmation by the will of what concerns one ultimately, but faith is not a creation of the will. In the ecstasy of faith the will to accept and to surrender is an element, but not the cause. And this is true also of feeling. Faith is not an emotional outburst: this is not the meaning of ecstasy. Certainly, emotion is in it, as in every act of man's spiritual life. But emotion does not produce faith. Faith has a cognitive content and is an act of the will. It is the unity of every element in the centered self. Of course, the unity of all elements in the act of faith does not prevent one or the other element from dominating in a special form of faith. It dominates the character of faith but it does not create the act of faith.

This also answers the question of a possible psychology of faith. Everything that happens in man's personal being can become an object of psychology. And it is rather important for both the philosopher of religion and the practical minister to know how the act of faith is embedded in the totality of psychological processes. But in contrast to this justified and desirable form of a psychology of faith there is another one which tries to derive faith from something that is not faith but is most frequently fear. The presupposition of this method is that fear or something else from which faith is derived is more original and basic than faith. But this presupposition

cannot be proved. On the contrary, one can prove that in the scientific method which leads to such consequences faith is already effective. Faith precedes all attempts to derive it from something else, because these attempts are themselves based on faith.

3. THE SOURCE OF FAITH. We have described the act of faith and its relation to the dynamics of personality. Faith is a total and centered act of the personal self, the act of unconditional, infinite and ultimate concern. The question now arises: what is the source of this all-embracing and all-transcending concern? The word "concern" points to two sides of a relationship, the relation between the one who is concerned and his concern. In both respects we have to imagine man's situation in itself and in his world. The reality of man's ultimate concern reveals something about his being, namely, that he is able to transcend the flux of relative and transitory experiences of his ordinary life. Man's experiences, feelings, thoughts are conditioned and finite. They not only come and go, but their content is of finite and conditional concern—unless they are elevated to unconditional validity. But this presupposes the general possibility of doing so; it presupposes the element of infinity in man. Man is able to understand in an immediate personal and central act the meaning of the ultimate, the unconditional, the absolute, the infinite. This alone makes faith a human potentiality.

Human potentialities are powers that drive toward actualization. Man is driven toward faith by his awareness of the infinite to which he belongs, but which he does not own like a possession. This is in abstract terms what concretely appears as the "restlessness of the heart" within the flux of life.

The unconditional concern which is faith is the concern about the unconditional. The infinite passion, as faith has been described, is the passion for the infinite. Or, to use our first term, the ultimate concern is concern about what is experienced as ultimate. In this way we have turned from the subjective meaning of faith as a centered act of the personality to its objective meaning, to what is meant in the act of faith. It would not help at this point of our analysis to call that which is meant in the act of faith "God" or "a god." For at this step we ask: What in the idea of God constitutes divinity? The answer is: It is the element of the unconditional and of ultimacy. This carries the quality of divinity. If this is seen, one can understand why almost every thing "in heaven and on earth" has received ultimacy in the history of human religion. But we also can understand that a critical principle was and is at work in man's religious consciousness, namely, that which is really ultimate over against what claims to be ultimate but is only preliminary, transitory, finite.

The term "ultimate concern" unites the subjective and the objective side of the act of faith—the *fides qua creditur* (the Faith through which one believes) and the *fides quae creditur* (the faith which is believed). The first is the classical term for the centered act of the personality, the ultimate concern. The second is the classical term for that toward which this act is directed, the ultimate itself, expressed in symbols of the divine. This distinction is very important, but not ultimately so, for the one side cannot be without the other. There is no faith without a content toward which it is directed. There is always something meant in the act of faith. And there is no way of having the content of faith except in the act of faith. All speaking about divine matters which is not done in the state of ultimate concern is meaningless. Because that which is meant in the act of faith cannot be approached in any other way than through an act of faith.

In terms like ultimate, unconditional, infinite, absolute, the difference between subjectivity and objectivity is overcome. The ultimate of the act of faith and the ultimate that is meant in the act of faith are one and the same. This is symbolically expressed by the mystics when they say that their knowledge of God is the knowledge God has of himself; and it is expressed by Paul when he says (I Cor. 13) that he will know as he is known, namely, by God. God never can be object without being at the same time subject. Even a successful prayer is, according to Paul (Rom. 8), not possible without God as Spirit praying within us. The same experience expressed in abstract language is the disappearance of the ordinary subject-object scheme in the experience of the ultimate, the unconditional. In the act of faith that which is the source of this act is present beyond the cleavage of subject and object. It is present as both and beyond both.

This character of faith gives an additional criterion for distinguishing true and false ultimacy. The finite which claims infinity without having it (as, e.g., a nation or success) is not able to transcend the subject-object scheme. It remains an object which the believer looks at as a subject. He can approach it with ordinary knowledge and subject it to ordinary handling. There are, of course, many degrees in the endless realm of false ultimacies. The nation is nearer to true ultimacy than is success. Nationalistic ecstasy can produce a state in which the subject is almost swallowed by the object. But after a period the subject emerges again, disappointed radically and totally, and by looking at the nation in a skeptical and calculating way does injustice even to its justified claims. The more idolatrous a faith the less it is able to overcome the cleavage between subject and object. For that is the difference between true and idolatrous faith. In true faith the ultimate concern is a concern about the truly ultimate; while in idolatrous faith preliminary, finite realities are elevated to the rank of ultimacy. The inescapable consequence of idolatrous faith is "existential disappointment," a disappointment which penetrates into the very existence of man! This is the dynamics of idolatrous faith: that it is faith, and as such, the centered act of a personality; that the centering point is something which is more or less on to the periphery; and that, therefore, the act of faith leads to a loss of the center and to a disruption of the personality. The ecstatic character of even an idolatrous faith can hide this consequence only for a certain time. But finally it breaks into the open.

9 / SUMMARY

Existentialists, writes F. H. Heinemann in this concluding selection, show the diversity of form and expression found within other philosophic schools. Yet they are "children of the same age," all involved in the same predicament, which to them is one of crisis. Thus in spite of their diversity, they are united in attitude and situation, protesting in their individual ways against tendencies in the present age. Sympathetic yet critical, Heinemann sees this protest as a challenge to all philosophy. Its function is to release us from the predominance of analysis and rationalism, and to stir us to a revaluation of the traditional problems of men. So seen, he concludes, existentialism remains an important, though perhaps not final, expression of our day.

THE CHALLENGE OF EXISTENTIALISM

F. H. Heinemann (1889-   )

So far we have considered some existentialist philosophers. We had to discuss them just as they are in their diversity and particularity, and some readers may well have wondered whether they are not so different as human beings, so particular in their language and thought and sometimes so antagonistic to each other that one is unable to see what they have in common. "Even if we agree to call them existentialists," one may object, "we fail to see what that existentialism is on which they agree." We have therefore to return to our starting-point and to

repeat the question: What is existentialism? Can this question be answered at all? If it is meant to imply the demand for a real definition, it cannot, for there is no single entity or essence to which this word corresponds. There is not *one* philosophy called existentialism, but several philosophies with profound differences. It is not even possible to make a clear-cut distinction between German philosophers of existence and French existentialists, for Marcel is nearer to Jaspers than to Sartre and therefore rightly calls one of his books *Philosophy of Existence;* Sartre is nearer to Heidegger than to Marcel, and Heidegger would like to form a class of his own as ek-sistentialist. There is no set of principles common to them all, nor do they share a well-defined method comparable to the dialectic of the Hegelians. Nevertheless they belong to-

The selection is from F. H. Heinemann, *Existentialism and the Modern Predicament* (London: A. & C. Black, Ltd., 1953; New York: Harper & Brothers, 1958), pp. 165-174, 179-180. Copyright © 1953, 1958 by F. H. Heinemann. Used by permission of A. & C. Black, Ltd.

gether. Children of one and the same age, they are faced with the same challenge to which they have to respond, and are involved in the same predicament. Though their answers are not identical, they move in parallel directions and are, even if opposed to each other, internally related. In other words, the term "existentialism" points to a certain state of mind, to a specific approach or attitude, to a spiritual movement which is of significance in present circumstances and to a specific mode of thought, in any case to something which is alive.

It is a fundamental mistake to assume that what cannot be defined does not exist. On the contrary, anything which is alive cannot be exhausted by definition. I do not deny for a moment that the emphasis on form, *Gestalt,* definition and measurement was of the greatest importance for the development of European science. But we should never forget that life is inexhaustible and that often the formless, which cannot be defined or measured, is the most valuable part of living beings. It is possible to define existentialism in three ways. The first is by ostensive definition, *i.e.* by pointing to existentialists and their books and by saying that what they are doing is existentialism. That we have done. The second is to describe the situation to which they respond and to interpret these philosophies as an expression of the *Zeitgeist.* The third is to change the form of the question and to search for their *function* rather than for their *essence.*

It can hardly be doubted that these philosophies are specific expressions of the *Zeitgeist,* albeit of the first half of the twentieth century. They express something of that which many feel without being able to formulate it. True, it is the feeling of a minority, but of a minority that counts, because it belongs to the intellectual élite. Whilst the majority accepted, voluntarily or forced, the pseudo-philosophies of Marx-

ism, Bolshevism and Fascism, the existentialists defended the rights of the person. It would, however, be incorrect to interpret existentialism as the antithesis to Marxism and Fascism, for on the one hand its battlefront is broader, and on the other, individual existentialists may well be Marxists or Fascists.

The Marxists are therefore not right if they try to explain existentialism away as a last desperate attempt of a declining bourgeoisie, which just before its ultimate submergence clings to an overemphasized individualism as to a life-belt. Existentialism is not the philosophy of a class, and the problems which it discusses transcend the boundaries of a specific group; they are simply human and they reappear within dictatorial states, even in a more pressing, though perhaps insoluble form. Anyone in Russia or her satellite states who wants to be himself in order to live his own life, express his own thought, and practise his own religion, has to experience the agony of existentialist problems. The Bolshevists hate the existentialists as the potential revolutionaries of the future. In fact, the existentialists are philosophers of resistance. They attempt to resist the collectivizing trend, bound up with machine production, which seems to lead in any society, whether democratic, fascist or socialist, to a depersonalization of man. This resistance takes various forms. Kierkegaard criticizes the modern tendency towards equality and the levelling brought about by public opinion and the rise of the masses. Jaspers protests against the absorption of man by the machinery of the modern welfare state, Marcel against the increased socialization of life, against the extension of the powers of the State, and against the substitution of the registration card for the person. Most of the French existentialists were members of the Resistance, in deadly opposition to the Nazi oppressors.

The philosophies of existence are philosophies of liberation rather than philosophies of freedom. They attempt to liberate man from the domination of external forces, of society, of the state, and of dictatorial power. They want to set man's authentic self free from the shackles of the unauthentic self. We saw that they experience freedom (Sartre) and that they may formulate a philosophy of freedom (Berdyaev).

Existentialism is in all its forms a philosophy of crisis. It expresses the crisis of man openly and directly, whereas other schools, like that of the Logical Positivists, express it indirectly and unconsciously. For this reason, the fact of estrangement in its enormous complexity and many-sidedness became central with them. Today it pervades the relations of persons as well as of groups, of classes and races rather than of nations and religious sects. Science and the arts are out of harmony. Science claims to contain the whole of true knowledge. Art, religion and speculative philosophy cannot accept this claim, and contend that wisdom, nurtured by the experience of generations, may be of greater significance than abstract science. Some schools, like those of Gurdieff and Ouspensky, go still further. They reject science as a guide to human action, and build their "Teaching" on esoteric wisdom allegedly coming down to them from primeval times. Hegel's idealistic and Marx's materialistic alienation have led to institutional alienation. Human institutions—the state, the government, the civil service, the party, the factory—have become impersonal and anonymous powers of enormous strength which the individual tries in vain to master. Thence arises the growing sense of frustration, anxiety and despair, which pervades the Western hemisphere. At the back of it all is man's estrangement from Nature, deeply felt by Rousseau and the Romantics; but chiefly that estrangement from God, which is in a certain sense the source of all these troubles and therefore remains a recurrent theme from Kierkegaard to Marcel,

and is present, even when not discussed, as in the case of Sartre.

Alienation ends in absurdity, because under its domination the acts of individuals and groups become unco-ordinated. Shall we ridicule or praise Sartre and Camus because of their revelation of *homo absurdus* and of the absurd universe? It is not the universe that is absurd, but man, who projects his absurdity into the world. Nothing is absurd except feelings, thoughts, interpretations, actions or productions of man. Many products of contemporary art and literature are undoubtedly absurd, and in that they are a true mirror of our time. It would, however, be unfair to our age to single it out in this manner. Absurdity is at all times a possibility for human beings though not for animals. It is the price man has to pay for the inexhaustibility and indefiniteness of his nature. If, however, it *actually* dominates him, it points to a *cul-de-sac*, it indicates that a point has been reached where the direction has to be changed. The absurd man needs no refutation, he is his own *reductio ad absurdum*. However, genius and madness, exceptional gifts and absurdity, may co-exist. It would therefore be a mistake to reject existentialist doctrines as absurdities; for they merely reveal the fact that life on this planet is on the point of becoming absurd. Wherever one looks, whether at the lives of individuals, communities or nations, one cannot help noticing them. The only trouble is, that we fail to see how absurd we ourselves and some of our actions are becoming. Sometimes I cannot help wondering whether Shakespeare's Puck is still making an ass of many a man who remains quite unaware of his transformation. Are examples really necessary? Everyone knows them: the policy of unconditional surrender followed after a short time by a rearmament of Japan and Germany; the demolition of factories in these countries, which had to be reconstructed after a few months; the United Nations broken up into two hostile camps waging a cold war against each other; and the piling up of arms in both camps for the preservation of peace, but which in very fact enhances the danger of war. "Absurdity of absurdities, all is absurd," seems to be the motto of the contemporary world.

But even if it be granted that existentialism has a representative value by expressing the crisis of our time in its phase of absurdity, the question remains: What then is existentialism? This is the point where we have to change the form of our question. Instead of asking, "What is the essence of existentialism?" we now ask, "What is its function in present circumstances?"

Its first function is to bring about a revaluation of problems and to liberate us from certain traditional problems whether they are material or purely formal and technical. The existentialists maintain that the philosophers of the past overlooked the most pressing problems of man and of human existence. What is the good, they would say, of talking about a transcendent realm of values, if these are not realized here and now in human persons? What alone matters are problems that are lived, directly experienced, suffered and intimately connected with our being; problems in which we are engaged, which form part of ourselves, which we cannot escape. It is a change in the quality of problems, brought about by the climate of the age. The existentialists reject the starting-point of modern philosophers, from Descartes to the present time, *e.g.* the thesis that nothing but the data of my consciousness are given to me. However these data are interpreted, either with Descartes as "ideas" in their three forms, with Locke as simple ideas, with Hume as impressions, or with Kant as a "chaos of sensations," they are in each case abstractions. Whitehead is right, these philosophers are the victims of the fallacy of misplaced concreteness, they falsely assume that their data are concrete, whereas in fact they are abstract. If these philosophers try to prove or disprove, on the basis of their hypotheses, the existence or non-existence of material objects, of other minds, or of God, they are discussing pseudo-problems. On this point, that is in rejecting certain problems as pseudo-problems, the existentialists are in agreement with the logical positivists. They go, however, much further. They would say that the attempt of the latter to reduce all problems to linguistic problems may again lead to the replacement of real problems by pseudo-problems.

The existentialists have here the function of liberating us from the predominance of analysis. Nobody denies the importance of analysis, but analysis as such is not enough. Analysis is the breaking up of a material or ideal whole into its parts. It can only break down, but not build up. It has been too easily assumed that the model of arithmetical analysis may be applied in psychology and epistemology, *i.e.* that just as all numbers may be broken down into prime numbers, so all our ideas may be analyzed into simple ideas. That is what I call the fallacy of simplicity. An analysis into simpler elements is possible, but the so-called simple ideas prove to be very complex, if they are not mere abstractions. Each field of inquiry demands a different form of analysis adequate to its problems. Since in psychology and epistemology the whole is more than its parts, the whole, the totality, the overriding meaning disappears in this sort of analysis. The analysts are inclined to disregard synthesis altogether, in spite of the fact that analysis and synthesis are strictly correlative; or if they acknowledge it, they interpret it in a superficial manner as a "collection of ideas." There is a second sense which may be given to analysis. *Analyser, c'est traduire*, said Hippolyte Taine. In fact, if I am of the opinion that nothing but sense-data are given to me, I have to translate statements about external objects into statements about my sensations. I do not wish to discuss this standpoint here. I can only stress one point. The analysis of ethical statements in the first half of the twentieth century has resulted in greater disagreement than ever before, and we are told that "in some cases disagreement about issues so fundamental arose that certain schools of thought find it unrewarding, if not impossible to communicate with each other." That this should be the case is easily understandable if one notices the arbitrariness of these translations. Stevenson, *e.g.*, would analyze the proposition "this action is right" into: "I approve of it. Do so likewise!" This analysis seems to be completely arbitrary, because the criterion on which the approval is based remains undefined. The danger in all these translations is that they are not equivalent, *i.e.* that they substitute something else foreign to the original meaning. In fact, in both kinds of analysis the negative tendency prevails. In this situation the existentialist would seem to fulfil a useful function by raising the following questions: Is the analysis of ethical statements really the only function of a moral philosopher? Is it not more important to clarify the condition of man, to reveal the danger in which the persons find themselves, to appeal to them to make their own decision and to take the responsibility for their actions, and to discuss the criteria on which the rightness of an action is based? And, generally speaking, is analysis enough? Should we not go on to meta-analysis, *i.e.* to an analysis of analysis on a higher level? Should we not analyze the analyzers? Is it not time to see that analysis without the corresponding synthesis is condemned to remain barren and fruitless? Should we not restrict the sphere of influence of analysis within the realm of philosophy and science? The existentialists remind us that there may be some concrete problems of primary importance which are not discussed by analytic science

and by analytic philosophy. They concern the existence of human persons.

All the existentialists stressed the fact of alienation. Did they succeed in overcoming self-estrangement? The problem of estrangement is, as we saw, multi-dimensional. We have therefore to ask whether there is one solution to it, or whether its different aspects call for diverse remedies. Before attempting an answer, the preliminary somewhat unusual question has to be pondered: Is it at all possible to get rid of this affliction? Will not an element of it always remain because of its having, so to say, metaphysical roots? Is it perhaps our permanent fate to remain foreigners on this earth, in spite of our being at home on it? Is this not even more true of man within the Universe? Though a creature of this world, he nevertheless remains foreign in it. Responding consciously and unconsciously to rays from sun and stars, he does not understand the message they may convey. Cosmic alienation is even greater than earth alienation. Pantheists and Yogis may believe that they are nearer to the Unity of all beings than to their neighbors and to the earth, but that is a matter of subjective experience and not of verifiable fact. The highest degree of estrangement, *i.e.* a complete break and an unbridgeable gulf, and the lowest degree, where no feeling of difference is left, are seldom realized, but they mark the limits between which the pendulum of our feeling oscillates. There is a limit to our understanding of other persons. In their inner life they all remain, to a certain degree, foreign to us. Is it to be wondered at that this feeling increases if we meet animals, plants, stones or stars?

From this it follows that alienation cannot be completely eliminated, it can only be reduced to reasonable terms. All we can do is to remove it from the foreground to the background and deprive it of its central position and of its emotional power, but we have to acquiesce in the fact that alienation somehow belongs to our heritage. It brings, moreover, certain advantages with it. It allows us to keep aloof from others in cases where we do not wish to identify ourselves with their doings. In due degree it is to be welcomed so long as it remains less intense than the opposed feeling of togetherness and participation. Normal alienation is healthy, abnormal alienation is morbid, because if dominant it becomes an impediment to creative work, destroying normal relations and transforming trust into mistrust. Therefore all those solutions which assume the possibility of a complete elimination of estrangement seem to be over-simplifications. Neither Hegel's return of the Mind to itself, nor Marx's proletarian revolution, nor Kierkegaard's repetition understood as a restitution of the *status pristinus,* nor Marcel's absolute hope which does not leave room for any sort of despair, offer a definitive solution of the problem, for in spite of them alienation remains. . . .

Existentialism points here to an urgent problem, or rather to a series of problems, but offers no solution, partly because the problems are so complex and many-sided that no simple solution is possible, and partly because they are, to a certain extent, in principle insoluble. . . .

But whatever the attitude of the individual philosopher to these problems may be, even if he should think that they are not his concern, he should still accept the challenge of existentialism. It should help him to overcome the non-existential philosophy of our time. "Non-existential philosophy" is concerned with words or with symbols and their manipulation, with the clarification of scientific propositions or with talk. The linguistic philosophers started with the rejection of metaphysical problems as pseudo-problems, but, alas! they did not foresee that one day they themselves might be enmeshed in linguistic pseudo-problems which

they discuss at great length. Linguistic analysis and the distinction of different kinds of symbols are important, but not enough. Words and symbols are only means to an end, and not the end itself. They cannot serve as a final substitute for thinking, not even as the substitute signs of algebra and symbolic logic. A philosopher cannot help asking what they mean. He knows quite well that the word *reality* has different meanings. But even a hard-boiled Logical Positivist can hardly deny that one of these meanings is predominant in the problem of reality when, *e.g.,* a bomb has fallen near him and smashed his leg. He should see that philosophy has something to do with man. It should be an expression of the whole man and not merely of his intellect. It demands a decision of his will as well. His philosophy should be a response to the challenge of his time. He should not try to evade it, and he should not imagine that he could render it non-existent by doing so. Does he perhaps not see what the challenge of our time is? Can he really overlook it? Or does he not wish to see it for the simple reason that he himself is infected with the mortal disease of our age? Whatever formula one may choose, dehumanization of man, annihilation of man, or the question whether man will survive in the face of nihilistic destruction of all human and moral values, the facts are indisputable. Once more the human world resembles the valley full of bones which Ezekiel saw in his vision. And again is the question put to us: "Son of man, can these bones live?" The integration of the diffused and disintegrated parts into a whole, the rehumanization of man, that is the task with which we are confronted. One cannot expect a philosopher to put new breath into dead bones, but one can expect him to remind human beings of what it means to be man. In short, what we need is not Philosophies of Existence, but Existential Philosophers.

BIBLIOGRAPHICAL NOTE

A number of fine surveys of existentialist thought have been written; among them are F. H. Heinemann, *Existentialism and the Modern Predicament* (New York, 1958), which includes bibliographical materials; H. J. Blackham, *Six Existentialist Thinkers* (New York, 1959); Marjorie Grene, *Dreadful Freedom* (Chicago, 1948; reissued as *Introduction to Existentialism*); Robert Grimsley, *Existentialist Thought* (Cardiff, Wales, 1955); and Emmanuel Mounier, *Existentialist Philosophies* (New York, 1949). The student will want, however, to consult the writings of existentialists themselves, and these surveys will direct him to the major sources. A brief sample of them, additional to the writings from which the selections in this text are taken, is given here. R. Bretall, *A Kierkegaard Anthology* (Princeton, 1946), is useful for a first orientation, although it should be supplemented by further reading in Kierkegaard. Among Jaspers' works available in English are *Way to Wisdom* (London, 1951), *The Perennial Scope of Philosophy* (New York, 1949), and *Reason and Existenz* (New York, 1955). Werner Brock's *Existence and Being* (Chicago, 1949) contains four of Heidegger's essays together with a long introductory study of Heidegger's thought. Also available in English translation is Heidegger's *An Introduction to Metaphysics* (New Haven, 1959). Sartre's major philosophical work, *Being and Nothingness* (New York, 1956), is available in English, along with many of his literary pieces and shorter essays. Many editions of Pascal and Nietzsche are in print. Finally, mention should be made of three other writers of major importance. Gabriel Marcel has attempted to produce a Roman Catholic form of existentialism; for one of his major works, see *The Mystery of Being*, 2 vols. (Chicago, 1950, 1951). The Russian Nicholas Berdyaev, whose works are available in English through Geoffrey Bles, Ltd., has produced a personalistic existentialism. His *Dream and Reality* (London, 1950) contains both a good introduction to his own thought and a bibliography of his other writings. And Albert Camus, French novelist, essayist, and Nobel prize winner, has written many stirring books, including *The Myth of Sisyphus* (New York, 1955) and *The Rebel* (New York, 1956).

GLOSSARY

Many of the key terms met in the readings are defined in the following selected glossary. Its aim is not so much completeness—which would be impossible here—as helpfulness. For further elaboration of these and related words, the student should consult a standard philosophical lexicon or dictionary.

Absolute idealism: monistic variant of idealism. The real is one inclusive mind or self, the "Absolute."

Agnosticism: position holding that ultimate propositions are, for mankind, undecidable.

Analysis: a philosophical procedure, variously characterized, for solving problems by translation or resolution to simpler parts.

Analytic: a statement whose denial involves a contradiction; or, a statement whose truth follows, with the help of definitions, from logical principles alone.

A posteriori: lit., "after experience." Used with reference to knowledge derived from experience.

A priori: lit., "before experience." Used with reference to knowledge or concepts supposedly gained independently of experience.

Art: generally, any manipulation of objects to serve human purposes. Fine art is manipulation to produce an esthetic experience.

Axiology: a branch of philosophy that investigates problems of value.

Category: a principle of explanation, usually considered ultimate in the area of experience to which it applies.

Cause: an event, process, or object productive of change in another. Additionally, in Aristotle, a principle.

Coherence: theory that the criterion of truth is systematic entailment of propositions; also, that the nature of truth is such a coherent system.

Common good: the good for society, as distinguished from the individual good.

Concept: a term defining what is common to the objects to which it applies.

Cosmology: a division of metaphysics; lit., study of the cosmos.

Deduction: type of inference where the evidence for the conclusion is exhaustively given in the premises.

Definition: a statement articulating the meaning of a term. May be of many kinds.

Dialectic: relating to the interrelationships of concepts.

Efficient cause: in Aristotle, the cause productive of a thing or its changes.

Emotive meaning: a noncognitive form of meaning having an emotional basis and designed to arouse or express emotion.

Empiricism: the theory that knowledge is derived from and tested in experience.

Epistemology: lit., theory of knowledge.

Essence: the principle in a being that makes it to be *what* it is.

Esthetics: normative investigation of art and the beautiful.

Ethics: normative science of human conduct.

Existence: the act whereby some essence *is*. Also, the field of human struggle and decision.

Existential proposition: a proposition asserting or denying the existence of some subject.

Existentialism: a philosophical position directed toward articulating human existence.

Final cause: in Aristotle, the end toward which a being or change is directed.

Form, formal cause: the structure or pattern of anything.

Generalization: a proposition covering all instances of the items being referred to.

Historicism: theory making all knowledge and experience relative to historical circumstance. In Karl Popper, the theory that social science is impossible.

Hypothesis: proposition suggesting a resolution of a problem.

Ideal: a definition of a value.

Idealism: most generally, the theory that reality is mind or the mind-like.

Induction: an inference whose conclusion is derived from a set of particulars.

Inference: a conclusion drawn from premises.

Instrumentalism: alternative name for pragmatism; the theory that mind and ideas are instruments in adjustment.

Intention, intentional act: the reference of consciousness to some specified object.

Logic: the study of arguments.

Logical empiricism: alternative name for logical positivism.

Logical form: the pattern or structure of arguments, as isolated and studied by logicians.

Logical positivism: school holding that all empirical statements are scientific and that the task of philosophy is analysis.

Material cause: in Aristotle, that out of which a being comes.

Materialism: metaphysical theory that matter is the ultimately real.

Metaphysics: philosophical inquiry into being or reality.

Natural law: in ethics, a principle of right believed to be derived from the nature of man.

Natural theology: theology based on nature or reason rather than on revelation. Sometimes also called rational theology.

Naturalism: philosophical position holding that nature is all there is, —there is no supernatural being, realm, or entity.

Necessary condition: that without which an event cannot occur.

Norm, normative: having reference to what ought to be as against what is; also, what is taken as a true ideal.

Ontology: division of metaphysics concerned with the meaning of being.

Panpsychism: a pluralistic form of idealism; reality is held to be a society of minds or mindlike entities.

Pantheism: a religious position that identifies God and nature.

Particular: opposed to universal; that which is taken as a unit or individual.

Personalism: a variant of idealism that holds that the real is personal or a person.

Phenomenalism: theory that limits human knowledge to phenomena or appearances.

Phenomenology: philosophical discipline directed toward describing the structures of experience.

Philosophy: lit., "love of wisdom." Generally concerned with comprehensive problems, be they of the nature of analysis, description, evaluation, or reality as a whole.

Philosophy of religion: a normative investigation of the truth of religious beliefs and the value of religious practices.

Positivism: generally, the theory that limits valid knowledge to scientific knowledge.

Pragmatism: position in philosophy that defines meaning and knowledge in terms of their function in experience, with reference to adjustment and the resolution of problematic situations.

Primary quality: quality or attribute of an object that is definable in mathematical terms.

Proposition: the meaning of a declarative sentence; an assertion that may be true or false.

Rational psychology: branch of metaphysics that investigates the being of mind; distinguished from empirical psychology.

Rational theology: division of metaphysics that investigates the being and attributes of God on the basis of reason and experience alone. Sometimes called natural theology.

Rationalism: epistemological view that holds that reason is the source and criterion of truth.

Realism: metaphysical view that the real consists of independently existing substances; in epistemology, the theory that the object of knowledge is independent of the act of knowing.

Reductive: as used of explanation, the view that "higher" levels of experience are to be explained through "lower" ones.

Religion: concern about the status of values, devotion to what is believed to be the source of value, and suitable expression of this concern and devotion.

Science: in classical thought, an organized body of knowledge. Currently used chiefly only of the experimental sciences.

Secondary quality: quality or attribute of an object that is dependent on the perceiving mind for its existence.

Sense-datum: term used for that which is experienced in an act of perceiving. Usually distinguished from a physical object.

Skepticism: a position that doubts or denies the power of intellect to know reality or ultimate truths.

Social philosophy: a normative inquiry into the principles underlying social process.

Soul: in Aristotle, the form of a living body that makes it live.

Substance: the real thing referred to by the demonstrative "this."

Sufficient condition: a condition in the presence of which an effect occurs.

Syllogism: an argument wherein two premises necessitate a conclusion. The basis of classical logic.

Synthetic: a statement referring to actual states of affairs; one whose truth can be determined only by recourse to experience. Opposed to analytic.

Teleology: study or doctrine of ends and purposes; also the belief in natural purposes.

Theism: religious position that believes God to be a living, conscious being.

Theology: a systematic inquiry into the being and attributes of God.

Transcendent: having reference to what is beyond experience.

Universal: a concept or proposition holding for the entire class to which it refers.

Value: whatever is enjoyed, desired, esteemed, or prized.

Verifiability theory of meaning: theory that the meaning of a synthetic proposition lies in its reference to possible empirical confirmation.

Virtue: a habit of right action; in classical thought, it may be either moral or intellectual.

Wisdom: traditionally, knowledge of first principles and their application to experience.

INDEX

Italic page numbers refer to definitions in the Glossary.

403